BIRT
A Field Guide

Third Edition

BIRT
A Field Guide
Third Edition

Diana Peh • Nola Hague • Jane Tatchell

✦Addison-Wesley

Upper Saddle River, NJ • Boston • Indianapolis • San Francisco
New York • Toronto • Montreal • London • Munich • Paris • Madrid
Capetown • Sydney • Tokyo • Singapore • Mexico City

The publisher offers excellent discounts on this book when ordered in quantity for bulk purchases or special sales, which may include electronic versions and/or custom covers and content particular to your business, training goals, marketing focus, and branding interests. For more information, please contact:

> U.S. Corporate and Government Sales
> (800) 382-3419
> corpsales@pearsontechgroup.com

For sales outside the United States please contact:

> International Sales
> international@pearsoned.com

Visit us on the Web: informit.com

Library of Congress Control Number: 2010943257

ISBN-13: 978-0-321-73358-0
ISBN-10:   0-321-73358-4

Text printed on recycled paper in the United States at Courier in Stoughton, Massachusetts.
First printing, January 2011

Contents

Chapter 19   Laying Out and Formatting a Chart 453

Application development tools and technology have come a long way since the late 1970s, when I took my first job out of college in Hewlett-Packard Company's IT (Information Technology) department. Of course, IT was not the term we used to refer to the discipline back then; our preferred acronym was EDP (Electronic Data Processing).

And maybe that difference between simply "processing" data and delivering "information" was reflected in our development tools. We worked on TTY terminals connected to 16-bit mini-computers over 2400 baud lines. We used simple line editors to make changes to our COBOL programs, and we kept our application data in non-relational hierarchical databases. Debugging was COBOL WRITE statements, and source code control was keeping full copies of every version on tape or in separate directories.

Reports for our applications were typically afterthoughts, and they were done by hand in the same technology we used to develop the base application, i.e., COBOL. We designed them—when we did design—by laying them out in pencil on the report design pads that IBM had developed for RPG and COBOL programmers. Because we created them without much forethought, and because junior programmers like me often got the assignment of coding them, our users often found them inadequate, and the cost of making changes to accommodate their true requirements was high.

But while today's application developer may scratch his or her head in wonder at the primitive tools and technologies we employed in building our base applications in the late 1970s, he or she may not find my description of our approach to report development so very unfamiliar.

JSP = COBOL and Banded Report Writers = Report Design Pads

The majority of Java developers still hand-code reports for their applications using JavaServer Page (JSP) technology. This is analogous to our approach of hand-coding them in COBOL and has all the same downsides: high development cost, low user satisfaction, and inflexible, high-cost maintenance.

A minority of Java developers do use tools to develop reports; however, almost all of these tools—be they commercial or open source—are what's known as "banded report writers," and they support a design metaphor that has essentially evolved from the old IBM report pads. Each section in the report writer—header, detail, footer—corresponds to a section in the report with the detail sections repeating as needed to accommodate rows from the data source.

Because they were created before the advent of the internet, banded report writers are not intuitive to web application developers, who are most comfortable with the web page-oriented design metaphor that one finds in modern graphical web development tools. In addition, web concepts—such as tables, graphical object containment and inheritance, cascading style sheets (CSS), and scripting in web-oriented languages like Java and JavaScript—are not supported.

Enter BIRT

The Eclipse Foundation's Business Intelligence and Reporting Tools (BIRT) project takes report development into the age of the internet. Based on industry-leading Eclipse IDE and Rich Client Platform (RCP) technology, BIRT was built from the ground up for web applications.

As Senior Vice President of Engineering for Actuate Corporation, I'm proud of the leading role my company has played in the project. We've leveraged our 16+ years of experience in the reporting and business intelligence space and put to work a significant number of full-time developers (or "committers," in Eclipse Foundation parlance) on the development of the platform. In fact, Ohloh, the open-source rating website, calculates that it would cost over $21M to hire a team to write the project from scratch. But more important than the investment is the result: BIRT is an extensible, full-featured reporting platform that is ready for use in and integration with production applications.

An impressive list of commercial adopters justifies this claim. BIRT is used extensively in IBM's Rational and Tivoli product lines, in Borland's Silk and Together product lines, in the Sybase IQ analytics server, in the Zend Platform to enable reporting in PHP, and by SPSS.

Likewise, enterprise IT developers and system integrators have embraced BIRT and are using it in important business applications. In fact, a survey done by an independent market research firm found that BIRT is used by about 1,000,000 developers worldwide.

All of these constituencies—ISVs, IT, and SI developers—contribute to the Eclipse Foundation BIRT community, which is a vibrant one. The BIRT newsgroup is especially active and BIRT is one of the most searched-for terms on the Eclipse website. Feedback from the community has helped to drive project priorities, give direction on feature implementation, uncover defects, and once in a while, deliver some "attaboys" to the project team. Here are just a few comments posted by developers in the Eclipse BIRT newsgroup:

"I had installed BIRT the other day just to check it out and barely went through the introductory tutorial. Today I was able to drag and drop my way to replacing a broken report (600 lines of somebody else's perl) and all I can really say is it was almost too easy."

"I've gotten through what I think is a complex development and I'm impressed with exactly how much BIRT can do."

"BIRT is an inspiring piece of work that I chose over Crystal Reports."

"I find BIRT much easier to use and customize than JasperReports/iReport."

"I think BIRT is one of the best reporting tools today."

"Lots of credit to the BIRT crosstab team. The crosstab feature looks great."

"I will recommend BIRT and its community for other people."

"We love BIRT."

I hope that you will leverage the information in this book to become a successful member of the BIRT community as well. And, in the off chance that you are standing in a bookstore aisle, having picked up this book with no idea what BIRT is all about, may I suggest that you rush home—after buying the book, of course—and download the software from the Eclipse BIRT website:

`http://www.eclipse.org/birt`

Take it from me—it's the best way to prevent yourself from being lumped into the same category as 1970s COBOL programmers!

Mark Coggins
Senior Vice President of Engineering, Actuate Corporation

About this book

BIRT is a powerful reporting platform that provides end-to-end reporting solutions, from creating and deploying reports to integrating report capabilities into other enterprise applications. Two companion books, *BIRT: A Field Guide* and *Integrating and Extending BIRT*, cover the breadth and depth of BIRT's functionality.

Using BIRT Report Designer's rich set of tools, report developers can create many reports, simple and sophisticated, without programming. This book teaches report developers how to create reports using the graphical tools of BIRT Report Designer. Report developers who want to go beyond the graphical tools to customize the report-generation process or incorporate complex business logic in their reports should read the second book, *Integrating and Extending BIRT*.

This third edition, newly revised for BIRT 2.6, adds updated examples and covers all the new features in cross tabs, charts, page management, and data sharing.

Who should read this book

This book is intended for people who have a basic need for reporting and data presentation. You need not be an expert at creating reports nor do you need years of programming experience. Familiarity with the following subjects, however, is useful:

- HTML, for formatting report content
- SQL, for writing basic queries to extract data from a database for a report
- JavaScript, for writing basic expressions to manipulate data in the report

This book provides many examples of formatting with HTML, and writing SQL queries and JavaScript expressions, but it is not designed to teach you HTML, SQL, or JavaScript.

Contents of this book

This book is divided into several parts. The following sections describe the contents of each of the parts.

Part I, Installing BIRT

Part I introduces the currently available BIRT reporting packages, other components, and the steps to install and update the packages. Part I includes the following chapters:

- *Chapter 1, Introducing BIRT Report Designers.* BIRT provides a number of separate packages for BIRT Report Designer as downloadable archive (.zip) files on the Eclipse web site. This chapter describes the components that make up each of the available report designer packages and additional packages that enhance the designer technology and environment.

- *Chapter 2, Installing a BIRT Report Designer.* BIRT provides two report designers as separate packages, which are downloadable archive (.zip) files on the Eclipse web site. This chapter describes the steps required to install and update each of the available report designers. The chapter also shows how to troubleshoot installation problems and install a language pack that provides localization support.

Part II, Getting Started

Part II provides an overview of the report creation process and introduces the report design environment. Part II includes the following chapters:

- *Chapter 3, Learning the Basics.* This chapter presents fundamental concepts of reporting and provides a tutorial. Report developers learn that the report design process begins with a paper and pencil sketch of the proposed report layout and continues through specifying data, laying out the report, formatting, previewing, and testing. In addition, this chapter orients the reader to the software. To accomplish that objective, the chapter provides a tutorial that walks the reader through a creation of a complete report.

- *Chapter 4, Planning Your Report.* This chapter explains the planning process in greater detail. Planning is essential to creating effective and efficient reports. A thorough understanding of user requirements and objectives makes the development process smoother and achieves better results. This chapter discusses the types of requirements and other information that a report developer should consider when determining how to set up, format, and distribute a report.

Part III, Accessing and Binding Data

Part III discusses the tasks necessary to connect to an external data source, extract, and prepare data for use in a report. Part III includes the following chapters:

- *Chapter 5, Connecting to a Data Source.* Report data comes from many different information systems. An important step in developing a report is ensuring you can connect to a system that provides data. This chapter explains how to access data in JDBC databases, text files, XML documents, and web services.

- *Chapter 6, Retrieving Data.* Data sources typically contain more data than is needed in an effective report. This chapter explains how to define data sets to retrieve only the data required for a report. Specifically, this chapter describes retrieving data from JDBC databases, text files, XML sources, and web services.

- *Chapter 7, Binding Data.* The data sets you create retrieve the data you want to use in a report. Before you can use or display this data in a report, you must first create the necessary data bindings. A data binding defines an expression that specifies what data to display. This chapter explains how to create and manage data bindings.

Part IV, Designing Reports

Part IV describes the tasks that a report developer completes to design reports using BIRT Report Designer. Part IV includes the following chapters:

- *Chapter 8, Laying Out a Report.* A report developer places and arranges report data on a page to determine how report users view the information. This chapter provides an overview of the layout model and describes the report elements that BIRT Report Designer provides for organizing and displaying data. This chapter also describes techniques for creating report sections and placing report elements.

- *Chapter 9, Displaying Text.* Much of the information in any report is textual. Textual information can be static text or values derived from data set fields. Text can be as short as a single word, or span paragraphs or pages. This chapter describes the different types of textual elements that BIRT Report Designer provides, and how to use each type of element.

- *Chapter 10, Formatting Report Content.* Formatting different types of data within a report improves the clarity and visual appeal of the report. This chapter describes many formatting techniques, including how to change the display of dates, numbers, or currency values, format report elements based on conditions, and adjust the spacing between report elements.

- *Chapter 11, Sorting and Grouping Data.* Almost all reports require that a report developer structure the data that comes into the report. Grouping and sorting are two ways of structuring data to ensure that the critical relationships among various pieces of information in a report are apparent to the report user. For example, a report developer can use grouping and sorting with sales data to organize the data by region, then by office, and finally by sales representatives. This chapter also includes a tutorial.

- *Chapter 12, Aggregating Data.* One of the key features of any report is the ability to display summary, or aggregate, information. For example, a sales report can show the overall sales total, sales subtotals by product type, region, or sales representative, average sales amount, or the highest or lowest sales amounts. This chapter describes the common types of aggregate calculations, and explains how to write aggregate expressions and where to place them in a report.

- *Chapter 13, Writing Expressions.* To obtain the necessary data for a report, it is often necessary to use expressions to manipulate the raw data that comes from a data source. This chapter explains how to write JavaScript expressions and provides many examples of manipulating data, including how to convert numbers to strings, combine values from multiple data set fields, search and replace string values, get parts of a string, and calculate the time between two dates.

- *Chapter 14, Filtering Data.* Often the data from a data set includes information that is not relevant in a particular report. To exclude this extraneous information from the report, a report developer filters the data to use only the data that pertains to the report. This chapter discusses how to use BIRT Report Designer to filter data and how to enable filtering in the external data set.

- *Chapter 15, Enabling the User to Filter Data.* A report developer can use parameters to enable report users to determine which part of the data they see in the report. For example, in a report of nationwide sales figures, filtering can be used to display the data for a user-specified region. This chapter shows how to set up a report that enables a user to specify parameter values to determine what data appears in a report. This chapter also shows how to design report parameters to improve their usability and presentation.

- *Chapter 16, Building a Report That Contains Subreports.* This chapter provides examples of building and organizing subreports in a report. This chapter also includes a tutorial that provides an example of a master-detail report. This tutorial illustrates and reviews many of the topics from earlier chapters. A reader can complete the tutorial and practice applying the basic principles to build a more complex report that includes both side-by-side subreports and data set parameters.

- *Chapter 17, Using a Chart.* The graphical presentation of summary data is another way of improving the effectiveness of a report. A chart can serve as a report in itself or provide a synopsis of more complex data that appears in a report. Charts often provide an additional view of the data, highlighting or extending the information that appears in a report. This chapter introduces the types of charts that a developer can create and discusses the steps that are required to add a chart to a report. The chapter includes a tutorial that introduces a reader to the chart features.

- *Chapter 18, Displaying Data in Charts.* Setting up chart data differs somewhat from selecting typical report data and requires some specific knowledge about how to process data to produce effective charts. To modify which data appears and the arrangement of the data in the chart, you must use series, grouping, and axis settings. This chapter discusses how to link data to a chart, use the chart builder to filter data, plot the data by defining *x*- and *y*-axes, and sort and group data. You also learn how to create a combination chart and a meter chart.

- *Chapter 19, Laying Out and Formatting a Chart.* Like chart data, the steps to lay out and format a chart are distinct from the layout and formatting options for a typical report. This chapter explains how to work with the visual elements of a chart to produce the desired appearance. The tasks include positioning elements in the chart area, adding and formatting titles and labels, and changing the style of the series elements available in each chart type.

- *Chapter 20, Presenting Data in a Cross Tab.* A cross tab is ideal for presenting summary data in a compact row-and-column matrix that looks similar to a spreadsheet. This chapter explains how to prepare data for a cross tab and how to build a cross tab. The chapter also includes a tutorial that provides an example of building and formatting a cross tab.

- *Chapter 21, Presenting Different Views of the Same Data.* A report is often more effective when it presents key data in both graphical and textual formats. This chapter explains how report elements can share and display the same data, and provides examples for building dashboard reports.

Part V, Enhancing Reports

Part V discusses features you can add to a report to improve usability and increase productivity when working with suites of reports. Part V includes the following chapters:

- *Chapter 22, Designing a Multipage Report.* Most reports display on multiple pages. Often, report developers want to specify where page breaks occur and they want to display information, such as page numbers and report titles, on every page. This chapter explains how to control pagination in a report and how to design a page layout.

- *Chapter 23, Adding Interactive Viewing Features.* To make a report more useful, you can add interactive features, such as hyperlinks or bookmarks. This chapter describes how to create and use bookmarks and tables of contents. It also describes how to add interactive features, such as highlighting and tooltips, to charts.

- *Chapter 24, Building a Shared Development Framework.* To support a consistent appearance for a suite of reports, BIRT provides two ways to share the report development among designers. A report library contains standard report elements, such as data sources, a company logo, or a set of styles. A report template combines report elements from libraries or the BIRT palettes to provide a predefined layout and master page. Report developers who use these tools increase their productivity.

- *Chapter 25, Localizing Text.* To support international data or produce reports that can be viewed in multiple locales or languages requires planning and an understanding of the issues that are associated with working with resource files. This chapter provides an overview of the localization process and procedures for localizing text in a report.

Glossary contains definitions of terms that are useful to understanding all parts of the book.

Typographical conventions

Table P-1 describes the typographical conventions that are used in this book.

Table P-1   Typographical conventions

Item	Convention	Example
Code examples	Monospace font	`String Name = "M. Barajas";`
File names	Initial capital letter, except where file names are case-sensitive	SimpleReport.rptdesign
Key combination	A + sign between keys means to press both keys at the same time	Ctrl+Shift
Menu items	Capitalized, no bold	File
Submenu items	Separated from the main menu item with a small arrow	File➤New
User input	Monospace font	`2011`

Acknowledgments

John Arthorne and Chris Laffra observed, "It takes a village to write a book on Eclipse." In the case of the BIRT books, it continues to take a virtual village in four countries to create these two books. Our contributors, reviewers, Addison-Wesley editorial, marketing, and production staff, printers, and proofreaders are collaborating by every electronic means currently available to produce the major revisions to these two books. In addition, we want to acknowledge the worldwide community of over one millions Java programmers using BIRT and the individuals who have completed over ten million downloads of the multiple versions of the software. Their enthusiastic reception to the software creates an opportunity for us to write about it.

We want to thank Greg Doench, our acquisitions editor, who asked us to write a book about BIRT and has been supportive and enthusiastic about our success. Of course, we want to acknowledge the staff at Addison-Wesley who worked on the first edition and this revision. In particular, we would like to acknowledge John Fuller, Michelle Housley, Anne Jones, Mary Kate Murray, Julie Nahil, Stephane Nakib, Elizabeth Ryan, Sandra Schroeder, Beth Wickenhiser, and Lara Wysong. We also want to thank Mike Milinkovich at the Eclipse Foundation and Mark Coggins at Actuate Corporation for continuing to provide the forewords for the books.

We particularly want to acknowledge the many, many managers, designers, and programmers too numerous to name who have worked diligently to produce, milestone by milestone, the significant upgrades to BIRT, giving us a reason for these two books. You know who you are and know how much we value your efforts. The following engineers have been of particular assistance to the authors: Linda Chan, Hank Christensen, Yasuo Doshiro, Wenbin He, Rima Kanguri, Nina Li, Wenfeng Li, Yu Li, Zhiqiang Qian, Pierre Tessier, Mingxia Wu, Gary Xue, Jun Zhai, and Lin Zhu. In addition, we want to acknowledge the support and significant contribution that was provided by Paul Rogers. Dan Melcher's and Daniel O'Connell's insights into the techniques for building reusable components can be applied to building internationalized reports. Working examples demonstrating these techniques are to be found at:

http://reusablereporting.blogspot.com/

Creating this book would not have been possible without the constant support of the members of the extended Developer Communications team at Actuate Corporation. Many of them and their families sacrificed long personal hours to take on additional tasks so that members of the team of authors could create this material. In particular, we wish to express our appreciation to other writers who contributed original material to these books. Terry Ryan pulled together the terminology in the glossary that accompanies each of the books. Kris Hahn assisted the writers by replacing screenshots and reworking content under direction. In addition, Frances Buran, Bruce Gardner, Mike Hovermale, C. J. Walter-Hague, and Forest White all contributed to the success of the books.

Actuate's active student intern program under the Executive Sponsorship of Dan Gaudreau, Chief Financial Officer, made it possible for Daniel Heinrich, Maziar Jamalian, Tori Marroquin, Gene Sher, and James Turner to support the projects in Developer Communications.

Installing BIRT

1

Introducing BIRT Report Designers

There are two designer applications that you can use to create BIRT reports:

- BIRT Report Designer
  A tool that a report developer uses to build a BIRT report design and preview a report. BIRT Report Designer is a set of Eclipse plug-ins that includes BIRT Report Engine, BIRT Chart Engine, and BIRT Demo Database. This tool supports Java and JavaScript customization. BIRT Report Designer requires multiple Eclipse platform components and a Java Development Kit (JDK).

- BIRT RCP Report Designer
  A simplified tool that a novice report developer uses to build a BIRT report design and preview a report. BIRT RCP (Rich Client Platform) Report Designer includes BIRT Report Engine, BIRT Chart Engine, and BIRT Demo Database without the additional overhead of the full Eclipse platform. This tool supports JavaScript customization, but does not support Java customization or debugging.

Understanding BIRT components

BIRT Report Designer 2.6 consists of the following components:

- Eclipse Software Development Kit (SDK) 3.6
  The SDK is a framework that supports the development of plug-ins and extensions to the Eclipse platform. The SDK includes the core platform, the Java Development Tools (JDT), and the Plug-in Developer Environment (PDE).

- Data Tools Platform (DTP) 1.8.0
  The DTP is a set of development tools used to develop plug-ins that access data sources and retrieve data.

- Eclipse Modeling Framework (EMF) 2.6.0
  The EMF supports the development of BIRT charts. The EMF includes the Service Data Objects (SDO), which is a graph-structured data object that supports applying changes to a graph back to the data source.

- Graphical Editing Framework (GEF) 3.6.0
  The GEF is an Eclipse plug-in that the BIRT Report Designer user interface requires. This framework provides a rich, consistent, graphical editing environment for an application running on the Eclipse Platform.

- Eclipse Web Tools Platform (WTP) 3.2
  The WTP is a set of Eclipse plug-ins that support deploying the BIRT report viewer to an application server. The package includes source and graphical editors, tools, wizards, and APIs that support deploying, running, and testing.

Understanding Eclipse BIRT packages

Eclipse BIRT provides the following packages. These packages do not include the required Java 1.5 JDK.

- Report Designer Full Eclipse Install (All-in-One)
  Contains BIRT and the Eclipse Integrated Development Environment (IDE). This all-in-one installation is the easiest way to install BIRT.

- Report Designer
  Contains only BIRT for installing in an existing Eclipse Integrated Development Environment (IDE).

- RCP Report Designer
  Contains a simplified version of BIRT without the Eclipse IDE.

- Software Development Kit (SDK)
  Contains the source code for the BIRT plug-ins, documents, and examples.

- Report Engine
  Contains the run-time version of BIRT for installing in a J2EE application server.

- Chart Engine
  Contains the stand-alone library that supports embedding a chart in a Java application.

- BIRT Web Tools Integration

Contains the plug-ins required to use the BIRT Web Project Wizard in a Web Tools Project, including the source code.

- BIRT Source Code

  Contains the BIRT source code for a specific build. All source code is in a plug-in format ready to import into a workspace to build BIRT. These plug-ins are the required libraries for a standard BIRT installation. Additional libraries may be necessary. For example, this package does not include the Data Tools Platform (DTP) source code.

- BIRT Samples

  Contains sample reports and charts, plus application examples that use the Chart, Report Engine, and Design Engine APIs.

- BIRT Demo Database

  Contains the package for defining and loading the demonstration database into Apache Derby and MySQL, including SQL and data files. The demonstration database package is a convenient way to install the Classic Models database schema and data in the Apache Derby and MySQL systems. The package does not include any BIRT software. The Report Designer and the RCP Report Designer packages include the demonstration database for Apache Derby.

  The demonstration database supports the following Apache and MySQL versions:

  - Apache Derby version 5.1 or higher

  - MySQL Connector/J version 3.1 or MySQL client version 4.x

About types of BIRT builds

The Eclipse BIRT download site makes several types of builds available for BIRT. The following list describes these builds:

- Release build

  A production build that passes the complete test suite for all components and features. Use the release build to develop applications.

- Milestone build

  A development build that provides access to newly completed features. The build is stable, but it is not production quality. Use this type of build to preview new features and develop future reporting applications that depend on those features.

- Stable build

  A development build that is stable, but passes a reduced test suite. New features are in an intermediate stage of development. Use a stable build to preview new features.

- Nightly build

  The Eclipse BIRT development team builds BIRT every night. As BIRT is an open-source project, these builds are available to anyone. These builds are unlikely to be useful to a report developer.

  If a certain feature that you require does not work in a nightly build, you can provide feedback to the development team by filing a bug report. Later, you can download a new build to confirm that the fix solves the problem that you reported.

2

Installing a BIRT Report Designer

Installing BIRT Report Designer adds a report design perspective to the Eclipse Integrated Development Environment (IDE). To install aBIRT Report Designer, download an archive file from the Eclipse web site and extract it in your existing Eclipse environment. BIRT Report Designer is available for various Linux and Microsoft Windows platforms. The following sections describe how to install BIRT Release 2.6.

Installing BIRT Report Designer Full Eclipse Install

If you are new to Eclipse and BIRT, download and install BIRT Report Designer Full Eclipse Install (All-in-One) package to start developing and designing BIRT reports immediately. This package includes the Eclipse Integrated Development Environment (IDE), BIRT Report Designer, and all other required Eclipse components. You must also download and install Java JDK 1.5.

Complete the following procedure to download this installation package on a Windows or Linux system.

How to install BIRT Report Designer All-in-One

1 Using your browser, navigate to the main BIRT web page at:

    http://www.eclipse.org/birt/phoenix

2 From BIRT Project, choose Download BIRT 2.6.

3 From BIRT Report Downloads, choose All-in-One.

4 On BIRT Report Downloads, select the Download Link that meets your requirements, for example, Windows 64-bit.

Eclipse downloads - mirror selection appears. This page shows all the sites that provide this download file.

5 Choose the download site that is closest to your location.

The BIRT Report Designer all-in-one archive file downloads to your system.

6 Extract the archive file to a hard drive location that you specify.

The extraction creates a directory named eclipse at the location that you specify.

To test the BIRT Report Designer installation, start Eclipse, then start BIRT Report Designer as described in the following procedure. BIRT Report Designer is a perspective within Eclipse.

How to test the BIRT Report Designer installation

1 Start Eclipse.

2 Close the welcome window. In the Eclipse Window menu, choose Open Perspective➤Report Design. If Report Design does not appear in the Open Perspective window, choose Other. A list of perspectives appears. Choose Report Design.

Eclipse displays the BIRT Report Designer perspective.

Installing BIRT RCP Report Designer

BIRT RCP Report Designer is a stand-alone report design application that enables report developers to produce reports in both web and PDF formats. This application uses the Eclipse Rich Client Platform (RCP) to provide a report design environment that is less complex than the full Eclipse platform. If you need the project-based environment that the full Eclipse platform provides, return to the section on installing BIRT Report Designer. BIRT RCP Report Designer runs on Windows only.

To install BIRT RCP Report Designer, download and extract an archive file. The following examples use Release 2.6.

Complete the following procedure to download and install BIRT RCP Report Designer on a Windows system.

How to install BIRT RCP Report Designer

1 Using your browser, navigate to the main BIRT web page at:

`http://www.eclipse.org/birt/phoenix`

2 From BIRT Home, choose Download 2.6.

3 From BIRT Report Downloads, choose RCP Designer.

Eclipse downloads - mirror selection appears. This page shows all the sites that provide this download file.

4 Choose the download site that is closest to your location.

The BIRT RCP Report Designer archive downloads to your system.

5 Extract the archive file to a hard drive location that you specify.

The extraction creates a directory named birt-rcp-report-designer-2_6_0 at the location that you specify.

To test the installation, start BIRT RCP Report Designer as described in the following procedure.

How to test the BIRT RCP Report Designer installation

1 Navigate to the birt-rcp-report-designer-2_6_0 directory.

2 To run BIRT RCP Report Designer, double-click BIRT.exe. BIRT RCP Report Designer appears.

Troubleshooting installation problems

Installing a BIRT report designer is a straightforward task. If you extract the archive file to the appropriate location and the required supporting files are also available in the expected location, your BIRT report designer will work. One of the first steps in troubleshooting an installation problem is confirming that all files are in the correct location.

Verify that the /eclipse/plugins directory contains JAR files whose names begin with org.eclipse.birt, org.eclipse.emf, and org.eclipse.gef. The following sections describe troubleshooting steps that resolve two common installation errors.

Avoiding cache conflicts after you install a BIRT report designer

Eclipse caches information about plug-ins for faster start-up. After you install or upgrade BIRT Report Designer or BIRT RCP Report Designer, using a cached copy of certain pages can lead to errors or missing functionality. The symptoms of this problem include the following conditions:

- The Report Design perspective does not appear in Eclipse.

- You receive a message that an error occurred when you open a report or use the Report Design perspective.

- JDBC drivers that you installed do not appear in the driver manager.

The solution is to remove the cached information. The recommended practice is to start either Eclipse or BIRT RCP Report Designer from the command line with the -clean option.

To start Eclipse, use the following command:

```
eclipse.exe -clean
```

To start BIRT RCP Report Designer, use the following command:

```
BIRT.exe -clean
```

Specifying a Java Virtual Machine when starting BIRT report designer

You can specify which Java Virtual Machine (JVM) to use when you start a BIRT report designer. This specification is important, particularly for users on Linux, when path and permission problems prevent the report designer from locating an appropriate JVM to use. A quick way to overcome such problems is by specifying explicitly which JVM to use when you start the BIRT report designer.

On Windows and Linux systems, you can either start a BIRT report designer from the command line or create a command file or shell script that calls the appropriate executable file with the JVM path. The example in this section uses BIRT Report Designer on a Windows system.

How to specify which JVM to use when you start a BIRT report designer

On the command line, type a command similar to:

```
eclipse.exe -vm $JAVA_HOME/jdk1.5/bin/java.exe
```

Installing a language pack

All BIRT user interface components and messages are internationalized through the use of properties files. BIRT uses English as the default language, but supports other languages by installing a language pack that contains the required properties files. BIRT 2.6 provides one language pack, NLpack1, which supports the following languages:

- French
- German
- Spanish
- Japanese
- Korean
- Simplified Chinese

The following instructions explain how to download and install the language pack for BIRT 2.6 on Windows.

How to download and install a language pack

To download and install a language pack, perform the following steps:

1 Using your browser, navigate to the BIRT language pack web page at:

   `http://www.eclipse.org/babel/downloads.php`

2 From Babel Language Packs for Galileo, download the language pack for the product that you need.

3 Extract the language pack archive file into the directory above the Eclipse directory.

   For example, if C:/eclipse is your Eclipse directory, extract the language pack into C:/.

4 Start Eclipse and choose Window➤Preferences➤Report Design➤Preview.

5 Select the language of choice from the drop-down list in Choose your locale.

6 Restart Eclipse.

If Windows is not running under the locale you need for BIRT, start Eclipse using the -nl <locale> command line option, where <locale> is a standard Java locale code, such as es_ES for Spanish as spoken in Spain. A list of locale codes is available at the following URL:

`http://www.oracle.com/technetwork/java/javase/locales-137662.html`

Eclipse remembers the locale you specify on the command line. On subsequent launches of Eclipse, the locale is set to the most recent locale setting. To revert to a previous locale, launch Eclipse using the -nl command line option for the locale to which you want to revert.

Updating a BIRT Report Designer installation

Because BIRT Report Designer is a Java-based application, updating an installation typically requires replacing the relevant files. Eclipse supports the update process for BIRT Report Designer by providing the Update Manager. BIRT RCP Report Designer is a stand-alone product, so you must replace the existing version with a newer version.

This section describes the steps required to update the following BIRT packages:

- Report Designer
- RCP Report Designer

You can use the Eclipse Update Manager to find and install newer major releases of BIRT Report Designer.

How to update a BIRT Report Designer installation using the Update Manager

1 In Eclipse, choose Help→Check for Updates.

2 In Available Updates, choose Select All then choose Next.

3 In Update Details, choose Next.

4 In Review Licenses, accept the license agreement terms and choose Finish.

5 When the update completes, restart your computer.

How to update BIRT Report Designer manually

1 Back up the workspace directory if it is in the eclipse directory structure.

2 To remove the BIRT files, use one of the following techniques:

- To prepare for a new all-in-one installation, remove the entire eclipse directory.

- To prepare for only a BIRT Report Designer installation, remove only the BIRT components.

    1 Navigate to the eclipse\features directory.

    2 Delete all JAR files and subdirectories with birt in their names.

    3 Navigate to the eclipse\plugins directory.

    4 Delete all JAR files and subdirectories with birt in their names.

3 Download and install BIRT Report Designer as described earlier in this book.

4 Restore the workspace directory, if necessary.

5 Restart BIRT Report Designer with the -clean option:

```
eclipse.exe -clean
```

Updating BIRT RCP Report Designer installation

Unlike BIRT Report Designer, BIRT RCP Report Designer is a stand-alone application. To update this application, you delete the entire application and reinstall a newer version. If you created your report designs and resources in the birt-rcp-report-designer-<version> directory structure, you must back up your workspace directory and any resources that you want to keep before you delete BIRT RCP Report Designer. After you install a newer version of the application, you can copy your files back to the application directory structure.

As a best practice, do not keep your workspace in the birt-rcp-report-designer-<version> directory structure. Keeping your workspace in a different location enables you to update your installation more easily in the future.

How to update BIRT RCP Report Designer

1 Back up the workspace directory and any other directories that contain report designs, libraries, and other resources, if they are in the birt-rcp-report-designer-<version> directory structure.

2 Delete the birt-rcp-report-designer-<version> directory.

3 Download and install BIRT RCP Report Designer as described earlier in this book.

4 Restore the directories that you backed up in step 1, if necessary.

5 Restart BIRT RCP Report Designer with the -clean option:

```
BIRT.exe -clean
```

Getting Started

Learning the Basics

This chapter provides an overview of the report design process and environment. The chapter also includes step-by-step procedures for building your first report.

About BIRT reports

A BIRT report is a structured document that displays data from an external information system, such as a database or application. Data in the report is organized and formatted so that it is meaningful and useful to the person who reads the report. A BIRT report is not a document that you type, like an essay or research paper, although you could use BIRT Report Designer to create such documents.

Using BIRT Report Designer, you can create operational reports, such as a bill of materials, a purchase order, or an invoice. You can also create reports that provide real-time information about business performance, such as the number of calls handled by your customer service organization, the number of problems handled, categorized by levels of complexity, and the number of repeat calls made by the same customer. You can use BIRT to create client-facing reports, such as account statements and transaction details. Any time that you need to gather, analyze, summarize, and present data from an information system, a report is the solution.

Overview of the report design process

Designing a report involves the following tasks. You do not have to perform all the tasks in the order in which they are presented here, but if you are new to BIRT Report Designer or learning how to design reports, you can use the following task list as a starting point:

- Plan the report.
- Start a new report design.
- Specify the data to use.
- Lay out the report.
- Format the report.
- Design a master page.
- Preview and test the report.

For those who do not have report development expertise, it is important to understand that the process of creating a report is iterative rather than linear. You typically perform each task multiple times and in different orders. You might specify the data to use, lay out data, preview the report, then modify the data set, change the layout, preview the report again, and so on, until you are satisfied with the report's contents and appearance.

Planning the report

Before creating a report, identify the information that you want the report to provide and decide how to present that information. It is important to think through these details, then draw a mock-up on paper, which you use to get feedback from your report users. Most people cannot visualize what a report could be without a paper and pencil sketch. Planning saves time in the long run because you do not waste time creating a polished report that contains the wrong information or layout. More frequently, you discover in this review process that the customer wants much more and can now articulate those requirements more successfully.

Starting a new report design

If you are using BIRT Report Designer, start Eclipse, and create a new project, if you have not already done so. Eclipse requires that all files are organized in a project. No project is required if you are using BIRT Rich Client Platform (RCP) Report Designer. After you create the project, create a new report using one of the following techniques:

- Start with a report template.
- Start with a blank report.

Specifying the data to use

A report can access data from a wide variety of sources, including databases, text files, XML documents, and web services. To set up the report to access data, complete the following tasks in this order:

- In BIRT Report Designer, choose the type of data source.

- Specify how to connect to the data source.

- Create a data set that identifies the data to extract from the data source.

Laying out the report

There are many ways to present information in a report. Different users have different expectations about how to visualize the data, and different types of layouts work better for different types of data. A report can display information in a tabular list, a cross tab, a series of paragraphs, a pie chart, a bar chart, a hierarchical list, or a series of subreports. These different layouts can be combined and customized. Laying out a report entails placing data on the page and organizing it in a way that helps the report user to grasp and analyze the information.

Formatting the report content

After laying out data in a report, format the report to give it a professional and polished appearance. Typical formatting tasks include highlighting certain data, applying styles to data, adjusting the spacing between rows of data, and conditionally hiding sections. You can also apply conditional formatting to data. One basic example is to display numbers in different colors depending on their values. Highlighting data makes the report more accessible to users. Key information stands out in the report, and users can absorb the information in layers.

Designing a master page

When you create a new report, BIRT Report Designer uses a default master page. The master page specifies default values for page size, orientation, and margins. It also defines a default page header and footer, where you can display page numbers or the date. You can modify the master page to design a custom page layout.

Previewing and testing the report

You should preview and test the report as you design it. The most important item to test is your data set. Verify that the data retrieved from the data source is what you expect before you start laying out the report. As you lay out and format the report, check the report output throughout the design process. If you add code, test and debug it as you go.

About the report design environment

BIRT Report Designer provides a flexible environment that meets the needs of both beginning report developers and experienced report developers who want the power of programming. It provides the following features:

- Report templates that include instructions to help new report developers get started quickly

- Customizable views that enable report developers to tailor the environment to their style of working

- User-friendly tools for designing, debugging, and previewing reports

- Sample reports that demonstrate how to use various product features

- Accessibility features, such as access to all report design functionality from the keyboard instead of the mouse

This section introduces the report design environment. If you are using BIRT Report Designer for the first time, reviewing the topics in this section can help you learn how to use BIRT Report Designer more effectively.

Procedures in this book apply to both BIRT Report Designer and BIRT RCP Report Designer unless the instructions explicitly state which platform to use. Both platforms provide the same reporting functionality. BIRT Report Designer appears within the Eclipse Workbench and therefore requires the installation of Eclipse. BIRT RCP Report Designer does not require all the Eclipse-specific tools because it is designed for report developers who want only the reporting functionality.

Starting BIRT Report Designer

The steps you take to start BIRT Report Designer depend on whether you are using BIRT Report Designer or BIRT RCP Report Designer. To start the designer, follow the instructions that are appropriate to the designer that you use.

How to start BIRT Report Designer

1 Start Eclipse by navigating to the Eclipse directory and performing one of the following tasks:

- If you are using a Microsoft Windows system, run eclipse.exe.

- If you are using a UNIX or Linux system, run eclipse.

2 In Workspace Launcher, shown in Figure 3-1, specify a workspace in which to store your report projects.

- To create a workspace in the default location, choose OK.

- To specify a different location, choose Browse to select a different folder, then choose OK.

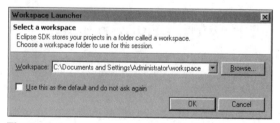

Figure 3-1   Workspace Launcher

3 From the main menu of Eclipse Workbench, choose Window→Open Perspective→Other→Report Design to start BIRT Report Designer. The application window displays the Report Design perspective, as shown in Figure 3-2.

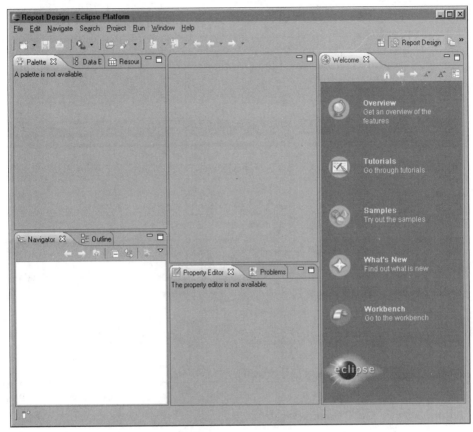

Figure 3-2   BIRT Report Designer

The Report Design perspective shows all the tools, which Eclipse calls views, for creating and managing reports. A perspective is an Eclipse mechanism for organizing the initial set and layout of views in the application window.

If you are new to the Eclipse environment, read the Eclipse online documentation at http://www.eclipse.org/documentation for information about perspectives, views, and other Eclipse user interface topics.

How to start BIRT RCP Report Designer

Start the Report Designer by navigating to the BIRT RCP Report Designer directory then running BIRT.exe. This application appears similar to BIRT Report Designer. BIRT RCP Report Designer, however, does not show the Navigator view and does not include menu items that provide access to Eclipse-specific tools.

Report design views

The BIRT Report Designer views provide tools that you use to build and customize a BIRT report design, preview the report, and debug the report. Figure 3-3 shows the views that open by default in the Report Design perspective.

Each view is a window you can close, resize, minimize, or maximize. You can also move each view to a different location, either inside or outside the application window. Change or rearrange the set of views to fit the way you work or to fit in the available screen space.

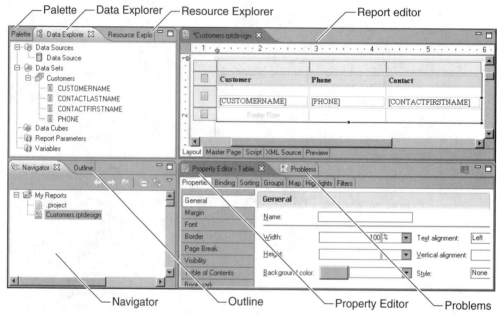

Figure 3-3   BIRT Report Designer views

Report editor

This window is where you design and preview your report. You can open multiple reports in the report editor. The report editor has five pages, which you access by choosing the tabs at the bottom of the report editor. The pages are

- Layout editor, where you create and edit your report design. Figure 3-3 shows the layout editor.

- Master Page, which shows items, such as the date and page number, that appear on every page.

- Script editor, where you add JavaScript code to your report. You can create many reports without programming. Typically, you write code only if you want to change the way in which BIRT generates a report.

- XML Source, which shows the XML content that BIRT Report Designer generates when you create a report.

- Previewer, which runs your report and displays the output.

Palette

The palette shows all the elements that you can use in a report to organize and display data. To lay out a report, you can drag elements from the palette and drop them in the report page in the layout editor.

Data Explorer

Data Explorer shows the data sources, data sets, and report parameters that your report uses. Use Data Explorer to create, edit, or delete these items. You can also use Data Explorer to add data set fields to your report.

Resource Explorer

Resource Explorer shows the shared resources available to your reports. Resources can include images, style sheets, and libraries. A library is a collection of report elements that can be used by more than one report. Use Resource Explorer to view the resources you can use in a report or to insert report elements from a library in a report.

Property Editor

Property Editor displays the properties of the report element currently selected in the layout editor. It organizes properties by functional categories. Use it to apply style or format settings to the contents of your report.

Navigator

Navigator shows all your projects and the reports within each project. Use it to manage your report files. Each project is a directory in the file system. Using Navigator, you can open files, delete files, rename files, or move files from one project to another. If you add files to a project directory through the file system, for example, through Windows Explorer, you need to refresh the project in Navigator to update the list of reports.

BIRT RCP Report Designer does not organize report files in projects. Therefore, it does not include a Navigator view.

Outline

Outline shows the structure of your report as a tree view. It shows the hierarchy of elements in a format that is similar to the outline view of a Microsoft Word or PowerPoint document. You expand or collapse parts of the report by choosing the plus (+) or minus (–) signs. Outline also shows all the resources that are used by or defined in a report, including data sources, data sets, libraries, and styles. You can select items in Outline to edit, delete, rename, or copy them.

Problems

Problems displays messages about errors in the report designs in the current project. It describes the error, says which report file contains the error, provides the location of the file, and indicates the line numbers in which the error occurs.

Tutorial 1: Building a simple listing report

This section provides step-by-step instructions for building a report that lists customer names, phone numbers, and contact names. The report uses data from the sample database that is supplied with BIRT Report Designer, Classic Models. Figure 3-4 shows a portion of the finished report.

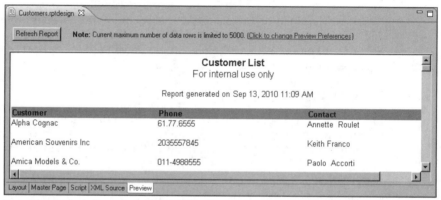

Figure 3-4   Report listing customer names, phone numbers, and contacts

In this tutorial, you perform the following tasks:

- Create a new project. If you are using BIRT RCP Report Designer, you do not complete this step.

- Create a new report.

- Build a data source.

- Build a data set.

- Lay out the report to display each row of the data set.

- Sort the data.

- Format the report to enhance its appearance.

- Create a report title.

Task 1: Create a new project

Eclipse organizes files by projects. You can create one project to organize all your reports or create multiple projects to organize your reports by categories. For each project that you create, Eclipse creates a directory in your file system.

If you are using BIRT RCP Report Designer, this task does not apply to you.

1 Choose File→New→Project. New Project, which appears in Figure 3-5, displays the types of projects that you can create.

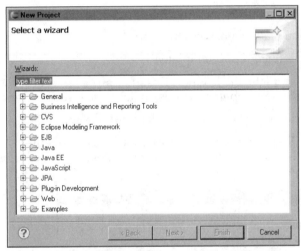

Figure 3-5   New Project

2 Expand Business Intelligence and Reporting Tools, select Report Project, then choose Next.

3 In New Report Project, in Project name, type the following text, as shown in Figure 3-6:

My Reports

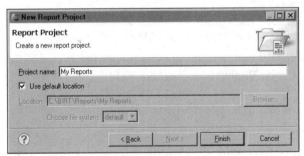

Figure 3-6   New Report Project

4 To add the project, choose Finish. You can now see the project in the Navigator view, as shown in Figure 3-7.

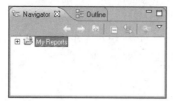

Figure 3-7   A project in the Navigator view

Task 2: Create a new report

You can create a report in the following ways:

- Start with a blank report design.

- Use a predefined report template.

  For each template, BIRT Report Designer provides a cheat sheet, which contains step-by-step instructions, to help you create the report.

For this tutorial, you start with a blank report design.

1 Choose File➔New➔Report. New Report appears. Figure 3-8 shows the window that appears in BIRT Report Designer. New Report is slightly different in BIRT RCP Report Designer.

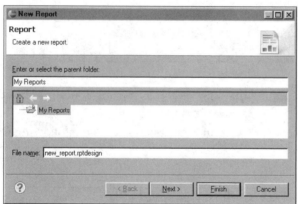

Figure 3-8   New Report in BIRT Report Designer

2 In BIRT Report Designer, in the tree view of the available folders, select the project that you created. This step applies only to BIRT Report Designer users.

3 Type the following text as the file name:

`Customers.rptdesign`

4 Choose Next. New Report provides options for starting with a blank report and several report templates, as shown in Figure 3-9.

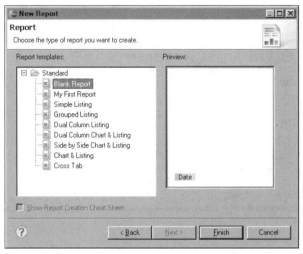

Figure 3-9   Report templates in New Report

5 Select Blank Report, then choose Finish. Your new report appears in the main window. This window displays the layout editor, as shown in Figure 3-10. The layout editor shows an empty report page.

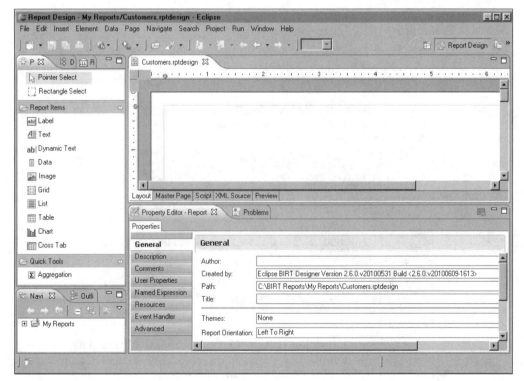

Figure 3-10   Blank report design

The remainder of this tutorial provides the detailed steps for creating the customer report.

Task 3: Build a data source

Before you begin designing your report in the layout editor, you build a BIRT data source to connect your report to a database or other type of data source. When you build a data source, you specify the driver class, data source name, and other connection information that is specific to the type of data source. For this tutorial, you use the sample database, Classic Models, that is already configured for use with BIRT Report Designer. You do not need to specify the connection information for this sample database.

1 Choose Data Explorer. If you use the default report design perspective, Data Explorer is to the left of the layout editor, next to Palette, as shown in Figure 3-11. If Data Explorer is not open, choose Window→Show View→Data Explorer.

Figure 3-11 Data Explorer

2 Right-click Data Sources, then choose New Data Source from the context menu. New Data Source displays the types of data sources you can create, as shown in Figure 3-12.

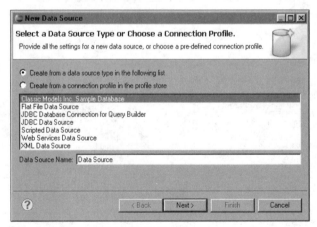

Figure 3-12 New Data Source

3 Select Classic Models Inc. Sample Database from the list of data source types. Use the default data source name, then choose Next. Connection information about the new data source appears.

4 Choose Finish. BIRT Report Designer creates a new data source that connects to the sample database. It appears within Data Sources in Data Explorer, shown in Figure 3-13.

Figure 3-13 Data Sources in Data Explorer

Task 4: Build a data set

Now, you are ready to build your data set. A data set identifies the data to retrieve from the data source. If your report connects to a JDBC data source, such as the sample database, you use a SQL SELECT statement to specify the data to retrieve.

1 In Data Explorer, right-click Data Sets, and choose New Data Set from the context menu.

2 In New Data Set, in Data Set Name, type the following text, as shown in Figure 3-14:

Customers

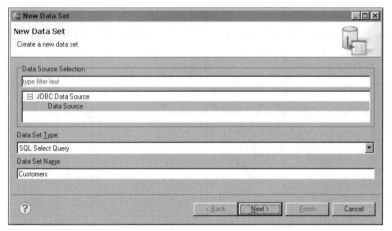

Figure 3-14 New Data Set

3 Use the default values for the other fields.

  ■ Data Source Selection shows the type and name of the data source that you created earlier.

  ■ Data Set Type indicates that the data set uses a SQL SELECT query.

4 Choose Next.

The Query page displays information to help you create a SQL query. Available Items lists all the schemas in the data source, including CLASSICMODELS, which you use for this tutorial and other reports you want to create with the sample database. You can click the plus (+) sign next to CLASSICMODELS to display the tables. The text area on the right side of this dialog shows the following required keywords of a SQL SELECT statement:

```
select
from
```

5 In the text area, type the following SQL SELECT statement to specify the data to retrieve:

```
select customerName,
contactLastName,
contactFirstName,
phone
from Customers
```

Although the data set editor shows table and column names in uppercase letters, you can type these names in the case you prefer because SQL is not case-sensitive. If you do not want to type the query, you can drag columns and tables from Available Items to the text area.

The SELECT statement that you created, which is shown in Figure 3-15, gets values from the CUSTOMERNAME, CONTACTLASTNAME, CONTACTFIRSTNAME, and PHONE columns in the CUSTOMERS table.

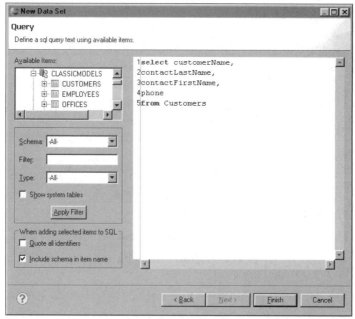

Figure 3-15   SQL SELECT statement in Edit Data Set

6 Choose Finish to save the data set. If you typed the query correctly, Edit Data Set appears. If you made a mistake, an error message appears before Edit Data Set opens. Edit Data Set displays the columns you specified in the query, and provides options for editing the data set.

7 Choose Preview Results to make sure the query is valid and that it returns the correct data. Figure 3-16 shows some of the data rows that the query returns.

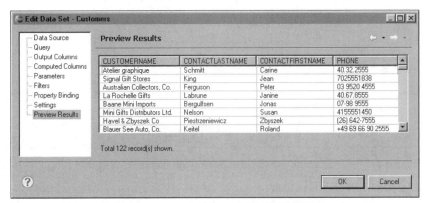

Figure 3-16   Data rows returned by a SQL SELECT statement

8 Choose OK.

Task 5: Lay out the report

In this procedure, you insert elements in the report page to display the data from the data set that you created previously. You start by inserting a table element, then you insert data elements in the table. It is important to understand the functionality that the table provides. The table:

- Iterates through all the data rows that a data set returns

- Enables you to lay out data easily in a row and column format

1 Choose Palette. The palette displays all the elements that you can place in a report.

2 Drag a table element from the palette, and drop it in the report in the layout editor. Insert Table prompts you to specify the number of columns and detail rows to create for the table. The dialog also prompts you to select a data set to bind with the table.

3 In Insert Table, specify the following values:

- In Number of columns, type 3.

- In Number of details, type 1.

- In Data Set, select Customers from the drop-down list.

Choose OK. A table appears in the layout editor.

4 Choose Data Explorer.

5 In Data Explorer, expand Data Sets, then expand Customers. The columns that you specified in the query appear below Customers.

6 Drag CUSTOMERNAME from Data Explorer, and drop it in the first cell in the table's detail row, as shown in Figure 3-17. The detail row displays the main data in the report. In the generated report, the detail row repeats to display all the data rows from the data set.

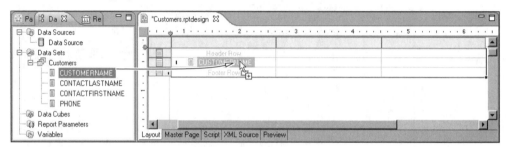

Figure 3-17   Dragging a column from Data Explorer and dropping it in a table cell

In the layout editor, the table cell in which you dropped the CUSTOMERNAME field contains a data element that displays [CUSTOMERNAME]. Above this data element is a label element that the layout editor automatically added to the header row. This label displays the field name as static text. It serves as the column heading. Figure 3-18 shows the data and label elements.

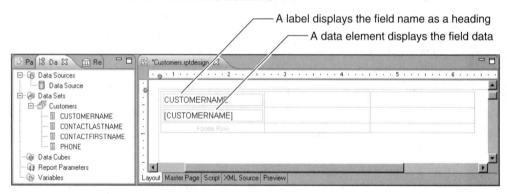

Figure 3-18   Data and label elements in a table

7 Drag PHONE from Data Explorer, and drop it in the second cell in the detail row.

8 Drag CONTACTFIRSTNAME, and drop it in the third cell in the detail row.

9 Drag CONTACTLASTNAME, and drop it in the third cell in the detail row, below CONTACTFIRSTNAME. The report page should look like the one shown in Figure 3-19.

Figure 3-19   Customer and contact information added to a table

10 Choose Preview, the tab at the bottom of the layout editor. BIRT Report Designer generates and displays the report in HTML format, as shown in Figure 3-20. Scroll down to see the entire report.

As Figure 3-20 shows, the data is correct, but it appears in random order. It makes more sense to sort the data alphabetically by customer name. The report's appearance also needs improvement.

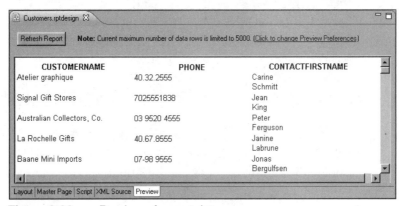

Figure 3-20   Preview of report data

Task 6:   Sort the data

When you first create and preview a report, the report displays the data rows in the order in which the query returns them. The order can vary, depending on many factors, such as how data was supplied in the data source. In most cases, you will want to change the order in which data appears in the report.

1 Choose Layout to return to the layout editor.

2 Open Property Editor, if necessary. If you use the default report design perspective, Property Editor appears below the layout editor. If it is not open, choose Window→Show View→Property Editor.

3 In the layout editor, select the table by selecting the Table tab in the lower left corner, as shown in Figure 3-21. This tab appears when you hover the mouse pointer over the lower left corner of the table.

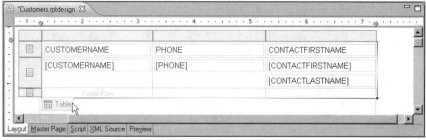

Figure 3-21   Selecting the table

Property Editor displays the properties for the table, as shown in Figure 3-22.

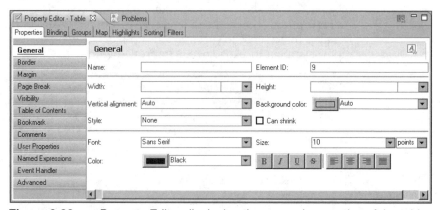

Figure 3-22   Property Editor displaying the general properties of the table

4 Choose the Sorting tab, then choose Add to specify a sort key.

5 In New Sort Key, specify the following values:

- In Key, select CUSTOMERNAME from the drop-down list.

- Use the default values for the other fields.

Figure 3-23 shows the sort definition.

Figure 3-23   Sort definition in New Sort Key

Choose OK. The Sort page displays the defined sort key.

6 Preview the report. The sorted data appears in ascending order by customer name, as shown in Figure 3-24.

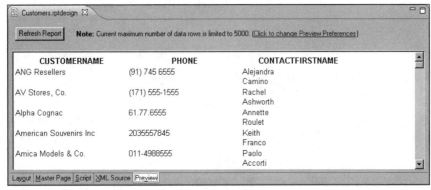

Figure 3-24 Data sorted by customer name

Notice that names with uppercase letters appear at the top of the list. BIRT sorts string data by UCS-2 code point values. In ASCII-based character sets, uppercase letters have lower code point values than lowercase letters. Therefore, uppercase letters appear before lowercase letters.

7 Sort the customer names case-insensitively so that ANG Resellers appears after American Souvenirs Inc., rather than before.

1 Choose Layout to return to the layout editor.

2 In the Sort page, shown in Figure 3-25, select the sort key, then choose Edit.

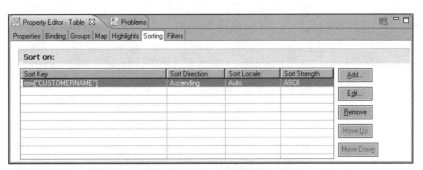

Figure 3-25 Sort key displayed on the Sort page

3 In Edit Sort Key, change the Sort Key expression to the following expression, then choose OK:

```
row["CUSTOMERNAME"].toUpperCase()
```

This expression uses the JavaScript toUpperCase( ) function to convert all the customer name values to uppercase before sorting. JavaScript function names are case-sensitive, so you must type toUpperCase( )

exactly as shown. References to column names are also case-sensitive. In this expression, row["CUSTOMERNAME"] is the correct name to use. If you type row["customername"], for example, BIRT Report Designer displays an error when you run the report. You can verify the capitalization of a column name by looking at the name that is displayed in Data Explorer.

8 Preview the report.

Task 7: Format the report

Now that you verified that the report displays the correct data in the correct order, you can turn your attention to improving the report's appearance. You perform the following tasks in this section:

- Edit the text of the column headings.

- Format the column headings.

- Display the contact first and last names on the same line.

- Increase the space between rows.

Edit the column headings

1 Choose Layout to return to the layout editor.

2 Double-click the first column heading, CUSTOMERNAME. The column heading is in the first row—the header row—of the table.

3 To replace all the highlighted text, start typing, then press Enter when you finish. To edit the text, click once to deselect the text, then position the cursor where you want to add or delete characters.

Replace CUSTOMERNAME with the following text:

Customer

4 Repeat steps 2 and 3 to change the second and third column headings to the following text:

Phone
Contact

The report design should look like the one shown in Figure 3-26.

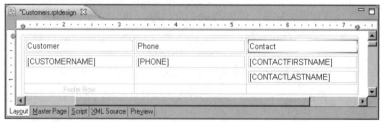

Figure 3-26   Revised column headings in a report design

Format the column headings

To format a report element, set its properties in one of the following two ways:

- Set an element's properties through Property Editor. Use this method to format only the selected element.

- Define a style that contains the desired properties, and apply the style to an element. Use this method to define format properties once and apply them to more than one element.

You might notice that in the report design, the column headings appear in plain text and are left-aligned. The generated HTML report, however, displays the column headings in bold and centered. This discrepancy occurs because BIRT uses the browser's default format for items placed in a table header.

In this procedure, you use the Property Editor to align the column headings to the left, and you define a style to add color to the header row.

1 To format the column headings using Property Editor:

    1 Select all the column headings. To select multiple elements, press and hold the Shift key as you click each element. Property Editor displays the properties for the selected elements, as shown in Figure 3-27.

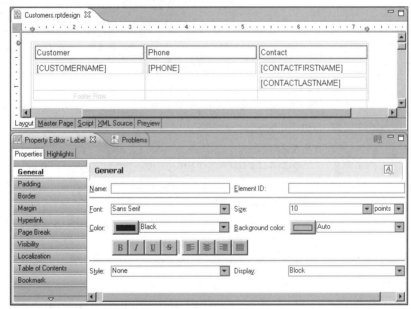

Figure 3-27   Properties for selected elements in Property Editor

    2 Choose the Left button to align the column headings to the left.

    3 Choose the B button to format the column headings as bold text.

4 Deselect the column headings by clicking the white space outside the table.

2 To add a background color to the header row, using a style:

1 From the main menu bar, choose Element➤Style➤New Style.

New Style appears, as shown in Figure 3-28. The left side displays the property categories. The right side displays the properties for the category that you select.

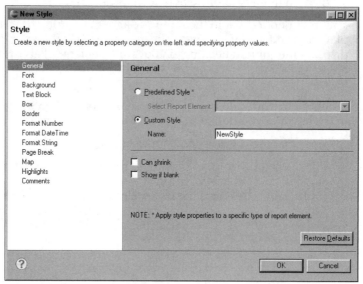

Figure 3-28   New Style

2 For Custom Style, type the following name for the style:

`table_header_row`

3 Choose Background from the list of property categories. New Style displays the background properties that you can set.

4 Specify a color for the Background Color property, using one of the following methods:

❑ Select the button next to the property, then select a color from the color palette that appears.

❑ Select a color from the drop-down list.

Choose OK.

5 In the layout editor, select the table. Selecting the table causes guide cells to appear at the top and left side of the table, as shown in Figure 3-29.

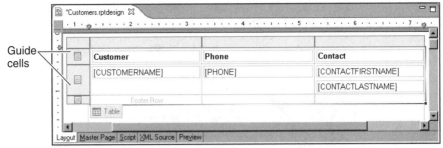

Figure 3-29 Guide cells at the top and left of a table

6 Select the guide cell next to the header row.

7 In Property Editor, choose Properties, then choose General to display the general properties for the row.

8 Apply the style that you just created by selecting table_header_row from the drop-down list next to Style. BIRT Report Designer applies the style to the header row and it appears in color.

3 Preview the report. The report should look like the one shown in Figure 3-30.

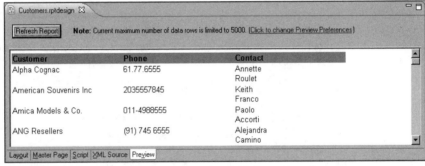

Figure 3-30 Report preview showing header row style

Display first and last names on the same line

When you place multiple elements in a single cell, BIRT Report Designer creates block-level elements. If you are familiar with HTML, you know that each block element starts on a new line. To display multiple elements on the same line, you need to set them as inline elements. Alternatively, you can concatenate the first and last name values to display in a single data element, as described in this procedure.

1 Choose Layout to return to the layout editor.

2 Delete the data element that displays [CONTACTLASTNAME].

3 Double-click the data element that displays [CONTACTFIRSTNAME].

Edit Data Binding, shown in Figure 3-31, shows information about the data associated with the current data element. In Expression, dataSetRow["CONTACTFIRSTNAME"] indicates that the data element displays data from the CONTACTFIRSTNAME field in the data set.

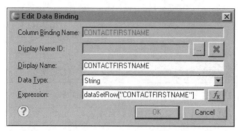

Figure 3-31   Edit Data Binding

 4 Click the expression builder button next to the Expression field.

The expression builder displays the expression in the text area at the top of the window.

5 To concatenate the first and last names, edit the expression as follows:

```
dataSetRow["CONTACTFIRSTNAME"] + " " +
    dataSetRow["CONTACTLASTNAME"]
```

Figure 3-32 shows this expression in the expression builder. The empty quotation marks (" ") add a space between the first name and last name. You can type the expression in the text area or double-click an item in the lower right of the window to insert it in the expression.

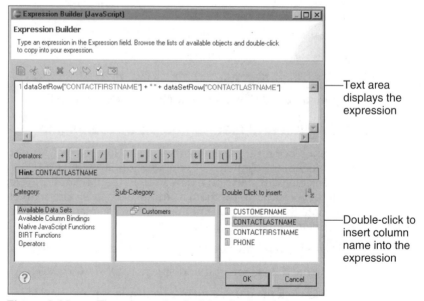

Figure 3-32   The expression builder displaying the expression to concatenate data

6 Choose OK to close the expression builder.

The edited expression appears in Edit Data Binding.

7 Choose OK to save the changes to the data element.

8 Preview the report. The report should look like the one shown in Figure 3-33.

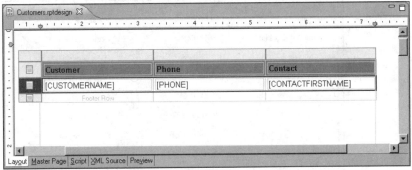

Figure 3-33 Report preview showing concatenated contact names

Increase the space between rows

The default layout adds a minimum space between table rows. Typically, you will want to adjust the spacing between rows.

1 Choose Layout to return to the layout editor.

2 Select the table's detail row, the middle row, as shown in Figure 3-34.

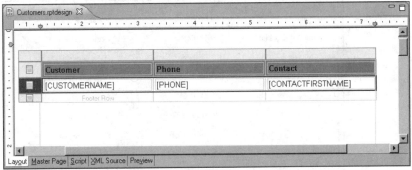

Figure 3-34 Selected table row in the layout editor

Property Editor displays the properties for the row. The title that appears in Property Editor shows the type of element that you select, so you should see Property Editor—Row.

3 In the General properties, set Height to 24 points. The height of the row increases, as shown in Figure 3-35.

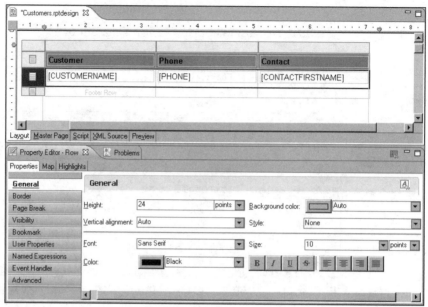

Figure 3-35   Row height set to 24 points

4 Preview the report. The report should look like the one shown in
Figure 3-36. There is more space between the rows of data.

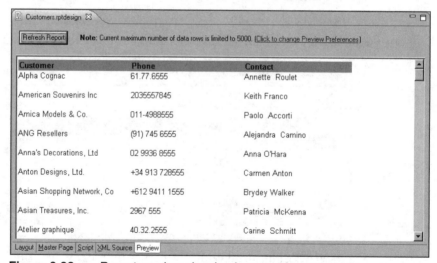

Figure 3-36   Report preview showing increased row spacing

Task 8:   Create a report title

All your report needs now is a title. To display a title, you can use either a
label element, a text element, or a data element. The following list describes
each type of element:

- The label element is suitable for short, static text, such as column headings.

- The data element is suitable for displaying dynamic values from a data set field or a computed field.

- The text element is suitable for multiline text that contains different formatting or dynamic values.

In this procedure, you use a text element and HTML tags to format the text. Note that you are not required to use HTML to create formatted text. If, however, you are well-versed in HTML or web design, you might prefer using HTML to create a block of formatted text.

1 Choose Layout to return to the layout editor.

2 Choose Palette.

3 Drag the text element from the palette, and drop it above the table.

4 In Edit Text Item, select HTML from the drop-down list that displays Auto.

When you select HTML, you can embed HTML tags or CSS properties in the text. You can type the tags or you can insert the commonly used HTML tags that the text editor provides.

5 Specify the following text in the text area, shown in Figure 3-37:

```
<CENTER><B><span style="font-size: larger">
Customer List
</B></span><BR>
<FONT size="small">For internal use only</FONT><BR><BR>
Report generated on <VALUE-OF>new Date()</VALUE-OF>
</CENTER><BR><BR>
```

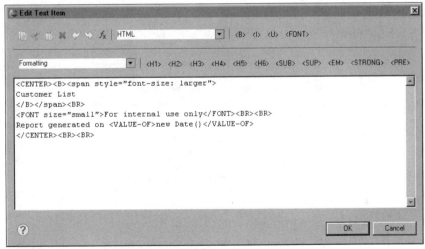

Figure 3-37 Text with HTML tags

6 Choose OK, then preview the report. The report should look like the one shown in Figure 3-38.

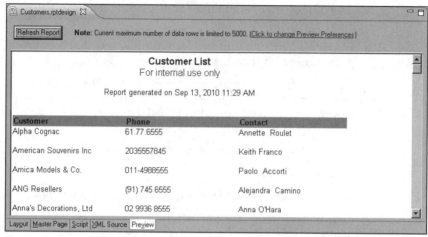

Figure 3-38 Report preview showing formatted report title

As you can see, using the text element with embedded HTML enables you to:

- Use different formatting for each line in a multi-line text block.
- Insert dynamic values, such as the current date.

Alternatively, you can use

- Two label elements to display the first and second lines of static text
- A data element to display the third line that contains the dynamic value

Next steps

You just built your first report and worked with some of the basic tools and features of BIRT Report Designer. There are many more tasks that you can accomplish to build more sophisticated reports. Some of these tasks, described in other chapters of this book, include

- Connecting to your own data source
- Creating charts
- Creating cross tabs
- Creating report parameters for user input
- Building reports that contain subreports
- Formatting report elements based on conditions
- Hiding report elements or sections based on conditions
- Adding hyperlinks to link your report to web locations or to link one report section to another

About report files and supported formats

In the tutorial, you created and formatted a report using graphical tools. This section describes the document model that BIRT Report Designer uses and how you can view the code behind the report. This section also describes how to save and preview a report in formats other than HTML.

Report design files

BIRT Report Designer uses a simple document model. When you create and save a report design, BIRT Report Designer creates just one file with the .rptdesign file-name extension. This file contains all the information that is necessary for generating a report.

Unlike many report design tools that generate files in proprietary formats, BIRT design files are written in XML. XML is a widely used markup language specification that was designed especially for web documents. Because BIRT uses XML to define the structure and contents of a report design, developers can leverage their knowledge of XML to get a deeper understanding of how BIRT constructs a report design. BIRT's suite of report-specific XML elements and properties is called Report Object Model (ROM).

You open a report design (.rptdesign) file with the report editor, which, by default, displays the report design in the layout editor. The layout editor provides a graphical view of the report design. If you wish, you can view the report design in the XML editor. This editor displays the XML that BIRT Report Designer generates when you create a report.

View the report design in the XML editor to see its XML code or to locate, by line number, an error that was reported in the Problems view. To understand the XML code, you can consult the ROM specification at the following location:

`http://www.eclipse.org/birt/phoenix/ref/`

How to open a report design

- If using BIRT Report Designer, use one of the following methods:

  - In Navigator, double-click the .rptdesign file.

  - Choose File➤Open File, then select the .rptdesign file from the file system.

  If someone sends you a .rptdesign file, first save the file in a project folder, then, in Navigator, right-click the project, and choose Refresh. This action updates the project folder to include the file, which you then open using one of these two methods.

- If using BIRT RCP Report Designer, choose File➤Open File, then select the .rptdesign file from the file system.

Eclipse saves your environment settings when you exit. If you keep a file open when you exit Eclipse, this file opens when you next start Eclipse.

How to view a report design in the XML editor

1 Open the report design file, using one of the procedures that is described in the previous section.

The layout editor displays the graphical view of the report, as shown in Figure 3-39.

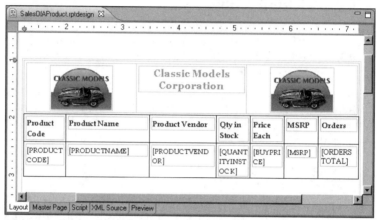

Figure 3-39   Report design in the layout editor

2 Choose the XML Source tab at the bottom of the report editor.

The XML editor displays the XML that defines the report design, as shown in Figure 3-40.

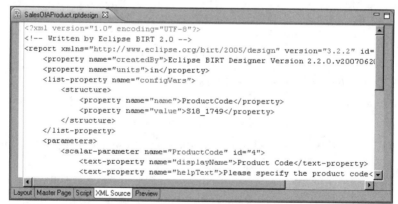

Figure 3-40   XML code for a report design

Report output formats

You can save and view a report in the following formats:

- HTML
- Microsoft Excel document (.xls)
- Microsoft PowerPoint document (.ppt)
- Microsoft Word document (.doc)
- PDF
- Postscript

In addition, users who receive reports can export the data to any of these common office software formats, then edit and redistribute the reports to other users.

Previewing a report

As you work on the design of a report, you typically want to see the report as it would appear to the report user. Using BIRT, you can easily preview a report in any of the supported output formats. You can also view the report in the BIRT report viewer. The report viewer, shown in Figure 3-41, is an interactive viewer that provides report users with the capability to jump to specific pages or to specific sections of a report, to run a report to get the latest data, to print a report, and to export a report to any of the supported output formats.

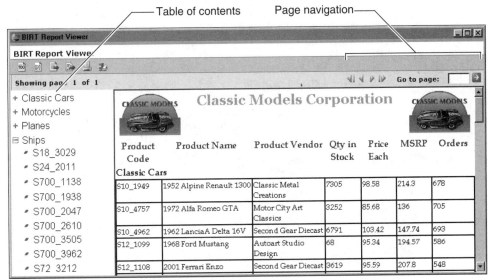

Figure 3-41   BIRT Report Viewer

The following list describes the ways to preview a report:

- To preview a report in BIRT Report Designer, choose the Preview tab at the bottom of the layout editor. The previewer displays the report in HTML format.

- To preview a report in the report viewer, choose Run→View Report→In Web Viewer.

- To preview a report as a Microsoft Word document, choose Run→View Report→As DOC.

- To preview a report in HTML format in a separate window, choose Run→View Report→As HTML.

- To preview a report in PDF format, choose Run→View Report→As PDF.

- To save a report as a PostScript file, choose Run→View Report→As POSTSCRIPT.

- To preview a report as a Microsoft PowerPoint document, choose Run→View Report→As PPT.

- To preview a report as a Microsoft Excel document, choose Run→View Report→As XLS.

Viewing sample reports

BIRT Report Designer includes many sample reports that you can open to review how various product features are implemented. These sample reports access data from the sample database, Classic Models, that ships with BIRT Report Designer, so you can run the reports and view them with actual data. The sample reports are grouped by feature and common report types, and they are accessible through two views called Chart Examples and Report Examples.

How to access the sample reports

1 Choose Window→Show View→Other.

2 In Show View, expand Report and Chart Design. The Chart Examples and Report Examples views appear in the list, as shown in Figure 3-42.

Figure 3-42   Show View displaying items under Report and Chart Design

3 Select the view you want to open. To open both views, select both Chart Examples and Report Examples (press the Shift key as you click each item), then choose OK.

The Chart Examples and Report Examples views appear next to the Property Editor and Problems views.

4 In Chart Examples or Report Examples, expand the categories to view the list of chart or report examples, and select the example you want to see. For example, to view a particular report in Report Examples, select the report design (.rptdesign).

As Figure 3-43 shows, the right side of the Report Examples view displays an image of the selected report's output, and provides a description of the report.

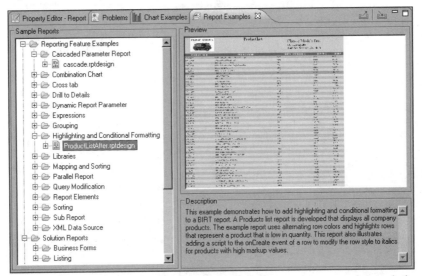

Figure 3-43   Report Examples view displaying an image and description of a selected report

5 Open a sample report in the report editor by selecting one of the icons on the title bar next to the Report Examples tab:

- If you have already created a report project to which you want to save the sample report, choose the icon on the left. Then, in Navigator, refresh the project folder, and open the report from the folder.

- If you have not created any report projects, choose the icon on the right. BIRT creates a project folder, places the report in the folder, and opens the report.

Planning Your Report

The tutorial in the previous chapter demonstrates how easy it is to build a report using BIRT, so it may be puzzling to see a chapter that recommends planning your report development. In practice, planning is an essential task, particularly when addressing more complex reporting requirements.

Planning helps clarify the report requirements and saves time in the long run because you do not waste time creating and fine-tuning a report that does not meet the users' needs. Before creating a report, you should have the following documents:

- A specification that describes the requirements for the report project

- A prototype, or mock-up, of the report

Ideally, these documents should be reviewed and approved by your report users to determine if the proposed layout meets requirements they may not be able to predict without seeing a mock-up on paper.

In organizations with large IT departments that have strong formal processes in place, report developers typically receive requests for new reports that are accompanied by a specification and perhaps a mock-up of the report. Sometimes, report developers discuss report requirements with the person who requested the report, and they develop the specification and mock-up together. Either way, both documents are essential planning tools before a report developer even starts BIRT Report Designer.

If you are responsible for writing the specification, identify the information that the report should provide and determine how best to present the information. This chapter provides guidelines for defining the specification and designing a mock-up of the report. If you receive a specification developed by someone else, use the guidelines to ensure that the specification covers all the information you need.

Identifying the content of the report

This step is the most important one in the planning process. To get started, answer the following questions:

- What is the purpose of the report?

  A purpose statement helps you determine the information that you need. It also gives the report a starting point.

  The following example is a sample purpose statement:

  > The purpose of this report is to show monthly sales by region, then by sales representatives, and to flag the representatives whose sales figures fall below a certain amount.

  Make the purpose statement as specific as possible. A vague requirement, such as a monthly sales report, does not help define the precise data requirements.

- Who is going to read the report?

  A report can be viewed by different types of users. For example, sales representatives, sales managers, and the vice president of sales can all use a sales report. Each type of user, however, is interested in different types of information and different levels of detail. Knowing the users of a report clarifies the data requirements.

- What data should appear in the report?

  Identify all the data that the report needs to include. It is important to have a complete list because the type and amount of data affects the report layout. Adding data in the late stages of report creation often can mean redesigning a layout to fit the new data.

- Where is the data coming from?

  Much of the information in a typical report is taken directly from data fields in a database, application, or text file. First, you need to know the source or sources of data for the report. Second, you need to understand how the data is structured. For example, if the data source is a database, you need to know what tables are in it, the relationships among tables, the columns in each table, the data types, and so on. If necessary, ask the database administrator for this information.

- Does any of the data need to be calculated?

  Some report data comes directly from data fields, such as sales representative names or addresses. Some information must be calculated, such as sales totals, or the percentage by which sales figures exceed or fall below a certain amount.

- How will the data be calculated?

  Some data can be calculated by performing a mathematical operation on data field values, such as multiplying Item.Quantity by Item.Price to get extended prices. Some data may need to be calculated by using a JavaScript function or a user-defined function.

- Do you want to enable the report user to specify what data to display?
  You can create a report that displays a specific set of data from the data source. You can also create a report that lets users specify what information they want to see. For example, rather than displaying sales data for all regions, create a report that prompts the user to specify a region for which the sales data appears in the report.

Determining how the report will be viewed

When designing a report, consider and test in the environment in which the report will be viewed because the environment affects how a report appears and prints.

Always design for the final delivery environment. This approach includes choosing the right fonts and colors, selecting the appropriate page size, fine-tuning the size of report fields and the space between them, and so on.

Consider the following questions:

- Which is more important, viewing online or printing the report?
  Recognize that there are differences between online and printed reports; decide which is more important, and design for that output. For example, printed reports vary in appearance depending on the printer producing the output. If a report is primarily viewed online, you can add interactive viewing features, such as hyperlinks or a dynamic table of contents.

- Will the report be viewed in HTML, a PDF file, or one of the other supported file formats?
  The appearance of the report differs depending on the file format. Pagination, for example, is a key difference between HTML and page-based file formats, such as PDF and Microsoft Word document (.doc). A report in PDF format, for example, appears on multiple pages of a fixed size. An HTML report, on the other hand, can appear on multiple pages or in one scrollable page, depending on what you specify.

- If distributing an HTML report, what browsers are you supporting?
  Different browsers can display results differently because they interpret HTML or CSS tags differently. If there are particular browsers that you must support, test the report in those browsers.

Considering international reporting requirements

BIRT Report Designer supports creating reports that contain international data for use in multiple locales. A locale defines a set of conventions for providing, displaying, and sorting data. Numbers, dates, and currencies appear differently in different locales. The following examples show dates in long date format when the locale is English (United States) and when the locale is German (Germany):

```
Tuesday, July 7, 2009
Dienstag, 7. Juli 2009
```

BIRT reports automatically display date, number, and currency data according to the locale to which the report user's machine is configured. You do not have to do anything special to display these types of data in multiple locales.

When designing a report for international users, consider the following questions:

- Will the report be viewed in one locale? If yes, which locale?

  If your report will be used in a specific locale, design and test the report using those locale settings.

- Will the report be viewed by users in multiple countries?

  If your report will be viewed by users in multiple countries, consider internationalizing the report so that it appears correctly in multiple locales. For example, rather than specifying text directly in a report design, you can create text strings in an external source and provide translations of those strings. Using this technique, called localization, the report displays text in the language that is specified by the locale of the user's machine.

  Testing report output in multiple locales is an important early stage in the report design process. Develop a small sample and send that to recipients who can test the output in that locale and, in particular, can test printed output for possible glitches in fonts and layout. Even decisions such as how names are to be displayed can be challenging if the report is to be viewed by users with differing language competencies.

Deciding the layout and format of the report

After you identify the report's purpose and content, you should have a good idea about organizing and presenting the information. Consider these questions:

- What is the overall layout for the report data?

  Data can appear in a single section or be presented in multiple sections. A simple listing of customer names and phone numbers, for example, can be presented in a two-column table. A financial statement, on the other hand, can be a multi-sectioned report that includes a form letter, a summary of accounts and balances, and transaction details for each account.

- Do you need to organize information into groups? If yes, how?

For example, a monthly sales report can display sales figures by region, by sales representative, or by both. To display both, you can group the information by region first, then list sales representatives for each region.

- How do you want to sort information?

  A report can present information in the order in which it is stored in the data source, in ascending order, or in descending order. The sort order affects the readability and usability of a report.

- Do you need to summarize the data? If yes, how?

  Reports that present numerical data, such as expense reports, financial statements, and earnings reports, always contain summary sections for totals, averages, or percentages. Decide if this summary information should appear in a table, a chart, a cross tab, or a combination of these display options.

- Do you want to highlight information based on certain conditions?

  It is common to use formatting to emphasize certain information. For example, if a report displays a long list of customers in alphabetical order, you can display the names of the top ten customers in blue.

- Do you need to display information in page headers and footers?

  Printed reports typically display information in the page header to help users navigate multi-page reports. For example, you can display the region name in the header, so users know that sales representatives on page n are part of region x. In the page footer, you can show the page number and the report's generation date. On the other hand, online reports that present data in one continuous page do not require page headers and footers.

- Are there corporate standards that you need to follow?

  If your company produces reports for external use, such as financial statements for clients, it is likely that a report that you create needs to use corporate styles. Corporate styles typically dictate the logos, security statements, fonts, and colors that you can use.

- Are there online style sheets that you can use?

  Most organizations maintain a corporate web site and frequently use CSS to format the look and feel of web pages. You can reuse CSS styles in your reports, which enables you to create reports with the corporate look without having to recreate the styles.

- Are there report templates you can use?

  Unless your organization is just starting up, report templates are probably available. If there are no formal templates, look at existing reports to see if you can reuse and adapt their layouts. If the organization is in start-up phase, examine the sample reports, and consider establishing standards for organizational reporting in common areas, such as budget variance, expenses, and vacation reporting.

Drawing a mock-up

After making the decisions that are described in the previous sections, you are ready to create a mock-up of the report. Use any tool with which you are comfortable, such as a word processor, graphics program, or pen and paper.

A mock-up should show approximately what the finished report will look like, including the report title, page header and footer information, and all the fields in the body of the report. Using a mock-up to get feedback and approval from your primary users can save you time. With this approval, you do not waste time creating a polished report that contains the wrong information or layout.

A mock-up is especially useful when you are first learning BIRT Report Designer. With a blueprint in hand, you can focus on using the tool, rather than trying to learn and design at the same time.

Considering reuse of report components

Rarely do you create just one report for a company. Often, you create reports for different departments or to meet your clients' varying reporting needs. You can approach report creation one report at a time, or you can plan and design a suite of reports. Consider these questions to evaluate which approach is more suitable:

- How many reports are you creating?

- Do the reports require common elements and styles, such as connections to the same data source, page headers and footers that display the same information, report titles in a particular font and color, or tables with a certain format?

- Do you work in a group with other report developers? If yes:

  - How similar are the report projects?

  - Do you need to collaborate on the designs?

If you create more than a couple of reports, and they contain many common elements, or if you work with other report developers on similar reports, you can streamline the report creation process by creating a collaborative and shared report development environment. Using BIRT Report Designer, you can:

- Create and store common report elements in a library, which all reports can use.

- Create report templates that define a basic report structure on which new reports can be based.

With careful planning, you can create rich sets of libraries and templates that provide you and other report developers with a head start when creating a new report.

Managing report design resources

A report design typically uses external resources, such as image files, report libraries, Java files, and resource files used for localization. If you work on a suite of reports that use multiple external files, you need a way to organize the files so that you can easily package and deploy them to an application server or migrate your reports to different machines.

BIRT Report Designer provides a resource folder as a way to organize all these external files for ease of deployment later. The default location of this resource folder is specified in the Preferences page, which you access by choosing Window→Preferences from the main menu, then choosing Report Design→Resource. On this page, you can specify a different path for the resource folder option.

When you publish a library or create a resource file in BIRT Report Designer, these files are automatically saved in the resource folder. To manage files that are created by other applications, such as image files, copy the files into the resource folder before creating the report. Then, when you insert the images in the report, select the image in the resource folder.

Deciding how the report will be deployed

Planning the report design is one phase of the planning process. You also need a plan for deploying or distributing the report. Consider these questions:

- How will the report be distributed to users?
  - Will the report be deployed from an application?
  - Will the report be sent through e-mail?
- If the report will be deployed from an application, address these questions:
  - How will the report integrate with the application?
  - Will users need a secure login to access the report?
  - Will users view a generated report, or will users generate the report to view it with real-time data?

Depending on your deployment strategy, there are many other questions to answer and programming tasks to perform. For information on deployment and integration, see *Integrating and Extending BIRT* (Addison-Wesley, 2011).

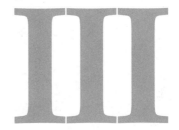
Accessing and Binding Data

5

Connecting to a Data Source

Enterprise report data is frequently stored in a variety of systems and formats. BIRT Report Designer provides wizards to set up access to the following types of data sources:

- JDBC data sources
- Text files
- XML documents
- Web services

A report, however, is not limited to using data from these data sources. Developers can write JavaScript or Java scripts to get data from Java objects, such as Enterprise JavaBeans. Developers can also use BIRT's Open Data Access (ODA) framework to write custom data drivers to access data from any source, including data stored in proprietary systems.

This chapter discusses how to use the wizards in BIRT Report Designer to set up access to a data source without programming. For information about writing scripts and developing custom data drivers, see *Integrating and Extending BIRT (Addison-Wesley, 2011)*.

About BIRT data sources

To access data for a BIRT report, you create and use a BIRT data source. A BIRT data source is an object that contains the information to connect to an underlying data source. Each type of data source requires different connection information. Use Data Explorer, shown in Figure 5-1, to create and manage BIRT data sources.

Figure 5-1   Data source in Data Explorer

You can create as many data sources as is necessary for a report. The data sources can be of different types. For example, a report can use data from a database and data from a flat file repository.

BIRT Report Designer provides default names that begin with Data Source for each data source in a report. For example, if you create three data sources, the default names are Data Source, Data Source1, and Data Source2. Specify descriptive names, such as SalesDB or BooksXml, so that you can identify easily the type or name of the data source.

Connecting to a database using JDBC

A report can access data from any database or other data source that uses a JDBC driver. Most relational databases, such as Oracle, SQL Server, or MySQL, use JDBC drivers. Make sure you have the appropriate JDBC driver for the database that you want to access. BIRT supports JDBC 3.0 drivers. Download the necessary drivers from a data source vendor or third-party web site.

Creating a JDBC data source

When creating a JDBC data source in BIRT, you select the driver class and provide a URL to connect to the database. If the database requires user authentication, provide a user name and a password. If the database to which to connect uses connection pooling, specify the path to the service. Many databases use a connection pool—a cache of database connection objects—to minimize the overhead of establishing a connection to the database. A connection pool optimizes database performance through the reuse of connections, which reduces the need to repeatedly open and close connections each time a report is run.

How to specify the connection information for a database or other JDBC data source

1   In Data Explorer, right-click Data Sources, then choose New Data Source.

2   In New Data Source, specify the following information:

    1   Select JDBC Data Source from the list of data source types.

2 In Data Source Name, type a name for the data source. The name must be unique in the current report. Figure 5-2 shows a default data source name.

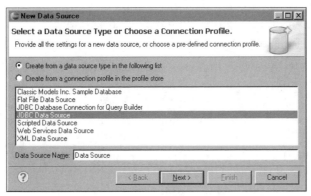

Figure 5-2   Creating a JDBC data source

3 Choose Next.

New JDBC Data Source Profile appears, as shown in Figure 5-3.

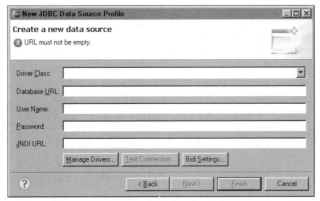

Figure 5-3   Defining JDBC connection information

3 Specify the connection information for the JDBC data source.

1 In Driver Class, choose a driver class from the drop-down list. If you do not see the driver class that you need, add the driver as described later in this chapter.

2 In Database URL, type the URL for the database, using the format that the driver requires. For a MySQL database, for example, the format is

```
jdbc:mysql://<host>:<port>/<database>
```

3 In User Name, type a valid user name to connect to the JDBC data source. This field can be left blank if the data source does not require a user name.

4   In Password, type a valid password to connect to the JDBC data source. This field can be left blank if the data source does not require a password.

5   In JNDI URL, type the full path to the connection pooling service, if applicable. The following path is an example:

    `java:comp/env/jdbc/MyDataSource`

    In the example, MyDataSource is the name of the JNDI database service.

4   To ensure that the connection information is correct, choose Test Connection. If Test Connection returns an error, repeat the preceding steps to correct the error. Then, test the connection again.

5   Choose Finish. The new JDBC data source appears under Data Sources in Data Explorer.

Managing JDBC drivers

Use the JDBC driver manager to install and manage drivers. You access the JDBC driver manager, shown in Figure 5-4, from the data source editor. To indicate which drivers are available for use, the JDBC driver manager displays symbols next to the file names in the JAR files list.

■   A symbol x indicates that a file, previously available to BIRT, is no longer in the JDBC drivers directory. Reports that use this driver cannot access the underlying data source. To solve this problem, you must restore the driver in the JDBC drivers directory.

■   An asterisk (*) indicates that a file does not exist in the original location from which you installed the driver. Reports that use this driver can still access the underlying data source as long as the driver is in the JDBC drivers directory.

■   A plus sign (+) indicates that a file has been restored to the JDBC drivers directory.

In Figure 5-4, the JDBC driver manager indicates that the JAR file is no longer in the JDBC drivers directory.

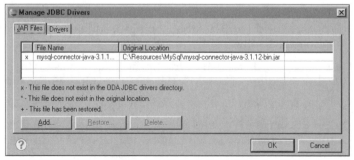

Figure 5-4   Managing JDBC drivers

Adding a JDBC driver

To install a JDBC driver, the JDBC driver manager prompts you to select the JAR file that contains the JDBC driver. The JAR file you select is copied to the following directory:

```
eclipse\plugins
    \org.eclipse.birt.report.data.oda.jdbc_<version>\drivers
```

The driver or drivers contained in the JAR file located in this directory are available to all your report designs.

How to add a JDBC driver

This procedure assumes you are creating a new JDBC data source, and you need to install a new driver because the driver that the database requires is not available in the list of drivers.

1 In New JDBC Data Source Profile, shown in Figure 5-5, choose Manage Drivers.

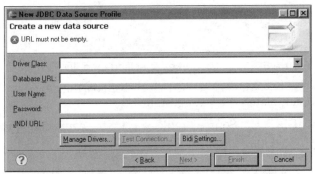

Figure 5-5   New JDBC Data Source Profile

2 In Manage JDBC Drivers, choose Add to install the JAR file that contains the driver.

3 Navigate to the directory that contains the JAR file. Select the JAR file and choose Open. Manage JDBC Drivers shows the new JAR file.

4 Choose Drivers to see the list of installed drivers, as shown in Figure 5-6.

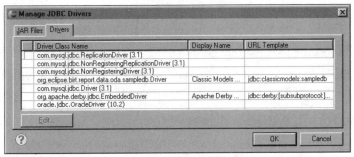

Figure 5-6   Viewing JDBC driver classes

5 Optionally, set the properties for a driver, using the following steps:

1 Select the new driver, then choose Edit.

2 In Edit JDBC Driver, specify the following information:

❑ In Driver Display Name, type a user-friendly name that describes the driver. This name appears in parenthesis next to the driver class name in Driver Class on New JDBC Data Source Profile.

❑ In URL Template, type the URL format that the driver requires. This URL format appears in Driver URL on New JDBC Data Source Profile.

Figure 5-7 shows an example of properties specified for a MySQL JDBC driver.

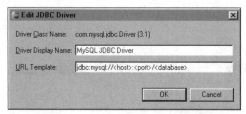

Figure 5-7 Properties specified for a JDBC driver

3 Choose OK. Manage JDBC Driver displays the new display name and URL template syntax suggestion.

6 In New JDBC Data Source Profile, specify the connection properties to connect to the JDBC data source. The Driver Class list displays the installed driver.

Deleting a JDBC driver

If you are upgrading a driver, delete the JAR file that contains the current driver before adding a new file. If the JAR file contains more than one driver, the driver manager deletes all drivers in the JAR file.

How to delete JDBC drivers in a JAR file

1 Right-click an existing JDBC data source, then choose Edit from the context menu. Edit Data Source appears.

2 Choose Manage Drivers to open the JDBC driver manager.

3 Select the JAR file that contains the driver, then choose Delete.

BIRT Report Designer removes the JAR file and any drivers that it contains from the JDBC drivers directory.

Restoring a JDBC driver

When you install a new version of BIRT Report Designer, the process replaces all the files in the eclipse directory and all the drivers installed in the JDBC drivers directory are lost. Reports that use a JDBC driver to access a data source display an error when you run them. Figure 5-8 shows an example of such an error. To solve this problem, use the JDBC driver manager to restore the drivers.

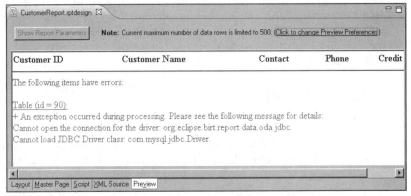

Figure 5-8   Report displaying a Cannot load JDBC Driver class error

How to restore a JDBC driver

1 In Data Explorer, right-click the JDBC data source, then choose Edit from the context menu. Edit Data Source appears.

2 In Edit Data Source, choose Manage Drivers to open the JDBC driver manager.

   The JDBC driver manager indicates that the driver used by the report no longer exists in the JDBC driver directory.

3 Select the JAR file to restore, then choose Restore. BIRT Report Designer restores the driver from the original location to the JDBC driver directory and replaces the x next to the file name with a plus sign (+), as shown in Figure 5-9.

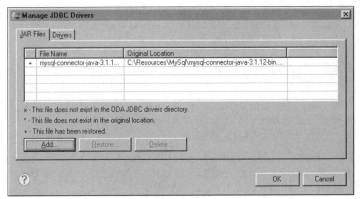

Figure 5-9   JDBC driver restored

Connecting to a text file

A BIRT report can access data from a text file, or flat file, that conforms to a defined and consistent structure. These files are typically generated by business systems and applications that create logs. These files can also be spreadsheets saved as comma separated values (CSV) files. Before using text file data in a report, make sure the file uses a valid structure, and if necessary, edit the text accordingly.

Text file structure

A text file used for report data must have the following structure:

- The first line of the text file can contain the names of the columns, separated by commas. If the first line does not contain column names, BIRT assigns default names, such as Column_1, Column_2, and so on.

- The second line of the file can specify the data types of the columns. See Table 5-1 for a list of supported data types. If you use the second line to specify data types, list the data types in the same order as the columns, and separate the data types with a comma, semicolon, tab, or pipe.

- The remaining lines in the file must contain values for the columns. The values can be separated by a comma, semicolon, tab, or pipe.

- Each line must contain the same number of fields.

- The file cannot include empty lines between records.

- Each record must occupy a separate line, delimited by a line break, such as CRLF or LF. The last record in the file can either include or omit an ending line break.

- Data in a field can be surrounded by more than one set of quotation marks. Quotation marks are required only if the data contains one or more commas within a field. A field can enclose single quotation marks and commas with double quotation marks, such as:

  `"He said, 'Yes, I do.'"`

- If a field without content has zero or more spaces, the field is treated as NULL and evaluated as NULL in comparison operations.

- The file name and extension can be any name that is valid for your operating system. Although TXT and CSV are typical, you do not have to use either as the file extension.

The following example shows a valid sample text file. The text file has two lines of metadata and three lines of data. The first line lists the column names, and the second line lists the data types.

```
FamilyName,GivenName,AccountID,AccountType,Created
STRING,STRING,INT,STRING,TIMESTAMP
"Smith","Mark",254378,"Monthly",01/31/2003 09:59:59 AM
"Johnson","Carol",255879,"Monthly",09/30/2004 03:59:59 PM
"Pitt","Joseph",255932,,10/01/2005 10:32:04 AM
```

Text file data types

Table 5-1 lists and provides information about the abbreviations you use for the data types.

Table 5-1   Supported data types in flat files

Abbreviation	Data type	Examples
BIGDECIMAL	java.sql.Types.NUMERIC	
DATE	java.sql.Types.DATE	YYYY-MM-DD or MM/DD/YYYY Examples: 2003-01-31 01/31/2003
DOUBLE	java.sql.Types.DOUBLE	
INT	java.sql.Types.INTEGER	
STRING	java.sql.Types.VARCHAR	
TIME	java.sql.Types.TIME	hh:mm:ss Examples: 12:59:59 AM 12:59:59 pm
TIMESTAMP	java.sql.Types.TIMESTAMP	YYYY-MM-DD hh:mm:ss.nnnnnn

Creating a flat file data source

When creating a flat file data source in BIRT, you specify its property values, such as the file location and the character set that the text file uses. You should also know how the text file is structured—whether the file uses commas, semicolons, tabs, or pipes to separate values, and whether the file specifies column names or data types.

How to specify the connection information for accessing a text file

1   In Data Explorer, right-click Data Sources, then choose New Data Source.

2   In New Data Source, supply the following information:

    1   Select Flat File Data Source from the list of data source types.

    2   In Data Source Name, type a name for the data source.

3 Choose Next. New Flat File Data Source Profile appears, as shown in Figure 5-10.

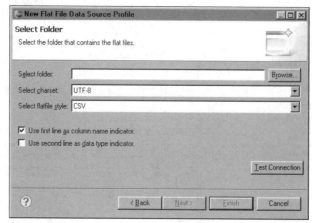

Figure 5-10 Selecting flat file directory and character set

3 Specify the following connection information for the text file:

1 In Select folder, type the location of the folder, or choose Browse to navigate to and select the folder.

2 In Select charset, select the character set that the text files in this folder use.

3 In Select flatfile style, select either CSV, SSV, PSV, or TSV for a file that uses comma-separated values, semicolon-separated values, pipe-separated values, or tab-separated values, respectively.

4 If the first line of the text file specifies the column names, select the following option:

```
Use first lines as column name indicator
```

5 If the second line of the text file specifies the column data types, select the following option:

```
Use second line as data type indicator
```

4 Choose Finish. The new flat file data source appears under Data Sources in Data Explorer.

Connecting to an XML file

XML is an open specification recommended by the World Wide Web Consortium, and has become a common mechanism for sharing structured data across different information systems. The XML document that a report accesses must be well-formed. To be well-formed, it must conform to the

XML 1.0, third edition specification. You can find more information about this specification at the following URL:

http://www.w3.org/TR/REC-xml/

When creating an XML data source in BIRT, you specify the location of the XML file. You can also specify the location of an XML schema. An XML schema contains a set of rules to which an XML file conforms. You can use the schema to validate the XML file.

How to specify the connection information for accessing an XML file

1 In Data Explorer, right-click Data Sources, then choose New Data Source.

2 In New Data Source, supply the following information:

   1 Select XML Data Source from the list of data source types.

   2 In Data Source Name, type a name for the data source.

   3 Choose Next.

   New XML Data Source Profile appears, as shown in Figure 5-11.

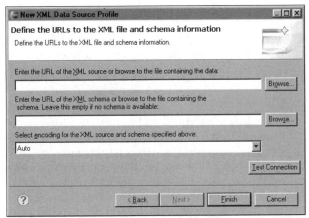

Figure 5-11   Defining XML source and schema information

3 Specify the following connection information:

   1 In the first field, type the location of the XML file, or choose Browse to navigate to and select the file.

   2 In the second field, type the location of the schema file, if one is available, or choose Browse to navigate to and select the file. A schema is not required.

   3 Select the type of encoding for the XML file and schema. Use Auto to specify that the data source detect the encoding type specified in the XML file or schema.

4 Choose Finish. The new XML data source appears under Data Sources in Data Explorer.

Connecting to a web service

Web services make software functionality available over the internet, using open and standard protocols, in the following manner:

- A web service defines a structured format for requests for its service and for the response the service generates.

- An application—a BIRT report, for example—makes a request for the web service over the internet.

- The web service performs an action and sends the results to the application.

The action can be calculating a monthly mortgage payment, retrieving stock quotes, converting currencies, getting the weather forecast for a particular city, or finding books by a particular author. If a report needs to present data that can only be generated by a program, you can save time and effort by looking for a web service that does the programming work and returns the data you need.

Web services use the following standard protocols:

- WSDL (Web Services Description Language) to describe the available services or operations provided by a web service

- SOAP (Simple Object Access Protocol) to transfer data

- XML to structure the data

Because web services are written and maintained by other developers, always examine the web service definition to ensure that the web service does what you need. You should also verify that the WSDL document is well-formed. Remember, too, that you have no control over web services created by others, and if a web service your report accesses is modified significantly or removed, the functionality no longer works in the report.

When creating a web service data source in BIRT, you typically need to specify only the location of the WSDL file. A well-formed WSDL file defines the available services, and typically, the information to connect to the SOAP server identified by a SOAP endpoint URL.

Alternatively, you can connect to the web service through a custom driver class. You would create and use a custom driver, if, for example, the web service does not provide a WSDL document.

How to specify the connection information for accessing a web service

This procedure shows how to connect to a public web service that returns the weather forecast for a specified U.S. zip code. You can get information about this web service at the following location:

```
http://www.webservicex.net/WS/WSDetails.aspx?CATID=12&WSID=68
```

1. In Data Explorer, right-click Data Sources, then choose New Data Source.

2. In New Data Source, supply the following information:

   1. Select Web Services Data Source from the list of data source types.

   2. In Data Source Name, type a name for the data source. For this example, type

      Weather_ws

   3. Choose Next.

3. In New Web Services Data Source Profile, in WSDL URL or Location, type the following URL, as shown in Figure 5-12:

   http://www.webservicex.net/WeatherForecast.asmx?WSDL

   For well-defined web services, you need only specify the URL to the WSDL document.

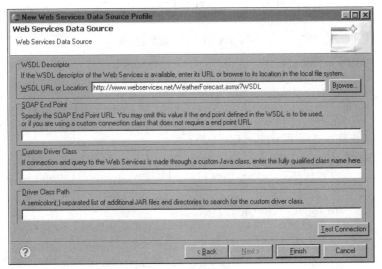

Figure 5-12   URL to WSDL specified

4. Choose Test Connection to verify the connection to the web service.

5. Choose Finish. The new web service data source, Weather_ws, appears under Data Sources in Data Explorer.

Creating reusable data sources

Each BIRT data source you create contains the connections properties required to connect to a database, flat file, XML document, or web service. Often, multiple reports require access to the same source. You might, for example, create a suite of reports that use data from the same corporate sales database. Rather than typing the same connection information repeatedly for each report, you can:

- Enter the connection information once in a file called a connection profile, then link the connection profile to any BIRT data source that requires that connection information.

- Create one BIRT data source, then store it in a library that all reports can access.

The basic principles behind both techniques are simple: define connection properties once, store the information in a shared location, and reuse the information in as many reports as needed. Another advantage that both techniques offer is the ability to update connection properties in one location and have the changes propagate to all reports.

This section describes how to create and use a connection profile. For information about sharing data sources in a library, see Chapter 24, "Building a Shared Development Framework."

Creating a connection profile

You use Data Source Explorer (not to be confused with Data Explorer) to create a connection profile. You can create a connection profile for any data source type, and you can create as many profiles as needed. For example, if your reports frequently access data from a particular database and a particular web service, you can create one connection profile for the database, and one for the web service.

BIRT saves all the connection profiles in a single file named ServerProfiles.dat. This file is saved in the .metadata folder in your current workspace. The path is

```
...\workspace\.metadata\plugins\
    org.eclipse.datatools.connectivity\ServerProfiles.dat
```

To share your connection profiles with other report developers, place ServerProfiles.dat in a central location. You can rename the file in the event that there are other ServerProfiles.dat files in the central location.

How to create a connection profile

1 Choose Window→Show View→Other.

2 In Show View, expand Data Management and select Data Source Explorer, then choose OK.

Data Source Explorer appears at the bottom of the application window.

3 In Data Source Explorer, expand ODA Data Sources.

Data Source Explorer lists the data source types and connection profiles, if any were defined previously. Figure 5-13 shows the list of data source types in Data Source Explorer.

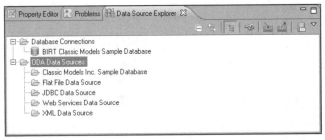

Figure 5-13   Data Source Explorer

4 Right click the data source type for which you want to create a connection profile, then choose New.

5 In New <data source type> Data Source Profile, type a name and description for the connection profile. Figure 5-14 shows an example of information specified for a JDBC connection profile.

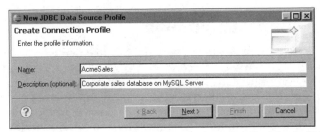

Figure 5-14   Name and description specified for a JDBC connection profile

Choose Next.

6 In New <data source type> Data Source Profile, specify the connection values to connect to the data source. Figure 5-15 shows an example of connection properties to connect to a JDBC data source.

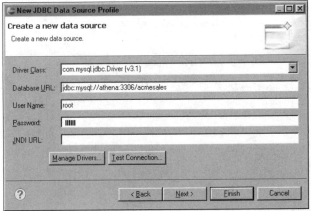

Figure 5-15   Connection properties for a JDBC data source

7 Choose Test Connection to verify the connection.

8 Choose Finish. The new connection profile appears in Data Source Explorer, as shown in Figure 5-16. It displays the name you specified when you created the connection profile.

Figure 5-16   Data Source Explorer displays the new JDBC connection profile

Using a connection profile

You have the option of creating a new data source using information stored in a connection profile. Using a connection profile saves time and reduces the potential for connection errors because all you need to do is supply the location of the profile. You do not need to know or remember all the required connection information, and, presumably, the connection profile has been tested. To use a connection profile created by another report developer, make sure you get the location of the profile.

How to create a data source that uses a connection profile

1 In Data Explorer, right-click Data Sources, then choose New Data Source.

2 In New Data Source, select Create from a connection profile in the profile store, as shown in Figure 5-17. Choose Next.

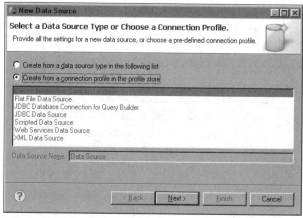

Figure 5-17   Creating a data source that uses a connection profile

3 In Connection Profile, in Connection Profile Store, specify the location of the file that contains the connection profiles. You can choose Browse to find and select the file. As described in the previous section, the default file name is ServerProfiles.dat, and BIRT saves this file, by default, in the .metadata folder in the workspace in use when the connection profile was created. The default path is

```
...\workspace\.metadata\.plugins\
     org.eclipse.datatools.connectivity\ServerProfiles.dat
```

4 After you specify the location of the .dat file, Connection Profile displays all the available profiles. Figure 5-18 shows an example of two connection profiles, SystemLogs and AcmeSales.

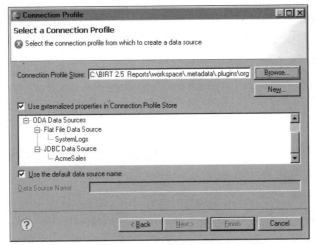

Figure 5-18   Connection Profile displays two predefined profiles

5 Select the connection profile to use.

By default, Use the default data source name is selected. If you selected the SystemLogs profile, the new data source is also named SystemLogs by default.

6 Optionally, specify a different name for the data source.

7 Choose Next. New <data source type> Data Source Profile displays in read-only text the connection information derived from the connection profile.

8 Choose Finish. The new data source appears under Data Sources in Data Explorer.

Setting connection properties when a report runs

When you first design and test a report, you create a BIRT data source that uses hard-coded information. All the procedures for creating data sources, described previously, used hard-coded information. For example, the procedure for creating a JDBC data source included providing a user name and password that the report uses to access a database. When the report is run, the database uses whatever roles and privileges are assigned to the hard-coded report user.

Production reports, however, cannot always use the hard-coded information specified at report design time. A typical example is prompting a report user to provide his credentials when he runs the report. Based on the specified credentials, the database authentication system determines the appropriate data to use to generate the report.

To support the setting of connection properties at report run time, the data source editor provides a feature called property binding. As its name suggests, this feature supports binding each connection property to a JavaScript expression that evaluates to a value that the report uses at run time.

Because each data source type requires different connection information, the Property Binding page displays a different set of connection properties for each data source type. The Property Binding page is available only when you edit an existing data source. It is not available when you create a new data source.

Figure 5-19 shows the Property Binding page for a JDBC data source.

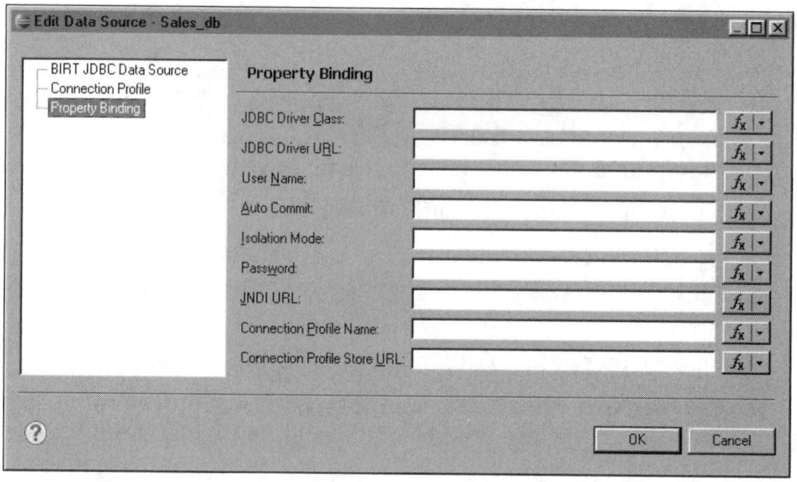

Figure 5-19   Property Binding page showing JDBC connection properties that can be set at run time

Figure 5-20 shows the Property Binding page for a flat file data source. Notice that, for both types of data sources, all the connection properties that you set at design time can also be set dynamically at run time. As the figures also show, if the data source uses a connection profile, you can dynamically assign a connection profile and its location at run time.

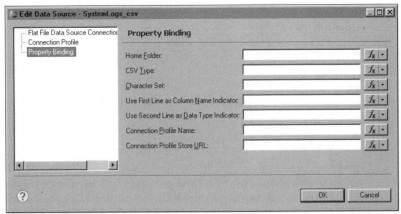

Figure 5-20 Property Binding page showing flat file connection properties that can be set at run time

The following sections show two examples of setting connection properties at run time.

Setting the folder path for text files at run time

To access a text file, one of the properties that you must specify is the path to the folder that contains the text file. There are cases when the path to the folder can be determined only at run time. Consider the following scenario: A log file named log.csv is generated daily. Each daily log is stored in an auto-generated folder whose name is the current date. Examples of the full path to these folders are as follows:

```
C:\Logs\2011-07-01
C:\Logs\2011-07-02
C:\Logs\2011-07-03
```

You design a report that displays data from log.csv. When the report is run, the report uses the log.csv data for the current day. For example, if the report runs on July 1, 2011, the flat file data source uses the log.csv file in the 2011-07-01 folder. If the report runs on July 2, 2011, the data source uses the log.csv file in the 2011-07-02 folder. The following procedure shows how to write a JavaScript expression that returns the full folder path value based on the current date.

How to set the folder path for text files at run time

This procedure assumes that you have already created a flat file data source.

1 In Data Explorer, right-click the flat file data source, then choose Edit.

2 In Edit Data Source, choose Property Binding. The Property Binding page displays the flat file connection properties that you can set at run time.

 3 Choose the expression builder button to the right of Home Folder.

4 In the expression builder, type the following expression:

```
function DF(n) {
return (n > 9 ? n : '0' + n);
}

var d = new Date();
shortDate = (d.getFullYear() + '-' + DF(d.getMonth() + 1) + '-'
  + DF(d.getDate()));

HomeFolder = "C:/Logs/"+shortDate;
```

The JavaScript functions, getFullYear( ), getMonth( ), and getDate( ), get the parts of the full date and time returned by new Date( ). The user-defined DF function formats the month and day parts of the date. The shortDate variable contains the date in 2009-01-01 format. The HomeFolder variable contains the full folder path, which is constructed by concatenating the static path with the shortDate variable.

5 Choose OK to save the expression.

Edit Data Source shows the JavaScript expression bound to the Home Folder property, as shown in Figure 5-21.

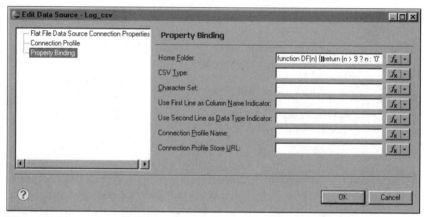

Figure 5-21   JavaScript expression bound to the Home Folder property

6 Choose OK to save your changes to the data source.

Setting the database user name and password at run time

When a report accesses data in a database, a typical action is to prompt the report user to type his user name and password at run time. You accomplish this action by using report parameters. Report parameters provide a mechanism for getting values at run time and passing the values to the report. For more information about report parameters, see Chapter 15, "Enabling the User to Filter Data."

The following procedure shows how to create report parameters and bind the parameters to the user name and password properties in a JDBC data source.

How to enable a user to provide a database user name and password when a report runs

This procedure assumes that you have already created a JDBC data source.

1 Create a report parameter to get the user name, using the following steps:

   1 In Data Explorer, right-click Report Parameters, then choose New Parameter.

   2 In New Parameter, supply the following information:

      ❑ In Name, type a name for the report parameter. For example:

      `username_param`

      ❑ In Prompt text, specify a word or sentence to prompt the report user to provide a user name value. For example:

      `User name`

      ❑ In Data type, select String.

   Figure 5-22 shows the completed report parameter definition.

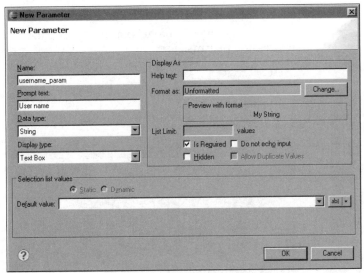

Figure 5-22   Report parameter to get the user name

   3 Choose OK. The username_param parameter appears under Report Parameters in Data Explorer.

2 Use the previous steps to create a report parameter to get the password. Use the following values to define the report parameter:

- In Name, type

  password_param

- In Prompt text, type

  Password

- In Data type, select String.

3 Choose OK. The password_param parameter appears under Report Parameters in Data Explorer.

4 Bind the user name property to the username_param report parameter.

   1 In Data explorer, right-click the JDBC data source, then choose Edit.

   2 In Edit Data Source, choose Property Binding. The Property Binding page displays the JDBC connection properties.

   3 Choose the expression builder button on the right of User Name.

   4 In the expression builder, perform the following tasks:

      ❑ Under Category, choose Report parameters. All appears under Sub-Category.

      ❑ Choose All. Under Double Click to insert, BIRT Report Designer displays the report parameters that you created.

      ❑ Double-click the username_param report parameter. The expression params["username_param"].value appears in the text area, as shown in Figure 5-23.

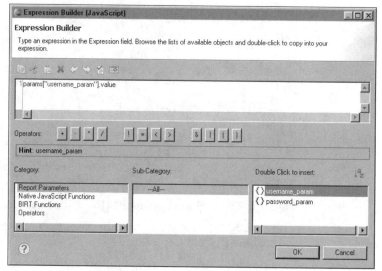

Figure 5-23   Choosing the username_param in the expression builder

❏ Choose OK. The expression builder closes. The report parameter expression appears in the User Name field, as shown in Figure 5-24.

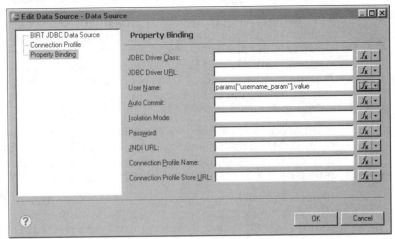

Figure 5-24   User Name property bound to the username_param report parameter

5   Using the previous steps, bind the password property to the password_param report parameter.

5   In Edit Data Source, choose OK.

6   Preview the report to confirm that the user is prompted for a user name and password. Figure 5-25 shows Enter Parameters, the dialog that prompts the user to enter a user name and password.

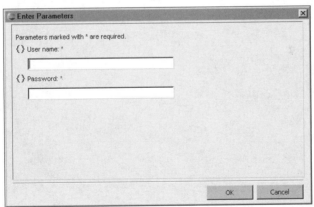

Figure 5-25   Enter Parameters prompts the user for a user name and password

The values that the user specifies are used to connect to the JDBC database.

Troubleshooting data source problems

BIRT Report Designer displays information about data source connection problems in several different places. Error reports can appear in the previewer, the problems view, the error log view, and as pop-up messages. Generally, BIRT Report Designer displays JDBC connection-related problems in pop-up error messages. If the connection information is syntactically correct, but the data source is not available, you see a pop-up message and entries in the error log view.

A list of errors appears in the Problems view if a data source is incorrectly defined. You cannot manually delete items from the Problems view. They display until you resolve the problem or delete the object that is creating the problem.

If you have problems connecting to a data source from BIRT Report Designer, try connecting using a data source manufacturer or third-party tool to confirm that the connection string works as expected. This troubleshooting exercise can help you determine whether to focus your troubleshooting on a driver or on the parameters that you have provided.

If you make changes to the connection parameters and BIRT Report Designer behaves as though it is still using the original values for the parameters, restart Eclipse using the -clean option. What has happened is that Eclipse is using cached information that contains the previous values. To clear the cache, exit Eclipse and restart using the -clean option.

6

Retrieving Data

After creating a BIRT data source to connect to a database, text file, XML file, or web service, you specify what data to retrieve. Data sources, especially databases, typically contain more data fields than are needed for a report. Retrieving excess data fields slows report generation. This chapter discusses how to create data sets to retrieve data from the different data source types.

About data sets

A data set is an object that defines all the data that is available to a report. To create a data set, you must have an existing BIRT data source. As with data sources, BIRT Report Designer provides wizards to create data sets. The first and the only required step in creating a data set is to select the data to retrieve from a data source. After this first step, you can optionally process the raw data as needed for the report. For example, you can change the names of columns, create computed columns, and define filters to provide a subset of the data to the report.

You can create as many data sets as are necessary for a report. Typically, you create at least one data set for each data source. For example, if you created a JDBC data source and an XML data source in a report, you would create a JDBC data set and an XML data set. You can also create multiple data sets that use a single data source. If, for example, a report displays sales data from the same database in a chart and in a table, you can create one data set to return data for the chart, and another data set to return data for the table. In this scenario, creating different data sets can improve performance because each data set retrieves only the specific data required by each report element. Alternatively, to use identical data, both items can share the same data set.

BIRT Report Designer provides a default name for each data set you create in a report. The names begin with Data Set. If you create two data sets, the default names are Data Set and Data Set1. You should use descriptive names, such as CorporateSalesDB or SupportLogXML, that enable you to identify easily the type of data that the data set provides.

Selecting data

BIRT uses data based on a relational model. A relational model organizes data in a two-dimensional table consisting of rows and columns, and a data set must return data in this format, as illustrated in Figure 6-1.

PRODUCTCODE	PRODUCTNAME	BUYPRICE	MSRP
S10_1678	1969 Harley Davidson Ultimate Chopper	48.81	95.7
S10_1949	1952 Alpine Renault 1300	98.58	214.3
S10_2016	1996 Moto Guzzi 1100i	68.99	118.94
S10_4698	2003 Harley-Davidson Eagle Drag Bike	91.02	193.66
S10_4757	1972 Alfa Romeo GTA	85.68	136
S10_4962	1962 LanciaA Delta 16V	103.42	147.74
S12_1099	1968 Ford Mustang	95.34	194.57
S12_1108	2001 Ferrari Enzo	95.59	207.8
S12_1666	1958 Setra Bus	77.9	136.67
S12_2823	2002 Suzuki XREO	66.27	150.62
S12_3148	1969 Corvair Monza	89.14	151.08
S12_3380	1968 Dodge Charger	75.16	117.44
S12_3891	1969 Ford Falcon	83.05	173.02
S12_3990	1970 Plymouth Hemi Cuda	31.92	79.8
S12_4473	1957 Chevy Pickup	55.7	118.5
S12_4675	1969 Dodge Charger	58.73	115.16
S18_1097	1940 Ford Pickup Truck	58.33	116.67

Figure 6-1   A data set returns data in a table consisting of rows and columns

A JDBC data source organizes data in exactly this way. Other types of data sources, such as XML and web services, do not. When creating a data set for these data sources, you map the data so that the data is organized in the structure that BIRT requires.

This section explains how to retrieve data from JDBC, flat file, XML, and web service data sources.

Using a SQL query to retrieve data from a JDBC data source

Typically, a JDBC data set retrieves data using a SQL query. SQL is a standard query language for requesting data from a database. This section discusses how to write a basic SQL query and how to combine data from multiple tables. In many cases, a basic knowledge of SQL is sufficient to retrieve the data a report requires.

Writing a basic SQL query

A SQL query consists of one or more statements. The first statement of a SQL query is the SELECT statement that specifies which columns to retrieve from the database. The SELECT statement contains two required clauses: SELECT and FROM. The SELECT clause lists the columns to retrieve. The FROM clause specifies the table from which to retrieve the selected columns of data.

The following is an example of a SQL statement that selects the firstname and lastname columns from a table called customers:

```
SELECT customers.firstname, customers.lastname
   FROM customers
```

A SQL SELECT query can also include other clauses that limit what data a query returns. Use the WHERE clause to specify criteria that results must meet and use ORDER BY to sort results. The following is an example of the same SQL statement, with the addition of the WHERE and ORDER BY clauses:

```
SELECT customers.firstname, customers.lastname
   FROM customers
   WHERE customers.country = 'Japan'
   ORDER BY customers.lastname, customers.firstname
```

Combining data from multiple tables

Typically, you have to select data from two or more tables to retrieve complete data for your report. This operation is called a join. You join tables in a database through a common column called a key.

For example, suppose you want to retrieve the orders for every customer. The database, however, stores customer information in a Customers table, and order information in an Orders table, as shown in Figure 6-2. Both tables contain a column called CustomerID. You can join the customers and the orders table using the CustomerID column.

Customers

CustomerID	CustomerName
01	Mark Smith
02	Maria Hernandez
03	Soo-Kim Young
04	Patrick Mason

Orders

OrderID	Amount	CustomerID
110	251.49	02
115	145.75	03
120	176.55	01

Figure 6-2   Database stores customer and order information in two tables

To retrieve order information for every customer, use the following SELECT statement:

```
SELECT Customers.CustomerName, Orders.Amount
FROM Customers, Orders
WHERE Customers.CustomerID = Orders.CustomerID
```

The WHERE clause in this example specifies that the query returns rows where the CustomerID in both tables match. Figure 6-3 shows the results that the SELECT statement returns.

Alternatively, use the JOIN keyword to select data from the two tables. The rest of this section describes the different types of joins you can use, and the results that each join returns. The following SELECT statement uses INNER JOIN and returns the same results shown in Figure 6-3:

```
SELECT Customers.CustomerName, Orders.Amount
FROM Customers
INNER JOIN Orders
ON Customers.CustomerID = Orders.CustomerID
```

CustomerName	Amount
Mark Smith	176.55
Maria Hernandez	251.49
Soo-Kim Young	145.75

Figure 6-3   Results returned by SELECT statement

The INNER JOIN clause returns all rows from both tables where the two CustomerID fields match. If there are rows in the Customers table that do not match rows in the Orders table, those rows are not listed. In the example, Patrick Mason is not listed in the result set because this customer does not have a matching order.

To obtain all the customer names, whether or not a customer has an order, use the LEFT JOIN clause, as shown in the following example:

```
SELECT Customers.CustomerName, Orders.Amount
FROM Customers
LEFT JOIN Orders
ON Customers.CustomerID = Orders.CustomerID
```

LEFT JOIN returns all rows from the first (left) table, even if there are no matches in the second (right) table. Figure 6-4 shows the results of the SELECT statement that uses the LEFT JOIN clause. Here, Patrick Mason is listed in the result set even though he does not have an order, because the record is in the first table.

CustomerName	Amount
Mark Smith	176.55
Maria Hernandez	251.49
Soo-Kim Young	145.75
Patrick Mason	

Figure 6-4   Results of a left join

Conversely, to retrieve all rows from the second table (the Orders table in our example), even if there are no matches in the first table (the Customers table), use the RIGHT JOIN clause, as shown in the following example:

```
SELECT Customers.CustomerName, Orders.Amount
FROM Customers
RIGHT JOIN Orders
ON Customers.CustomerID = Orders.CustomerID
```

In our example, all the rows in the second table match rows in the first table, so the result is the same as in Figure 6-3. If, however, the Orders table had contained rows that did not have matches in the Customers table, those rows would also have been returned.

To retrieve all customer names and orders from both tables, even if there are no matching values, you can use the FULL OUTER JOIN clause, as shown in the following example:

```
SELECT Customers.CustomerName, Orders.Amount
FROM Customers
FULL OUTER JOIN Orders
ON Customers.CustomerID = Orders.CustomerID
```

In our example, the result is the same as in Figure 6-4. All the customer names and all the order amounts are returned. Some databases do not support FULL OUTER JOIN. In most cases, you can get the same results using the UNION operator.

Note that in all the examples, the SELECT statements specify the columns being joined: Customers.CustomerID and Orders.CustomerID. You must specify the columns to join. If you do not, the result is what is commonly referred to as a cartesian join. In a cartesian join, all rows in the first table are joined with all rows in the second table. If the first table has 1000 rows and the second table has 10,000 rows, the cartesian join returns 10,000,000 rows, a result you rarely want.

The inner, left, and right joins are the most common types of joins. For more information about these joins and others that your database supports, see the database manufacturer's documentation.

How to create a SQL query to retrieve data from a JDBC data source

This procedure assumes you have already created the JDBC data source that this data set uses.

1   In Data Explorer, right-click Data Sets, then choose New Data Set.

2   In New Data Set, specify the following information:

   1   In Data Source Selection, under JDBC Data Source, select the data source to use.

   2   In Data Set Type, select SQL Select Query.

   3   In Data Set Name, type a name for the data set.

   4   Choose Next.

   Query displays the information to help you create a SQL query. Available Items lists the items in the data source.

3   To see the tables in a database, expand the database, as shown in Figure 6-5.

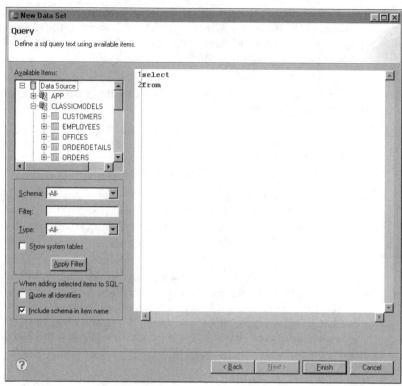

Figure 6-5   Viewing a schema

You can use the following filter options to display specific schemas or objects. Choose Apply Filter after specifying the filters.

- In Schema, select an item to display only objects from that schema.

- In Type, select the type of objects—tables, views, or stored procedures—to display.

- In Filter, type one or more letters to display only the objects that have names beginning with those letter or letters. You can also use SQL filter characters for the database that you are using. For example, on some databases, an underscore (_) matches any single character, and the percent sign (%) matches any sequence of characters.

4 To display the columns in a table or view, click the plus sign (+) next to a table or view name.

5 In the text area, type a SQL statement that indicates what data to retrieve from the JDBC data source. Alternatively, drag tables, views, and columns from Available Items to the text area to insert their names in the SQL statement at the insertion point, as shown in Figure 6-6.

For some databases, if a table or column name contains spaces or SQL reserved words, you must enclose the name in quotation marks (" "). If you drag and drop tables and columns, and those items need to be enclosed in double quotation marks, select the Use identifier quoting option. When this option is selected, the data set editor inserts the quotation marks around a table or column name when you drop it in the text area.

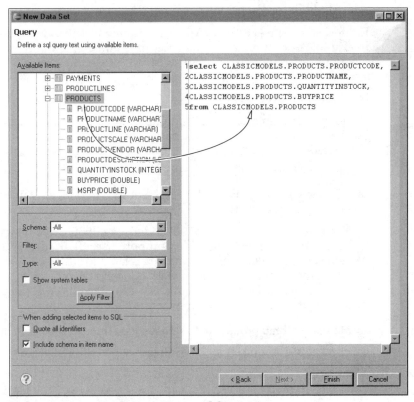

Figure 6-6   Adding a table to a SQL query

6 Choose Finish. Edit Data Set displays the columns specified in the query, and provides options for editing the data set.

Using a stored procedure to retrieve data from a JDBC data source

BIRT Report Designer also supports using a stored procedure to retrieve database data. As its name suggests, a stored procedure is a procedure that is stored in a database. A stored procedure consists of SQL statements used to execute operations or queries on a database. A stored procedure can:

- Return a result set, which is a set of rows.

- Accept input parameters, which are parameters used to pass data to the stored procedure. For example, a stored procedure runs a query that returns the customer name and credit limit for a specified customer ID. In this case, the stored procedure defines an input parameter to get the customer ID.

■ Use output parameters to return values. The stored procedure described in the previous point uses two output parameters to return the name and credit limit for a specified customer ID.

To run a stored procedure, use the call statement. The following statement is an example of running a stored procedure named getEmployeeData that contains no parameters. This type of stored procedure typically returns a result set.

```
{call getEmployeeData()}
```

The following is an example of running a stored procedure named getClientData that contains three parameters. The first and second parameters are output parameters, and the third is an input parameter.

```
{call getClientData(?, ?, 103)}
```

Each ? character is a placeholder for the output parameter value that the stored procedure returns.

BIRT relies on the capabilities of the underlying JDBC driver in its support for stored procedures. For more robust support, use a JDBC driver that fully implements the JDBC interfaces that are related to stored procedures, including those that provide its metadata. The jTDS project on SourceForge.net, for example, provides a pure Java (type 4) JDBC 3.0 driver for Microsoft SQL Server, which supports stored procedures.

How to use a stored procedure to retrieve data from a JDBC data source

This procedure assumes you have already created the JDBC data source that this data set uses.

1 In Data Explorer, right-click Data Sets, then choose New Data Set.

2 In New Data Set, specify the following information:

    1 In Data Source Selection, select the JDBC data source to use.

    2 In Data Set Type, select SQL Stored Procedure Query.

    3 In Data Set Name, type a name for the data set. Choose Next.

    Query displays a template for executing a stored procedure.

3 In Available Items, navigate to the stored procedure. Select the stored procedure, and drag it to the text area. The stored procedure name appears at the insertion point. Type the arguments if the stored procedure uses parameters.

    Figure 6-7 shows a stored procedure selected in Available Items. The stored procedure has three parameters. The text area displays the call statement to run the stored procedure.

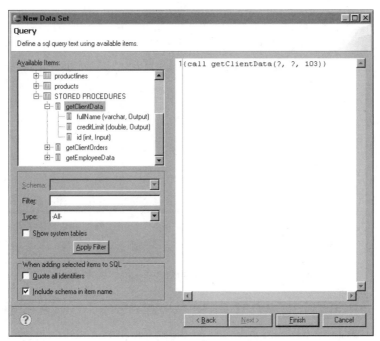

Figure 6-7   Displaying stored procedures in a database

4 Choose Finish to save the data set.

5 Verify the results returned by the stored procedure, using one of the following steps:

■ If the stored procedure returns a result set, choose Preview Results to see the data rows. If a stored procedure returns multiple result sets, select the result set you want by specifying the result set's name or number. To do so, choose Settings and, in Result Set Selection, specify the result set. Figure 6-8 shows an example of selecting the second result set.

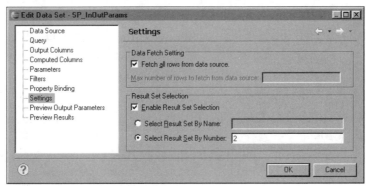

Figure 6-8   Selecting a result set

- If the stored procedure returns output parameter values, choose Preview Output Parameters. Figure 6-9 shows an example of the values returned by the stored procedure shown in Figure 6-7.

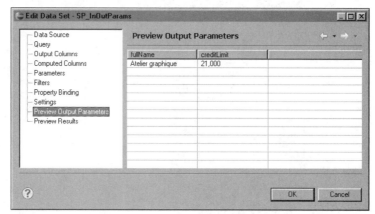

Figure 6-9 Previewing output parameter values

Specifying what data to retrieve from a text file

The previous chapter described the structure of data in a text file and provided an example. In the example, the structure of column names followed by rows of values resembles values stored in the table structure required by BIRT reports. This resemblance in data structure makes it easy to select the data to retrieve from a text file. The data set wizard displays the column names from the text file, and you select the columns that contain the data you want.

How to create a data set to retrieve data from a text file

This procedure assumes you have already created the flat file data source that this data set uses.

1 In Data Explorer, right-click Data Sets, then choose New Data Set.

2 In New Data Set, specify the following information:

1 In Data Source Selection, select the flat file data source to use. Data Set Type displays Flat File Data Set.

2 In Data Set Name, type a name for the data set.

3 Choose Next.

3 In Select Columns, in File filter, select the file-name extension of the text file.

4 In Select file, select a text file from the drop-down list. The left pane displays the columns that are available in the selected file.

5 Select the columns to retrieve, and move them to the right pane. You can select columns in either of the following ways:

- Select a column, then choose the arrow button.

- Press Shift while you click to select multiple columns, then choose the arrow button.

Figure 6-10 shows an example of all columns selected from a text file.

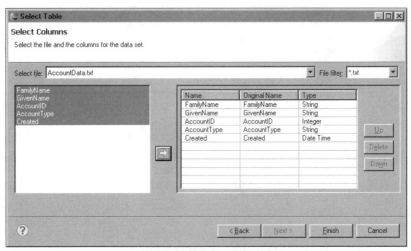

Figure 6-10   Selecting columns from a text file

6 Choose Finish to save the data set. Edit Data Set displays the columns you selected, and provides options for editing the data set.

Specifying what data to retrieve from an XML data source

As discussed previously, BIRT reports must use data that is structured as a table consisting of rows and columns. XML documents use elements and attributes to present data. The data set wizard enables you to map a top-level XML element as a data set row, and other XML elements or attributes as columns. The wizard uses XPath expressions to define the paths to elements and attributes. XPath is a query language used to access parts of an XML document.

When you select an element or attribute to map to a row or a column, the wizard generates the corresponding XPath expression. If you are familiar with XPath syntax and you want to do more than the basic mapping, you can write your own XPath expressions.

This section describes the most common ways to write an XPath expression to use an element or attribute as a row or column in an XML data set. This section is not a substitute for formal XPath user documentation. Examples in this section refer to the following sample XML document:

```
<?xml version="1.0"?>
<library>
   <book category="COOKING">
      <title lang="es">The Spanish Cook Book</title>
      <author name="Miguel Ortiz" country="es"/>
      <year>2005</year>
   </book>
   <book category="CHILDREN">
      <title lang="en">Everyone is Super Special</title>
      <author name="Sally Bush" country="us"/>
      <year>2005</year>
   </book>
   <audio format="CD" category="MUSIC">
      <title lang="en">We All Sing Perty</title>
      <artist name="Mary Rogers" country="us"/>
      <year>2005</year>
   </audio>
   <audio format="CD" category="MUSIC">
      <title lang="en">The Bluest Blues</title>
      <artist name="Barry Sadley" country="us"/>
      <year>2005</year>
   </audio>
</library>
```

The most important syntax rules to consider when writing XPath expressions to define rows and columns are as follows:

- Any path that starts with a forward slash (/) is an absolute path to an element.

- Any path that starts with two forward slashes (//) selects an element at any location.

- The XPath expression that defines the row mapping can use either of the previous path syntaxes. The following XPath expression selects all book elements that are children of library:

  /library/book

  The following XPath expression selects all book elements at any location:

  //book

- For attribute paths, use a single forward slash or left and right brackets. For example, the following paths are equivalent:

  title/@lang
  title[@lang]

- To define an element's attribute as a column, use either of the following syntax forms:

  author/@name
  author[@name]

- To define a table-level attribute as a column, use either of the following syntax forms:

  ```
  /@category
  [@category]
  ```

- To filter data rows, use either of the following predicate expression syntaxes:

  - Single-position predicates in the abbreviated form. The following example selects the first author listed:

    ```
    author[1]
    ```

  - Single-equality conditions based on an attribute value. For example, select an element by using the value of an attribute of the element. In the following example, only books that are in English are selected:

    ```
    title[@lang='eng']
    ```

- XPath functions are not supported.

How to create a data set to retrieve data from an XML document

This procedure assumes you have already created the XML data source that this data set uses.

1 In Data Explorer, right-click Data Sets, then choose New Data Set.

2 In New Data Set, specify the following information:

   1 In Data Source Selection, select the XML data source to use. Data Set Type displays XML Data Set.

   2 In Data Set Name, type a name for the data set.

   3 Choose Next.

3 In New XML Data Set, specify the XML source in one of the following ways:

   - To use the file specified in the XML data source, select Use the XML file defined in data source.

   - To select a file that is not specified in the data source, select the second option. In the text box, type the path to the XML file, or choose Browse to navigate to and select an XML file.

   Choose Next.

4 Define the row mapping, using the following steps:

   1 In XML Structure, navigate to the XML element that represents a data set row, and select the element. Choose the right arrow.

   The Select or edit the XPath expression dialog displays an XPath expression that corresponds to the element you selected, as shown in Figure 6-11.

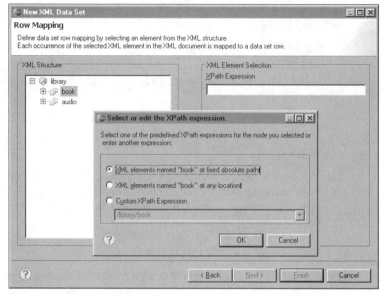

Figure 6-11   Creating an XML data set

2 Select one of the generated XPath expressions or type another
   expression. For example, you can type a filter expression to retrieve
   only rows that meet a certain condition, as shown in the following
   example:

   `/library/book/author[@country='us']`

   Choose OK, then choose Next.

5 Define the column mapping, using the following steps:

   1 In XML structure, navigate to and select the XML element or attribute
      that represents a column, then choose the right arrow. Column
      Mapping displays the default column mapping properties for the
      element or attribute you selected. Figure 6-12 shows an example of the
      default column mapping for an attribute named category.

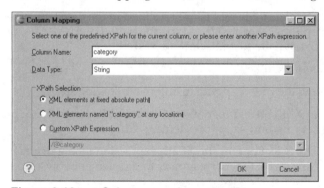

Figure 6-12   Column mapping properties

2 Select one of the generated XPath expressions or type another expression. Choose OK.

6 Repeat the preceding steps for every column to add to the data set. Figure 6-13 shows an example of column mappings defined in a data set.

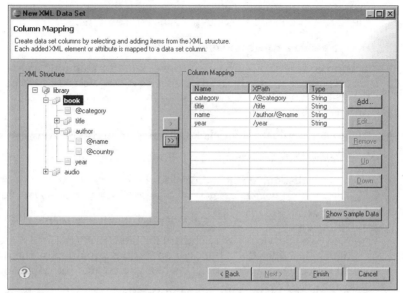

Figure 6-13   Mapping columns for an XML data set

7 Choose Finish to save the XML data set. Edit Data Set displays the columns, and provides options for editing the data set.

Specifying what data to retrieve from a web service

A web service provides application functionality from a remote server, which makes the creation of a web service data set more complex than the other data set types. While the wizard guides you through the steps to supply the necessary information, it helps to understand generally how the data set communicates with a web service. The data set performs the following tasks:

■ It sends a SOAP request to the web service. The request specifies the action you want the web service to perform and the parameter values to use when performing the action. For example, the request can be to run a mortgage calculator, and the parameter values to send are the loan years, interest rate, loan amount, annual tax, and annual insurance.

■ The data set specifies the format of the SOAP response to use when the web service sends data back to the report.

■ Finally, the data set specifies the data that the web service should return. For example, in the case of a mortgage calculator, you can choose to get just the total monthly mortgage payment, or get additional data, such as monthly principal and interest, monthly tax, and monthly insurance.

The data set wizard constructs the SOAP request and response based on the web service operation and schema you select. For well-defined web services, you can use the generated SOAP request and response without any modifications, so while knowledge of SOAP can be helpful, it is typically not required. The wizard also displays, in XML format, all the data that the operation can return, so all you do is select the data that you want to use in the report, then map the data to rows and columns.

How to create a data set to retrieve data from a web service

This procedure shows how to retrieve data from a public web service that returns the weather forecast for a specified U.S. zip code. This procedure uses the web service data source, Weather_ws, for which the creation procedure is provided in the previous chapter.

1 In Data Explorer, right-click Data Sets, then choose New Data Set.

2 In New Data Set, specify the following information:

   1 In Data Source Selection, select the web services data source, Weather_ws. Data Set Type displays Web Services Data Set.

   2 In Data Set Name, type a name for the data set, then choose Next.

   New Web Services Data Set displays the URL to the WSDL document, which describes the services or operations provided by the web service. You specified the WSDL URL when you created the data source.

3 Expand the WSDL URL. Expand WeatherForecastSoap, then select GetWeatherByZipCode, as shown in Figure 6-14.

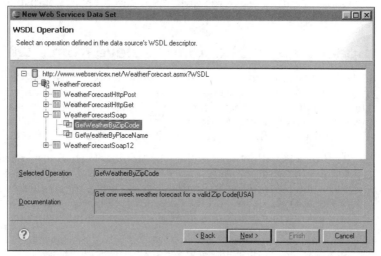

Figure 6-14   Selecting the GetWeatherByZipCode operation under WeatherForecastSoap

Choose Next.

New Web Services Data Set displays the parameter used by the GetWeatherByZipCode operation, as shown in Figure 6-15. The parameter, selected by default, defines the zip code for which to return the weather forecast.

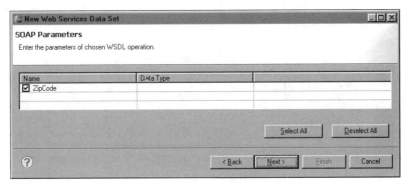

Figure 6-15   Parameters and specified default values

Choose Next.

BIRT generates a SOAP request template based on the WSDL document and your parameter selection, as shown in Figure 6-16. The body section of the SOAP request tells the web service to run the GetWeatherByZipCode operation, using the value of the ZipCode parameter. The parameter notation, &?ZipCode?&, indicates that a value can be inserted in the SOAP request at run time.

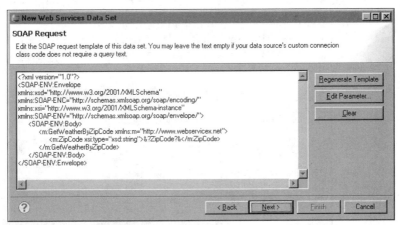

Figure 6-16   SOAP request template

4   Specify a value for the ZipCode parameter, using the following steps:

1   Choose Edit Parameter.

2   In SOAP Request, select the ZipCode parameter, then choose Edit.

3   In Edit parameter property, in Default Value, type a zip code, such as 94044. Choose OK.

5 Choose OK to save your changes to the SOAP request.

Choose Next. New Web Service Data Set displays the options for constructing a SOAP response, as shown in Figure 6-17.

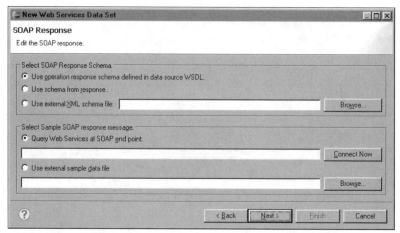

Figure 6-17   Options for constructing a SOAP response

6 Choose Next to accept the default options, which is the typical case for most well-defined web services.

New Web Services Data Set displays an XML structure of the web service.

7 Select an element to map to a data set row, using the following steps:

1 In XML Structure, expand all the items, then select GetWeatherByZipCodeResult, as shown in Figure 6-18. GetWeatherByZipCodeResult defines the data returned by the weather forecast service.

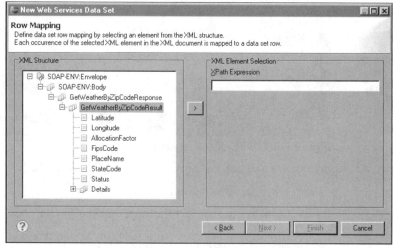

Figure 6-18   Select an element to map as a table

2 Click the > button.

The Select or edit the XPath expression dialog, shown in Figure 6-19, prompts you to select a generated XPath expression, or to write a custom XPath expression. The expression defines the path to the selected XML element.

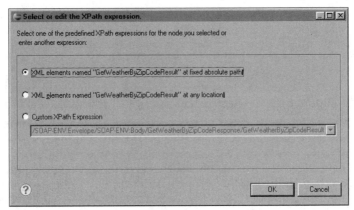

Figure 6-19   Options for specifying an XPath expression

3 Choose OK to accept the generated XPath expression selected by default.

4 Choose Next.

8 In Column Mapping, select the elements to map to columns.

1 In XML Structure, under GetWeatherByZipCodeResult, expand Details, then WeatherData.

The GetWeatherByZipCodeResult operation returns several categories of data. For this example, assume that you want to retrieve only the following data: Day, MaxTemperatureF, and MinTemperatureF.

2 Select the Day element. Click the > button to create the XPath expression that maps the selected element as a column, then choose OK.

3 Select MaxTemperatureF and repeat the previous step to map it to a column.

4 Select MinTemperatureF and map it to a column.

9 Choose Finish.

10 In Edit Data Set, choose Preview Results.

The data set returns the date, and the maximum and minimum temperatures for zip code 94044, as shown in Figure 6-20.

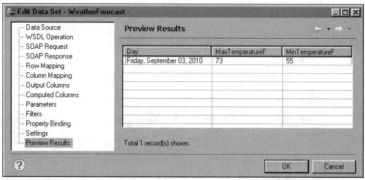

Figure 6-20   Results returned by the web service data set

When you use this data in a report, each time the report is run, the data set gets the weather forecast for the current day and for zip code 94044. While this data may be all you want to display in your report, the typical case when using a web service is to enable the report user to supply parameter values at run time. In the weather forecast example, you can make the report more interesting by prompting the user to specify the zip code for which to get weather information. For many web services, such as a mortgage calculator or a currency converter, incorporating web service data in the report makes sense only if users can specify parameter values to get the data they want.

The solution is to create report parameters to prompt the user for values. The user-specified values are then passed to the data set, which, in turn, passes those values to the web service through the SOAP request. The procedure for implementing this solution is described next. The procedure describes how to create a basic report parameter. For detailed information about report parameters, see Chapter 15, "Enabling the User to Filter Data."

How to enable a user to provide parameter values to a web service

This procedure continues with the weather forecast example.

1 Create a report parameter to get the zip code at run time, using the following steps:

    1 In Data Explorer, right-click Report Parameters, then choose New Parameter.

    2 In New Parameter, supply the following information:

       ❑ In Name, type a name for the report parameter. For example:

          `zipcode_reportparam`

       ❑ In Prompt text, specify a word or sentence to prompt the report user to provide a zip code. For example:

          `Weather forecast for this zip code`

       ❑ In Data type, select String.

       ❑ Use the default values for the other attributes.

Figure 6-21 shows the completed report parameter definition.

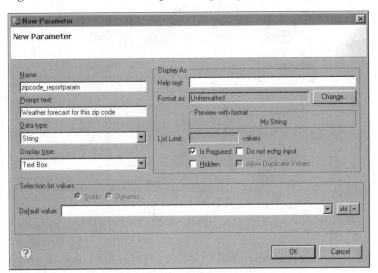

Figure 6-21   Report parameter to get the zip code

3   Choose OK. The zipcode_reportparam parameter appears under Report Parameters in Data Explorer.

2   Edit the data set parameter and link it to the report parameter.

1   In Data Explorer, right-click the web service data set, then choose Edit.

2   In Edit Data Set, select Parameters. As Figure 6-22 shows, the Parameters page displays the ZipCode parameter defined in the GetWeatherByZipCodeResult operation. The parameter's default value is set to 94044, which is the value specified when you defined the data set.

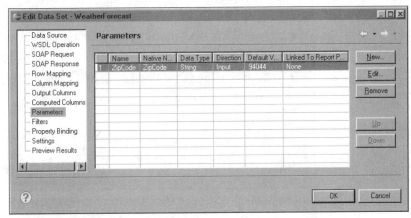

Figure 6-22   Data set parameter

3   Select the ZipCode parameter, then choose Edit.

4   In Edit Parameter, in Linked To Report Parameter, select
    zipcode_reportparam, as shown in Figure 6-23, then choose OK.

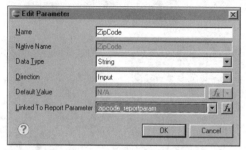

Figure 6-23   Link the data set parameter to the report parameter

3   Choose OK to save your changes to the data set.

4   Test the web service functionality in a report.

1   Drag the web service data set from the Data Explorer and drop it in the
    layout editor. BIRT creates a table and data elements to display the
    weather data, as shown in Figure 6-24.

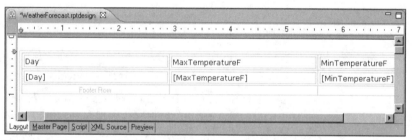

Figure 6-24   Report design to display the weather forecast data

2   Choose Preview. Enter Parameters displays the report parameter to get
    the zip code value.

3   Type a zip code, as shown in Figure 6-25. Do not include quotation
    marks. Choose OK.

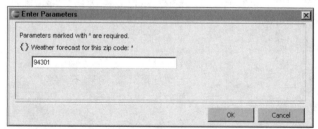

Figure 6-25   Zip code specified for the report parameter

The report displays weather data for that zip code. Figure 6-26 shows
an example.

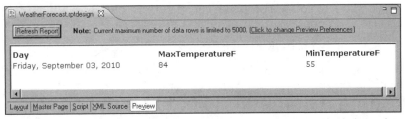

Figure 6-26   Report displays weather data for the specified zip code

Viewing and changing output columns

Use the Output Columns page of the data set editor to view the list of columns selected for retrieval, and to specify an alias or display name for each column. BIRT Report Designer uses the display name in Data Explorer and for the column headings in a table. For example, you can give a column named $$CN01 a display name of Customer Name. This display name makes the column easier to identify in Data Explorer and more user-friendly in the column heading of a table.

If you are creating a report for multiple locales, you can localize each display name by providing a resource key in the Display Name Key property. A resource key is a text string in an external source that is translated, or localized, into different languages. For more information about resource keys and localization, see Chapter 25, "Localizing Text."

Specify an alias to use a shorter or more recognizable name when referring to the column in code. For example, give a column named $$CN01 an alias of custName so that you can write row["custName"] instead of row["$$CN01"]. If you do not specify a display name for the column, BIRT Report Designer displays the alias in Data Explorer and for the column headings in a table.

How to view and change output columns

1   Choose Output Columns from the left pane of Edit Data Set. Output Columns displays the names and types of the columns, as shown in Figure 6-27.

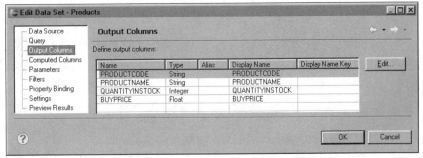

Figure 6-27   Viewing the output columns for a data set

2 To edit the properties of an output column, select the column name, then choose Edit. Edit Output Column displays the properties you can set.

3 Choose OK to save the edits.

Adding a computed field to a data set

A data set can contain computed data as well as data that is returned from a data source. Computed data displays the result of an expression, typically involving one or more columns from a data source. For example, if each row that is returned from the data source contains a price and a quantity, you can create a computed field that calculates the total amount paid, using the following expression:

```
row["pricequote"] * row["quantity"]
```

You can also concatenate values from multiple fields, using the + operator, or calculate values using JavaScript functions. The expression builder provides a list of operators and functions that you can use to build expressions.

You can also define a computed field in the report layout. Defining computed fields in the data set is, however, the preferred approach. Defining the computed field in the data set separates business logic from the presentation of the data. Defining the computed field in the data set also enables you to verify the results of the calculation in the Preview Results page of Edit Data Set. You can determine whether the expression for the computed field is correct before using the field in the report design. Figure 6-28 shows the Preview Results page including the results of a computed field, Total_cost.

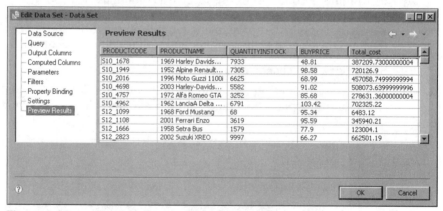

Figure 6-28 Preview Results including the results of a computed field, Total_cost

How to add a computed field to a data set

1 In Edit Data Set, choose Computed Columns.

2 Choose New to create a new computed field.

3 In New Computed Column:

1 In Column Name, type a name for the computed field.

2 In Data Type, select a data type appropriate for the data returned by the computed field.

3 To perform a calculation on all the rows in the data set, in Aggregation, select an aggregate function. If performing an aggregate calculation, you can optionally specify a filter expression in Filter to determine which rows to include in the calculation.

4 In Expression, specify the expression to calculate the desired value. You can either type the expression or use the expression builder to construct the expression. To use the expression builder, complete the following steps:

❏ Choose the expression builder button to open the expression builder. In Category, select Available Data sets, then select your data set. Double-click an item to add it to the text area at the top. Figure 6-29 shows how to create an expression for a computed column.

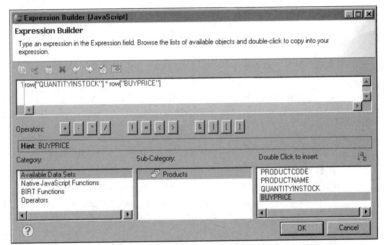

Figure 6-29 Creating an expression for a computed column

❏ Choose OK to save the expression. The expression appears in the Expression field in New Computed Column.

5 Choose OK to save the computed field. Computed Columns displays the computed field and the expression you defined.

4 Choose Output Columns to see all the columns that are specified in the data set. The computed field appears on this page.

5 Choose Preview Results to confirm that the computed field returns the correct data.

6 Choose OK to save your changes to the data set.

Joining data sets

The capability to join data sets is a useful and easy way to combine data from two data sources. For example, you can combine data from two XML files, or combine data from a text file with data from a database table. Before joining data sets, you must create the individual data sets. For example, to combine data from an XML file with data from a text file, you must first create the XML data set and the text file data set.

Joining data sets is similar to joining tables in a database, described earlier in "Combining data from multiple tables," but with the following two limitations:

- You can join only two data sets. In a database, you can join more than two tables.

- You can create only four types of joins: inner, left outer, right outer, and full outer.

The four types of joins you can use to join data sets yield the same results as the similarly-named database joins. The following list summarizes the function of each join type:

- Inner join returns rows from both data sets where the key values match.

- Left outer join returns all rows from the first data set, even if there are no matches in the second data set.

- Right outer join returns all rows from the second data set, even if there are no matches in the first data set.

- Full outer join returns all rows from both data sets, even if there are no matches in either data set.

Like the database joins, you must specify a column on which to join the two data sets. Joining two data sets creates a BIRT object called a joint data set. Just as you can with a regular data set, you can add computed columns and filters to a joint data set, and preview the results it returns. Once you understand the concepts of joining data sets, you can be creative about combining data from more than two sources, assuming that the data from the various sources relate in some way.

Although each joint data set can join only two data sets, you can use a joint data set as one or both of those data sets. For example, you can create joint data set A and joint data set B, then join both of them. Doing so, in effect, combines data from four data sets. Figure 6-30 illustrates this concept.

As Figure 6-30 also shows, each data set can return data from different types of sources. You could also use joint data sets to join multiple tables in a single database. For performance reasons, however, this technique is not recommended. Where possible, you should always join multiple tables through the SQL SELECT statement, as described earlier in this chapter.

You should create joint data sets only to:

- Combine data from disparate data sources.
- Combine data from non-relational data sources, such as XML or text files.

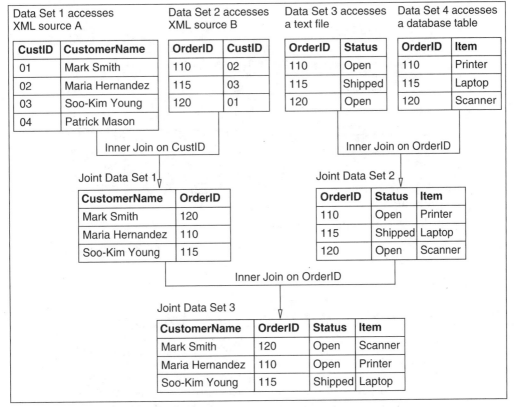

Figure 6-30   Combining data from four data sets

How to join data sets

1 In Data Explorer, right-click Data Sets, and choose New Joint Data Set.

2 Select the first data set for the joint data set from the drop-down list at the left of New Joint Data Set. The columns of the first data set appear in the panel below your selection.

3 Select the second data set for the joint data set from the drop-down list at the right of New Joint Data Set. The columns of the second data set appear.

4 Select the columns to join. Select one column from the first data set, and one column from the second data set.

   Typically, you select the columns that are common to both data sets. BIRT Report Designer does not prevent you from selecting two unrelated columns. Doing so, however, typically does not provide the correct results. Figure 6-31 shows an example of a joint data set definition.

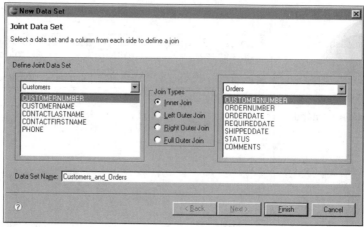

Figure 6-31   Joint data set definition

5 Select a join type, then choose Finish.

6 In Edit Data Set, choose Preview Results to see the rows returned by the joint data set.

Verifying the data returned by a data set

After creating a data set, always use Preview Results to verify that the data set returns the expected data. Figure 6-32 shows an example of a result set returned by a JDBC data set. By default, Preview Results shows up to 500 data rows. If you expect the data set to return more than 500 data rows and you want to see all the rows, increase the number of rows that Preview Results displays. Doing so, however, can increase the amount of time it takes to display the results.

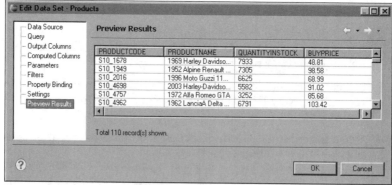

Figure 6-32   Previewing the results of a data set

How to change the number of rows that appear in Preview Results

1 Choose Window→Preferences.

2 In Preferences, click the plus sign (+) beside Report Design to expand the item.

3 Choose Data Set Editor.

4 In Number of rows to display, type the maximum number of rows to display, then choose OK.

Specifying the data to retrieve at run time

In all the procedures for retrieving the different types of data, described previously, the data you select is hard-coded at design time. Some reports, however, require the ability to display a different set of data based on run time criteria, such as user login or the data source that a report user selects.

As you may recall from the previous chapter, the data source editor provides a feature called property binding to support the setting of connection properties at run time. Similarly, the data set editor provides the property binding feature to support the selection of data at run time.

Figure 6-33 shows the Property Binding page for a JDBC data set. The Query Text property is where you specify an expression that determines at run time what data to select. The Query Text property is also available to the flat file and web services data set.

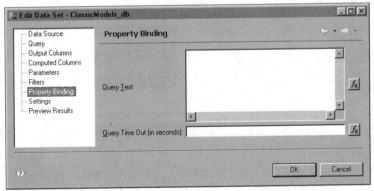

Figure 6-33   Property Binding page for a JDBC data set

About the Query Text property

When selecting data, whether by writing a SQL query, selecting a text file and columns, selecting XML elements, or specifying a SOAP request, BIRT stores that information in a property named queryText. Choose the XML Source tab on the report editor to see the XML source that BIRT generates when you create a report.

Figure 6-34 shows the part of the XML source that defines the value of the queryText property. In the example shown, the report uses data from the sample database, ClassicModels. The queryText property contains the SQL SELECT statement that specifies the data to retrieve.

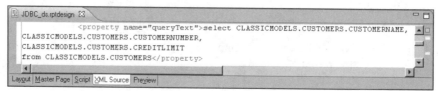

Figure 6-34   Report's XML source showing the queryText property for a JDBC data set

Figure 6-35 shows an example of a report's XML source, where the report uses data from a text file named ProductionData.csv. Although the flat file data set does not use a SQL query to select data, the queryText property contains a statement similar to a SQL query.

Figure 6-35   Report's XML source showing the queryText property for a flat file data set

Figure 6-36 shows the queryText property for a report that uses a web service data set. This property contains the SOAP request template.

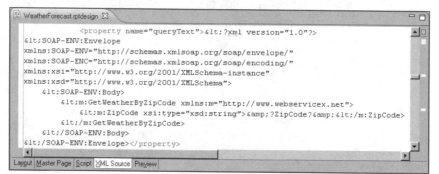

Figure 6-36   Report's XML source showing the queryText property for a web service data set

Specifying a value for the Query Text property

The Query Text property on the Property Binding page of the data set editor is the same as the queryText property in the report source file. The value you specify on the Property Binding page updates the queryText property in the source file, and must use the same format you see in the report source file. In

addition, you must enclose the value you type in double quotation marks
(" ").

The following example shows the correct syntax for specifying a Query Text
value for a JDBC data set:

```
"select CUSTOMERNAME, CUSTOMERNUMBER from CUSTOMERS where COUNTRY
   = 'Australia'"
```

The following example shows the correct syntax for specifying a Query Text
value for a flat file data set:

```
"select Date, Open, High from StockHistory.csv"
```

The previous examples showed the syntax for a Query Text value, but both
examples specified static data. Typically, when you specify a value for the
Query Text property, you use variables or JavaScript expressions that
evaluate to a specific value at run time.

The following example shows how to select a text file at run time. The
JavaScript expression params["pTextFileName"] refers to a report parameter
whose value evaluates to a file name specified at run time.

```
"select PRODUCTNAME, QUANTITYINSTOCK, MSRP from " +
   params["pTextFileName"]
```

The following example shows how to select from a database the customer
rows for a particular country. The country value is specified by the user at
run time through the report parameter p_Country.

```
"select CUSTOMERNAME, CUSTOMERNUMBER, COUNTRY from CUSTOMERS where
   COUNTRY =  " + "'" + params["p_Country"] + "'"
```

Binding Data

The data set or data sets that you create provide the data you want to use in a report. Before you can use or display this data in a report, you must first create the necessary data bindings. As the first tutorial demonstrated, to display the data in a report, you simply drag data set fields from Data Explorer to a table in the layout editor. Each time you insert a data set field, BIRT creates a data binding.

This data binding, called a column binding, defines an expression that specifies what data to display. The column binding also defines a name that report elements use to access data. To view the column bindings that BIRT creates for each data set field that you place in a table, select the table, then, in Property Editor, choose the Binding tab. Figure 7-1 shows an example of column bindings created for each data set field in a table.

Understanding column bindings

For each piece of data to display or use in a report, there must be a column binding. For this discussion, note that data refers to dynamic data, and not the static text that you type for a label. Dynamic data is data from a data set, or data that is calculated from a function or a formula. The data is dynamic because the values are not fixed at design time.

The default column binding, which BIRT Report Designer creates for a data set field, uses the data set field name as the name of the column binding. In Figure 7-1, the expression defined for the first column binding is dataSetRow["CITY"]. This expression indicates that the column binding accesses data from the data set field, CITY. In the layout editor, the column-binding name appears within square brackets ([]) in the report, as shown in Figure 7-1.

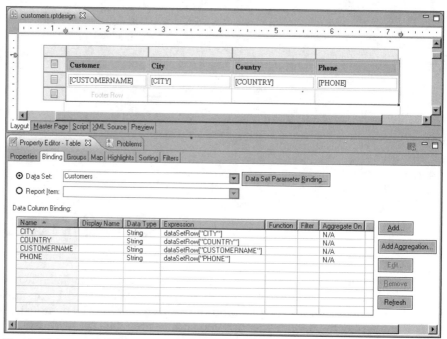

Figure 7-1   Table's Binding page showing four column bindings

Column bindings form an intermediate layer between data set data and report elements—such as chart, data, dynamic text, and image elements—that display data. Figure 7-2 illustrates this concept. Report elements can access data only through column bindings.

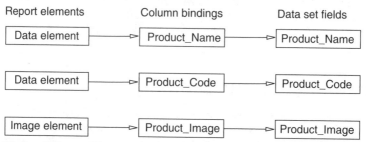

Figure 7-2   Report elements access data set data through column bindings

The preceding examples show column bindings that access data in a data set. Column bindings can also access data derived from functions or user-defined formulas. For example, you can use a data element to display the current date derived from the JavaScript Date object. You would create a column binding that uses the following expression:

```
new Date()
```

Figure 7-3 shows this column binding definition.

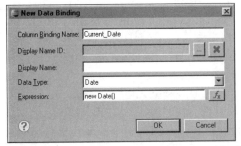

Figure 7-3   User-defined column binding

Descriptive names

One of the benefits of using column bindings is that you control the names used in the report. Instead of displaying data set field names, which are often not descriptive enough, or formulas, which can be long, you can specify short and descriptive names. If you share report designs with other report developers, descriptive names make that design much easier to understand. Modifying and maintaining a report design that has user-friendly names is easier.

Dynamic updates of calculated data

Another advantage of column bindings becomes apparent when working with calculated data. When a report needs to display a series of related calculated data, column bindings enable you to create and update calculations easily. For example, assume a report contains the following four data elements:

- The first data element uses column binding, Order_Total, which uses the SUM function, and the following expression to calculate the sum of all order line items:

  ```
  dataSetRow["pricequote"] * dataSetRow["quantity"]
  ```

- The second data element uses column binding, Sales_Tax, which refers to the previous column binding, Order_Total, to calculate the sales tax. The expression defined for the Sales_Tax column binding is

  ```
  row["Order_Total"] * 0.08
  ```

  Without using column bindings, the second data element must use the SUM function and the following longer expression to calculate sales tax:

  ```
  (dataSetRow["pricequote"] * dataSetRow["quantity"]) * 0.08
  ```

- The third data element uses column binding, Shipping_Charge, which also refers to the first column binding, Order_Total, to calculate the shipping charge. The expression defined for the Shipping_Charge column binding is

  ```
  row["Order_Total"] * 0.02
  ```

Again, without using column bindings, the third data element must use the SUM function, and the following lengthier expression to calculate the shipping charge:

```
(dataSetRow["pricequote"] * dataSetRow["quantity"]) * 0.02
```

- The fourth data element uses column binding, Invoice_Total, which refers to all the previous column bindings to calculate the grand total. The expression defined for the Invoice_Total column binding is

```
row["Order_Total"] + row["Sales_Tax"] + row["Shipping_Charge"]
```

Without column bindings, the expression would be more complicated:

```
(dataSetRow["pricequote"] * dataSetRow["quantity"]) +
   ((dataSetRow["pricequote"] * dataSetRow["quantity"]) * 0.08)
   +
   ((dataSetRow["pricequote"] * dataSetRow["quantity"]) * 0.02)
```

You have already seen how column bindings make expressions shorter and more readable. Now, consider the case where you need to update one calculation that is used by other calculations. Suppose you need to change how Order_Total is calculated, from:

```
dataSetRow["pricequote"] * dataSetRow["quantity"]
```

to:

```
(dataSetRow["pricequote"] * dataSetRow["quantity"]) -
   dataSetRow["discount"]
```

Because the second, third, and fourth data elements use Order_Total in their calculations, without using column bindings, you must manually edit those calculations as well. For example, without using column bindings, you would have to revise the expression for the fourth element as follows:

```
((dataSetRow["pricequote"] * dataSetRow["quantity"]) -
   dataSetRow["discount"]) +
   ((dataSetRow["pricequote"] * dataSetRow["quantity"]) * 0.08) +
   ((dataSetRow["pricequote"] * dataSetRow["quantity"]) * 0.02)
```

By using column bindings, any change to the first calculation automatically applies to the second, third, and fourth calculations. By modifying only one expression instead of three, your work is faster and less error-prone.

Creating column bindings

As discussed previously, when you drag a data set field from Data Explorer to a table in the layout editor, BIRT creates the column binding. When you bind a table to a data set, BIRT also creates a column binding for each field in the data set.

For other cases, when inserting a dynamic text, text, image, or data element from the palette, you manually create the column binding if you want the element to display dynamic data. If the information to display is static—for example, a specific image stored in a file system, or literal text—then column binding is not applicable.

How to create a column binding

This procedure shows an example of creating a column binding for a data element.

1 Drag a data element from the palette and drop it in the report.

2 In New Data Binding, create a new column binding:

   1 In Column Binding Name, specify a unique name for the column binding.

   2 In Display Name, optionally specify a different name to display in the report design. If you leave this property blank, the report design displays the Column Binding Name value.

   3 In Data Type, select a data type appropriate for the data returned by the expression you specify next.

   4 In Expression, specify the expression that indicates the data to return, using one of the following methods:

      ❑ Type the expression directly in the Expression field.

      ❑ If you need help constructing the expression, choose the expression builder button to launch the expression builder. Figure 7-4 shows an expression in the expression builder that combines the values of two data set fields selected from the Customers data set.

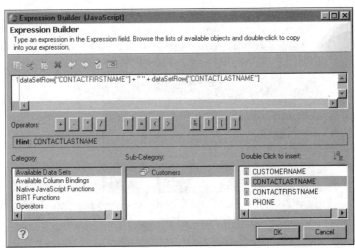

Figure 7-4   The expression builder showing a column-binding expression

Choose OK when you finish constructing the expression. Figure 7-5 shows an example of a column-binding definition.

Figure 7-5   New column-binding definition

5   Choose OK to save the column binding.

In the layout editor, the report design displays [Contact_Name] in the location where you inserted the data element, indicating that the data element uses the column binding you defined.

3   Preview the report. The data element displays the data defined in the column binding expression.

Editing and deleting column bindings

Be careful when editing or deleting column bindings. More than one element can use a column binding, and a column binding can refer to other column bindings. Earlier in this chapter, you saw examples of how a change to a calculated-data expression cascaded to other expressions. The ease with which you can dynamically update formulas that refer to column bindings also requires that you be aware of those dependencies.

To minimize errors, BIRT allows you to edit the data type, display name, and the expression, but not the name of the column binding. Figure 7-6 shows Edit Data Binding, which opens when you double-click a data element in the report. The value in Column Binding Name is read-only.

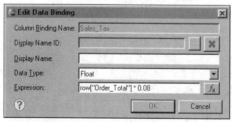

Figure 7-6   Edit Data Binding showing the definition of a column binding

If you could edit the name of the column binding, expressions in other column bindings that refer to that column binding would no longer be valid, unless you also update all expressions to refer to the renamed column binding. For example, as Figure 7-6 shows, the expression in Sales_Tax refers to a column binding named Order_Total. If you could rename Order_Total, the expression in Sales_Tax, row["Order_Total"] * 0.08, would refer to a column binding that no longer exists.

Deleting a column binding that is used by multiple elements results in errors in the report design. Consider the following scenario:

You drop a data set field, COUNTRY, in a table. BIRT Report Designer creates a column binding named COUNTRY that refers to the data set field. You create a sort condition to display rows alphabetically by country names. The sort expression uses the COUNTRY column binding. Later, you decide not to display the COUNTRY values in the report. You delete the [COUNTRY] data element from the table. To maintain an accurate list of column bindings used in the table, you also delete the COUNTRY column binding from the table's Binding page. When you run the report, BIRT displays an error message because the sort expression still refers to the COUNTRY column binding, which no longer exists.

Before you edit or delete a column binding, consider these guidelines:

- A change to a column binding's expression applies to other column bindings that refer to that column binding.

- A column binding can be used in a variety of expressions, not just by data elements that display field values in the report. For example, expressions used to sort, group, filter, or highlight data also refer to column bindings.

If you delete a column binding, preview the report immediately to make sure you have not introduced any errors. If the report no longer generates, use the Undo functionality to restore the report to its previous state.

Copying data elements

Another action to be careful about is copying and pasting data elements. In a report that displays the same or similar data in multiple places, the natural inclination is to copy the data element and paste it elsewhere in the report. For example, you want to display the order ID in two places: the detail row and header row of a table. You already inserted the order ID data element in the detail row, so you copy the data element and paste it in the header row. When you run the report, the order ID appears in both places.

Later, you decide to add static text, Order Number:, to the order ID value that appears in the header row. You double-click the data element in the header row, and change the expression in the Edit Data Binding dialog from:

```
dataSetRow["ORDERNUMBER"]
```

to

```
"Order Number: " + dataSetRow["ORDERNUMBER"]
```

When you choose OK to save the change, BIRT prompts you to choose one of the following options:

- Create a new column binding for the selected data element. This option enables you to make changes only to the selected data element.

- Update both data elements to use the new expression.

Figure 7-7 shows the message that BIRT displays when you edit an expression for a column binding that is used by multiple data elements.

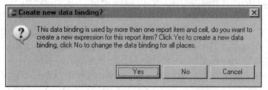

Figure 7-7   Options for editing a column-binding expression

When you copy and paste a data element, all the copies refer to a single instance of the column binding. Because this behavior is not apparent, BIRT asks how you want a change in a column binding's expression or data type to be processed. Otherwise, you might assume that selecting a data element and editing its column binding information affects only the selected data element.

More about column-binding expressions

When writing an expression for a column binding, the expression can refer to data set fields, other column bindings, functions, and operators. The expression builder simplifies writing an expression by displaying the available items—data set fields, column bindings, functions, and so on.

The items available in the expression builder change depending on where you define the column binding. For example, if you insert a data element in a table that contains other column bindings, the data element can access those column bindings. If you insert a data element directly on the report page, the data element cannot access column bindings defined for the table or any other report element.

When you select an item in the expression builder, the expression builder adds the item to the expression with the proper syntax. When a column-binding expression refers to a data set field, the syntax is

```
dataSetRow["datasetField"]
```

When a column-binding expression refers to another column binding, the syntax is

```
row["columnBinding"]
```

If you use the expression builder to construct column-binding expressions, you do not need to remember what syntax to use. You will find it helpful, though, to understand what each syntax means because the expression examples that appear throughout the book use both syntaxes.

Designing Reports

Laying Out a Report

You can present information in a report in many ways, for example, in a tabular list, a nested list, a chart, a series of text blocks, or a series of subreports. More complex report layouts can use a variety of these different presentations in a single report. Laying out a report entails placing data on the page and organizing the information in a way that helps a user to read and understand the information in the report.

Because there are infinite ways to lay out a report, it helps to work from a paper design. If you try to design and create the report layout at the same time, you can lose track of the data that you want to place in the report, or you can finish laying out one part of the report before realizing that you can better present the data using another layout.

Before you begin to lay out a report, verify in Data Explorer that the data set or data sets return the data that you want to use in your report. In many cases, the layout of a report is driven by the data.

Understanding the layout model

Like most documents, reports tend to be very structured. A report typically consists of distinct sections or a series of content blocks, as shown in Figure 8-1. BIRT Report Designer provides an intuitive way to lay out a report. A visual layout editor displays a page to which you add content, such as data fields, charts, pictures, or text blocks, in each section of the report.

A section can consist of one or multiple elements. The first section of a report, for example, is typically the report title. This section might contain just one text element. Another section, which displays a list of customer records, might contain four data fields and four column headings. More complex sections can contain multiple subsections to display items such as multiple lists that appear side by side or a combination of lists, charts, and text blocks. A key concept to understand about sections is that each section is a horizontal block of content.

You lay out the contents of each section of a report in the same way that you read a report— start from the top of the report and go from left to right until the end of the report. By dividing a report into sections, you can manipulate each section independently. For example:

- Use a different set of data for each section.

- Size and format each section independently.

- Specify page breaks before or after each section.

- Conditionally show or hide each section.

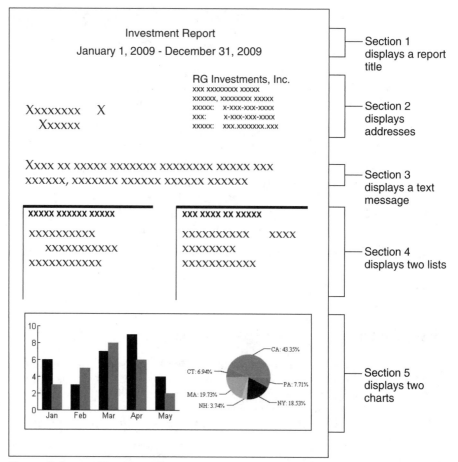

Figure 8-1   Report sections

About the report layout elements

BIRT Report Designer provides a variety of elements for building a report. To lay out a report, drag report elements from the palette and drop them on the page in the layout editor. Report elements fall into two general categories:

- Elements that display information
- Elements that organize multiple elements in a section

Table 8-1 provides a summary of the report elements that you can use to lay out your report. Details about using these report elements appear later in this chapter or elsewhere in this book.

Table 8-1   Report layout elements

Report element	Description
Label	Displays a piece of static text.
Text	Displays text that can contain HTML formatting and dynamic values.
Dynamic text	Displays memo or CLOB (Character Large Object) data from a data set field. The data typically consists of large amounts of text.
Data	Displays a computed value or a value from a data set field.
Image	Displays any image that a web browser supports.
Grid	Organizes multiple report elements in a static table. The number of rows in a static table is fixed at design time.
Table	Organizes data from a data set in a dynamic table. The number of rows in a table is determined by the number of data rows returned by the data set when the report is run.
List	Organizes data from a data set in a variety of layouts. By contrast, a table element organizes elements in a row-and-column format only.
Chart	Displays data from a data set in a variety of chart types, including pie charts, bar charts, and line charts.
Cross tab	Displays summary, or aggregate, data in a row-and-column matrix that is similar to a spreadsheet.

Overview of the layout process

To lay out a report, follow these general steps:

- Identify the sections in the report.
- For each section, insert either:

- A single report element, such as a text element

- A container element to organize multiple report elements in a section

- For sections that contain multiple elements, insert report elements in each container. You can insert containers within a container to create nested sections. Preview each section as you complete it. If you wait until you finish laying out the report before verifying the output, and there are errors, it can be difficult to determine which part of the report causes the problems.

Creating the sections of a report

Most sections in a report contain multiple elements. BIRT Report Designer provides three types of containers for organizing elements in a section:

- Grid

- Table

- List

The following sections describe each container element.

Organizing elements in a grid

Use a grid to arrange static elements, such as text and pictures, in a section. The grid is similar to the HTML table in a web page. It is ideal for creating report title sections and page headers and footers, as shown in Figure 8-2 and Figure 8-3.

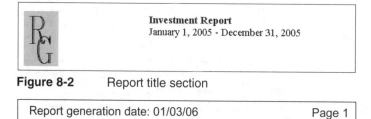

Investment Report
January 1, 2005 - December 31, 2005

Figure 8-2   Report title section

Report generation date: 01/03/06   Page 1

Figure 8-3   Report footer section

When you place a grid on the page, the layout editor displays a row-and-column structure, such as the one shown in Figure 8-4. By default, all the columns have the same width, and all the rows have the same height.

The grid layout automates the task of aligning blocks of content. When you place report elements in the cells, the report elements are automatically aligned horizontally and vertically. If you have used other reporting tools that provide a free-form layout editor that lack this capability, you will appreciate the automatic alignment feature that the grid provides. Placing report elements and then aligning them manually is time-consuming.

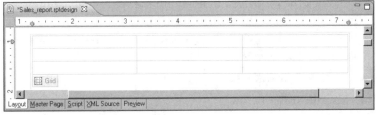

Figure 8-4 Row-and-column structure of a grid

You can add, delete, and resize rows and columns in the grid, as needed. Figure 8-5 shows a report title section that consists of a picture and two text elements, arranged in a grid with one row and two columns of different sizes.

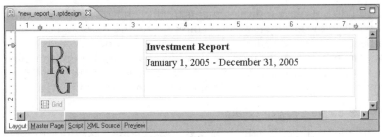

Figure 8-5 Grid displaying resized rows and columns

You can also format individual rows, columns, and cells to customize their size, color, borders, and text alignment. Chapter 10, "Formatting Report Content," describes these tasks.

Adding rows and columns

When you insert a grid, you specify a number of rows and columns. Depending on the number of report elements that you place in the grid, you might need to add rows or columns later.

How to add a row or column

1 In the layout editor, hover the mouse pointer over the bottom left corner of the grid until you see the Grid tab, then choose the tab. Guide cells appear at the top and left side of the grid, as shown in Figure 8-6.

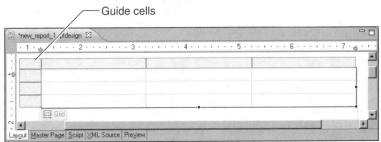

Figure 8-6 Guide cells support adding rows and columns

2   Right-click the guide cell in line with the space where you want to add a row or column.

3   Choose one of the following items from the context menu to add a row or column in the desired location:

- Insert➤Row➤Above

- Insert➤Row➤Below

- Insert➤Column to the Right

- Insert➤Column to the Left

Deleting rows and columns

If you do not place report elements in all of the grid's rows or columns, you can delete the empty rows and columns. Empty rows and columns have different effects on different output formats. By default, empty rows do not appear as blank space in HTML and PDF formats. If you want an empty row to appear as blank space in these formats, set the row to a specific size. Empty rows and columns, however, appear as blank space in DOC and XLS formats.

How to delete a row or column

1   In the layout editor, hover the mouse pointer over the bottom left corner of the grid until the Grid tab appears, then choose the tab. Guide cells appear at the top and left side of the grid.

2   Right-click the guide cell of the row or column to delete, then choose Delete from the context menu. If the row or column contains elements, the elements are also deleted.

Organizing elements in a table

Use a table to display dynamic data in a row-and-column format. Dynamic data is data from a data source, such as a database or XML document. The data is dynamic because the values are not fixed in the report design. Instead, when the report runs, the report connects to the data source, retrieves the specified data, and displays the current data. Figure 8-7 shows an example table that displays customer names and phone numbers from a data source.

Customer	Phone
Alpha Cognac	61.77.6555
American Souvenirs Inc	2035557845
Amica Models & Co.	011-4988555
ANG Resellers	(91) 745 6555
Anna's Decorations, Ltd	02 9936 8555
Anton Designs, Ltd.	+34 913 728555
Asian Shopping Network, Co	+612 9411 1555
Asian Treasures, Inc.	2967 555
Atelier graphique	40.32.2555

Figure 8-7   Table data in a generated report

When you place a table on the page, the layout editor displays a row-and-column structure, such as the one shown in Figure 8-8.

Like the grid, the table layout automates the task of aligning report elements. Unlike the grid, the table iterates through all the data rows that a data set returns to display the dynamic list of data.

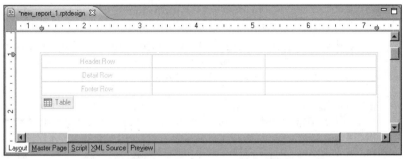

Figure 8-8   Row-and-column structure of a table

Note that a table can display data from one data set only. When you create a data set, ensure that it returns all the data that you want to display in a table. If the data that you need is stored in two database tables, write a query that joins the two tables. Alternatively, create two data sets and use two tables, one table for each data set.

Deciding where to place elements in a table

The table contains three types of rows in which you place report elements. Table 8-2 describes the types of information that you typically place in each row.

Table 8-2   Table row descriptions

Table row	Description
Header	Elements that you place in the header row appear at the beginning of the table. If the data in the table appears on multiple pages, the contents of the header display at the top of every page. You can display the header contents only once, at the beginning of the table, by turning off the table's Repeat Header property.
	Place elements in the header to display the following:
	■ A title
	■ Column headings, such as Customer Name, Address, and Phone, above the data in a customer list
	■ Summary information, such as the number of customers in the list

(continues)

Table 8-2   Table row descriptions *(continued)*

Table row	Description
Detail	Elements that you place in the detail row represent the dynamic data in the table. The detail row displays each row from the data set. For example, display the main data, such as customer names, addresses, and phone numbers, in a customer list.
Footer	Elements that you place in the footer row appear once, at the end of the table. For example, display summary information, such as totals.

Figure 8-9 shows a table layout for displaying a list of customer names and their phone numbers. The finished report displays the list that appears in Figure 8-7.

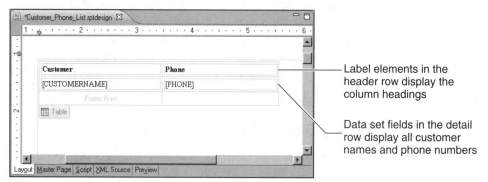

Figure 8-9   Table layout for customer names and phone numbers

Binding a table to a data set

When you place a data set field in a table, BIRT Report Designer:

- Binds, or associates, the data set with the table. By binding these items, the table has the information that it needs to iterate through the data rows that the data set returns.

- Creates a column binding, which binds the data set field with a named column.

- Creates a data element that uses the column binding to display data from the data set field.

You can view this binding information on the table's binding properties page. To access this information, select the table, then choose the Binding tab at the top of Property Editor. Figure 8-10 shows the binding properties page.

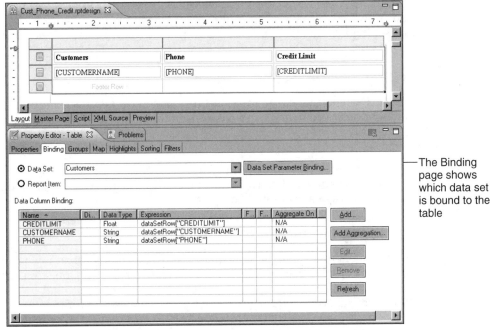

The Binding page shows which data set is bound to the table

Figure 8-10 Property Editor's Binding page for a selected table

You can also use this page to bind a table manually to a data set. The easier approach, however, is to place a data set field in the table and let BIRT Report Designer do the binding. If you are not placing data set fields in the table, but are inserting other types of elements, such as dynamic text elements or image elements that need to access data set data, then you need to manually bind the data set to the table before inserting those elements in the table.

A table can be bound to only one data set. BIRT Report Designer prevents you from inserting a field from a different data set. If you change the data set binding after you place fields in the table, you need to delete the fields because the table no longer has information about them.

If you do not change the data set binding, and you delete all the fields from a table, the table maintains its binding to the data set. To insert fields from a different data set into a table, you need to change the table's data set binding first. Deleting all the fields from the previous data set does not remove the original binding.

How to bind a data set to a table

1 In the layout editor, hover the mouse pointer over the bottom left corner of the table until the Table tab appears, then choose the tab.

2 Choose the Binding tab at the top of Property Editor. The Data Set field shows either the name of the data set that is currently bound to the table or None if no data set is bound to the table.

3 From the Data Set drop-down list, select a data set. BIRT Report Designer binds the data set to the table. It also creates a column binding for each data set field. Elements placed in the table can now access all the fields in the data set.

Adjusting table rows and columns

You can add, delete, and resize rows and columns in the table as is necessary. You add and delete table rows and columns in the same way that you add and delete grid rows and columns. These tasks are described earlier in this chapter.

A table can contain any number of header, detail, and footer rows. For example, you can add two header rows, one to display summary information and the other to display column headings.

Organizing elements in a list

Use a list element to display dynamic data in any format other than rows and columns. For example, use the list element to create form letters, one for each customer in a data set. Figure 8-11 shows an example PDF report that displays a series of form letters. Each letter is the same except for the recipient's name, which is dynamically derived from a customer name field.

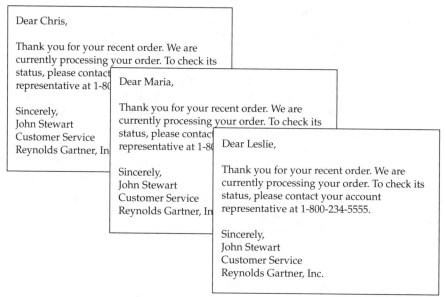

Figure 8-11   The list element supports the creation of form letters using dynamic data

When you place a list on the page, the layout editor displays the structure that appears in Figure 8-12.

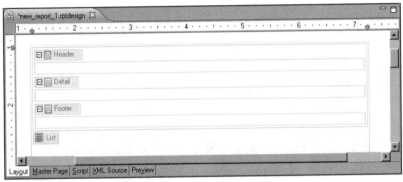

Figure 8-12   List structure

Deciding where to place elements in a list

Like the table, the list iterates through all the data rows that a data set returns to display data. Table 8-3 describes the three areas in a list.

Table 8-3   List area descriptions

List area	Description
Header	Elements that you place in Header appear once, at the beginning of the section. For example, display introductory information, such as a description of the report.
Detail	Elements that you place in Detail display dynamic data. The amount of data that appears is determined by the number of data rows that your data set returns. For example, print a letter for each customer in the data set.
Footer	Elements that you place in Footer appear once, at the end of the section. For example, display summary information, such as the number of records in the report.

Figure 8-13 shows a list layout that displays a form letter for each customer. The form letter is created using a text element that contains HTML formatting. The generated report displays the form letters that appear in Figure 8-11.

Figure 8-13 shows the most basic use of the list element. Typically, you use the list element to present data in more complex layouts. For example, you need a report that consists of many subreports. Each subreport goes to a single customer and consists of a cover letter, a summary account statement, and a detailed statement. To create this type of report, you define data sets that return each customer and the required account information, use grids and tables to create each section of the subreport, and place all the sections in a list element. For an example that shows the use of a list to organize subreports, see Chapter 16, "Building a Report That Contains Subreports."

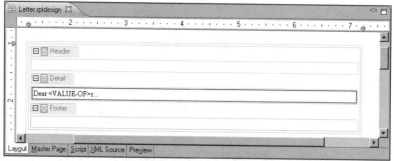

Figure 8-13   List element containing a text element in the detail area

Binding a list to a data set

Like the table, a list must be bound to a data set if the elements within the list need to access data set data. The binding principles and procedures for the table are the same for the list.

Placing report elements

You can place report elements in a page using one of the following methods:

- Drag an element from the palette and drop it in the page.

- Use the Insert menu to select an element to place.

- Drag a data set field from Data Explorer and drop it in a table, grid, or list. BIRT Report Designer inserts a data element to display the contents of the data set field.

When you drag an element from the palette, two cursors appear in the layout editor, as shown in Figure 8-14. The arrow cursor tracks your mouse movement. The straight cursor moves to the left or bottom of an existing report element when you move the mouse pointer around on the page. Watch the straight cursor. It shows where the element is placed when you release the mouse button.

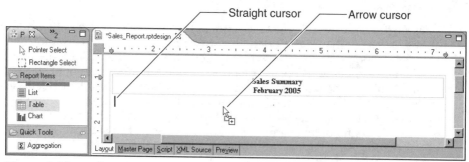

Figure 8-14   Straight cursor and arrow cursor indicate placement of an element

If you drop the element when the straight cursor is below an element, the new element appears on the next line, after the existing report element. Figure 8-15 shows the new element in the design.

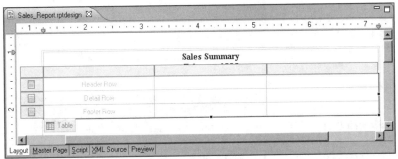

Figure 8-15　Inserted element placed beneath existing text element

Placing report elements side by side

By default, the layout editor does not allow you to place report elements side by side directly on the page. For example, you cannot place two labels, two tables, or a picture and a text element next to one another. The layout editor inserts the second element below the first one. To place multiple elements horizontally across the page, place them in a container element, such as a grid or table. Alternatively, use Property Editor to change the Display property of the elements from Block to Inline.

Inserting a data set field

Most of the information in a report is derived from data set fields. The report displays this data as it is stored in the data source. For example, in a customer orders report, you place customer name, order number, item, quantity, and price fields in the report.

To insert all the fields in a data set, choose Data Explorer, expand Data Sets, then drag the data set, and drop it in the page. BIRT Report Designer creates a table and the required column bindings, and places all the fields in the detail row of the table. The fields appear in the order in which they appear in the data set.

Often, however, you do not want to insert all the fields, or you want to insert them in a particular order. To place individual data fields, first insert a container element, typically a table, in which to place the fields. Although you can place data fields in a grid or directly on the page, you typically place fields in the detail row of a table or a list. If you place a field in a grid or in the page, only one value appears in the generated report. Unlike a table or list, the grid and page do not go through all the data rows in a data set.

To access and insert data set fields, choose Data Explorer, expand Data Sets, and select the data set. Then drag data set fields from Data Explorer and drop them in the container, as shown in Figure 8-16.

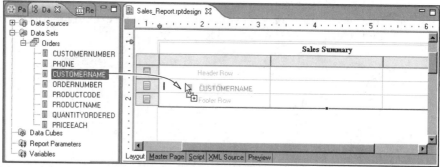

Figure 8-16   Use Data Explorer to insert data set fields in the report

Inserting a computed field

A computed field displays the result of an expression rather than stored data. For example, a database stores the prices of order items and the quantities that were ordered. To display the extended prices, specify the following expression to calculate the values:

```
row["pricequote"] * row["quantity"]
```

Table 8-4 lists other examples of when to use computed fields and the types of expressions that you can specify.

Table 8-4   Examples of expressions in computed fields

Uses for computed fields	Examples of expressions

Display data that concatenates values from multiple fields	The following expression displays a customer's first and last names, which the data source stores in two fields:
	
	`row["firstname"] + " " + row["lastname"]`
	
	The following expression displays a full address by concatenating values from four fields in the data source:
	
	`row["address"] +", " + row["city"] + ", " + row["state"] + " " + row["postalcode"]`

Display data using a JavaScript or BIRT function	The following expression uses the JavaScript Date object to return the current date:
	
	`new Date()`
	
	The following expression uses the BIRT BirtDateTime.diffDay( ) function to return the number of days between two dates:
	
	`BirtDateTime.diffDay(row["orderdate"], row["shippeddate"])`

Table 8-4 Examples of expressions in computed fields

Uses for computed fields	Examples of expressions
Display data that is calculated from multiple fields	The following expression calculates a customer's available credit: `row["creditlimit"] - row["balance"]`

JavaScript is a case-sensitive language. You must type keywords, function names, and any other identifiers with the correct capitalization. For example, type the Date( ) function as Date( ), not date( ) or DATE( ). If you need help constructing expressions using the correct syntax, choose objects, functions, and operators from the lower part of the expression builder. For more information about writing expressions or using the expression builder, see Chapter 13, "Writing Expressions."

You can create a computed field using either of the following techniques:

- Define the computed field in the data set.

- Define the computed field in the report layout.

The first technique is preferable because:

- You can test the results of the calculation by choosing Preview Results in the data set editor.

- The computed field is available to any table, list, or chart that uses the data set. It appears in the list of fields for that data set.

- BIRT Report Designer processes the computed values once, rather than multiple times, if the same computed field is used in multiple places in the report.

To create a computed field in the report layout, drag a data element from the palette, and drop it in the desired location. Then, in New Data Binding, create a column binding that defines the expression that returns the computed values. Figure 8-17 shows an example of a column binding that defines an expression, which uses the BirtDateTime.diffDay( ) function.

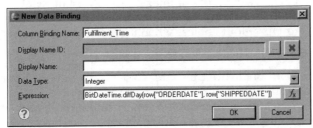

Figure 8-17 A column binding that defines an expression

If you insert the data element directly on the page or in a grid, and you want to write an expression that refers to a data set field, first bind the data element to the appropriate data set. On the other hand, if you insert the data element in a table or a list, the data element has access to the data set bound to the table or list.

Inserting an image

Images add visual appeal to reports. You can add a company logo or pictures of merchandise, or use icons instead of text labels. These images can originate from a file system, a web server, or a data source. Images are often used as decoration, but you can also use them as data. A product database, for example, might contain images of each item. If you create a report with product information, you can add product images to the report.

Figure 8-18 shows a report that displays two types of images: a static image of a company logo, and dynamic images stored in a database.

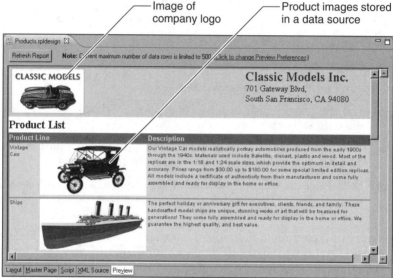

Figure 8-18   Report displaying two types of images

BIRT supports the following types of image files: BMP, GIF, ICO, JFIF, JPE, JPEG, JPG, PNG, TIF, and TIFF. To display an image, insert the image element in your report. You have four choices when inserting an image. You can:

- Link the image from any location to the report.

- Link the image from the BIRT resource folder to the report. The resource folder is a central location for external files used by reports. Rather than link images from various locations, you may find it more convenient to store all image files in the resource folder because packaging resource files for deployment is much easier.

- Embed the image in the report.

- Refer to the data set field that contains the images.

Use one of the first three methods to display a specific, or static, image. Typically, you display a static image once, so you insert the image directly on the report page, in a grid cell, or in the header row of a table. Use the fourth method to display a set of images returned by a data set. In this case, you probably want to display all the images in the data set field, so insert the image element in the detail row of a table.

When displaying a static image, decide whether to link or embed the image. Visually, there is no difference between a linked image and an embedded image. The difference is how changes to the image file affect what the report displays. If you link the image, any change to the original image file is reflected in the report. If you embed the image, changes to the original image file have no effect on the image that appears in the report. Use the guidelines in Table 8-5 to determine whether to link or embed an image in a report.

Table 8-5   Guidelines for linking and embedding images

When to link	When to embed
You expect to modify the original image, and you want the report to reflect future changes.	You expect to modify the original image, but you do not want the report to reflect future changes.
You do not expect to move or delete the original image file. Moving or deleting the image file breaks the link.	The original image file might be moved or deleted without your knowledge.

How to insert a linked image

1   Drag the image element from the palette, and drop it in the desired location on the page. Edit Image Item appears, as shown in Figure 8-19.

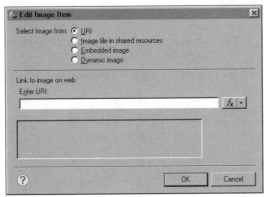

Figure 8-19   Edit Image Item dialog

2   To link to an image stored in the resource folder:

   1   In Select Image from, select Image file in shared resources.

   2   Choose Browse to find the image file in the designated resource folder.

3 Select the image file, and choose OK.

4 Choose Insert to insert the image in the report.

3 To link to images for which URIs are stored in a database, use the following procedure. The procedure assumes you have already created a data set that includes the field, which stores the URIs to the images.

   1 In Edit Image Item, in Select Image from, select URI.

   2 Under Enter URI, choose the expression builder button.

   3 In the expression builder, select the data set field that stores the locations of the images, then choose OK. Figure 8-20 shows an example of selecting a data set field named URL, which stores the URLs to images.

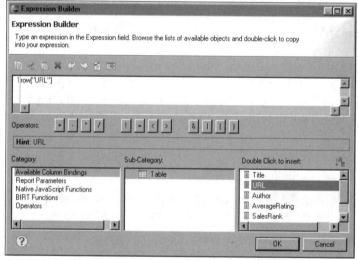

Figure 8-20   The expression builder showing a selected data set field that stores the URLs to images

In Edit Image Item, Enter URI displays the expression that refers to the data set field.

   4 Choose Insert to insert the image in the report.

4 To link to an image stored in any other location:

   1 In Edit Image Item, in Select Image from, select URI.

   2 Under Enter URI, specify the location of the image file, using one of the following methods:

   ❑ To type a specific URL, choose the arrow button next to the expression builder button, and choose Constant. Type the URL.

   The following is an example of a URL for a file in a remote location:

   `http://mysite.com/images/companylogo.jpg`

The following is an example of a URI for a file that is on the local file system:

```
file:///c:/myprojects/images/companylogo.jpg
```

Specify a local file system location only for testing in the early stages of report development. A deployed report cannot access resources on a local machine.

❑ To specify an expression that evaluates to a URL at report run time, choose the expression builder button to construct the expression.

3 Choose Insert to insert the image in the report.

How to insert an embedded image

1 Drag the image element from the palette, and drop it in the desired location on the page.

2 In Edit Image Item, in Select Image from, select Embedded image. If you previously inserted images, Edit Image Item displays the names of those images, as shown in Figure 8-21.

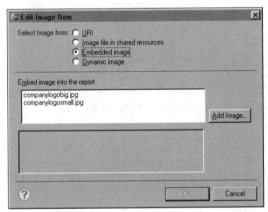

Figure 8-21   New Image Item showing embedded image names

3 To embed a new image, choose Add Image.

4 In Open Image File, find and select the image to embed, then choose Open. Edit Image Item displays the image.

5 Choose OK. The image appears on the page.

How to insert images that are stored in a data source

1 In Data Explorer, create a data set that includes the image field.

2 In the layout editor, insert a table element on the page.

3 Bind the table to the data set in the following manner:

1 Select the table and, in Property Editor, choose Binding.

2 In the Binding page, in Data Set, choose the data set that contains the image field. BIRT creates a column binding for each field in the data set.

4 Drag the image element from the palette, and drop it in the detail row of the table.

5 In Edit Image Item, select Dynamic image.

6 Choose Select Image Data. Select Data Binding displays the column bindings available to the image element, as shown in Figure 8-22. The image element has access to all the column bindings defined for the table, its container.

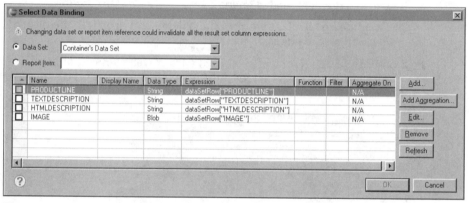

Figure 8-22 Select Data Binding showing column bindings

7 Select the column binding that references the image field by clicking the check box next to the column binding. Choose OK.

In Edit Image Item, under Enter dynamic image expression, an expression that refers to the selected column binding appears, as shown in Figure 8-23.

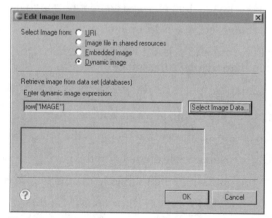

Figure 8-23 New Image Item showing the dynamic image expression

8 Choose OK. The image element appears on the page in the layout editor. It shows an X. The actual images appear only when the report is generated.

Resizing an image

The image element displays an image at its actual size. If you cannot change the size of the original image, you can resize the image element in the report. Note, however, that images are designed to display optimally at a specific size. Resizing an image in the report typically results in the degradation of its appearance.

To resize an image, select the image element, then in Property Editor, select General. Specify a width and height for the image element. Typically, you want to resize an image so that its aspect ratio is maintained to avoid stretching the graphic out of proportion. To maintain an image's aspect ratio, specify the width and height as a percentage of the original size. For example, setting both the width and height to 80%, as shown in Figure 8-24, reduces the image size to 80% of the original size.

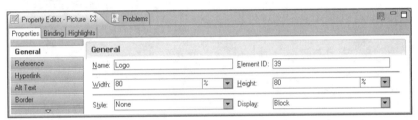

Figure 8-24 Setting the width and height of an image element

Providing a text alternative

A standard practice in HTML document design is to display a text alternative for an image. Sometimes, a document cannot access or display an image, or a user configures the browser to not display images. In these cases, rather than not display anything, the report should display a textual description of the missing image. The rule of thumb is that the text alternative should always describe the content of the image, but the description should also be short and succinct.

To specify a text alternative, select the image element, then in Property Editor, under Properties, choose Alt Text. In Alternative text, type the text to display in place of a missing image. For an image of a company logo, for example, type Company logo, as shown in Figure 8-25.

Figure 8-25 Providing a text alternative for an image

To display the text in the language determined by the locale of the user's machine, specify a resource key in Alternative text key. A resource key is a value that maps to translated strings. For information about resource keys and displaying text in different languages, see Chapter 25, "Localizing Text."

Displaying Text

A report typically presents most of its information in textual format. In fact, it is safe to assume that all reports contain text. Even if a report consists primarily of charts or pictures, it uses text to label charts, display titles, describe the charts or pictures, and so on.

Textual information can be any of the following:

- Static text, which is text that the report displays exactly as you type it in the design. Use static text in a report title, column headings, or to write a summary about the report.

- String, number, or date values that are derived from data set fields. Typically, the majority of information in a report comes from data set fields.

- String, number, or date values that are derived from JavaScript expressions. Reports often contain information that is calculated, such as the report-generation date, or the number of records in a report table.

Textual information can be as short as a single word, or span multiple paragraphs, even pages. BIRT Report Designer handles all lengths of text elegantly. When you insert a textual element, you do not need to calculate an element size to make it large enough to display all the text. BIRT Report Designer dynamically adjusts the height of elements to accommodate their contents.

Types of textual elements

To support the wide variety of text that a report can display, BIRT Report Designer provides a rich set of textual elements. Table 9-1 describes these elements.

Table 9-1   Descriptions of BIRT textual elements

Textual element	Use to
Data	Display dynamic values that are derived from data set fields, computed fields, or JavaScript expressions. You can add literal, or static, text to the dynamic data. Doing so, however, changes the entire expression to a string, and, if the dynamic value is a number or a date, you can no longer format it as a number or a date.
Dynamic text	Display memo or Character Large Object (CLOB) data from a data set field. This type of data typically consists of large amounts of text that contain HTML formatting.
Label	Display a small amount of static text, such as a report title or column heading.
Text	Display the following types of user-specified text: ■ Multiline text ■ HTML text that contains multiple style formats, for example, text with paragraph styles, such as bulleted lists and numbered lists, or text formats, such as bold or italics ■ Text that combines static text with dynamic values, such as a form letter that includes customer names and addresses that are stored in a data source ■ Interactive content driven by code, which you specify using the <script> tag

Figure 9-1 and Figure 9-2 show a report using textual elements. Figure 9-1 shows the finished report. Figure 9-2 shows the design in the layout editor.

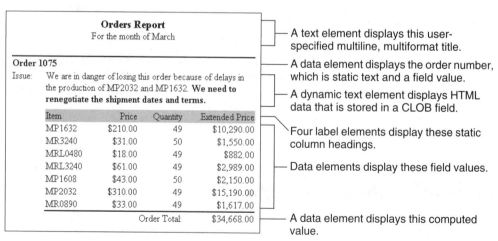

Figure 9-1   Textual elements in a report

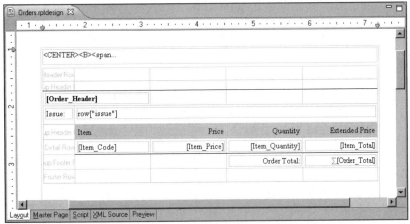

Figure 9-2   Textual elements in the report design

Deciding which textual element to use

In many cases, you can use several textual elements to accomplish the same task. For example, you can use a label element, a text element, or a data element to display a static report title like the one in the following example:

```
Sales Report for Quarter One, 2011
```

When you apply complex formats or combine static text with dynamic data, you need to use the appropriate textual element to achieve the best results. This section provides guidelines and examples for determining the best textual element to use for different purposes. The rest of this chapter provides details about using each element, except the data element, which is described in the previous chapter.

Formatting words differently in a static string

The previous example showed how you can use a label, text, or data element to display a static title. To format words in the title differently, as shown in the following example, you must use the text element. In the example, some words appear as plain text and some in bold. With the label and data elements, formats apply to the entire string.

```
Sales Report for Quarter One, 2011
```

Combining static text with dynamic data

To display the following text, where Order Total: is static text, and the number is a dynamic, or calculated, value, use a text element or a data element:

```
Order Total: 74050
```

To format the dynamic value so that it appears as a currency value with comma separators and decimal places, as shown in the following example, use the text element. The text element enables you to format different parts of text differently.

```
Order Total: $74,050.00
```

Alternatively, use a label element and a data element to display the preceding text. Use the label element to display the static text portion, Order Total:, and the data element to display the dynamic portion, as shown in Figure 9-3. When the data element consists of just the number value, you can use the Format Number property to format the number.

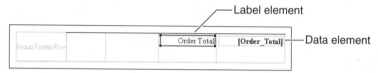

Figure 9-3   Label and data elements in the layout editor

Figure 9-4 shows the output of the preceding report design.

Figure 9-4   Label and data elements in a report

The difference between using the label and data elements and using the text element is how you control the space between the static text and the dynamic value. Using the text element, you can easily specify one character space between the two. If you use the label and data elements, the spacing is determined by various factors, such as text alignment and column widths. In the previous example, the label element and data element are both right-aligned.

Displaying dynamic data that contains HTML tags

Many data sources store large amounts of text that contain internal formatting, as shown in the following example. Data like this is typically stored in CLOB fields.

```
<html><b>Customer log 04/12/05 13:45:00</b><br>Customer called
to enquire about order. He says order 2673-9890 was supposed
to arrive on 04/10/05. Records show that the order is on
backorder. Customer says he received no notification about the
status of his order. He wants to cancel the order if it is not
shipped by 04/15/05.<br><i>Action Items:</i><ul><li>Call
distributor about delivery status. <li>Send email to customer
about delivery status.</ul></html>
```

To display the text with the specified HTML formats, use the text element or the dynamic text element. To combine static text with dynamic text, use the text element. If you add static text to the dynamic text element, for example,

"Customer Issue: " + row["Issue"], the dynamic data appears in the report exactly as it appears in the field, including the HTML tags.

Figure 9-5 shows how the text element displays the static text, Customer Issue:, with the dynamic text. The text element converts the HTML tags to formatting and layout attributes. For example, text within the <b> and </b> tags appears in bold.

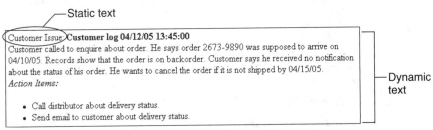

Figure 9-5   Static and dynamic text in a text element

Figure 9-6 shows how the dynamic text element displays the text when you add static text to the dynamic text. The HTML tags appear because the content is converted to string type.

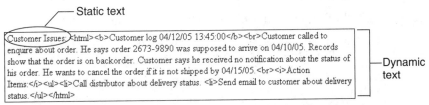

Figure 9-6   Static and dynamic text in a dynamic text element

Displaying dynamic data that a JavaScript expression returns

An expression is any valid combination of literals, variables, functions, or operators that evaluates to a single value. Both the text element and the data element can display the results of any valid JavaScript expression, including multiline expressions, such as the one in the following example:

```
if (row["creditScore"] > 700){
    displayString = "Your loan application has been approved."
    }
else{
    displayString = "Your loan application has been denied."
    }
```

Using a dynamic text element

You can place a dynamic text element directly on the page or in any of the container elements. Typically, you place it in a table or a list because the dynamic text element displays CLOB data from a data set field, and only the table and list elements iterate through the rows in a data set.

Unlike most data set fields, you do not simply drag a CLOB field from Data Explorer and drop it in the table or list. You can, but if the CLOB data is HTML text, the data element displays the contents of the field exactly as it appears, including the HTML tags. The dynamic text element, on the other hand, is designed to correctly display data that is stored as HTML.

As with any element that displays data set data, you must create a column binding that refers to the data set field. The column binding, in turn, needs access to the data set. If you insert the dynamic text element in a table or list that is already bound to a data set, the column binding has access to the data set. If the table or list is not bound with a data set, first bind the table or list with the data set.

How to use a dynamic text element

1 Make sure the table or list in which you want to insert a dynamic text element is bound to the data set that contains the CLOB data. To verify or create the data set binding, perform the following tasks:

    1 Select the table or list.

    2 In Property Editor, choose the Binding tab.

    3 In the Binding page, in Data Set, select the data set. BIRT creates a column binding for each field in the data set.

2 Drag the dynamic text element from the palette, and drop it in the table or list.

3 In the expression builder, choose Available Column Bindings, choose the table under Sub-Category, then double-click the column binding that refers to the data set field that contains the CLOB data. Choose OK to save the expression.

4 In the layout editor, select the dynamic text element. In Property Editor, choose the Properties tab. Property Editor displays the properties of the dynamic text element.

5 Choose General properties, then choose one of the following values for Content type:

    ■ Auto

       Choose this value if you do not know the format of the field contents. If the content contains HTML tags, BIRT Report Designer interprets it as HTML and displays the content correctly. If the content is plain text, BIRT Report Designer displays it correctly also.

    ■ HTML

       Choose this value if you know that all the field contents are HTML.

    ■ Plain

Choose this value to display the field contents exactly as they appear in the data source. If the content contains HTML tags, BIRT Report Designer displays the HTML tags.

6   Preview the report to verify that the report displays the text from the specified data set field.

Using a label element

You can place a label directly on the page or in any of the container elements. When you insert a label, the layout editor displays an empty label with a cursor in it, as shown in Figure 9-7.

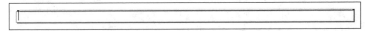

Figure 9-7   Empty label in the layout editor

Start typing the text to display, then press Enter when you finish.

Figure 9-8 shows the result.

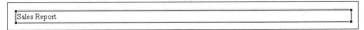

Figure 9-8   Label text in the layout editor

You can edit the text in the label by double-clicking the label or by selecting the label and pressing F2, then typing the new text.

You can change the format of the text by selecting the label, then setting the desired style properties in the property editor. For example, you can specify a different font, text alignment, size, or color. These properties apply to the entire text string. You cannot, for example, set one word to bold and another to italic. If variable formats are a requirement, use a text element instead.

Using a text element

You can place a text element directly on the page or in any of the container elements. When you insert a text element, the layout editor displays the text editor, as shown in Figure 9-9.

First, decide what type of text you want to create. You have three choices:

■   Auto

■   Plain text

■   HTML

HTML enables you to create highly formatted text using HTML tags or CSS properties. The text can contain placeholders for data set field values and expressions, which enable you to mix static text with dynamically generated values. Plain text and auto, on the other hand, cannot contain internal formatting or dynamic values. A text element that is set to plain text or auto functions like a label element.

Select the type
of text to create

For HTML text, you can use
any of these and other tags

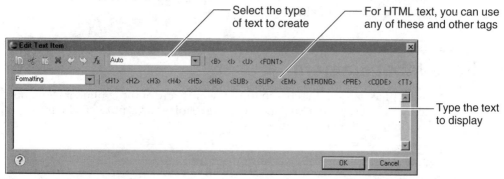

Type the text
to display

Figure 9-9   Edit Text Item

After selecting the text type, type the text to display in the report. If you selected HTML, you can use HTML tags or CSS properties in the text. Type the tags manually, or insert the commonly used HTML tags that the text editor provides.

The following sections provide a few examples of text you can create using a text element of HTML type.

Applying multiple style formats to text

Using HTML, you can format individual words and lines in a text element. The following example shows two lines with different font sizes and styles.

Text that you supply:

```
<CENTER><B><span style="font-size: larger">
Shipped Orders Report
</B></span><BR>
<FONT size="small">For the month of March</FONT></CENTER>
```

Output:

Combining a JavaScript expression and static text

BIRT Report Designer provides a useful tag, VALUE-OF, which you use to insert a dynamic value in a text element. Using the VALUE-OF tag, you can insert any JavaScript expression.

The following example shows static text combined with a value that a JavaScript function returns.

Text that you supply:

```
Report generated on <VALUE-OF>new Date()</VALUE-OF>
```

Output:

```
Report generated on Jan 19, 2010 12:30 PM
```

The following example shows static text combined with a conditional expression and a field value expression.

Text that you supply:

```
Dear <VALUE-OF>row["Sex"] == "M" ? "Mr." : "Ms."</VALUE-OF>
    <VALUE-OF>row["Name"]</VALUE-OF>,
```

Output:

```
Dear Mr. Scott Johnson,
Dear Ms. Ella Parker,
```

As the example shows, a conditional expression can have one of two values based on a condition. The syntax for this conditional expression is

```
condition ? value1 : value2
```

If the condition is true, the expression has the value of value1; otherwise, it has the value of value2.

Alternatively, you can use an if...else statement within the VALUE-OF tag. The following text displays the same results as the preceding conditional expression:

```
Dear <VALUE-OF>if(row["Sex"] == "M"){
Title = "Mr."
}
else{
Title = "Ms."
}</VALUE-OF>
<VALUE-OF>row["Name"]</VALUE-OF>,
```

Combining a value from a data set field and static text

The following example shows how to use the VALUE-OF tag to insert dynamic values that data set fields return.

Text that you supply:

```
Dear <VALUE-OF>row["contact_firstname"]</VALUE-OF>,
<p>
Thank you for your recent order. Order <VALUE-OF>
    row["orderID"]</VALUE-OF> will be shipped by <VALUE-OF>
    row["shipByDate"]</VALUE-OF>.
```

Output:

Dear Bob,

Thank you for your recent order. Order 1115 will be shipped by Apr 17, 2009 12:00AM.

You can display field values in a text element only if the following requirements are met:

- The text element has access to the data set that contains the fields.

  - If you place the text element directly on the page, you must bind the text element to the data set that contains the field value. To do so, select the text element, choose the Binding tab in the property editor, then select the data set to which to bind. Placing the text element directly on the page, however, displays only one value.

  - If you place the text element in the detail row of a table or a list to display all values of a data set field, bind the table or list to the data set.

- A column binding is created for each data set field. The column binding refers to the data set field. The VALUE-OF tag refers to the column binding.

Formatting dynamic values in a text element

The previous examples show how to use the VALUE-OF tag to insert dynamic values that a JavaScript function or a field returns. Sometimes the returned values are not in the desired format. You can reformat the values using the format attribute, as shown in the following example.

Text that you supply:

```
<VALUE-OF format="MM-dd-yy">new Date()</VALUE-OF><br>
<VALUE-OF format="$#,###.00">row["orderTotal"]</VALUE-OF><br>
<VALUE-OF format="(@@@) @@@-@@@@">row["phone"]</VALUE-OF>
```

Output:

```
04-17-05
$321,000.00
(415) 123-5555
```

The format pattern must be enclosed in quotation marks. You can use any format pattern that the Format Number, Format DateTime, and Format String properties support. For information about these properties, see Chapter 10, "Formatting Report Content."

Displaying data set field values that are stored as HTML text

Sometimes values in a data set field contain HTML text. If you insert such a field in a report, BIRT Report Designer displays the content of the field exactly as it appears in the data source, including the HTML tags. To display the text with its intended formatting, use a text element or a dynamic text element instead of a data element. As described earlier in this chapter, the text element enables you to add static text to the dynamic text, whereas the dynamic text element displays all the HTML tags if you add static text.

To use the text element, select HTML as the text type, then use the VALUE-OF tag to insert the value of the field, and set the format attribute to HTML, as shown in the following example.

Text that you supply:

```
Notes: <VALUE-OF format="html">row["CustomerNotes"]</VALUE-OF>
```

Output:

```
Notes: The customer wants email confirmation for his orders.
```

Displaying text from right to left

Most languages use a writing system in which text flows from left to right. In a few languages, text flows from right to left. These languages, used mostly in the Middle East, include Arabic, Farsi, and Hebrew. BIRT supports the display of text in both directions, a feature known as bidirectional (Bidi) text.

Bidirectional text consists of predominantly right-to-left text with some left-to-right text embedded in paragraphs, such as an Arabic report with addresses, acronyms, or proper names in English. Figure 9-10 shows an example of such a report. As the report shows, the general flow of text is right to left, but numbers and English words are written from left to right.

Classic Models, Inc.

العملاء الجدد لعام 2009 في منطقة آسيا والمحيط الهادئ

إجمالي مبلغ التمويل : 797,400$

أستراليا

مبلغ الائتمان	مدينة	زبون
117,300.00 $	ملبورن	Australian Collectors, Co.
107,800.00 $	شمال سيدني	Anna's Decorations, Ltd
51,600.00 $	جنوب بريسبان	Australian Gift Network, Co
60,300.00 $	على Waverly	Australian Collectables, Ltd

نيوزيلندا

مبلغ الائتمان	مدينة	زبون
88,000.00 $	أوكلاند	Down Under Souveniers, Inc
77,700.00 $	أوكلاند	GiftsForHim.com
86,800.00 $	ويلنجتون	Extreme Desk Decorations, Ltd
110,000.00 $	أوكلاند	Kelly's Gift Shop

سنغافورة

مبلغ الائتمان	مدينة	زبون
97,900.00 $	سنغافورة	Handji Gifts& Co

Figure 9-10   Report displaying Arabic text from right to left

Typically, when designing a report to display bidirectional text, you set the text flow direction at the report level. You can, however, also set text flow direction at the element level. In the rare case where a report displays significant sections of text in multiple languages, this capability enables you to display some sections in right-to-left and some in left-to-right. For example, if a report is mostly in Arabic, but some sections are in English, you can set the report's text direction as right-to-left and the text elements that display English text as left-to-right.

Setting text flow direction for a report

To create a report that displays text from right to left, all you do is change one report property setting. Select the report, and in the General properties of Property Editor, set the Report Orientation property to Right to Left. Figure 9-11 shows a report design and Property Editor displaying the report's general properties, including the Report Orientation property.

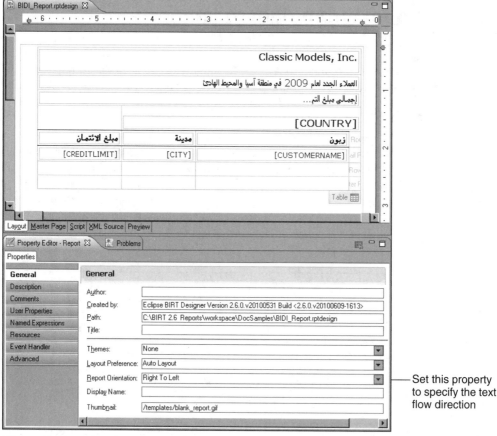

Figure 9-11   Setting a report design's orientation to Right to Left

Notice in the layout editor that, aside from the text flow, the user interface elements are now also in the opposite direction. The scroll bar, typically on the right of the window, is on the left. The vertical ruler, typically on the left side of the window, is on the right. The table shifts to the right side of the page, and the table tab and row information move to the right side of the table. These direction changes make it easier to design a right-to-left report.

If you want all new reports to use the right-to-left orientation by default, set the Default Report Orientation property in Preferences, as shown in Figure 9-12. To access this property, select Window➤Preferences, and choose Report Design—Bidirectional Properties.

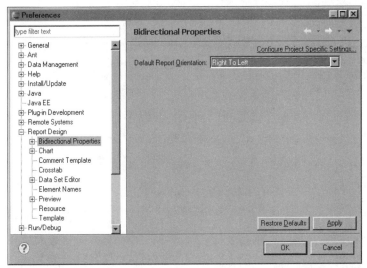

Figure 9-12   Setting the default report orientation for all new reports

Alternatively, set the Default Report Orientation property for new reports in a specific project or projects, rather than for all reports in the workspace. To do so, in the page shown in Figure 9-12, choose Configure Project Specific Settings, select the desired project or projects, and set the Default Report Orientation property.

Setting text flow direction for an element

Use this functionality judiciously. A report that changes the direction of text too much can be confusing and difficult to read. If the information is in two languages that use different text flow directions, consider translating the content so that it is in one language. If that is not possible, minimize the number of times the text direction changes and try to place sections contiguously by language.

To set the text direction for an element, select the element, and in Property Editor, under Properties, choose Advanced. In the Advanced properties page, expand Text, and set the Text direction property, as shown in Figure 9-13.

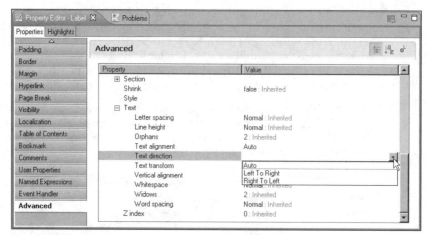

Figure 9-13   Setting text direction for a selected element

Formatting Report Content

Formatting is what you do to make a report visually appealing and effective. Format a report, for example, to highlight certain data, change the display of dates, numbers, or currency values, adjust the spacing between report elements, or display data based on a specified condition or output format.

BIRT Report Designer provides many options for customizing the appearance of report elements. Using various formatting properties, you can change the alignment, color, font, size, and other properties of these report elements. You can also add background colors, draw borders around elements, and so on.

Familiarity with CSS is useful because BIRT follows the CSS specification as closely as possible. Many of the formatting properties available in BIRT Report Designer are the same as CSS formatting properties.

The formatting options are available through the following views:

- Property Editor
  This view organizes commonly used properties by functional categories. The properties that appear vary depending on which report element you are formatting. Figure 10-1 shows some of the categories of properties that are available through Property Editor.

- Properties
  This view shows a list of the properties that you can set for an element, as shown in Figure 10-2. You can choose to list the properties by category or in alphabetical order. This view also shows more complex properties that are not available in Property Editor. The default application window layout does not display the Properties view. To display it, choose Window➤Show View➤Properties.

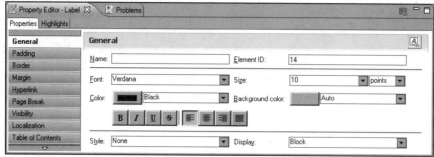

Figure 10-1   Property Editor showing categories of properties for a label element

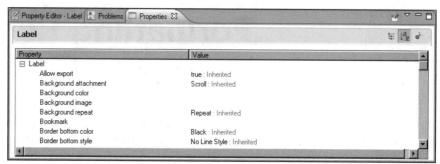

Figure 10-2   Properties view showing the properties for a label element

Formatting data

Format the data in a report element by selecting the element, then setting property values using Property Editor or the Properties view. If you apply a format using Property Editor, the format choices appear in the Properties view. Similarly, if you update a format using the Properties view, the change is reflected in Property Editor.

You can customize how data appears by modifying the following settings:

- Formats of numbers, text, dates, and times

  BIRT Report Designer provides common format styles in which to display numbers, currency, or date values. If you do not choose a format, BIRT Report Designer displays the data as it appears in the data source. Specify format styles by setting the Format Number, Format DateTime, and Format String properties.

- Font typeface, point size, and color

  When choosing fonts, remember that for the report user to view the report with the chosen fonts, the fonts must be installed on the user's system. If the report will be distributed widely, select default fonts that are installed on all systems. Specify font attributes by setting the font properties in the General category of Property Editor.

- Text style
  BIRT Report Designer provides the standard styles: bold, italic, underline, and strike through. These styles are available under the General category in Property Editor.

- Text alignment
  BIRT Report Designer provides the standard ways to align text: left-aligned, centered, right-aligned, and justified. These settings are available under the General category in Property Editor.

Formatting numeric data

You can display numeric data in a variety of formats. For example, you can display numbers with decimal values, in scientific notation, or with a currency symbol. By default, reports display numeric data according to the locale configured on the user's machine. For example, a number that appears as 5015.75 in the English (United States) locale appears as 5015,75 in the French (France) locale. If you want some numeric data always to appear in a specific locale's format, set the locale for that data element.

You can apply number formats only to decimal, float, or integer data types. Number formats have no effect on numbers that are string type. For example, a Customer_ID field can be defined as string type and display number values, such as 325. Number formats have no effect on these values.

Display numeric data using either a text element or a data element, depending on what you want to accomplish. When you drag a data set field from Data Explorer and drop it on the report page in the layout editor, BIRT Report Designer creates a data element to display the values of the data set field. The procedure for formatting data differs for a data element and a text element, as described in the following sections.

Formatting numeric data in a data element

Specify the format of numeric data in a data element by setting the data element's Format Number property, as shown in Figure 10-3.

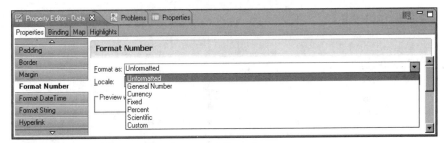

Figure 10-3   Format Number property values

Choose a format and, optionally, a locale. Use the locale's Auto value to display the data according to the locale set on the user's machine.

Table 10-1 lists the available number formats and provides examples of how the formatted data appears. The examples in the table reflect the English (United States) locale. If you select a different locale, the data displays differently. When selecting a number format, you can set additional formatting options, such as the number of decimal places, the inclusion of a thousands separator, a currency symbol, and so on.

Table 10-1   Examples of number formats

Format type	Example of data display
General Number	3200 or 3200.5 or 3200.75, depending on the original value. Whole numbers and numbers with up to three decimal places appear in their original format.
Currency	$3,200.50 or ¥3200 or 3,200€, depending on the symbol, symbol position, decimal place, and thousands separator values you set.
Fixed	3200 or 3200.5 or 3,200.48, depending on the decimal place and thousands separator values you set.
Percent	65% or 65.7% or %65, depending on the symbol position and decimal place values that you set. This format multiplies the original value by 100 and adds the percent (%) symbol.
Scientific	3.20E03 or 3E03, depending on the decimal place value you set.

You can also define your own formats. For example, you can specify the number of digits after the decimal or add literal characters to the numbers. To define a custom format, you use special symbols to construct a format pattern. BIRT Report Designer supports the Java numeric formatting defined by the DecimalFormat class. For details about the supported formatting symbols, see the Javadoc for DecimalFormat.

Table 10-2 shows examples of custom format patterns and their effects on numeric data displayed in the English (United States) locale.

Table 10-2   Results of custom number format patterns

Format pattern	Data in the data set	Result
0000.00	12.5	0012.50
	124.5	0124.50
	1240.553	1240.55
#.000	100	100.000
	100.25	100.250
	100.2567	100.257

Table 10-2 Results of custom number format patterns

Format pattern	Data in the data set	Result
$#,###	2000.00 20000.00	$2,000 $20,000
ID #	15	ID 15

Formatting numeric data in a text element

To insert dynamic data in a text element, use the VALUE-OF tag. To format the dynamic data, include a format attribute that specifies the format, as shown in the following examples. You must enclose the format value in double quotation marks (" ").

```
<VALUE-OF format="$#,###.00">row["orderTotal"]</VALUE-OF>
<VALUE-OF format="#.000">row["unitTotal"]</VALUE-OF>
```

You can use any format pattern that the Format Number property supports, as described in the preceding section.

Formatting date-and-time data

You can display date-and-time data in different formats. You can, for example, display dates and times in short, medium, or long formats. By default, reports display date-and-time data according to the locale configured on the user's machine. For example, a short date that appears as 5/7/09 in the English (United States) locale appears as 07.05.09 in the German (Germany) locale. If you want some dates to always appear in a specific locale's format, set the locale for that data element.

Display date-and-time data using either a text element or a data element, depending on what you want to accomplish. When you drag a data set field from Data Explorer and drop it on the report page in the layout editor, BIRT Report Designer creates a data element to display the values of the data set field. The procedure for formatting data differs for a data element and a text element, and is described in the following sections.

Formatting date-and-time data in a data element

Specify the format for date-and-time data in a data element by setting the element's Format DateTime property. As Figure 10-4 shows, BIRT Report Designer provides many common date-and-time formats from which to choose. Optionally, choose a locale. Use the locale's Auto value to display the data according to the locale set on the user's machine.

You can also define your own date-and-time formats. For example, you can specify two-digit months, use two digits for the year, or add the day of the week. To define a custom format, use special symbols to construct a format pattern. BIRT Report Designer supports the Java formatting defined by the SimpleDateFormat class. For details about the supported formatting symbols, see the Javadoc for SimpleDateFormat.

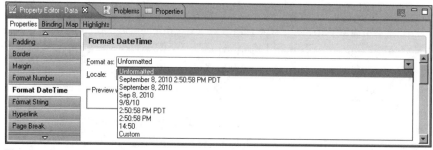

Figure 10-4   Format DateTime property values

Table 10-3 shows examples of custom format patterns and their effects on a date that is stored as 4/15/2009 in the data source.

Table 10-3   Results of custom date format patterns

Format pattern	Result
MM-dd-yy	04-15-09
E, M/d/yyyy	Wed, 4/15/2009
EEEE, M/dd/yy	Wednesday, 4/15/09
MMM d	Apr 15
MMMM	April
yyyy	2009
W	3 (the week in the month)
w	16 (the week in the year)
DD	105 (the day in the year)

Specify custom formats if a report will be viewed in only one locale because custom formats always display date or time data in the specified format. For example, if you use the format MM-dd-yy, the date January 10, 2006, always appears as 01-10-06, regardless of the locale in which the report is viewed. For locales in which dates are displayed in day-month-year format, a 01-10-06 date is interpreted as October 1, 2006.

Formatting date-and-time data in a text element

To insert dynamic data in a text element, use the VALUE-OF tag. To format the dynamic data, include a format attribute that specifies the format, as shown in the following examples:

```
<VALUE-OF format="MM-dd-yyyy">row["orderDate"]</VALUE-OF>
<VALUE-OF format="M/d/yy hh:mm:ss">new Date()</VALUE-OF>
```

You can use any format pattern that the Format DateTime property supports, as described in the preceding section.

Formatting string data

Typically, you format string data to fix inconsistent or poorly formatted data that is retrieved from the data source. The data source, for example, can store names with inconsistent capitalization or phone numbers in 1234567890 format. To fix these problems, specify the desired string format.

Display string data using either a text element or a data element, depending on what you want to accomplish. When you drag a data set field from Data Explorer and drop it on the report page in the layout editor, BIRT Report Designer creates a data element to display the values of the data set field. The procedure for formatting data differs for a data element and a text element, and is described in the following sections.

Formatting text in a data element

Specify a text format by setting the data element's Format String property, as shown in Figure 10-5.

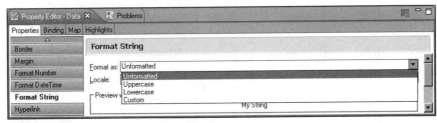

Figure 10-5   Format String property values

Table 10-4 describes the available string formats.

Table 10-4   Examples of string formats

Format type	Description	Example of data display
Lowercase	Converts the string to lowercase	smith
Uppercase	Converts the string to uppercase	SMITH

You can also define custom string formats using special symbols. Table 10-5 describes these symbols.

Table 10-5   Symbols for defining custom string formats

Symbol	Description
>	Converts string characters to uppercase.
<	Converts string characters to lowercase.
@	Character placeholder. Each @ character displays a character in the string. If the string has fewer characters than the number of @ symbols in the format pattern, spaces appear.

(continues)

Table 10-5   Symbols for defining custom string formats *(continued)*

Symbol	Description
@	Placeholders are filled from right to left, unless you specify an exclamation point (!) at the beginning of the format pattern. See Table 10-6 for examples.
&	Same as @, except that if the string has fewer characters, spaces do not appear. See Table 10-6 for examples.
!	Specifies that placeholders are to be filled from left to right. See Table 10-6 for examples.

Table 10-6 shows examples of custom format patterns and their effects on text data.

Table 10-6   Results of custom string format patterns

Format pattern	Data in data source	Result
(@@@) @@@-@@@@	6175551007 5551007	(617) 555-1007 ( ) 555-1007
(&&&) &&&-&&&&	6175551007 5551007	(617) 555-1007 () 555-1007
!(@@@) @@@-@@@@	6175551007 5551007	(617) 555-1007 (555) 100-7
!(&&&) &&&-&&&&	6175551007 5551007	(617) 555-1007 (555) 100-7
!(@@@) @@@-@@@@ + ext 9	5551007	(555) 100-7 + ext 9
!(&&&) &&&-&&&& + ext 9	5551007	(555) 100-7 + ext 9
>&&&-&&&&&-&&	D1234567xy	D12-34567-XY
<&&&-&&&&&-&&	D1234567xy	d12-34567-xy

Formatting text data in a text element

To insert dynamic data in a text element, use the VALUE-OF tag. To format the dynamic data, include a format attribute that specifies the format, as shown in the following examples:

```
<VALUE-OF format="(@@@) @@@-@@@@">row["phone"]</VALUE-OF>
<VALUE-OF format=">">row["custName"]</VALUE-OF>
```

You can use any format pattern that the Format String property supports, as described in the preceding section.

Copying formats

To format a report element in the same way as another element, right-click the element from which to copy the format, then choose Copy Format.

Right-click the element to which you want to apply the format, then choose Paste Format. The Copy Format and Paste Format commands are useful shortcuts to format a report quickly in the early stages of report development.

Formatting with styles

Styles support providing a consistent appearance to multiple report elements. Styles are dynamic. Changing a style applies the changes to all report elements using that style. Although you can set the appearance of each report element individually, this task can take a while, especially if you frequently change the appearance of multiple elements. Using the Copy Format and Paste Format commands speeds the process, but only up to a point. Each time you update the format of similar report elements, you change and copy the format of one element, and then select the other elements, one at a time, to paste the new format. When selecting elements, you must also take care to reformat only the intended items. BIRT Report Designer solves these problems by providing a style mechanism that is similar to HTML CSS and Microsoft Word styles.

A style is a named set of formatting characteristics that you can apply to a report element to change its appearance quickly. Applying a style applies an entire group of formats—font size, color, alignment, borders, and so on—in one step. For example, you want to format all column headings in a report as Arial, small, blue, and center-aligned. Instead of formatting each heading in four separate steps, apply a style to achieve the same result in a single step.

Using styles, you can:

- Create a consistent appearance for similar report elements.

- Update the appearance of a set of report elements by changing a single style.

When you first create a report, it does not contain any styles. The report displays elements with default formatting values. To use styles to format report elements, you must first create the styles. If you have designed web pages and use a CSS file that defines styles, you can reuse those styles in your reports.

Creating styles

BIRT Report Designer styles are a hybrid of CSS and Microsoft Word styles. You can use the following methods:

- Create a named style, and apply it to a report element.
  For example, you can create a style called ColumnHeading, then apply the style to all column headings in a report. This approach is like using Microsoft styles in that you create a Body Text style then apply this style to selected paragraphs.

- Apply style properties to predefined style names, or selectors.

  These predefined style names correspond to the different types of report elements. For example, you can apply style properties to a style called table-header, and all table headers in a report will be formatted accordingly. This technique is like using CSS in that you associate styles with HTML elements, such as <H1> or <P>.

You will find it useful to create styles using both techniques. The first technique is useful for creating specialized styles for different types of text content, such as important notes, offer notices, or copyrights. The second technique provides a powerful way to define style properties once for a container element and have those properties cascade to the container's contents. For example, to apply a default format, such as the Arial typeface, to all elements in a report, apply the format to the predefined style name, report. After doing so, all text in the report appears in Arial.

Table 10-7 lists the predefined style names for which you can set style properties.

Table 10-7   Predefined style names

Predefined style name	Applies style properties to...
chart	All elements in a chart. Use the predefined chart style to set general formats that you want to apply to all charts, such as boxes around all charts, or a particular font family to use as the default. To format each element in a chart, use the formatting options in the chart builder.
crosstab	All parts of a cross tab, and all elements in a cross tab.
crosstab-cell	Cross tab cells, including elements within them.
crosstab-column-header	The part of the cross tab that displays the column headings, excluding the total headings.
crosstab detail	The part of the cross tab that displays the aggregate values.
crosstab-header	The entire row and column header area of the cross tab.
crosstab-row-header	The part of the cross tab that displays the row headings, excluding the total headings.
data	Data elements.
grid	Grids, including elements within them. For example, if you specify a background color, the entire grid displays the specified color.
image	Image elements.
label	Label elements.
list	Lists, including elements in them.
list-detail	Detail area of lists, including elements in that area.
list-footer	Footer area of lists, including elements in that area.

Table 10-7   Predefined style names

Predefined style name	Applies style properties to...
list-group-footer-n	A specific group footer (1–9) in lists that contain groups of data.
list-group-header-n	A specific group header (1–9) in lists that contain groups of data.
list-header	Header area of lists, including elements in that area.
page	The report's master page.
report	All elements in the report. The report is the topmost container. Any formatting you set for this style applies to everything in a report.
table	Tables, including elements in them.
table-detail	Detail rows of tables, including elements in the rows.
table-detail-cell	Cells in the detail rows of tables.
table-footer	Footer rows of tables, including elements in the rows.
table-footer-cell	Cells in the footer rows of tables.
table-group-footer-n	A specific group footer (1–9) in tables that contain groups of data.
table-group-footer-cell	Cells in the group footer rows of tables.
table-group-header-n	A specific group header row (1–9) in tables that contain groups of data.
table-group-header-cell	Cells in the group header row of tables.
table-header	Header rows of tables, including elements in the rows.
table-header cell	Cells in the header rows of tables.
text	Text elements.
text-data	Dynamic text elements.
TOC-level-n	A specific level (0–9) in a hierarchical table of contents. For reports that contain groups of data, BIRT automatically creates a table of contents, which users can use to jump to different parts of the report.

If creating styles using the cascading model, it is best to design a set of styles from the top-level container down. At the top level, define style properties that you want to apply to all elements, then add style properties at each successive level. For example:

- Use the report style to specify a default font family and font size for the entire report.

- Use the table style to specify a default font size and text alignment for all data in tables.

- Use the table-header style to specify bold font and a background color for table headers.

Any element you insert in a table header inherits the style properties from the report, table, and table-header styles. Any element you insert in a table detail inherits style properties from the report and table styles. Figure 10-6 shows the results of applying the cascading concept to styles.

Not all style properties cascade. For example, the background color, margins, borders, and padding properties do not cascade from a container to the elements within it. In these cases, cascading the style does not make good design sense. For example, it does not make sense to cascade border values because designs typically use different border values for different elements. A design might use a border around a table without using borders around rows, columns, cells, or elements in cells.

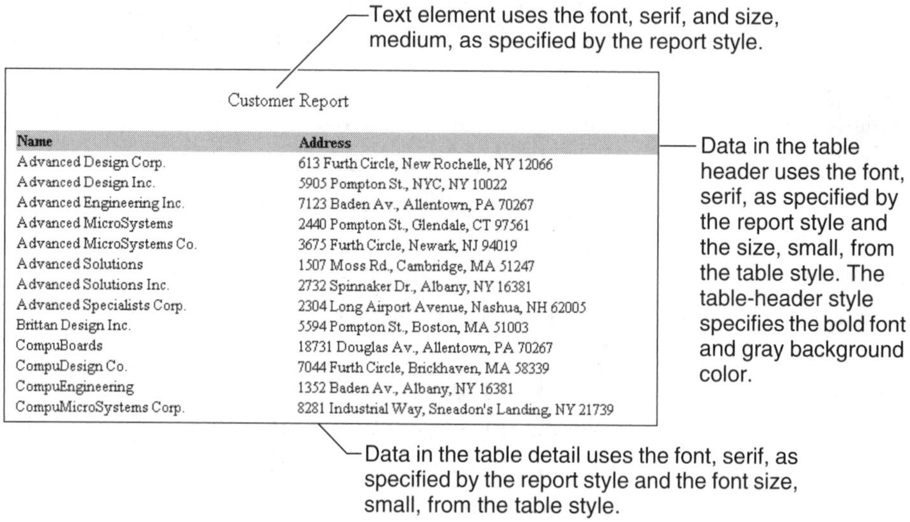

Text element uses the font, serif, and size, medium, as specified by the report style.

Data in the table header uses the font, serif, as specified by the report style and the size, small, from the table style. The table-header style specifies the bold font and gray background color.

Data in the table detail uses the font, serif, as specified by the report style and the font size, small, from the table style.

Figure 10-6   Report that shows the use of cascading styles

For details about each property, including the cascading rule, see the ROM Styles specification document, which is available at the following URL:

http://www.eclipse.org/birt/phoenix/ref/

How to create a style

1 In the layout editor, select the report element to which you want to apply a style. To create a style but not apply it to any elements, click in an empty area on the report page.

2 Choose Element➤Style➤New Style. New Style appears, as shown in Figure 10-7. The left side displays the property categories. The right side displays the properties for the category that you select.

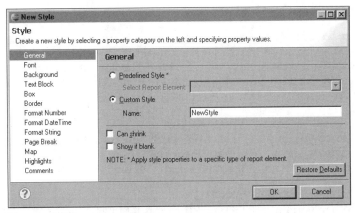

Figure 10-7   New Style

3 Specify one of the following settings:

- To apply style properties to a specific type of report element, select Predefined Style, and select a style from the drop-down list.

- To create a user-named style, select Custom Style, and specify a unique descriptive name. Ensure that the name is not the same as any of the predefined style names. If you specify a name that is the same as a predefined style, your custom style takes precedence, and you can no longer use the predefined style to apply cascading styles.

4 Set the desired style properties by selecting a property category on the left and specifying property values.

5 When you finish setting style properties, choose OK to save the style. If you selected an element before you created the style, BIRT Report Designer applies the style to that element.

The custom styles and predefined styles that you define appear in Outline, as shown in Figure 10-8. Any time you want to change a style, access it from this view.

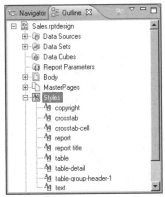

Figure 10-8   Styles in Outline

Reusing CSS styles

Most organizations maintain web sites, and most of the web pages on these sites use CSS to define the look and feel of the pages. As a report designer, you can reuse the styles from CSS files. The benefits of reusing styles are obvious—you save time by not having to reinvent the styles, and your reports reflect the standard style. You can reuse CSS styles in two ways:

- Import the styles into your reports.

  When you import styles from a CSS file, BIRT Report Designer copies the styles to the report. Subsequent changes to styles in the CSS file have no effect on the imported styles in the report.

- Link the CSS file to your reports.

  When you link a CSS file to the report, any changes made to the CSS file are reflected in the report.

Import styles if you expect the styles in the original CSS file to change, but you do not want the report to use the future style changes. If you do not have any control over the original CSS file, extensive style changes in the file, such as font sizes, line spacing, or text alignment, can alter a precisely designed report in undesirable ways.

Link a CSS file to your report if you are the author of the CSS file, and you want to maintain and update the styles in all your reports by modifying a single CSS file.

BIRT Report Designer supports the CSS2 specification. Not all CSS2 properties, however, are supported. For a list of unsupported properties, see the Style and CSS specification document, which is available at the following URL:

```
http://www.eclipse.org/birt/phoenix/ref
```

Styles that use unsupported properties are available to a report. The unsupported properties, however, do not have an effect when applied to a report element.

Importing styles

You can import any number of styles from a CSS file. If you import a style whose name matches the name of an existing style in the report, BIRT Report Designer appends a number to the name of the imported style. For example, if a report contains a style named TopLevelHeading, and you import a style with the same name, the imported style's name changes to TopLevelHeading1.

Imported styles appear in the list of available styles with all the styles that are created with BIRT Report Designer. You apply an imported style to a report element, edit the style's properties, or delete it in the same way that you do with a style that was created using BIRT Report Designer.

How to import styles

1 Select the layout editor.

2 Choose Element→Style→Import CSS Style.

3 In Import CSS Styles, in File Name, specify the name of the CSS file from which to import styles. Choose Browse to find the file. Import CSS Styles displays all the styles defined in the CSS file. Figure 10-9 shows an example of the styles in a CSS file named base.css.

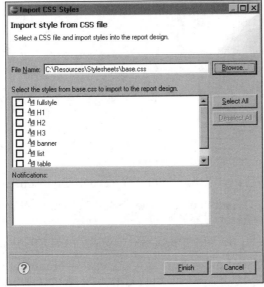

Figure 10-9 Examples of styles defined in a CSS file

4 Select the styles that you want to import. To import all the styles, choose Select All.

5 When you finish making your selections, choose Finish. BIRT Report Designer copies the styles to the report. The imported styles appear in the Styles list in Outline.

Linking a CSS file

Linking a CSS file to a report is a two-step process.

1 Place the CSS file in the BIRT resource folder. The resource folder is a central location for external files used by reports.

2 Link the CSS file in the resource folder to the report.

As with styles that you create or import, the styles in a linked CSS file also appear in the list of styles in Outline. The difference is that these styles are read-only. You cannot edit or delete these styles within BIRT Report Designer. Changes can be made only in the CSS file and these changes propagate to all reports linked to the CSS file.

If a style in a linked CSS file has the same name as a style that already exists, the existing style has precedence. In the layout editor, the list of styles available to apply to a report element shows only the existing instance of the style.

How to link a CSS file

1   In Resource Explorer, right-click Shared Resources, then choose Add Resource, as shown in Figure 10-10.

Figure 10-10   Choose Add Resource

2   In Add Resource, specify the CSS file to place in the resource folder.

    1   In Source File, type the path to the CSS file, or choose Browse to locate and select the file.

    2   In File Name, optionally type a new name for the CSS file.

    3   In Folder, the read-only path value shows the location of the BIRT resource folder. Add the CSS file to this root folder, or choose Browse to select a subfolder in which to place the CSS file.

    Figure 10-11 shows an example of values specified in Add Resource.

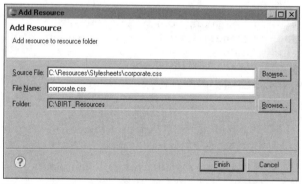

Figure 10-11   Add Resources with values supplied

4   Choose Finish. The CSS file appears in Resource Explorer, and it is available to any report design. Expand the file to display all styles, as shown in Figure 10-12.

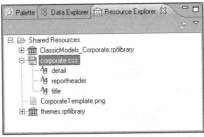

Figure 10-12   Resource Explorer showing the styles in a CSS file

3   Link the CSS file to the report by performing the following tasks:

   1   Choose Outline.

   2   Right-click Styles, then choose Use CSS File, as shown in Figure 10-13.

Figure 10-13   Choose Use CSS File

   3   In Use CSS, choose Browse to select the CSS file to link to the report. The Browse dialog, shown in Figure 10-14, displays the resource folder and the CSS files in the folder.

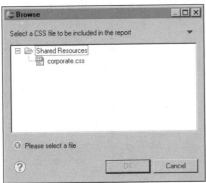

Figure 10-14   Browse showing the CSS file in the resource folder

   4   Select the CSS file, then choose OK. Use CSS displays the selected CSS file and the styles in that file, as shown in Figure 10-15.

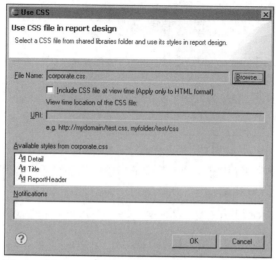

Figure 10-15　Use CSS showing the selected CSS file and its styles

5　Optionally, link a CSS file at report view time, using the following steps. Use this option to apply HTML-only selectors, such as :link and :visited to customize the style of hyperlinks.

　　1　Choose Include CSS file at view time.

　　2　In URI, type the location of the CSS file. Type a full or relative URL.

6　Choose OK. The linked CSS file and its styles appear under Styles in Outline, as shown in Figure 10-16. The style names appear in gray, indicating that they are not defined in the report design, but rather, are linked from an external file.

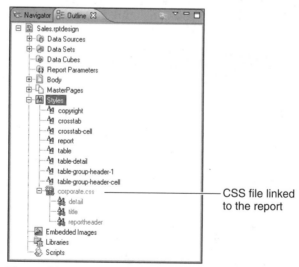

Figure 10-16　Outline showing a linked CSS file and its styles

Applying a style

After you link a CSS file, or create or import styles for a report, you can apply styles to specific report elements. To apply a style to a report element, right-click the report element, choose Style→Apply Style, then select one of the styles in the list. The list displays all the available styles. Choose None to remove the style that is currently applied to the report element.

If you set style properties to predefined style names, such as table-header or table-footer, BIRT Report Designer applies the style properties to all those types of report elements. You cannot selectively apply predefined styles to only some elements of that type.

Modifying a style

One of the most powerful features of styles is the ease with which you can change the look of a report. If you decide to change fonts or font sizes in the entire report, all you do is modify the style that controls the font properties. To modify a custom or imported style, in Outline, expand Styles, right-click the style, then choose Edit Style. All report elements that use that style are automatically updated to use the new formatting.

To modify styles in a linked CSS file, edit the CSS file that resides in the BIRT resource folder. When you save the edits, the report reflects the style changes.

Deleting a style

You can delete any style at any time. You should, however, delete only the styles that your report elements no longer need. If you delete a style that is applied to a report element or elements, the affected elements lose the formats that the style applied. Before deleting a style that is in use, BIRT Report Designer displays the names of the elements that are affected and prompts you to cancel or confirm the deletion. To delete a style, choose Outline. Under Styles, right-click the style to delete, then choose Delete.

You cannot delete individual styles in a linked CSS file. You can, however, unlink the CSS file from the report by right-clicking the file, then choosing Delete. BIRT unlinks the file without displaying a warning, even if there are report elements using styles in the CSS file. These report elements revert to their unformatted state, and when you preview the report, BIRT Report Designer displays an "Errors in Report" message. You can still preview a report with this type of error, but the message appears every time you choose Preview. To fix the problem, select the elements that used the deleted style, and set the Style property to None.

Formatting data based on conditions

When you format a report element, the format applies to all instances of the element in the generated report. For example, if you specify that an item price appears in the Arial typeface and blue, all item prices in the generated report appear in Arial and blue. This type of formatting is called absolute formatting. The appearance of the element is set when you design the report.

You can change the format of an element according to its value or the value of another element. For example, you can specify that item prices appear in green if the value exceeds $1,000.00 and in a default color if the value is equal to or less than $1,000.00. This type of formatting is called conditional formatting. In the report, the appearance of each item generated from a conditionally formatted element is set only at the point when the report runs.

The following examples are some common uses of conditional formatting:

- Show numbers in a different color if they are negative.

- Highlight delinquent accounts by using a different typeface or font style.

- Highlight the top ten customers by displaying their names in a colored box.

Creating a formatting rule

BIRT Report Designer provides an easy way to apply conditional formatting to report elements. Use the Highlights page of Property Editor to create a formatting rule that defines when and how to change the appearance of an element. When creating a formatting rule, specify the following information:

- The condition to meet in order to apply a format, for example, row["OrderTotal"] Greater than 50000.

- The format to apply, for example, font color = blue. You can also specify a style to apply.

Figure 10-17 shows an example of a formatting rule.

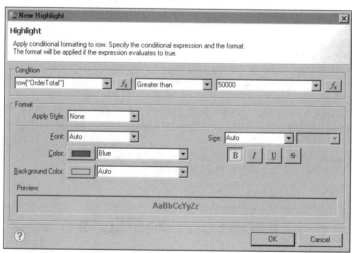

Figure 10-17   New Highlight showing a formatting rule

How to create a formatting rule

1 In the layout editor, select the report element to format conditionally.

2 Choose the Highlights tab in Property Editor. The Highlights page appears, as shown in Figure 10-18. It is empty if you have not yet specified any formatting rules for the selected element.

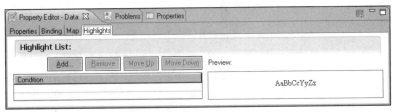

Figure 10-18 Highlights page

3 Choose Add to add a new formatting rule.

4 In New Highlight, create the rule for applying a particular format to the report element by completing the following steps:

　1 Think of the rule in plain English first. For example:

```
If the order total is greater than $50,000.00, then set
the font color to blue and the font style to bold.
```

　There are two parts to the rule: If (condition) and Then (format). The New Highlight dialog helps you specify the condition and format parts of the rule by breaking them down to more specific parts.

　2 Specify the condition part of the rule by completing the following steps:

　　1 In the first field, specify the first part of the conditional expression. Using the example rule, this part is order total:

　　　❑ If the order total values come directly from the selected element, from the drop-down list, choose Value of this data item.

　　　❑ If the order total values come from another data element, choose that element's column binding name from the drop-down list.

　　2 In the second field, specify the second part of the conditional expression by selecting an option from the list. Using our example rule, this part is Greater than.

　　3 In the third field, specify the third part of the conditional expression. Using our example rule, this part is a value of 50000, as shown in Figure 10-19.

Figure 10-19 Elements of the conditional expression

You have now completed the condition part of the rule, which specifies the following:

```
If row["OrderTotal"] is greater than 50000
```

3 Specify the format part of the rule, which is "then set the font color to blue and the font style to bold," by completing the following steps:

❏ Choose Color, then select a color from the color picker.

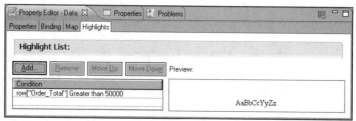 ❏ Choose B to select the Bold format, as shown in Figure 10-20.

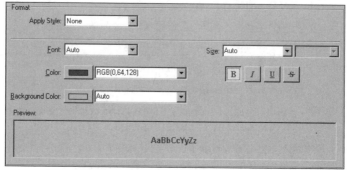

Figure 10-20   Elements of the formatting expression in New Highlight

❏ Alternatively, if you created a style named order_data_highlight, for example, that specifies the formats, you can select the style from the list of styles next to Apply Style.

4 Choose OK to save the highlight rule.

The rule that you created appears in Highlight List, as shown in Figure 10-21. The rule takes effect the next time you run the report.

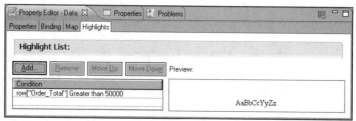

Figure 10-21   Highlight List

5 Preview the report to test your formatting rule.

Modifying a formatting rule

To modify a formatting rule, use the same highlight tool that you use to create the rule. Select the element for which you want to modify the formatting rule, choose the Highlights tab in Property Editor, then double-click the rule to modify. You can change any part of the rule, such as the condition that triggers the formatting or the format properties to apply. The modified rule takes effect the next time you run the report.

Creating multiple formatting rules

You can create multiple formatting rules for an element. For example, you can create three rules to set the values of an order total data element to one of three colors, depending on the dollar amount. Figure 10-22 shows an example.

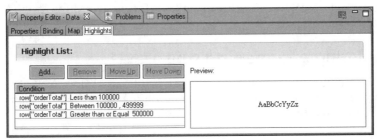

Figure 10-22 Highlights page showing multiple format rules for an element

You can create any number of rules, and you can base conditions on the value of the selected element or on the value of other elements. Using the previous example, you can also change the color of the order total value based on the value of another data element, such as order ID. Figure 10-23 shows this example.

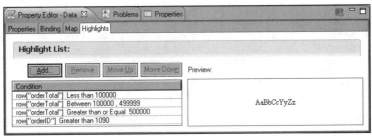

Figure 10-23 Conditional format for orderTotal based on the value of orderID

For each row of data, BIRT Report Designer evaluates the rules in the order in which they appear in the list of rules. As it evaluates each rule, BIRT Report Designer applies the specified format properties if the condition is met. If multiple rules with different conditions use the same format property, the later rule can override the format that the earlier rules specify.

Consider the following example:

- The first rule sets order total values to red if they are less than 100000.

- The fourth rule sets order total values to blue if the order ID is larger than 1090.

If an order total value is 50000 and the order ID is 2000 (the conditions in both rules are true), the order total value appears in blue, not red, because the fourth rule supersedes all rules before it. If, however, the fourth rule sets order total values to italics rather than to blue, the value appears in red and italics.

When creating multiple rules for an element, plan the rules carefully. Consider the effect of individual rules and how the order of the rules changes the results. Test thoroughly to verify that the report displays the results that you expect. If necessary, change the order of the rules by selecting a rule and moving it up or down the list using the Move Up or Move Down buttons on the Highlights page.

Deleting a formatting rule

All formatting rules that you create for an element take effect when you run the report. If you do not want a formatting rule to apply to an element, delete the rule from the Highlights page of the selected element.

Alternating row colors in a table

If a table displays many rows, it can be hard to read the data. A common solution is to use alternating colors for the rows, as shown in Figure 10-24.

Customer	Address	Phone
Atelier graphique	54, rue Royale, Nantes, 44000, France	40.32.2555
Signal Gift Stores	8489 Strong St., Las Vegas, NV 83030, USA	7025551838
Australian Collectors, Co.	636 St Kilda Road, Level 3, Melbourne, Victoria 3004, Australia	03 9520 4555
La Rochelle Gifts	67, rue des Cinquante Otages, Nantes, 44000, France	40.67.8555
Baane Mini Imports	Erling Skakkes gate 78, Stavern, 4110, Norway	07-98 9555
Mini Gifts Distributors Ltd.	5677 Strong St., San Rafael, CA 97562, USA	4155551450
Havel & Zbyszek Co	ul. Filtrowa 68, Warszawa, 01-012, Poland	(26) 642-7555
Blauer See Auto, Co.	Lyonerstr. 34, Frankfurt, 60528, Germany	+49 69 66 90

Figure 10-24 Conditional formatting that displays rows in alternating colors

To create this effect, use the conditional formatting feature, as described in the preceding section. In the example shown, if the row number is even, set a darker color as the row's background color. If the row number is odd, leave the row's background color unchanged from its default.

Note that BIRT counts the first row as 0, so what appears as the first row is actually row 0, what appears as the second row is actually row 1, and so on. In other words, the rows that appear to be odd-numbered rows in the generated report are technically even-numbered rows, and vice versa. In the report that appears in Figure 10-24, the gray color applies to even-numbered rows.

How to alternate row colors

1 Select the detail row in the table, as shown in Figure 10-25.

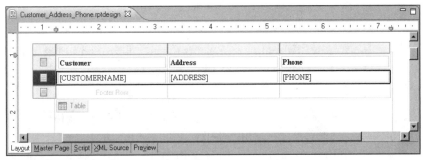

Figure 10-25 Detail row selected

2 In General properties in Property Editor, choose a color for Background Color, or use the default value, Auto. This color is the default color for the detail rows.

3 Choose the Highlights tab in Property Editor to create a formatting rule to apply a different color to alternate rows.

4 In the Highlights page, choose Add to create a formatting rule.

5 In New Highlight, specify an expression in the first field:

   1 Next to the first field, choose the expression builder button.

   2 In the expression builder, select Available Column Bindings, then select Table, then double-click RowNum. The following expression appears in the text area, as shown in Figure 10-26.

```
row.__rownum
```

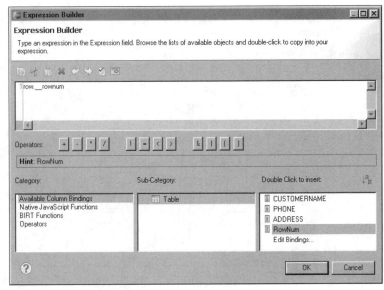

Figure 10-26 The expression builder showing the row.__rownum expression

3 Change the expression to:

```
row.__rownum % 2
```

row.__rownum represents the current row number. The modulus (%) operator returns the remainder of a division. 2 specifies the number by which to divide. Using this expression, even-numbered rows return 0, and odd-numbered rows return a non-zero value.

4 Choose OK to save the expression. The expression appears in the first field in New Highlight.

6 In the second field, choose either Equal to or Not Equal to:

- To apply the formatting rule to even-numbered rows, choose Equal to.

- To apply the formatting rule to odd-numbered rows, choose Not Equal to.

7 In the third field, type the following number:

```
0
```

0 specifies the value to compare to the result of the expression, row.__rownum % 2. This value completes the condition part of the formatting rule as follows:

```
If row.__rownum % 2 Equal to (or Not Equal to) 0
```

8 Specify the color to assign to the even- or odd-numbered rows by choosing a color for Background Color. Figure 10-27 shows an example of a completed format rule. The rule sets the background color of even-numbered rows to silver.

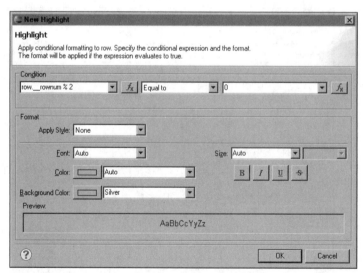

Figure 10-27   New Highlight dialog showing a complete format rule

Choose OK.

9 Preview the report. The detail rows should appear in alternating colors.

Use row.__rownum and the % operator with different values to alternate colors for a different number of rows. For example, the following highlight expressions change the row color for every three and every five rows, respectively:

```
row.__rownum % 6 Greater than or Equal 3
row.__rownum % 10 Greater than or Equal 5
```

Specifying alignment of content in a table or grid

Content in a table or grid aligns horizontally and vertically. When you place elements in the cells of a table or grid, BIRT Report Designer, by default, aligns content as follows:

- Aligns text horizontally to the left
- Aligns content vertically to the cell's baseline

Aligning text horizontally

You can change the horizontal alignment of text by setting the text-alignment property to one of the following values: left, right, center, or justify. This property is equivalent to the CSS text-align property.

You can align content by applying the text-alignment property to individual data elements, to cells, to an entire row, or to the entire table or grid. To align all text in a table in the same way, set the text-alignment property at the table level. To align all text in a particular row, set the property at the row level.

Figure 10-28 shows the results of using the different property values.

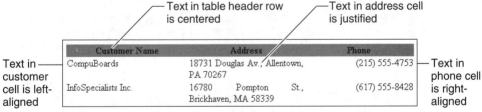

Figure 10-28   Text-alignment properties

Aligning content vertically

You can change the vertical alignment of content by setting the vertical-alignment property to one of the following values: top, middle, bottom. You can align content vertically by applying the vertical-alignment property to a row, to individual cells, or to a content element.

Set the vertical-alignment property on a row to align vertically all elements in the row at the same position. Figure 10-29 shows the results of setting a row's vertical-alignment property to middle. All the labels in the row, which has a specified height, appear in the center vertically.

Figure 10-29   Vertical-alignment property setting for a row

Set the vertical-alignment property on a cell to control the vertical position of elements in the cell. Figure 10-30 shows the results of using a different vertical-alignment value for each grid cell that contains a label.

Figure 10-30   Vertical-alignment property settings for cells that contain one element

Figure 10-31 shows the results of using a different vertical alignment value for each cell that contains two inline elements. An inline element is one that has no line break before or after it, and for which the Display property is set to inline. Two inline elements in a cell appear side by side on a single line.

Figure 10-31   Vertical-alignment property settings for cells that contain multiple elements

---

Adjusting the spacing of content in a report

The default layout adds a minimum amount of space between elements in a report. After laying elements in a report, preview the report in the desired output format to see if you need to adjust the spacing between contents. Reports render differently in the different output formats.

One key difference is the effect of empty grid and table rows in the generated report. In DOC, PPT, and XLS formats, empty rows appear as blank space. For example, if a grid has three rows, but only one row contains content, the DOC, PPT, and XLS reports display two blank lines. In HTML and PDF, an empty row does not appear as blank space unless you set the row to a specific height.

Figure 10-32 shows the default spacing for report elements in a report design. As the figure shows, a table contains columns of equal width unless you specify explicit column widths. Similarly, the table occupies as much space horizontally as is available unless you specify a value for the table width. The available, or printable, area is determined by the page size and margin sizes of the master page.

Figure 10-32 Default spacing in a report design

Figure 10-33 shows the report output in HTML. The default layout displays rows of content with very little space between them. The data is displayed in three columns of equal size. The address data fills the second column and is truncated to fit on one line.

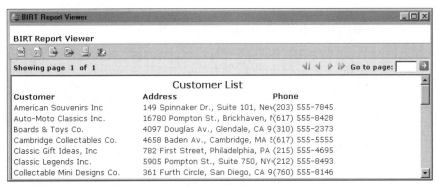

Figure 10-33 Default spacing in an HTML report

Figure 10-34 shows the same report in PDF format. The PDF report looks similar to the HTML report. The data also appears in three columns of equal size with minimal space between the rows and columns, and data in the address column is truncated.

Customer List

Customer	Address	Phone
American Souvenirs Inc	149 Spinnaker Dr., Suite 101,	(203) 555-7845
Auto-Moto Classics Inc.	16780 Pompton St.,	(617) 555-8428
Boards & Toys Co.	4097 Douglas Av., Glendale, CA	(310) 555-2373
Cambridge Collectables Co.	4658 Baden Av., Cambridge,	(617) 555-5555
Classic Gift Ideas, Inc	782 First Street, Philadelphia,	(215) 555-4695
Classic Legends Inc.	5905 Pompton St., Suite 750,	(212) 555-8493
Collectable Mini Designs Co.	361 Furth Circle, San Diego, CA	(760) 555-8146

Figure 10-34 Default spacing in a PDF report

To display the entire address, you can increase the width of the column or the height of the row. A more practical solution, especially for lengthy blocks of data, is to specify that the text wrap onto as many lines as needed.

To adjust the spacing of content in a report, use one of the following techniques:

- Resize the rows or columns of a table or grid to adjust spacing of content in a table or grid.

- Insert an empty row or column in a table or grid, and specify a specific size for the row or column.

- Resize the margins, borders, and padding of elements.

The first two techniques provide more predictable results. The padding and margin properties can yield varying results in different web browsers, depending on how the browser interprets these properties.

Wrapping text onto multiple lines

As the HTML and PDF reports in Figure 10-33 and Figure 10-34 show, by default, content in data elements appear in one line. Data that does not fit within the column is truncated. Figure 10-35 shows an alternative format where text wrapping is applied and the text appears on multiple lines.

Figure 10-35   Text in address column wraps onto multiple lines

How to specify text wrapping

1 Select the data element that displays the text.

2 In Property Editor, choose Properties, then choose Advanced.

3 Change Text—Whitespace from No Wrapping to Normal, as shown in Figure 10-36.

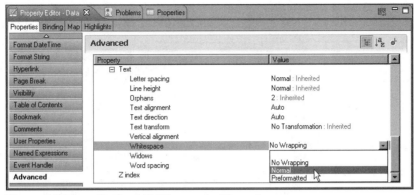

Figure 10-36 Setting Whitespace to Normal

Resizing rows and columns

The quickest way to change the size of a row or column is to drag the row or column boundary to the desired height or width. You can also resize a row or column by setting a specific row height or column width.

When setting a row height, preview the report to ensure that the results are what you want. The row height you specify is a fixed height. If the content cannot fit within the specified height, content is truncated.

How to resize a column or row by dragging its boundary

1 Select the tab at the bottom left corner of the grid or table. Guide cells appear at the top and left sides of the grid or table.

2 In the guide cell area, select a row or column boundary, and drag it until the row or column is the desired size, as shown in Figure 10-37.

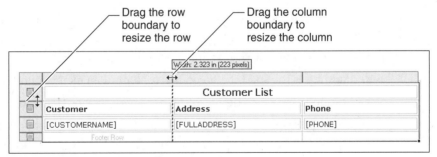

Figure 10-37 Resize rows or columns by dragging boundaries

How to specify a row height

1 Select the tab at the bottom left corner of the grid or table. Guide cells appear at the top and left sides of the grid or table.

2 Select the guide cell of the row to resize.

3 In Property Editor, under Properties, choose General. Property Editor displays the general properties of the row, as shown in Figure 10-38.

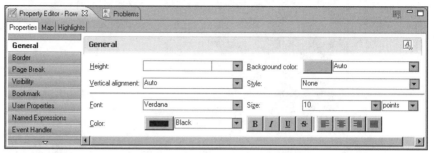

Figure 10-38 Property Editor showing row properties

4 Specify a value for Height. You can specify different units of measurements, including inches, centimeters, millimeters, and points.

How to specify a column width

1 Select the tab on the bottom left corner of the grid or table. Guide cells appear at the top and left sides of the grid or table.

2 Select the guide cell of the column to resize.

3 In Property Editor, under Properties, choose General.

4 Specify a value for Width. You can specify different units of measurements, including inches, centimeters, millimeters, and a percentage of the total grid or table width.

Resizing margins, borders, and padding of elements

As in CSS, BIRT Report Designer provides three properties to define the horizontal and vertical space between elements:

- Border is a visible or invisible line around the element.

- Padding is the space between the content of an element and the border.

- Margin is the space between the border and other elements.

Figure 10-39 shows how margins, borders, and padding work together.

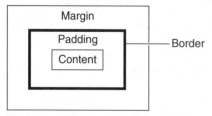

Figure 10-39 Properties that define the space between elements

You can use the padding and margin properties of an element to adjust the horizontal and vertical spacing of content in a report. Figure 10-40 shows how to set a label element's Padding Bottom property to increase the spacing between the report title and the table below it.

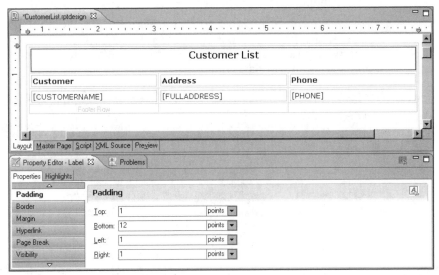

Figure 10-40 Use the Padding Bottom property to specify the spacing below an element

Figure 10-41 shows the report output. You can get the same result by increasing the table's Margin Top property.

Customer List		
Customer	**Address**	**Phone**
American Souvenirs Inc	149 Spinnaker Dr., Suite 101, New Haven, CT 97823	(203) 555-7845
Auto-Moto Classics Inc.	16780 Pompton St., Brickhaven, MA 58339	(617) 555-8428
Boards & Toys Co.	4097 Douglas Av., Glendale, CA 92561	(310) 555-2373

Figure 10-41 Report output showing the result of the Padding Bottom setting

Specifying auto-expand layout for HTML output

As described previously, by default, the contents of a report display in a fixed-width area determined by the page and margin sizes set in the master page. While this behavior is standard for page-based formats, such as PDF and DOC, it is not always desirable for HTML output. Typically, HTML documents are formatted to display content that adjusts to the size of the browser window.

If you are designing an HTML report and you want the report to expand or contract with the browser window or the BIRT report viewer window, set the report's Layout Preference property to Auto Layout. The Auto Layout setting changes the layout of HTML output only and has no effect on the other output formats.

Compare the reports in Figure 10-42 and Figure 10-43. Figure 10-42 shows a report in which Layout Preference is set to Fixed Layout. The table and column widths do not have specified values, so BIRT creates a table with columns of equal widths.

Figure 10-42   HTML report in which Layout Preference is set to Fixed Layout

Figure 10-43 shows the same report, but the Layout Preference property is set to Auto Layout. The table does not have a fixed width, nor do the columns in the table. The content fills the area in the window.

BIRT Report Viewer

BIRT Report Viewer

Showing page 1 of 1   Go to page:

Customer List

Customer	Address	Phone
American Souvenirs Inc	149 Spinnaker Dr., Suite 101, New Haven, CT 97823	(203) 555-7845
Auto-Moto Classics Inc.	16780 Pompton St., Brickhaven, MA 58339	(617) 555-8428
Boards & Toys Co.	4097 Douglas Av., Glendale, CA 92561	(310) 555-2373
Cambridge Collectables Co.	4658 Baden Av., Cambridge, MA 51247	(617) 555-5555
Classic Gift Ideas, Inc	782 First Street, Philadelphia, PA 71270	(215) 555-4695
Classic Legends Inc.	5905 Pompton St., Suite 750, NYC, NY 10022	(212) 555-8493
Collectable Mini Designs Co.	361 Furth Circle, San Diego, CA 91217	(760) 555-8146
Collectables For Less Inc.	7825 Douglas Av., Brickhaven, MA 58339	(617) 555-8555
Corporate Gift Ideas Co.	7734 Strong St., San Francisco, CA 94217	(650) 555-1386
Diecast Classics Inc.	7586 Pompton St., Allentown, PA 70267	(215) 555-1555
Diecast Collectables	6251 Ingle Ln., Boston, MA 51003	(617) 555-2555

Figure 10-43   HTML report in which Layout Preference is set to Auto Layout

How to specify auto-expand layout for an HTML report

1 In the layout editor, click in an empty area of the report page.

2 In Property Editor, in the report's general properties, set Layout Preference to Auto Layout, as shown in Figure 10-44.

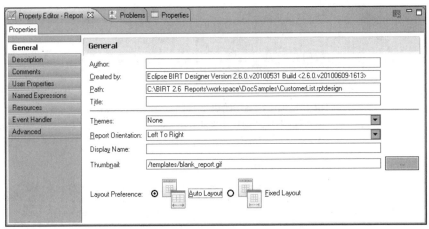

Figure 10-44 Property Editor showing the general properties of the report, including the Layout Preference property

3 Make sure there are no values specified for the width property of the table or any of the columns. Specific width values create a fixed-width report.

Displaying data values in one row

For typical listing reports, data is best presented in rows and columns in a table, as shown in numerous examples. If, however, a table displays data from one field only and the field contains a few values, you can improve the presentation by displaying all the values in one row. Compare the following layouts for displaying the locations of sales offices.

Layout 1:

```
Sales Offices:
London
New York
Paris
```

Layout 2:

```
Sales Offices: London, New York, Paris
```

The first layout uses a table conventionally. Figure 10-45 shows the report design. The table's header row contains a label to display the column heading, Sales Offices. The detail row contains the CITY field, which displays each city value in a separate row.

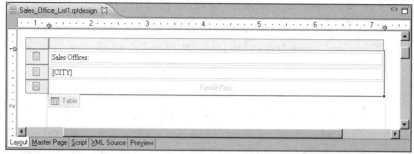

Figure 10-45   Table layout to display cities, each in a separate row

The second layout also uses a table. In this design, shown in Figure 10-46, the table's header row contains a text element. This text element displays the static text, Sales Offices:, and refers to a column binding that returns the list of cities. The column binding uses the CONCATENATE function to join all the city values into a single string value.

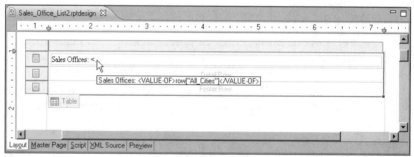

Figure 10-46   Table layout to display cities in one row

How to display data values in one row

1 Insert a table and bind it to the data set that contains the field from which to display values.

2 Create a column binding to return all the field values in a single string.

   1 Select the table, and in Property Editor, select the Binding tab.

   2 In the Binding page, choose Add Aggregation.

   3 In Aggregation Builder, specify the following information:

      ❑ In Column Binding Name, type a name to identify the column binding.

      ❑ In Function, select CONCATENATE from the drop-down list. Aggregation Builder selects String as the data type.

      ❑ In Expression, select the field from which to concatenate values.

      ❑ In Separator, optionally type a character or characters to insert between each value. A common separator is a comma followed by a space. You must enclose the separator value in double quotation marks (" "), as shown in the following example:

" , "

❑ In Max length, specify the maximum number of characters returned, including the separator characters. If you do not set a value for this property, CONCATENATE returns all the values in the field.

❑ In Show all values, type true to include duplicate values. If you do not set a value for this property, CONCATENATE excludes duplicate values.

Figure 10-47 shows the column binding defined for the report example shown in Figure 10-46.

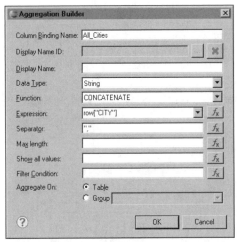

Figure 10-47   Definition of column binding using the CONCATENATE function

3 In the table's header row, insert a text or data element to display the string returned by the column binding. Figure 10-48 shows the contents of the text element used in the report example shown in Figure 10-46.

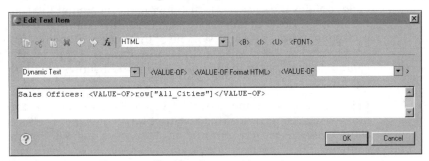

Figure 10-48   Text specified for the text element

Displaying content across multiple columns

Grid and table columns enable you to align report elements easily and neatly. Often, however, you need to display text or data across multiple columns to enhance the report's appearance. For example, compare the layout of the reports in Figure 10-49 and Figure 10-50.

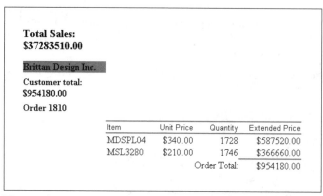

Figure 10-49   Report data displayed within five columns

Total Sales:
$37283510.00

Brittan Design Inc.

Customer total:
$954180.00

Order 1810

Item	Unit Price	Quantity	Extended Price
MDSPL04	$340.00	1728	$587520.00
MSL3280	$210.00	1746	$366660.00
		Order Total:	$954180.00

Total Sales: $37283510.00

Brittan Design Inc.

Customer total: $954180.00

Order 1810

Item	Unit Price	Quantity	Extended Price
MDSPL04	$340.00	1728	$587520.00
MSL3280	$210.00	1746	$366660.00
		Order Total:	$954180.00

Figure 10-50   Report data spans multiple columns

In the first report, data appears in a five-column table. The first column of the table contains the sales total, customer name, customer total, and order number. The order details occupy the rest of the columns. To fit five columns, each column is fairly narrow. Some of the content in the first column wraps onto two lines. If you increase the width of the first column, the second column moves too far to the right. Figure 10-51 shows the design for the first report.

In the second report, the sales total, customer name, and customer total span multiple columns, so that the text appears on one line. The second column starts farther to the left, eliminating extra space on the left of the detailed content.

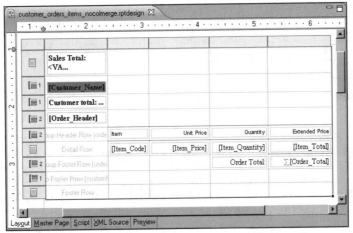

Figure 10-51 Report design without column spanning

Figure 10-52 shows the design for the second report.

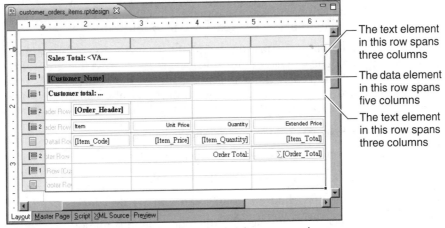

The text element in this row spans three columns

The data element in this row spans five columns

The text element in this row spans three columns

Figure 10-52 Report design that uses column spanning

To display table or grid content across multiple columns, merge the cells.

How to merge table or grid cells

1 Select the cells to merge by using Shift-click. A border appears around the selected cells, as shown in Figure 10-53.

Figure 10-53 Cells selected for merging

2 Right-click within the border, then choose Merge Cells from the context menu. The cells merge into one, as shown in Figure 10-54.

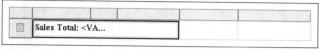

Figure 10-54 Merged cells

Specifying alternate values for display

Data in a data source can sometimes be cryptic or appear in abbreviated form. For example, gender values may be M or F rather than male or female. Credit rankings may be 1 to 5 rather than excellent, good, average, fair, or poor.

BIRT Report Designer supports the display of alternate values if you do not want to use the original values in a report. You use a data element's map property to create rules for mapping data values. Create one map rule for each data value you want to replace. For example, to map M and F to Male and Female, respectively, create two map rules.

You can replace a data value with a literal text value. Alternatively, if the report will be viewed in multiple locales, replace a data value with a resource key. A resource key is a text string in an external source that is translated, or localized, into different languages. For information about resource keys and localization, see Chapter 25, "Localizing Text."

How to map data values to different display values

1 Select the data element for which to replace values.

2 In Property Editor, choose the Map tab.

3 In Map List, choose Add to create a map rule.

4 In New Map Rule, specify the following information:

   1 In the first field, specify the expression that refers to the data set field for which you want to replace values. You can select, from the drop-down list, Value of this data item. The following is an example of an expression:

     `row["creditrank"]`

   2 In the second field, select an operator from the list. For example:

     `Equal to`

   3 In the third field, specify the value to replace. For example:

     `"A"`

   You must enclose string values in quotation marks (" ").

4 Specify the value that you want to display, using one of the following options:

❏ Under "Then display following value:", type the text to display. For example:

Excellent

❏ Specify a resource key. Choose Browse to select a resource key. You can access resource keys only if you have assigned a resource file to the report.

Figure 10-55 shows an example of a completed map rule, which replaces the value A with the value Excellent.

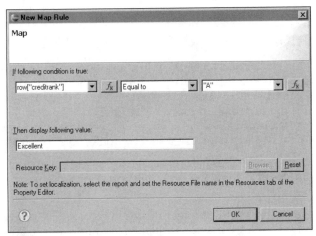

Figure 10-55   A map rule

5 Choose OK. The rule that you created appears in Map List. When you select the rule, the display value appears in the box at the right, as shown in Figure 10-56.

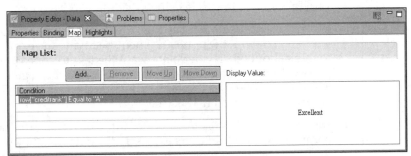

Figure 10-56   Map rule and its display value in Property Editor

6 Repeat steps 3 through 5 to create additional rules, one for each data value to replace. Figure 10-57 shows an example of three map rules created for the selected data element.

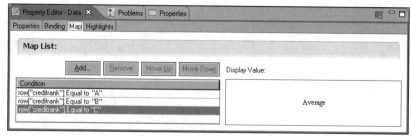

Figure 10-57   Three map rules for an element

5   Preview the report to check the results of the map rules.

Hiding elements based on conditions

In most cases, you add an element to a report in order to display the contents of the element. There are many good reasons, however, for hiding report elements conditionally. Using an element's Visibility property, you can customize the information that a report displays. You can hide an element based on the output format or on a specific condition. You specify a condition by writing a Boolean expression that evaluates to either true or false.

The following examples describe cases for conditionally hiding an element. The examples also show the Boolean expressions to apply to the Visibility property.

- Display a text message only for certain records. Assume you want the report to display a message when an account balance falls below a certain amount, such as $1,000.00. First, create a text element that displays something like "Your account balance is below the minimum balance required to waive the service fee." Then, conditionally hide the text element by setting its Visibility property to the following expression:

  ```
  row["accountbalance"] > 1000
  ```

  When the expression returns true, the text element is hidden. Notice that you have to think the opposite when specifying the expression. You have to think about when you do not want the text to appear, rather than when you do. In this example, you want to display a message when the balance is less than $1,000.00. Therefore, you hide the text element when the balance is greater than $1,000.00.

- Display a text message if a report returns no data. If the report uses parameters to prompt users to specify the data that they want to view, and it is possible for the report to return nothing, you can display a message, such as "No records found." To accomplish this task, perform the following steps:

  - Create a column binding, named Row_Count, for example, that uses the aggregate function, COUNT, to get the number of data rows in a table. Remember, for each piece of computed data to use or display in a report, there must be a column binding.

- Create a text or label element that displays the "No records found" message, then conditionally hide the element by setting its Visibility property to the following expression:

```
row["Row_Count"] != 0
```

The expression row["Row_Count"] refers to the Row_Count column binding that computes the number of rows. When Row_Count returns zero, the "No records found" message appears. Because an aggregate function processes all data rows in a table, you must place the text or label element in the header or footer row of the table. For information about using aggregate functions, see Chapter 12, "Aggregating Data."

- Display different pictures, depending on the values of a field. To add visual interest to a report, you want to display two stars next to an order total that equals or exceeds $10,000.00, one star for totals between $5,000.00 and $10,000.00, and nothing for totals less than $5,000.00. Create two pictures—one with two stars and the other with one star—and insert them next to the element that displays the order number. Use the following expression to hide the two-star picture conditionally. The expression hides the two-star picture when the order total is less than $10,000.00.

```
row["ordertotal"] <= 10000
```

Use the following expression to hide the one-star picture conditionally. The expression hides the one-star picture if the order total is less than $5,000.00 or more than $10,000.00.

```
row["ordertotal"] < 5000 || row["ordertotal"] > 10000
```

- Display different report sections, depending on the values of a field. For example, your staff are either full-time employees or contractors. You want to display different sets of information for these two groups. Create two report sections, one to show full-time employee information and another to show contractor information. Use the following expression to hide the section containing full-time employee information conditionally when the employee record is for a contractor.

```
row["classification"] == "fulltime"
```

Use the following expression to hide the section containing contractor information conditionally when the employee record is for a full-time employee.

```
row["classification"] == "contractor"
```

The Visibility property also provides you with the option to:

- Hide an element, depending on the output format. For example, hide an element for HTML output and display it for the other output formats.

- Specify different visibility conditions for different output formats. For example, hide an element in HTML if its value is *x* and hide an element in PDF if its value is *y*.

How to hide an element conditionally

1 Select the element to hide conditionally.

2 In Property Editor, under Properties, choose Visibility. The Hide Element option appears, as shown in Figure 10-58.

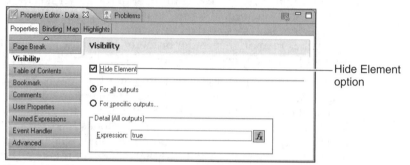

Figure 10-58 Hide Element option in Property Editor

3 Select Hide Element to specify that this element be hidden. If you want the element, such as an empty row, to always be hidden, this selection is all you need to do. To hide the element conditionally, specify the condition as well.

4 Select the report format to which to apply the hide condition.

- To apply the hide condition for all report formats, select For all outputs.

- To apply the hide condition for certain report formats, select For specific outputs. Also select this option to apply different conditions, depending on the report format.

5 Specify the hide condition by performing the following tasks:

    1 Open the expression builder.

    2 In the expression builder, create an expression that specifies the hide condition. Remember, think about when to hide the element, not when to display it. For example, to display the text message, Jumbo, when a loan amount exceeds $363,000.00, conditionally hide the text element using the following expression:

```
row["LoanAmount"] < 363000
```

    This expression hides the text message when loan amounts are less than $363,000.00.

    3 Choose OK.

6 Preview your report to test the conditional visibility.

Sorting and Grouping Data

When you first create a report and preview the data, the report displays the data in the order in which the data source returns it. The order varies based on how data was entered in the data source and how you joined tables in the query.

In most cases, you will want to change the order in which data appears in a report. A customer phone list, for example, is easier to use if it is in alphabetical order. A sales report is more useful if it presents sales figures from highest to lowest, or the reverse, depending on whether the focus is on top or low performers.

Compare the reports shown in Figure 11-1.

Report displays unsorted data

Customer	Phone
Signal Engineering	(203) 555-7845
Technical Specialists Co.	(203) 555-9545
SigniSpecialists Corp.	(212) 555-1957
Technical MicroSystems Inc.	(212) 555-7413
InfoEngineering	(212) 555-1500
Advanced Design Inc.	(212) 555-8493
Technical Design Inc.	(212) 555-7818
Design Solutions Corp.	(212) 555-3675
TekniSystems	(201) 555-9350
InfoDesign	(201) 555-2343
Computer Systems Corp.	(201) 555-8624
SigniDesign	(201) 555-5888
Advanced MicroSystems Co.	(201) 555-3722
TeleMicroSystems	(201) 555-5171

Report sorts data by customer name

Customer	Phone
Advanced Design Corp.	(914) 555-6707
Advanced Design Inc.	(212) 555-8493
Advanced Engineering Inc.	(215) 555-3197
Advanced MicroSystems	(203) 555-4407
Advanced MicroSystems Co.	(201) 555-3722
Advanced Solutions	(617) 555-3842
Advanced Solutions Inc.	(518) 555-9644
Advanced Specialists Corp.	(603) 555-8647
Brittan Design Inc.	(617) 555-2480
CompuBoards	(215) 555-4753
CompuDesign Co.	(617) 555-2663
CompuEngineering	(518) 555-3942
CompuMicroSystems Corp.	(914) 555-9081
CompuSolutions Co.	(201) 555-9867

Figure 11-1   Reports showing unsorted and sorted data

The report on the left displays customer names in the order in which the data set returns them. The customer names appear in a seemingly random order. The report on the right displays the customer names sorted in alphabetical order.

Now, compare the reports in Figure 11-2. The report on the left sorts the data alphabetically by customer name. The report on the right also sorts the data alphabetically by customer name, but adds an additional sort criterion, by state. This report first groups the data by state, then within each state, the report sorts data by customer name.

Report sorts data by customer name

Report groups customers by state

Customer	Phone
Advanced Design Corp.	(914) 555-6707
Advanced Design Inc.	(212) 555-8493
Advanced Engineering Inc.	(215) 555-3197
Advanced MicroSystems	(203) 555-4407
Advanced MicroSystems Co.	(201) 555-3722
Advanced Solutions	(617) 555-3842
Advanced Solutions Inc.	(518) 555-9644
Advanced Specialists Corp.	(603) 555-8647
Brittan Design Inc.	(617) 555-2480
CompuBoards	(215) 555-4753
CompuDesign Co.	(617) 555-2663
CompuEngineering	(518) 555-3942
CompuMicroSystems Corp.	(914) 555-9081
CompuSolutions Co.	(201) 555-9867

Customer	Phone
CT	
Advanced MicroSystems	(203) 555-4407
Design Design	(203) 555-1450
Signal Engineering	(203) 555-7845
SigniSpecialists	(203) 555-2570
Technical Boards	(203) 555-2373
Technical Specialists Co.	(203) 555-9545
MA	
Advanced Solutions	(617) 555-3842
Brittan Design Inc.	(617) 555-2480
CompuDesign Co.	(617) 555-2663
Computer MicroSystems Corp.	(508) 555-7307
Design Engineering Corp.	(617) 555-6274

Figure 11-2   Reports showing two different sorting techniques

As you can see from the examples, sorting and grouping are two essential ways to organize data for more effective viewing and analysis.

Sorting data

As the previous section shows, sorting data displays report data in a more meaningful order. Without sorting, a report can be much less usable, as the first report in Figure 11-1 shows.

You can sort data in ascending or descending order, and you can sort by as many fields as you like. For example, you can sort a list of customers by credit rank, then by customer name.

Figure 11-3 shows the first six data rows in three lists. The first list is unsorted, the second sorts data by credit rank, and the third sorts data first by credit rank, then by customer name.

A field that you use to sort data is called a sort key. For example, the third list in Figure 11-3 has two sort keys—the credit field and the customer name field.

Credit	Customer
B	Signal Engineering
A	Technical Specialists Co.
C	SigniSpecialists Corp.
A	Technical MicroSystems Inc.
A	InfoEngineering
A	Advanced Design Inc.

Data unsorted

Credit	Customer
A	Technical Specialists Co.
A	Technical MicroSystems Inc.
A	InfoEngineering
A	Advanced Design Inc.
A	Technical Design Inc.
A	Design Solutions Corp.

Data sorted by credit rank

Credit	Customer
A	Advanced Design Inc.
A	Advanced MicroSystems
A	Advanced MicroSystems Co.
A	Advanced Solutions
A	Advanced Solutions Inc.
A	Advanced Specialists Corp.

Data sorted by credit rank, then by customer name

Figure 11-3   Three examples of sorting data in a listing report

Ways to sort data

Sort data in one of two ways:

- Specify sorting in the data set query so that the database processes the data before sending the results to BIRT. Databases are efficient at sorting data, especially if they have indexes to optimize sorts. For that reason, use the query to sort data whenever possible.

- Sort data in BIRT. Use this method if the data source, such as a text file, does not support sorting.

How to sort data through the query

1   In Data Explorer, create a new data set, or edit an existing one.

2   In the query text area, write an ORDER BY clause in the SELECT statement. For example, the following statement returns customer information and sorts rows by credit rank, then by customer name:

```
SELECT Customers.customerName,
Customers.phone,
Customers.creditRank
FROM Customers
ORDER BY Customers.creditRank, Customers.customerName
```

3   Choose Preview Results to verify the data that the query returns. The rows should be sorted by the fields in the ORDER BY clause.

4   Choose OK.

How to sort data in BIRT

The instructions in this section assume that you already inserted data in a report.

1   In the layout editor, select the table element or list element that contains the data that you want to sort. Property Editor displays the properties for the table or list.

Figure 11-4 shows an example of a selected table and the table's general properties.

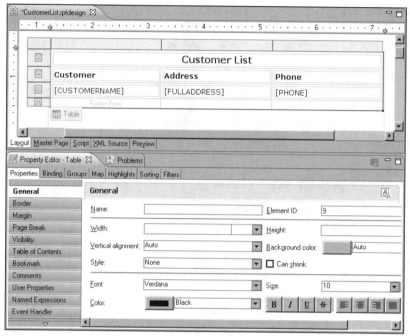

Figure 11-4   Properties for a selected table

2 In Property Editor, choose the Sorting tab.

3 In the sorting page, shown in Figure 11-5, choose Add to specify the criteria on which to sort the rows.

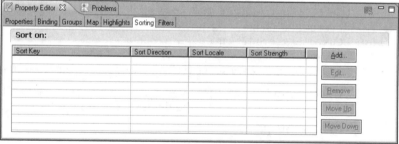

Figure 11-5   Sorting page of Property Editor

4 In New Sort Key, specify the following information:

    1 In Key, complete one of the following steps:

       ❑ To specify a field to sort by, select a field from the drop-down list.

       ❑ To specify an expression by which to sort the data, choose the expression builder button, then provide an expression.

    2 In Direction, specify the sort order by selecting Ascending or Descending.

3   In Locale, select a language. The language determines the sorting, or collation, attributes that conform to local conventions. Select Auto to sort data according to the locale set on the user's machine.

4   In Strength, select a collation strength, also known as a collation level. The collation strength determines whether accent marks, case, or punctuation are considered when sorting strings.

Figure 11-6 shows an example of a sort definition.

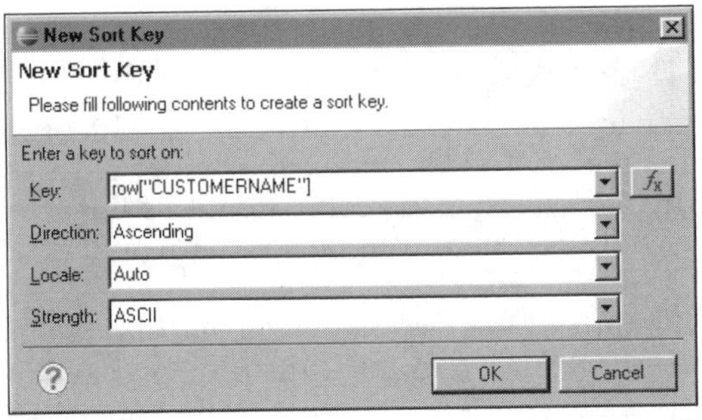

Figure 11-6   Sort expression in New Sort Key

Choose OK. The Sorting page displays the sort key that you defined for the selected table or list.

5   Preview the report. The data in the details section appears in a different order.

Setting the sort strength

BIRT supports locale-sensitive sorting and provides six strengths, or levels, of string comparisons, described in Table 11-1. The strength specifies what type of difference needs to exist between two letters or strings for them to be considered different.

Table 11-1   Sort strengths

Strength	Description
ASCII	Collates by the ASCII values of the letters. Differences in case and accents are significant. For example: A < B < a < à
Primary	Different base letters are considered a primary difference. Use Primary to ignore case and accents. For example: a = A = à < b < c
Secondary	Different accented forms of the same base letter are considered a secondary difference. Use Secondary to ignore case. For example: ab = Ab < àb < ac

(continues)

Table 11-1   Sort strengths *(continued)*

Strength	Description
Tertiary	Case differences and different accented forms of the same base letter are considered Tertiary differences. For example: ao < Ao < aò
Quaternary	When punctuation is ignored at the previous strengths, use Quaternary to differentiate strings with and without punctuation. For example: ab < a-b < aB
Identical	When all other strengths are equal, the Identical strength is a tie-breaker. The Unicode code point values of the NFD form of each string are compared. Use this strength sparingly as it decreases performance and is rarely needed.

The effect of applying the different strengths depends on the locale. Each language has its own rules for determining the proper collation order. For example, in some languages, such as Danish, certain accented letters are considered to be separate base characters. In most languages, however, an accented letter has a secondary difference from the unaccented version of that letter. The following example shows the difference in sorting when the collation strength is secondary, but the locales are different:

Danish	German
a	A
A	a
â	â
Ä	B
B	Ä

Sorting string data ignoring capitalization

By default, BIRT sorts string data according to ASCII values, so uppercase letters precede lowercase letters. For example, "Z" appears before "a." The following list of values is an example of an ASCII sort:

```
ANG Resellers
AV Stores, Co.
Alpha Cognac
Anna's Decorations, Ltd
abc Shops
```

Typically, users prefer to view a list of names in simple alphabetical order, without regard to capitalization. To display string values in case-insensitive alphabetical order, set the collation strength to primary or secondary.

Alternatively, use JavaScript's toUpperCase( ) or toLowerCase( ) function to convert the values to all uppercase or all lowercase before sorting. The following expression is an example of a sort key expression that you specify:

```
row["CUSTOMERNAME"].toUpperCase()
```

Using this expression, the previous list of values appears alphabetically as:

```
abc Shops
Alpha Cognac
ANG Resellers
Anna's Decorations, Ltd
AV Stores, Co.
```

Grouping data

It is common for reports to present data that is organized into meaningful groups. For example, rather than displaying a basic list of sales orders, an orders report can group orders by customers. In addition to providing a more effective way to view data, grouped reports have other advantages over reports that are not grouped.

When grouping data, you can:

- Add titles or other text at the beginning of each group.

- Add averages, counts, subtotals, or other summary information at the beginning or end of each group.

- Insert a page break before or after each group.

- Generate a table of contents that displays the values of every group. The table of contents supports navigating to specific locations in the report.

- Remove duplicate field values.

Compare the reports in Figure 11-7 and Figure 11-8. The report in Figure 11-7 displays customer order information in a simple list. The data rows are sorted by customer name, then by order number. Notice the repeated customer name and order ID information.

Customer	Order ID	Item	SKU Price	Quantity	Total Price
Brittan Design Inc.	1810	MSL3280	$210.00	1746	$366,660.00
Brittan Design Inc.	1810	MDSPL04	$340.00	1728	$587,520.00
CompuBoards	1075	MP2032	$310.00	49	$15,190.00
CompuBoards	1075	MP1632	$210.00	49	$10,290.00
CompuBoards	1900	MP2032	$310.00	13	$4,030.00
CompuBoards	1900	MP1632x	$221.00	13	$2,873.00
CompuBoards	1900	MSL3290	$300.00	13	$3,900.00
CompuBoards	1900	MDSPL04	$340.00	13	$4,420.00
CompuBoards	1900	MPL1632	$303.00	13	$3,939.00
CompuBoards	1900	MVL1664	$320.00	13	$4,160.00
CompuBoards	1900	MPL2032	$650.00	13	$8,450.00
CompuDesign Co.	1615	MSL3290	$300.00	386	$115,800.00
CompuDesign Co.	1615	MPL1632	$610.00	384	$234,240.00
CompuDesign Co.	1660	MP1632s	$290.00	306	$88,740.00

Figure 11-7   Report showing data in a simple list

The report in Figure 11-8 shows data from the same data set. Unlike the first report, it groups the data rows by customers and order numbers, removing the repeated customer names and order numbers. The customer name and order totals appear at the beginning of each customer group. The order number appears at the beginning of each order group, and a subtotal appears at the end of each order. When the report is displayed in the BIRT report viewer or in PDF format, a table of contents appears to the left of the report.

The report in Figure 11-8 uses the customer and order ID fields to create two groups. The customer group is the outer, or top, group. The orders group is within the customer group. There is no limit to the number of groups that a report can contain. For example the sample report can contain two additional groups, one to organize customers by state, and another to organize states by region. Practically, however, a report that contains too many groups can make the report difficult to read.

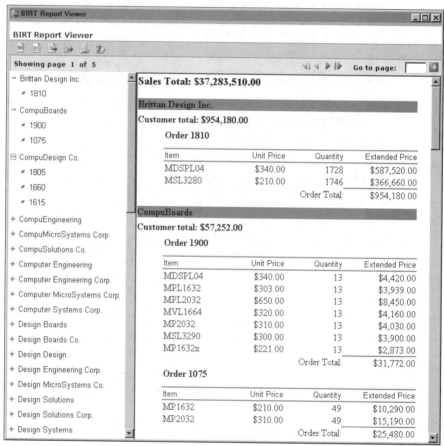

Figure 11-8   Viewing a report that shows customers, orders, and items

How to group data

The instructions in this section assume that you already inserted data in a report.

1 In the layout editor, select the table element or list element that contains the data that you want to group.

2 In Property Editor, choose the Groups tab, then choose Add. New Group, shown in Figure 11-9, displays the properties you can set for the group.

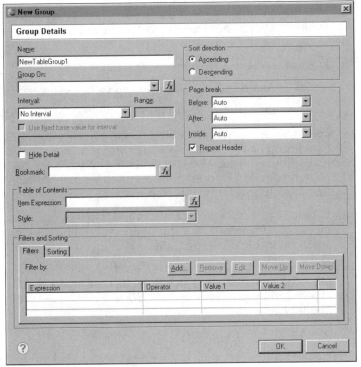

Figure 11-9   New Group

3 Specify the properties of the group.

- In Name, type a name for the group. The name identifies the group and appears in the Edit Group context menu, so you can easily find a specific group for editing later.

- In Group On, select the field on which you want to group. The drop-down list displays all the fields associated with the table. You can group on a field in the table or a field that you have not used in the table. To group on a field that you have not used in the table, you must first create the column binding. For information about column binding, see Chapter 7, "Binding Data."

- In Interval, you can select a grouping interval, then specify a range. You can also specify the initial value to use for calculating numeric intervals. For information about grouping by intervals, see "Grouping data by intervals," later in this section.

- In Hide Detail, specify whether or not to display the detail rows. Select this option to display only summary data in the group's header or footer rows.

- In Table of Contents—Item Expression, specify the expression that returns the values to display in the auto-generated table of contents. By default, the group values appear in the report's table of contents.

- In Table of Contents—Style, select a style to apply to the values in the table of contents. For information about styles and how to create them, see Chapter 10, "Formatting Report Content."

- In Sort Direction:

  □ Select Ascending to sort the group values in ascending order.

  □ Select Descending to sort the group values in descending order.

- For Page Break, you can control where page breaks occur. To display each group of data on its own page, insert a page break before or after each group. You can also specify if the group header appears at the top of each page. For information about setting page breaks, see Chapter 22, "Designing a Multipage Report."

- In Filters, you can specify a filter condition to select group values that meet a certain criteria. For information about filtering group values, see Chapter 14, "Filtering Data."

- In Sorting, you can specify that the group values be sorted by a field other than the field on which the data is grouped. For information about sorting group values, see "Sorting data at the group level," later in this chapter.

Choose OK to save the group.

The table includes two new rows, group header and group footer, as the example in Figure 11-10 shows. BIRT Report Designer places a data element in the group header. This data element displays the values of the field (PRODUCTCODE, in this example) on which the group is based.

Product	Price	Quantity	Total	
[PRODUCTCODE]				← Group header row
[PRODUCTCODE]	[PRICEEACH]	[QUANTITYORDERED]	[EXTENDEDPRICE]	
Group Footer Row				← Group footer row
Footer Row				

Figure 11-10   Group header and group footer rows in a table

4   Preview the report. The data is organized in groups.

5   To create additional groups, repeat all the previous steps.

Grouping data by intervals

When you create a group, BIRT's default behavior is to group data by a single value, such as a customer name, an order ID, or a date. In the detailed orders report shown in Figure 11-8, each customer name starts a new group, and each order ID starts a new group within the customer group.

Sometimes, it is more useful to group data by a specific interval. A sales report, for example, can present sales by quarters, rather than by dates. Similarly, you can group data in a shipping report by weeks or months, rather than by dates.

Compare the reports in Figure 11-11 and Figure 11-12. The report in Figure 11-11 groups shipping information by dates.

Shipping Schedule

Ship by	Order ID	Customer name
01/02/2006	1440	Advanced Engineering
01/02/2006	1445	Technical Design Corp.
01/03/2006	1355	Signal MicroSystems
01/04/2006	1400	InfoSpecialists Inc.
01/05/2006	1320	CompuDesign Co.
01/09/2006	1410	Brittan Design Inc.
01/10/2006	1420	Exosoft Corp
01/11/2006	1250	Technical Solutions Inc.
01/11/2006	1325	SigniMicro Systems
01/12/2006	1500	CompuBoards

Figure 11-11 Dates grouped by single date values

The report in Figure 11-12 groups the same shipping information by weeks.

Weekly Shipping Schedule

Week of 01/02/2006

Ship by	Order ID	Customer name
01/02/2006	1440	Advanced Engineering
01/02/2006	1445	Technical Design Corp.
01/03/2006	1355	Signal MicroSystems
01/04/2006	1400	InfoSpecialists Inc.
01/05/2006	1320	CompuDesign Co.

Week of 01/09/2006

Ship by	Order ID	Customer name
01/09/2006	1410	Brittan Design Inc.
01/10/2006	1420	Exosoft Corp
01/11/2006	1250	Technical Solutions Inc.
01/11/2006	1325	SigniMicro Systems
01/12/2006	1500	CompuBoards

Figure 11-12 Dates grouped into weekly intervals

As the reports show, grouping by interval provides the following benefits:

- Organizes a long report into shorter, more readable pieces
- Summarizes data further for more effective analysis

The following sections describe in more detail how to group date-and-time, numeric, and string data by intervals.

Grouping string data by intervals

When grouping string data by interval, the interval you specify is a sequence of characters of a particular length. For example, if a customer group sorts customers by name, you can group customers by the first letter of their names, or the first two letters, or the first three letters, and so on. Figure 11-13 shows the results of grouping names by the first letter, the first two letters, and the first three letters. Lines separate the groups.

Grouping by first letter   Grouping by two letters   Grouping by three letters

Customers	Customers	Customers
Accere	Accere	Accere
Accor	Accor	Accor
Acer	Accuview	Accuview
Acme	Acer	
Adamark	Acme	Acer
Advair		
Aegis	Adamark	Acme
Altria	Advair	
		Adamark
BayView	Aegis	
Baywater		Advair
	Altria	
		Aegis
	BayView	
	Baywater	Altria
		BayView
		Baywater

Figure 11-13   Results of grouping string data by intervals

Group by the first letter to group names by letters of the alphabet. In a customer list, for example, you might want to group all customers whose names begin with A under the heading A, all customers whose names begin with B under the heading B, and so on.

Group by multiple letters to group items whose names contain special prefixes for classification or categorization. A computer parts vendor, for example, might use the prefix ME for all memory chips, CP for CPU boards, MO for monitors, and so on. In this case, creating a computer parts list that groups names by the first two letters lends itself to logical groupings by part type.

How to group string data by intervals

1 Create a group using the instructions in "How to group data," earlier in this chapter.

2 Set the Interval field in the group editor to Prefix.

3 Set Range to the number of characters by which to group.

Grouping numeric data by intervals

When grouping numeric data by intervals, the interval you specify is a range of numbers. For example, if an order group sorts orders by numeric ID, you can group the orders by intervals of 10, 50, 100, 1000, and so on.

The interval that is best for any set of numeric data depends on the range of numeric values. If the numbers range from 100 to 200, it makes sense to group in intervals of 10. If the numbers range from 100 to 1000, you might want to group in intervals of 100.

Figure 11-14 shows the results of grouping numbers by intervals of 10, 100, and 1000. Lines separate the groups.

Grouping by 10s   Grouping by 100s   Grouping by 1000s

Order ID
1070
1080
1085
1095
1340
1345
1405
2005
2030
3015

Order ID
1070
1080
1085
1095
1340
1345
1405
2005
2030
3015

Order ID
1070
1080
1085
1095
1340
1345
1405
2005
2030
3015

Figure 11-14   Results of grouping numeric data by intervals

Groups are calculated from the first value in the data set. If the first number is 1070, and you use an interval of 10, the first group contains values from 1070 to 1079, the second group contains values from 1080 to 1089, and so on. In the example report that shows a grouping interval of 1000, the numbers 2005 and 2030 are not in a separate group, which is what you might expect, because the first group contains numbers from 1070 to 2069. The second group contains numbers from 2070 to 3069.

Rather than using the first data set value as the starting, or base, value for determining the grouping of numbers, you can specify a different base value to group numbers in more predictable ranges. Compare the two reports in Figure 11-15.

A base value of 1000 provides better results than a base value of 1070 when grouping by intervals of 1000. Rather than grouping numbers in groups of 1070–2069 and 2070–3069, the second report uses more logical groups of 1000–1999 and 2000–2999.

Grouping by 1000s
No base value specified

Grouping by 1000s
Base value of 1000

Order ID
1070
1080
1085
1095
1340
1345
1405
2005
2030
3015

Order ID
1070
1080
1085
1095
1340
1345
1405
2005
2030
3015

Figure 11-15   Results of grouping with and without a base value of 1000

How to group numeric data by intervals

1 Create a group using the instructions in "How to group data," earlier in this chapter.

2 Set the Interval field in the group editor to Interval.

3 Set Range to the desired grouping interval.

4 To specify a starting value to use for calculating groups, select Use fixed base value for interval, and specify a number.

Grouping date-and-time data by intervals

When grouping date-and-time data by intervals, you group data by time periods, such as hours, days, weeks, months, and so on. Grouping by time periods is useful for reports that display information that has a time or schedule focus, such as weekly shipping schedules or quarterly sales figures.

The reports in Figure 11-16 show the results of grouping dates by weeks, months, and quarters. The lines separate the groups. By default, weekly groups start on Mondays, monthly groups start on the first date of the month, and quarterly groups are January 1–March 31, April 1–June 30, July 1–September 30, and October 1–December 31. If you group by year, the groups start on January 1 and end on December 31.

To use a value other than the default start value for date-and-time groups, specify a different base value to group dates in different ranges. For example, an organization's fiscal year is October 1 to September 30. To group ten years' worth of data into groups by fiscal year rather than by calendar year, set the interval to month and the range to 12, then specify a base value such as 1995-10. You must use the year-month format. The report displays the data in the following groups: October 1, 1995–September 30, 1996; October 1, 1996–September 30, 1997; October 1, 1997–September 30, 1998; and so on.

A base value should have the same granularity as that of the interval. As the previous example shows, if you set the interval to month, you specify a base value that includes the year and the month. If you set the interval to day, specify a base value that includes the year, month, and day.

Grouping by weeks

Ship Dates
January 9, 2006
January 15, 2006
January 30, 2006
February 5, 2006
March 7, 2006
April 5, 2006
April 12, 2006
June 18, 2006
June 30, 2006
July 7, 2006
October 1, 2006

Grouping by months

Ship Dates
January 9, 2006
January 15, 2006
January 30, 2006
February 5, 2006
March 7, 2006
April 5, 2006
April 12, 2006
June 18, 2006
June 30, 2006
July 7, 2006
October 1, 2006

Grouping by quarters

Ship Dates
January 9, 2006
January 15, 2006
January 30, 2006
February 5, 2006
March 7, 2006
April 5, 2006
April 12, 2006
June 18, 2006
June 30, 2006
July 7, 2006
October 1, 2006

Figure 11-16   Results of grouping date-and-time data by intervals

How to group date-and-time data by intervals

1 Create a group using the instructions in "How to group data," earlier in this chapter.

2 Set the Interval field in the group editor to one of the time period values, such as Year, Month, Week, Day, or Hour.

3 Set Range to the number of units to include in each group. For example, if the selected interval is Week, specify 2 as the range to group data in two-week periods.

4 To specify a different starting value to use for calculating groups, select Use fixed base value for interval, then specify a date.

Sorting data at the group level

When you create a group, the default setting specifies sorting the group values by the grouping field in ascending order. For example, if you create an order ID group, the default setting is to sort order ID values in ascending order. You can, however, sort the group values by a different field. For example, rather than sort group values by order ID, you can sort by order total.

Sorting at the group level is different from sorting at the detail row level. To sort at the detail row level, specify the sorting criteria in the Sorting page in Property Editor. To sort at the group level, specify the sorting criteria in the Groups page.

The report in Figure 11-17 groups sales data by product code. The group header, highlighted by a gray background, displays the product code and the sales total. The product code group uses the default sorting, which sorts by product code in ascending order, such as S10_1678, S10_1949, and so on.

S10_1678			$6,702.15
Order Number	Quantity Sold	Price Per Unit	Order Total
10211	41	$90.92	$3,727.72
10223	37	$80.39	$2,974.43
S10_1949			**$16,769.28**
Order Number	Quantity Sold	Price Per Unit	Order Total
10206	47	$203.59	$9,568.73
10215	35	$205.73	$7,200.55
S10_2016			**$7,996.11**
Order Number	Quantity Sold	Price Per Unit	Order Total
10201	24	$116.56	$2,797.44
10223	47	$110.61	$5,198.67

Figure 11-17 Results of sorting group values in ascending order

The reports in Figure 11-17 and Figure 11-18 contain the same data. The report in Figure 11-18 sorts the data by the product sales total in ascending order, rather than sorting by product code.

S10_1678			$6,702.15
Order Number	Quantity Sold	Price Per Unit	Order Total
10211	41	$90.92	$3,727.72
10223	37	$80.39	$2,974.43
S10_2016			**$7,996.11**
Order Number	Quantity Sold	Price Per Unit	Order Total
10201	24	$116.56	$2,797.44
10223	47	$110.61	$5,198.67
S10_1949			**$16,769.28**
Order Number	Quantity Sold	Price Per Unit	Order Total
10206	47	$203.59	$9,568.73
10215	35	$205.73	$7,200.55

Figure 11-18 Results of changing the sort order of groups

By changing the field on which groups are sorted, you can choose the information to emphasize. As Figure 11-18 shows, the report can group sales data by product code but list them in order of sales total, which is often a more useful way to present sales information.

How to sort data at the group level

1 Create a group using the instructions in "How to group data," earlier in this chapter. Figure 11-19 shows the group editor. You can specify sorting in two ways. The first way is to specify sorting by the grouping field. The second way enables you to specify a different field by which to sort and also enables you to specify a sort expression.

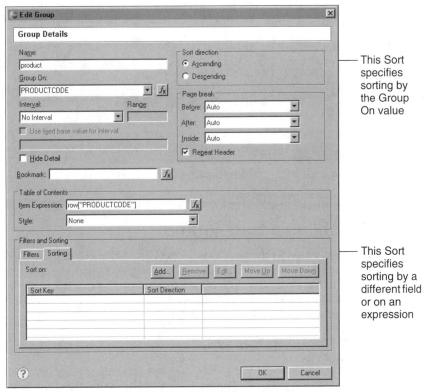

This Sort specifies sorting by the Group On value

This Sort specifies sorting by a different field or on an expression

Figure 11-19 Sorting options in Edit Group

2 In Filters and Sorting, choose Sorting.

3 Choose Add to specify a sort key.

4 In New Sort Key, specify the sort criteria. This procedure is described earlier in this chapter. Figure 11-20 shows an example of a sort definition that sorts group values by sales totals in ascending order.

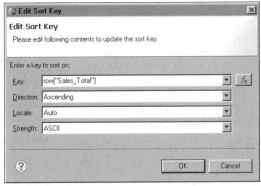

Figure 11-20 New Sort Key, displaying a sort definition

5 Choose OK to save the sort definition. The sort definition appears in the Sorting section of Edit Group, as shown in Figure 11-21.

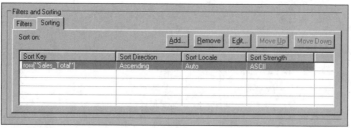

Figure 11-21   Sorting expression in Edit Group

6 Preview the report.

Disabling group sorting

As mentioned in the previous section, by default, BIRT sorts group values in ascending order. You can disable this sorting if you want to group the data rows in the order the data set returns them. For example, if you use the ORDER BY clause in a SQL query to sort data, disabling sorting in BIRT prevents unnecessary processing and improves performance.

How to disable group sorting

1 Select the table or list.

2 In Property Editor, choose the Properties tab, and choose Advanced.

3 Set the Sort By Groups property to false. Figure 11-22 shows how to select the value from a drop-down list.

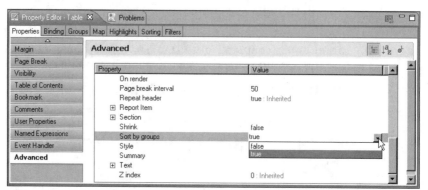

Figure 11-22   Changing the Sort By Groups value

Creating multiple groups

When creating multiple groups, the order in which you create them determines how the report groups data. Before you create groups, think about their order. For example, if you want to group data by state, then by city, create the groups in that order. In other words, state is the table or list element's first, or top-level, group, and city is the second, or inner, group.

The reports in Figure 11-23 show the results of creating the state and city groups in different orders.

Report groups data by state, then by city   Report groups data by city, then by state

CT			Albany		
	Bridgewater			NY	
		Design Design			CompuEngineering
		SigniSpecialists			Signal MicroSystems
	Glendale				Technical Systems Corp.
		Advanced MicroSystems			Advanced Solutions Inc.
		Technical Boards	Allentown		
	New Haven			PA	
		Signal Engineering			InfoBoards
		Technical Specialists Co.			Technical Design Corp.
MA					CompuBoards
	Boston				Advanced Engineering Inc.
		Technical Systems Inc.			TekniMicroSystems Co.
		Design Systems	Boston		
		Brittan Design Inc.		MA	
		TeleBoards Co.			Technical Systems Inc.
		Design Engineering Corp.			Design Systems

Figure 11-23   Results of creating groups in two different orders

The first report shows the output when the state group is the top-level group. The second report shows the output when the city group is the top-level group. Data in the first report is organized logically. The report shows each state in alphabetical order, then the cities are sorted alphabetically within each state. On the other hand, data in the second report is sorted by city first, which results in repeated state headings that are organized in seemingly random order.

Figure 11-24 shows the report design for the first report. The state field appears in the group header 1 row, and the city field appears in the group header 2 row.

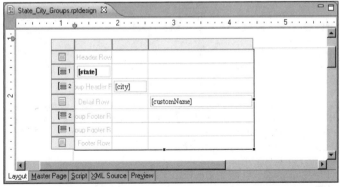

Figure 11-24   Report design grouping data by state, then by city

Create groups using any of the following procedures. The procedure you use depends on whether you are creating all the groups for the first time or adding groups to an existing group structure.

- To create groups that follow the order of creation, use one of the following procedures:

  - Select the table or list, then choose Element➤Group➤Insert Group➤Below from the main menu to create each group. For example, if you create a state group first and a city group second, the state group is the top-level group, and the city is the inner group.

  - Select the table or list, then choose the Groups tab on Property Editor. Like the previous technique, the order in which you create the groups determines the order in which data is grouped.

- To add a group at the topmost level, right-click the table or list, then choose Insert Group➤Above from the context menu. For example, if you already created a state group and a city group, use Insert Group➤Above to add a country group as the top-level group.

- To add a group at the lowest level, right-click the table or list, then choose Insert Group➤Below from the table or list's context menu. For example, if you already created a state group, choose Insert Group➤Below to add a city group as the inner group.

- To add a group between two existing groups, use one of the following procedures:

  - Right-click the group row above which to create the new group, then choose Insert Group➤Above.

  - Right-click the group row below which to create the new group, then choose Insert Group➤Below.

All the techniques display the Edit Group dialog box used to define the properties of a group. If you inadvertently create groups in the wrong order, you can easily change the order of the groups. It is not necessary to delete and recreate the groups.

Changing the order of groups

The Groups page in Property Editor shows all the groups in a particular table or list. Use this page, shown in Figure 11-27, to change the order of groups, or to add, edit, and delete groups.

You cannot change the order of groups by moving data elements in the layout editor. This action affects only the display position of the data values. Compare the report designs in Figure 11-25. The state and city data elements are transposed by dragging and dropping in the layout editor.

Now compare the corresponding report output, shown in Figure 11-26.

State data element placed in group header 1
City data element placed in group header 2

State data element moved to group header 2
City data element moved to group header 1

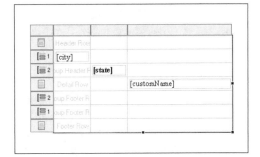

Figure 11-25   Report designs having transposed state and city elements

The first report shows data sorted by state, then by city. The second report displays the city values above the state values. The report data, however, is still sorted by state first, then by city.

```
CT                                       Bridgewater
      Bridgewater                                CT
            Design Design                              Design Design
            SigniSpecialists                           SigniSpecialists
      Glendale                                   CT
            Advanced MicroSystems                      Advanced MicroSystems
            Technical Boards                           Technical Boards
      New Haven                                  CT
            Signal Engineering                         Signal Engineering
            Technical Specialists Co.                  Technical Specialists Co.
MA                                       Boston
      Boston                                     MA
            Technical Systems Inc.                     Technical Systems Inc.
            Design Systems                             Design Systems
            Brittan Design Inc.                        Brittan Design Inc.
            TeleBoards Co.                             TeleBoards Co.
            Design Engineering Corp.                   Design Engineering Corp.
      Brickhaven                                 MA
            Signal Design Corp.                        Signal Design Corp.
            InfoEngineering                            InfoEngineering
            InfoSpecialists Inc.                       InfoSpecialists Inc.
```

Figure 11-26   Reports showing the effect of transposing state and city elements

How to change the order of groups

1   Select the table or list for which you want to re-order groups.

2   In Property Editor, choose the Groups tab. The Groups page displays the groups defined in the table or list, as shown in Figure 11-27.

    This page displays the group names in the order in which the report currently groups the data.

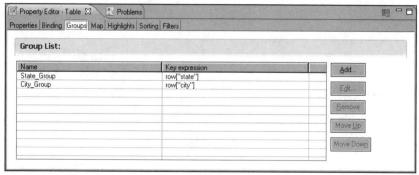

Figure 11-27 Groups page

3 Select a group from the list, then choose Move Up or Move Down to move the selected group up or down the list. In the layout editor, the data elements change positions to reflect the new grouping order.

4 Repeat the previous step until you finish changing the order of groups.

Adding group headings

Adding a descriptive heading that appears at the beginning of each group identifies the data within the group. When you create a group, BIRT Report Designer inserts a data element in the group header row to serve as the group heading. This data element displays the values of the field on which the group is based. For example, when grouping data by state, the data element displays a state name for each group.

Unlike column headings, which are static, group headings change based on the content of the group. If a report groups data by customers, for example, you can display the customer name at the beginning of each group. For a customer list that groups names by the first letter, the titles for the groups are A, B, C, and so on. For a shipping schedule that groups data by weeks, the titles for the groups could be Week of 01/02/06, Week of 01/09/06, and so on.

The reports in Figure 11-28 show examples of headings that change with each group. Bold text highlights the group headings. Group headings are necessary to show where one group ends and another begins. Remove the A and B headings from the Customers report, for example, and the report looks like a list sorted alphabetically. You can add a line or space between groups to indicate a change in group, but a descriptive heading makes it easier for users to find information in the report.

Inserting group header rows

If you deleted a group header row from a table, you can re-insert the row. You can also insert additional group header rows to display header information on two lines, for example, a group title on the first line, and summary information on the next line.

Customer Orders	Customers	Weekly Shipping Schedule
Advanced Design	**A**	**Week of 01/02/06**
Order 1010		
Item Quantity Price	Accere	Ship date Order ID
M12 2 $60.00	Accor	01/02/06 1015
M15 1 $55.00	Acer	01/03/06 1025
Order 1015	Acme	01/03/06 1026
Item Quantity Price	Adamark	01/04/06 1020
R50 1 $20.00	Advair	01/05/06 1022
...	**B**	01/06/06 1030
Advantix Inc	BayView	
Order 1050	Beaucoup	**Week of 01/09/06**
...	...	Ship date Order ID
		01/09/06 1029

Figure 11-28   Examples of group headings that change

How to insert a group header row

The procedure for inserting a group header row depends on whether the table already contains a group header row or not.

- If the table does not contain a group header row, use the following procedure:
  1 Select the table.
  2 Right-click the Table tab, then choose Insert Group Header or Footer➤<group>➤Header.

- If the table contains a group header row and you want to add another group header row, use the following procedure:
  1 Select the table.
  2 Right-click the group header row, then choose Insert➤Row➤Above to insert a row above the current row, or choose Insert➤Row➤Below to insert a row below the current row.

Displaying group headings in the detail row

Headings in a group header row appear above the detail rows. Sometimes, a report looks better if the headings appear in the first detail row of each group. Compare the examples in Figure 11-29. The example on the left shows the group headings, which are order numbers, in a row above the detail rows. The example on the right shows the group headings in the detail row.

To display group headings on the same line as the first detail row, drop the cell that contains the heading using the Drop property. Do not just move the group heading to the detail row because it would be repeated for every row. To drop a cell, observe the following rules:

- There must be an empty cell below the cell that contains the group heading. Otherwise, the cell content overwrites the content in the cell below it.

Group headings (order numbers)
appear above the detail rows

Group headings (order numbers)
appear in the first detail row

Order 10200		
	S24_1785	$3,285.81
	S32_1374	$2,831.85
	S32_4289	$1,764.45
		$7,882.11
Order 10202		
	S32_2206	$901.53
	S32_4485	$2,530.84
		$3,432.37

Order 10200	S24_1785	$3,285.81
	S32_1374	$2,831.85
	S32_4289	$1,764.45
		$7,882.11
Order 10202	S32_2206	$901.53
	S32_4485	$2,530.84
		$3,432.37

Figure 11-29   Two ways to display group headings

- If a table contains multiple group header rows, you can drop only cells in the group header row directly above the detail row.

- You can only drop cells in a group header row. You cannot drop cells in a detail or group footer row.

You can drop a group header cell so that it spans the detail rows, or all the rows in the group, including the group footer row. The difference is visible only if the group header cell has a border or background color. Compare the examples in Figure 11-30.

Group header cell (shown with gray
background) dropped to the detail rows

Group header cell dropped to all rows
in the group

Order 10200	S24_1785	$3,285.81
	S32_1374	$2,831.85
	S32_4289	$1,764.45
		$7,882.11
Order 10202	S32_2206	$901.53
	S32_4485	$2,530.84
		$3,432.37

Order 10200	S24_1785	$3,285.81
	S32_1374	$2,831.85
	S32_4289	$1,764.45
		$7,882.11
Order 10202	S32_2206	$901.53
	S32_4485	$2,530.84
		$3,432.37

Figure 11-30   Reports showing different settings for the Drop property

The example on the left drops the group header cell to the detail rows. The example on the right drops the group header cell to all the rows in the group. Notice that the cell color in the example on the left extends to the last detail row, whereas the cell color in the example on the right extends to the group footer row. If the cell did not have a background color, the output would look the same whether you set the cell's Drop property to Detail or All. The order numbers always appear in the first detail row of each group.

Figure 11-31 shows the portion of the report design that generates the previous example output.

How to drop a group heading to the detail row

1   Select the cell that contains the group heading to drop. The cell directly below it must be empty.

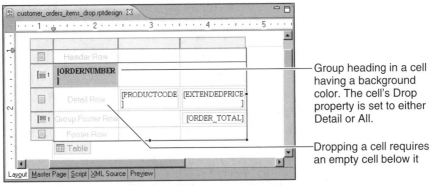

Figure 11-31 Report design that generates a dropped cell

2 In Property Editor, under Properties, choose General.

3 In Drop, select one of the following values:

- Detail—Select this value to drop the group heading so that it spans only the detail rows.

- All—Select this value to drop the group heading so that it spans all the rows in the group, including the group footer row.

These values display a difference in the generated report only if the cell has borders or background color.

4 Preview the report. The group heading appears in the first detail row of each group.

Specifying expressions for group headings

Unlike column headings, which display static text, you specify expressions for group headings because the heading values are dynamic. In other words, the value changes based on the group's content. Use a data set field, a computed field, or a text element that includes dynamic values, depending on the value to display.

Typically, you use a computed field to combine a field value and static text. Sometimes, you use a JavaScript function to display the values you need. The following list shows some examples of expressions used for group headings:

- To display the customer name as the group heading, use the customer name field as the expression. For example:

```
dataSetRow["customerName"]
```

- To display a group heading that combines static text with a field, insert a data element, and use an expression such as the one in the following example:

```
"Order " + dataSetRow["orderID"]
```

- To create headings (A, B, and so on) for a customer list that is grouped by the first letter, insert a data element, and use the JavaScript charAt( ) function to get the first letter of the name in each group. For example:

```
dataSetRow["customerName"].charAt(0)
```

- To create headings that display the names of months (January, February, and so on) for each group of dates, insert an HTML text element, and use the following expression:

```
<VALUE-OF format="MMMM">row["shipByDate"]</VALUE-OF>
```

Tutorial 2: Grouping report data

This tutorial provides instructions for grouping customer data by credit limit. It uses the report from Tutorial 1: "Building a simple listing report," in Chapter 3, "Learning the Basics." The first tutorial shows how to build a simple report that lists customers in alphabetical order. This report builds on the first one and organizes customers into credit limit groups of $50,000.00, such as 0–49999, 50000–99999, 100000–149999, and so on.

In this tutorial, you perform the following tasks:

- Open the report design.
- Save the report as a new file.
- Add the credit limit field to the data set.
- Add credit limit data to the report.
- Group customer data by credit limit.
- Display credit limit ranges in the group header.
- Display aggregate information.
- Format the report.
- Preview the report in the BIRT report viewer.
- Display credit limit ranges in the table of contents.

Task 1: Open the report design

In the first tutorial, you created Customers.rptdesign in a project folder named My Reports. Open that report using one of the following procedures depending on the designer you are using:

- In BIRT Report Designer, open the file through Navigator, using the following steps:

  1 If necessary, open Navigator by choosing Window➤Show View➤Navigator. Navigator shows all the project folders and report files you create.

2 Navigate to the My Reports folder, then double-click Customers.rptdesign.

- In BIRT RCP Report Designer, use the main menu to open the file.

  1 Choose File→Open File.

  2 Navigate to and select Customers.rptdesign, then choose Open.

The file opens in the layout editor, as shown in Figure 11-32.

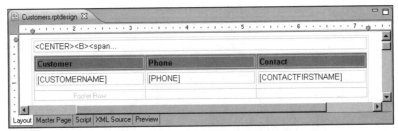

Figure 11-32   Customer report design in the layout editor

Task 2:   Save the report as a new file

Rather than editing directly the report created in the first tutorial, save Customers.rptdesign as a new file. This approach ensures you have a file to return to if you have problems completing this tutorial.

1 Choose File→Save As. Save As displays the file's current name and location.

2 In File name, change Customers.rptdesign to Customers_grouped.rptdesign, then choose Finish. BIRT Report Designer makes a copy of Customers.rptdesign. The new report appears in the layout editor.

Task 3:   Add the credit limit field to the data set

In order for the report to display credit limit data, add the CREDITLIMIT field to the data set.

1 Choose Data Explorer, expand Data Sets, then double-click Customers. Edit Data Set displays the SQL query for the Customers data set.

2 In the query, add a comma (,) after phone.

3 On the next line, add the following text:

```
creditLimit
```

The modified query should look like the one shown in Figure 11-33.

4 Choose Preview Results to verify that the query returns rows that include credit limit information.

5 Choose OK to save the data set.

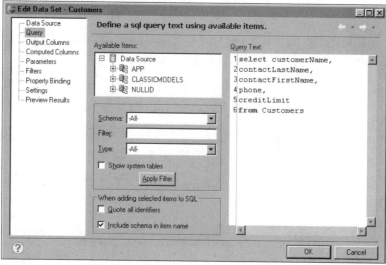

Figure 11-33   Query showing creditLimit field added

Task 4:   Add credit limit data to the report

Use this procedure to insert the credit limit field in the existing table.

1   In the layout editor, select the table by selecting the Table tab. Guide cells appear at the top and left side of the table.

2   Right-click the guide cell above the first column, then choose Insert▶Column to the Left, as shown in Figure 11-34.

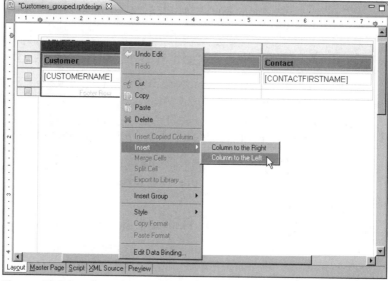

Figure 11-34   Inserting a column to the left of an existing column

A new column appears.

3 Drag the CREDITLIMIT field from Data Explorer, and drop it in the detail row cell next to [CUSTOMERNAME].

In the layout editor, the table displays the added field, as shown in Figure 11-35. The table also shows the label element that the layout editor automatically added to the header row. This label serves as the column heading and displays the field name as static text.

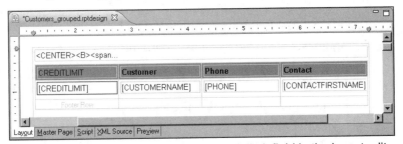

Figure 11-35 Result of adding the credit limit field in the layout editor

4 Edit the CREDITLIMIT label so that it displays Credit Limit.

5 Format the Credit Limit label to look like the other labels in the table header.

   1 Right-click the Customer label, and select Copy Format.

   2 Right-click the Credit Limit label, and select Paste Format.

6 Preview the report. The report should look like the one shown in Figure 11-36.

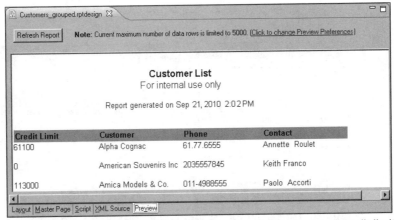

Figure 11-36 Report preview showing the result of adding credit limit

Some of the customers have a credit limit of 0. These are new customers who have not yet been approved for a line of credit.

Task 5: Group customer data by credit limit

The report is currently sorted alphabetically by customer name. Recall that in the first tutorial, you specified that the rows in the table be sorted by customer name. In this procedure, you group the data by credit limit in intervals of 50,000. When grouping data, BIRT sorts the rows into groups first, then it sorts the rows within each group, assuming that there is a sort condition specified at the table level. Completing this task sorts the data rows within each credit limit group by customer name.

1. Choose Layout to return to the layout editor.

2. Right-click the Table tab, and choose Insert Group→Above.

3. In New Group, follow these steps to specify grouping by credit limit in intervals of 50000:

    1. In Name, type the following text:

       credit_group

    2. In Group On, select CREDITLIMIT from the drop-down list.

    3. In Interval, select Interval from the drop-down list.

    4. In Range, type 50000.

    5. Use the default values for the other options. Choose OK. The table in the report design displays a group header and a group footer row, as shown in Figure 11-37. The table also shows the data element that the layout editor automatically added to the group header row. This data element serves as the group heading and, in the generated report, displays the first credit limit value of each group.

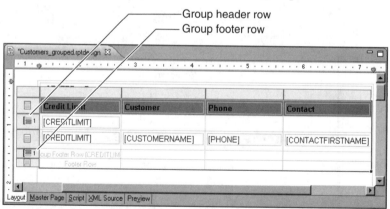

Figure 11-37 Group header and group footer rows in a report design

4. Select the [CREDITLIMIT] data element in the group header row. Do not select the [CREDITLIMIT] data element in the detail row.

5. In Property Editor, under Properties, in General, choose the B button to format the group heading as bold text.

6 Preview the report. Scroll down the report to view all the data. The report organizes data into four credit limit groups. At the beginning of each group, the following numbers appear in bold: 0, 61100, 113000, 227600. These numbers match the first credit limit value of each group. Within each group, customer names are sorted in alphabetical order. Figure 11-38 shows one of the four credit limit groups.

The group header displays the first value in each group

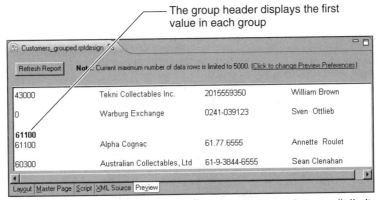

Figure 11-38   Report preview showing one of the four credit limit groups

Task 6: Display credit limit ranges in the group header

Rather than display the first value of each group in the group header, the report is easier to navigate if it displays the credit limit range for each group, as follows:

```
0 - 49999
50000 - 99999
100000 - 149999
```

This procedure shows how to write a JavaScript expression to display these credit limit ranges. The procedure also shows how to create a column binding with which to associate the JavaScript expression.

1 Choose Layout to return to the layout editor.

2 Delete the [CREDITLIMIT] data element in the group header.

3 Insert a new data element in its place by right-clicking the cell and choosing Insert→Data. New Data Binding prompts you to create a column binding for the new data element.

4 Specify a name and expression for the column binding. Use the default data type, String.

> **1** In Column Binding Name, type the following name:
>
> CREDIT_GRP_HEADER

> **2** Open the expression builder to write a JavaScript expression.

3 In the expression builder, type the following expression:

```
for(i=50000; i<300000; i+=50000){
    if( row["CREDITLIMIT"] < i ){
        rangeStart = i-50000;
        rangeEnd = i-1;
        break;
    }
}
displayString = rangeStart + " - " + rangeEnd;
```

Choose OK. The expression appears in the Expression field on New Data Binding, as shown in Figure 11-39.

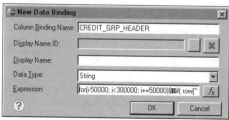

Figure 11-39   Column binding defined

4 Choose OK to save the column binding for the data element. In the layout editor, the data element displays the column binding name, [CREDIT_GRP_HEADER].

5 Select the data element. In Property Editor, under Properties, in General, choose B to format the group heading as bold text.

6 Preview the report. The group headers display the credit limit ranges. Figure 11-40 shows the 50000 - 99999 group header.

Figure 11-40   Report preview showing credit limit ranges

Task 7:   Display aggregate information

One of the benefits of grouping data is that you can add summary information at the beginning or end of each group. Summary information is also known as aggregate information. In this procedure, add the following aggregate information to the report:

- The number of customers in each group
- The number of all customers listed in the report

Display the number of customers in each group

1 Choose Layout to return to the layout editor.

2 In the palette, under Quick Tools, drag an aggregation element and drop it in the second cell in the group footer row. Elements that are in the group footer appear at the end of every group.

3 In Aggregation Builder, specify the following values:

  1 In Column Binding Name, type the following name:

    GRP_TOTAL_CUSTOMERS

  2 In Function, select COUNT. BIRT selects the appropriate data type, integer.

  3 In Aggregate On, select Group and credit_group. This value indicates that the COUNT function returns the number of rows in each credit limit group.

    Figure 11-41 shows the complete definition for the aggregation element.

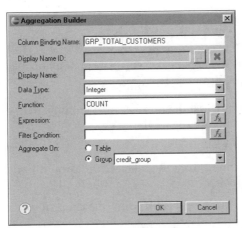

Figure 11-41 Aggregation Builder displaying values for getting the count of customers in each credit limit group

4 Choose OK. In the report design, shown in Figure 11-42, the aggregation element displays the sigma symbol followed by the column binding name.

  Σ [GRP_TOTAL_CUSTOMER]

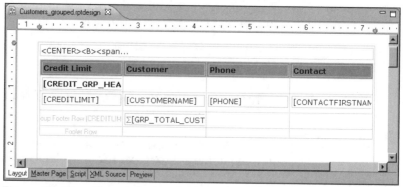

Figure 11-42 Report design displaying the aggregation element

4 Preview the report. The report displays the number of customers at the end of each group. Figure 11-43 shows the number of customers, 37, for the first credit limit group.

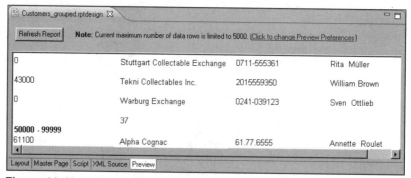

Figure 11-43 Report preview showing a count for each group

5 Choose Layout to return to the layout editor.

6 Instead of displaying just the number of customers in each group, display the following text before the total:

```
Customers:
```

1 Drag a text element from the palette, and drop it in the first cell in the group footer row.

2 In Edit Text Item, select HTML from the drop-down list that displays Auto.

3 Specify the following text in the text area, shown in Figure 11-44:

```
Customers: <VALUE-OF>row["GRP_TOTAL_CUSTOMERS"]</VALUE-OF>
```

In a text element, the <VALUE-OF> tag supports the display of dynamic data. The expression, row["GRP_TOTAL_CUSTOMERS"], is a reference to the column binding you created to return the number of customers in each credit limit group.

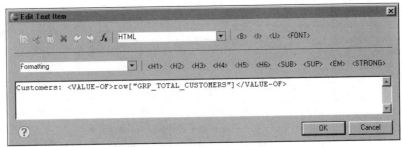

Figure 11-44   Text specified for the text element

    4 Choose OK to save the edits to the text element.

7 Preview the report.

8 Scroll to the bottom of the first credit limit group. The report should look like the one shown in Figure 11-45. The group footer displays the following information:

    Customers: 37   37

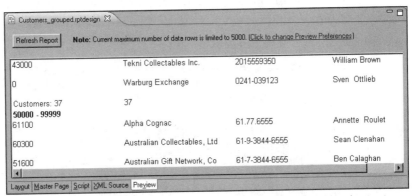

Figure 11-45   Report preview showing the text displayed by the text element

9 Choose Layout to return to the layout editor.

10 Delete the aggregation element from the second cell in the group footer row to remove the second total, which is now redundant.

Display the total number of customers in the report

In the previous procedure, you added aggregate data by inserting the aggregation element from the palette. This time, you add aggregate data by creating a column binding through the table's Binding page.

1 Select the table.

2 In Property Editor, choose the Binding tab. The Binding page, as shown in Figure 11-46, displays all the column bindings used by elements in the table.

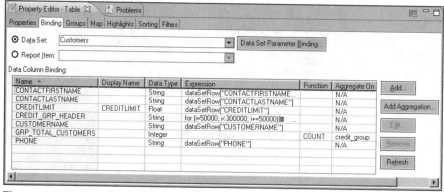

Figure 11-46 Column bindings displayed

3 Choose Add Aggregation to create a new column binding that defines an aggregate expression.

4 In Aggregation Builder, specify the following values:

   1 In Column Binding Name, type the following name:

   TOTAL_CUSTOMERS

   2 In Function, select COUNT.

   3 In Aggregate On, select Table. This value indicates that the COUNT function returns the number of rows in the table. Figure 11-47 shows the complete definition for the aggregation element.

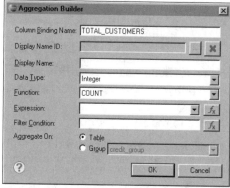

Figure 11-47 Aggregation Builder displaying values for getting the count of customers in the table

   4 Choose OK. The new column binding, TOTAL_CUSTOMERS, is available for use by any element in the table.

5 Select the table, if necessary. Guide cells appear at the top and left side of the table.

6 Right-click the guide cell on the left of the first row, Table - Header, then choose Insert→Row→Above. A new table header row appears above the row that displays the column headings. The new row appears in color because it inherits the properties of the row below it.

7 Select the new row. In Property Editor, under Properties, in General, set Background color to white.

8 Drag a data element from the palette, and drop it in the first cell in the new table header row.

9 In New Data Binding, create a new column binding:

1 In Column Binding Name, type the following name:

`CUSTOMER_TOTAL`

2 In Data Type, use the default, String.

3 In Expression, choose the expression builder button.

4 In the expression builder:

❑ Type the following text:

`"Number of customers: " +`

❑ In the lower pane of the expression builder, select Available Column Bindings, select Table, then double-click TOTAL_CUSTOMERS, the column binding you created to get the number of customers in the table. The expression, row["TOTAL_CUSTOMERS"] appears after the text you typed in the text area, as shown in Figure 11-48.

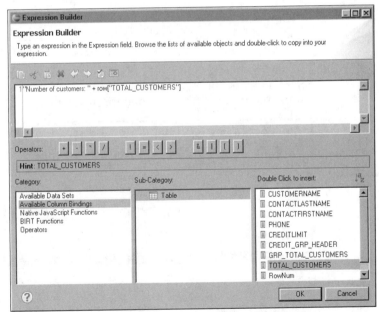

Figure 11-48   The expression builder displaying the expression that refers to the TOTAL_CUSTOMERS column binding

❑ Choose OK. The expression appears in the Expression field on New Data Binding, shown in Figure 11-49.

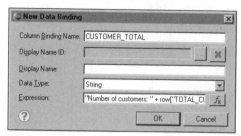

Figure 11-49   Column binding defined

5   Choose OK to save the column binding. The report design should look like the one shown in Figure 11-50.

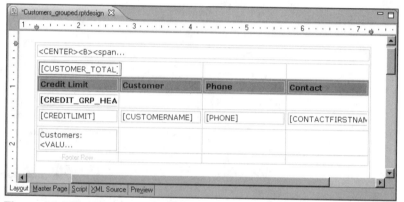

Figure 11-50   Report design showing a total count for customers

10 Preview the report. The report displays the number of customers at the beginning of the table, as shown in Figure 11-51. The text is centered within the column. You re-format this text later.

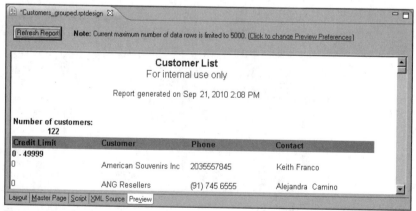

Figure 11-51   Report preview showing a total number of customers

Task 8:   Format the report

Now that the report displays the correct data, focus on improving the report's appearance. You perform the following tasks in this section:

- Adjust the column widths.

- Remove credit limit data from the detail rows.

- Display group headings on the first row of each group.

- Separate each group with a line.

- Display the number of customers text on one line.

Adjust the column widths

When you insert a table, BIRT creates columns with equal widths. In this report, you can improve the layout by decreasing the width of the credit limit column, and increasing the width of the customer column. If you view the entire report, you see that some of the customer names extend to the edge of the column and one name is truncated.

1 Choose Layout to return to the layout editor.

2 Select the table.

3 Select the first column and decrease its width to 1.5 inches either by dragging the column boundary or setting its Width property.

By decreasing the width of the first column, the width of the second column increases.

4 Preview the report.

The spacing of data is improved, as shown in Figure 11-52.

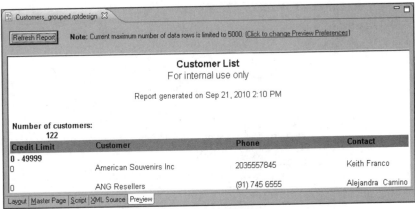

Figure 11-52   Report preview showing adjusted column widths

Remove credit limit data from the detail rows

To verify that data appears in the correct credit limit groups, it is useful to display each customer's credit limit. Now that you have verified the data, delete the individual credit limit information from the report.

1 Choose Layout to return to the layout editor.

2 Delete the [CREDITLIMIT] data element from the detail row.

3 Preview the report. It should look like the one shown in Figure 11-53.

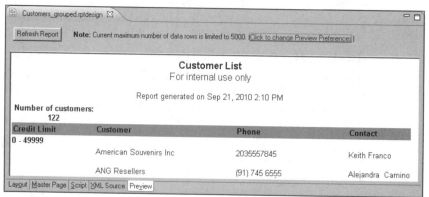

Figure 11-53   Report preview showing credit limit data removed for each row

Display group headings on the first row of each group

The credit limit group headings appear in their own rows, above the detail rows of each group. In this procedure, drop the group headings so that they appear in the first detail row of each group.

1 Choose Layout to return to the layout editor.

2 Select the cell that contains the group heading, as shown in Figure 11-54. Be sure to select the cell and not the data element in the cell.

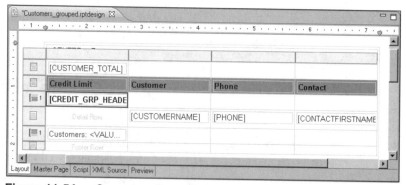

Figure 11-54   Group heading cell selected

3 In the General properties of Property Editor, set Drop to Detail. In the report design, the group heading still appears above the detail row because technically the element is still in the group header row.

4 Preview the report. The group headings appear in the first row of each group, as shown in Figure 11-55.

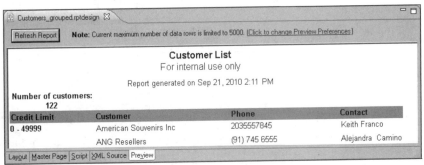

Figure 11-55 Report preview showing dropped group headings

Separate each group with a line

Drawing a line to separate each group makes it easier to see each data group.

1 Choose Layout to return to the layout editor.

2 Select all the cells in the group footer row. To select multiple cells, press the Shift key as you click each cell.

3 In Property Editor, under Properties, choose Border, then set the border properties, as follows:

- Set Style to a solid line.

- Set Color to Black.

- Set Width to Thin.

- Choose the button that shows the bottom border.

4 Add more space between the line and text above it. While the cells are still selected, choose the Padding properties in Property Editor, and set Bottom to 6.0 points, as shown in Figure 11-56.

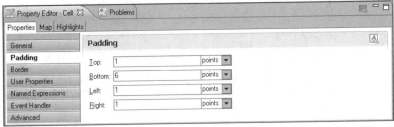

Figure 11-56 Property Editor showing padding values for selected cells

5 Preview the report. A line appears at the end of each group, as shown in Figure 11-57.

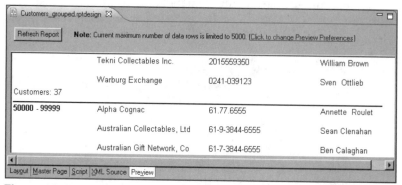

Figure 11-57 Report preview showing a line between groups

Display the number of customers text on one line

The text at the top of the table appears centered within the first column. In this procedure, you format the text so that it appears left-aligned and on one line.

1 Choose Layout to return to the layout editor.

2 Using Shift-click, select the first and second cells in the top table header row, as shown in Figure 11-58.

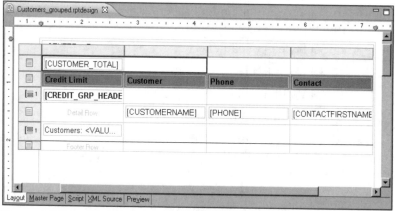

Figure 11-58 Two cells in the top table header row selected

3 Right-click the selected cells, and choose Merge Cells.

4 Select the [CUSTOMER_TOTAL] element in the merged cell, and in the General properties of the Property Editor, choose the B button and the Left button.

5 Preview the report. It should look like the one shown in Figure 11-59.

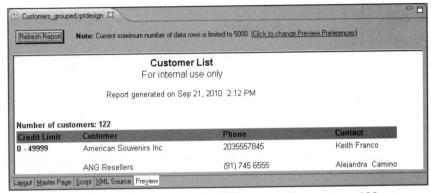

Figure 11-59 Report preview showing Number of customers: 122 on one line

Task 9: Preview the report in the BIRT report viewer

So far, you have been checking the report output in the BIRT Report Designer previewer. This time, use the report viewer to see what the report looks like when it is deployed. The report viewer provides additional functionality, including the capability to navigate to specific sections of a report using a table of contents. When a report contains groups, BIRT generates a table of contents, using the group values to show the hierarchy of the report.

1 Choose Run→View Report→In Web Viewer. The report appears in the report viewer.

 2 Choose the table of contents button in the toolbar to display the table of contents. The table of contents displays the first value in each of the four credit limit groups. When you select a value, the report displays the corresponding section of the report. If you select 113000, for example, the report shows the customer rows in the 100000 - 149999 credit limit range, as shown in Figure 11-60.

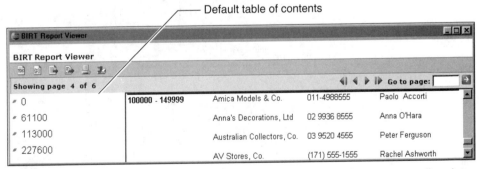

Figure 11-60 Select a value in the table of contents to view the corresponding data

Task 10: Display credit limit ranges in the table of contents

Rather than display the first value of each credit limit group, the table of contents makes more sense if it displays the same credit limit range values as the report. You accomplish this task by using the same JavaScript expression that you used previously to display credit limit ranges (0 - 49999, 50000 - 99999, and so on) in the group header.

1   Return to BIRT Report Designer.

2   In the layout editor, select the table, then choose the Groups tab in Property Editor.

3   Double-click credit_group in the list of groups.

Edit Group, shown in Figure 11-61, displays the properties of the group. Under Table of Contents, Item Expression is set, by default, to the grouping field, row["CREDITLIMIT"].

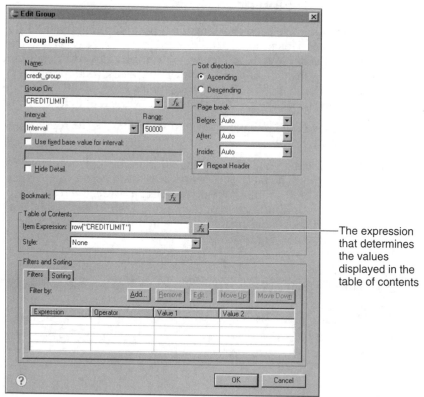

The expression that determines the values displayed in the table of contents

Figure 11-61   Edit Group displaying the properties of credit_group

4   Choose the expression builder button, and, in the expression builder, replace the row["CREDITLIMIT"] expression with the following expression. This expression is the same column-binding expression that is

used by the data element, [CREDIT_GRP_HEADER], in the group header. Rather than typing the expression again, you can copy it from the data element and paste it here.

```
for(i=50000; i<300000; i+=50000){
    if( row["CREDITLIMIT"] < i ){
        rangeStart = i-50000;
        rangeEnd = i-1;
        break;
    }
}
displayString = rangeStart + " - " + rangeEnd;
```

Choose OK to save the expression.

5 In Range, type 50000. You specified this value in Task 5:, "Group customer data by credit limit," but a bug in BIRT 2.6 removes this value each time you open the group editor.

6 Choose OK to save the edits to the group.

7 Preview the report in the report viewer to verify the change in the table of contents. The table of contents displays the credit limit ranges, as shown in Figure 11-62.

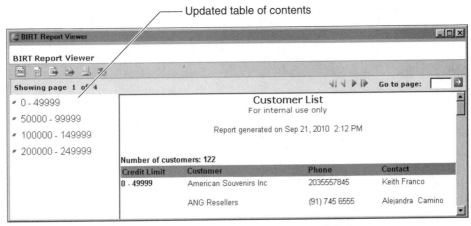

Figure 11-62 Updated table of contents displaying credit limit ranges

12

Aggregating Data

One of the key features of any report is the ability to display summary, or aggregate, information. For example, a sales report can show the overall sales total; sales subtotals by product type, region, or sales representatives; average sales figures; or the highest and lowest sales figures.

Aggregating data involves performing a calculation on a set of values rather than on a single value. For a simple listing report, aggregate calculations are performed on values in a specific field, over all the data rows in the report. The listing report in Figure 12-1 displays aggregate data at the end of the report.

Customer	Payment Date	Check Number	Amount
Saveley & Henriot, Co.	16 January 2004	FU793410	$49,614.72
Men 'R' US Retailers, Ltd.	18 January 2004	DG700707	$21,053.69
Osaka Souveniers Co.	19 January 2004	CI381435	$47,177.59
Auto Canal+ Petit	28 January 2004	HJ217687	$49,165.16
Euro+ Shopping Channel	30 January 2004	HJ32686	$59,830.55
Double Decker Gift Stores, Ltd	31 January 2004	PO860906	$7,310.42
Corrida Auto Replicas, Ltd	06 February 2004	NA377824	$22,162.61
Auto Associés & Cie.	10 February 2004	EP227123	$5,759.42
West Coast Collectables Co.	13 February 2004	PB951268	$36,070.47
Frau da Collezione	17 February 2004	LL427009	$7,612.06
Handji Gifts& Co	28 February 2004	LA318629	$22,474.17
Signal Collectibles Ltd.	29 February 2004	PT550181	$12,573.28
Clover Collections, Co.	01 March 2004	NM916675	$32,538.74

Summary Information

Number of records: 13
Average payment: $28,718.68
Largest payment: $59,830.55
Smallest payment: $5,759.42

— Aggregate data

Figure 12-1   A simple listing report that displays detail and aggregate data

In the example, BIRT calculates the average payment in the report by adding the values in the Amount field in every row, then dividing the total by the number of rows. Similarly, BIRT returns the largest and smallest payment amounts by comparing the amount values in every row in the report.

For a report that groups data, as shown in Figure 12-2, you can display aggregates for each group of data rows, as well as for all the data rows in the report.

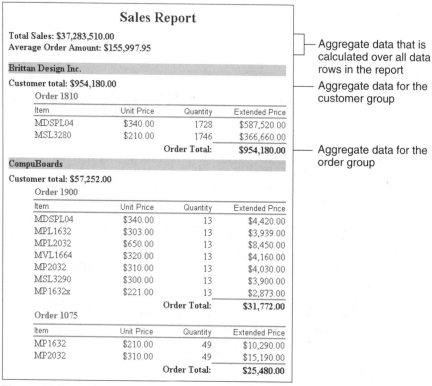

Figure 12-2   A grouped report that displays detail and aggregate data

Types of aggregate calculations

BIRT provides a wide range of functions that perform aggregate calculations. Table 12-1 describes these functions.

Table 12-1   Aggregate functions

Aggregate function	Description
AVERAGE	Returns the average (mathematical mean) value in a set of values. For example, if a set contains values 5, 2, 7, and 10, AVERAGE returns 6.

Table 12-1   Aggregate functions *(continued)*

Aggregate function	Description
CONCATENATE	Joins the values in a set of values. For example, if a set contains values Belgium, Denmark, and France, CONCATENATE returns BelgiumDenmarkFrance. You can optionally specify a separator to insert between the values, the maximum length of the returned string, and whether to include duplicate values in the returned string.
COUNT	Counts the number of rows. If a set contains values 5, 2, 7, and 10, COUNT returns 4.
COUNTDISTINCT	Counts the number of unique values in a set of values. If a set of values contains values 5, 2, 5, 7, and 10, COUNTDISTINCT returns 4.
FIRST	Returns the first value in a set of values. If a set of values contains values 5, 2, 7, and 10, FIRST returns 5.
IS-BOTTOM-N	Returns a Boolean value that indicates if a value is one of the bottom n values. If a set of values contains 5, 2, 7, and 10, and you specify 2 as the n value, IS-BOTTOM-N returns true for values 5 and 2, and false for values 7 and 10.
IS-BOTTOM-N-PERCENT	Returns a Boolean value that indicates if a value is one of the bottom n percent values. If a set of values contains 5, 2, 7, and 10, and you specify 25 (percent) as the n value, IS-BOTTOM-N-PERCENT returns true for 2, and false for 5, 7, and 10.
IS-TOP-N	Returns a Boolean value that indicates if a value is one of the top n values. If a set contains values 5, 2, 7, and 10, and you specify 2 as the n value, IS-TOP-N returns false for 2 and 5, and true for 7 and 10.
IS-TOP-N-PERCENT	Returns a Boolean value that indicates if a value is one of the top n percent values. If a set of values contains 5, 2, 7, and 10, and you specify 25 (percent) as the n value, IS-TOP-N-PERCENT returns false for 5, 2, and 7, and true for 10.
LAST	Returns the last value in a set of values. If a set of values contains values 2, 5, 7, and 10, LAST returns 10.
MAX	Returns the largest value in a set of values. If a set of values contains values 5, 2, 7, and 10, MAX returns 10. For string values, MAX returns the last value alphabetically. For date values, MAX returns the latest date.
MEDIAN	Returns the median, or mid-point, value in a set of values. If a set of values contains values 5, 2, 7, and 10, MEDIAN returns 6.

(continues)

Table 12-1   Aggregate functions *(continued)*

Aggregate function	Description
MIN	Returns the smallest value in a set of values. If a set of values contains values 5, 2, 7, and 10, MIN returns 2. For string values, MIN returns the first value alphabetically. For date values, MIN returns the earliest date.
MODE	Returns the mode, which is the value that occurs most often in a set of values. If a set of values contains values 5, 2, 5, 7, and 10, MODE returns 5.
MOVINGAVE	Returns the moving average for a set of values over a specified interval or number of values. This type of calculation is typically used for analyzing trends of stock prices. For example, you can display the moving average of stock prices over three days. If a set of values contains values 5, 2, 5, 7, and 10, and you specify 3 as the interval, MOVINGAVE returns null, null, 4, 4.66, and 7.33 for each row, respectively.
PERCENTILE	Returns the percentile value in a set of values, given a specified percent rank. For example, you can get the score that represents the 50th percentile of all scores on a test. If a set of values contains 50, 75, 80, 90, and 95, and you specify a percent rank of 0.9 (to get the 90th percentile value), PERCENTILE returns 93.
PERCENTRANK	Returns the rank of a value as a percentage of all the values in a set. The return value ranges from 0 to 1. If a set of values contains 50, 75, 80, 90, and 95, PERCENT-RANK returns 0, 0.25, 0.5, 0.75, and 1 for each row, respectively.
PERCENTSUM	Returns the percentage of a total. If a set of values contains 50, 75, 80, 90, and 95, the sum of the values is 390. PERCENT-SUM returns 0.128 (50/390), 0.192 (75/390), 0.205 (80/390), 0.231 (90/390), and 0.244 (95/390) for each row, respectively.
QUARTILE	Returns the quartile value in a set of values, given a specified quart (0 - 4). MIN, MEDIAN, and MAX return the same value as QUARTILE when quart is equal to 0, 2, and 4, respectively. If a set of values contains 50, 75, 80, 90, and 95, and you specify a quart of 2, QUARTILE returns 80.
RANK	Returns the rank of a value in a set of values. The rank of a value ranges from 1 to the number of values in the set. If two values are identical, they have the same rank. You can rank values in ascending or descending order. In descending order, the highest value is ranked 1. In ascending order, the lowest value is ranked 1. If a set of values contains 50, 75, 80, 90, and 95, and you specify descending order, RANK returns 5, 4, 3, 2, and 1 for each row, respectively.

Table 12-1   Aggregate functions *(continued)*

Aggregate function	Description
RUNNINGCOUNT	Returns the row number, up to a given point, in the report. If a set of values contains 50, 75, 80, 90, and 95, RUNNINGCOUNT returns 1, 2, 3, 4, and 5 for each row, respectively.
RUNNINGSUM	Returns the total, up to a given point, in the report. If a set of values contains 50, 75, 80, 90, and 95, RUNNINGSUM returns 50, 125, 205, 295, and 390 for each row, respectively.
STDDEV	Returns the standard deviation of a set of values. Standard deviation is a statistic that shows how widely values are dispersed from the mean value. If a set of values contains 50, 75, 80, 90, and 95, STDDEV returns 17.536.
SUM	Adds all the values in a set of values. If a set of values contains 50, 75, 80, 90, and 95, SUM returns 390.
VARIANCE	Returns the variance of a set of values. Variance is a statistical measure that expresses how large the differences between the values are. The variance increases as the differences between the numbers increase. If a set of values contains 50, 75, 80, 90, and 95, VARIANCE returns 307.5. If a set of values contains 5, 2, 5, 7, and 10, VARIANCE returns 8.7.
WEIGHTEDAVE	Returns the weighted average value in a set of values, given weights specified in another set of values. In a weighted average, some numbers carry more importance (weight) than others. Grades are often computed using a weighted average. For example: Score Weight (counts toward n% of grade) 50 10 75 25 80 15 90 30 95 20 Given this set of scores and weights, WEIGHTEDAVE returns 81.75.

Placing aggregate data

Where you place aggregate data is essential to getting the correct results. For aggregate calculations, such as SUM, AVERAGE, MAX, and MODE, which process a set of values and return one value, you typically insert the aggregate data in the following places in a table:

- At the beginning of a group, in the group header row

- At the beginning of a table, in the header row

- At the end of a group, in the group footer row

- At the end of the table, in the footer row

You can place this type of aggregate data in a table's detail row, but the data would not make much sense because the same aggregate value would appear repeatedly for every row in the group. On the other hand, insert aggregate calculations, such as RUNNINGSUM, MOVINGAVE, PERCENT-RANK, and RANK, in the detail row of a table. These functions process a set of values and return a different value for each row.

The report in Figure 12-3 groups data rows by customer, then by order ID. It displays totals for each order, totals for each customer, and a grand total of all sales. At the detail level, the report displays the running total for each line item.

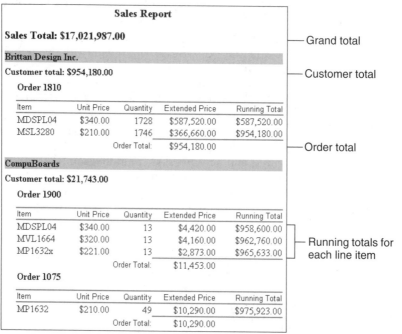

Figure 12-3   Report showing totals for groups and running totals for detail rows

To display the aggregate data as shown in the preceding report example, place the aggregate data in these locations:

- To display the grand total at the beginning of the report, place the aggregate data in the table's header row.

- To display the customer total at the beginning of each customer group, place the aggregate data in the customer group's header row.

- To display the order total at the end of each order group, place the aggregate data in the order group's footer row.

- To display the running totals, place the aggregate data in the table's detail row.

Figure 12-4 shows the report design.

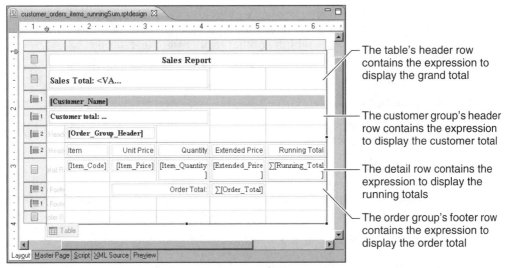

The table's header row contains the expression to display the grand total

The customer group's header row contains the expression to display the customer total

The detail row contains the expression to display the running totals

The order group's footer row contains the expression to display the order total

Figure 12-4 Aggregate calculations in a report design

Creating an aggregation

As with all dynamic or computed data, you must create a column binding for each aggregation. To display the aggregate data, use a text or data element that refers to the column binding. BIRT Report Designer provides a tool, Aggregation Builder, to help create the column binding and the aggregation. Figure 12-5 shows Aggregation Builder displaying default values.

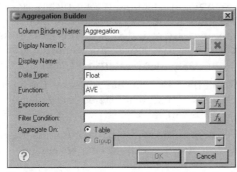

Figure 12-5 Aggregation Builder showing default values

Access Aggregation Builder, using one of the following procedures:

- In the palette, under Quick Tools, drag the aggregation element and drop it in the desired location in a table. Use this procedure to display just the aggregate value, for example, 55. The aggregation element is a shortcut to inserting a data element and associating it with a column binding that defines the aggregation.

- Select the table in which to place aggregate data, choose the Binding tab in Property Editor, then choose Add Aggregation. Use this procedure to use the aggregate value within another expression, for example, to:

  - Display the aggregate value with static text, as shown in the following example:

    ```
    Number of rows: 55
    ```

  - Use the aggregate value in a conditional expression, as shown in the following example:

    ```
    row["Order_Total"] Greater Than or Equal 10000
    ```

When defining an aggregation in Aggregation Builder, take care to provide the required information properly, or the report generates unexpected results. Table 12-2 describes the information required for all aggregations.

Table 12-2   Required information for defining an aggregation

Property	Description
Column Binding Name	Use a short but descriptive name that describes the aggregate value that is returned by the column binding, for example, Grand_Total, Customer_Total, and Order_Total. Every column binding in a report must have a unique name.
Data Type	Most aggregate values are numbers, so you typically select either decimal, float, or integer as the data type. The type you select depends on the type of the values being aggregated, and on the level of precision the report requires. For example, the decimal type is often used for currency values. If you select integer instead, the numbers are rounded, which is less precise. If performance is more important than a high level of precision, use float instead of decimal.
Function	Select the function that performs the aggregate calculation you want. The functions are described in Table 12-1.
Expression	Select the data set field that contains the values to aggregate, or specify an expression.

Table 12-2 Required information for defining an aggregation

Property	Description
Aggregate On	Select the data rows to include in the aggregate calculation.
	■ Select Table to perform the calculation over all the data rows in the table.
	■ Select a specific group to perform the calculation over the data rows in that group.
	Selecting the wrong item produces incorrect results. For example, if you place aggregate data in a customer group header, but select Table as the Aggregate On value, the customer group header displays the aggregate value for the table, not the aggregate value for the customer group.

Most aggregate functions require only the information described in Table 12-2. Some functions, such as IS-TOP-N, MOVINGAVE, QUARTILE and WEIGHTEDAVE, require additional information, which appears in Aggregation Builder after you select the function. For information about the additional information to supply for these functions, read the function descriptions in Table 12-1.

The rest of this section describes how to create the aggregations to calculate the subtotals and totals that appear in the report example in the previous section.

Displaying the grand total in the table's header row

In the report example, a text element displays the sales grand total, using the following combination of static text and dynamic data:

```
Sales Total: $17,021,987.00
```

First, calculate the sales grand total by defining the aggregation in a column binding. Then, insert a text element that uses this column binding.

How to calculate the grand total

1 Select the table that contains the report data.

2 In Property Editor, choose the Binding tab. The Binding page displays all the column bindings defined and used by elements in the table.

3 In the Binding page, choose Add Aggregation.

4 In Aggregation Builder, specify the following information:

   1 In Column Binding Name, type the following name for the column binding:

   ```
   Grand_Total
   ```

2 In Data Type, use the default, Float, as the type of the aggregate value.

3 In Function, select SUM.

4 In Expression, select the data set field, Extended_Price, that contains the values to sum.

5 In Aggregate On, select Table to perform the aggregate calculation over all the rows in the table. Figure 12-6 shows the complete definition.

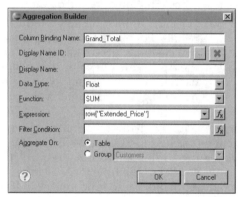

Figure 12-6   Aggregation Builder displaying values for getting the sales total for the table

6 Choose OK. The Grand_Total column binding is now available to any report element you place in the table.

How to use the column binding in a text element

1 Drag a text element from the palette and drop it in the table header row.

2 In Edit Text Item, select HTML from the drop-down list that displays Auto.

3 Type the following text, as shown in Figure 12-7:

```
Sales Total: <VALUE-OF format=$#,###.00>row["Grand_Total"]
</VALUE-OF>
```

Figure 12-7   Text, containing static text and dynamic data, specified for the text element

The expression, row["Grand_Total"], refers to the column binding you created to calculate the sales grand total.

4 Choose OK to save the expression specified for the text element.

Displaying the customer total in the customer group header

In the report example, a text element displays the customer total, using the following combination of static text and dynamic data:

```
Customer Total: $954,180.00
```

Just as you did to calculate and display the sales grand total, first, calculate the customer total by defining the aggregation in a column binding. Then, insert a text element that uses this column binding.

Figure 12-8 shows the definition of the column binding and aggregation in Aggregation Builder. The aggregation uses the SUM function to add all the values in the Extended_Price field, for all rows in each customer group.

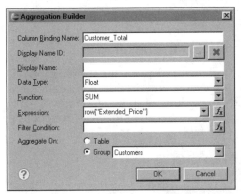

Figure 12-8   Aggregation Builder displaying values for getting the sales total for each customer group

The text element in the customer group header row contains the following expression to display the customer totals:

```
Customer Total: <VALUE-OF format=$#,###.00>row["Customer_Total"]
    </VALUE-OF>
```

Displaying the order total in the order group footer

In the report example, a data element displays the order total. Unlike the previous procedures in which text elements are used to display static text with the aggregate value, the data element is used to display just the order total value.

In this case, drag the aggregation element from the palette, and drop it in the order group footer. In Aggregation Builder, specify the values as shown in Figure 12-9. The aggregation uses the SUM function to add all the values in the Extended_Price field, for all rows in each order group.

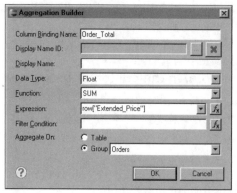

Figure 12-9   Aggregation Builder displaying values for getting the total for each order group

In the report design, the data element displays the sigma symbol followed by the column binding name, as shown in the following example:

Σ[Order_Total]

Displaying the running total in the detail rows

In the report example, a data element displays the running total. Drag the aggregation element from the palette, and drop it in the detail row. In Aggregation Builder, specify the values as shown in Figure 12-10. This time, use the RUNNINGSUM function, rather than the SUM function, and aggregate on all the rows in the table.

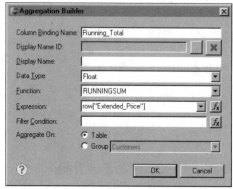

Figure 12-10   Aggregation Builder displaying values for getting the running total for each detail row

Viewing the column bindings for the report

Figure 12-11 shows the column bindings defined for the table that contains all the report data. Review the four column bindings that define aggregations. The Aggregate On values indicate the level at which aggregate calculations apply. The ALL value indicates that the aggregate calculation is applied to all rows in the table. The Customers and Orders values indicate that the aggregate calculations are applied to rows in the Customers group and to rows in the Orders group, respectively. The N/A value indicates that the expression is not an aggregate expression.

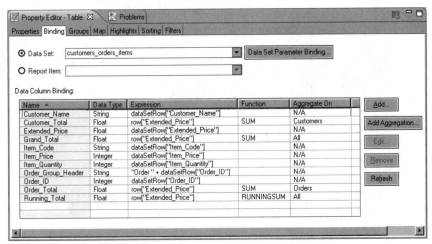

Figure 12-11   Column bindings used by elements in the table

Filtering aggregate data

When calculating aggregate data, you can specify a filter condition to determine which rows to factor in the calculation. For example, you can exclude rows with missing or null credit limit values when calculating an average credit limit, or include only deposit transactions when calculating the sum of transactions.

To specify a filter condition when aggregating data, in Aggregation Builder, specify a filter expression that evaluates to true or false. The following examples of aggregations include filter conditions:

- If summing the values in the Extended_Price field, adding the following filter expression returns the sum of extended prices for item MSL3280 only:

```
row["itemCode"] == "MSL3280"
```

- If averaging the values in the orderAmount field, adding the following filter expression returns the average order amount for closed orders only:

```
row["orderStatus"] == "Closed"
```

Figure 12-12 shows an example of an aggregation in Aggregation Builder that includes a filter condition. The aggregation returns the sales total for item MSL3280.

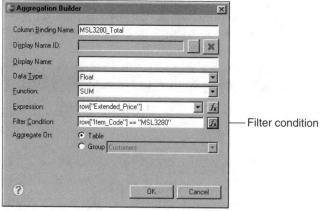

Figure 12-12   Aggregation definition that includes a filter condition

Excluding null values from an aggregate calculation

When calculating the sum of a numeric field, it does not matter if some of the rows contain null values for the specified numeric field. The results are the same, regardless of whether the calculation is 100 + 75 + 200 or 100 + 75 + 0 (null) + 200. In both cases, the result is 375. Note that null is not the same as zero (0). Zero is an actual value, whereas null means there is no value.

Some aggregate calculations, however, return different results when null values are included or excluded from the calculation. The average value returned by the calculation without the null value in the previous example is 125, which is calculated as (100 + 75 + 200)/3. The average value of the calculation with the null value, however, is 93.75, which is calculated as (100 + 75 + 0 + 200)/4. Similarly, COUNT returns a different number of total rows, depending on whether you include or exclude rows with null values for a specified field.

By default, aggregate functions include all rows in their calculations. To exclude rows in which a specified field contains null values, specify a filter condition, as described in the following examples:

- If averaging the values in a transactionAmount field, adding the following filter condition performs the aggregate calculation on rows where the transaction amount is not null:

  ```
  row["transactionAmount"] != null
  ```

- If counting the number of new customers in a report, adding the following filter condition counts only rows in which the creditLimit field has no value (indicating new customers):

  ```
  row["creditLimit"] == null
  ```

Counting unique field values in a set of rows

A field can contain duplicate values. Sometimes, you want to get the count of distinct values. For example, a table displays a list of customers and their countries, as shown in Figure 12-13. The table lists 12 customers from 4 different countries and a customer for which the country is not available.

Customers with orders over 10K	
Customer	Country
American Souvenirs	USA
Land of Toys Inc.	USA
Porto Imports	
La Rochelle Gifts	France
Gift Depot	USA
Dragon Souvenirs	Singapore
Saveley & Henriot, Co.	France
Technics Stores Inc.	USA
Osaka Souvenirs Co	Japan
Diecast Classics Inc	USA
Collectable Mini Designs	USA
Mini Wheels Co	USA

Figure 12-13   A table that lists customers and their countries

If you insert a data element that uses COUNT in the header or footer row of the table, COUNT returns 12, the number of rows in the table. However, if you want to get the number of countries, use COUNTDISTINCT instead.

In the example report, COUNTDISTINCT returns 5, not 4 as you might expect, because like the other aggregate functions, COUNTDISTINCT counts rows with null values. The third row in the table contains a null value for country. To get the real count of countries that are listed in the table, add a filter condition to the aggregation, as follows:

```
row["country"] != null
```

This condition counts only rows in which the country value is unique and not null.

Calculating percentages

To provide more meaningful analysis, a report that displays subtotals and totals frequently also displays percentages. For example, if a report groups revenues by regions for a given quarter, it is useful to know both the actual revenue for each region and the percentage of revenues generated by each region.

Some percentages are calculated at the detail level, where each number in a row is calculated as a percentage of the total of all rows in a group. Some percentage calculations require aggregate values from two different groups of data. For example, a report displays each regional sales total as a percentage of the total national sales. To calculate this aggregate data for each region, two totals are required:

- The total of all sales in each region
- The overall total of sales across all regions

Figure 12-14 shows an example of a report that displays sales data that is grouped by state, then by product.

Sales By State and Product

Total Sales: $149,833.76

California		$51,172.72	34.15%
Product Code	Total Units	Amount	% of Total Amount
S10_1678	152	$12,652.59	24.73%
Order 10145	45	$3,445.20	27.23%
Order 10159	49	$3,986.15	31.50%
Order 10168	36	$3,410.64	26.96%
Order 10201	22	$1,810.60	14.31%
S10_2016	125	$13,044.24	25.49%
Order 10145	37	$3,872.79	29.69%
Order 10159	37	$3,740.70	28.68%
Order 10168	27	$2,633.31	20.19%
Order 10201	24	$2,797.44	21.45%
S10_4698	146	$25,475.89	49.78%
Order 10145	33	$5,112.69	20.07%
Order 10159	22	$3,749.24	14.72%
Order 10168	20	$3,214.80	12.62%
Order 10201	49	$9,394.28	36.88%
Order 10362	22	$4,004.88	15.72%
Massachusetts		**$25,758.16**	**17.19%**
Product Code	Total Units	Amount	% of Total Amount
S10_1678	78	$6,821.58	26.48%
Order 10285	36	$3,445.20	50.50%
Order 10388	42	$3,376.38	49.50%
S10_2016	97	$11,145.67	43.27%
Order 10285	47	$5,198.67	46.64%
Order 10388	50	$5,947.00	53.36%
S10_4698	48	$7,790.91	30.25%
Order 10285	27	$4,496.85	57.72%
Order 10388	21	$3,294.06	42.28%

This aggregate value displays a state's total sales as a percentage of the overall sales

This aggregate value displays a product's total sales as a percentage of the state's total sales

These aggregate values display each order's sales as a percentage of the product's total sales

Figure 12-14 Percentage calculations in a grouped report

This report shows the following three percentage calculations:

- A state's total sales as a percentage of the overall sales
- A product's total sales as a percentage of the state's total sales
- An order's sales as a percentage of the product's total sales

Figure 12-15 shows the report design.

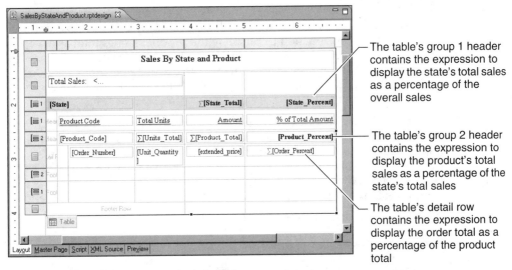

The table's group 1 header contains the expression to display the state's total sales as a percentage of the overall sales

The table's group 2 header contains the expression to display the product's total sales as a percentage of the state's total sales

The table's detail row contains the expression to display the order total as a percentage of the product total

Figure 12-15   Percentage calculations in a report design

Calculating each order total as a percentage of the product sales total

As the report in Figure 12-14 shows, the order information appearing in the report's detail rows is grouped by product code. The amount of each order is displayed in the Amount column. The percent number that appears next to each amount represents that order's total as a percentage of the product's sales total.

To display that value for each order, insert an aggregation element in the detail row, then use the PERCENT-SUM function, as shown in Figure 12-16. The Aggregate On value is Product group, which indicates that each aggregate value is a percentage of the total of the rows in a product group.

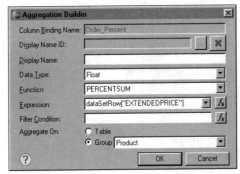

Figure 12-16   The Order_Percent column binding uses the PERCENTSUM function

Calculating the product's sales total as a percentage of a state's sales total

Unlike the previous percentage calculation, the example report does not use the PERCENT-SUM function to calculate the product's sales total as a percentage of a state's sales total. You use PERCENT-SUM only for values in the detail row. You cannot use this function to calculate percentage values that require data from two different groups, which, in this example, are the product and state groups.

The report shown in Figure 12-15 uses two column bindings, Product_Total and State_Total, to calculate a product's sales total and a state's sales total, respectively. These column bindings are then used in an expression in another column binding, Product_Percent, to calculate the product's sales total as a percentage of a state's sales total. Insert a data element, then specify the expression. As Figure 12-17 shows, the expression in Product_Percent is

```
row["Product_Total"]/row["State_Total"]
```

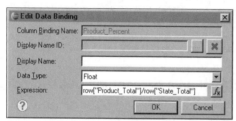

Figure 12-17   The Product_Percent column binding uses the Product_Total and State_Total column bindings in an expression

Calculating the state's sales total as a percentage of the overall sales total

The report shown in Figure 12-15 uses two column bindings, Grand_Total and State_Total, to calculate the overall sales and a state's sales total, respectively. These column bindings are used in an expression in another column binding, State_Percent, to calculate the state's sales total as a percentage of the overall sales total. As Figure 12-18 shows, the expression in State_Percent is

```
row["Product_Total"]/row["State_Total"]
```

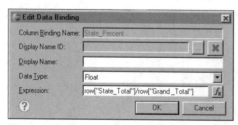

Figure 12-18   The State_Percent column binding uses the State_Total and Grand_Total column bindings in an expression

Displaying the percentage values in the correct format

The values returned by the previous calculations range from 0 to 1. To display a value, such as 0.8, as 80%, use the following procedure:

1 Select the data element that displays the percentage value.

2 In Property Editor, choose Format Number, then choose the Percent format.

3 Choose the settings, including the number of decimal places and the placement of the percent symbol. Figure 12-19 shows an example of specifying the percent format for numbers in a data element.

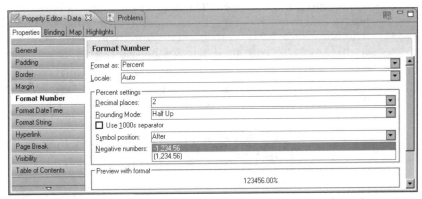

Figure 12-19   Percent format specified for numbers in a data element

Creating a summary report

Reports typically display both detail and aggregate data. A summary report is a report that shows only aggregate data. Summary reports, such as the top ten products or sales totals by state, provide key information at a glance and are easy to create. Figure 12-20 shows an example of a report that displays sales data by state. This report is the summary version of the report shown in Figure 12-14.

Sales By State		
Total Sales: $149,833.76		
California	$51,172.72	34.15%
Massachusetts	$25,758.16	17.19%
New Jersey	$18,021.37	12.03%
New York	$37,053.19	24.73%
Pennsylvania	$17,828.32	11.90%

Figure 12-20   Summary report showing sales data by state

Hiding details

When creating a report that contains data in detail rows and aggregate data in header or footer rows, you can change such a report to a summary report by hiding the contents in the detail rows. To hide these contents, use one of the following techniques:

- Choose the group that contains the details to hide, and in the group editor, select the Hide Detail option.

- Select the row that contains the details, and use the Visibility property to hide the contents of the row.

While both techniques provide the flexibility of maintaining two versions of a report, the first technique is more intuitive. In a report that contains more than one group, however, using the Visibility property gives you more control over which group details to hide.

Consider the example sales report that groups order data by state and product. To show only the state totals, as shown in Figure 12-20, you choose the top-level group, state, then select the Hide Detail option, as shown in Figure 12-21.

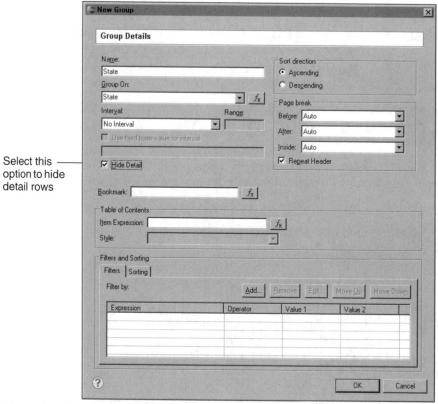

Figure 12-21   Select Hide Detail to hide all data within the state group

Hiding the details from the state group recursively hides all data within the state group; the report hides product groups and the order details within each product group. You may want to hide only the product groups, but still show the order details within the product groups, however, as shown in Figure 12-22. You can get this output only by selecting specific sections and using the Visibility property to hide the selected sections.

Sales By State			
Total Sales: $149,833.76			
California		$51,172.72	34.15%
Order 10145	45	$3,445.20	
Order 10159	49	$3,986.15	
Order 10168	36	$3,410.64	
Order 10201	22	$1,810.60	
Order 10145	37	$3,872.79	
Order 10159	37	$3,740.70	
Order 10168	27	$2,633.31	
Order 10201	24	$2,797.44	
Order 10145	33	$5,112.69	
Order 10159	22	$3,749.24	
Order 10168	20	$3,214.80	
Order 10201	49	$9,394.28	
Order 10362	22	$4,004.88	
Massachusetts		$25,758.16	17.19%
Order 10285	36	$3,445.20	
Order 10388	42	$3,376.38	
Order 10285	47	$5,198.67	
Order 10388	50	$5,947.00	
Order 10285	27	$4,496.85	
Order 10388	21	$3,294.06	
New Jersey		$18,021.37	12.03%
Order 10251	59	$5,533.61	
Order 10251	44	$5,076.28	
Order 10251	43	$7,411.48	
New York		$37,053.19	24.73%
Order 10107	30	$2,440.50	
Order 10237	23	$2,113.01	
Order 10329	42	$3,376.38	
Order 10107	39	$4,128.54	

Figure 12-22 Report showing the top-level state data and the order details, but not the product groups

Figure 12-23 shows the report design that generates the output in Figure 12-22. In the design, the following rows have their Visibility property set to hide the rows:

- Group 1 header row, which displays the column headings for the product summary data

- Group 2 header row, which displays the product summary data

Figure 12-23 shows the group 2 header row selected in the layout editor, and the Hide Element option selected for the Visibility property in Property Editor.

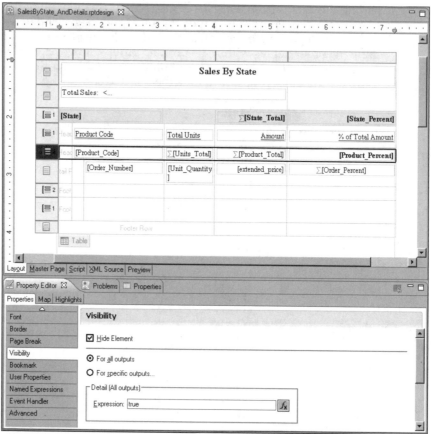

Figure 12-23 Report design with the product group row selected, and the row's Visibility property set to hide the row

Creating a top *n* report

To create a top *n* or bottom *n* summary report, insert the aggregate data in the header or footer row. Then create a filter for the group that contains the data, and use a filter condition, as shown in the following examples:

```
//Show only the top ten orders
row["Total_Sales"] Top n 10
```

```
//Show only orders in the top ten percent
row["Total_Sales"] Top Percent 10
```

```
//Show only the lowest five orders
row["Total_Sales"] Bottom n 5
```

```
//Show only orders in the bottom one percent
row["Total_Sales"] Bottom Percent 1
```

Figure 12-24 shows a top ten report. Figure 12-25 shows the report design.

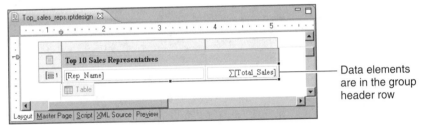

Top 10 Sales Representatives	
Gerard Hernandez	$1,258,577.81
Leslie Jennings	$1,081,530.54
Pamela Castillo	$868,220.55
Larry Bott	$732,096.79
Barry Jones	$704,853.91
George Vanauf	$669,377.05
Peter Marsh	$584,593.76
Loui Bondur	$569,485.75
Andy Fixter	$562,582.59
Steve Patterson	$505,875.42

Figure 12-24   Top ten report

Figure 12-25   Top ten report design

The data elements that display the sales representative names and their sales totals are in a group header row. This report groups sales data rows (not shown in the report) by sales representatives. To display only the top ten sales representatives, a filter is specified in the group definition, as shown in Figure 12-26.

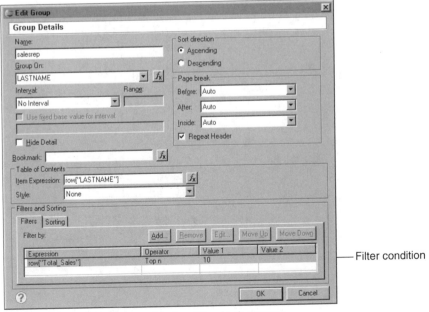

Figure 12-26   Defining a top ten filter in the group

13

Writing Expressions

You can create many reports using data that comes directly from a data source simply by dragging the data set fields from Data Explorer to the report. Sometimes, however, you want to display information that is not in the data source, or you want to display data differently from the way it appears in the data source. You might also want to sort data using a formula, rather than sorting on an existing field. For these cases, and many others, write expressions using JavaScript.

An expression is a statement that produces a value. An expression can be a literal value, such as:

```
3.14
"It is easy to create reports with BIRT"
```

When you drag a field into the report, BIRT Report Designer creates a column binding with the correct expression. The expression specifies the name of the field from which the report displays values. For example, the following expressions get values from the customerName field and the phone field, respectively:

```
dataSetRow["customerName"]
dataSetRow["phone"]
```

An expression can contain any combination of literal values, fields, operators, variables, and functions that evaluates to a single value. In the following examples, the first expression combines static text with a field, the second uses a JavaScript function, and the third multiplies the values of two fields:

```
"Order Total: " + row["orderTotal"]
row["orderDate"].getYear()
row["itemQuantity"] * row["itemPrice"]
```

This chapter describes some common uses and examples of expressions in reports. This chapter does not describe all the functions, objects, or operators that you can use in expressions. If you are new to JavaScript, you will find it useful to read a book about JavaScript.

Basic concepts

This section describes some of the basic concepts you need to understand and remember when writing JavaScript expressions. Understanding these concepts helps you avoid some common mistakes.

Data types

One of the fundamental concepts to understand is data types. Data types are the types of values—numbers, strings, and Booleans, for example—that can be represented and manipulated in any programming language. Every database field has a certain data type, every piece of report data has a certain data type, and every expression you create returns a value of a particular data type.

This concept is important because if an expression does not handle data types properly, errors occur or the report returns unexpected results. For example, you cannot perform mathematical calculations on numbers if they are of string type, and you cannot convert values in a date field to uppercase characters.

If writing an expression to manipulate a data set field, verify its type, particularly if the field values are numbers. Numbers can be of string or numeric type. For example, databases typically store zip codes and telephone numbers as strings. Item quantities or prices are always of numeric type so that the data can be manipulated mathematically. IDs, such as customer IDs or order IDs are usually of numeric type so that the data can be sorted in numeric order, such as 1, 2, 3, 10, 11, rather than in alphanumeric order, such as 1, 10, 11, 2, 3.

To see the data type of a field, open the data set in Data Explorer, and choose Output Columns. Output Columns displays the fields in the data set and their types, as shown in Figure 13-1.

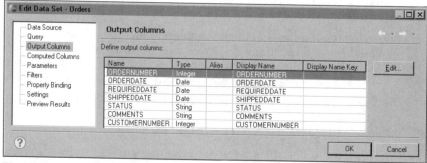

Figure 13-1   Output Columns

Case sensitivity

JavaScript is a case-sensitive language. This feature means that a keyword, a function name, a variable name, or any other identifier must always be typed using the correct capitalization. For example, you must type the getDate( ) function as getDate( ), not as GetDate( ) or getdate( ). Similarly, myVar, MyVar, MYVAR, and myvar are four different variable names.

Data set field names are case-sensitive. When referring to a data set field in an expression, specify the field name with the same capitalization that the data source driver uses to identify the field. As mentioned previously, Output Columns in the data set editor shows the fields. If you use the expression builder to write an expression, select a field to insert in the expression to ensure that the correct field name is used.

Multiline expressions

An expression can contain multiple lines, as shown in the following example:

```
firstInitial = row["customerFirstname"].charAt(0);
firstInitial + ". " + row["customerLastname"];
```

The expression looks like lines of program code because it is. Expressions can be small pieces of code that do something. The expression in the previous example does the following tasks:

- It extracts the first character of a string value in a customerFirstname field and assigns the value to a variable named firstInitial.

- Then, it combines the firstInitial value, a period, a space, and the value in a customerLastname field.

An expression can contain as many lines as needed. Just remember that an expression returns a single value. If an expression contains several lines, it returns the results of the last line. The previous expression returns a value, such as T. Robinson.

The lines are called statements, and they are separated from each other by semicolons. If you place each statement on a separate line, as shown in the example, JavaScript allows you to leave out the semicolons. It is, however, good practice to use semicolons to separate statements.

Using the expression builder

The expression builder, shown in Figure 13-2, is a tool you use to create, modify, and view expressions. It provides a list of the objects, functions, and operators that you can include in expressions. The expression builder is particularly useful when you are learning how to write expressions in JavaScript and discovering which BIRT and JavaScript functions are available.

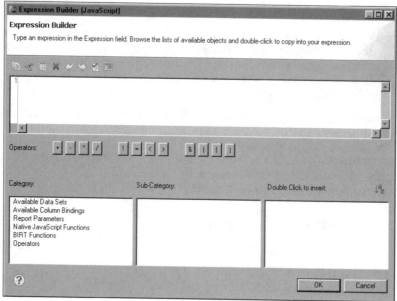

Figure 13-2　　The expression builder

The expression builder is accessible when you need to specify an expression, such as when you create a computed field in Data Explorer, when you filter data, when you insert a data element, when you specify a data series for a chart, or when you want to display dynamic data in a text element.

You open the expression builder by choosing the button that appears in Figure 13-3.

Figure 13-3　　The expression builder access button

Creating an expression

The expression builder consists of two parts:

- The top part of the expression builder is where you create or edit an expression. When you choose objects from the bottom part, they appear in this area. You can also type an expression directly in this area.

- The bottom part provides a hierarchical view of the column bindings, report parameters, variables, JavaScript functions, BIRT functions, operators, and data set fields that you can select to build an expression. The items that appear under Category vary, depending on the context of the expression. When you select an item in Category, its contents appear in Sub-Category. When you select an item in Sub-Category, its contents— which you insert in an expression—appear in the box that is the farthest to the right. Figure 13-4 shows an example.

Figure 13-4   Functions for String class

Table 13-1 provides descriptions of the items in the expression builder's Category column.

Table 13-1   Categories in the expression builder

Item	Description
Available Column Bindings	Displays the column bindings—references to data set fields or computed data—that are available to the current report element. An element can access column bindings that are defined on the element itself and on the element's container.
Available Data Sets	Displays the data set or data sets that are available to the current report element. Expand the data sets to select fields to use in an expression. Data set fields are accessible only when you create a column-binding expression or when you create a computed field in the data set editor.
Report Parameters	Displays the report parameters that you created using Data Explorer. Report parameters are typically used to get input from users when they run the report.
Native JavaScript Functions	Displays native JavaScript functions by objects, such as String, Date, Math, and so on. Use these functions to manipulate or calculate data.
	For summary information about a function, hover the mouse over the item to display a tooltip. For detailed information, see a JavaScript book.
BIRT Functions	Displays the JavaScript functions that are defined by BIRT. The functions are categorized by objects, such as BirtDateTime, BirtMath, and Finance. Use these functions to calculate data.
	For summary information about a function, hover the mouse over the item to display a tooltip. For detailed information, see "Scripting Reference" in BIRT's online help.
Operators	Displays types of JavaScript operators, such as Assignment, Comparison, Computational, and Logical.

(continues)

Table 13-1   Categories in the expression builder *(continued)*

Item	Description
Variables	Displays the report variables that you created using Data Explorer. A report variable has global scope. It is available to any element in the report.

Validating an expression

When you finish creating an expression in the expression builder, choose Validate, as shown in Figure 13-5, to verify the expression. If the expression is syntactically correct, the expression builder displays the message, No syntax error was found in current script. If the expression contains an error, the expression builder displays a message that describes the error.

Choose Validate to verify an expression

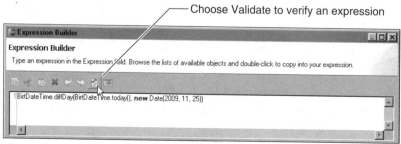

Figure 13-5   Verifying an expression

Manipulating numeric data

Numeric data is probably the most commonly manipulated type of data. Expressions can perform a basic operation, such as multiplying a price field by a quantity field to calculate an extended price, or more complex calculations, such as a financial calculation that returns the depreciation value of an asset. Use Aggregation Builder to calculate aggregate information, such as totals, averages, medians, modes, and so on, as discussed in Chapter 12, "Aggregating Data."

Both JavaScript and BIRT provide a wide range of functions for manipulating numeric data. In the expression builder, look under Native JavaScript Functions—Number and Math, and under BIRT Functions—BirtMath and Finance. The following sections describe common number-manipulation tasks and provide examples of expressions.

Computing values from multiple numeric fields

If a report primarily displays values from numeric fields, it most likely contains computed values as well. An invoice, for example, typically shows the following computed values:

- Extended prices that display the product of unit price * quantity for each line item

- Sales tax total that displays the product of extended prices * tax rate

- Invoice total that displays the sum of extended prices + shipping + sales tax

Order of operations

When a calculation involves more than two numbers and different operators, remember the order of operations, which is the order in which operators are evaluated. Consider the following math expression:

```
55 + 50 + 45 * 2
```

If you performed each operation from left to right in the following steps:

```
55 + 50 = 105
105 + 45 = 150
150 * 2 = 300
```

the answer would be 300.

If you specify the math expression in a data element, BIRT Report Designer returns 195, which is the correct answer. The difference in answers lies in the order of operations. This concept is one that you might remember from math class. Multiplication and division are evaluated first from left to right across the expression. Then, addition and subtraction are evaluated from left to right across the expression. Using the previous example, the expression is evaluated as follows:

```
45 * 2 = 90
55 + 50 = 105
105 + 90 = 195
```

To perform the addition before the multiplication, enclose the addition part within parentheses, as follows:

```
(55 + 50 + 45) * 2
```

The following list describes examples of expressions that compute values from multiple numeric fields:

- The following expression calculates a total price after deducting a discount and adding an 8% tax that applies to the discounted price:

  ```
  (row["extendedPrice"] - row["discount"]) +
      (row["extendedPrice"] - row["discount"]) * 0.08
  ```

- The following expression calculates an invoice total, which includes the total of all extended prices, an 8% sales tax, and a 10% shipping and handling charge:

  ```
  row["salesTotal"] + (row["salesTotal"] * 0.08) +
      (row["salesTotal"] * 0.10)
  ```

- The following expression calculates a gain or loss in percent:

```
(row["salePrice"] - row["unitPrice"])/row["unitPrice"] * 100
```

Division by zero

If you divide the value of one numeric field by another and the denominator value is 0, the result is infinity (∞).

For example, if the following expression:

```
row["total"]/row["quantity"]
```

evaluates to:

```
150/0
```

the data element that contains the expression displays ∞.

The return value is infinity because dividing a number by zero is an operation that has no answer. Mathematicians consider this operation undefined, illegal, or indeterminate.

If you do not want the infinity symbol to appear in the report, you can replace it with a string value, such as Undefined, or replace it with an empty string ("") to display nothing. The infinity symbol is a numeric value; therefore, you must convert it to a string before replacing it with a different string.

The following expression replaces ∞ with Undefined:

```
// Convert number to a string
x = row["total"]/row["quantity"] + ""
// Replace ∞ with the word Undefined
x.replace("Infinity", "Undefined")
```

Alternatively, use the BirtMath function, safeDivide( ). The safeDivide( ) function takes three arguments: the number to divide, the divisor, and the value to return if the result of the division is infinity. The following expression uses safeDivide( ) to divide row["total"] by row["quantity"] and to return Undefined for an infinity value:

```
BirtMath.safeDivide(row["total"], row["quantity"], "Undefined")
```

Converting a number to a string

Convert a number to a string using one of the following techniques:

- Use the JavaScript toString( ) function.

- Add an empty string ("") to the number.

The following expressions yield the same result. If the value of orderID is 1000, both expressions return 10005.

```
row["orderID"].toString() + 5
row["orderID"] + "" + 5
```

Any time you combine a literal string with a number, JavaScript converts the number to a string. Be aware of this fact, especially if you want to also manipulate the number mathematically. For example, the following expression changes orderID to a string:

```
"Order ID: " + row["orderID"]
```

To perform a calculation and add a literal string, do them in separate steps. Perform the calculation first, then append the string, as shown in the following example:

```
orderIDvar = row["orderID"] + 10;
"Order ID: " + orderIDvar;
```

If the value of orderID is 1000, the expression returns

```
Order ID: 1010
```

Manipulating string data

Often, a data source contains string or text data that is not in the right form for a report. For example, you want to sort a report by last name, but the data source contains last names only as part of a full name field. Or, conversely, you want to display full names, but the data source stores first names and last names in separate fields.

Both JavaScript and BIRT provide a wide range of functions for manipulating strings. In the expression builder, look under Native JavaScript Functions—String, and under BIRT Functions—BirtStr. The following sections describe some of the common string-manipulation tasks and provide examples of expressions.

Substituting string values

Sometimes, you need to substitute one string value for another. Perhaps data was added to the data source inconsistently. For example, some addresses contain "Street," and some contain "St.". You can replace entire string values or just parts of a string by using the replace( ) function in JavaScript.

The replace( ) function searches for a specified string and replaces it with another string. It takes two arguments: the string to replace, and the new string. The following expression searches for "St." in an address field and replaces it with "Street":

```
row["address"].replace("St.", "Street")
```

To search for and replace multiple strings in a single field, add as many replace( ) functions as needed to the expression, as shown in the following example:

```
row["address"].replace("St.", "Street").replace("Ave.", "Avenue")
   .replace("Blvd", "Boulevard")
```

As with any global search-and-replace operation, be aware of unintended string replacements. For example, the row["address"].replace("St.", "Street") expression replaces St. Mary Road with Street Mary Road. In this case, rather than just searching for "St.", you need to search for "St." at the end of a line. To perform this type of search, specify a string pattern to search, rather than a literal string. For more information about searching for patterns, see "Matching string patterns," later in this chapter.

To replace entire strings, rather than just a part of the string, you can use the mapping feature instead. The mapping feature is ideal for replacing known sets of values. For example, a gender field contains two values, M or F. You can map the M value to Male, and F to Female. For more information about mapping values, see "Specifying alternate values for display" in Chapter 10, "Formatting Report Content."

Combining values from multiple fields

Each field in a database often represents a single piece of information. For example, a customer table might contain these fields: customerFirstname, customerLastname, addressLine_1, addressLine_2, city, state, zip, and country.

You can create a customer report that uses data from all these fields by dragging each field to a table cell. The generated report, however, does not look professional because the spaces between the pieces of data are uneven, as shown in Figure 13-6.

Name		Address					
Jean	King	8489 Strong St.		Las Vegas	NV	83030	USA
Susan	Nelson	5677 Strong St.		San Rafael	CA	97562	USA
Julie	Murphy	5557 North Pendale Street		San Francisco	CA	94217	USA
Kwai	Lee	897 Long Airport Avenue		NYC	NY	10022	USA
Jeff	Young	4092 Furth Circle	Suite 400	NYC	NY	10022	USA

Figure 13-6   Report with separate field values

The solution is to combine, or concatenate, the first and last names and place the concatenated name in a single table cell. Similarly, concatenate all the address-related fields and place the full address in a single table cell. In JavaScript, concatenate string values using the + operator.

For the name, add a literal space (" ") between the name fields so that the first and last name values do not run together. For the address, add a comma and space between all the fields, except between state and zip. For these fields, add only a space between them.

For this example, use the following expression to display the full customer name:

```
row["customerFirstname"] + " " + row["customerLastname"]
```

Use the following expression to display the full address:

```
row["addressLine1"] + ", " + row["addressLine2"] + ", " +
    row["city"] + ", " + row["state"] + " " + row["zip"] + ", " +
    row["country"]
```

The report now looks like the one shown in Figure 13-7.

Name	Address
Jean King	8489 Strong St., null, Las Vegas, NV 83030, USA
Susan Nelson	5677 Strong St., null, San Rafael, CA 97562, USA
Julie Murphy	5557 North Pendale Street, null, San Francisco, CA 94217, USA
Kwai Lee	897 Long Airport Avenue, null, NYC, NY 10022, USA
Jeff Young	4092 Furth Circle, Suite 400, NYC, NY 10022, USA

Figure 13-7   Report with combined field values

Several addresses display the word null because the addressLine2 field contains no data. In a database, a null value means no value was supplied. In cases where you concatenate fields that might contain no data, you need to remove the word null from the returned string value. This task is described in the next section.

Removing null values from combined fields

When concatenating string values, JavaScript converts null values to the word null. The example report in Figure 13-7 displayed addresses with the word null when the addressLine2 field did not contain a value, for example:

```
8490 Strong St., null, Las Vegas, NV 83030, USA
```

Remove the word null by using the replace( ) function. In this example, use replace( ) in the expression to search for "null, " and replace it with an empty string. You should also search for the comma and space after null to remove the extra comma and space that is added after the addressLine2 field. If you search only for "null" you get the following results:

```
8490 Strong St., , Las Vegas, NV 83030, USA
```

Use the following expression to remove null values from a concatenated address:

```
(row["addressLine1"] + ", " + row["addressLine2"] + ", " +
    row["city"] + ", " + row["state"] + " " + row["zip"] + ", " +
    row["country"]).replace("null, ","")
```

Searching for and replacing "null, " does not, however, take into account missing values in the state and country fields. The state value does not have a comma after it, so you need to search for "null ". The country value does not have a comma or space after it, so you need to search for "null".

To replace null values in the state and country fields, add two more replace( ) functions to the expression, as follows:

```
(row["addressLine1"] + ", " + row["addressLine2"] + ", " +
   row["city"] + ", " + row["state"] + " " + row["zip"] +
   ", " + row["country"]).replace("null, ","").replace("null
   ","").replace("null","")
```

Removing spaces from the ends of strings

When combining values from multiple fields, the resulting string can
sometimes contain extra spaces, as shown in the following example:

```
Carine  Schmitt
```

The string has an extra space between the first name and the last name
because the first name value contains a space after the name, and the
following expression inserts the second space:

```
row["customerFirstname"] + " " + row["customerLastname"]
```

To remove spaces from strings, use the BirtStr functions, trim( ), trimLeft( ),
or trimRight( ). The trim( ) function removes both leading and trailing space
characters, trimLeft( ) removes leading space characters, and trimRight( )
removes trailing space characters.

The following expression uses trim( ) to remove all leading and trailing
spaces from both firstName and LastName fields:

```
BirtStr.trim(row["firstName"]) + " " +
   BirtStr.trim(row["lastName"])
```

Getting parts of a string

Sometimes, you want to display only a portion of a string. For example:

- An address field stores a full address, but you want to display only the zip
  code or the state.

- A name field stores a full name, and you want only the first or last name.

- An e-mail field stores e-mail addresses, and you want only the user name
  that precedes the @ symbol.

Depending on the content of the string and which part of a string you need—
the first part, the last part, or a part after or before a particular character—the
expression that you specify varies. The JavaScript functions you are likely to
use in the expression include the functions shown in Table 13-2.

Table 13-2   Getting information about a string

Function	Use to
charAt( )	Get the character at the specified position of a string. Note that in JavaScript, the first character starts at 0, not 1.
indexOf( )	Find the first occurrence of a specified character and return its position in the original string.

Table 13-2 Getting information about a string

Function	Use to
lastIndexOf( )	Find the last occurrence of a specified character and return its position in the original string.
length	Get the length of a string. Note that length is a property of a string, not a function, so do not use parentheses, ( ), after the keyword, length.
substr( )	Return a substring of a specified length, starting from a particular position in the original string.

The following examples show how to get different parts of a string. Assume a customerName field stores names in first name and last name format, such as Robert Allen.

- To get the first name:

  - Use indexOf( ) to get the position of the space character that separates the first name from the last name.

  - Use substr( ) to get the first name, starting from the first character and for a specified length. The first character for JavaScript starts at 0, not 1. The length to specify is equal to the position of the space character, and not the position of the space character minus 1, as you might think. Consider the name Robert Allen. Logically, the space between the first and last names is the seventh character, but JavaScript counts its position as six. To return the first name, Robert, excluding the space, you want substr( ) to return six characters.

  The following expression returns the first name:

  ```
  spaceCharPosition = row["customerName"].indexOf(" ");
  newStringtoDisplay =
      row["customerName"].substr(0, spaceCharPosition);
  ```

- To get the last name, use indexOf( ) and substr( ) again. The difference is the arguments that you specify for substr( ). To get the last name, start from the character after the space, and the number of characters that you want is the length of the entire string minus the length up to the space.

  The following expression returns the last name:

  ```
  spaceCharPosition = row["customerName"].indexOf(" ");
  newStringtoDisplay =
      row["customerName"].substr(spaceCharPosition + 1,
      row["customerName"].length - spaceCharPosition);
  ```

- To get the first name initial and the last name, for example, R. Allen, to display in the report:

  - Use the expression in the previous example to get the last name.

- Add a statement that gets the first letter in the customerName field. You can use substr(0,1) to get only the first character. Alternatively, use charAt(0), which returns a character in a specified position of a string.

- Add a statement to combine the first name initial, a period, a space, and the last name.

The following expression returns the first name initial and last name:

```
firstNameInitial = row["customerName"].charAt(0);
spaceCharPosition = row["customerName"].indexOf(" ");
lastName = row["customerName"].substr(spaceCharPosition + 1,
    row["customerName"].length - spaceCharPosition);
newStringtoDisplay = firstNameInitial + ". " + lastName;
```

Matching string patterns

The previous section described some techniques for getting parts of a string for display. Sometimes you need to match patterns, rather than literal substrings, in string values. For example, use pattern-matching to:

- Filter rows to display only customers whose last names start with a particular string pattern.

- Search for string patterns, using wildcard characters, and replace with a different string.

To perform pattern-matching, use regular expressions. A regular expression, also known as regexp, is an expression that searches for a pattern within a string. Many programming languages support regular expressions for complex string manipulation. JavaScript regular expressions are based on the regular expression features of the Perl programming language with a few differences.

In JavaScript, a regular expression is represented by the RegExp object, which you create by using a special literal syntax. Just as you specify a string literal as characters within quotation marks, you specify a regular expression as characters within a pair of forward slash (/) characters, as shown in the following example:

```
var pattern = /smith/;
```

This expression creates a RegExp object and assigns it to the variable pattern. The RegExp object finds the string "smith" within strings, such as smith, blacksmith, smithers, or mark smith. It does not match Smith or Mark Smith because the search is case sensitive.

You can perform complex pattern-matching by using any number of special characters along with the literal string to search. Table 13-3 shows a few examples of regular expressions that contain special characters. There are many more special characters that you can use in a regular expression, too many to summarize in this section.

Table 13-3   Examples of regular expressions

Regular expression	Description
/y$/	Matches any string that contains the letter "y" as its last character. The $ flag specifies that the character to search for is at the end of a string. Matches: Carey, tommy, johnny, Fahey. Does not match: young, gayle, faye.
/^smith/i	Matches any string that starts with "smith". The ^ flag specifies that the string to search for is at the beginning of a string. The i flag makes the search case insensitive. Matches: Smith, smithers, Smithsonian. Does not match: blacksmith, John Smith.
/go*d/	Matches any string that contains this pattern. The asterisk (*) matches zero or any number of occurrences of the character previous to it, which is "o" in this example. Matches: gd, god, good, goood, goodies, for goodness sake. Does not match: ged, gored.
/go?d/	Matches any string that contains this pattern. The question mark (?) matches zero or one occurrence of the character previous to it, which is "o" in this example. Matches: gd, god, godiva, for god and country. Does not match: ged, gored, good, for goodness sake.
/go.*/	Matches any string that contains "go" followed by any number of characters. The period (.) matches any character, except the newline character. Matches: go, good, gory, allegory.
/Ac[eio]r/	Matches any string that contains "Ac" followed by either e, i, or o, and r. Matches: Acer, Acir, Acor, Acerre, National Acer Inc. Does not match: Aceir, Acior, Aceior.

The RegExp object provides several functions for manipulating regular expressions. The following is an example of using a regular expression with the test( ) function to test for customer names that start with "national":

```
var pattern = /^national/i;
var result = pattern.test(row["customerName"]);
```

The first statement specifies the string pattern to search. The second statement uses the test( ) function to check if the string pattern exists in the customerName field value. The test( ) function returns a value of true or false, which is stored in the result variable.

If you are familiar with regular expressions in other languages, note that some of the syntax of JavaScript regular expressions differs from the syntax of Java or Perl regular expressions. Most notably, JavaScript uses forward slashes (/ /) to delimit a regular expression, whereas Java and Perl use quotation marks (" ").

Using pattern-matching in filter conditions

In BIRT Report Designer, regular expressions are particularly useful when creating filter conditions. For example, a filter condition can contain a regular expression that tests whether the value of a string field matches a specified string pattern. Only data rows that meet the filter condition are displayed. For example, you can create a filter to display only rows where a memo field contains the words "Account overdrawn", where a customer e-mail address ends with ".org", or where a product code starts with "S10".

When using the filter tool in BIRT Report Designer to specify this type of filter condition, use the Match operator, and specify the regular expression, or string pattern, to match. Figure 13-8 shows an example of specifying a filter condition that uses a regular expression.

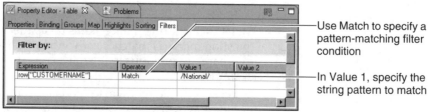

Figure 13-8   Example of regular expression

In this example, the filter condition is applied to a table in the report design. In the generated report, the table displays only customers whose names contain the word National. You can learn more about filtering data in the next chapter.

Using pattern-matching to search and replace string values

So far, this chapter has described some of the syntax that is used to create regular expressions. This section discusses how regular expressions can be used in JavaScript code to search for and replace string values.

Recall that in "Substituting string values," earlier in this chapter, we used replace( ) to search for a specified string and replace it with another. Sometimes, you need the flexibility of searching for a string pattern rather than a specific string.

Consider the example that was discussed in that earlier section. The row["address"].replace("St.", "Street") expression replaces St. Mary Road with

Street Mary Road. To avoid these types of erroneous search-and-replace actions, use the following expression to search for "St." at the end of a line. The $ flag specifies a match at the end of a string.

```
row["address"].replace (/St.$/, "Street")
```

Consider another example: A report displays the contents of a memo field. You notice that in the content, the word JavaScript appears as javascript, Javascript, and JavaScript. You want JavaScript to appear consistently in the report. To do so, write the following expression to search for various versions of the word and replace them with JavaScript:

```
row["memoField"].replace("javascript", "JavaScript")
    .replace("Javascript", "JavaScript")
```

This expression searches for the specified strings only. It would miss, for example, JAVASCRIPT or javaScript. You can, of course, add as many versions of the word you can think of, but this technique is not efficient.

An efficient and flexible solution is to use a regular expression to search for any and all versions of JavaScript. The following expression replaces all versions of JavaScript with the correct capitalization, no matter how the word is capitalized:

```
row["memoField"].replace(/javascript/gi, "JavaScript")
```

The g flag specifies a global search, causing all occurrences of the pattern to be replaced, not just the first. The i flag specifies a case-insensitive search.

Converting a string to a number

A data source can store numbers as strings. Telephone numbers, zip codes, user IDs, and invoice numbers are some of the numbers that might be stored as strings. To manipulate these numbers mathematically, you need to convert them to a numeric type using the parseInt( ) or parseFloat( ) JavaScript function.

The following example converts an invoice ID to an integer and adds 10 to it:

```
parseInt(row["invoiceID"]) + 10
```

If invoiceID is 1225, this expression returns 1235. If parseInt( ) is not used to convert invoiceID to a real number, the result of adding 10 to invoiceID is 122510.

Converting a string to a date

A data source sometimes stores dates as strings. Reports, however, typically need to sort, format, or manipulate these values as dates. For example, values of date type are sorted in date order, such as 2/18/2010, 2/19/2010, 2/20/2010, 2/21/2010 rather than in alphanumeric order, such as 2/18/2010, 2/19/2010, 2/2/2010, 2/20/2010. In addition, unlike date strings, you can manipulate values of date type mathematically, for example, calculate the difference between two dates.

To convert dates from string to date type, pass a supported date format to the JavaScript Date object, as shown in the following example:

```
var datestring = "01/15/2010"; //Variable with MM/dd/yyyy format
new Date(datestring); //Pass the date format to the Date object
```

JavaScript supports the following date formats for string to date conversions:

- MM/dd/yyyy (for example: 10/15/2010)

- MMMM dd, yyyy (for example: October 15, 2010)

- MMM dd, yyyy (for example: Oct 15, 2010)

- yyyy/MM/dd (for example: 2010/10/15)

If a data source stores dates as strings in one of those formats, the string to date conversion is simple. The following example converts values in the OrderDate field to the date type:

```
var datestring = row["OrderDate"];
new Date(datestring);
```

Manipulating date-and-time data

Both JavaScript and BIRT provide a wide range of functions for manipulating dates. In the expression builder, look under Native JavaScript Functions—Date, and under BIRT Functions—BirtDateTime. The following sections describe some of the common date-manipulation tasks and provide examples of expressions.

Displaying the current date

A report typically displays the date on which it is generated, so that users can tell if the data in the report is up-to-date. To display the current date, use one of the following expressions in a data element:

```
new Date()
BirtDateTime.now()
BirtDateTime.today()
```

BirtDateTime.now( ) and new Date( ) return the current date and time. BirtDateTime.today( ) returns the current date and a time value of midnight, 12:00 AM.

When the report is run, the current date appears in the format that is determined by the locale setting on the user's system and by the data type you select when you define the data element. For example, if the locale is English (United States) and you select the Date Time data type, the date appears as follows for new Date( ) and BirtDateTime.now( ):

```
Jan 19, 2009 10:30 PM
```

For BirtDateTime.today( ), the date appears as follows:

```
Jan 19, 2009 12:00 AM
```

To display only the date portion, use any of the three functions and select the Date data type. The following value appears when you specify the Date data type:

```
Jan 19, 2009
```

To display only the time portion, use new Date( ) or BirtDateTime.now( ) and select the Time data type. The following value appears when you specify the Time data type:

```
10:30:45 PM
```

To display the date in a different format, such as 01/19/09, use the data element's Format DateTime property to apply the desired format.

Getting parts of a date or time as a number

You can use the JavaScript date functions, such as getDay( ), getMonth( ), and getYear( ), to get the day, month, or year of a specified date field. Similarly, using the getHours( ), getMinutes( ), and getSeconds( ) functions, you can get the hour, minute, or second of a specified time field.

All these functions return values as numbers. For example, getDay(row["orderDate"]) returns 1 for a date that falls on Monday. Except for getDate( ), which returns the day of the month, the range of return values for the other functions start at 0. The return values for getMonth( ), for example, are between 0, for January, and 11, for December. Similarly, getDay( ) returns 0 for Sunday and 6 for Saturday.

To display parts of a date in a different format, for example, display the month as a word such as January, February, and so on, use Property Editor to set the data element's Format DateTime property to the desired format.

Calculating the time between two dates

It is often useful to calculate and display the number of days, months, or years between two dates. For example, a data source might store two dates for each order record—the date on which the order was placed and the date on which the order was shipped. To provide information about order fulfillment trends, use BIRT's BirtDateTime functions to calculate and display the number of days between the order date and the ship date, as follows:

```
BirtDateTime.diffDay(row["orderDate"], row["shippedDate"])
```

You can also display the number of hours between the two dates, using the following expression:

```
BirtDateTime.diffHour(row["orderDate"], row["shippedDate"])
```

Use a different BirtDateTime function, depending on the range of time between two dates. For example, you would not use

BirtDateTime.diffMonth( ) to calculate the amount of time between order dates and ship dates because if orders are usually shipped within two weeks, BirtDateTime.diffMonth( ) would often return 0.

Calculating a date

You can add or subtract a specified amount of time to, or from, a date to calculate a new date. For example, the following information is stored for each order record: the date on which the order was placed and the shipment time in days. You want to calculate the date that customers can expect to receive their orders. Given those two fields, calculate the new date by adding the number of shipping days to the date on which the order was placed. Use BIRT's BirtDateTime.addDay( ) function to calculate the new date. The addDay( ) function takes two arguments: the starting date and the number of days to add.

The following expression shows how to calculate the expected delivery date:

```
BirtDateTime.addDay(row["orderDate"], row["shipTime"])
```

You can also calculate a new date by adding a specified number of seconds, minutes, hours, weeks, months, quarters, or years. Use the corresponding add<time period> function. The following expression uses the addMonth( ) function to add two months to each value in the startDate field and return the date:

```
BirtDateTime.addMonth(row["startDate"], 2)
```

To subtract a specified amount of time, specify a negative number for the second argument, as shown in the following example:

```
BirtDateTime.addMonth(row["startDate"], -2)
```

Using specific dates in an expression

When creating an expression that contains a specific date, you can use any of the following expressions to represent a date:

```
new Date(2009, 0, 31)
"2009-01-31"
"2009-01-31 15:30:30"
```

All the expressions represent January 31, 2009. The first expression creates a JavaScript Date object. Months in a JavaScript Date object start at 0, so January is month 0. If you cannot remember the correct date expression to type, use the calendar tool in the expression builder to select a date, as shown in Figure 13-9. The date you select appears in the following format:

```
"2009-04-15 11:22:15.872-0800"
```

By default, the time portion of the date expression uses the current time, including the milliseconds. The -800 part of the expression indicates the time zone in the RFC 822 4-digit time zone format.

Choose to open the calendar

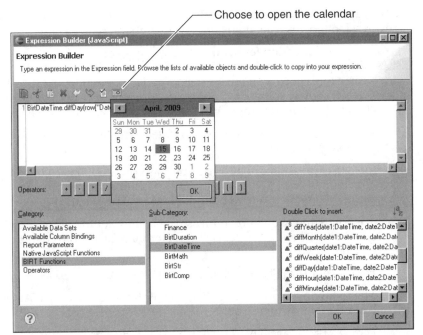

Figure 13-9 Use the calendar tool in the expression builder to select a date

The following examples show expressions that include specific dates. The first expression returns the number of days from the current date to Christmas:

```
BirtDateTime.diffDay(BirtDateTime.today(), "2009-12-25")
```

The following expression calculates expected delivery dates. If the order date is after December 22, 2009, add the standard shipping time plus three days to the orderDate date; otherwise, add the standard shipping time.

```
if (row["orderDate"] >= "2009-12-20"){
    BirtDateTime.addDay(row["orderDate"], row["ShipTime"] + 3)
    }
else{
    BirtDateTime.addDay(row["orderDate"], row["ShipTime"])
    }
```

Using Boolean expressions

A Boolean expression returns one of two values: true or false. The following expressions are basic Boolean expressions:

```
row["sales"] > 5000
row["state"] == "CA"
row["orderDate"] >= new Date(2005, 4, 30)
```

The first expression tests if the sales value is greater than 5000. If so, the expression returns true. If it is not, the expression returns false.

The second expression tests if the state value is equal to CA. If the value is CA, the expression returns true; if not, the expression returns false. For Boolean expressions, you must use comparison operators. As the second expression shows, you use ==, not the assignment operator, =. The expression row["state"] = "CA" returns CA. It does not return a true or false value.

The third expression tests if the order date is greater than or equal to the date May 30, 2005.

A Boolean expression can be as complex as you need. It can contain a combination of && (AND) and || (OR). The following expressions are examples of complex, or compound, Boolean expressions:

- The following expression returns true if an order total is greater than or equal to 5000 and an order ID is greater than 2000. Both conditions must be true.

```
row["orderTotal"] >= 5000 && row["orderID"] > 2000
```

- The following expression returns true if the state is CA or WA. Only one condition needs to be true.

```
row["state"] == "CA" || row["state"] == "WA"
```

- The following expression returns true if three conditions are true:

  - The state is CA or WA.

  - The order total is greater than 5000.

  - The order ID is greater than 2000.

```
(row["state"] == "CA" || row["state"] == "WA") &&
   (row["orderTotal"] > 5000 && row["orderID"] > 2000)
```

Use a Boolean expression to:

- Conditionally display a report element.

- Specify conditions with which to filter data.

- Specify conditions with which to perform particular tasks. For example, use a Boolean expression in an if statement to do something when the expression is true and to do something else when the expression is false, as shown in the following example:

```
if (row["creditScore"] > 700) {
   displayString = "Your loan application has been approved."
   }
else{
   displayString = "Your loan application has been denied."
   }
```

You seldom use a Boolean expression on its own unless you want to display true or false in the report.

14

Filtering Data

Data sources typically contain large amounts of data. Reports usually need only a specific subset of data that meets certain conditions. You can select specific records to use in a report by using filters. For example, rather than get information about all customers, you can create filters to select customers in a certain region or customers with a certain credit rank. You can also design filters that provide the report user with the opportunity to specify the filter conditions when the report runs. This chapter discusses creating filters for which you specify the conditions at design time.

Filtering opportunities

Generally, one goal in developing reports with acceptable performance is to limit the amount of data in a report to just the data that meets the report users' requirements. You limit, or filter, data in different ways depending on the type of data source and the type of report.

The first opportunity to set a filter is to use any filtering techniques provided by the data source. For example, JDBC-compliant databases allow users to run SQL queries that use restrictive WHERE clauses. In fact, best practices recommend designing databases with filtering in mind. You can achieve optimal report performance by filtering data while it is still in the database.

After BIRT retrieves the data from the data source, there are several more opportunities for filtering. Base the decision on where and when to filter on efficiency. For example, instead of creating two data sets that return similar data, one for populating a table and another for populating a chart, create one data set for use by both the table and the chart.

You can use a combination of filtering techniques. For example, if accessing data from a database, you can write a query that filters some rows and use other filtering techniques to filter additional rows.

Figure 14-1 shows the effects of filtering at different points in processing data.

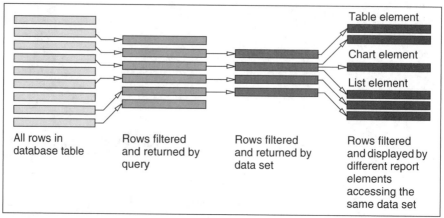

| All rows in database table | Rows filtered and returned by query | Rows filtered and returned by data set | Rows filtered and displayed by different report elements accessing the same data set |

Figure 14-1   Filtering opportunities

Specifying conditions on row retrieval

If a report accesses data from a database or an XML data source, you can specify filter conditions to retrieve a certain set of data from the data source. By filtering at the data source level and retrieving a limited number of rows, you improve performance. The larger the number of rows a data set returns, the more memory and resources BIRT uses to store and process the rows. This section covers some typical ways to filter data in a database and XML data source.

Filtering database data

When creating a JDBC data set, use a SQL SELECT statement to specify which rows to retrieve from the database. To select only rows that meet certain criteria, add a WHERE clause to the SELECT statement. The WHERE clause consists of the keyword WHERE, followed by a search condition that specifies which rows to retrieve.

For example, the following statement returns only customers from the USA:

```
SELECT customerName
FROM Customer
WHERE country = 'USA'
```

As another example, the following statement returns only customers from USA and whose credit limit exceeds $10,000.00:

```
SELECT customerName
FROM Customer
WHERE country = 'USA'
AND creditLimit > 10000
```

In the following example, the statement returns all customers from USA or Canada:

```
SELECT customerName
FROM Customer
WHERE country = 'USA'
OR country = 'Canada'
```

How to filter the rows to retrieve from a JDBC data source

This procedure assumes that you have already created a JDBC data set using a SQL query or stored procedure.

1 In Data Explorer, double-click the data set to which to add a filter condition.

2 In Edit Data Set, add a WHERE clause to the SELECT statement to specify a filter condition.

   For examples and information about the types of filter conditions that you can specify, see the next section.

3 Choose Preview Results to verify that the query returns only the rows that meet the filter condition.

Types of SQL filter conditions

Table 14-1 describes the types of SQL filter conditions and provides examples of filter conditions that are used in WHERE clauses.

Table 14-1   Examples of filter conditions in the WHERE clause

Type of filter condition	Description	Examples of WHERE...

Comparison	Compares the value of one expression to the value of another expression	`quantity = 10`
		`custName = 'Acme Inc.'`
		`custName > 'P'`
		`custState <> 'CA'`
		`orderDate > {d '2005-06-30'}`

(continues)

Table 14-1   Examples of filter conditions in the WHERE clause *(continued)*

Type of filter condition	Description	Examples of WHERE...

Range	Tests whether the value of an expression falls within a range of values. The test includes the endpoints of the range.	`price BETWEEN 1000 AND 2000`
		`custName BETWEEN 'E' AND 'K'`
		`orderDate BETWEEN`
		`   {d '2005-01-01'}`
		`   AND {d '2005-06-30'}`

Membership	Tests whether the value of an expression matches one value in a set of values	`officeCode IN (101,103,104)`
		`itemType IN ('sofa',`
		`   'loveseat', 'endtable',`
		`   'clubchair')`
		`orderDate IN`
		`   ({d '2005-10-10'},`
		`   {d '2005-10-17'})`

Pattern-matching	Tests whether the value of a string field matches a specified pattern	`custName LIKE 'Smith%'`
		(% matches zero or more characters)
		`custName LIKE 'Smiths_n'`
		(_ matches one character)
		`custState NOT LIKE 'CA%'`

Null value	Tests whether a field has a null, or missing, value	`manager IS NULL`
		`shipDate IS NULL`
		`shipDate IS NOT NULL`

SQL provides many other operators and options that you can use to create more complex search conditions. For more information about the WHERE clause, see the SQL documentation for your JDBC database.

Filtering XML data

When creating an XML data set, you specify what data to retrieve from an XML data source by mapping XML elements and attributes to data set rows and columns. To map an XML element to a row or to a column, you specify an XPath expression. XPath is a query language for accessing parts of an XML document.

Figure 14-2 shows an example of a row mapping defined in an XML data set. The XPath expression is /library/book.

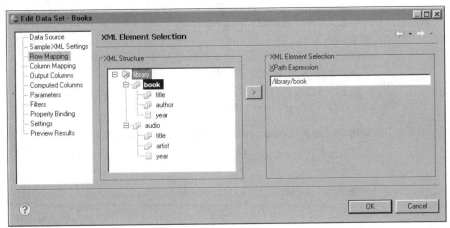

Figure 14-2   Row mapping for an XML document

Figure 14-3 shows an example of column mappings defined in an XML data set. The XPath expressions define the paths to the elements or attributes.

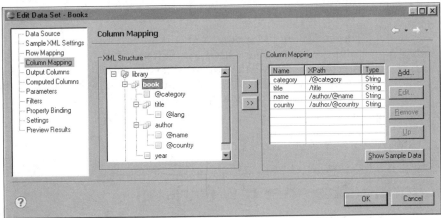

Figure 14-3   Column mappings and the data rows returned by the XML data set

To retrieve only data rows that meet certain criteria, specify the value to search for in the row mapping XPath expression. The following XPath expression, for example, specifies that only rows where the book category is Children should be retrieved:

```
/library/book[@category="Children"]
```

When filtering data with an XPath expression, observe the following limitations:

- You can specify only one value on which to search. You cannot, for example, search for categories Children and Cooking.

- You can filter on XML attributes only, not XML elements. The XML structure in the Column Mapping page displays XML attributes with the @ symbol. In the Column Mapping page shown in Figure 14-3, for example, @category, @lang, @name, and @country are attributes, whereas title, author, and year are elements.

For more advanced filtering capabilities, use BIRT Report Designer's filter tool, which is described later in this chapter.

How to define a filter on row retrieval for XML data sets

1 In Data Explorer, double-click the XML data set to which to add a filter condition.

2 In Edit Data Set, choose Row Mapping.

3 Modify the XPath expression to specify the filter condition. The following expressions are examples of XPath filtering expressions:

```
/library/book[@category="Children"]
/library/book/author[@country="uk"]
```

The value you specify within the double quotation marks (" ") must match exactly the value in the XML document.

4 Choose Column Mapping, and edit the column mappings so that the paths are compatible with the modified row mapping. Rather than directly edit the XPath expressions, you may find it easier to delete the existing column mappings, then create new ones by selecting the element or attribute in the XML data structure and choosing the right arrow.

5 Choose Preview Results to confirm that the filter returns only rows that match the specified value.

Filtering data after row retrieval

It is recommended to filter at the data source when possible. There are cases, however, when you cannot. BIRT provides options for filtering data that complement, and in some cases, replace filtering provided by data sources. For example, if a report uses a flat file data source, you can filter data in BIRT only.

In addition, if using SQL to modify an existing database query is problematic, you can specify the filter conditions using JavaScript expressions instead of SQL. BIRT Report Designer provides a graphical tool to help you build these filter conditions.

Deciding where to filter in BIRT

You can create a filter in any or all of the following places:

- The data set

- A report element, such as a table, list, chart, or cross tab

- A group

The first opportunity to filter data in BIRT is on the data set level. Use this technique if only one report element uses the data set or if you want all report elements that use the data set to use the same set of rows.

Next, you can filter on a report element. Edit the report element filter properties to specify conditions for displaying only certain data rows. Use this technique if multiple tables, lists, and charts use the same data set, but you want each report element to display a different set of rows.

For example, consider a data set that returns data for all customers in the USA. You use this data set for two elements, such as a table and a list. Specify a different filter condition for each element to limit further the rows to display. The table element, for example, can filter the rows to display only customers from California. The list element can filter the rows to display only customers from New York. Figure 14-4 illustrates this concept.

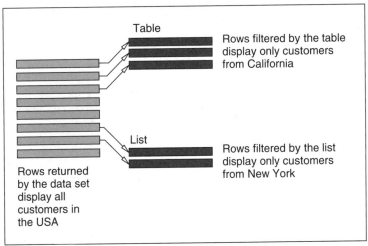

Figure 14-4   Filters applied to a data set, a table, and a list

Finally, you can filter on a group of data. If grouping data in a table or list, you can edit the filter properties of each group. Filter at the group level if a table or list displays rows in groups and you want to display only certain groups. For example, a sales report groups orders by customer. Rather than showing data for all customers, you can specify a filter to display only customers that have order totals above a certain amount, or specify a filter to display only the top three customers.

Figure 14-5 compares three reports that use the same data set but different group filters. The first report shows all customer groups. The second report uses a filter at the customer group level to show only customers whose order totals exceed $100,000.00. The third report uses a filter at the customer group level to show the top three customers with the highest order totals.

Report shows all customer groups

Corporate Gift Ideas Co.	$102,908.44
Order 10159	$37,872.32
Order 10162	$25,345.98
Order 10381	$28,734.69
Order 10384	$10,955.45
Gift Depot Inc.	$83,274.15
Order 10172	$19,318.08
Order 10263	$40,618.93
Order 10413	$23,337.14
Land of Toys Inc.	$105,499.28
Order 10107	$9,347.60
Order 10248	$34,077.36
Order 10292	$23,510.33
Order 10329	$38,563.99
Muscle Machine Inc	$146,063.02
Order 10127	$45,049.74
Order 10204	$47,609.95
Order 10267	$20,314.44
Order 10349	$33,088.89
Online Diecast Creations Co.	$93,495.72
Order 10100	$8,563.71
Order 10192	$40,586.41
Order 10322	$44,345.60
The Sharp Gifts Warehouse	$133,390.92
Order 10250	$40,517.12
Order 10400	$29,589.38
Order 10407	$48,904.14

Report applies a filter on the customer group to show customers whose order totals exceed $100,000.00

Corporate Gift Ideas Co.	$102,908.44
Order 10159	$37,872.32
Order 10162	$25,345.98
Order 10381	$28,734.69
Order 10384	$10,955.45
Land of Toys Inc.	$105,499.28
Order 10107	$9,347.60
Order 10248	$34,077.36
Order 10292	$23,510.33
Order 10329	$38,563.99
Muscle Machine Inc	$146,063.02
Order 10127	$45,049.74
Order 10204	$47,609.95
Order 10267	$20,314.44
Order 10349	$33,088.89
The Sharp Gifts Warehouse	$133,390.92
Order 10250	$40,517.12
Order 10257	$14,380.28
Order 10400	$29,589.38
Order 10407	$48,904.14

Report applies a filter on the customer group to show customers with the top three order totals

Land of Toys Inc.	$105,499.28
Order 10107	$9,347.60
Order 10248	$34,077.36
Order 10292	$23,510.33
Order 10329	$38,563.99
Muscle Machine Inc	$146,063.02
Order 10127	$45,049.74
Order 10204	$47,609.95
Order 10267	$20,314.44
Order 10349	$33,088.89
The Sharp Gifts Warehouse	$133,390.92
Order 10250	$40,517.12
Order 10257	$14,380.28
Order 10400	$29,589.38
Order 10407	$48,904.14

Figure 14-5 Three reports that apply filters on the group level to display different results from the same data set

You can specify filter conditions at all three levels if necessary. Filtering at each level serves a different purpose, can yield different results, and can have different rules. Use the following guidelines to decide where to filter data for a report:

- When filtering at the data set level, BIRT filters rows that are retrieved from the data source.

- When filtering at the report element level, BIRT filters rows that are returned by the data set that is bound to the report element.

- When filtering at the group level, BIRT filters only rows in that particular group. In the reports shown in Figure 14-5, you can filter on customer names and order totals only. You cannot filter on order number because that data is in a different group. Typically, a filter at the group level uses an aggregate expression.

- Filters that use aggregate data can be specified only at the group level. The second report shown in Figure 14-5 uses the following filter condition:

  ```
  row["Customer_Total"] Greater than 100000
  ```

  The third report uses the following filter condition:

  ```
  row["Customer_Total"] Top n 3
  ```

  In these filter conditions, row["Customer_Total"] refers to a column binding that calculates customer order totals, using the SUM aggregate function. If you use aggregate data in a filter at the data set or report element level, BIRT Report Designer displays an error message.

- Some filter conditions provide the same results whether they are applied at the data set, report element, or group level. In the reports shown in Figure 14-5, to display only customers whose names start with M or a later letter, you can specify the following filter condition at the data set, table, or group level, and the reports display the same data:

  ```
  row["customerName"] Greater than "M"
  ```

Types of BIRT filter conditions

Just as with the data source filtering, design different types of BIRT filter conditions depending on how you want to search for data rows. For example, you can specify that BIRT returns rows when the value of a particular field matches a specific value, when the field value falls within a range of values, when the field value matches a string pattern, or when the field value is null.

The filter tool displays operators as English words instead of the actual operators. For example, the tool displays Equal, Greater than, Greater than or Equal, and Not Equal to, instead of ==, >, >=, and !=. Table 14-2 describes the types of filter conditions supported by the filter tool. The table also contains numerous examples of expressions you can create using the operators. Most operators can be used with different data types.

Be aware that the filter tool provides two pattern-matching operators: Like and Match. The Like operator enables users who are familiar with SQL to specify pattern-matching expressions using SQL syntax. The Match operator enables users who are familiar with JavaScript to specify pattern-matching expressions using JavaScript's regular expression syntax.

Table 14-2   Examples of BIRT filter conditions

Type of filter condition	Description	Example as it appears in the filter tool

Comparison	Compares the value of a field to a specified value.	`row["quantity"] Less than 10`
		`row["custName"] Equal "Acme Inc."`
		`row["custName"] Greater than or Equal "P"`
		`row["custState"] Not Equal "CA"`
		`row["orderDate"] Less than or Equal "06/30/05"`

Null value	Tests whether a field has a value or not.	`row["manager"] Is Null` `row["shipDate"] Is Not Null`
Range	Tests whether the value of a field falls within a range of specified values. The test includes the endpoints of the range.	`row["quantity"] Between 50 and 100` returns all quantities between 50 and 100, including 50 and 100. `row["custName"] Between "A" and "B"` returns all names that start with A. `row["custName"] Not Between "A" and "M"` returns all names that start with M and later letters. `row["orderDate"] Between "06/01/05" and "06/30/05"` returns all dates between these dates, including 06/01/05 and 06/30/05.

Conditional logic	Tests if a complete filter condition evaluates to true or false. Use to create a single filter condition that consists of multiple conditions.	`row["country"] == "USA"||`
		`   row["country"] == "Canada"`
		`   Is False`
		returns all countries except the USA and Canada.
		
		`row["orderStatus"] == "Open"||`
		`   row["orderTotal"] > 100000`
		`   Is True`
		returns all orders with open status and all orders with totals exceeding 100000.

Table 14-2   Examples of BIRT filter conditions

Type of filter condition	Description	Example as it appears in the filter tool
Pattern-matching test, using JavaScript syntax	Tests whether the value of a string field matches a specified pattern called a regular expression.	`row["custName"] Match /Smith/` returns names that contain the substring Smith. `row["creditRank"] Match /[AB]/` returns credit ranks A or B `row["productCode"] Match /^S10/` returns product codes that begin with S10.
Pattern-matching test, using SQL syntax	Tests whether the value of a string field matches a specified pattern that uses SQL syntax.	`row["custName"] Like '%Smith%'` returns names that contain the substring Smith `row["productCode"] Like 'S10%'` returns product codes that begin with S10.
Top or bottom *n* logic	Tests if the value of a specified field is within the top or bottom *n* values.	`row["age"] Top Percent 5` returns ages in the top five percent `row["age"] Bottom Percent 5` returns ages in the bottom five percent. `row["orderTotal"] Top n 10` returns the top ten orders. `row["orderTotal"] Bottom n 10` returns the bottom ten orders.

Creating a filter condition

The procedure for creating a filter condition is the same whether you create it at the data set, report element, or group level. The difference is how you access the filter tool.

When creating a filter condition, you specify the following information:

- The expression to evaluate, typically a single field, such as row["grade"]

- The operator that specifies the type of filter test, such as Equal to

- The value for which to search, such as "A"

You can create more complex filter conditions that include JavaScript functions or scripts. For example, you can specify computed values for the expression and value portions of the filter. The following example shows a multiline expression in the expression part. The expression returns a customer's first name from the customerName field, which stores full names.

```
spaceCharPosition = row["customerName"].indexOf(" ");
stringToGet = row["customerName"].substr(0, spaceCharPosition);
```

If you combine this expression with the Equal to operator and specify a value of "John", the filter condition extracts the first name from the customerName field, compares the first name to John, and returns only rows where this condition is true.

The expressions and values that you specify in a BIRT filter condition must use JavaScript syntax, unless you use the LIKE operator. As described in Table 14-2 in the previous section, when specifying a value for a filter condition that uses the LIKE operator, specify a string pattern that uses SQL syntax.

If you filter data using both the SQL query and BIRT Report Designer's filter tool, be careful not to confuse SQL syntax with JavaScript syntax when specifying the filter condition. For example, it is easy to confuse the use of single quotation marks (' ') and double quotation marks (" "). SQL requires single quotation marks for string and date constants, but JavaScript requires double quotation marks. Another example is the comparison operator. Use = for SQL and == for JavaScript.

How to filter at the data set level

1 In Data Explorer, right-click the data set from which to filter rows, then choose Edit. Edit Data Set displays the query for the data set, as shown in Figure 14-6.

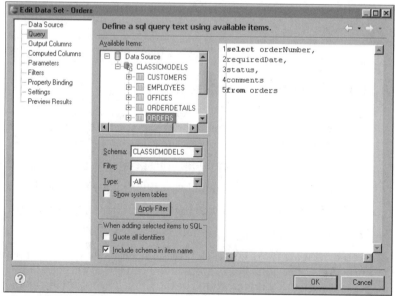

Figure 14-6 Edit Data Set displaying the query

2 Choose Filters from the left side of the window. Edit Data Set displays filter information, as shown in Figure 14-7.

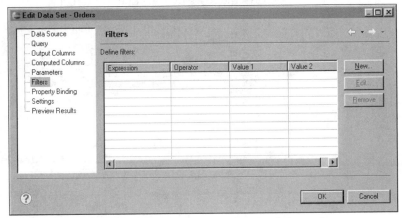

Figure 14-7   Edit Data Set displaying filtering information

3 Choose New to create a filter condition.

4 In New Filter Condition, specify the following values:

- In the first field, select a field from the drop-down list. Alternatively, open the expression builder to create a more complex expression.

- In the second field, select an operator from the drop-down list.

- In the third field, specify the value to search. Type the value, select from the list of values, or use the expression builder to create a more complex value expression. If you select the Is True, Is False, Is Null, or Is Not Null operator, a value is not required.

- In the fourth field, which appears only if you select the Between or Not Between operator, specify a value. Figure 14-8 shows an example of a filter condition.

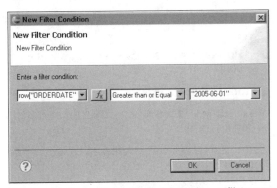

Figure 14-8   New Filter displaying a filter condition

Choose OK to save the new filter condition.

5 To create additional filter conditions for the data set, repeat steps 3 and 4. Figure 14-9 shows two examples of filter conditions created for a data set. Figure 14-10 shows the rows that the data set returns.

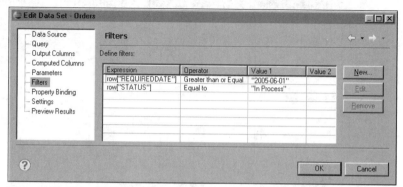

Figure 14-9   Edit Data Set displaying the filter conditions for the data set

6 Choose Preview Results to verify the results that filtering the data set returns. If you specified multiple filter conditions, the data set returns only rows that match all filter conditions, as shown in Figure 14-10. To return rows that match any one of the filter conditions, create a single filter condition that contains an OR expression, then select the Is True operator. This task is described later in this chapter.

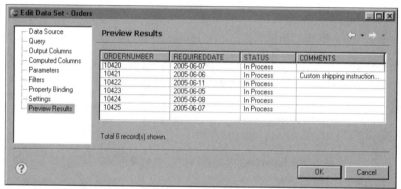

Figure 14-10   Preview Results shows only rows that meet both filter conditions

How to filter at the report element level

These instructions assume you already created a report that uses an element to display data from a data set.

1 In the layout editor, select the table, cross tab, chart, or list from which to filter data. Property Editor displays the properties of the selected element, as shown in Figure 14-11.

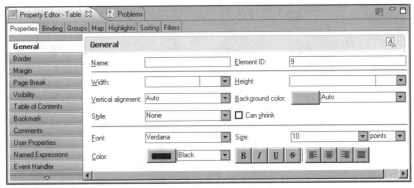

Figure 14-11 Table properties

2 In Property Editor, choose the Filters tab. Property Editor displays the Filters page.

3 Choose Add to create a filter condition.

4 In New Filter Condition, specify the filter condition, then choose OK. For detailed steps, see the previous section.

5 Figure 14-12 shows some examples of filter conditions specified for a table.

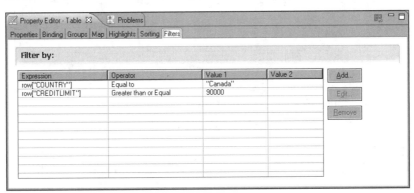

Figure 14-12 Filter conditions for a table

6 Preview the report to verify the results. If you specified multiple filter conditions, the report displays only rows that match all filter conditions.

How to filter at the group level

These instructions assume that you have already created a table that displays data from a data set, and created a group or groups to organize the data.

1 In the layout editor, select the table that contains the data to filter.

2 In Property Editor, choose the Groups tab. Property Editor displays the groups that you defined for the table.

3 Double-click the group for which you want to filter data. Edit Group displays the properties of the group. Figure 14-13 shows an example.

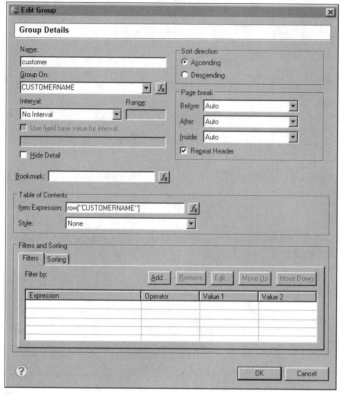

Figure 14-13 Edit Group

4 Under Filters and Sorting, choose the Filters tab.

5 Choose Add to create a filter condition.

6 In New Filter Condition, specify the filter condition, then choose OK. Figure 14-14 shows an example of a filter condition defined for a group.

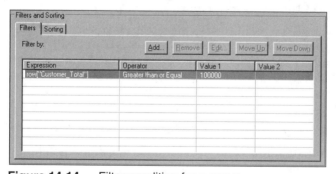

Figure 14-14 Filter condition for a group

7 Choose OK.

8 Preview the report to verify the results. The report displays a different set of group values.

Creating multiple filter conditions

The filter tool supports the creation of any number of conditions for filtering data. BIRT evaluates each condition and includes only data rows that meet all the conditions. For example, assume the following two conditions were created with the filter tool:

```
row["orderTotal"] Larger Than 10000
row["country"] Equal "USA"
```

In this example, BIRT includes a row only if the value in the orderTotal field is greater than 10000 and the value in the country field is equal to USA. In other words, creating two filter conditions is equivalent to specifying the following JavaScript expression:

```
row["orderTotal"] > 10000 && row["country"] == "USA"
```

The following rows meet the specified filter conditions:

```
Country    Order ID    Order Total

USA        1001        12000
USA        1010        15000
USA        1035        18500
USA        1155        25000
USA        1200        12000
USA        1455        20500
```

To return a row if it meets any one of multiple conditions, create a single filter condition that uses the OR (| |) operator to combine multiple conditions. For example, to include a row where either orderTotal exceeds 10000 or country is USA, create an expression that compares to true, as follows:

```
row["orderTotal"] > 10000 || row["country"] == "USA" Is True
```

For expressions that compare to true or false, you must use the comparison operator. As the previous example shows, use ==, not the assignment operator, =. Figure 14-15 shows how the filter condition appears in the filter tool. Note that you select Is True as the operator.

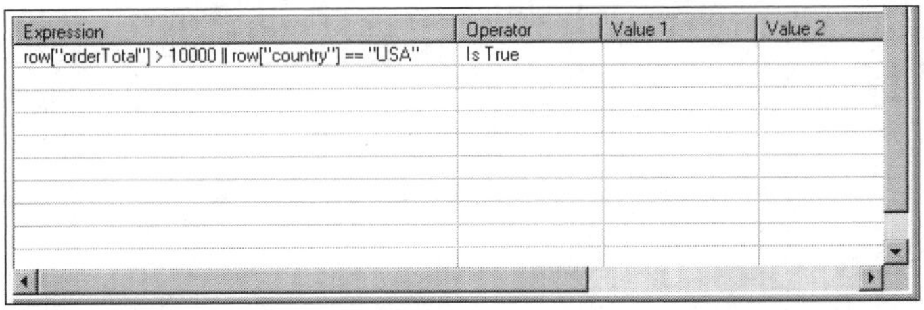

Figure 14-15   Filter condition that uses the OR and Is True operators

In this example, the following rows meet the specified filter condition:

Country	Order ID	Order Total
Belgium	1020	21000
France	2005	14500
USA	1425	5000
USA	1750	7500
USA	1001	12000
USA	1010	15000
USA	1035	18500
USA	1155	25000
USA	1200	12000
USA	1455	20500

Enabling the User to Filter Data

When you create a report, you build a data set and typically specify filter criteria to display a certain set of data in the report. When a user views the report, the user sees the information that you selected. As users become familiar with the report and recognize its potential as an analytical tool, they may want to view the data in different ways. For example, in a sales report, a user may want to view only sales in a particular region, or sales over a certain amount, or sales that closed in the last 30 days.

The solution for this type of ad hoc reporting requirement is for the report to prompt the user to provide information that determines what data to display. You make this solution available by creating report parameters.

About report parameters

Report parameters collect information that determines the data to display in the report when the report runs. Typically, you use report parameters to prompt a report user to specify what data to display before BIRT generates the report. You can also use report parameters in more creative ways. For example, a web application can use a user's login information to set the value of an account number report parameter programmatically. Then the web application can generate a report for that particular account.

Using report parameters, you can:

■ Generate on-demand reports.
  You can create a single report design that generates specialized reports, on demand, to meet the different needs of report users. For example, you can prompt users to select what sections of a report to generate.

- Design a report once, and use the same design to display different data that is based on specific criteria.

  Report parameters are essential tools for time-sensitive reports. Consider a monthly sales report. When first creating the report, you build a query to retrieve sales data for the month of January only. Without report parameters, you must modify the query manually for every month. By creating a report parameter that prompts for the month for which to display sales information, you can create one report and run it each month to refresh its data.

- Manage large reports.

  Report parameters are also useful for managing large reports. Consider a report design that generates a detailed report that displays all itemized sales orders for all customers in all cities in every country. The report includes more information than most users want. To limit the scope of the report, you can use report parameters that ask the user to specify a customer name, a city, or a country for which to display sales orders.

Enter Parameters, shown in Figure 15-1, displays the report parameters when the user runs the report. The user chooses the parameter values, and BIRT generates a report according to those choices.

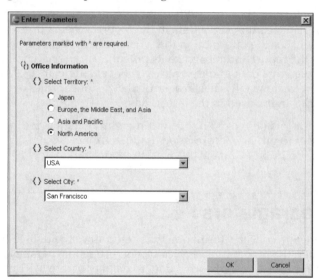

Figure 15-1   Enter Parameters

Planning to use report parameters

Before creating parameters for a report, decide what field values the report user needs to be able to specify and how to prompt the user for those values.

- Think of the different ways in which a user may need to filter the information. Create one report parameter for each question that you want the user to answer. Theoretically, you can create a parameter for each piece of data in the data source. To ensure that report parameters are not overwhelming for the user, limit the parameters to important fields.

- When creating more than one report parameter, consider the interaction of the values. For example, if you create two parameters to get the values of state and sales total, decide whether to return rows only if both values in the row match or if either value matches.

- When creating many report parameters, organize them in logical groups. For example, create two groups of parameters to organize customer parameters, such as customer name, city, and state, in one group and order parameters, such as order ID, order date, and order amount, in another group.

- Use short, descriptive text prompts, but ensure the text is not ambiguous. For example, Customer State is clearer than State.

- Do not assume that the user knows how the data is stored in the data source. For example, a user might not know that an order-status field takes three values: Open, Closed, and In Evaluation. Without this knowledge, the user does not know what value to enter for an order-status parameter. To improve usability, create a drop-down list or radio buttons for the user to select a value instead of requiring the user to type a value. Figure 15-1 provides an example of a simple, but effective, parameter presentation.

User filtering options

Filtering on user-specified values can occur either at query run time, or after BIRT retrieves data from the data source. The filtering option available to a report depends on the data source. User filtering at query run time is supported for JDBC and XML data sources. If a report uses other types of data sources, you can define filters only after BIRT retrieves data from the data source. You define these filters at either the data set, table-element, or list-element level.

Enabling user filtering at query run time

As described previously, a report parameter enables or requires users to specify a value that determines the data to include in a report. When they run a report that uses a JDBC data source, BIRT updates the SQL query with these values before retrieving any data. The data source then returns only the rows that match the user-specified values.

To enable users to filter database data, complete the following tasks in the recommended order. For detailed information about these tasks, see the corresponding topics later in this section.

- Create report parameters to prompt the user to specify values that determine what rows to retrieve.

- Insert parameter markers in the SQL query.

- Create a data set parameter to supply a value for each parameter marker.

- Bind the data set parameter to the report parameter, so that the data set parameter gets the user-specified value from the report parameter and passes it to the SQL query.

- Determine how to present the report parameters.

- Test the report parameters.

Creating a report parameter

Report parameters provide a mechanism for passing values into a report. You can create a report parameter to prompt the report user to specify a value for a particular field. Alternatively, you can use a hidden report parameter to pass a value into the report on a programmatic basis. For instance, a hidden parameter can be used to pass a customer's account code into a report if you do not want a customer to look at any account data but her own.

Report parameters have global scope, which means they are available to the entire report and any report element can access a report parameter's value. To enable user filtering, bind the report parameter to a corresponding data set parameter.

When creating a report parameter, you perform two main tasks:

- Define the basic properties of the parameter: its name and data type.

- Design the presentation of the parameter to the user. Consider the following tasks:

  - Specifying whether users type a value or select a value from a list box or radio buttons

  - Providing a default value

  - Displaying a descriptive text prompt

  - Organizing report parameters in logical groups

How to create a basic report parameter

1 In Data Explorer, right-click Report Parameters, and choose New Parameter.

New Parameter appears, as shown in Figure 15-2.

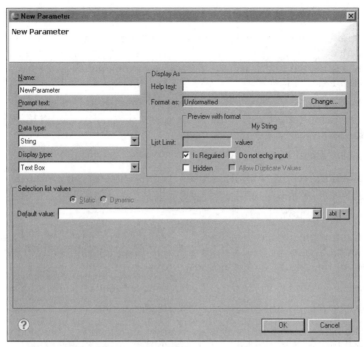

Figure 15-2 New Parameter

2 Specify the following basic properties:

1 In Name, type a name for the parameter. It is good practice to use a prefix, such as RP, in the name to help distinguish report parameters from other parameter types, such as data set parameters. For example, a report parameter used to filter on a quantityinstock field might be named RP_quantityinstock. The value you specify in Name appears as the prompt to the report user if you do not specify a value for the next property, Prompt text. Rather than specify only a Name value for the parameter, you should use a technically descriptive value in Name, and provide a user-friendly value in Prompt text.

2 In Data type, select a data type for the parameter.

The data type that you select for the report parameter determines the formatting options that are available if you choose to provide a default value or a list of values for the report parameter. The data type of the parameter does not have to match the data type of the field in the data source. Values in an orderID field, for example, can be stored as integers in the data source, but the report parameter that is associated with this field can be of string type.

3 Choose OK.

The parameter appears under Report Parameters in Data Explorer.

Inserting a parameter marker in the SQL query

After creating a report parameter, insert a parameter marker in the WHERE clause of the SQL query of the data set. The parameter marker, represented by a question mark (?), indicates where you want BIRT to insert the parameter value.

For example, to ask the user to specify the threshold inventory quantity for a restocking report, insert the ? parameter marker in the WHERE clause, as shown in the following example:

```
WHERE quantityinstock < ?
```

When the report runs, if the user specifies 500 for quantityinstock, BIRT replaces ? with 500 and sends the following filter condition to the data source:

```
WHERE quantityinstock < 500
```

If you write a filter condition that uses more than one field, consider the interaction of the field values. Each of the following WHERE clauses, for example, returns a different set of rows:

```
WHERE quantityinstock < ? AND productvendor = ?
```

```
WHERE quantityinstock < ? OR productvendor = ?
```

The first clause returns only those rows in which both the quantityinstock and the productvendor values match the values that replace the ? markers. The second clause returns more rows. It returns rows in which the quantityinstock value is less than the value that replaces the quantityinstock ? marker and rows in which the productvendor value matches the value that replaces the productvendor ? marker.

Before completing all of the steps to enable filtering, test the filter conditions by specifying actual values in the WHERE clause to verify that the results meet your expectations.

SQL supports many options and operators for specifying filter conditions. For complete information about writing WHERE clauses and SQL statements in general, consult a book about SQL.

How to insert a parameter marker in the SQL query

This procedure assumes that you already created a data set.

1 In Data Explorer, right-click the data set for which you want to edit the query, then choose Edit. Edit Data Set displays the query.

2 Add a WHERE clause with one or more parameters, as shown in the following examples:

```
WHERE quantityinstock < ?
```

```
WHERE quantityinstock <= ? AND productvendor = ?
```

```
WHERE quantityinstock <= ? OR productline LIKE ?
```

Figure 15-3 shows an example of a query with two parameter markers.

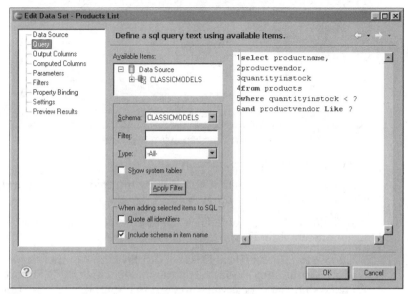

Figure 15-3 Query with two parameter markers

At this point, you are ready to define a data set parameter for each
? parameter marker. The next section describes this task.

Defining a data set parameter and binding it to the report parameter

A data set parameter passes a value that replaces the ? parameter marker in
the WHERE clause of the query when the query is run. You must define one
data set parameter for each parameter marker in the query's WHERE clause.
If you do not, BIRT displays an error.

The order of the data set parameters is critical. SQL uses the positions of the
? parameter markers in the WHERE clause to determine which data set
parameter matches which ? marker. For example, you must define two data
set parameters if you specify the following WHERE clause:

```
WHERE quantityinstock < ? and productvendor LIKE ?
```

The first data set parameter must pass a value to quantityinstock < ?, and the
second parameter must pass a value to productvendor LIKE ?. In Figure 15-4,
the order of these parameters matches the order of the parameter markers in
the example WHERE clause.

If you change the WHERE clause, you must update the data set parameters
accordingly. For example, if you change the order of the parameter markers
in the WHERE clause, you must change the order of the data set parameters.
If you remove a parameter marker, you must delete the corresponding data
set parameter.

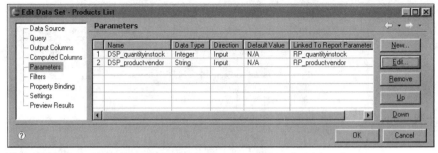

Figure 15-4 Edit Data Set displaying two data set parameters

How to define a data set parameter

This procedure assumes that you already inserted a parameter marker in the SQL query, as described previously.

1 In Data Explorer, double-click the data set for which you want to create parameters. Edit Data Set displays the query.

2 Choose Parameters. Edit Data Set displays the Parameters page. This page displays placeholder data set parameters, which BIRT Report Designer creates for each ? parameter marker in the WHERE clause of the query.

3 Edit each data set parameter. Select a parameter and choose Edit.

4 In Edit Parameter, specify the following information:

   1 In Name, type a name for the data set parameter. It is good practice to use a prefix, such as DSP, to differentiate the data set parameter from other parameter types, such as report parameters.

   2 In Data type, select a data type for the parameter.

   3 In Direction, choose Input. This value means that the parameter is an input parameter.

   4 In Linked To Report Parameter, select the report parameter to bind to this data set parameter.

   Figure 15-5 shows an example of a data set parameter definition where the data set parameter, DSP_quantityinstock, is linked to a report parameter, RP_quantityinstock.

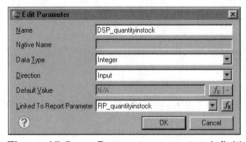

Figure 15-5 Data set parameter definition

5 Choose OK.

5 Repeat steps 3 and 4 to define additional data set parameters for any other parameter markers in the SQL query.

6 To save the changes to the data set, choose OK.

7 Test the parameters to verify that the query is updated with user-specified values and that the report shows the results you expect.

1 Choose Preview.

2 If Enter Parameters does not appear, choose Refresh Report.

Enter Parameters displays all the report parameters you created. Figure 15-6 shows example report parameters, RP_quantityinstock and RP_productvendor. The parameter names appear because values were not supplied for the Prompt text property.

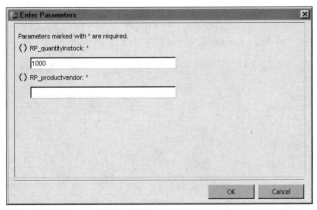

Figure 15-6   Enter Parameters

3 Specify a value for each parameter, then choose OK.

If you completed all the tasks that were described earlier in this chapter, the WHERE clause of the query incorporates the specified values, and the report displays the rows that match the WHERE clause.

Creating a SQL query at run time

The previous sections described how to create a report parameter and a data set parameter. The sections also described how to bind both types of parameters to replace a ? marker in the WHERE clause of a SQL query with a report parameter value. This technique works well when the WHERE clause uses a filter condition that substitutes one value for each ? marker.

You cannot, however, use this technique for a WHERE clause that uses a membership filter condition, as shown in the following example:

```
WHERE city IN ('San Francisco', 'San Jose', 'Los Angeles')
```

The following WHERE clause accepts only one value to replace the ? marker:

```
WHERE city IN (?)
```

For cases such as this, where you need to update a WHERE clause with multiple report parameter values for a single ? marker, use the data set's property binding feature to update the entire query at run time.

How to update a query at run time

1 In the Query page of a data set, write a SQL query, such as:

```
SELECT CustomerName FROM customers
```

2 Create three report parameters, for example, City1, City2, and City3.

3 In Edit Data Set, choose Property Binding, and write the following query text to use the values from the three report parameters, as shown in Figure 15-7:

```
"SELECT CustomerName from customers where customers.City IN ( "
   +  "'" + params["City1"] + "' , '" + params["City2"] +
"' , '" + params["City3"] + "' )"
```

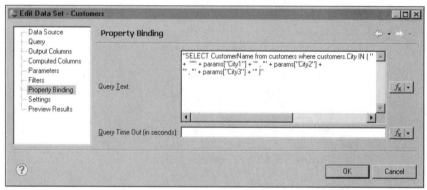

Figure 15-7   Property Binding showing the dynamic query

The query you specify in Property Binding replaces the query you specified on the Query page.

4 Choose OK to save the changes to the data set.

Enabling user filtering after data retrieval

This option is available for all data sources, including JDBC, XML, and text file, but filtering at query run time using data set parameters is the preferred approach for JDBC for performance reasons.

Though the goal in enabling users to filter at query run time and after BIRT retrieves the data is the same, the steps are different. To enable users to filter after data retrieval, complete the following tasks in the recommended order.

For detailed information about these tasks, see the corresponding topics later in this section.

- Create report parameters to prompt a user to specify field values that determine what data to display.

- Create one filter condition for each field for which you want the user to supply a value. Set the value of each filter condition to a report parameter to dynamically update the filter condition with the parameter value.

- Determine how to present the report parameters.

- Test the report parameters.

Creating a report parameter

The procedure for creating a report parameter is the same whether enabling user filtering at query run time or after data retrieval. Follow the steps described earlier in this chapter.

Updating a filter condition when the report runs

Typically, when you specify a filter condition to display only certain data in a report, you specify the value on which to search, as in these examples:

```
row["quantityinstock"] Less than 500
row["productvendor"] Equal to "Exoto Designs"
```

To enable a user to filter data when the report runs, specify the report parameter value as the filter value. The following expressions are examples of filter conditions for which values are set to report parameter values:

```
row["quantityinstock"] Less than
    params["RP_quantityinstock"].value
```

```
row["productvendor"] Equal to params["RP_productvendor"].value
```

When the user runs the report and supplies a value for the report parameter, BIRT dynamically updates the filter condition with the parameter value and generates a report that displays only the specified data.

How to update a filter condition dynamically when the report runs

This procedure assumes that you already created a report design that contains a table or list to display data from a data set and uses one or more report parameters. This procedure uses the parameter to filter the values that the table displays.

1 In the layout editor, select the table element or list element to filter.

2 In Property Editor, choose the Filters tab.

3 Choose Add to create a new filter condition.

4 In New Filter Condition, specify the filter condition.

1 In the first field, select a field from the drop-down list. Alternatively, open the expression builder to create a more complex expression.

2 In the second field, select an operator from the drop-down list.

3 In the third field, specify the name of the report parameter that you created. You can use the expression builder to select the report parameter from the list of report parameters in the report design, as shown in Figure 15-8.

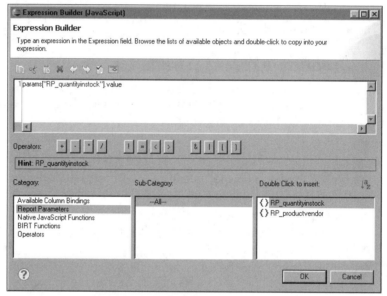

Figure 15-8   Using the expression builder to select a report parameter

Choose OK to apply the expression to the filter condition. New Filter Condition displays the completed filter condition, as shown in Figure 15-9.

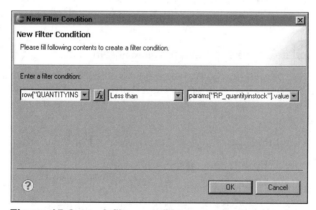

Figure 15-9   A filter condition

4 Choose OK to save the filter condition.

The filter condition appears on the Filters page in Property Editor, as shown in Figure 15-10.

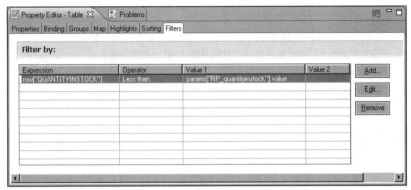

Figure 15-10   Filter condition set to a report parameter

5 Preview the report.

Enter Parameters appears and displays the report parameters that you created. Figure 15-11 shows an example.

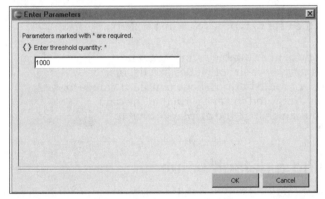

Figure 15-11   Enter Parameters showing a report parameter

6 Specify values for the report parameters, then choose OK.

The report displays data that matches the values that you specified.

Designing the presentation of report parameters

After verifying that the report parameters generate the report that you expect, focus on the presentation of the parameter information. You can make the parameters more user-friendly by setting their display properties. Table 15-1 lists the ways in which you can enhance the usability and appearance of report parameters. Details about each technique are presented in subsequent sections.

Table 15-1   Techniques for enhancing report parameter usability

To apply this technique	Use this property
Use a prompt that describes clearly what value a user enters. For example, display text, such as: `Enter the state's abbreviation`	Prompt text
Provide a default value that generates a well-presented report in the event that a user does not supply a value. A default value also functions as an example.	Default value
Provide helpful information about a report parameter. A user sees this information when he hovers the mouse over the parameter. For example, for a customer ID parameter, provide information, such as: `Type a number between 100 and 500`	Help text
Create a list box, a combo box, or a set of radio buttons that display values for the user to select, instead of requiring the user to type a value in a text box.	Display type
Display values in a suitable format if a report parameter displays a list of values in a list box, a combo box, or radio buttons. For example, if values for sales totals are stored in #### format in the data source, you can change the display format to $#,###.00.	Format As

Providing a default value

BIRT does not require you to specify a default value for each report parameter. Typically, however, you should provide one. If you do not, the user must specify a value to generate the report. It is particularly important to specify a default value if you present the report parameter as a text box in which the user has to type a value, rather than a list box from which the user selects a value.

The default value can be any value from the data set field that is bound to the report parameter. You should, however, specify a value that most users would select, such as Active for an account status. Another option is to specify a value that appears most often. If the field contains unique values, such as an order ID or a customer ID, it is typical to specify the first ID as the default value, particularly when using a list box or combo box to display a list of values.

When setting the default value, you can type a literal value or write an expression. For example, to display the current date as the default value for a date parameter, use the expression new Date( ).

How to provide a default value for a report parameter

This procedure assumes that you already created a report parameter.

1   In Data Explorer, expand Report Parameters, then double-click the report parameter to edit.

    Edit Parameter displays the current property settings for the selected report parameter. Figure 15-12 shows an example of a report parameter with no value specified for Default value.

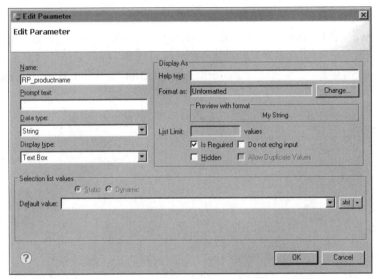

Figure 15-12   Property settings for a report parameter

2   Depending on the display type that you select, complete one of these tasks:

    ■   If the display type is text box, in Default value, type a value or an expression. To type a value, choose the Constant button. To create an expression, choose the expression builder button.

    ■   For all other display types, specify a list of values to display, then select one value as the default value.

3   Choose OK.

Providing the user with a list of values

List boxes, combo boxes, and radio buttons are ideal mechanisms for providing a list of values to a user. The differences between these user interface elements are as follows:

- Radio buttons occupy as many lines in the Enter Parameters dialog as there are values. For ease of use, a set of radio buttons should contain fewer than 10 entries.

- The list box and combo box appear similar to the user. Both save space in the Enter Parameters dialog. The list box takes up only one line, and the combo box takes up two lines in Enter Parameters. For ease of use, a list box or combo box should contain fewer than 100 values.

- In addition to presenting a list of values, the combo box also supports the user typing a value. This feature is useful for supplying a string pattern. For example, instead of selecting a specific name for a customer name parameter, the user can type M% to get all customers whose names start with M. This technique assumes that the user is familiar with SQL pattern-matching syntax.

- The list box supports the selection of multiple values. The combo box and radio buttons support the selection of only one value.

Figure 15-13 shows an example of an Enter Parameters dialog that displays a list box, combo box, and radio buttons.

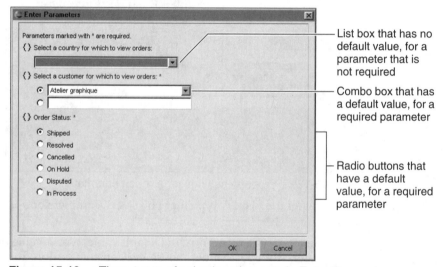

Figure 15-13   Three types of selection elements in Enter Parameters

You can create two kinds of lists: static and dynamic.

- In a static list of values, you specify the values to display to the report user during report design. Creating a static list provides more control over the list of values. For example, you might want to present only certain values to the user, or localize the values. If you create a static list of values, however, you have to update the list manually to match the values in the data source.

- In a dynamic list of values, BIRT retrieves the values from the data source when the report runs. Create a dynamic list for values that are frequently updated in the data source, such as new customer names, product names, or order numbers.

For a list box or a combo box, you can create either a static or a dynamic list of values. For a set of radio buttons, you can only create a static list.

Creating a static list of values

To create a static list of values for a list box, combo box, or a set of radio buttons, use one or both of the following techniques:

- Import values from a data set field.

- Type each value to display.

To display all the unique values in a data set field, which is the typical case, import the values from the data set field. You can type the values, but this task would be tedious. Type a value only to display a value that is not in the data set field, such as ranges of values (0–100, 101–200, and so on).

To import all values from a data set field, first create a data set that retrieves the values. The query in the following example retrieves the unique values from the country field in the Customers table. You would specify this simple query to populate a parameter list with all the country names.

```
SELECT DISTINCT country
FROM Customers
```

Sometimes the values in a data set field are not in a suitable form or descriptive enough for report users. For example, the values in a territory field might use abbreviations, such as NA, EMEA, or APAC. For such cases, it is preferable to display the full names to the user. You do so by providing alternate values in the Display Text property.

If you are creating a report to be viewed in multiple locales, you can localize each parameter value by providing a resource key in the Display Text Key property. A resource key is a text string in an external source that is translated, or localized, into different languages. For more information about resource keys and localization, see Chapter 25, "Localizing Text."

How to specify static report parameter values

This procedure assumes that you already created a report parameter.

1 In Data Explorer, expand Report Parameters, then double-click the report parameter to edit.

   Edit Parameter displays the property settings for the report parameter.

2 For Display type, choose Combo Box, List Box, or Radio Button.

   Edit Parameter displays the Selection list values table and the Import Values button, as shown in Figure 15-14. The Selection list values table is where you specify the values to display in the list box, combo box, or radio buttons.

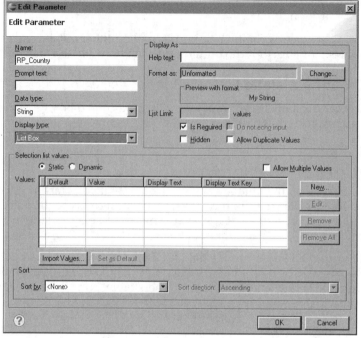

Figure 15-14　Selection values table and Import Values button in Edit Parameter

3　In Selection list values, use the default value, Static.

4　To import values from a data set field, perform the following tasks:

　1　Choose Import Values. Import Values displays the first data set in the report and the values of the first field in the data set, as shown in Figure 15-15.

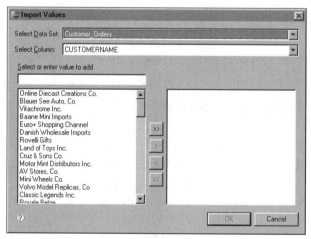

Figure 15-15　Import Values

2   In Select Data Set, choose the data set that returns the field values to display in the list box, combo box, or radio buttons. Typically, this data set is one that you create specifically to populate the parameter's list of values.

3   In Select Column, choose the field that contains the values to use.

4   Select the values to import.

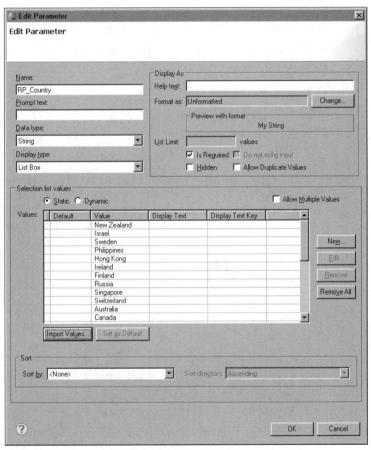

   ❏   To import all values, choose the double right arrow (>>) button.

   ❏   To import a particular value, select the value, and choose the right arrow (>) button.

   Choose OK. Edit Parameter displays the imported values in the Selection list values table, as shown in Figure 15-16.

Figure 15-16   Imported values in Edit Parameter

5   To provide descriptive labels for users to choose, other than the value in Value, perform the following steps:

1 Double-click the item in the Selection list values table.

2 In Edit Selection Choice, in Display Text, type the text that you want to display to the user. Figure 15-17 shows an example of displaying United Kingdom for the value, UK.

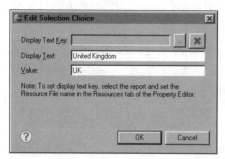

Figure 15-17 Specifying the text to display

3 Choose OK to save the change. The Selection values table displays the updated value.

6 To add values manually, complete the following steps for each value:

1 Next to the Selection list values table, choose New.

2 In New Selection Choice:

    1 In Display Text, type the text prompt to display to the user.

    2 In Value, type the value to pass to the SQL query or the filter condition. Figure 15-18 shows an example of a user-defined value that appears as All Customers on the Enter Parameter dialog when the user runs the report. When the user selects this value, % is passed to the SQL query.

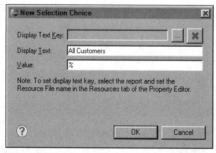

Figure 15-18 Creating a new value

3 Choose OK. The new value is added to the Selection list values table.

7 To designate a value as the default value, select the value, then choose Set as Default.

8 To specify how the values should be sorted when presented to the user:

1 Under Sort, in Sort by, select one of the following values:

- ❏ Select None, the default, to display the values in natural order, which is the order of items in the Value column of the Selection list values table.

- ❏ Select Display Text to display in ascending or descending order the values in the Display Text column.

- ❏ Select Value Column to display in ascending or descending order the values in the Value column.

2 In Sort direction, select either Ascending or Descending.

9 Choose OK to save your changes to the report parameter.

Creating a dynamic list of values

You can create a dynamic list of values for a list box or a combo box. First, create a data set that retrieves the values with which to populate the list. The query in the following example retrieves all the unique values from the customername field in the Customers table. Specify this simple query in a data set to populate a parameter list with all the customer names.

```
SELECT DISTINCT customername
FROM Customers
```

For a report design using dynamic lists, BIRT retrieves values from the data source when the report runs. You cannot predict during the design process how many values the list box or combo box displays when the user runs the report. If you are concerned about the list getting too long, specify a maximum number of values to display. This solution, however, is not practical because the list displays the first value up to the specified maximum number, and omits the rest of the values.

You can display alternate values if you do not want to display the actual field values. You cannot, however, specify an alternate display value for each individual value because you do not know at design time the precise list of values. Instead, you specify an expression that applies to all the values. For example, you can prepend values with static text by using an expression, such as:

```
"Order " + dataSetRow["Ordernumber"]
```

How to specify dynamic report parameter values

This procedure assumes that you already created a report parameter.

1 In Data Explorer, expand Report Parameters, then choose the report parameter to edit. Edit Parameter displays the property settings for the report parameter.

2 In Display type, choose Combo Box or List Box.

3 In Selection list values, choose Dynamic. Edit Parameter displays additional fields, as shown in Figure 15-19.

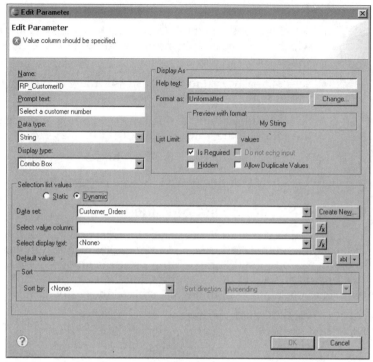

Figure 15-19 Dynamic parameter options in Edit Parameter

4 In Data set, choose the data set that returns the field values to display in the list box or combo box.

5 In Select value column, select the field that contains the values to pass to the SQL query or filter condition at run time.

6 Optionally, in Select display text, select a field that contains the values that you want to display to the user. For example, the values to pass to the SQL query or filter condition are from the customernumber field, but you want to display values from the customername field to the user. You can also use the expression builder to specify an expression to display custom values. The following example shows how to use an expression to combine values from two fields:

```
dataSetRow["ORDERNUMBER"] + "--" + dataSetRow["CUSTOMERNAME"]
```

From this expression, BIRT provides meaningful values to the user, such as:

```
10100--Online Diecast Creations, Co.
10101--Blauer See Auto, Co.
```

7 Optionally, in Default value, select a value to use as the default.

8 Optionally, in List Limit, specify the maximum number of values to display.

9 Choose OK to save your changes to the report parameter.

Enabling the user to select multiple values

You can provide the user with the option of selecting one value, multiple values, or all the values in a list. To provide this option, you must select the list box as the parameter display type and create a BIRT filter that uses the report parameter values.

How to enable the selection of multiple values

This procedure assumes that you already created a report parameter.

1 In Data Explorer, expand Report Parameters, then choose the parameter to edit.

2 In Edit Parameter, in Display type, choose List Box.

3 Create a static or dynamic list of values, using the steps provided in the previous sections.

4 Select Allow Multiple Values.

5 Choose OK to save your changes to the report parameter.

6 Create a filter at the data set, table, or list level. To define the filter condition:

- Select the field to filter.

- Select the In operator.

- Specify the report parameter as the filter value.

Figure 15-20 shows an example of a filter condition that returns data rows where the PRODUCTVENDOR field contains the value or values in the RP_productvendor report parameter.

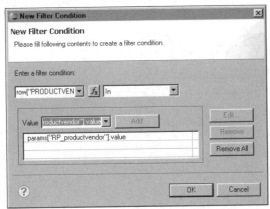

Figure 15-20   A filter condition that uses report parameter values

Formatting report parameter values

By default, the default values that you specify and the values that you import to display in a list box, combo box, or radio buttons appear exactly as they are stored in the data source. Sometimes, the values are not in a format that is appropriate for display. For example, US telephone numbers might be stored in ########## format. It is preferable to display these values in another format, such as (###) ###-####.

To specify a different format, use the Format As property. Format a report parameter value in the same way that you format a value that a data element displays. Either select from a list of common formats, or specify a custom format pattern.

Note that you can reformat values for display purposes only. You cannot use the Format As property to require a user to type values in a particular format. In addition, the property setting does not affect the format of the data in the report.

How to format a report parameter value

This procedure assumes that you already created a report parameter.

1 In Data Explorer, expand Report Parameters, then choose the report parameter to edit. Edit Parameter displays the current property settings.

2 In Format as, choose Change. Change is not available for report parameters of Boolean type.

3 In Format Builder, specify the format to use.

   1 In Format as, choose one of the predefined formats, or choose Custom to define your own format pattern. Additional fields appear, depending on the data type of the parameter and the format that you selected. A sample formatted value appears in Preview with format. Figure 15-21 shows the additional fields that are available for a report parameter of float type when Currency format is selected.

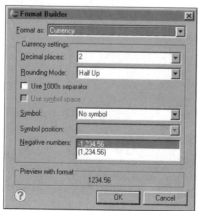

Figure 15-21   Format Builder for currency data

2 Type or select values for any additional fields that are available for that parameter data type and format.

3 When you finish specifying the format, choose OK.

Enabling the user to specify null or blank values

You can provide users who are database-savvy with the option of selecting rows when a field has a null value. Databases use a null value to indicate that there is no data in that field. A user might find it useful, for example, to view customer data where a customer's credit-limit field is null, because null in this field means that the customer account is new, and a credit limit has not been set. For string data, a null value is not the same as a blank value or an empty string (" "), which is an actual value. Blank values apply to string fields only. Null values apply to all data types.

You can create a report parameter that provides users the option to match null and blank values. Figure 15-22 shows Enter Parameters displaying two parameters that provide the null and blank value options. The Threshold Quantity parameter uses a text box, and the Product Vendor parameter uses a list box. To specify a null value for the first parameter, the user selects Null Value. To specify a blank value for the second parameter, the user selects the empty item at the top of the list.

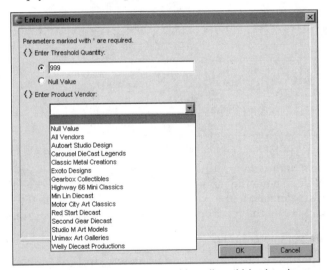

Figure 15-22   Parameters with null and blank values

How to enable a user to specify a null or blank value

This procedure assumes that you already created a report parameter.

1 In Data Explorer, expand Report Parameters, then choose the parameter to edit.

2 In Edit Parameter, in Display type, select Text Box, List Box, Combo Box.

3 To enable a user to specify a null or blank value for the report parameter, deselect Is Required.

Organizing report parameters in groups

If you create many parameters or want to provide the user with a prompt for certain sets of parameters, use parameter groups to organize report parameters. For example, you could create a parameter group to contain the report parameters for a specific table or data set.

When prompting the user to supply parameter values, the Enter Parameters dialog displays the parameter group name and the parameters within that group. Figure 15-23 shows two parameter groups, Office Information and Product Information. Each group contains multiple report parameters.

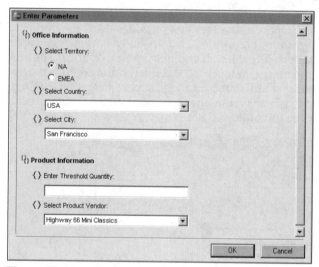

Figure 15-23   Parameter groups with multiple parameters in each group

You can create a parameter group before or after creating the report parameters. If you create the report parameters first, you can drag them from the report parameters list to the parameter group. If you create the parameter group first, you create the report parameters in the parameter group.

How to create a parameter group

1 In Data Explorer, right-click Report Parameters, and choose New Parameter Group. New Parameter Group appears.

2 In Name, specify a unique name for this parameter group.

3 In Display Name, specify the name that the Enter Parameters dialog displays when it prompts a user for parameter values.

Figure 15-24 shows an example.

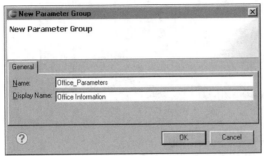

Figure 15-24   Create a display name for a parameter group

4 Choose OK. BIRT Report Designer creates the new parameter group and displays it in Report Parameters in Data Explorer, as shown in Figure 15-25.

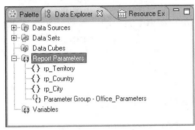

Figure 15-25   New parameter group in Data Explorer

5 Add report parameters to the parameter group in one of two ways:

- Move an existing parameter to the parameter group. From the report parameters list in Data Explorer, drag an existing parameter, and drop it in the parameter group.

- Create a new parameter in the parameter group. In Report Parameters, right-click the parameter group name, and choose New Parameter.

Figure 15-26 shows three report parameters in a parameter group called Office_Parameters.

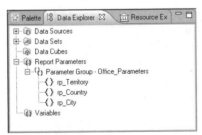

Figure 15-26   Parameter group containing three parameters

Figure 15-27 shows the Enter Parameters dialog, which displays the new parameter group and its three report parameters.

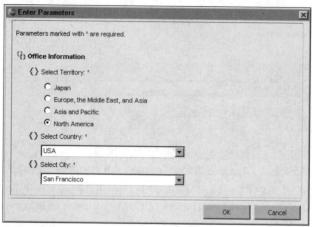

Figure 15-27   Office Information parameter group in Enter Parameters

Enter Parameters displays parameter groups and report parameters in the order in which they appear in the report parameters list. To display the groups or report parameters in a different order, change the order in Data Explorer.

Creating cascading report parameters

Cascading parameters are report parameters that have a hierarchical relationship, as shown in the following three examples:

```
Product Type        Territory          Mutual Fund Type
   Product          Country               Fund Class
                      City                   Fund
```

In a group of cascading parameters, each report parameter displays a set of values. When the report user selects a value from the top-level parameter, the selected value determines the values that the next parameter displays, and so on.

The advantages of cascading parameters are obvious in comparison with the alternative technique, which is the creation of separate and independent parameters. Consider the Territory-Country-City example. If you create three separate parameters, the territory parameter displays a list of all territories, the country parameter displays all countries, and the city parameter displays all cities. Figure 15-28 shows independent parameters as they appear to the report user.

The user has to traverse three long lists to select the values, and there is a potential for user errors. The user can inadvertently select invalid combinations, such as Japan, USA, Paris.

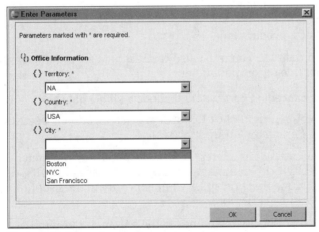

Figure 15-28   Independent parameters

Cascading parameters, on the other hand, display only relevant values based on user selections. For example, the territory parameter displays all the territories, and when the report runs, the user selects a territory, such as NA (North America), then the country parameter displays only countries in the sales territory of North America. Similarly, when the user selects USA, the city parameter displays only cities in the USA. Figure 15-29 shows cascading parameters as they appear to the report user.

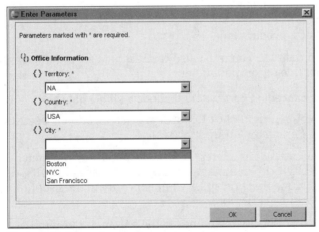

Figure 15-29   Cascading parameters

Before creating cascading report parameters, you must first create the data set or data sets that return the values to display in the cascading parameter lists. The query in the following example retrieves all the values from the territory, country, and city fields of the Offices table. Specify this query in a data set used to populate the Territory-Country-City parameter lists.

```
SELECT Offices.territory,
Offices.country,
Offices.city
FROM Offices
```

In this example, the Territory-Country-City cascading parameter uses a single data set to populate all the parameter lists because the fields are in the same table. If, however, the fields are in different tables or different data sources, you can create multiple data sets, where each data set provides the values for each report parameter in the cascading parameter group. When creating multiple data sets for cascading parameters, you must link the data sets through a common field to create the appropriate dependency relationships.

For example, the data set for the top-level report parameter contains the following query to retrieve all the values from the productline field in the Productlines table:

```
SELECT Productlines.productline
FROM Productlines
```

The data set for the second report parameter contains the following query to retrieve the values from the productname field in the Products table. The product name values to get depend on the product line value that the user selects at run time. The WHERE clause gets the value of the product line value at run time.

```
SELECT Products.productname
FROM Products
WHERE Products.productline = ?
```

In this second data set, you must also create a data set parameter and bind it to the product line report parameter.

How to create cascading parameters that use a single data set

1 In Data Explorer, right-click Report Parameters, and choose New Cascading Parameter Group.

2 In New Cascading Parameter Group, in Cascading Parameter Group Name, specify a different name if you do not want to use the default name. The name that you specify appears only in the list of report parameters in Data Explorer.

3 In Prompt text, specify the name for the parameter group that appears in the Enter Parameters dialog.

4 Select Single Data Set.

5 Create the report parameters for this group of cascading parameters.

   1 In Parameters, choose Add. In Add Cascading Parameter Group, specify the following values:

      ❑ In Name, type the parameter name.

❑ In Data Set, select the data set that returns the values to populate all the parameter lists.

❑ In Value, select the field that contains the values to pass to the SQL query or filter condition at run time.

❑ In Display Text, optionally select a field that contains the values that you want to display to the user. For example, the values to pass to the SQL query or filter condition are from the productcode field, but you want to display values from the productname field to the user.

❑ Choose OK.

2 In Properties, set the other properties for this report parameter, including the prompt text, display type, and default value.

3 To create the next report parameter, choose Add, and follow the same steps to set up all levels of the cascading parameter group. Figure 15-30 shows sample values in New Cascading Parameter Group.

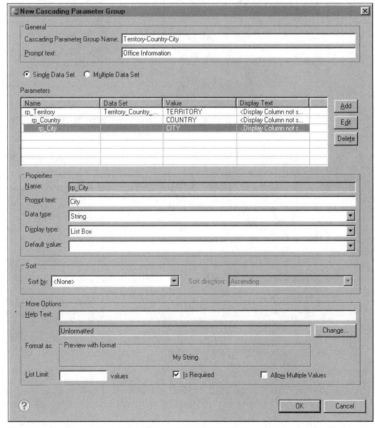

Figure 15-30   A cascading parameter that uses a single data set

6 When you finish creating all the report parameters in the group, choose OK. The cascading parameters appear in Report Parameters in Data Explorer.

How to create cascading parameters that use multiple data sets

This procedure assumes that you created all the data sets that return the values to display in the cascading parameter lists.

1 In Data Explorer, right-click Report Parameters, and choose New Cascading Parameter Group.

2 In New Cascading Parameter Group, in Cascading Parameter Group Name, you can specify a different name. The name that you specify appears only in the list of report parameters in Data Explorer.

3 In Prompt text, specify the name for the parameter group that appears in the Enter Parameters dialog.

4 Select Multiple Data Set.

5 Create the report parameters for this group of cascading parameters.

  1 In Parameters, choose Add. In Add Cascading Parameter Group, specify the following values:

  ❑ In Name, type the parameter name.

  ❑ In Data Set, select the data set that returns the values to populate the top-level parameter.

  ❑ In Value, select the field that contains the values to pass to the SQL query or filter condition at run time.

  ❑ In Display Text, optionally select a field that contains the values that you want to display to the user. For example, the values to pass to the SQL query or filter condition are from the productcode field, but you want to display values from the productname field to the user.

  ❑ Choose OK.

  2 In Properties, set the other properties for this report parameter, including the prompt text, display type, and default value.

  3 To create the next report parameter, choose Add, and follow the same steps to set up all the levels in the cascading parameter group.

6 When you finish creating all the report parameters in the group, choose OK. The cascading parameters appear under Report Parameters in Data Explorer.

7 Add data set parameters to the dependent data sets and bind them to the appropriate report parameters from the cascading parameter group.

1 In Data Explorer, right-click the data set that supplies the values for the second parameter in the cascading parameter group, then choose Edit. Edit Data Set displays the query.

2 Add a WHERE clause to the SQL query to filter the values of the data set based on the value of the top-level parameter. Figure 15-31 shows an example.

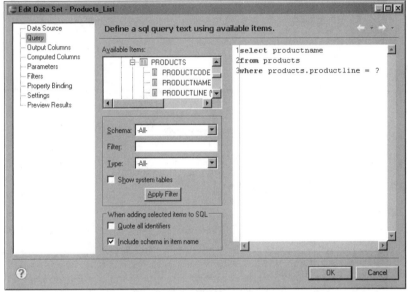

Figure 15-31 Query using WHERE clause to get a value at run time

3 Create a data set parameter to supply a value for the parameter marker in the SQL query.

   1 Choose Parameters.

   2 Select the placeholder data set parameter, then choose Edit.

   3 In Edit Parameter, specify a name for the data set parameter, and link it to the top-level report parameter, as shown in the example in Figure 15-32.

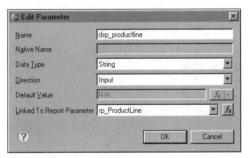

Figure 15-32 Linking a data set parameter to a report parameter

4 Choose OK to save the edits to the data set parameter.

4 In Edit Data Set, choose OK to save the changes to the data set.

5 Follow the same steps for subsequent data sets in the cascading parameter group to establish dependencies for all levels in the group.

Figure 15-33 shows an example of cascading parameters based on the product line and product data sets.

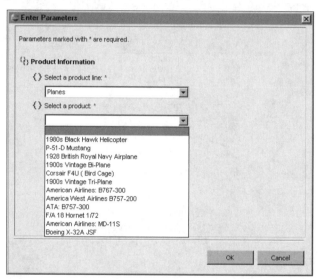

Figure 15-33 Selecting values for cascading parameters

Changing the order in which report parameters appear

By default, report parameter groups and report parameters are displayed to the user in the order in which they appear under Report Parameters in Data Explorer. The groups and parameters in the report parameters list, in turn, appear in the order in which you created them. You can change the order of groups and report parameters.

How to change the order in which report parameters appear

1 Choose Data Explorer.

2 Expand the report parameters list to display the list of parameter groups and report parameters.

3 Select a report parameter group or a report parameter, and drag it to a new position in the list.

Figure 15-34 shows an example of moving the rp_State report parameter to the top of the list.

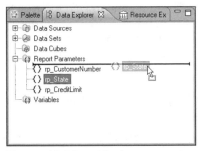

Figure 15-34   Moving a report parameter

4   Repeat the previous step to organize all the report parameter groups and report parameters in the desired order.

Testing the report parameters

It is important to test all the report parameters to verify that they work the way that you intend and that they meet user needs. Testing entails running the report, supplying different report parameter values, and checking the generated report carefully. Use the following guidelines:

- Test each report parameter as you create it.

  If you create many report parameters, it is best to test each parameter as you create it. If you wait until you create all the report parameters before you begin testing, it is much harder to debug errors in the output because it is not immediately clear which parameter causes the problem.

- Run the report without specifying any parameter values.

  The result of running a report without specifying any parameter values should be a report with information in it. If the OK button on the Enter Parameters dialog is unavailable, at least one report parameter that is currently empty requires the user to specify a value. Ensure that you provide a default value for each required parameter. A report parameter requires a value unless you deselect the Is Required option.

- Test each value in a list box, combo box, or series of radio buttons.

  If you manually created the values that these items display, rather than importing values from the data set field, test each value to confirm that the output is correct. If the report appears with no data, it means that no records matched the selection, which indicates one of three possibilities:

  - There are no rows that contain the selected value.

  - The value is not valid. For example, you might have created the value Closed for an order-status field, but the value in the data source is actually Shipped.

  - Another parameter causes the problem.

To debug the first two possibilities, review the data in the data source. Debugging the third possibility requires more effort if the report contains many other report parameters. As suggested earlier, you can avoid this situation if you always test parameters, one at a time, as you create them.

How to test report parameters

1 In the layout editor, choose Preview. Enter Parameters displays the report parameters that you created.

2 Specify a value for the report parameters. Choose OK. The report appears.

3 Review the report data carefully.

4 Test each report parameter with a different value by first choosing Show Report Parameters, then providing another value.

5 Repeat step 4 until you are certain that the report displays the correct data.

Tutorial 3: Creating and using report parameters

This tutorial provides instructions for building a report that lists products, their vendors, and quantities in stock. Rather than display all the products in stock, the report shows only products that need to be re-stocked. Because the number at which inventory is considered low can change with time, the report uses a report parameter that prompts the user to specify the minimum stock threshold when the user runs the report. The report also uses a report parameter that lets the user select a particular vendor or all vendors for the products that need re-stocking.

In this tutorial, you perform the following tasks:

- Create a new report.

- Build a data source.

- Build a data set.

- Lay out the data.

- Create a report parameter that prompts for a minimum product quantity.

- Create a report parameter that prompts for a vendor name.

- Edit the query.

- Create data set parameters and bind them to the report parameters.

- Test the report parameters.

- Provide the option to select all vendors.

- Create a title that uses the report parameter values.

Task 1: Create a new report

1 In Navigator, right-click the My Reports project you created in the first tutorial, then choose New→Report.

2 In New Report, type the following text as the file name:

Inventory.rptdesign

3 Choose Finish. The layout editor displays a blank report.

Task 2: Build a data source

Before you begin designing your report in the layout editor, create a data source to connect your report to the Classic Models sample database.

1 Choose Data Explorer.

2 Right-click Data Sources, and choose New Data Source from the context menu.

3 Select Classic Models Inc. Sample Database from the list of data sources. Use the default data source name, then choose Next. Connection information about the new data source appears.

4 Choose Finish. BIRT creates a new data source that connects to the sample database. It appears within Data Sources in Data Explorer.

Task 3: Build a data set

In this procedure, you build a data set to retrieve data from the Products table in the Classic Models database.

1 In Data Explorer, right-click Data Sets, and choose New Data Set.

2 In New Data Set, type the following text for Data Set Name:

Products

Use the default values for the other fields, then choose Next.

3 In Query, type the following query. Alternatively, drag the fields from the Products table, and drop them in the text area.

```
select productname,
productvendor,
quantityinstock
from Products
```

4 Choose Finish to save the data set. Edit Data Set displays the columns you specified in the query, and provides options for editing the data set.

5 Choose Preview Results to confirm that the query is valid and that it returns the correct data. You should see the results that appear in Figure 15-35.

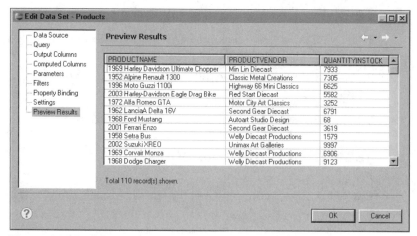

Figure 15-35   Data rows returned by the Products data set

6 Choose OK to save the data set.

Task 4: Lay out the data

In this procedure, you create a layout that displays the data in a simple row-and-column format.

1 Drag the Products data set from Data Explorer, and drop it in the layout editor. BIRT Report Designer creates a table that contains all the data set fields and corresponding labels, as shown in Figure 15-36.

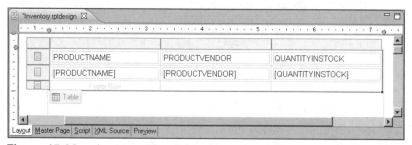

Figure 15-36   Layout editor displaying product data in a table

2 Edit and format the labels in the table's header row (the first row).

1 Double-click PRODUCTNAME. Change the text to:

```
Product Name
```

2 Press Enter to accept the change.

3 Similarly, edit the PRODUCTVENDOR and QUANTITYINSTOCK labels so that they appear as follows:

```
Vendor
Quantity In Stock
```

4 Select the row that contains those labels.

5 In Property Editor, in General properties:

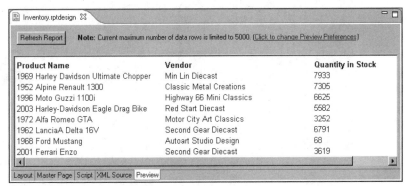

❏ Choose B to format all the label text as bold text.

❏ Choose the Left button to align the labels to the left.

3 Preview the report. It should look like the one shown in Figure 15-37.

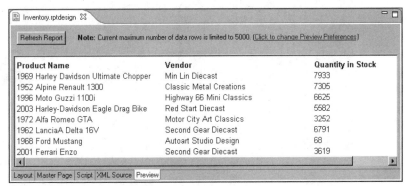

Figure 15-37 Report preview

Task 5: Create a report parameter that prompts for a minimum product quantity

In this procedure, you create a report parameter that prompts the user to specify a minimum quantity of stock. The report displays only rows where the quantity in stock is less than or equal to the user-specified value.

1 Choose Layout to resume editing the report.

2 In Data Explorer, right-click Report Parameters, then choose New Parameter.

3 Specify the following property values for the report parameter:

1 In Name, type the following text:

RP_quantityinstock

2 In Prompt text, type the following text:

Display products whose quantity in stock is less than or equal to this number

3 In Data type, select Integer.

4 In Display type, use the default, Text box.

5 In Default value, type the following amount:

1000

Figure 15-38 shows the complete parameter definition.

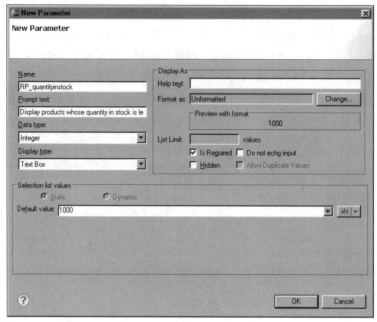

Figure 15-38   Properties for RP_quantityinstock report parameter

4 Choose OK to save the report parameter.

5 Preview the report. As shown in Figure 15-39, Enter Parameters appears, displaying the prompt text and the default parameter value that you specified when you created the report parameter.

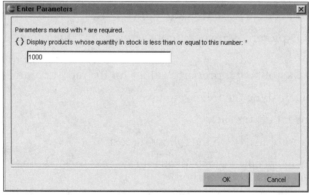

Figure 15-39   Enter Parameters displaying the RP_quantityinstock parameter

Choose OK. The report output shows all products. The report does not display only products with quantities less than or equal to 1000 because you have not yet bound the report parameter to the data set.

Task 6: Create a report parameter that prompts for a vendor name

In this procedure, you create a report parameter that prompts the user to select a particular vendor or all vendors for the products for which the quantity in stock matches the user-specified value.

1 Choose Layout to resume editing the report.

2 In Data Explorer, right-click Report Parameters, then choose New Parameter.

3 Specify the following property values for the report parameter:

1 In Name, type the following text:

    RP_productvendor

2 In Prompt text, type the following text:

    Display products for this vendor

3 In Data type, select String.

4 In Display type, select List Box.

In New Parameter, Selection list values displays options for providing a list of values to the user.

5 Under Selection list values, choose Dynamic.

This option creates a list of values dynamically. BIRT retrieves the values from the data source when the report runs. This technique ensures that the values displayed are always current.

Under Selection list values, Data Set displays Products, which is the only data set created for the report so far.

4 Create a new data set to retrieve the vendor names to display in the list box.

1 Choose Create New, next to the Data set field.

2 In New Data Set, in Data Set Name, type the following name:

    Vendors

Choose Next.

3 In Query, type the following query:

    select productvendor
    from Products

4 Choose Finish to save the data set. Edit Data Set displays the columns specified in the query, and provides options for editing the data set.

5 Choose Preview Results to confirm that the query is valid and that it returns the correct data. Figure 15-40 shows the rows returned by the query. Notice that some vendor names are listed multiple times.

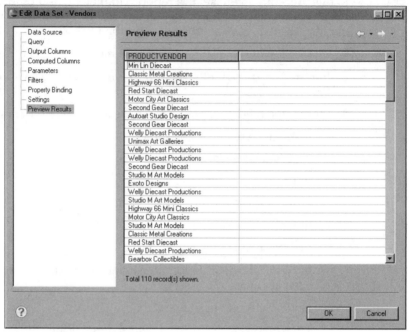

Figure 15-40 Data rows returned by the Vendors data set

6 Choose OK to save the data set.

5 Specify the values to display in the list box.

  1 In New Parameter, in Data set, select Vendors, the data set you created in the previous step.

  2 In Select value column, select PRODUCTVENDOR.

  3 In Select display text, select PRODUCTVENDOR.

6 Specify how the values should be sorted.

  1 Under Sort, in Sort by, select PRODUCTVENDOR.

  2 In Sort direction, select Ascending.

7 Ensure that Allow Duplicate Values is not selected. Remember that the Vendors data set returned some vendor names multiple times. Deselecting the Allow Duplicate Values option displays each name once in the list box.

Figure 15-41 shows the complete definition of the RP_productvendor report parameter.

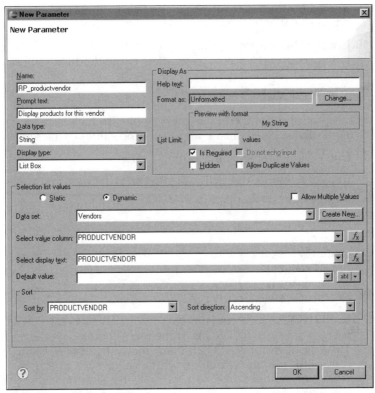

Figure 15-41 Complete definition of the RP_productvendor report parameter

8 Choose OK to save the report parameter.

9 Preview the report. Enter Parameters appears, as shown in Figure 15-42. The RP_productvendor parameter appears as a list box with the first value in the list selected by default.

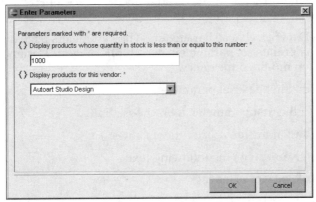

Figure 15-42 Enter Parameters displaying both report parameters

View the values in the list box. The values are sorted in ascending alphabetical order, and there are no duplicate values.

10 Choose OK. The report output still shows all products because you have not yet bound the report parameters to the Products data set.

Task 7: Edit the query

In this procedure, you edit the query in the Products data set so that it is dynamically updated at run time to use the values of the report parameters.

1 Choose Layout to resume editing the report.

2 In Data Explorer, right-click the Products data set, and choose Edit.

3 Edit the query to add a WHERE clause as follows:

```
select productname,
productvendor,
quantityinstock
from Products
where quantityinstock <= ?
and productvendor Like ?
```

The WHERE clause contains two parameter markers, ?, which indicate where you want BIRT to insert the report parameter values at run time. The Like operator is a SQL pattern-matching option. Using Like, you can replace the parameter marker with a value, such as A%, to return rows where the vendor name starts with A. In a later procedure, you see the flexibility of using the Like operator instead of the = operator.

Task 8: Create data set parameters and bind them to the report parameters

In this procedure, you define two data set parameters that correspond to the ? markers in the query. You then bind each data set parameter to the appropriate report parameter. At run time, the data set parameters get the values from the report parameters, and pass the values to the query.

1 In Edit Data Set, choose Parameters. The Parameters page displays two placeholder data set parameters, which BIRT Report Designer created when you modified the query.

2 Define the first data set parameter.

   1 Select the first parameter, then choose Edit.

   2 In Edit Parameter, specify these values:

     ❑ In Name, type the following text:

       `DSP_quantityinstock`

     ❑ In Data Type, select Integer.

▫ In Direction, select Input.

▫ In Linked to Report Parameter, select RP_quantityinstock. This option binds the data set parameter to the RP_quantityinstock report parameter.

Figure 15-43 shows the complete data set parameter definition.

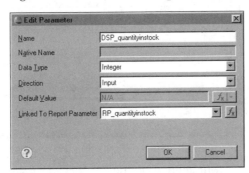

Figure 15-43   Definition of the first data set parameter

3 Choose OK to save the data set parameter. The Parameters page displays the edited data set parameter.

3 Define the second data set parameter.

1 Select the second parameter, then choose Edit.

2 In Edit Parameter, specify these values:

▫ In Name, type the following text:

DSP_productvendor

▫ In Data Type, select String.

▫ In Direction, select Input.

▫ In Linked to Report Parameter, select RP_productvendor.

Figure 15-44 shows the complete data set parameter definition.

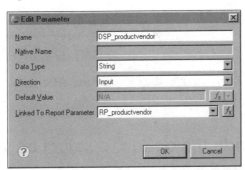

Figure 15-44   Definition of the second data set parameter

3 Choose OK to save the data set parameter.

The Parameters page, shown in Figure 15-45, displays the edited data set parameters.

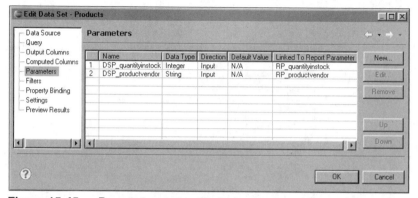

Figure 15-45 Parameters page displaying the two data set parameters

4 Choose OK to save your changes to the Products data set.

Task 9: Test the report parameters

In this procedure, you test that the query is updated with the report parameter values.

1 Choose Preview. In Enter Parameters, use the default values and choose OK. Figure 15-46 shows the report output.

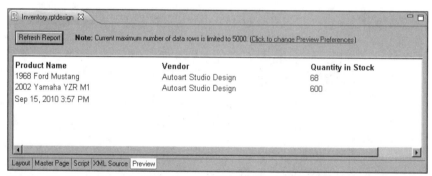

Figure 15-46 Report displays rows that match the default report parameter values

2 Choose Refresh Report to run the report using different parameter values. The report does not display any rows if none of the rows match the values you supply.

Task 10: Provide the option to select all vendors

The query and the design of the report parameters require the user to specify a minimum stock quantity and a specific vendor. The report displays only products meeting the specified minimum stock quantity and for the selected vendor. In this procedure, you provide the user with the option of selecting all vendors, so that the report displays all products—supplied by any vendor—that meet the specified minimum quantity. To provide this option, you modify the RP_productvendor report parameter to display an All Vendors value, and to send the appropriate value to the query.

1 Choose Layout to resume editing the report.

2 In Data Explorer, expand Report Parameters, right-click RP_productvendor, then choose Edit.

3 In Edit Parameter, under Selection list values, choose Static. This option supports creating user-defined values, whereas the dynamic option does not.

The properties under Selection list values change to reflect the change from dynamic to static values.

4 Specify the values to display in the list box.

   1 Choose Import Values. Import Values displays the first data set in the report, Products, and the values of the first field in the data set, PRODUCTNAME.

   2 In Select Data Set, select Vendors.

   3 In Select Column, select PRODUCTVENDOR. Import Values displays the values for the field.

   4 Choose >> to import all values from the field.

   Figure 15-47 shows the selections you make in Import Values.

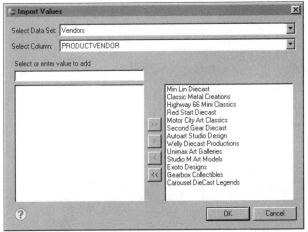

Figure 15-47   Import Values showing the data set field values to import

5 Choose OK. Edit Parameter displays the imported values in the Values table, as shown in Figure 15-48.

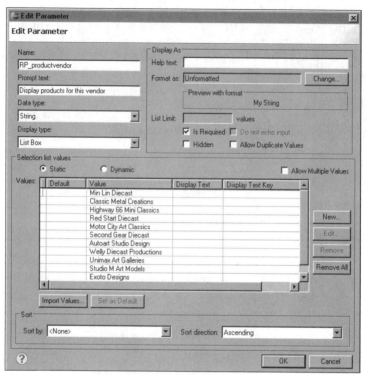

Figure 15-48 Edit Parameter displaying the values that appear in the list box

5 In Edit Parameter, add a new value to display in the list box.

1 Choose New next to the Values table.

2 In New Selection Choice:

❑ In Display Text, type the following text:

All Vendors

❑ In Value, type the following character:

%

Figure 15-49 shows the definition of the new value.

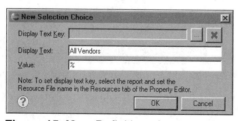

Figure 15-49 Definition of a new value

In SQL, % is a wildcard character that matches any sequence of characters. When the user selects All Vendors, the WHERE clause in the Products query is updated as follows:

```
WHERE ...
and productvendor Like %
```

This query returns all rows that have any productvendor value.

❑ Choose OK to save the new value definition.

In Edit Parameter, the new value appears at the bottom of the Values table.

6 Designate the new value as the default value.

1 In the Selection values table, scroll to the bottom of the list.

2 Select the % value.

3 Choose Set as Default.

7 Specify how the values should be sorted when presented to the user.

1 Under Sort, in Sort by, select Value Column. This sort displays All Vendors at the top of the list in the list box because the value % appears before A.

2 In Sort direction, select Ascending.

8 Choose OK to save your changes to the report parameter.

9 Test the report parameter.

1 Choose Preview. Enter Parameters appears, as shown in Figure 15-50. All Vendors is the first value in the list, and this value is selected by default.

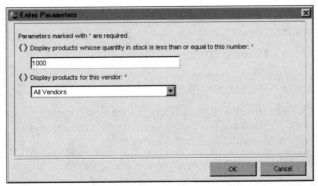

Figure 15-50   Enter Parameters displaying the updated vendor parameter

2 Provide values for the parameters.

□ For the first parameter, type the following number:

500

□ For the second parameter, use All Vendors.

Choose OK.

The generated report should look like the one shown in Figure 15-51. The report displays products, supplied by any vendor, where the quantity in stock is less than or equal to 500.

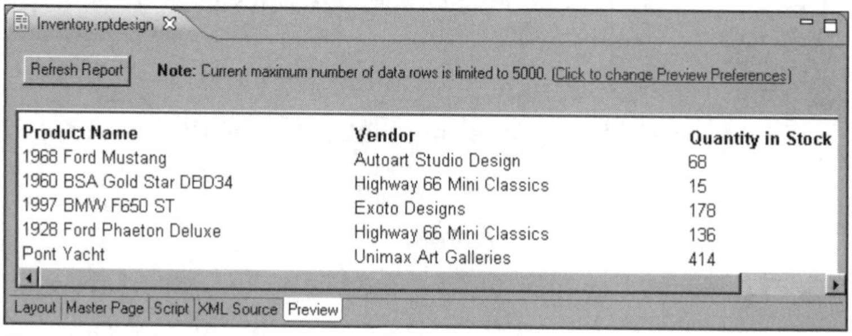

Figure 15-51 Report displays rows that match the specified report parameter values

Task 11: Create a title that uses the report parameter values

Report parameters can be used for purposes other than filtering data. In this procedure, you add a report title that displays a report parameter value.

1 Choose Layout to resume editing the report.

2 Insert a text element at the top of the report.

3 In Edit Text Item, in the field with the value Auto, select HTML from the drop-down list.

4 Type the following text:

```
Products with inventory less than
    <VALUE-OF>params["RP_quantityinstock"].value</VALUE-OF>
```

The <VALUE-OF> tag supports displaying a dynamic value. The expression params["RP_quantityinstock"].value refers to the value of the RP_quantityinstock report parameter.

5 Choose OK to save the edits to the text element.

6 Preview the report. Use the current parameter values.

The report title displays the following text:

```
Products with inventory less than 500
```

16

Building a Report That Contains Subreports

A report can contain multiple reports called subreports. A subreport is a report that appears inside another report. BIRT supports many ways of arranging subreports within a report, such as:

- Displaying multiple reports, one after another. For example, you can display the top ten customers, top ten sales managers, and top ten products.

- Displaying multiple reports next to one another. For example, you can display general employee information and employee salary history.

- Displaying one report within another. For example, you can display detailed mutual fund performance within general fund information.

BIRT also supports combining any of these configurations. Each subreport can access a different data source, use data from its own set of tables, and specify its own data selection criteria. Subreports can be linked to one another, meaning that the data of one report determines what data appears in the other. Alternatively, subreports can be independent of each other.

Always create, lay out, and test each subreport before creating the next one, and verify that the subreport displays the correct data. If you skip intermediate testing, it can be difficult, if you have problems, to determine which subreport causes an error.

Creating the report structure

This section describes some general principles and provides a few examples for organizing subreports in a report. The three report elements that you use to organize subreports are the table, list, and grid. Reports with complex layouts typically use all three of these container elements.

- The table iterates through the rows in a data set and displays the data in row and column format. For some reports, a subreport consists of data that is organized in a table.

- The list also iterates through the rows in a data set. The list, however, provides much greater flexibility for arranging data. A report that contains multiple linked subreports typically uses a list as the top-level container. Within the list, subreport data can be organized in tables.

- The grid is a static table that organizes elements in rows and columns. In a report that includes subreports, use a grid to align multiple tables horizontally or to add space between tables. For example, to display two subreports next to one another, create two tables to display the data for the subreports, then insert both tables in a grid to align the subreports.

Building a report with independent subreports

Figure 16-1 shows an example of a report that has four unlinked subreports. Each Top 10 subreport displays a different set of data. Each subreport is a table with data elements. The tables are arranged in a grid so that they appear side by side.

Top 10 Products	
1992 Ferrari 360 Spider red	$276,839.98
2001 Ferrari Enzo	$190,755.86
1952 Alpine Renault 1300	$190,017.96
2003 Harley-Davidson Eagle Drag Bike	$170,686.00
1968 Ford Mustang	$161,531.48
1969 Ford Falcon	$152,543.02
1980s Black Hawk Helicopter	$144,959.91
1998 Chrysler Plymouth Prowler	$142,530.63
1917 Grand Touring Sedan	$140,535.60
2002 Suzuki XREO	$135,767.03

Top 10 Sales Representatives	
Gerard Hernandez	$1,258,577.81
Leslie Jennings	$1,081,530.54
Pamela Castillo	$868,220.55
Larry Bott	$732,096.79
Barry Jones	$704,853.91
George Vanauf	$669,377.05
Peter Marsh	$584,593.76
Loui Bondur	$569,485.75
Andy Fixter	$562,582.59
Steve Patterson	$505,875.42

Top 10 Customers	
Euro+ Shopping Channel	$820,689.54
Mini Gifts Distributors Ltd.	$591,827.34
Australian Collectors, Co.	$180,585.07
Muscle Machine Inc	$177,913.95
La Rochelle Gifts	$158,573.12
Dragon Souveniers, Ltd.	$156,251.03
Down Under Souveniers, Inc	$154,622.08
Land of Toys Inc.	$149,085.15
AV Stores, Co.	$148,410.09
The Sharp Gifts Warehouse	$143,536.27

Top 10 Cities	
Madrid	$979,880.77
San Rafael	$591,827.34
NYC	$497,941.50
Auckland	$292,082.87
Singapore	$263,997.78
Paris	$240,649.68
San Francisco	$199,051.34
New Bedford	$190,500.01
Nantes	$180,887.48
Melbourne	$180,585.07

Figure 16-1   Unlinked subreports

Figure 16-2 shows the design for the report that appears in Figure 16-1.

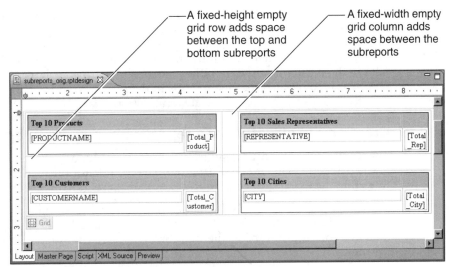

A fixed-height empty grid row adds space between the top and bottom subreports

A fixed-width empty grid column adds space between the subreports

Figure 16-2   Report design for unlinked subreports

Building a report with linked subreports

The preceding section described subreports that are not linked to each other. The subreports run independently and do not coordinate their data. Sometimes, however, you need to create reports that are linked to one another, such as a detailed customer-issues report in a customer report, or a list of top ten stocks in a fund report. Figure 16-3 shows these two example reports.

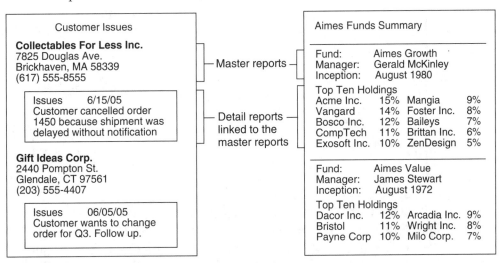

Figure 16-3   Two reports containing linked subreports

As each example report shows, one report is nested in another, creating a master report and detail report relationship. Each report accesses data from a different table or data source, and the reports are linked by a common field value, such as customer ID or mutual fund name. The value of the linking field in the master report determines the data that appears in the detail report. For example, if the customer ID in the master report is 112, the detail report displays the issues for the customer whose ID is 112.

Creating the structure of a report with linked subreports

The master-detail report examples in the previous section use the list element as the primary organizational structure. The list iterates through the data rows that the data set returns, and supports the structure of nested reports.

Within the list, a grid aligns the data in both reports. The data for the master report is placed in the grid in the detail area of the list. The grid aligns the data in a column, and the list iterates through the master report's data rows. The detail report uses a table to iterate through its data rows.

This structure assumes that the master and detail reports use different data sets and that each data set accesses data from a different table or data source. Figure 16-4 shows the report design for the Customer Issues master-detail report that appears in the previous section.

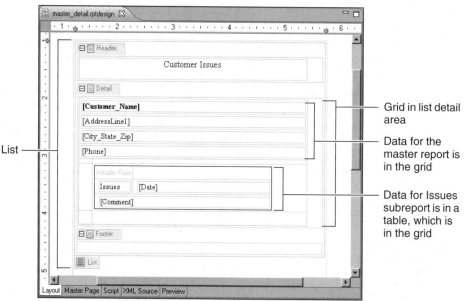

Figure 16-4   Report design for linked subreports using the list element

An alternate design technique is to use two tables, one nested in the other. Place data for the master report in the detail rows of the outer table. Place data for the detail report in a table, and place the table in the detail row of the outer table. Figure 16-5 shows this alternate report design.

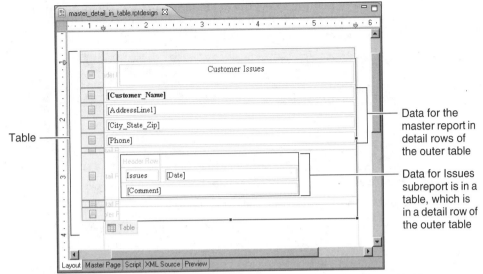

Figure 16-5   Report design for linked subreports using nested tables

Labels in figure:
- Table
- Data for the master report in detail rows of the outer table
- Data for Issues subreport is in a table, which is in a detail row of the outer table

Linking master and detail reports

Master and detail reports must be linked by a common field. In the customer-issue example report, the linking field is the customer ID. To link the reports, perform the following tasks:

1   For the detail report's data set, create a SELECT statement with a parameter marker in a WHERE clause. For example:

```
SELECT *
FROM issues
WHERE issues.customerNumber = ?
```

2   Create a data set parameter. Figure 16-6 shows the definition of a parameter in the data set that the detail report uses. Supply a specific value as the parameter's default value so that you can test the query.

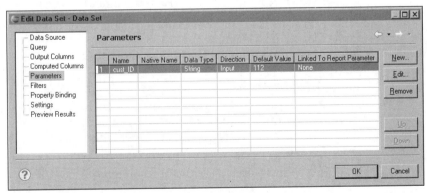

Figure 16-6   Data set parameter definition

3 In the layout editor, select the detail table, and use the property editor's Binding page to bind the detail report's data set parameter to the linking field in the master report. Figure 16-7 shows an example of this binding.

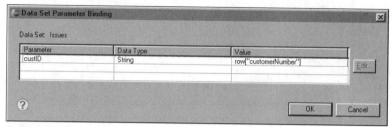

Figure 16-7   Data set parameter bound to the linking field

When the report runs, BIRT performs the following tasks:

- When the master report processes a customer row, it passes the customer number value to the data set parameter defined for the detail report.

- The data set parameter passes this customer number value to the detail report's query and dynamically updates the WHERE clause.

- The detail report displays the issues data for that customer number.

The previous steps repeat until the master report processes all its customer rows.

Tutorial 4: Building a report containing side-by-side subreports

This section provides step-by-step instructions for building a report that displays a list of customers. For each customer, the report displays order and payment information. The order information and payment information are in separate, adjacent subreports. The customer report is the master report, which is also called the outer report. The orders and payments subreports are the detail reports, which are also called the inner reports.

Each report accesses data from a different table in the sample database, Classic Models. The customer report, orders subreport, and payment subreport use data from the Customers, Orders, and Payments tables, respectively.

A common field, CUSTOMERNUMBER, links the reports. The value of the linking field in the master report determines what data appears in the detail reports. For example, if the customer number in the master report is 173, the detail reports display the order and payment information for the customer whose ID is 173.

Figure 16-8 shows a portion of the finished report.

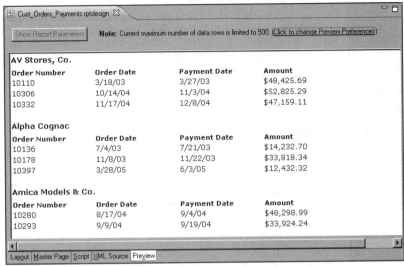

Figure 16-8 Customers master report including orders and payments subreports

In this tutorial, you perform the following tasks:

- Create a new report.
- Build a data source.
- Build a data set for the customer report.
- Build a data set for the orders subreport.
- Build a data set for the payments subreport.
- Create the customer master report.
- Create the orders subreport.
- Link the orders subreport to the customers master report.
- Create the payments subreport.
- Link the payments subreport to the customers master report.
- Display only customers that have orders or payments.
- Display the subreports next to one another.
- View the outline of the report.
- Format the report.

Task 1: Create a new report

If you are using BIRT Report Designer, this task assumes you have already created a project for your reports. If you are using BIRT RCP Report Designer, there is no requirement for a project.

1 Choose File→New→Report.

2 In New Report, select a project in which to store your report.

3 Type the following text as the file name:

Cust_Orders_Payments.rptdesign

4 Choose Finish. A blank report appears in the layout editor.

Task 2: Build a data source

Before you begin designing the report in the layout editor, you create a data source to connect the report to the Classic Models database.

1 Choose Data Explorer.

2 Right-click Data Sources, and choose New Data Source from the context menu.

3 Select Classic Models Inc. Sample Database from the list of data sources, use the default data source name, then choose Next. Connection information about the new data source appears.

4 Choose Finish. BIRT Report Designer creates a new data source that connects to the sample database. The new data source appears within Data Sources in Data Explorer.

Task 3: Build a data set for the customer report

In this procedure, you build a data set to indicate what data to retrieve from the Customers table. The customer report that you create later uses this data set.

1 In Data Explorer, right-click Data Sets, and choose New Data Set.

2 In New Data Set, type the following text for data set name:

Customers

Use the default values for the other fields.

- ▪ Data Source Selection shows the name of the data source that you created earlier.

- ▪ Data Set Type specifies that the data set uses a SQL SELECT query to retrieve the data.

3 Choose Next.

4 In Query, in Available Items, expand CLASSICMODELS, then expand the Customers table. The columns in the Customers table appear.

5 Use the following SQL SELECT statement to indicate what data to retrieve. You can type the column and table names, or you can drag them from Available Items to the appropriate location in the SELECT statement.

```
SELECT Customers.customerName,
Customers.customerNumber
FROM Customers
```

This statement that you created, which is shown in Figure 16-9, gets values from the CUSTOMERNAME and CUSTOMERNUMBER columns in the Customers table.

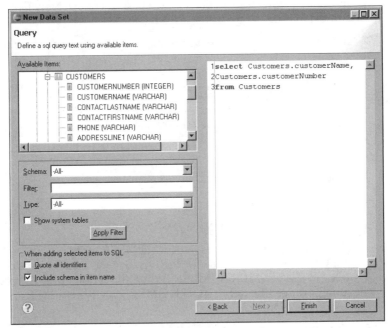

Figure 16-9   Query for Customers data set

6   Choose Finish to save the data set.

7   In Edit Data Set, choose Preview Results to confirm that the query returns the correct data. Figure 16-10 shows some of the data rows that the data set returns.

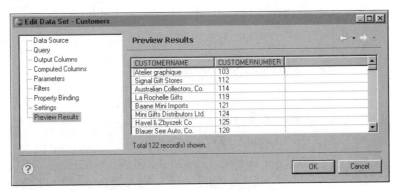

Figure 16-10   Data preview

8 Choose OK to save the data set.

Task 4: Build a data set for the orders subreport

In this procedure, you build a data set to indicate what data to extract from the Orders table. The orders subreport that you create later uses this data set.

1 In Data Explorer, right-click Data Sets, and choose New Data Set from the context menu.

2 In New Data Set, type the following text for the data set's name:

Orders

3 Use the default values for the other fields, then choose Next.

4 In Query, in Available Items, expand CLASSICMODELS, then expand the Orders table to display the columns in the table.

5 Use the following SQL SELECT statement to indicate what data to retrieve:

```
SELECT Orders.orderNumber,
Orders.orderDate
FROM Orders
WHERE Orders.customerNumber = ?
```

This statement selects the ORDERNUMBER and ORDERDATE columns from the Orders table. The WHERE clause has a parameter marker for the value of CUSTOMERNUMBER. When the report runs, the orders subreport gets the current CUSTOMERNUMBER value from the customers report.

6 Choose Finish to save the data set.

7 In Edit Data Set, create a data set parameter to supply the CUSTOMERNUMBER value in the WHERE clause.

   1 Choose Parameters from the left side of the window. Edit Data Set displays a default parameter definition.

   2 Choose Edit to modify the parameter definition.

   3 In Edit Parameter, specify the following values, as shown in Figure 16-11:

      ❑ Name: CustID

      ❑ Data Type: Integer

      ❑ Direction: Input

      ❑ Default value: 103

         103 is one of the values in the CUSTOMERNUMBER column. A default value is required for BIRT Report Designer to run the query for testing purposes.

❏ Linked To Report Parameter: None

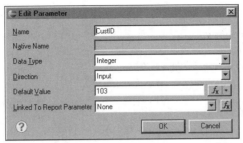

Figure 16-11 Edited parameter definition

4 Choose OK to confirm your edits to the parameter definition. The parameter definition appears in Edit Data Set.

8 Choose Preview Results to confirm that the query returns the correct data. Figure 16-12 shows the data rows that the data set returns for customer number 103.

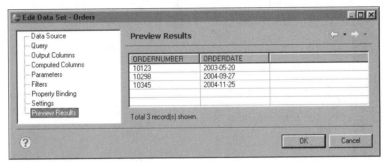

Figure 16-12 Data preview for the orders subreport

9 Choose OK to save the changes to the data set.

Task 5: Build a data set for the payments subreport

In this procedure, you build a data set to indicate what data to extract from the Payments table. The payments subreport that you create later uses this data set.

1 In Data Explorer, right-click Data Sets, and choose New Data Set from the context menu.

2 In New Data Set, type the following text for the data set's name:

Payments

3 Use the default values for the other fields, then choose Next.

4 In Query, in Available Items, expand CLASSICMODELS, then expand the Payments table to display the columns in the table.

5 Use the following SQL SELECT statement to indicate what data to retrieve:

```
SELECT Payments.paymentDate,
Payments.amount
FROM Payments
WHERE Payments.customerNumber = ?
```

This statement selects the PAYMENTDATE and AMOUNT columns from the Payments table. The WHERE clause has a parameter marker for the value of CUSTOMERNUMBER. When the report runs, the payments subreport gets the current CUSTOMERNUMBER value from the customers report.

6 Choose Finish to save the data set.

7 In Edit Data Set, create a data set parameter to supply the CUSTOMERNUMBER value for the WHERE clause.

   1 Choose Parameters. Edit Data Set displays a default parameter.

   2 Choose Edit to modify the parameter definition.

   3 In Edit Parameter, specify the following values:

      ❑ Name: CustID

      ❑ Data Type: Integer

      ❑ Direction: Input

      ❑ Default value: 103

      ❑ Linked To Report Parameter: None

   4 Choose OK to confirm your edits to the parameter definition.

8 Choose Preview Results to confirm that the query returns the correct data. Figure 16-13 shows the data rows that the data set returns for customer number 103.

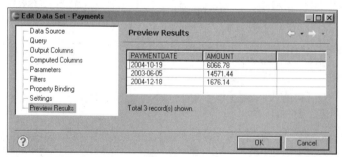

Figure 16-13   Data preview for the payments subreport

9 Choose OK to save the changes to the data set.

Task 6: Create the customer master report

You use a list element to create the master report and organize the orders and payments subreports within it. The list iterates through the customer data rows and creates the related orders and payments subreports for each record. For the sake of simplicity, the customer report displays just the customer name. It can, of course, display additional data, such as customer address, phone number, and credit limit.

1 Drag a list element from the palette, and drop it in the report. The list element appears in the report, as shown in Figure 16-14.

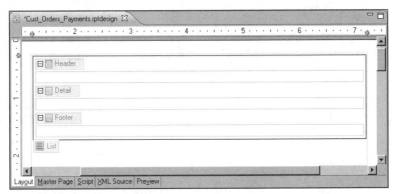

Figure 16-14   List element

2 Associate, or bind, the list with the Customers data set.

1 In Property Editor, choose the Binding tab.

2 In Data Set, select Customers from the drop-down list.

BIRT creates a column binding for each column in the Customers data set. Figure 16-15 shows the binding information for the list.

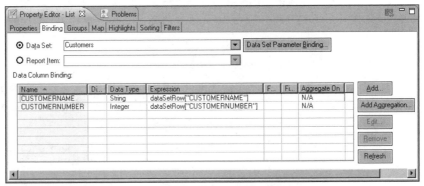

Figure 16-15   Binding information for the list element

3 Choose Data Explorer, expand Data Sets, then expand Customers. The columns that you specified in the query appear below Customers.

4 Drag CUSTOMERNAME from Data Explorer, and drop it in the detail area of the list. Figure 16-16 shows what the report design looks like so far.

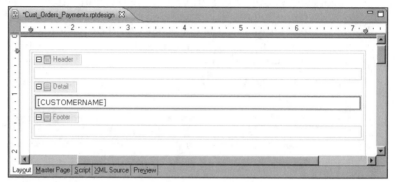

Figure 16-16 Data set field in the list element

5 Preview the report. The report should look like the one shown in Figure 16-17. The report lists all the customer names in the order in which the data set returns them.

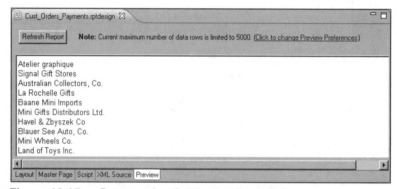

Figure 16-17 Data preview for the master report

6 Sort the customer names in ascending order.

1 Choose Layout to resume editing the report.

2 In the layout editor, select the list element. Hover the mouse pointer over the bottom left corner to locate the List tab, then choose the tab.

3 In Property Editor, choose the Sorting tab.

4 In the Sort page, choose Add to create a sort expression.

5 In New Sort Key, specify the following values, as shown in Figure 16-18. Then, choose OK.

❏ In Key, select CUSTOMERNAME from the drop-down list.

❏ Use the default values for the other fields.

Figure 16-18 Sort definition

7 Preview the report.

Task 7: Create the orders subreport

The orders subreport lists the orders for each customer in a row and column format. It displays the order number and date of each order. To iterate through the Orders data set rows and display them in a row and column format, you use the table element.

1 Choose Layout to resume editing the report.

2 Drag a table element from the palette, and drop it below the [CUSTOMERNAME] data element, in the detail area.

3 In Insert Table, specify the following values:

- In Number of columns, type 2.

- In Number of details, type 1.

- In Data Set, select Orders from the drop-down list.

Choose OK. A table appears in the detail area of the list, as shown in Figure 16-19.

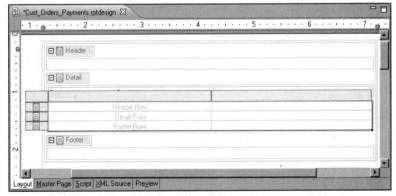

Figure 16-19 Table inserted in the detail area of the list

4 Choose Data Explorer, expand Data Sets, then expand Orders. The columns that you specified in the query appear below Orders.

5 Drag ORDERNUMBER from Data Explorer, and drop it in the first cell of the table's detail row.

In the layout editor, the table cell containing the dropped data set field contains a data element that displays [ORDERNUMBER]. Above this data element is a label element that the layout editor adds to the header row. This label displays the field name as static text and serves as the column heading.

6 Drag ORDERDATE from Data Explorer, and drop it in the second cell in the detail row. The report design should look like the one shown in Figure 16-20.

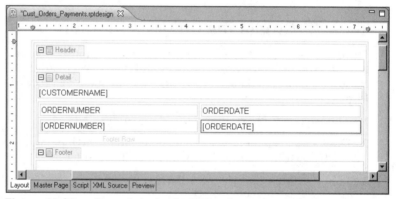

Figure 16-20 Report design including the orders subreport

7 Sort the order rows by order number.

  1 Select the Orders table.

  2 In Property Editor, choose Sorting.

  3 In the Sort page, choose Add to create a sort expression.

  4 In New Sort Key, specify the following values, then choose OK:

   ❑ In Key, select ORDERNUMBER from the drop-down list.

   ❑ Use the default values for the other fields.

8 Preview the report. The report should look like the one shown in Figure 16-21.

The same order records appear for every customer because you specified a default value of 103 for customerNumber when you created the data set parameter, CustID. Using this default value, the orders subreport always displays the order records for customer 103. The solution is to update the value of the CustID parameter dynamically each time the customer row in the master report changes. This procedure is described in the next task.

The column headings appear in bold and are centered because BIRT Report Designer uses the browser's default format for elements placed in a table header. You reformat these elements in a later task.

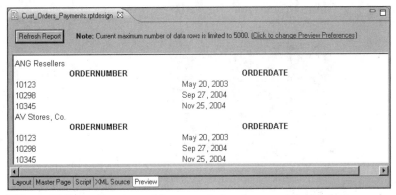

Figure 16-21   Preview of the report showing repeated order records

Task 8: Link the orders subreport to the customers master report

You link the orders subreport to the customers master report by binding the CustID parameter to the CUSTOMERNUMBER data set field in the customers report. Each time the customers report reaches a new customer row, the CustID parameter is updated with the new CUSTOMERNUMBER value.

1 Choose Layout to resume editing the report.

2 Select the Orders table.

3 In Property Editor, choose Binding.

4 In the Binding page, choose Data Set Parameter Binding.

Data Set Parameter Binding displays the CustID parameter, as shown in Figure 16-22. Its value is set to the default, 103, which you specified when you created the data set parameter.

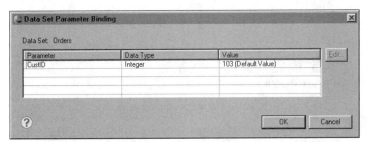

Figure 16-22   Data Set Parameter Binding for the Orders table

5 Change the parameter value to the CUSTOMERNUMBER field in the customers report.

1 Select the parameter, then choose Edit. Edit data set parameter binding, shown in Figure 16-23, prompts you to specify a new parameter value.

Figure 16-23 Edit data set parameter binding

 2 Choose the expression builder button that appears to the right of the Value field.

3 In the expression builder, choose Available Column Bindings, choose List, then double-click CUSTOMERNUMBER. The expression builder displays the expression, row["CUSTOMERNUMBER"], as shown in Figure 16-24.

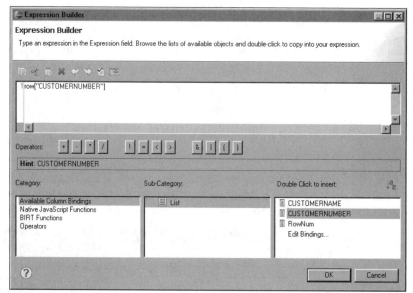

Figure 16-24 CUSTOMERNUMBER field in the expression builder

Choose OK to save the expression and close the expression builder.

4 In Edit data set parameter binding, choose OK to accept the new parameter value. Dataset Parameter Binding displays the new value of row["CUSTOMERNUMBER"] for the CustID parameter, as shown in Figure 16-25.

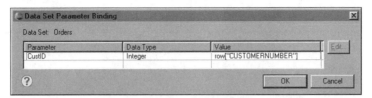

Figure 16-25   Updated data set parameter binding

6 Choose OK to save the changed data set parameter binding.

7 Preview the report. It should look like the one shown in Figure 16-26.

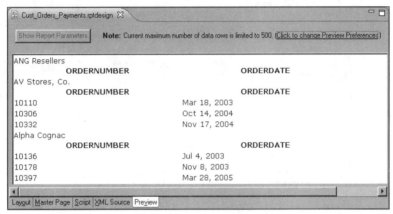

Figure 16-26   Preview of the report shows correct orders data

Now different order records appear for different customers. Not all customers have order records. To display only customers that have orders, you change the query for the customers report. This task is described later in Task 11: "Display only customers that have orders or payments."

Task 9:   Create the payments subreport

The payments subreport shows, in a row and column format, the payments that each customer made. It displays the payment date and amount paid. To iterate through the Payments data set rows and display them in a row and column format, you use a table element. This time, you use an alternate and quicker method to insert the table and the data set fields in the table.

1 Choose Layout to resume editing the report.

2 Choose Data Explorer, and expand Data Sets.

3 Drag the Payments data set, and drop it below the orders subreport, in the detail area of the list.

BIRT Report Designer inserts a table in the report, and places all the data set fields in the detail row of the table. BIRT Report Designer also inserts labels in the header row of the table. The report design should look like the one shown in Figure 16-27.

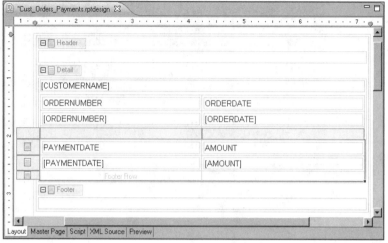

Figure 16-27 Report design including the payments subreport

4 Sort the payment rows by payment date.

1 Select the Payments table.

2 In Property Editor, choose Sorting.

3 In the Sort page, choose Add to create a sort expression.

4 In New Sort Key, specify the following values, then choose OK:

    ❑ In Key, select PAYMENTDATE from the drop-down list.

    ❑ Use the default values for the other fields.

5 Preview the report. The report should look like the one shown in Figure 16-28.

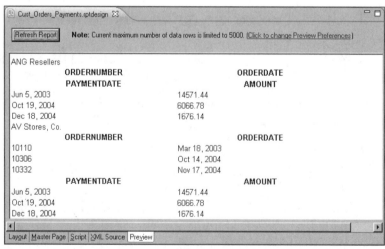

Figure 16-28 Report preview showing repeated payment records

The same payment records repeat for every customer because you specified a default value of 103 for customerNumber when you created the parameter, CustID, for the Payments data set. Just as you did for the orders subreport, you need to dynamically update the value of the CustID parameter for each customer in the master report.

Task 10: Link the payments subreport to the customers master report

You link the payments subreport to the customers master report by binding its CustID parameter to the CUSTOMERNUMBER field in the customers report.

1 Choose Layout to resume editing the report.

2 Select the Payments table.

3 In Property Editor, choose the Binding tab.

4 In the Binding page, choose Data Set Parameter Binding. Data Set Parameter Binding displays the CustID parameter. Its value is set to the default, 103, which you specified when you created the data set parameter.

5 Change the parameter value to the CUSTOMERNUMBER field in the customers report.

   1 Select the parameter, then choose Edit. A dialog prompts you specify a parameter value.

   2 Choose the expression builder button that appears on the right of the Value field.

   3 In the expression builder, choose Available Column Bindings, choose List, then double-click CUSTOMERNUMBER. The expression builder displays the expression row["CUSTOMERNUMBER"]. Choose OK to save the expression and close the expression builder.

   4 In Edit data set parameter binding, choose OK to accept the new parameter value. Data Set Parameter Binding displays the new value of row["CUSTOMERNUMBER"] for the CustID parameter, as shown in Figure 16-29.

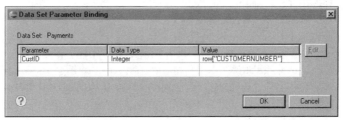

Figure 16-29　Modified data set parameter binding for the Payments table

6 Choose OK to save the changed data set parameter binding.

7 Preview the report. Now the report displays different payment records for different customers. Not all customers have payment records. To display only customers that have payments or orders, you change the query for the customers report.

Task 11: Display only customers that have orders or payments

The database contains customers that do not have orders or payments. The query for the customers report returns all customers. When you run the report, there are customer rows that show only the column headings for the Orders and Payments tables, as shown in Figure 16-30.

ANG Resellers
| ORDERNUMBER | ORDERDATE |
| PAYMENTDATE | AMOUNT |
AV Stores, Co.

Figure 16-30   Report showing no order or payment data for one customer

You can exclude customers that do not have orders or payments by changing the query for the customers report.

1 Choose Layout to resume editing the report.

2 In Data Explorer, expand Data Sets, right-click Customers, then choose Edit.

3 Add the following SQL lines to the end of the existing query:

```
WHERE
EXISTS
(SELECT Orders.customerNumber
FROM Orders
WHERE Customers.customerNumber =
Orders.customerNumber)
OR
EXISTS
(SELECT Payments.customerNumber
FROM Payments
WHERE Customers.customerNumber =
Payments.customerNumber)
```

The WHERE EXISTS clause checks the Orders and Payments tables for customerNumber values that match the customerNumber values in the Customers table. Only rows that have matching customerNumber values are selected. The complete query should look like the one shown in Figure 16-31.

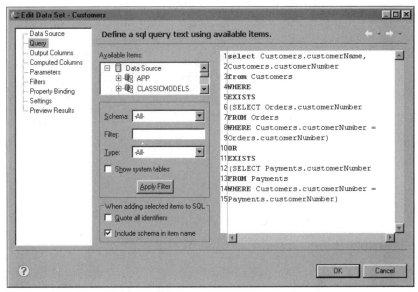

Figure 16-31   Updated SELECT query in Edit Data Set

4   Choose Preview Results to verify that the query returns rows, then choose OK to save the change to the data set.

5   Preview the report. Scroll down the report to check the output. The report no longer displays customers that do not have orders or payments.

Task 12: Display the subreports next to one another

Now that the subreports display the correct data, you can focus on laying out the subreports next to one another. Placing two tables next to one another does not work because BIRT Report Designer creates block-level elements, which means that each element starts on a new line. To display side-by-side tables, you insert the tables in a grid. The grid enables you to align elements easily.

1   Choose Layout to resume editing the report.

2   Drag a grid element from the palette, and drop it into the Detail row, between the [CUSTOMERNAME] data element and the Orders table. Before you drop the grid, make sure the straight cursor appears on the left side of the Orders table.

Insert Grid prompts you to specify the number of columns and rows for the grid.

3   In Number of columns, type 2 and in Number of rows, type 2, then choose OK. A grid with two columns and two rows appears in the layout editor.

4 Move the Orders table to the first cell in the first grid row. To do so, select the Table tab in the bottom left corner of the table, then drag the table and drop it in the grid cell.

5 Move the Payments table to the second grid cell. The report layout should look like the one shown in Figure 16-32.

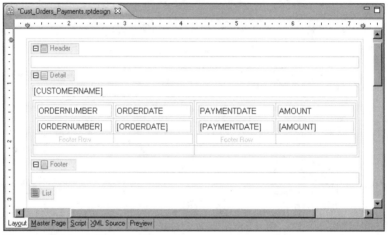

Figure 16-32 Side-by-side subreports in the report design

6 Preview the report. The report should look like the one shown in Figure 16-33.

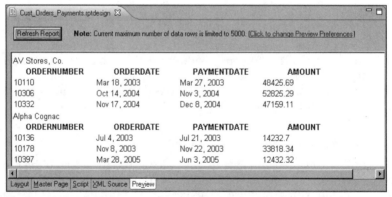

Figure 16-33 Report preview showing side-by-side subreports

Task 13: View the outline of the report

This report contains several levels of nested elements. At the top-most level is the list element. Within the list is a grid, which contains two tables. Within each table are data elements. The layout editor shows the borders of container elements and data elements, but for a container using several levels of nested elements, it can be difficult to see and select individual elements.

To get a clear view of the hierarchy of elements, use the Outline view. Figure 16-34 shows the outline of the report, which appears when the layout editor is selected. Select Body, then expand each item to view all the elements in the report.

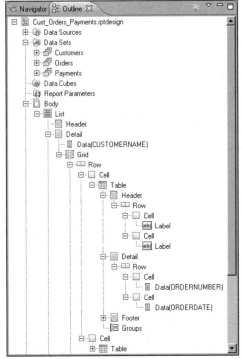

Figure 16-34 Outline of the report

If you have difficulty selecting an element in the layout editor, select the element in the Outline view. When you select an element in Outline, the element is selected in the layout editor.

Task 14: Format the report

Now that the report displays the correct data and layout, you can turn your attention to improving the report's appearance. You perform the following tasks in this section:

■ Highlight the customer names.

■ Edit and format the column headings.

■ Change the date formats.

■ Change the number formats.

■ Increase the vertical space between elements.

Highlight the customer names

1 In the layout editor, select the [CUSTOMERNAME] data element.

2 Choose the Properties tab of Property Editor.

3 Choose General from the list under Properties. Property Editor displays the general formatting properties of the data element.

 4 Choose B to format the data as bold text.

Edit and format the column headings

When you insert a data set field in a table, BIRT Report Designer adds a label that has the data set field name in the header row. Often, data set field names are not in a form that is appropriate for reports, and need to be changed.

1 Double-click the first column heading in the Orders table. The text is highlighted.

2 Replace ORDERNUMBER with the following text, then press Enter:

```
Order Number
```

3 Repeat the previous steps to change the rest of the column headings to the following text:

```
Order Date
Payment Date
Amount
```

4 Create a style to format the column headings, using the following steps:

    1 Choose Element➤Style➤New Style from the main menu.

    2 In New Style, choose Predefined Style, then select table-header from the drop-down list.

    3 Choose Font from the list of style properties on the left.

        ❑ In Size, type 8, and use points as the measurement unit.

        ❑ In Weight, select Bold.

    4 Choose Text Block from the list of style properties. In Text Alignment, select Left.

    5 Choose OK.

5 Preview the report.

Change the date formats

When you insert a data element of date data type, BIRT Report Designer displays dates according to your system's locale setting. You can select a different date format if you do not want to use the default format. In this procedure, you create a style that changes the format of ORDERDATE and PAYMENTDATE values from Jun 3, 2005 to 6/3/05.

1 Choose Layout to resume editing the report.

2 Select the data element that displays [ORDERDATE].

3 Choose Element➤Style➤New Style from the main menu.

4 In New Style, for Custom Style, type the following name:

Date_data

5 Choose Format DateTime from the list of style properties.

6 Choose the m/d/yy format from the drop-down list, as shown in Figure 16-35. The values in the drop-down list dynamically update using the current date.

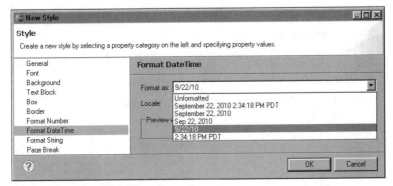

Figure 16-35   DateTime formats

7 Choose OK. BIRT applies the Date_data style to the [ORDERDATE] data element.

8 Apply the Date_data style to the payment date data element. Right-click the [PAYMENTDATE] data element, then choose Style➤Apply Style➤Date_data.

9 Preview the report. The dates have changed from Mar 18, 2003 format to 3/18/03 format, as shown in Figure 16-36.

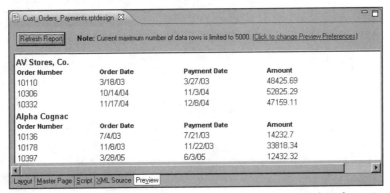

Figure 16-36   Report preview displaying the changed date formats

Change the number formats

When you insert a data element of a numeric data type, BIRT Report Designer displays numbers according to your system's locale setting. You can select a different number format if you do not want to use the default format. In this procedure, you create a style that changes the amount values format from 48425.69 to $48,425.69.

1 Choose Layout to resume editing the report.

2 Select the data element that displays [AMOUNT] in the Payments table.

3 Choose Element➤Style➤New Style from the main menu. New Style displays properties in the general category.

4 For Custom Style, type the following name:

Currency_data

5 Choose Format Number from the list of style properties.

6 Specify the following formatting attributes:

- For Format as, select Currency from the drop-down list.

- Select Use 1000s separator.

- For Symbol, select $ from the drop-down list.

- Use the default values for the other attributes.

Figure 16-37 shows the specified currency format.

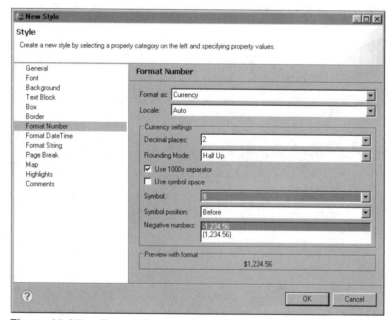

Figure 16-37   Format Number properties

7 Choose OK to save the style. The Currency_data style is applied to the [AMOUNT] data element, as indicated by the element's Style property in Property Editor.

8 Preview the report. The numbers appear in the currency format, as shown in Figure 16-38.

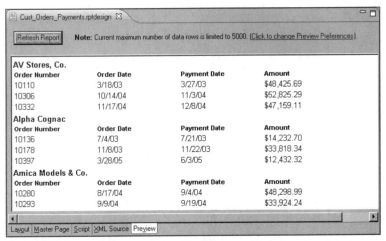

Figure 16-38 Currency format in the report preview

Increase the vertical space between elements

In this procedure, you increase the space between the customer name and the rows before and after it. To adjust the vertical space between elements, use any of the following techniques:

- Increase the top or bottom padding or margins of elements.

- Organize the elements in a grid and adjust the heights of the grid rows.

- Organize the elements in a grid and use empty rows with specified heights to provide space between elements.

Padding and margins property values can yield different results in different web browsers. Using a grid to format the layout is easier and provides more predictable results. This procedure uses the third technique.

1 Choose Layout to resume editing the report.

2 Place the [CUSTOMERNAME] data element in the grid that contains the two tables by completing the following steps:

    1 Select the grid. Hover the mouse pointer over the bottom left corner until the Grid tab appears, then choose the tab. Guide cells appear at the top and left of the selected grid.

    2 Right-click the guide cell on the left of the grid's first row, then choose Insert→Row→Above, as shown in Figure 16-39.

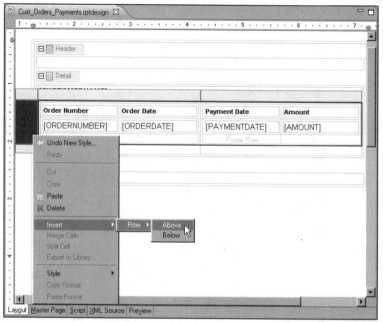

Figure 16-39   Inserting a new grid row

A new row appears above the selected row.

3 Move the [CUSTOMERNAME] data element from its current location to the first cell of the new grid row.

3 Using the procedures described earlier for adding a row, add a new grid row below the row that contains the [CUSTOMERNAME] data element.

4 Select the grid, then select the second row in the grid, as shown in Figure 16-40.

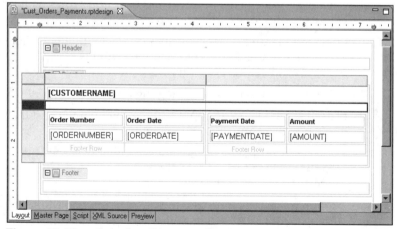

Figure 16-40   Selecting the second row

5 In General properties, set the row's height to 3 points, as shown in Figure 16-41.

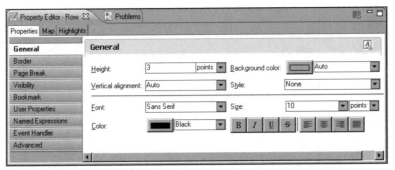

Figure 16-41 Setting the row height property

6 Select the fourth row in the grid, and set its height to 12 points.

7 Preview the report. There is more space above and below the customer name. The report should look like the one shown in Figure 16-42.

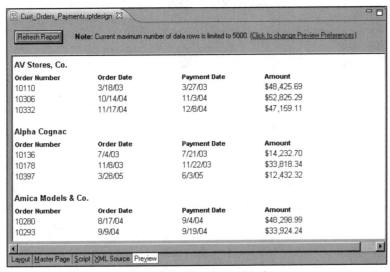

Figure 16-42 Report preview showing added space

17

Using a Chart

A chart is a graphical representation of data or the relationships among sets of data. Charts display complex data in an easy-to-assimilate format. Use the BIRT Report Designer chart builder to create a chart for a report. The chart builder facilitates selecting a chart type and sub-type, organizing the data into visual elements, and formatting the elements. Visual elements can include bars in a bar chart, points and trend lines in a line chart, and dials in a meter chart to name a few.

To create an effective chart, begin by deciding what data to display and then select the chart type that best presents that data. For example, to show the growth of a company's business units over time, use a chart that tracks data along an axis, such as a line chart or a bar chart. To show scientific X-Y data, use a scatter chart.

This chapter discusses the types and sub-types of charts available in the BIRT Report Designer, provides a tutorial in which you use the BIRT sample database, Classic Models, and includes a tour of the design interface. As you complete the tutorial, you learn the essential chart-building tasks.

Surveying the types of charts

BIRT supports a number of different types of charts. Some chart types present certain data better than other types. For example, a line chart can effectively show how numeric data changes over time. A bar chart is a good choice for comparing a limited number of individual items. A colorful pie chart can add interest to a report by showing the size of a small number of items, proportional to the sum.

The following sections describe the main chart types.

About area charts

An area chart displays data values graphically as a set of points that are connected by lines. A different color designates each series. If you include several series on an area chart, the chart displays overlapping filled areas. The area chart in Figure 17-1 shows the percentage of orders and the corresponding unit volume for trains, ships, and planes over three months.

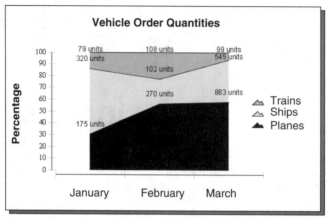

Figure 17-1   Area chart

The area chart emphasizes change along the category axis. A stacked or percent stacked area chart also shows the relationship of parts to a whole. In Figure 17-1, a percent stacked area chart shows how percentages of order quantities of different vehicles relate to each other over time.

About bar charts

A bar chart typically displays data values as a set of vertical columns, but the axis can be flipped to display horizontal bars, as shown in Figure 17-2.

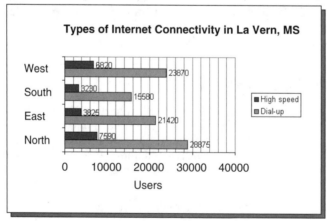

Figure 17-2   Bar chart using horizontal bars

When you flip the axes to create vertical instead of horizontal columns, the layout of the information changes such that the eye can easily compare the value differences between two types of internet connectivity.

A bar chart is useful to show data changes over a period of time or to illustrate comparisons among items. Like an area chart, stacked and percent stacked bar charts can also show the relationship of individual items to a whole.

About tube, cone, and pyramid charts

Tube, cone, and pyramid charts are variations of the bar chart that use tubular, conical, and triangular risers instead of bars. You can specify different types of risers within the same chart to distinguish types of data, as shown in Figure 17-3. The bar riser represents unit volume and the pyramid riser represents dollar volume.

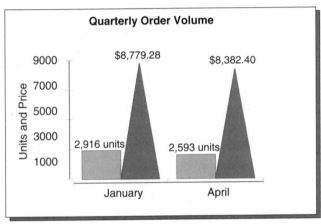

Figure 17-3   Bar-pyramid chart

Use a bar, tube, cone, or pyramid chart to display data values as a set of vertical or horizontal columns. Use a combination of risers to differentiate separate sets of information.

About line charts

A line chart displays data as a sequence of points, connected by a line. For example, the line chart in Figure 17-4 shows sales values for chips and boards over time. Figure 17-4 also shows trends in data over four quarters.

In addition to the main chart types, you can choose a number of subtypes. The area, bar, cone, line, pyramid, and tube are main chart types that have a stacked subtype and a percent stacked subtype. After selecting one of the main chart types, you can choose its stacked subtype to position positive or negative values above or below the origin of the chart. Alternatively, you can choose a percent stacked subtype to show the contribution of individual items to the whole.

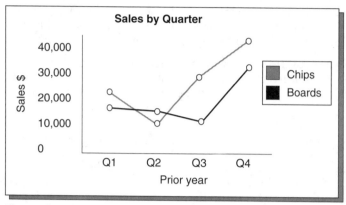

Figure 17-4　　Line chart

About meter charts

A meter chart uses a needle to point to values on a circular or semicircular dial. You use a meter chart to create a gauge or dashboard display. To emphasize settings on the dial, divide the meter background into sections called dial regions. Adjust the dial settings in the same way as you adjust an axis, resulting in many options for arranging and emphasizing the dial data. Figure 17-5 shows a meter chart that contrasts the speed of two products.

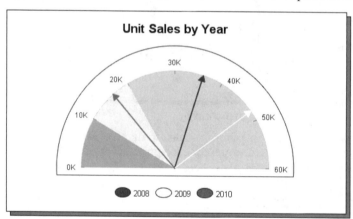

Figure 17-5　　Meter chart

A meter chart is best used to emphasize a small number of values.

About pie charts

A pie chart shows the relationships of parts to the whole. The shading and colors of sectors in a pie chart supports straightforward comparison of values. For example, the chart in Figure 17-6 shows the percentage revenue for multiple product lines. In this example, the size of the sectors for the 6 product lines ranges from 8 percent to 34 percent of total revenue.

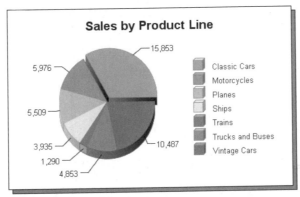

Figure 17-6   Pie chart

About scatter charts

A scatter chart shows data as points. Scatter charts display values on both axes. For example, the chart in Figure 17-7 compares two sets of numerical data for certain sports cars: the top speed and the price. You can see from the chart how performance increases in relation to price.

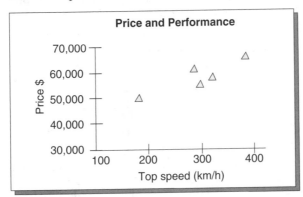

Figure 17-7   Scatter chart

A scatter chart shows the relationships among the numeric values of multiple data series. A typical use of a scatter charts is to display scientific data.

About bubble charts

A bubble chart resembles a scatter chart, but it uses bubbles instead of data points. Use a bubble chart instead of a scatter chart to represent three numeric values per data point. Two numeric values define the position of a bubble on the plot area. A third numeric value defines the size of the bubble. Use color-coding to differentiate among category values, such as product lines. For example, the bubble chart in Figure 17-8 plots the retail against the wholesale prices of products, calculates the discount, and uses the size of the bubbles to show the amount of the discount.

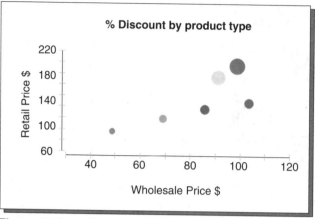

Figure 17-8   Bubble chart

A typical use of a bubble chart is to present financial data.

About stock charts

A stock chart shows four sets of numeric data values as points on a time continuum, such as days of the week. Figure 17-9 shows a sample stock chart.

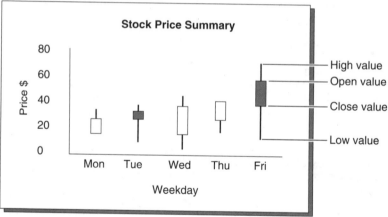

Figure 17-9   Stock chart

Stock values appear as a candlestick, a box with lines extending up and down from the ends. Open and close values mark the upper and lower edges of the box. High and low values mark the upper and lower points of the line. The default appearance of the bar depends on the chart values. If the open value is higher than the close value, the box is shaded. If the close value is higher than the open value, the box is white. You can change the color of the shaded boxes.

Although a stock chart typically displays stock price data, you can also use a stock chart to show scientific data, such as temperature changes over time.

About difference charts

A difference chart typically shows variation between two sets of data by shading the areas between points of comparison. You can format the series of values to display positive areas in one color and negative areas in another, as shown in Figure 17-10. The dark-shaded spike in the chart represents an unusual delay beyond the request date for shipment of order 10165. The light-shaded areas represent shipments made earlier than requested.

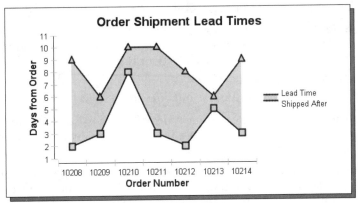

Figure 17-10   Difference chart

Use a difference chart to show deviation between two sets of data values.

About Gantt charts

A Gantt chart graphically presents project scheduling information by displaying the duration of tasks. One axis contains the time series, and the other contains tasks. Figure 17-11 uses color-coded bars to show the planned duration of the stages to complete the tasks. The bars use colors to differentiate Stage 1 and Stage 2.

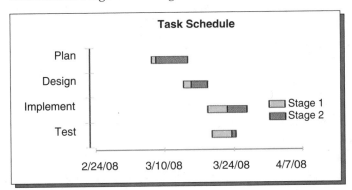

Figure 17-11   Gantt chart

Gantt charts use symbols on bars to mark beginning and ending dates.

Tutorial 5: Creating a stand-alone chart

This tutorial covers the following topics:

- Using the chart builder. You use the chart builder to create or modify a chart. The chart builder organizes tasks and shows your progress.

- Selecting a chart type. You review the types and subtypes, so you know the different presentation possibilities for displaying your data.

- Setting chart output formats. By default, the chart builder creates a chart in Scalable Vector Graphics (SVG) format. You can also create a chart in a static image file format, such as BMP or PNG.

- Providing data for a chart. You create a data source and data set, then, in the chart builder, you specify that data set for the chart.

- Plotting chart data. The various types of charts use data differently. You can drag and drop columns from the Chart Preview to areas of the Select Data page to define how to plot the data.

- Formatting a chart. In the tutorial, you format some parts of a pie chart, such as leader lines and data labels, using settings such as text style, position, and visibility. Other chart types offer different formatting options. You can manipulate the scale or placement of data on an axis or in a pie or meter to show information effectively.

The tutorial provides step-by-step instructions to build a report that displays order totals organized by product line. The report presents information graphically in a pie chart. In this case, the chart is the entire report.

To create a chart, complete the following tasks:

- Set up the report design file and data. Create a new report, data source, and data set.

- Add the chart element to the report design. Insert a chart element into a report and select a chart type.

- Provide data for the chart. Link the chart to a data set and build the expressions that the chart uses.

- Change the chart title.

- Refine the chart appearance. Remove the chart legend and modify the labels that identify each sector.

- Preview the chart.

Task 1: Set up and query the data source

Before you start to design a chart, you must create a report design file for the chart, then set up the data source and data set that the chart uses. These tasks are discussed in detail in earlier sections of this book and in a tutorial in which you build a sample report. This tutorial builds on that knowledge. This task shows how to select the data to build a sample pie chart.

1 To create a new report, choose File➤New➤Report.

2 Name the new report design Chart.rptdesign. Choose Finish.

3 Build a data source using the sample database, Classic Models.

4 Build a data set for the chart. Use the following data set name:

ChartData

Use the following SQL SELECT statement:

```
SELECT Products.ProductLine,
sum(OrderDetails.QuantityOrdered)
FROM OrderDetails,
Products
WHERE Products.ProductCode=OrderDetails.ProductCode
GROUP BY Products.ProductLine
ORDER BY Products.ProductLine
```

This SELECT statement obtains values from the ProductLine column in the Products table, groups the results by product line, and calculates the sum of the order quantities for each group.

5 Choose Finish, then Preview Results to validate the query. By creating the SELECT statement correctly, you see the data shown in Figure 17-12.

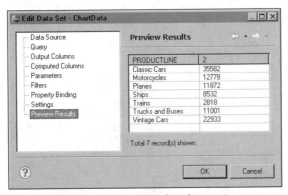

Figure 17-12   Previewing the data set

The first column lists product line names. The second column shows the total orders for each product line. BIRT uses sequential numbers to name generated columns, such as the sum column named 2 in Figure 17-12.

6 To rename the sum column to be more descriptive, choose Output Columns. Select column 2, then choose Edit. In Edit Output Columns, use the following settings:

1 In Alias, type:

TotalOrders

2 In Display Name, type:

TOTALORDERS

3 Choose OK.

7 To close Edit Data Set, choose OK.

Task 2: Add the chart to the report

In this task, use the palette to add a chart element, and select a chart type.

1 Choose Palette, then drag the chart element to the blank report design. The chart builder appears, as shown in Figure 17-13.

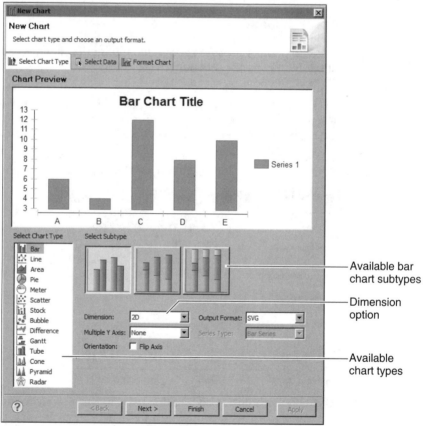

Figure 17-13 Selecting the chart type

The lower part of the Select Chart Type page displays the different types of charts that you can create. Some chart types include several subtypes, giving you a wide range of available types. Choosing a chart type on Select Chart Type displays the available subtypes for that type of chart. By default, these subtypes create two-dimensional charts. The selected Dimension option affects the available subtypes.

2 In the Select Chart Type list, select Pie. The chart builder shows a symbol of a pie chart in the Subtype area, as shown in Figure 17-14. Pie charts have only one subtype, so you see only one option in the Subtype area.

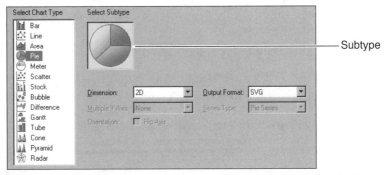

Figure 17-14   Viewing the two-dimensional subtype for a pie chart

Task 3: Provide data for a chart

In task 1, you created the data source connection and data set that you need. After selecting the data set to use, you must set up the expressions that the chart uses to represent the data graphically. Each type of chart uses data differently. For a pie chart, you must select data expressions that specify:

- The data values represented by sectors in the pie. In this tutorial, you use an expression that creates one sector for each product line value.

- The size of each sector. In this tutorial, the number of orders determines the size of each product-line sector.

You can use different techniques to provide a data expression in a chart. The easiest way to specify the data to use is to drag a column from Data Preview to a field. You can also type the expression or use expression builder to create an expression.

1 To navigate to the page you use to provide data, choose Select Data. The upper half of Select Data, shown in Figure 17-15, provides a chart preview.

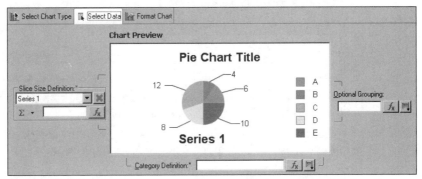

Figure 17-15   Previewing the chart in the upper section of Select Data

Chart Preview displays a rough sketch of the chart for design purposes. The final published version looks more elaborate and complete, particularly if you choose to use live data for previews. In Chart Preview, the chart builder uses either live data from your data set or randomly generated sample data, depending on how you set the Enable Live Preview preference.

2 In the lower half of the Select Data page, select:

```
Use Data from
```

This report design includes only one data set. Select ChartData from the drop-down list. Select the Show data preview option if it is not selected. In the lower half of the chart builder, as shown in Figure 17-16, Data Preview displays some of the data from the data set.

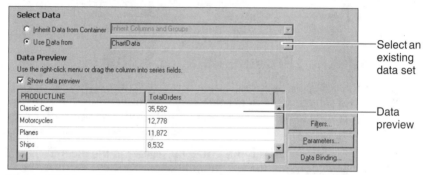

Select an existing data set

Data preview

Figure 17-16   Selecting a data set in the lower section of Select Data

3 In Data Preview, select the PRODUCTLINE column heading, and drag it to the empty Category Definition field, as shown in Figure 17-17.

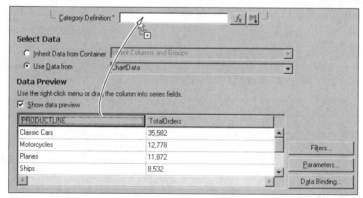

Figure 17-17   Supplying a category definition

A slice appears in the pie chart for each item in the category. The following expression appears in Category Definition:

```
row["PRODUCTLINE"]
```

4 To set the size of each sector, select the TotalOrders column header, and drag it to the empty field in Slice Size Definition, as shown in Figure 17-18.

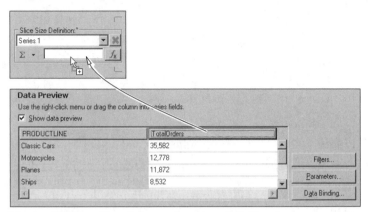

Figure 17-18   Supplying a slice size definition

The following expression appears in Slice Size Definition:

```
row["TOTALORDERS"]
```

In Data Preview, the TotalOrders column is colored to show that the chart uses the column. The image in Chart Preview changes to reflect the data you specified. The product lines are now the chart categories. The size of the sectors represents the total orders for each product line category.

Task 4: Enlarge the chart and preview the report

You usually need to enlarge a chart after you finish designing it in the chart builder. The size of the default pie chart cannot accommodate all the Classic Model data, so you resize the chart in the layout editor. You need to look at a preview in the report editor to ensure that the size of the chart is appropriate.

1 To close the chart builder, choose Finish. The chart element appears in the layout editor, as shown in Figure 17-19.

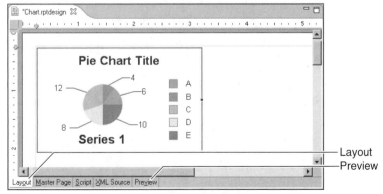

Figure 17-19   Chart element displayed in the layout editor

2 Choose Preview to preview the report in the report editor. The chart appears small, relative to the report page. Also in this case, the chart element is too small to accommodate all the legend data. The preview truncates the some of the labels and you cannot see Vintage Cars at all.

Figure 17-20 Previewing cramped chart before enlargement

3 To make the chart bigger so that all the data is visible and not so cramped, choose Layout, and enlarge the chart element to approximately 5 inches wide and 3 inches tall. To enlarge the chart, select it, then drag the handles that appear in the borders of the chart element, as shown in Figure 17-21.

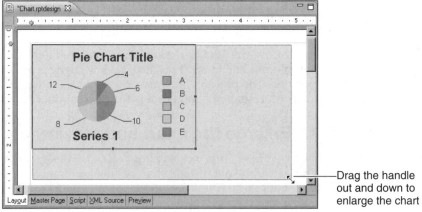

Figure 17-21 Enlarging a chart element

4 Choose Preview to show the chart in the previewer again. The chart appears as shown in Figure 17-22.

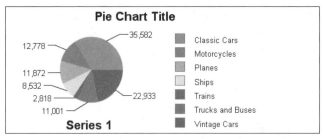

Figure 17-22 Previewing chart after enlargement

Compare the preview in Figure 17-22 with the preview in Figure 17-20, where Vintage Cars data is not visible.

The chart now uses the correct data, but the layout is not very attractive. You need to format the chart to make it visually appealing and to emphasize the points that you want. The remaining procedures in this tutorial help you to modify the chart. Some of the changes that you make include creating a new title, adjusting the data labels, and removing the legend.

Task 5: Change the chart and value series titles

Currently, the chart displays a default title. You provide new text for the title. The chart also displays a default title for the value series. Because there is only one value series in the chart, the number of orders, no title is necessary. You hide the series title.

1 Choose Layout to return to the layout editor, then double-click the chart element in the layout editor to open the chart builder.

2 Choose Format Chart. In the navigation list, choose Title. The title properties appear in the lower pane of the chart builder, as shown in Figure 17-23.

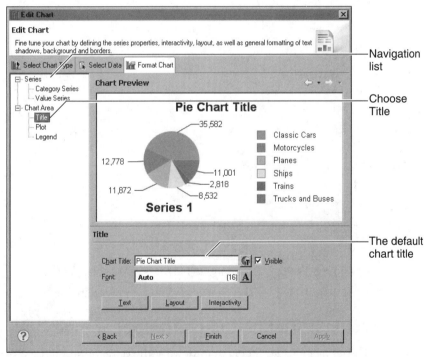

Figure 17-23 Preparing to add a chart title in the chart area section

3 In Chart Title, type:

```
Orders by Product Line
```

4 Choose Value Series from the navigation list. The value series properties appear, as shown in Figure 17-24.

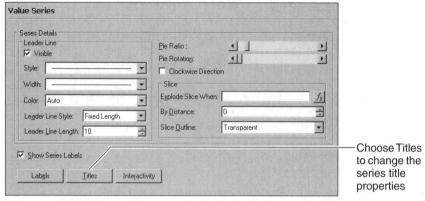

Figure 17-24   Value series properties

5   In the value series properties, choose Titles. Titles appears, as shown in Figure 17-25.

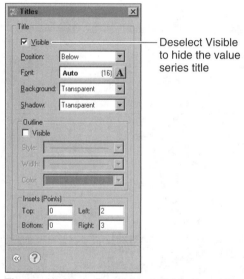

Deselect Visible to hide the value series title

Figure 17-25   Preparing to hide the value series title

6   Deselect Visible. The chart preview no longer shows the value series title.

Task 6:   Refine the chart appearance

The chart includes labels that identify the data value each sector presents. A legend identifies which product line each sector represents. Though the legend includes useful information, it also takes up space and reduces the size of the pie, so you may have to make a trade-off. One possibility is to remove the legend and use sector labels to display the product line information. Using the sector labels instead of a legend is a better choice when report users cannot easily distinguish colors. Each data label displays category information and value information. In this case, the category information is the sector name and the value information is the total number of orders for the sector.

In the following example, the label identifies the motorcycles sector:

`Motorcycles: 12,778`

1 To modify the legend, choose Legend from the navigation list at the left.

2 Deselect Visible, as shown in Figure 17-26.

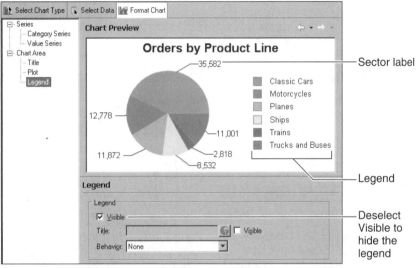

Figure 17-26 Legend section of Format Chart

3 Now you can add the legend information to the sector labels. Navigate to the Value Series formatting section, then choose Labels. Series Labels appears, as shown in Figure 17-27.

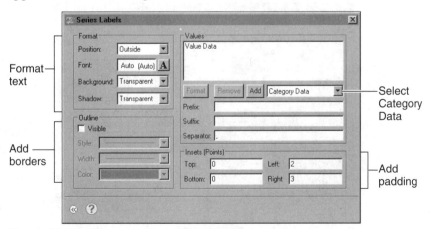

Figure 17-27 Series Labels formatting options

4 To add the section name to the label, ensure that Category Data appears in the drop-down list in the Values area, then choose Add. Category Data appears below Value Data in the list, as shown in Figure 17-28.

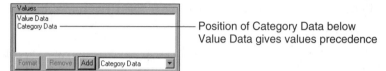

Position of Category Data below Value Data gives values precedence

Figure 17-28   Adding Category Data to a label

You need to rearrange the label data, so the Category Data, which are the product line names, appear before the values in the chart labels. For example, you want the label to read Classic Cars, 35,582 instead of 35,582, Classic Cars.

5 Select Value Data, and choose Remove.

6 In the drop-down list, select Value Data, and choose Add, as shown in Figure 17-29.

—Select Value Data

Figure 17-29   Selecting Value Data from the drop-down list

Now the labels display information in the correct order, but you still need to change the label appearance. When you use more than one kind of information in a label, you can use a separator between the different sections. The default separator is a comma.

7 To change the separator, in Separator, type a colon (:) then a space, as shown in Figure 17-30.

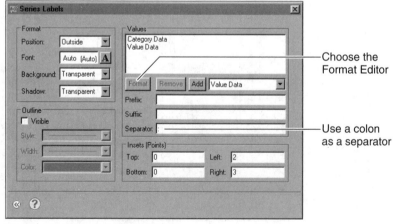

Choose the Format Editor

Use a colon as a separator

Figure 17-30   Adding a label separator

To change the number format of the value part of the label, select Value Data in Values, then choose the Format Editor. In Edit Format, you can change the format of date-and-time or numerical data.

8 Select Standard, then change the value in Fraction Digits to 0, as shown in Figure 17-31.

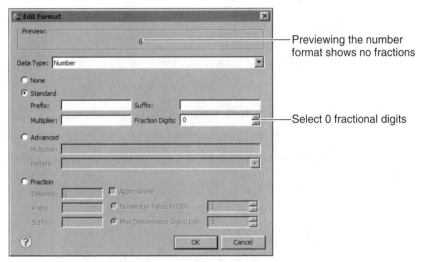

Previewing the number format shows no fractions

Select 0 fractional digits

Figure 17-31   Modifying the standard number format

Choose OK to close Edit Format.

A   **9** To change the formatting attributes of the label text, choose Font Editor, as shown in Figure 17-32.

Choose Font Editor to change style

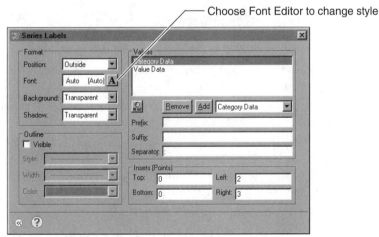

Figure 17-32   Opening Font Editor from Labels

Edit Font appears.

1 In Font, select Tahoma. Then, in Size, type 11, as shown in Figure 17-33.

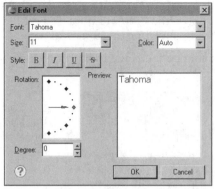

Figure 17-33 Edit Font

2 Choose OK, and close Series Labels.

10 Now set a consistent length for the leader lines that connect the labels to the sectors. Figure 17-34 indicates where to find the leader line settings.

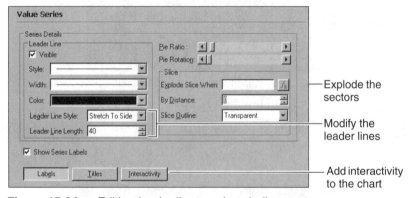

Figure 17-34 Editing leader lines and exploding sectors

1 In Leader Line Style, accept the default, Fixed Length. Change Leader Line Length to 20.

2 To separate the pie sectors so that a set amount appears between them, in Slice, set By Distance to 3.

To make the chart more useful to the report users, you can add interactive features, such as hyperlinks and highlighting, as described in later sections of this book. You can add interactive features to the chart area, legend, marker lines, and to other parts of the chart.

You have finished creating and formatting the chart.

11 To close the chart builder and see the chart element in the layout editor, choose Finish. Then, choose Preview to preview the chart.

The chart appears as shown in Figure 17-35. The completed chart shows the category names for each sector as well as the sector values. The size and organization of the chart make quick analysis possible, while still providing detailed data. For example, the user can immediately see that the largest pie sector is Classic Cars, which has 35,582 orders, followed by Vintage Cars, which has 22,933. The two car sectors are larger than all other sectors combined. Other product-line groups, such as Trains, do not contribute significant numbers of orders.

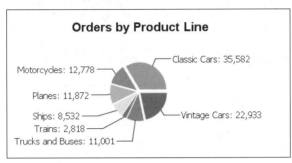

Figure 17-35   Completed tutorial chart

Exploring the chart builder

The tutorial that you just completed introduced the chart builder. As you saw in the tutorial, the chart builder has the following main pages:

- Select Chart Type
  In this page, you determine the type of chart and basic structural attributes such as orientation and the dimension of the chart.

- Select Data
  In this page, you specify the data that the chart displays.

- Format Chart
  In this page, you modify the appearance of the data that the chart displays, such as the range of values an axis displays, or the visual elements of the chart, such as the color of the lines in a line chart.

You access these pages by choosing the buttons at the top. You then complete the mandatory tasks, as well as some tasks that are optional, such as formatting the labels. This section describes the chart builder pages.

The most common task that you complete on Select Chart Type is selecting a chart type and subtype, as you did in the tutorial. You can also use Select Chart Type to modify the subtype you choose. You can show some charts in two dimensions, two dimensions with depth, or three dimensions, and you can flip the axes of some charts to a horizontal position. Select Chart Type is also where you can determine the output format of the chart. Figure 17-36 shows the options that appear on Select Chart Type.

Creating a chart with depth or three dimensions

All chart types offer two-dimensional rendering in which the chart shape appears flat against the chart background. Some BIRT charts have subtypes with depth, which use three-dimensional effects to create the appearance of depth. Finally, some charts have three-dimensional subtypes, which arrange multiple series elements along a third axis in addition to the typical x- and y-axes. You select the chart type, dimension, and subtype in Select Chart Type, as shown in Figure 17-36.

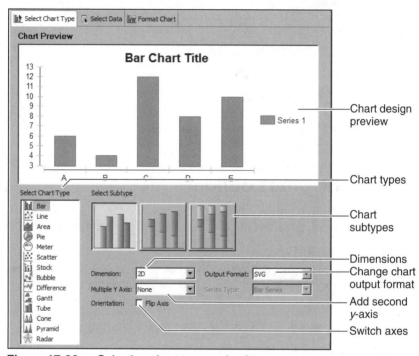

Figure 17-36 Selecting chart type and subtype

Figure 17-37 shows the difference between a bar chart with depth and a three-dimensional bar chart. In the first chart, the bars have the appearance of three-dimensional objects, and multiple series appear side by side on the x-axis. Three-dimensional charts display multiple series from front to back, as shown in the second chart in Figure 17-37.

Figure 17-37 Depth and three-dimensional bar charts

Table 17-1 lists the dimension options available for each chart type.

Table 17-1   Dimension options for chart types

Chart type	Dimension options		
	2D	2D with Depth	3D
Area	✓	✓	✓
Bar	✓	✓	✓
Bubble	✓	–	–
Cone	✓	✓	✓
Difference	✓	–	–
Gantt	✓	–	–
Line	✓	✓	✓
Meter	✓	–	–
Pie	✓	✓	–
Pyramid	✓	✓	✓
Scatter	✓	–	–
Stock	✓	–	–
Tube	✓	✓	✓

Using chart subtypes

In the chart builder, choosing a chart type and dimension displays any available subtypes. For example, bubble, difference, Gantt, and scatter charts do not have subtypes. Area, bar, cone, pyramid, tube, and line charts have the following subtypes:

- Either overlay or side-by-side

  A side-by-side bar, cone, pyramid, or tube chart arranges risers that represent each series beside one another, as shown in Figure 17-38. The number of series determines the width of the riser.

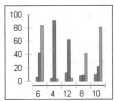

Figure 17-38   Side-by-side subtype for a two-dimensional bar chart

An overlay line or area chart arranges lines or areas that represent each series independently, one over another, as shown in Figure 17-39.

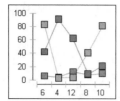

Figure 17-39   Overlay subtype for a two-dimensional line chart

- Stacked

A stacked chart arranges the data points from one series on top of the data points of another series, as shown in Figure 17-40.

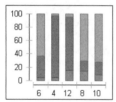

Figure 17-40   Stacked subtype for a two-dimensional bar chart

- Percent stacked

A percent stacked chart is similar to a stacked chart, except the total of the data points in a category fills the entire plot area for a category, as shown in Figure 17-41. The value of each data point is a percentage of the total of all data points for that category.

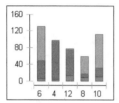

Figure 17-41   Percent stacked subtype for a two-dimensional bar chart

Understanding chart output formats

There are four output formats available: BMP, JPEG, PNG, and SVG. By default, the chart builder creates a chart in SVG format. SVG is a vector-graphics markup language that describes two-dimensional graphics in XML. SVG enables report developers to include more accessible, searchable, and interactive images in their reports. For example, the legend interactive features that BIRT charts include use the SVG format to enable highlighting and hiding series data.

SVG files are typically smaller than image files in other formats and produce high-resolution images. For example, if your chart uses a photograph as a background image, you will likely want to use JPEG or PNG format, because those formats display photographic images particularly well. Some web browsers, for example, Firefox version 1.5 and later, provide support for SVG images. Internet Explorer version 8 or earlier requires a plug-in to support SVG. You must use the SVG format if you want your chart to be interactive.

The following procedure explains how to change the chart output format.

How to change the chart output format

1 In the chart builder, choose Select Chart Type.

2 In Output Format, select an option, such as PNG or BMP, as shown in Figure 17-42. Choose Finish.

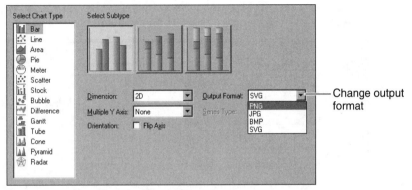

Figure 17-42   Output format option on Select Chart Type

Using a chart in a table

You can create a report that consists only of a chart, or you can incorporate a chart with other elements, such as tables, lists, and images. You can specify a chart data set that is different from the data set that you use for the rest of the report. For example, a chart that you place in a customer list could show the total sales for each customer. The customer list might use one set of data, such as customer names and addresses, whereas the chart uses a data set that returns the sales totals.

A chart that you place in a table typically uses the same data set as the table. In a table that groups data, you would usually want the chart to use the same grouping setup as the table.

You usually place a chart element in the following places:

■ A table header or footer. The chart displays data for the entire data set.

■ A group header or footer. Each group section includes a chart, and each chart displays data for its group section.

■ A detail row. Each detail row in the completed report includes a chart, and each chart displays data for its detail row.

For example, after placing a chart in a table header, select the Inherit Data from Container option. The container is the table. When you place a chart in a group header or footer and specify this option, the chart uses all data for the group. After selecting the option to inherit data from the container, select the inheritance mode, as shown in Figure 17-43. Available inheritance modes are:

■ Inherit columns and groups

The chart displays one data point for each section created by the section or table. Aggregation, grouping, or sorting are not available.

■ Inherit columns only

The chart receives the detail data rows used by the section or table. Aggregation, grouping, and sorting are available.

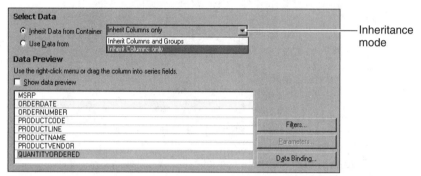

Figure 17-43   Setting the chart to inherit data from its container

Figure 17-44 shows the design for a report that includes Classic Models database order information that is grouped by product line, such as classic cars, motorcycles, and ships. The report uses a chart to present the order totals graphically.

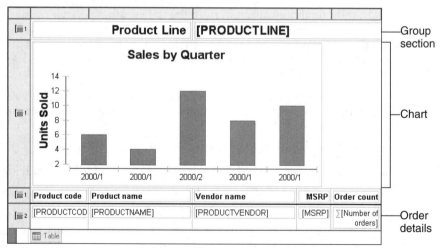

Figure 17-44   Report design including a chart in a group section

Figure 17-44 shows that the group section uses a header, row["productLine"]. The report positions the chart above the order details.

When you preview the chart, the data for a productLine group consists of one section. Each group provides a chart before listing the order details. Figure 17-45 shows the order details for the product line, ships. Details include ship product codes, names, vendors, and other details.

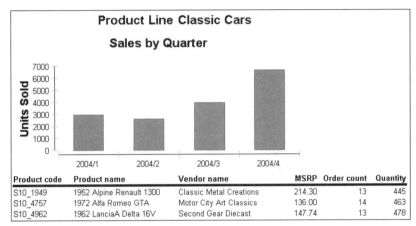

Product code	Product name	Vendor name	MSRP	Order count	Quantity
S10_1949	1952 Alpine Renault 1300	Classic Metal Creations	214.30	13	445
S10_4757	1972 Alfa Romeo GTA	Motor City Art Classics	136.00	14	463
S10_4962	1962 LanciaA Delta 16V	Second Gear Diecast	147.74	13	478

Figure 17-45   Report including a chart in a group section

Chapter

18

Displaying Data in Charts

You use the same kind of data sources for a chart as you do for other report items. You can open a connection to a data source and create the data set for a chart from the Data Explorer, or you can use an existing data set. You learned to create a data set in Task 4: "Build a data set" in Tutorial 1: "Building a simple listing report." The next section describes how to specify a data set used by another report item or a container.

How you retrieve and arrange data in a chart can be different from the way that you use data elsewhere in BIRT. As you learned in the chart tutorial, you provide expressions that organize the data into visual elements, such as bars or lines. After you preview the chart, you may think that you need additional or different data to make the meaning of the chart complete or clear. For example, you can group data values or use chart axis settings to modify the formatting, range, or scale of the data that the chart displays.

Linking data to a chart

Use the chart builder to link a data set to a chart and plot the data. Choose Select Data, then select one of the following options to link data to a chart, as shown in Figure 18-1:

- Inherit Data from Container
  Retrieves data from the data set that is bound to the container, such as a grid or table in which the chart appears.

- Use Data from
  Retrieves data from a data set, a cube, or another report item's result set.

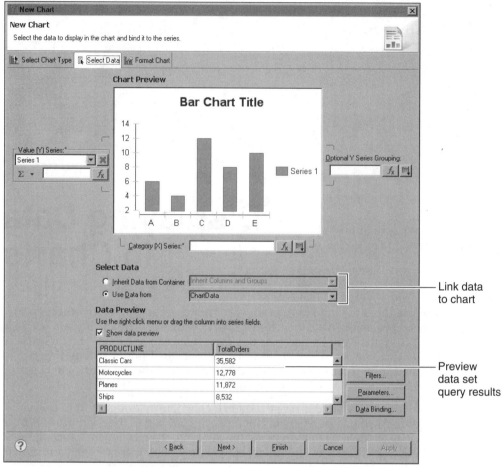

Figure 18-1   Select Data page of the chart builder

After linking data to the chart, Data Preview displays actual data. If you select Show data preview, you see column headings and up to six rows of data by default. To reduce the previewing time, deselect Show data preview. You then see column headings only. Inspect the data preview to verify that the data meets your needs. You can exclude values by filtering data or by using a parameter to return only certain data.

As described later in this chapter, you can drag and drop data columns from Data Preview to the upper half of the Select Data page to plot the data. For example, use this technique to specify which axis of a bar chart uses which column of data.

If there is no data available then you can select a message to appear in its place. In Format Chart, select Chart Area➤Chart Visibility and accept the default message or enter appropriate text, as shown in Figure 18-2.

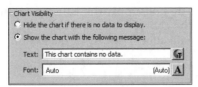

Figure 18-2   Empty chart message

Linking to data from a container

To inherit data from a container, first place a chart element in the cell of a table or list. In Inherit Data from Container, select one of the following options:

- Inherit Columns and Groups
- Inherit Columns

Selecting data inherited from the report container ensures integration of the chart with the report. For example, the chart changes when the table that contains it receives updates.

Linking to data from a data set, data cube, or report item

Generally, you define a data set or data cube using the Data Explorer before you start building a chart. Performing these tasks in the Data Explorer is a best practice because it gives you optimal control and performance. After setting up the data, open the chart builder and select the chart type, as you did in the tutorial in Chapter 17, "Using a Chart." Now you are ready to link data to the chart.

To use data from an existing data set, data cube, or report item, place a chart element anywhere in a report, and select Use Data from. Select from the list, as shown in Figure 18-3.

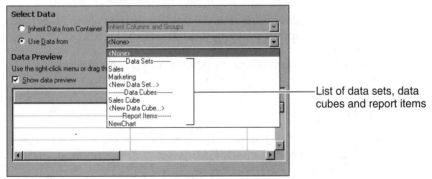

Figure 18-3   Using data from a data set, cube, or report item

If existing data sets and data cubes do not supply the data values that you need, and you do not want to exit the chart builder and start over, select the option to create a new data set or data cube. Use any of the existing data sources connected to your report.

Understanding the axes of a chart

Most charts have horizontal and vertical axes, called the x-axis and y-axis. These axes usually display the following types of values:

- Category series
  A set of values that lie on the x-axis. Category series can be of any data type.

- Value series
  A set of values that lie on the y-axis. A value series can be of the numeric, date, or date-and-time data type, depending on the chart type.

Generally, a chart displays a single category on the x-axis, and one or more value series on the y-axes. An axis displays additional value series or group values for a category series parallel to the x-axis. The series that is parallel to the x-axis often appears in depth or three dimensions. Certain charts, such as pie and meter charts, do not have any axes.

About the axes

Typically, you plot text or date-and-time data on the category (x) axis, which has regular segments that do not correspond to numerical values. If there are too many categories to fit within the finite limitations of the chart, you can use grouping. For example, group sales by quarter. By default, category values appear in the same order as they occur in the data source, unless sorted in another order by the query. You can sort the values in ascending or descending order using Edit Group and Sorting.

Typically, you plot numeric or date-and-time data on a value (y) axis. A value axis does not support plotting text data. A value axis positions data relative to the axis marks. The value of a data point determines where it appears on a value axis. Like data on the category axis, you can group and sort data on the value axis. Value series grouping defines sets of values.

Defining the axes

After you select the data set, you define how the chart builder uses data from the data set to plot the chart. The options you use in the upper half of the Select Data page, shown in Figure 18-4, define the axes.

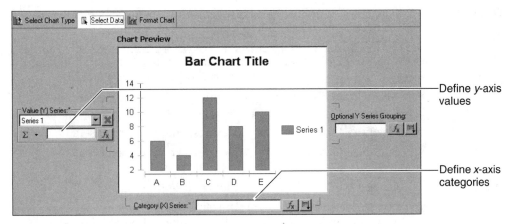

Define y-axis values

Define x-axis categories

Figure 18-4   Defining axes values in Select Data

Plotting different chart types

In the Select Data page, the Category (X) Series, or Category Definition, option plots data on the *x*-axis. The value series option plots data on the *y*-axis. The options differ slightly in name and function, depending on the chart type. For example, when you create a meter chart, which has no axes, you define the position of a needle on the dial instead of defining a *y*-axis. When you create a pie chart, you define the size of the slices instead of the *y*-axis. Table 18-1 describes the differences in plotting options in the Select Data page for chart types.

Table 18-1   Differences in *x*- and *y*-axis plotting options for chart types

Chart type	Option name	Description
Area, bar, cone, difference, line, pyramid	Category (X) Series	Arranges data on *x*-axis. Can group, sort, and aggregate data.
	Value (Y) Series	Plots values on *y*-axis.
Bubble	Category (X) Series	Plots values on the *x*-axis. Can group, sort, and aggregate data.
	Y Value and Size	Plots values on *y*-axis and defines the size of the bubbles.
Meter	Category Definition	Requires a blank string " ": quotation mark, space, quotation mark.
	Meter Value Definition	Defines values of the dial and position of the needle. Creates multiple meters.

(continues)

Chart type	Option name	Description
Alternate meter subtype	Category Definition	Requires a blank string " ": quotation mark, space, quotation mark.
	Meter Value Definition	Defines values of the dial and position of the needle.
Pie	Category Definition	Defines what slices represent.
	Slice Size Definition	Defines size of sectors. Creates multiple pies.
Scatter	Category (X) Series	Plots markers along *x*-axis. Groups data along *x*-axis.
	Value (Y) Series	Defines intersection of (*x*-*y*) value pairs. Defines multiple (*x*-*y*) value pairs.
Stock	Category (X) Series	Plots values along *x*-axis.
	Value (Y) Series	Defines four levels of data: high, low, open, close. Defines multiple sets of candlesticks.

Plotting the *x*- and *y*-axes

You can drag and drop the data columns from Data Preview to the category and value definition areas to plot the axes. The chart builder writes expressions for creating visual chart elements based on the data columns you drag and drop. You can then enhance the expressions to plot computed or filtered data. For example, you plot dates along the *x*-axis by dragging and dropping the ORDERDATE column from the data preview to Category (X) Series, as shown in Figure 18-5.

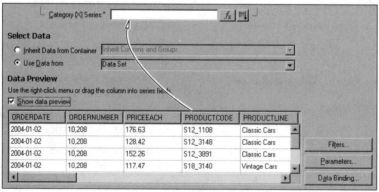

Figure 18-5   Defining the *x*-axis expression

You can specify that the chart builder plot X-Y data points using one column of data, such as order quantity, multiplied by another column, such as price.

You plot these data points by first dragging and dropping the order quantity column from Data Preview to Value (Y) Series, as shown in Figure 18-6.

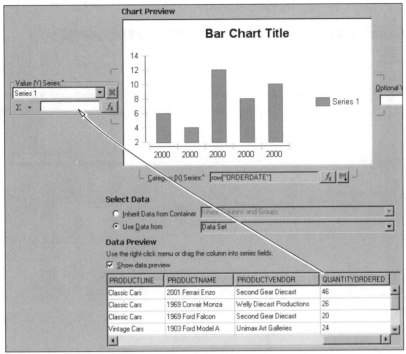

Figure 18-6   Defining the y-axis expression

 Next, open the expression builder to enhance the expression, as shown in Figure 18-7.

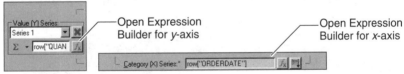

Figure 18-7   Opening the expression builder

In the expression builder, which is described earlier in this book, you can view and select the available column bindings to add code for the bindings to your expression. You can also add operators, JavaScript functions, and BIRT functions.

You need to type the portions of the following expression that you cannot drag and drop. For example, the first line of the following expression applies a filter to the query of the Classic Models database to return only classic car data. The second line computes the revenue for each order.

```
if(row["PRODUCTLINE"] == "Classic Cars"){
row["QUANTITYORDERED"] * row["PRICEEACH"]}
```

Using this expression to define the Value (Y) Series expression plots data points using order quantities times price.

Figure 18-8 shows the expression builder and available column bindings.

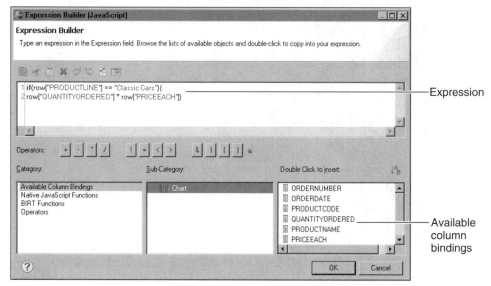

Figure 18-8   Expression builder

Grouping and sorting category data

When the expression returns too many categories to fit on the *x*-axis, on the meter, or in a pie, you need to use the grouping functionality in the chart builder, as shown in Figure 18-9.

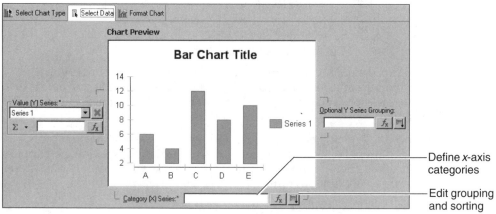

Figure 18-9   Defining *x*-axis categories and grouping and sorting

You can group text, numeric, or date-and-time data. For example, the Classic Models database includes all of these data types, as shown in Figure 18-10.

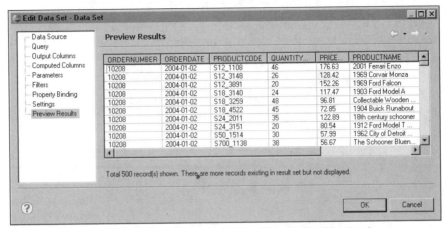

Figure 18-10   Previewing data types in the Classic Models database

Plotting every order across the *x*-axis creates so many bars that a user cannot read the values in the chart. To plot order information more clearly in a bar chart, group categories that appear on the *x*-axis by month, as shown in Figure 18-11.

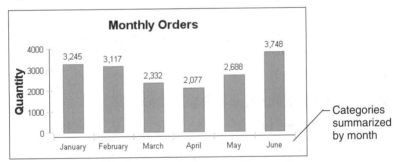

Figure 18-11   *X*-axis categories grouped by month

How to group categories on the *x*-axis

1 In the chart builder, in Select Data, choose Edit Group and Sorting. Figure 18-9 shows the location of Edit Group and Sorting.

2 In Data Sorting, select Ascending or Descending.

3 In Sort On, type or select a value.

4 In Grouping, select Enabled to see the grouping options shown in Figure 18-12.

5 Use the following options to set up a group:

   ▪ In Type, select Text, Numeric, or DateTime. If you select DateTime, you can specify the units to use to form the groups, such as Months.

- In Interval, select a number that represents the size of the groups to create. For example, to group three-row sequences of text data, select 3. To group numeric data in sections of four, select 4.

- In Aggregate Expression, select the function to use to aggregate the data in the group. You can select Average, Sum, Count, Distinct Count, First, Last, Minimum, and Maximum.

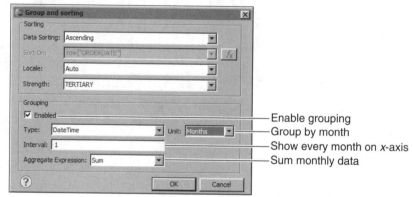

Figure 18-12   Grouping category data by month

Grouping date-and-time data

You can group date-and-time data by seconds, hours, minutes, days, weeks, months, or years. Use the interval option to perform selective plotting of group members. For example, to plot data for every other month, use an interval of 2.

Grouping textual data

You group textual data using an interval. The interval determines how many rows compose each group. For example, if you use an interval of 20, each group contains 20 rows of text from the database.

Grouping numeric data

You group numeric data by specifying the rows of data that compose the group. The chart builder uses a default interval of 0.5 to create numeric groups. If you change the setting to 20, the first group contains rows with values between 1 and 20, the second group contains rows with values between 21 and 40, and so on. If the chart does not include a value in a group section, that section does not appear in the report. If you group order numbers 150–300 using a value of 20, the first group section that appears in the chart is 141–160.

For example, Table 18-2 displays budget data for three cities.

Table 18-2   Data for a chart that uses category series grouping

Year	City	Budget
2008	Los Angeles	3485398
2008	Chicago	2783726
2008	New York	7322564
2009	Los Angeles	4694820
2009	Chicago	3196016
2009	New York	8008278
2010	Los Angeles	6819951
2010	Chicago	2569121
2010	New York	8085742

To group data using the Year field, you enable grouping, specify the data type of the field, and define a grouping interval. The data type that you select determines how the chart builder creates the groups as follows:

- If Year is a text field, selecting an interval value of 3 creates three groups. The first group includes the first three rows in the table, the second group contains rows four through six, and the third group contains the last three rows.

  When you group text values, you must use a regular grouping interval. You cannot create groups of varied sizes or use a field value to create a group. To create sensible groups in the chart, you must arrange the data in your data source before you create the chart. To use more complicated grouping, you should use your query to group data, then you can use those grouped values in the chart.

- If Year is a numeric field, selecting an interval value of 3 creates two groups. The first group includes the 1998 rows, because grouping by three from a base value of 1 creates one group that ends with 2008. The second group contains the 2009 and 2010 rows.

After you define how to create the groups, you must select an aggregate function that determines how the chart builder combines the values in each group.

Sorting category data

The category values appear in the chart in the order that the query returns them. You can sort the data so that it appears in a different order on an axis, in a dial, or in a pie. For example, you can show cities along the x-axis in alphabetical order. Similarly, you can show customer ranks in descending numeric order around a pie. Charts support sorting data in an ascending or a descending order. To sort data, in Select Data, choose Edit Group and Sorting. In Data Sorting, select Ascending or Descending, as shown in Figure 18-13.

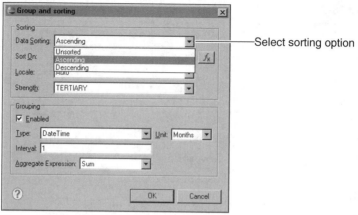

Select sorting option

Figure 18-13   Selecting a sorting option and enabling grouping

Grouping optional Y value data

You group Y values for different reasons, depending on the chart type, as described in Table 18-3.

Table 18-3   Using optional Y grouping for different chart types

Chart type	Reason for using optional Y grouping
Bar, cone, line, pyramid, tube	To summarize data into multiple sets of risers in the chart.
Area, difference	To summarize data into multiple areas in the chart.
Bubble	To identify bubbles using the legend.
Meter	To plot multiple meters.
Alternate meter subtype	To plot multiple dials.
Pie	To plot multiple pies.
Scatter	To plot multiple (x-y) value pairs.
Stock	To plot multiple sets of candlesticks.

To group y-axis values, you use Optional Y Grouping in the Select Data page of the chart builder.

Grouping Y values in a bar chart

The chart shown in Figure 18-14 groups Y values to plot multiple sets of bars representing the monthly sum of orders for three types of vehicles.

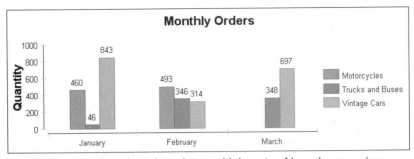

Figure 18-14   Bar chart that plots multiple sets of bars by grouping

Figure 18-15 shows the axes and grouping definitions used to create this chart.

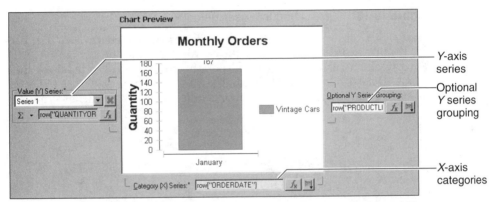

Figure 18-15   Axes and grouping definitions for plotting multiple sets of bars

Build the expressions shown in Table 18-4 by dragging columns from the data preview and dropping them in the three areas shown in Figure 18-15.

Table 18-4   Definitions of series in bar chart that uses grouping

Series	Expression
Value (Y) Series	`row["QUANTITYORDERED"]`
Category (X) Series	`row["ORDERDATE"]`
Optional Y Series Grouping	`row["PRODUCTLINE"]`

Grouping multiple *y*-axis values in a stock chart

In a stock chart, four different value series expressions provide the high, low, open, and close data. The category series expression arranges the values along the *x*-axis, typically along a date or time scale. To set up multiple sets of candlesticks, you can either define multiple value series definitions or use optional grouping. For example, the stock chart in Figure 18-16 presents stock data for two companies.

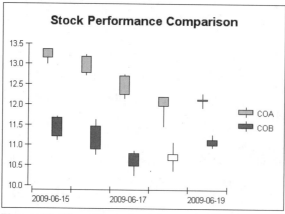

Figure 18-16   Stock chart that uses grouping

Figure 18-17 shows the expressions used to create the chart. The chart uses the *y*-value expressions to set up the candlesticks and the category X expression to arrange the candlesticks in chronological order along the *x*-axis. The expression, row["Symbol"], which you drag and drop in Optional Y Series Grouping, creates one set of candlesticks for each ticker symbol.

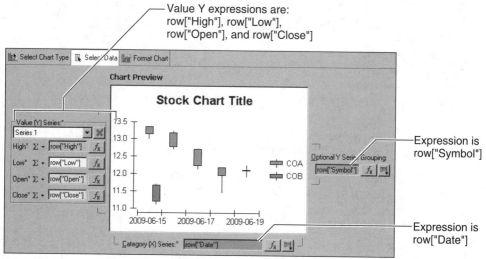

Figure 18-17   Data expressions for the stock chart

The data for the chart is shown in Table 18-5.

Table 18-5   Data for a stock chart that uses grouping

Symbol	Date	Open	High	Low	Close
COA	6/15/2009	13.36	13.36	13.01	13.15
COB	6/15/2009	11.67	11.70	11.12	11.21

Table 18-5   Data for a stock chart that uses grouping

Symbol	Date	Open	High	Low	Close
COA	6/16/2009	13.18	13.23	12.72	12.78
COB	6/16/2009	11.46	11.62	10.77	10.90
COA	6/17/2009	12.71	12.73	12.14	12.25
COB	6/17/2009	10.80	10.85	10.25	10.49
COA	6/18/2009	12.19	12.19	11.46	11.97
COB	6/18/2009	10.63	11.06	10.37	10.78
COA	6/19/2009	12.13	12.27	11.93	12.10
COB	6/19/2009	11.14	11.25	10.94	11.00

You can also use multiple sets of value series expressions to create multiple sets of candlesticks. For example, you can create the same chart using joined data. Table 18-6 contains the data for company COA stocks.

Table 18-6   Data for a stock chart using two sets of value series expressions

Date	COAOpen	COAHigh	COALow	COAClose
6/15/2009	13.36	13.36	13.01	13.15
6/16/2009	13.18	13.23	12.72	12.78
6/17/2009	12.71	12.73	12.14	12.25
6/18/2009	12.19	12.19	11.46	11.97
6/19/2009	12.13	12.27	11.93	12.10

Table 18-7 contains the data for company COB stocks used by the same chart.

Table 18-7   Data for the second series for a stock chart using two sets of value series expressions

Date	COBOpen	COBHigh	COBLow	COBClose
6/15/2009	11.67	11.70	11.12	11.21
6/16/2009	11.46	11.62	10.77	10.90
6/17/2009	10.80	10.85	10.25	10.49
6/18/2009	10.63	11.06	10.37	10.78
6/19/2009	11.14	11.25	10.94	11.00

To define multiple sets of candlesticks, you use the value series drop-down list. Select New Series, shown in Figure 18-18, and then either drag and drop columns from Chart Preview to the expression fields, or type code to create the series expressions. After you add one or more sets of expressions, you can use the drop-down list to navigate among them.

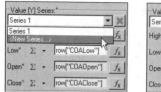 

Figure 18-18   Adding a stock chart value series

To create multiple sets of candlesticks, you use the following expressions to define the category and value series in the stock chart:

- The Category Series Definition is row["Date"].

- The first set of value series expressions uses row["COAHigh"], row["COALow"], row["COAOpen"], and row["COAClose"].

- The second set of value series expressions uses row["COBHigh"], row["COBLow"], row["COBOpen"], and row["COBClose"].

Using multiple *y*-axes

Charts support displaying data on more than one *y*-axis. Additional *y*-axes can use a different scale from the first *y*-axis. To create a second *y*-axis, use the Select Chart Type page. In Multiple Y Axis, select Secondary Axis or More Axes, as shown in Figure 18-19. The chart preview shows a second *y*-axis on the opposite side of the chart to the first *y*-axis after a selection of Secondary Axis. For a selection of More Axes, additional axes appear in the preview only after creation of each axis.

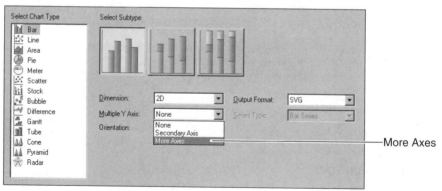

Figure 18-19   Using the Select Chart Type page to add a *y*-axis

After enabling multiple axes, specify data for all additional axes. Define the *y*-, but not the *x*-axis, of each additional axis. The category *x*-axis and optional grouping definitions apply to all *y*-axes. In Select Data, provide the expression for the second and any subsequent *y*-axes, as shown in Figure 18-20.

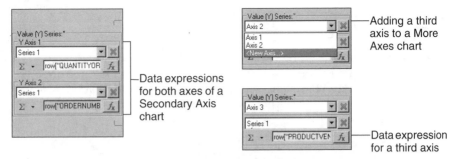

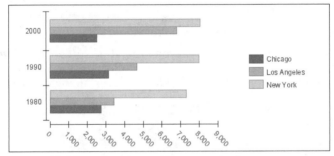

Adding a third axis to a More Axes chart

Data expressions for both axes of a Secondary Axis chart

Data expression for a third axis

Figure 18-20 Using Chart Data to add data for secondary *y*-axes

Transposing chart axes

Transposing the axes of a chart plots categories on the vertical axis and values on the horizontal axis. Figure 18-21 shows a bar chart using transposed axes.

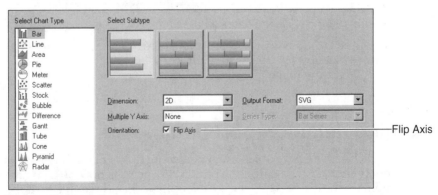

Figure 18-21 Bar chart with transposed axes

Two-dimensional charts and charts using depth support transposing axes. Three-dimensional charts do not support transposing axes. To transpose axes, navigate to the Select Chart Type page, then select Flip Axis, as shown in Figure 18-22.

Figure 18-22 Transposing the axes of a chart

Filtering data

You can limit the data that the chart displays by applying a filter. Usually, you filter data as you create a data set in Data Explorer. If you already started designing a chart, you can filter the data in the chart builder to prevent losing work on the chart. You choose Filters in the Select Data page, as shown in Figure 18-23.

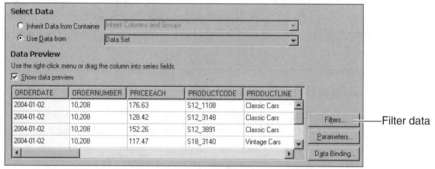

Figure 18-23   Options for filtering data from the chart builder

In Filters, shown in Figure 18-24, you construct the expression to filter the data. As you learned earlier in this book, you select the expression, operator, and values from the drop-down list, which contains only valid options.

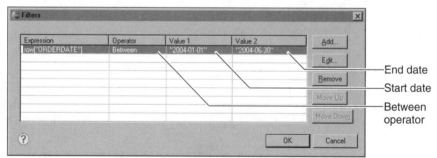

Figure 18-24   Filtering data by date

To define multiple filters, select <New Filter Here> in an empty row. Then, select set of options. To re-order a list of filters, select a filter, then use the up or down arrow to move the selected filter up or down the list.

Changing default report parameters

Earlier in this book, you learned how to include a parameter marker, ?, in the query defined for a data set. The marker specifies how BIRT dynamically updates the query when the user supplies a report parameter. If the data set linked to the chart includes a parameter marker in the query, you can review or change the default parameter value from the chart builder. From the Select Data page, choose Parameters. In Parameters, select the value to change it, as shown in Figure 18-25.

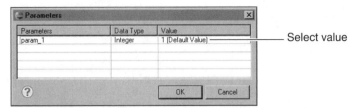

Figure 18-25   Changing the default parameter value from the chart builder

Creating data bindings

Data binding establishes a relationship between chart or report items and the underlying data source. When a user types a parameter in response to a prompt from the report, the data values of the chart or report item changes, and BIRT updates the chart or report.

From within the chart builder, you can add, edit, and delete data bindings using the data set linked to the chart. From the Select Data page, choose Data Binding. Select Data Binding, shown in Figure 18-26, appears.

Name	Display Name ID	Display Name	Data Type	Expression	Function	Filter	Aggregate On	
ORDERNUMBER			Integer	dataSetRow["ORDERNUMBE...			N/A	Add...
ORDERDATE			Date	dataSetRow["ORDERDATE"]			N/A	Add Aggregation...
PRODUCTCODE			String	dataSetRow["PRODUCTCODE"]			N/A	
QUANTITYORDERED			Integer	dataSetRow["QUANTITYORD...			N/A	Edit...
PRICEEACH			Float	dataSetRow["PRICEEACH"]			N/A	
PRODUCTNAME			String	dataSetRow["PRODUCTNAME"]			N/A	Remove
PRODUCTLINE			String	dataSetRow["PRODUCTLINE"]			N/A	
PRODUCTVENDOR			String	dataSetRow["PRODUCTVEND...			N/A	Refresh

Figure 18-26   Creating data bindings

Use Add, Edit, or Remove to perform the data binding tasks. Choose Add Aggregation to create a computed column using the aggregate functions described earlier in this book.

Previewing data and chart

From within the chart builder, you can see some of the data in the data set linked to the chart. Previewing sample data can help you decide which column to use to plot the x- and y-axis. For example, in Figure 18-27, Data Preview shows several columns of data from the Classic Models database that ships with BIRT.

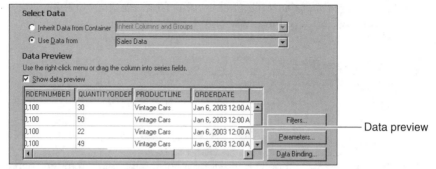

Figure 18-27   Previewing the data in the chart builder

Data Preview serves another important purpose as you define charts. You can drag and drop the columns from Data Preview to the value, category, and optional Y grouping definitions in the upper portion of Select Data.

As you set up the expressions that specify the data for your chart, Chart Preview presents a rough idea of how your published chart will look. Figure 18-28 shows the chart preview of a bar chart.

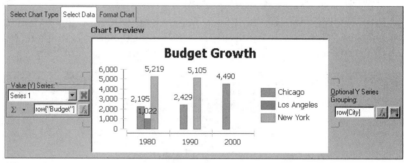

Figure 18-28   Previewing chart data on Select Data

You can change some characteristics of chart previews to improve performance. As you design a chart, the chart preview uses either live data, as shown in Figure 18-28, or randomly generated sample data, as shown in Figure 18-29. You can also change the number of data rows that appear in the chart builder. By default, the Data Preview section shows six rows of data. You can display more or fewer rows.

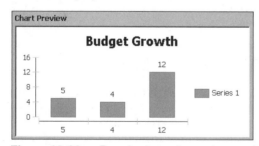

Figure 18-29   Bar chart preview using random data

How to change chart preview preferences

1 Choose Window→Preferences.

2 Expand Report Design. Select the Chart list item. Expand Chart and Field Assist, as shown in Figure 18-30. Field Assist and Content Assist preferences include options to flag required fields in the chart builder and to display hints for building an expression.

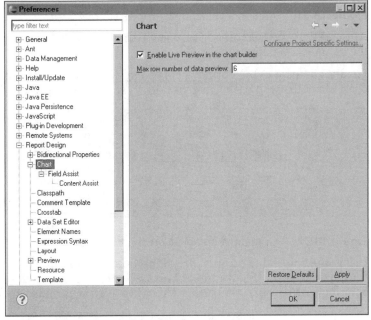

Figure 18-30 Chart page of Preferences

3 To have the chart builder use randomly selected data in the chart preview window, deselect Enable Live Preview.

4 To set the number of rows that Data Preview displays, type a value in the field.

5 Choose OK.

Creating a combination chart

A combination chart is a chart that incorporates two or more different chart types. You can combine the following chart types: area, bar, cone, pyramid, stock, tube, or line. Combination charts must use at least two value series, one for each of the chart types displayed.

To create the combination chart, first create a chart of one type, such as a bar chart. Next, define the value series expressions on the Select Data page. To provide more than one value series expression, use the value series drop-down list. Select New Series, then use the expression field to supply the series expression, as shown in Figure 18-31.

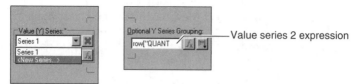

Figure 18-31　Adding a value series expression

After adding one or more series, use the drop-down list to navigate among the value series definitions.

Finally, navigate to the Format Chart page, and in the Series section, select a chart of another type, such as pyramid, as shown in Figure 18-32.

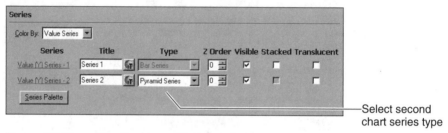

Figure 18-32　Creating a combination chart

Using multiple value series expressions, you can present more data on the chart. For example, Figure 18-33 shows a chart with one value series in which bars show order quantities and another in which pyramids show revenue.

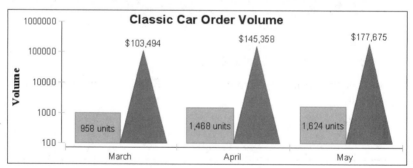

Figure 18-33　Combination bar and pyramid chart

The chart groups the dates by month and shows the unit order volume and revenue for classic cars over a three-month period.

To define the order in which the series appear on a combination chart, set the z-ordering rendering priority for the series. On the bar chart shown in Figure 18-34, the z-ordering priority causes the two bar series to display in front of the area chart.

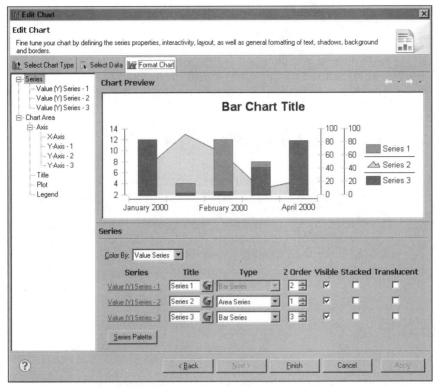

Figure 18-34   Z-order value

Defining a meter chart

A meter chart shows a data value as a needle that marks a position on a dial. You can create a chart that shows one or more needles on one dial or one that shows multiple dials, each displaying one needle. It is not possible to use multiple needles on multiple dials. Figure 18-35 shows two sample meter charts.

Figure 18-35   Meter charts using one and two meters

The meter value series specifies the needle value. The chosen expression determines where on the dial the needle appears. To show multiple needles or meters, use either multiple meter value series expressions or Optional Grouping.

A category definition is not essential to a meter chart. You must, however, provide an expression in the Category Definition field. You can type a space that is enclosed by quotation marks in this field to satisfy this requirement. The chart selects the first row returned by the meter value definition and uses the data from that row in the chart.

Using multiple meters in a chart

The meter value definition specifies the dial values and position of the needle. To show multiple meters, use either multiple meter value definitions or grouping. For example, Figure 18-36 is a standard meter chart. Standard meter charts use only one needle for each meter. The chart uses population as the needle value and city as a grouping field. Because the chart builder requires a value in the category field, provide a string containing a single space, " ", for the Category Definition.

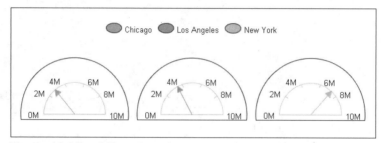

Figure 18-36   Meter chart that uses multiple meters

The chart in Figure 18-36 uses the data in Table 18-8.

Table 18-8   Data for a meter chart that uses grouping

City	Population
Chicago	2783726
Los Angeles	3485398
New York	7322564

The chart builder uses the expressions to position the needles and plot each population value as the position of a needle on the dial. The chart builder uses the values to position the dials, one for each meter, in the chart. The grouping sets up a meter for each city. The legend identifies the meters.

Using multiple dials in a chart

To show multiple dials, select the alternate subtype when you choose the chart type, as shown in Figure 18-37.

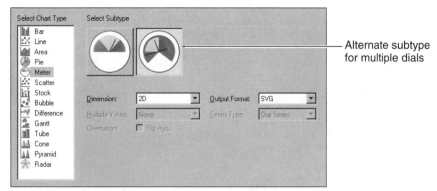

Alternate subtype
for multiple dials

Figure 18-37   Selecting the subtype, meter chart that uses multiple dials

You can also use multiple series definitions to create multiple meters or a meter with multiple needles. For example, the chart in Figure 18-38 is a superimposed meter chart that shows multiple needles in one meter. One needle shows the interior temperature, 201. The other needle shows the exterior temperature, 303.

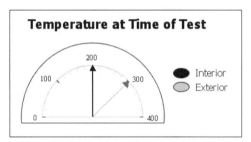

Figure 18-38   Super-imposed meter chart

The first meter value series expression is row["InteriorTemp"]. The second meter value series expression is row["ExteriorTemp"]. The chart does not use Optional Grouping. The Category Definition is a string containing a single space, " ".

To provide more than one meter value series expression, use the meter value series drop-down list. Select New Series, then use the expression field to supply the series expression. After adding one or more series, use the drop-down list to navigate among the meter value series definitions.

19

Laying Out and Formatting a Chart

Charts include many different visual elements, most of which are customizable. To clarify the presentation of data or to create a more pleasing composition, rearrange the chart layout. For example, change where the chart title appears or add padding between a series of bars and the axis on which they are arranged.

Before making changes to the layout of a chart, you must understand the parts making up a typical chart. Figure 19-1 identifies the elements of a basic bar chart, using different background colors to highlight the following areas:

- The plot containing all the parts of the chart

- The chart area containing the axes, their labels and titles, and the chart

- The legend containing information about the series displayed on the chart

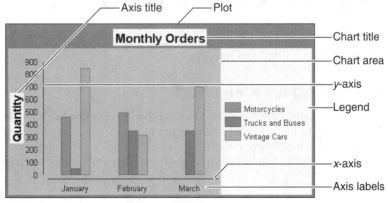

Figure 19-1   Elements of a chart

The color and style of these chart elements can be changed. For example, modify a chart to:

- Use a company's standard color scheme
- Outline or add a background color to the labels, legend, or plot
- Change the color and shape of the series elements, such as the sectors in a pie chart or the candlesticks in a stock chart
- Add gridlines that extend across the plot
- Add data point labels to show the exact value of bars in a bar chart

Overview of formatting

The following types of formatting changes are available for most charts:

- Setting chart area format attributes. Change the background color or outline of different chart areas or modify the padding between chart areas.
- Formatting numbers, dates, and times. Customize the appearance of dates and numbers in a chart, and add a prefix or suffix to numbers.
- Formatting the chart legend, plot, and title. Add color, an outline, and a shadow to highlight the plot, title, or legend.
- Formatting axis titles, markers, lines, and labels. Adjust the line style of an axis, and modify the text style, position, coloring, or outline of axis labels or titles.
- Formatting a series. Change the type of a series, such as line or bar, the color or style of the series markers, and the attributes specific to each series type.

Formatting specific types of charts

In addition to formatting options that apply to charts in general, the chart builder provides formatting options that apply to individual chart types or subsets of the available chart types.

Formatting an area chart

The style or color of the area borders can be changed or the borders themselves can be hidden. For example, Figure 19-2 shows a chart having standard lines bordering the areas on the left and curved lines bordering the areas on the right. Both charts in Figure 19-3 have no lines bordering the areas.

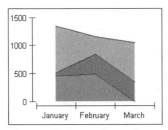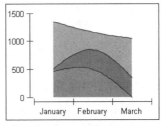

Figure 19-2   Area chart using different border line options

You can also add point markers that identify the data points that an area encloses. The legend uses the markers to identify the areas. Figure 19-3 shows one area chart that has markers and one that does not.

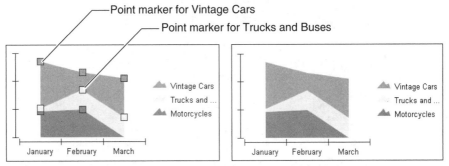

Figure 19-3   Area charts with and without point markers

To format lines and markers on an area chart, navigate to the Value (Y) Series section of Format Chart, then modify labels, lines, or markers, as shown in Figure 19-4. Line formatting affects marker borders as well as area borders.

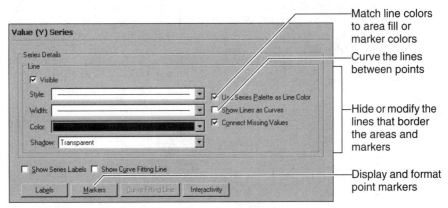

Figure 19-4   Format options for an area chart

Formatting a line or a scatter chart

Line and scatter charts use the same formatting attributes. By default, a line chart shows lines between data points, but a scatter chart shows only the data points. A scatter chart does support formatting to show lines between data points. To format a line or scatter-chart series, navigate to the Value (Y) Series section of Format Chart. The settings that can be modified for the chart lines and markers are shown earlier in Figure 19-4.

Formatting a bar chart

By default, a bar chart displays rectangles without outlines, but you can change the bars to cones, tubes, or pyramids, or add a bar outline. To format a bar chart, navigate to the Series section of Format Chart. Use the settings to modify the bars, as shown in Figure 19-5.

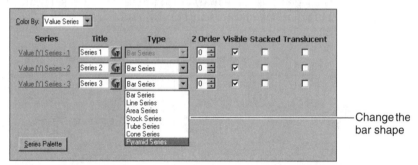

Figure 19-5   Formatting options for a bar chart series

To add an outline to the bars or other risers, navigate to the Value (Y) Series section of Format Chart. In Series Outline, select a color.

Formatting a bubble chart

Adding acceleration lines to bubble charts emphasizes their *y*-axis value, as shown by the dashed lines in Figure 19-6. You can also add various styles and colors of lines around the bubbles. In Figure 19-6, a thick black line around the bubbles makes them stand out.

Figure 19-6   Using acceleration lines and bubble borders

To change these colors and styles, navigate to the Value (Y) Series section of Format Chart. Use Series Details to add and format acceleration lines, or to add lines around the bubbles, as shown in Figure 19-7.

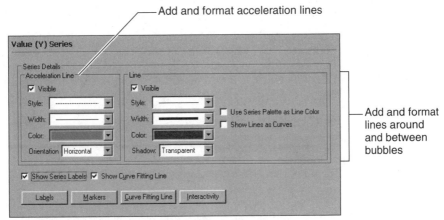

Figure 19-7   Bubble chart formatting options

Formatting a difference chart

Difference charts use fill areas to highlight differences in data. The chart can display positive differences in one color and negative differences in another. For example, use a difference chart to show how sales compare to quota over a period of time, where positive values represent sales in excess of quota and negative values represent sales below quota.

To show positive and negative differences, navigate to the Value (Y) Series section of Format Chart. Use Value (Y) Series to display and format positive and negative areas on the difference chart, as shown in Figure 19-8.

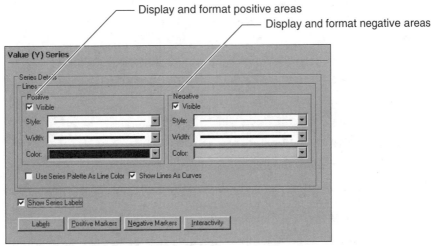

Figure 19-8   Displaying positive and negative fills on a difference chart

Formatting a Gantt chart

Gantt charts display project schedules using bars to show beginning and ending dates of multiple tasks. The colors of the bars represent the task status. Optionally, markers designate the start and end dates of tasks.

To add and format task markers and bars, navigate to the Value (Y) Series section of Format Chart. Use Value (Y) Series to change and resize the symbols that mark the start and end of a task. You can also specify the color, style, and size of symbol markers and task bars, as shown in Figure 19-9.

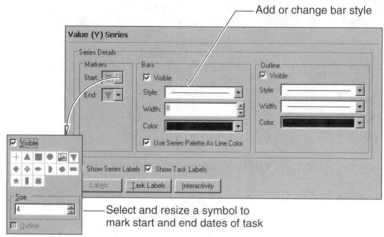

Figure 19-9   Formatting a Gantt chart

Formatting a meter chart

When you format a meter chart series, you work with the chart elements shown in Figure 19-10.

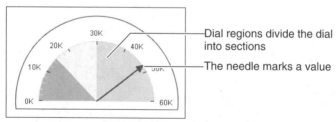

Figure 19-10   Elements of a meter chart

You can modify the following meter chart attributes:

- Dial size. Determine the size of the dial's radius as a proportion of the meter. Use start- and stop-angle settings to specify the portion of a complete circle that the meter comprises.

- Dial scale and tick marks. Set the range of values and the number or interval settings of tick marks.

- Dial-region size, color, and placement.

- Needle formats. Modify the style and width of the needle and its pointer.

- Multiple meter placement. If a chart uses multiple meters to present data, you can arrange the meters in rows or columns.

- Label settings. Show or hide labels for regions and for the chart data point.

Working with the dial size

To change the distance between the center of the chart and the outside of the dial, you change the dial radius. Use percentage settings to size the dial relative to the meter. For example, a setting of 50 creates a dial radius that is half the distance from the center of the meter to its outer boundary. In a chart that uses more than one value-series definition, you set a single dial radius that applies to all series. If different series contain different dial radius values, the dial uses the larger value.

To change the shape of a dial, you change the start- and stop-angle settings. The angles are measured counter-clockwise from the right. For example, in Figure 19-11, the dial uses a start setting of 20 and a stop setting of 160.

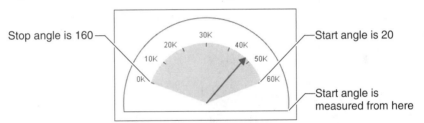

Figure 19-11   Start- and stop-angle settings in a semicircular meter

To set the size of a dial, navigate to the Value Series section of Format Chart. Use the Series Details to set or modify the dial size, as shown in Figure 19-12. You can also hide the dial labels using this page.

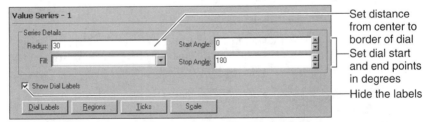

Figure 19-12   Dial size and label visibility settings

The start and stop settings of the dial affect the style of the meter. If both angle settings are between 0 and 180, the chart displays a half-circle. If either angle setting is less than 0 degrees or greater than 180 degrees, the chart displays a full circle. For example, the chart shown in Figure 19-13 uses a start angle of –20 and a stop angle of 200. The first value in the dial, 0, appears at 200 degrees, and the last, 60K, appears at –20 degrees.

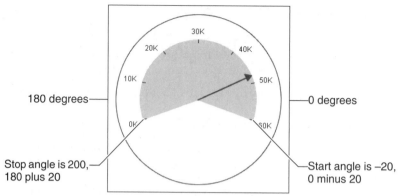

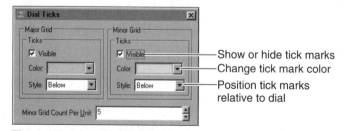

Figure 19-13   Start- and stop-angle settings in a full meter and full dial

Working with the dial scale and tick marks

The chart builder uses the available data to set a span for the dial, then it places tick marks at appropriate intervals. The dial scale defines the range of data values that the meter displays. To change the scale of a dial, navigate to the Value Series section of Format Chart, then choose Scale. Use the Scale settings to change the range or spacing of the data the dial displays, as shown in Figure 19-14.

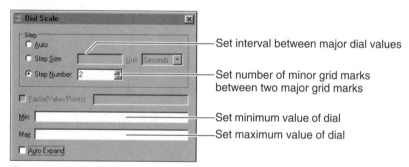

Figure 19-14   Dial scale options

To modify the tick marks on a dial, navigate to the Value Series section of Format Chart, then choose Ticks. Use the settings to modify the major or minor grid ticks, as shown in Figure 19-15.

Figure 19-15   Dial tick mark options

Working with needle formats

You can change the line style, width, and head style of a needle. Navigate to the Value Series section of Format Chart, then choose Needle to modify the needle appearance, as shown in Figure 19-16.

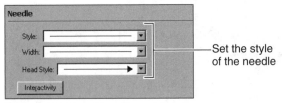

Set the style
of the needle

Figure 19-16   Needle style options

To change the color of a needle, select Series Palette, as shown in Figure 19-17.

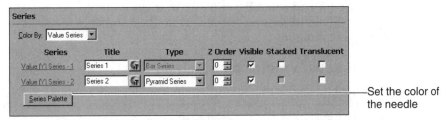

Set the color of
the needle

Figure 19-17   Changing needle color

Working with multiple meters

In a chart with multiple meters, you can position the meters by specifying how many columns to use to display them. For example, to use three meters to contrast the performance of two managers in one territory and one manager in another territory, specify a two-column grid. Using two columns for three meters produces the chart shown on the left in Figure 19-18. To arrange the meters horizontally, as shown on the right, specify three columns.

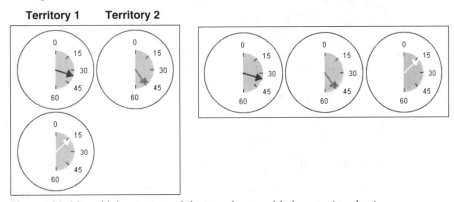

Figure 19-18   Using two- and three-column grids in a meter chart

To lay out the meters, navigate to the Chart Area section of Format Chart, then choose General Properties. In Grid Column Count, select the number of columns the chart uses to display the meters, as shown in Figure 19-19.

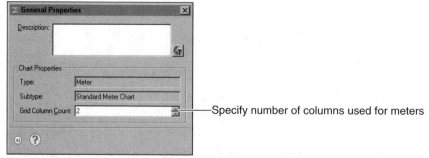
—Specify number of columns used for meters

Figure 19-19   Grid Column Count option

Specifying a grid column count of 1 arranges multiple meters vertically. Specifying a grid column count equal to the number of meters arranges the meters horizontally.

Working with meter chart labels

To format the labels that identify points on the dial, navigate to the Value Series section of Format Chart and choose Dial Labels. Use the settings shown in Figure 19-20 to format, outline, or pad the labels.

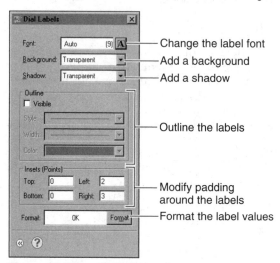
— Change the label font
—Add a background
—Add a shadow

— Outline the labels

— Modify padding around the labels
—Format the label values

Figure 19-20   Dial label options

Working with dial regions

To highlight the values on the dial, you use dial regions. Dial regions are similar to axis markers. You determine a start and an end value for each region. After you set up the regions, you can change the region color or outline. If regions overlap, the last region that you create takes precedence in formatting. You can also set the inner and outer radius of a region to specify the part of the dial showing the region's color. For example, Figure 19-21 shows a chart with two regions. The region on the left has an outer radius of 45. The region on the right has an inner radius of 30 and an outer radius of 60.

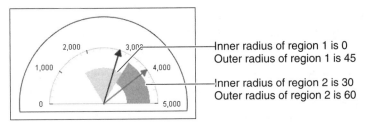

Figure 19-21   Regions in a dial

To add and format a dial region, navigate to the Value Series section of Format Chart, then choose Regions to use the options shown in Figure 19-22. To control the region's radius, set the distance from center of dial to the inner and outer edge of region.

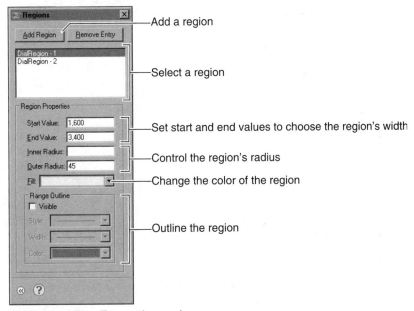

Figure 19-22   Formatting regions

Formatting a pie chart

You can modify the following characteristics of pie charts:

- Aspect ratio and rotation
  Change the aspect ratio to make a pie chart oval, and rotate the chart.

- Color and outline
  Select color and outline settings for each pie slice.

- Distance between pie slices
  Separate one or more slices of the pie from the rest of the chart.

- Leader lines
  Modify the appearance of leader lines or hide them.

- Presentation of multiple and grouped pie charts
  Improve the appearance of multiple pie charts by specifying a uniform size for individual pie charts. Arrange grouped pie charts in rows or columns.

Working with aspect ratio and rotation

Changing the aspect ratio of a pie chart makes it oval rather than circular, as shown in Figure 19-23. Rotating a pie chart changes the position of the slices.

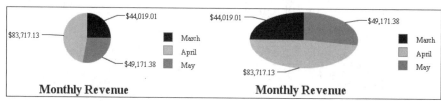

Figure 19-23   Pie chart displayed as a circle and an oval rotated 90 degrees

To modify aspect ratio or rotation, navigate to the Value Series section of Format Chart, shown in Figure 19-24.

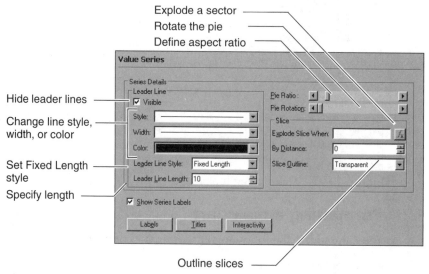

Figure 19-24   Formatting a pie chart

By default, Pie Ratio is set to an aspect ratio of 1, creating a circle. To create an oval, scroll to a higher or lower aspect ratio. An aspect ratio greater than 1 results in a vertically stretched oval, and an aspect ratio less than 1 creates a horizontally stretched oval. To rotate the chart, in Pie Rotation, scroll from a default value of 0.0 to the degrees by which to rotate the chart. The chart rotates in a counter-clockwise direction.

Working with leader lines

As shown in Figure 19-24, the line style, width, and color of leader lines can be modified in the same way as the formatting attributes of other lines in a chart. To specify the same length for all leader lines, select the leader-line style, Fixed Length. To hide the leader lines, deselect Visible.

Working with pie slices

You can outline each slice and change the outline properties. You can also select a color palette for the sectors. To outline pie-chart slices, navigate to the Value Series section of Format Chart, then use Slice Outline to select an outline color, as shown in Figure 19-24. You can also set the percentage of the plot area used to render the pie slices.

You can set a minimum value for pie slices. A slice with a value equal to or greater than the minimum appears as usual. Slices with values below the minimum are combined in a new remainders slice. You can create a label for the remainders slice to display in the legend.

You can set the minimum as a static value or as a percentage of the pie value. For example, you can show sales totals for a group of customers and combine customers with sales below $1,000,000.00 in a sector called Infrequent Orders, or you can combine customers with sales below two percent of the total sales.

To specify a minimum slice size, navigate to the Category Series section of Format Chart, then set up a minimum slice size equal to either a value related to slice size or to a percentage of the pie, as shown in Figure 19-25.

Figure 19-25   Minimum slice settings

Exploding pie slices

By default, pie slices are not offset from the chart. Slices appear joined to one another at the center of the chart, and leader lines connect slices and data labels, as shown in Figure 19-26.

To emphasize a slice, explode it. This action offsets the slice from the rest of the chart, as shown in Figure 19-27.

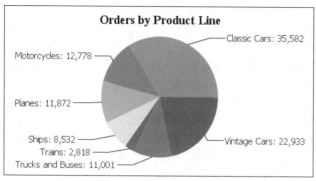

Figure 19-26   Using default formatting settings

First, decide which slices to explode. To explode all pie slices, specify the offset in By Distance. To explode specific pie slices, create an expression. For example, create an expression to explode only the slices that represent total orders under $3000.

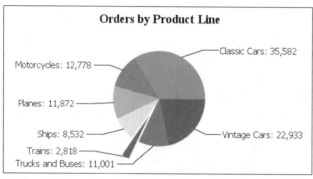

Figure 19-27   Exploding the Trains slice

 Navigate to the Value Series section of Format Chart. In Explode Slice When, open Expression Builder. Expression Builder includes a Variables category to facilitate creating the expression, as shown in Figure 19-28.

Use the Variables category to add variables, such as Value Data or Category Data, to the expression. For example, use the following expression to explode slices that have a value of less than 3000:

```
valueData<3000
```

In By Distance, provide the offset. For example, a value of 25 offsets exploded slices by twenty-five percent of the size of the original pie.

Arranging multiple pies

When you create a report that contains multiple pie charts, enhance the appearance of the report by making the pies a uniform size. Double-click one of the pie charts to open the chart builder. Navigate to the Chart Area section of Format Chart. In Coverage, type 50 to specify that the pie cover 50 percent

of the plotting area. Preview the report and compare the size of the pie you
scaled to others in the report. Experiment using different values until you
find the value that makes the pies a uniform size.

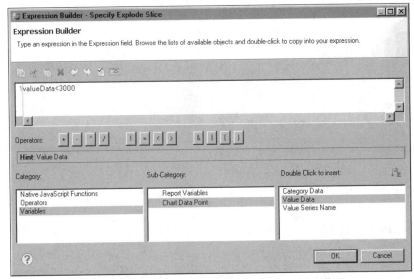

Figure 19-28   Building an expression to explode a pie slice

When you create a single chart that uses multiple pies, you can specify how
many columns to use to display them. For example, in Figure 19-29, the chart
on the left uses one column, so the chart builder positions the pies vertically,
one below the other, within the column. The chart on the right uses two
columns, so the chart builder positions pies in each of two columns.

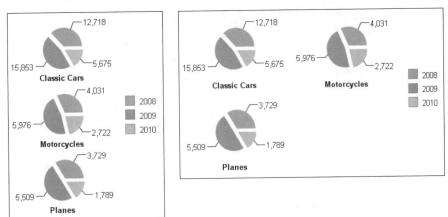

Figure 19-29   Pie charts using different column-count settings

To arrange multiple pies in a pie chart, navigate to the Chart Area section of
Format Chart, then choose General Properties. In Grid Column Count, select
how many columns to use to display the pies.

Formatting a stock chart

When you format a stock chart, change the color of the filled body of the candlestick using the Series Palette. You can also change the color and style of the shadows and hollow body, as shown in Figure 19-30.

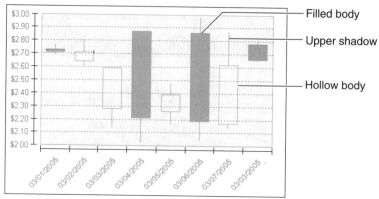

Figure 19-30   Stock chart

To format a stock-chart series, navigate to the Value (Y) Series section of Format Chart, then format the candlesticks, display series labels, or add a curve-fitting line, as shown in Figure 19-31.

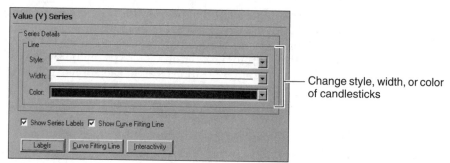

Figure 19-31   Stock-chart series options

Formatting a three-dimensional chart

When you format a three-dimensional chart, use axis rotation to change the orientation of the chart or use unit spacing to set the space between series. You can also change the wall and floor colors and set the series depth.

Working with chart rotation

You can rotate the axes of a three-dimensional chart. To rotate axes, use the following settings:

- The x-axis rotation controls how the chart tilts toward or away from the viewer.

- The *y*-axis rotation controls how the chart pivots left and right on the *y*-axis in the center of the chart.

- The *z*-axis rotation controls how the chart tilts up and down on the central *z*-axis.

By default, a three-dimensional chart uses an *x*-axis rotation of –20, a *y*-axis rotation of 45, and a *z*-axis rotation of zero. A chart that uses default rotation settings appears oriented like the one shown in Figure 19-32.

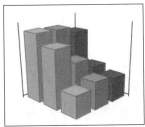

Figure 19-32   Three-dimensional chart using default axis rotation

Figure 19-33 shows the effects of changing each setting in the sample chart.

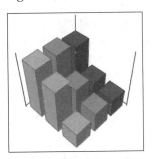  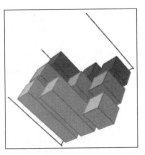

  x-axis rotation set to –45   *y*-axis rotation set to –45   *z*-axis rotation set to –45

Figure 19-33   Three-dimensional charts using different rotation settings

To change the rotation of an axis, navigate to the Chart Area section of Format Chart, then provide a rotation value, as shown in Figure 19-34.

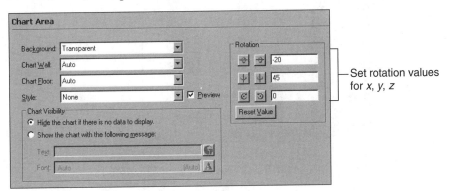

Figure 19-34   Setting rotation options

Working with the space between elements

To control the space between adjacent series in a three-dimensional chart, you use unit spacing. The unit-spacing value is the percentage of the series width that appears between each series. For example, the default unit spacing is 50. Consequently, the space between two series elements in the chart, such as two sets of bars, is approximately 50 percent of the width of one series element. Figure 19-35 presents the difference between two unit-spacing settings in a sample three-dimensional bar chart.

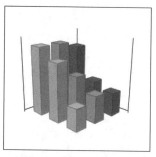 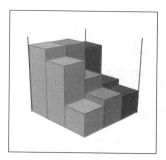

Unit spacing set to 100   Unit spacing set to 0

Figure 19-35   Charts using different unit-spacing settings

To change the spacing between adjacent series, navigate to the Chart Area section of Format Chart, then choose General Properties. In Unit Spacing, provide a value. The value specifies the percentage of the series width to use to separate series elements.

Setting the wall and floor colors

In a chart that has depth or a three-dimensional chart, you can modify the color of the chart wall and floor. The default wall and floor color setting is transparent. Figure 19-36 shows where the wall and floor appear in a two-dimensional bar chart with depth.

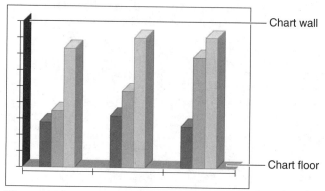

Chart wall

Chart floor

Figure 19-36   Wall and floor of a chart using depth

Figure 19-37 shows the locations of the wall and floor in a three-dimensional chart.

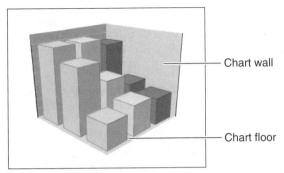

Chart wall

Chart floor

Figure 19-37 Walls and floor of a three-dimensional chart

To set the wall or floor color of a chart using depth or a three-dimensional chart, navigate to the Chart Area section of Format Chart. Use the settings shown in Figure 19-38 to set a wall or floor color.

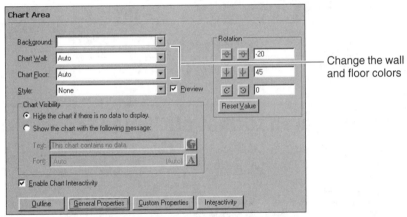

Change the wall and floor colors

Figure 19-38 Wall and floor color options

Setting the series depth of a chart

In a chart having depth or in a three-dimensional chart, you can specify how deep the chart bars stretch. For example, Figure 19-39 compares different series depths for a two-dimensional bar chart with depth. The upper chart uses a series depth of 10 points. The lower chart uses a series depth of 20 points. The units of measurement, such as points, for the series depth match the units that appear in the chart. You can specify the depth of lines that appear in a two-dimensional with depth pie chart.

To set the depth of series elements in a chart, navigate to the Chart Area section of Format Chart, then choose General Properties. Provide a value in Series Depth.

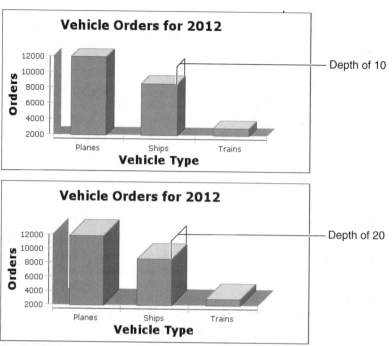

Figure 19-39   Comparing different depths of series elements

Setting chart area format attributes

You can add background color, an outline, and change the line style of the chart elements shown in Figure 19-40.

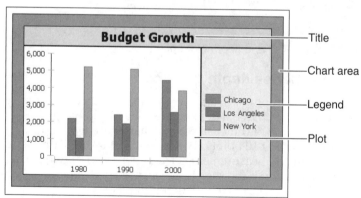

Figure 19-40   Parts of the chart included in Chart Area

To set the formatting attributes for these chart elements, access the Chart Area section of Format Chart. Figure 19-41 shows the location of Chart Area and the chart element sections.

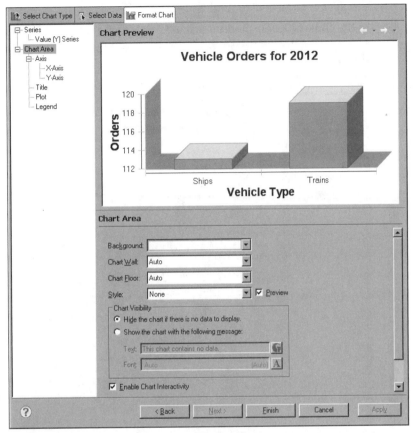

Figure 19-41   Formatting the area of a chart

Figure 19-42 highlights Chart Area in the navigation section of Format Chart. The navigation section for other chart types differs.

Figure 19-42   Navigating to a bar chart's Chart Area

Setting the background color for a chart

The background color of the chart can be a standard color, a custom color, or a color gradient. You can also use an image in the background. You can also use a transparent background. A transparent background displays the background color of the report page on which it appears.

How to set a chart's background color

1 In the chart builder, choose Format Chart, then navigate to the Chart Area section. Use the list on the left to navigate among sections. Figure 19-43 shows the Chart Area section.

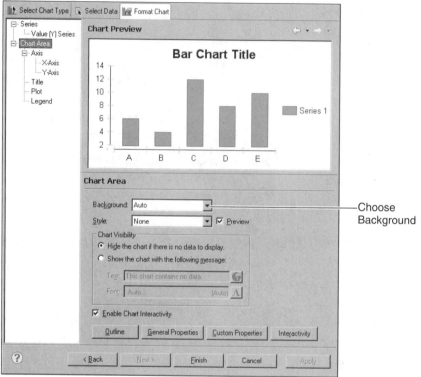

Figure 19-43   Background option in the Chart Area section

2 Choose Background. The color palette opens, as shown in Figure 19-44.

Figure 19-44   Color palette

3 Use the color palette to select a background color or image as follows:

- To use one of the basic colors, select a color from the palette.

- To use a transparent background, use the Opacity scroll tool to set the opacity to 0, then press Enter.

- To use a gradient color, choose Gradient. In Gradient Editor, select a start color, end color, and rotation for the gradient pattern, as shown in Figure 19-45.

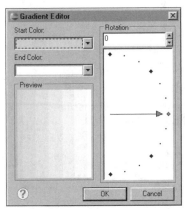

Figure 19-45   Setting colors and rotation for a gradient color

- To use a custom color, choose Custom Color to show the custom color list, then select a color.

- To use a background image, choose Image, then use Open to navigate to and select the image to use.

The background color or image appears in the chart builder.

4 To apply the color to the chart, choose Finish.

To define a custom color, on the color list, choose Define Custom Colors to show the custom color palette, as shown in Figure 19-46.

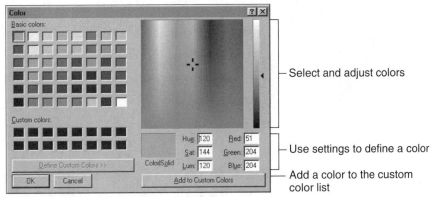

Figure 19-46   Color palette including custom color options

Use the options to select or define a custom color. When you finish, choose Add to Custom Colors, then choose OK.

Outlining a chart

An outline can distinguish the chart area from the rest of a report. To add an outline, navigate to the Chart Area section of Format Chart. Choose Outline to see the outline options, as shown in Figure 19-47.

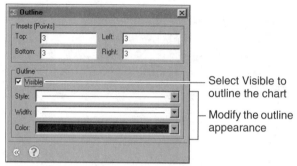

Figure 19-47   Setting a chart outline

Select Visible to add the outline, then use the Style, Width, and Color fields to change the appearance of the outline.

Adding padding around the chart

You can change the spacing around and within the chart using inset settings. To add more space, use a higher inset setting. For example, Figure 19-48 shows the effect of using two different chart top inset settings.

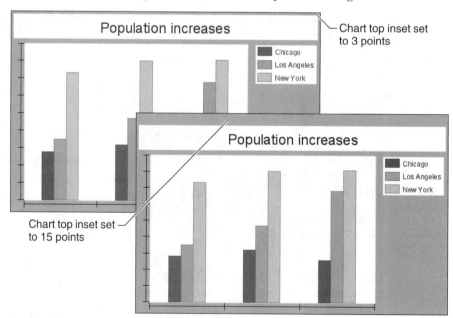

Figure 19-48   Charts using different inset settings

By default, inset values appear in points. To specify different units, such as pixels, inches, or centimeters, use Property Editor, as shown in Figure 19-49 to select the chart unit. The unit that you choose applies to chart settings, such as insets, or the width of series in three-dimensional charts and charts with depth.

Set units

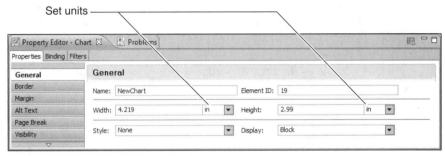

Figure 19-49   Changing units of measurement for the chart

To increase or decrease the number of units between chart elements, navigate to the Chart Area section of Format Chart, then choose General Properties and change the number of units, as shown in Figure 19-50.

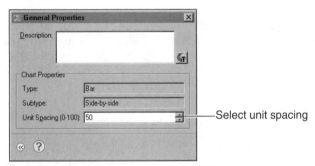

Select unit spacing

Figure 19-50   Setting the chart unit spacing option

To set chart area insets, navigate to the Chart Area section of Format Chart, then choose Outline to see inset options, as shown in Figure 19-51. Type a value in one or more of the Insets fields.

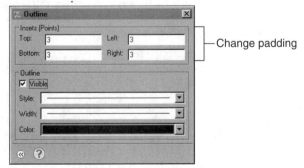

Change padding

Figure 19-51   Setting the inset options

Formatting the chart legend, plot, and title

When you create a chart, the chart builder inserts the legend, plot, and title using default placement and size. You can rearrange or format the legend, plot, or title. Each area includes a client area outside the axes in which data or text appears. For example, Figure 19-52 shows an outline around the legend. The text area in the legend uses a colored background.

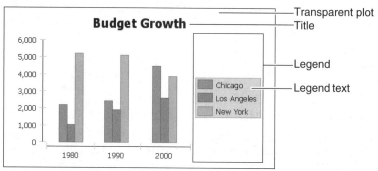

Figure 19-52   Legend areas

To highlight the plot, legend, or title, you can add a shadow behind that chart element. For example, Figure 19-53 shows a shadow behind title text. A shadow uses basic or custom colors. You cannot use a gradient color as a shadow.

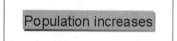

Figure 19-53   Title using shadow

You can change the location of these chart elements, add inset padding to separate a part from another part, or change the way a part resizes when the chart expands or contracts. You adjust the layout using the following settings:

- Anchoring
  To change where the plot, legend, or title appears, change the anchoring. For example, Figure 19-54 shows some of the different anchoring options for the legend text area within the legend area.

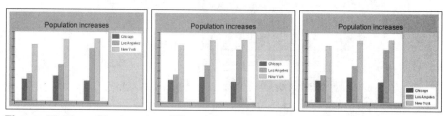

Figure 19-54   Charts using different legend anchor settings

Anchor positions are relative to the plot area. For example, the title in the first example chart in Figure 19-54 uses Top Right.

- Insets

  To adjust the padding around a chart area, modify the inset settings. For example, Figure 19-55 shows the effect of increasing the top inset setting for the plot. The chart on the right uses a higher inset setting, so there is more space between the top of the plot and other chart elements, such as the title.

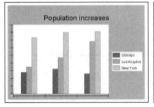 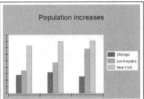

Figure 19-55   Charts using different plot inset settings

You also use inset settings to modify where the client area or text area appears within a chart area. For example, to change where series markers, such as bars in a bar chart, appear within the plot, change the plot client area insets. Figure 19-56 shows the effect of increasing the left inset for a bar chart plot client area. The chart on the right uses a higher inset setting, so more space appears between the plot client area, where the bars appear, and the edge of the rest of the plot.

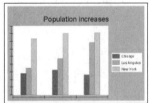 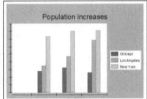

Figure 19-56   Charts using different plot client area inset settings

- Visibility

  You can hide the title and legend of a chart, as shown in Figure 19-57.

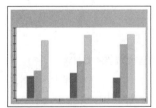

Figure 19-57   Chart not using a title or legend

The following sections describe how to arrange and format the chart plot, legend, and title.

Working with the plot area

When you adjust the plot area, you can modify the entire plot area, which includes the axes, or only the area that appears within the axes. Figure 19-58 shows the two sections of the plot in a sample bar chart. The lighter area shows the area including axes. The smaller, darker area shows the area within the axes. To use one color across the entire plot, select that color in both areas.

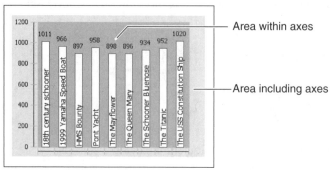

Figure 19-58   Plot areas

Setting the color, outline, or shadow for the plot

The default background color for the plot is transparent. You can also use a standard color, a custom color, a color gradient, or an image. Also, you can outline the plot and change the line color, style, and width. To highlight the plot area within the axes, you can use a shadow, similar to the one in Figure 19-59. You add a shadow by setting the Shadow option in Area Format.

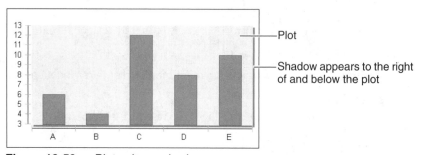

Figure 19-59   Plot using a shadow

Placing and adding space around the plot

You use anchor settings to modify where the plot appears within the chart and inset settings to determine how much padding appears between the plot and other chart features. You can use plot spacing settings to modify the space between the plot area and the chart axes. Plot spacing includes horizontal and vertical settings. For example, Figure 19-60 shows the effect of increasing the horizontal spacing in a bar chart. In the second chart, the space between the horizontal axis and the bottom edge of the plot is much larger. To change the spacing around the plot, you set inset and spacing options in Area Format.

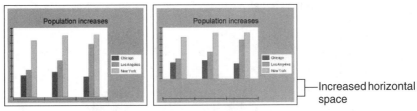

Increased horizontal space

Figure 19-60 Charts using different horizontal plot spacing

Specifying the plot size

You can use the height hint and width hint settings to suggest a minimum height and width for the plot. In most cases, BIRT Report Designer uses the values you supply to size the plot. If you set a plot size that is too large to fit in the total design space, or if other chart elements such as the legend or a title are too large to accommodate the suggested plot size, BIRT Report Designer ignores the settings.

A height or width hint is most useful in a report that uses multiple charts, such as a report with different chart elements or a report that includes a chart element in a group section. Because chart sizing is dynamic, one chart element can produce multiple charts with plots of different sizes, as shown in Figure 19-61.

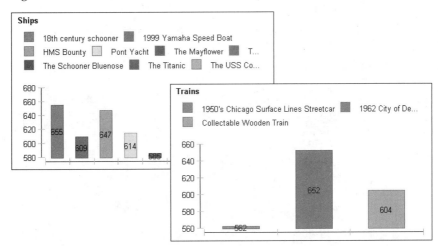

Figure 19-61 Charts created not using a height hint

Height and width hints help you to regulate the plot sizes in a group of charts. For example, the illustrations in Figure 19-62 show that charts using a value for the Height Hint setting maintain the same height.

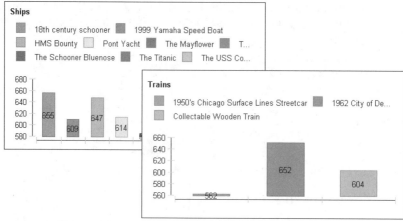

Figure 19-62   Effect of setting a height hint

The following procedures describe how to set the background color for a plot and how to include an outline or shadow and make adjustments in the size and placement of the chart.

To set a background color for the plot, navigate to the Plot section of Format Chart, shown in Figure 19-63. Choose Background for either Area Including Axes or Area Within Axes, then use the color picker to select a background color. To apply the color to the plot, choose Finish.

How to modify the plot area

1 Navigate to Plot in the Chart Area section of Format Chart.

   You see one of the two types of plot sections, as shown in Figure 19-63, depending on the type of chart.

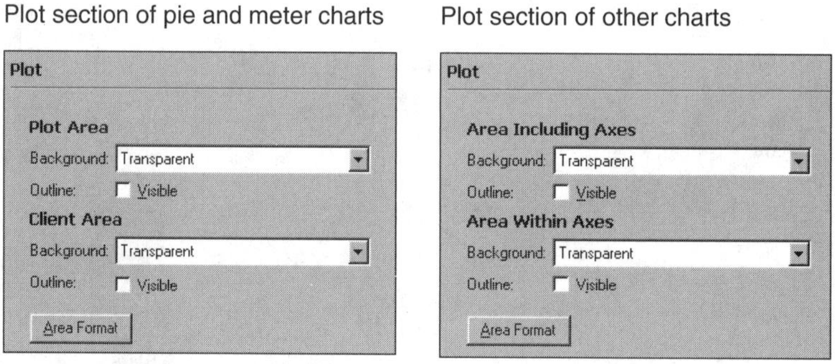

Plot section of pie and meter charts   Plot section of other charts

Figure 19-63   Plot section options in Format Chart

2 To make an outline of an area visible, select Visible in Outline for one or both areas.

3 To make other modifications to the area, choose Area Format. Figure 19-64 shows the options you can set using Area Format. Options that appear in

Area Format vary. Formatting options depend on the type of chart that you select.

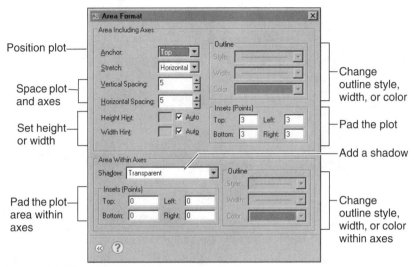

Figure 19-64   Options in Area Format

4 Modify any of the following options:

- The outline style, width, or color

- Padding to add space on any or all sides of the plot

- Shadow, using the color picker to select a shadow color

- Position of the plot

- Space between the vertical edge of the plot and the vertical axis

- Space between the horizontal edge of the plot and the horizontal axis

- Padding around the plot area enclosed by the 2D axes

- Constraints on the height or width of the plot block

5 When you are done, close Area Format, then choose Finish on the chart builder to save your changes.

Formatting the chart title text

You can modify the appearance of the title text in a number of ways. For example, you can change the font, size, color, style, or alignment of the text. You can also set the format to strike through or to rotate the title.

How to modify title text

1 Navigate to Title in the Chart Area section of Format Chart.

2 In Font, choose Font Editor to open the font editor.

3 Use the font editor settings shown in Figure 19-65 to modify the font.

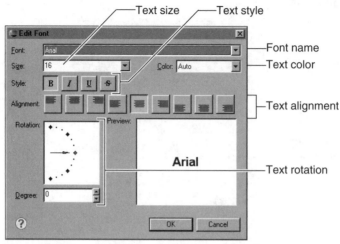

Figure 19-65   Font Editor options

4 To accept your changes, choose OK, and choose Finish on the chart builder.

Formatting the title area

When you apply a background color or outline to a chart title, you can work with the entire title area or with only the text area. Figure 19-66 shows the difference between the two areas in a sample chart.

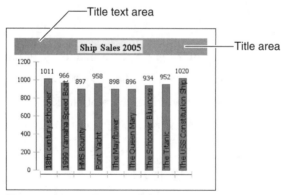

Figure 19-66   Title areas

If you apply a background color to the title area, the same color appears in the text area. Optionally, you can set a new background color or add a shadow to the text area. You cannot shadow the entire title area. To modify where the title appears within the chart, use anchor settings. To determine how much padding appears between the title or title text areas and other chart features, use inset settings.

To add a background color, outline, or shadow to the chart title text area, navigate to Title in the Chart Area section of Format Chart, then choose Text to see the options that are shown in Figure 19-67. Use the settings to modify the title text.

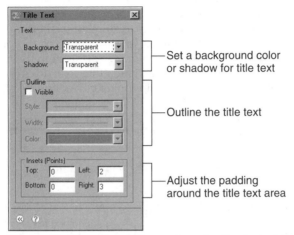

Figure 19-67   Formatting options for the text of the title

To add a background color or outline to the title area of the chart, or to position the title area, navigate to Title in the Chart Area section of Format Chart, then choose Layout to see the options shown in Figure 19-68.

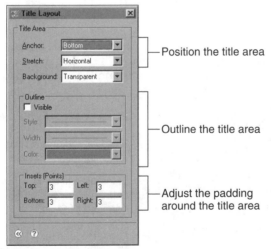

Figure 19-68   Formatting options for the title area

Working with the legend

By default, a chart displays a legend. The legend uses a transparent background and does not include an outline or a shadow. To highlight the legend area, add a background color, outline, or shadow. You can hide the legend or change its position in the chart area, add a legend title, or modify legend-text properties, such as the font size.

Setting the color, outline, or shadow for the legend

When applying a background color or outline to a chart legend, you can work with the entire legend area or with the text area only. Figure 19-69 shows the difference between the two areas in a sample chart. If you apply a background color to the legend area, the color also appears in the text area, unless you set a background color in the text area that overrides the legend area settings. You can add a shadow only to the text area, not the entire legend area.

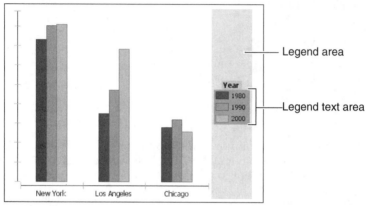

Figure 19-69   Legend areas

To format the legend, navigate to the Chart Area section of Format Chart and select Legend. First, select Visible in both places in the Legend section, as shown in Figure 19-70 to make the legend area and legend title visible. Then, choose either Title, Layout, or Entries.

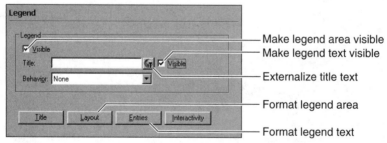

Figure 19-70   Options in the Legend section of a pie chart

To format the legend area, navigate to the Legend section of Format Chart, select Layout, then use Layout Legend, shown in Figure 19-71.

To prevent truncation of the legend, increase the wrapping width. Specify a maximum width for legend items. Items that extend beyond the wrapping width appear on multiple lines in the legend.

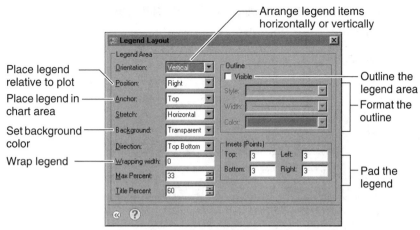

Arrange legend items
horizontally or vertically

Place legend
relative to plot

Place legend in
chart area

Set background
color

Wrap legend

Outline the
legend area

Format the
outline

Pad the
legend

Figure 19-71   Background option in Layout Legend

Placing and adding space around a legend

Use anchor settings to modify where the legend appears within the chart. To
determine how much padding appears between the legend or legend text
areas and other chart features, use the inset settings.

To adjust the position of the entire legend area, rather than the client area
where the legend items appear, change the legend-position setting. Position a
legend relative to the plot. For example, Figure 19-72 shows different legend
positions in a sample chart.

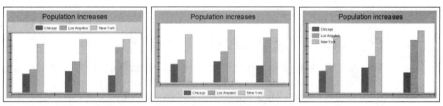

Figure 19-72   Legend positions, above, below, and inside the plot

You can also organize legend items within the legend client area. For
example, in Figure 19-73, the chart on the left shows legend items arranged
horizontally. The chart on the right shows legend items arranged vertically.
To adjust the positions of legend items in the legend-client area, set the
legend orientation.

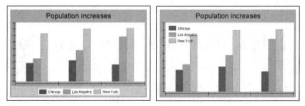

Figure 19-73   Horizontal and vertical legend orientation

Showing series item values in a legend

Typically, a legend displays only series item names. The legend can also display the values of series items. To display values in the legend, navigate to the Legend area of Format Chart, then select Show Value, as shown in Figure 19-74.

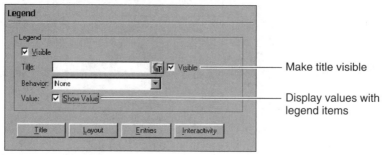

Figure 19-74 Displaying values in the legend

A pie chart always shows the legend values, so the Legend section of a pie chart does not include Show Value.

Formatting the legend text

You can change the font style and size of the legend text. For multiple series, add a separator line between the items in one series and the items in the next.

To format the legend text, navigate to the Legend section of Format Chart. Choose Entries, then choose Font Editor, as shown in Figure 19-75. Use the font editor to modify the font attributes.

Formatting a legend title

You can use a title for the chart legend. When you first add the title, the chart builder uses default font settings and the title appears above the list of legend items. You can change the font style and color of the title. You can also add a title outline, background color, or shadow, or position the title below, to the left, or to the right of the legend text.

To add and format the title of the legend, navigate to the Legend section of Format Chart. Figure 19-70 shows the Legend section options. Select Visible to show the title, then type the title text. To format the title, choose Title. Then use the settings shown in Figure 19-75 to format the title.

Formatting axis titles, markers, lines, and labels

In earlier sections you learned how to format the titles of the chart itself and of the legend. You can also add titles to axes, use markers to highlight points on the chart, modify the style and color of axis lines, and label the axes.

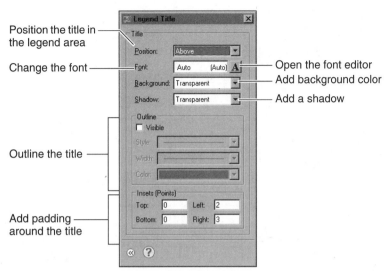

Position the title in the legend area

Change the font

Open the font editor

Add background color

Add a shadow

Outline the title

Add padding around the title

Figure 19-75   Legend title formatting options

You can hide or reposition an axis element and change its default appearance in Format Chart. For example, delete the title for an axis or move the axis tick marks. You can also change the color or style of an element, add an outline, or change the padding.

Working with an axis title

Chart types other than pie and meter can have *x*-axis or *y*-axis titles. To add and format an *x*-axis title, you navigate to the X-Axis section of Format Chart. Select Visible, shown in Figure 19-76. Then, type text in Title. To modify the position, outline, padding, or font style of the axis title, choose Title. Toggle between the *x*-axis or the *y*-axis to make title changes to one or the other by navigating to X-Axis or Y-Axis in the Chart Area.

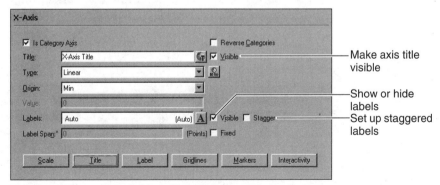

Make axis title visible

Show or hide labels

Set up staggered labels

Figure 19-76   Title field and labels in an axis section

In Axis Title, shown in Figure 19-77, you can position the title above or below an *x*-axis, or you can position the title to the left or right of a *y*-axis. You can outline the title, and add padding around it using Insets. You can change the size and style of the font, and add a shadow or a background color.

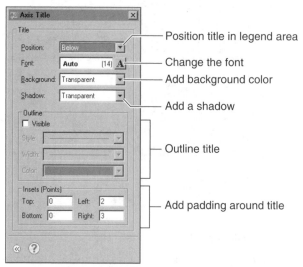

Position title in legend area

Change the font

Add background color

Add a shadow

Outline title

Add padding around title

Figure 19-77   Formatting options for an *x*-axis title

Working with axis markers

Axis markers highlight numbers or ranges on two-dimensional charts or charts with depth. You can use the following types of markers:

- A marker line is a line that extends across the plot from a point on the axis. You specify the axis and value from which to draw the line.

- A marker range is a rectangular area that highlights a range of values. You specify between which values and from which axis to draw the rectangle.

For example, Figure 19-78 shows a marker line and a marker range.

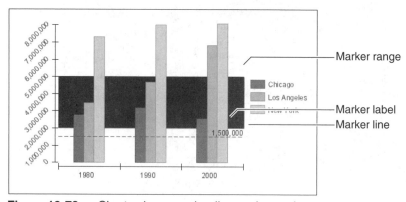

Marker range

Marker label

Marker line

Figure 19-78   Chart using a marker line and a marker range

Both markers highlight points on the *y*-axis. The marker line uses a label to show the marker value. You can change the style or color of the marker, change label text, or hide labels. Add a marker to an *x*-axis only if it shows numeric or date-and-time data. Adding a marker to an axis that shows text values as categories generally does not help users read the chart.

Adding an axis marker

To create and format an axis marker, navigate to the Format Chart section for the axis, then choose Markers to see the options shown in Figure 19-79.

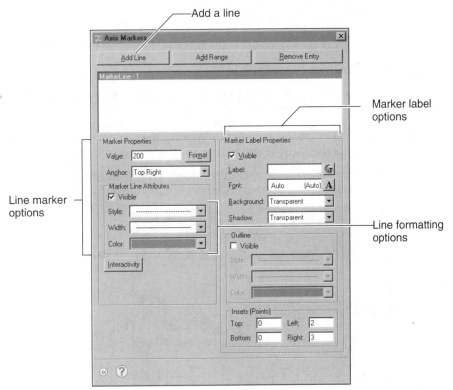

Figure 19-79   Axis Markers formatting options

Adding a marker line

To create a marker line, choose Add Line. The marker appears in the marker list. In Value, type the value at which the line should start.

Adding a marker range

To create an axis marker range, choose Add Range. Options to set range properties appear in Marker Properties. To set values that the range marker spans, type numeric values in Start Value and End Value.

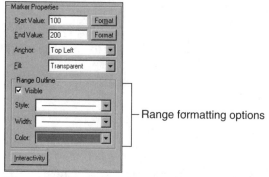

Figure 19-80   Range marker formatting options

Formatting axis markers

A marker displays a label to identify the axis point or range that the marker highlights. You can adjust the line style, width, and color of a marker line, or change the range fill color or outline of a marker range. You can also specify an image to be used as a marker on the chart. To format a marker line or range, use the formatting options shown in Figure 19-79 or Figure 19-80.

To hide or format a marker label, select a name from the marker list, then set the corresponding properties, as shown in Figure 19-81.

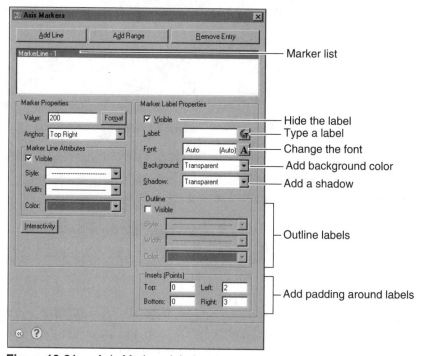

Figure 19-81   Axis Markers label options

Working with an axis line

To highlight intervals at which data values correspond to an axis, you can modify the line style of an axis and optionally, add tick marks. Major and minor tick marks highlight large and small intervals along an axis. An axis typically appears with major tick marks that are positioned across the axis at regular intervals, such as 5, 10, or 50 units. Major tick marks appear in a higher line weight than minor tick marks. You can change the position of tick marks relative to the axis line. For example, you can position tick marks to the left or right of a vertical axis or above or below a horizontal axis. Figure 19-82 shows different tick mark settings for a *y*-axis.

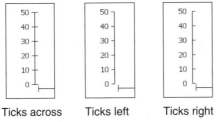

Ticks across   Ticks left   Ticks right

Figure 19-82   Tick mark positions

To make comparing series values easier, you can add gridlines to a chart. A gridline extends from an axis and spans the plot area. For example, the bar chart shown in Figure 19-83 uses *y*-axis gridlines to help a reader distinguish data points. When you add major or minor gridlines to an axis, the chart includes a gridline for each major or minor interval on the axis. Like tick marks, major gridlines appear in a higher line weight than minor gridlines.

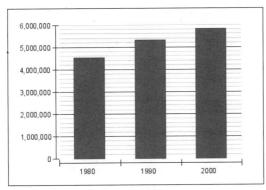

Figure 19-83   *Y*-axis gridlines

To modify an axis line, navigate to the Format Chart section for the axis, then choose Gridlines. Select options in Axis Gridlines to format the axis lines, tick marks, and gridlines. Figure 19-84 shows formatting options gridlines that extend from the *x*-axis of a 2D chart.

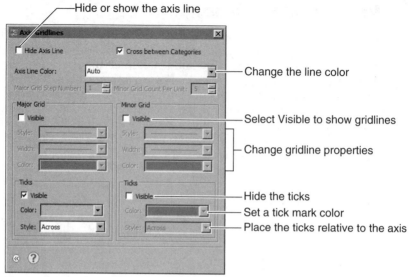

Hide or show the axis line

Change the line color

Select Visible to show gridlines

Change gridline properties

Hide the ticks

Set a tick mark color

Place the ticks relative to the axis

Figure 19-84   Axis Gridlines formatting options

To modify axis tick marks, navigate to the Format Chart section for the axis, then choose Gridlines. Use the Gridlines settings to format the tick marks, as shown in Figure 19-84. You can modify major or minor tick mark settings.

To add or modify gridlines, navigate to the Format Chart section for the axis, then choose Gridlines. Use the settings to add or change the axis gridlines, as shown in Figure 19-84. You can modify major or minor division settings.

Working with axis labels

By default, a chart displays labels to the left of a vertical axis and below a horizontal axis, as shown in Figure 19-85.

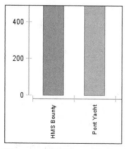

Figure 19-85   Default axis label positions

You can hide or reposition the labels on an axis. For example, you can show the labels on the *y*-axis to the right of the axis rather than the left, or rotate the labels on the *x*-axis so that they are easier to read. You can also modify the label font, add a background color, shadow, or outline, or change the padding around the labels.

Sometimes, a chart displays so many values on an axis that the label text overlaps and becomes illegible. In this case, the chart builder drops some of the axis labels. Figure 19-86 shows a chart in which labels have disappeared. In the chart, only three of four *x*-axis labels appear. The chart dropped the second label because it overlapped the neighboring labels.

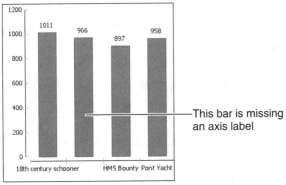

Figure 19-86   Chart displaying a missing *x*-axis label

To fix this problem, you can rotate the labels or stagger them, so they do not overlap. Figure 19-87 shows the two solutions on an *x*-axis. In the chart on the left, rotation of *x*-axis labels makes all the labels fit into the space. On the right, staggering labels displays all axis categories.

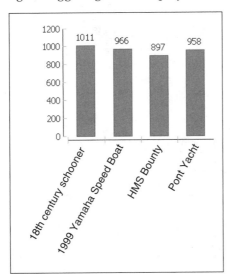

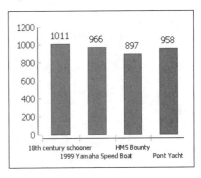

Figure 19-87   Rotated and staggered *x*-axis labels

You can also skip labels. For example, in Figure 19-88, the chart skips every other label. To skip labels, set the interval at which labels should appear. For example, to show every other label, use an interval of 2. To show every fifth label, use an interval of 5.

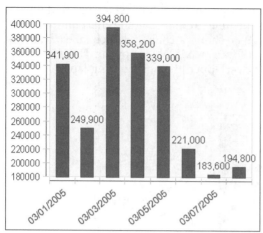

Figure 19-88   Chart showing skipped *x*-axis labels

To format axis labels, navigate to the Format Chart section for the axis, then choose Label. Use the Axis Label options, as shown in Figure 19-89.

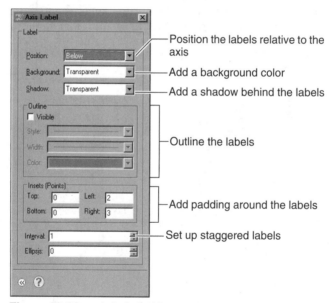

Figure 19-89   Axis Label formatting options

Defining the axis data type and number format

The axis data type and format determine how the chart builder arranges the data that appears on an axis. An axis has one of the following data types:

- Linear
  This axis type spaces values evenly.

- Logarithmic

  This axis type spaces values based on the ratio of their values. For example, values 1 and 10 are the same distance apart as 10 and 100.

- DateTime

  This axis type shows data on a date or time scale.

- Text

  This axis type displays text only and spaces words evenly. The location of a data point on a text axis does not indicate its size. Typically, a text axis is a category axis.

How to set the data type and format of an axis

1 In Format Chart, navigate to the axis section.

2 In Type, select a data type from the list, as shown in Figure 19-90.

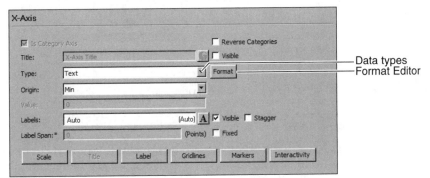

Data types
Format Editor

Figure 19-90   X-Axis section of Format Chart

3 Choose Format Editor.

The Edit Format dialog box displays options for the data type of the axis. Figure 19-91 shows options for the Date/Time data type.

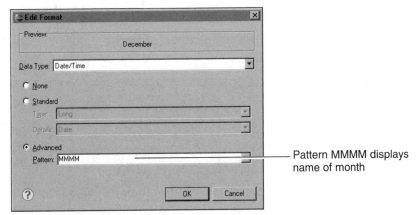

Pattern MMMM displays name of month

Figure 19-91   Editing the format of a date

Defining where one axis intersects the other

Typically, a chart displays each axis intersecting the opposing axis at the minimum value. Specifying an axis intersection setting defines the value at which the axis meets the opposing axis. Select one of the following values:

- Min to have the axis intersect the opposing axis at the opposing axis's minimum value. Figure 19-92 shows an *x*-axis intersecting the minimum value of the *y*-axis.

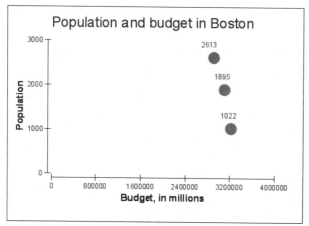

Figure 19-92   *Y*-axis Min intersection option

- Max to have the axis intersect the opposing axis at the opposing axis's maximum value. Figure 19-93 shows an *x*-axis intersecting the maximum value of the *y*-axis.

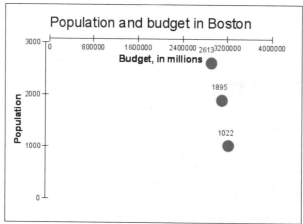

Figure 19-93   *Y*-axis Max intersection option

- Value to have the axis intersect the opposing axis at a value that you specify. Figure 19-94 shows an *x*-axis intersecting the *y*-axis at 1500.

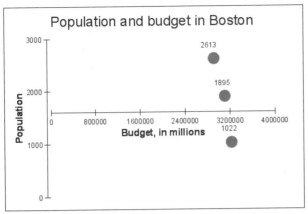

Figure 19-94   *Y*-axis Value intersection option

To set the intersection of an axis, on Format Chart, navigate to the page for that axis. In Origin, select Min, Max, or Value as the intersection setting. If you select Value, you must provide a value at which to join the axes.

Defining the scale of an axis

The scale of an axis determines the range of values displayed on a linear, logarithmic, or date-and-time axis. When you first create a chart, the chart builder selects a maximum and a minimum axis value to fit the data that the axis displays. Typically, the chart builder selects a minimum value that is just below the lowest axis value and a maximum value that is just higher than the highest axis value, rounding down or up to the nearest major unit, so the markings on the axis span the range of data that it displays.

You can change the following settings:

- The minimum and maximum values for an axis.

- The span between major grid values and the number of minor grid marks between major grid values on the axis. The distance between major grid marks is the step value. The number of minor grid marks is the minor grid count.

For example, in Figure 19-95, the axis on the left shows values from 0 to 1200. The step value is 200, so the major grid marks indicate values of 200, 400, and so on. The minor grid count is five grid marks for each major unit. The axis on the right shows values from 0 to 800. The step value is 100, so the major grid marks indicate 100, 200, and so on. The minor grid count is two grid marks for each major unit.

You can set the scale of value axes only. Category axes do not support scale changes. The following procedures describe how to set the scale of an *x*-axis. To set the scale of a *y*-axis, complete the same steps on the *y*-axis page. Most scale items appear in the Scale dialog. To set the number of minor grid marks per major unit, you use the Gridlines dialog.

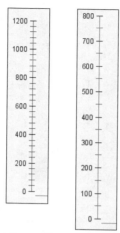

Figure 19-95   Axes using different scale options

To define the scale of an axis, in Format Chart, navigate to the axis section, then choose Scale. Use the Scale options to change the range and divisions of data on an axis. Figure 19-96 shows the scale options for a y-axis that uses a linear data type.

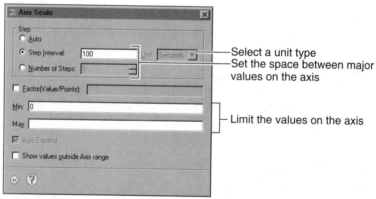

Figure 19-96   Scale options

To define the minor grid count, on Format Chart, navigate to the axis, then choose Gridlines. Use Minor grid count per unit to set the number of minor grid lines between major tick marks, as shown in Figure 19-97. You can use this setting only if Visible is selected.

Formatting a series

In addition to modifying the chart area element attributes, you can also format the chart series. Generally, the type of series determines the formatting options you can apply for that series. The following options are available:

- Formatting the color of value or category series elements
- Adding a trendline to value series of many chart types
- Adding a trendline to the category series in a scatter chart, because a scatter chart category series displays values.

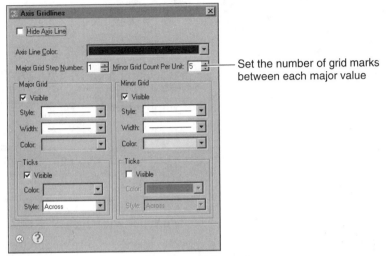

Figure 19-97   Setting the minor grid count

Stacking series

You can stack the value series that you display in a chart. In a stacked chart, the data points from one value series are arranged on top of the data points of another series. Stacking helps to show each data point's contribution to the total of all the data points in a category.

You can stack only area, bar, cone, pyramid, tube, and line series. To stack a series, navigate to the Series section of Format Chart, locate the series, then select Stacked.

Hiding a series

You can hide a series in a chart. A hidden series contributes data, but does not appear in the chart. For example, you might want to use a series to contribute to a trendline without displaying the series data points. Typically, you hide a value series rather than a category series.

To hide a series, navigate to the Series section of Format Chart, and deselect Visible for the series.

Making a series translucent

You can make a chart series translucent so you can see an image or color behind the chart data. For example, Figure 19-98 shows two versions of a chart that uses an image as the plot background. The chart on the left uses a solid series. The chart on the right uses a translucent series.

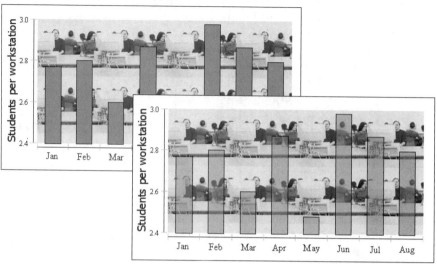

Figure 19-98   Bar charts using opaque series and translucent series

To make a series translucent, navigate to the Series section of Format Chart, and select Translucent for the series.

Setting the color palette for a series

You can specify which colors a series uses. Charts that have axes, such as line and stock charts, use varied colors to distinguish between different value series. When a bar chart uses more than one set of bars, the default behavior is to show each set in a different color. If a bar chart uses only one set of bars, the bars are the same color. Figure 19-99 and Figure 19-100 show charts using the default settings.

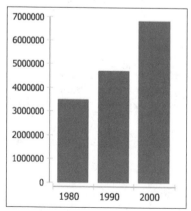

Figure 19-99   Default series colors for a chart using one value series

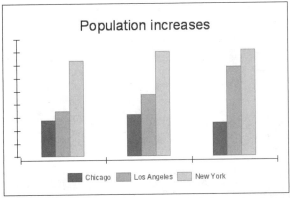

Figure 19-100 Default series colors for a chart using three value series

In charts that have axes, you can choose to color the chart by category series instead. This approach is useful when you have only one value series, but you want to show variously colored series elements, as in the chart in Figure 19-101. The chart uses one value series, but shows each bar in the series in a different color. Coloring the chart by category series also displays the category series items, rather than the value series items, in the legend.

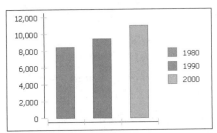

Figure 19-101 Varied colors in a chart using one value series

Pie charts and meter charts work differently. By default, a bar or a meter chart varies the category series colors to show each pie sector or needle in a different color, as shown in Figure 19-102.

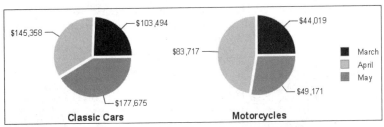

Figure 19-102 Pie chart colored by category series

When first created, a chart uses default colors for series elements. To select different colors, modify the series palette. The chart uses the colors selected in the selection order in the palette list. If the chart shows more series elements than there are colors in the palette, it uses some colors more than once.

To specify the colors used in the chart, navigate to the Series section of Format Chart, then choose Series Palette to see the options shown in Figure 19-103.

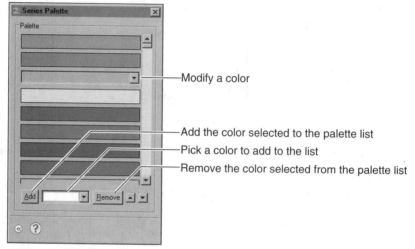

Figure 19-103   Series Palette

Use the following settings to modify the series palette:

- To set an element in the chart to use particular colors, find the color in the palette, and move that color to the top of the palette.

- To add a new color, select the color drop-down list to the right of Add, and use the color picker to select or create a color. When finished, choose Add.

- To remove a color, select the color in the list, and choose Remove.

- To modify a color, select it, then use the color picker to select or create a color.

When you finish adjusting the color palette, close Series Palette, then choose Finish in the chart builder.

You can also color by value series to show all the sectors in a pie or all the needles on a meter in the same color. For example, Figure 19-104 shows the same pie chart, colored by value series.

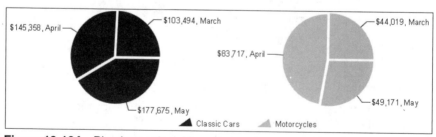

Figure 19-104   Pie chart colored by value series

To determine which data the legend displays, navigate to the Series section of Format Chart, then use Color By to select Value Series or Categories.

Formatting numbers, dates, and times

You can format numbers, dates, or times that the chart displays in a variety of ways. Format numbers and produce multiples of them in the following ways:

- Add a prefix, such as a currency symbol.

- Multiply values by a number, such as 100.

- Add a suffix to a number value, such as the word million.

- Determine the number of decimal places that numbers include.

- Specify a number format pattern, such as #.###, which formats numbers using a point as the thousands separator.

Format the following attributes of dates and times:

- Type. Use a standard format, including Long, Short, Medium, and Full.

- Details. Specify that the format is Date or Date Time.

- Pattern. Specify a pattern, such as MMMM to show only the month value or dddd to show only the day value, such as Wednesday.

How to format a number

1 In the chart builder, navigate to Values Series and choose Labels.

2 In Values, select Value Data, Category Data, or Percentile Value Data, as shown in Figure 19-105.

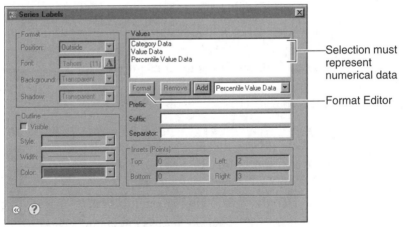

Figure 19-105   Selecting numerical data to format

3 Choose Edit Format.

If the selection you made in the previous step represents numerical data, Edit Format appears. If the selection you made in the previous step does not represent numerical data, Edit Format is not available.

4 From the Data Type drop-down list, choose Number to see the number format options. Figure 19-106 shows the options.

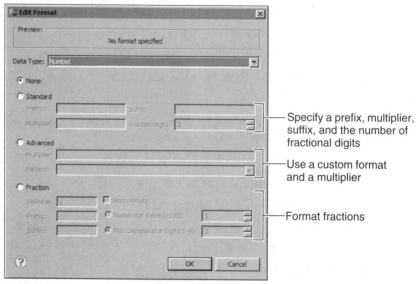

Figure 19-106 Format options for numeric data

5 To add a prefix, multiplier, or suffix, or to specify the number of decimal places, select Standard, then specify the following format settings:

- Type a value in Prefix to add a number prefix.

- Type a number by which to multiply expression values in Multiplier to multiply values by a number.

- Type the value in Suffix to add a number suffix.

- Select the number in Fraction Digits to specify the number of decimal places to use.

6 To use a custom number pattern, select Advanced, then specify the following format settings:

- Type the number by which to multiply expression values in Multiplier to multiply values by a number.

- Type the pattern string in Pattern to specify a number format pattern.

7 To use a custom fraction format, select Fraction, then specify the following format settings:

- A delimiter symbol, such as slash (/).

- A prefix, by typing the value in Prefix.

- A suffix, by typing the value in Suffix.

- Select Approximate to define guidelines for representing fractions rather than using the default, then provide a suggested numerator or the suggested maximum number of denominator digits. For example, to show fractions with single-digit denominators, such as 1/2 or 3/8, supply 1 as the maximum number of denominator digits.

8 When you finish defining the format, choose OK.

How to format a date and time

1 In the chart builder, navigate to Values Series and choose Labels.

2 In Values, select date-and-time data to modify, and choose Format Editor.

3 In Data Type, choose Date/Time. Figure 19-107 shows Date/Time options.

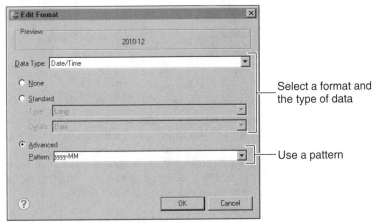

Figure 19-107 Format options for date-and-time data

4 To use a predefined format type, select Standard, then specify the following format options:

- Select a format value in Type.

- In Details, select Date or Date Time.

5 To use a custom format pattern, select Advanced, then type the custom format string in Pattern.

6 When you finish defining the format, choose OK.

Working with data points and data point labels

By default, a chart displays labels that identify value-series values, such as the height of a bar in a bar chart or the size of a sector in a pie chart.

To display different data in the labels, change the data point settings. The data point settings determine what text each label displays. Typically, the label shows the value-series value, such as the highest point of a line chart on the *y*-axis. You can also show where the point appears on the *x*-axis, use the series value to show to which group of data points a point belongs, or display the value as a percentage of the total value of all points in the chart.

For example, in Figure 19-108, the first chart uses a legend to show which bar represents each series. The second chart labels each bar with the city name.

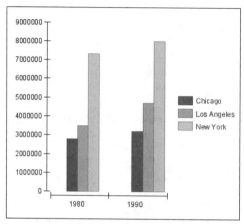 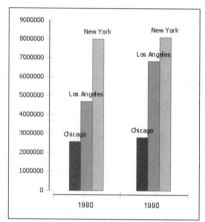

Figure 19-108　Bar charts using different label settings

After you decide the data to show in the labels, you can change the number format of the data points or add a prefix or a suffix to the label expression. You can also use a separator between values. For example, the chart in Figure 19-108 could display the city value and the year value, separated by a comma, such as Chicago, 1980. In a different chart, you could add a currency symbol before a value or append text, such as Orders.

To modify the data a label displays, navigate to the Value Series section of Format Chart, then choose Labels. Use the settings in Values, shown in Figure 19-109, to set up the data the label displays.

To format data point labels, navigate to the Value Series section of Format Chart, then choose Labels. Use the settings in Values to set up the data the label displays, as shown in Figure 19-109.

Adding and formatting a curve-fitting line

A curve-fitting line is a graphical representation of a trend in data. Use a curve-fitting line to detect patterns in data or to predict future values. For example, the chart in Figure 19-110 uses curve-fitting lines to highlight population trends in several cities. Use the trendlines to estimate population in the years after 2000. The population for Los Angeles, for example, is growing sharply, while the population in New York has increased less dramatically.

You use curve-fitting lines in both two-dimensional and two-dimensional with depth area, bar, bubble, line, scatter, and stock charts. You cannot use curve fitting with a three-dimensional chart. A curve-fitting line in a BIRT chart places each curve-fitting point based on the following factors:

- The location of the neighboring data points
- A weight function that takes into account all the data points that the curve-fitting line includes

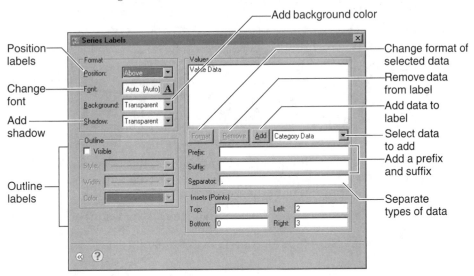

Figure 19-109 Label data settings

A curve-fitting line can look very different depending on the span and amount of data that you use. Before adding curve fitting to your chart, ensure you have enough data to show a meaningful trend.

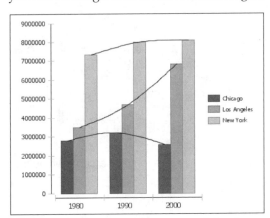

Figure 19-110 Chart using curve-fitting lines

To display a curve-fitting line, navigate to the Value Series section of Format Chart, then select Show Curve Fitting Line, as shown in Figure 19-111. By default, a curve-fitting line uses a thin black line. You can change the line style or color.

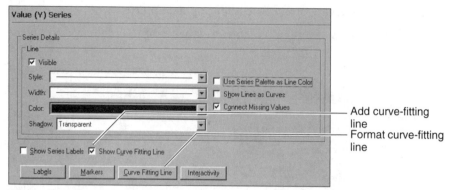

Figure 19-111   Show curve-fitting line option

To format a curve-fitting line, navigate to the Value Series section of Format Chart, and choose Curve Fitting Line, then use the settings to change the style, width, or color of the line, as shown in Figure 19-112.

To add labels to a curve-fitting line, navigate to the Value Series section of Format Chart, and choose Curve Fitting Line. In Label, select Visible, then use the settings on Curve Fitting Line to format the labels, as shown in Figure 19-112.

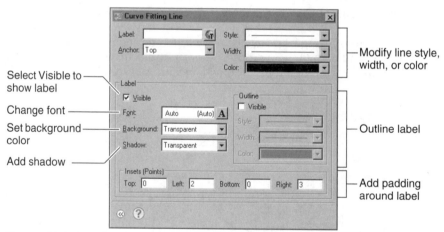

Figure 19-112   Labeling and formatting options for a curve-fitting line

Presenting Data in a Cross Tab

A cross tab displays data in a row-and-column matrix that looks similar to a spreadsheet. Like a spreadsheet, the cross tab is ideal for summarizing data in a compact and concise format. It displays summary, or aggregate, values such as sums, counts, or averages. The cross tab groups these values by one set of data listed down the left side of the matrix and another set of data listed across the top of the matrix.

Figure 20-1 shows a cross tab that displays sales totals by state and by product line. The cross tab uses data from three fields: state, productline, and extendedprice.

Values in the productline field form the columns

	Classic Cars	Motorcycles	Planes	Ships	Trains	Trucks and Buses	Vintage Cars	Grand Total
CA	$458,563.64	$162,710.57	$108,632.26	$66,758.95	$17,965.32	$167,896.48	$366,355.37	$1,348,882.59
CT	$89,671.28	$39,699.67	$41,142.34	$5,936.68	$9,548.53	$15,671.49	$14,101.07	$215,771.06
MA	$223,366.59	$91,024.09	$51,924.57	$71,419.40	$12,184.49	$58,487.98	$105,384.18	$613,791.30
NH	$69,150.35	--	--	--	--	$7,922.29	$39,376.65	$116,449.29
NJ	--	$35,116.44	$33,308.49	$4,346.26	--	--	$9,035.36	$81,806.55
NV	$58,718.89	--	--	--	--	--	$21,462.09	$80,180.98
NY	$260,619.73	$99,514.87	$24,647.66	$36,219.65	$15,033.47	$77,996.00	$62,342.28	$576,373.66
PA	$102,856.24	$39,025.09	$15,889.79	$4,983.38	$4,862.02	$37,483.09	$34,925.01	$240,024.62
Grand Total	$1,262,946.72	$467,090.73	$275,545.11	$189,664.32	$59,593.83	$365,457.33	$652,982.01	$3,273,280.05

Values in the state field form the rows

Each cell is an intersection of a row and column field, and displays the sales total by state and product line. Sales totals are calculated by summing values in the extendedprice field.

Figure 20-1   Cross tab displaying sales totals by state and product line

511

As Figure 20-1 shows, a cross tab typically uses data from at least three fields.

- One field populates the column headings in the cross tab. There is one column for each unique value in the field. In the example shown in Figure 20-1, there are five unique values in the productline field: Classic Cars, Motorcycles, Planes, Ships, and Trains.

- One field populates the row headings in the cross tab. There is one row for each unique value in the field. In the example, there are eight unique values in the state field: CA, CT, MA, NH, NJ, NV, NY, and PA.

- One field's values are aggregated, and these values populate the cells of the cross tab. In the example, each cell displays a sales total by product line and by state. The sales total is calculated using the SUM function on the values in the extendedprice field.

This chapter begins with a tutorial in which you build a cross tab similar to the one shown in Figure 20-1. The tutorial leads you through the essential tasks. The rest of the chapter expands on some of the concepts, such as data cubes, which are unique to cross tabs.

Tutorial 6: Creating a cross tab

This tutorial provides instructions for creating a cross tab that displays sales totals by state and product line. The cross tab uses data from the Customers, OrderDetails, and Products tables in the sample database, Classic Models.

In this tutorial, you perform the following tasks:

- Create a new report
- Build a data source
- Build a data set
- Set up data for the cross tab
- Add a cross tab to the report
- Add grand totals
- Format the cross tab

Task 1: Create a new report

1 Choose File➞New➞Report.

2 In New Report, select a project in which to save your report.

3 Type the following text as the file name:

   SalesByStateAndProductLine.rptdesign

4 Choose Finish. A blank report layout appears in the layout editor.

Task 2: Build a data source

Before you begin designing your report in the layout editor, create a data source to connect your report to the Classic Models database.

1 Choose Data Explorer.

2 Right-click Data Sources, and choose New Data Source.

3 Select Classic Models Inc. Sample Database from the list of data sources, use the default data source name, then choose Next. Connection information about the new data source appears.

4 Choose Finish. BIRT Report Designer creates a new data source that connects to the sample database.

Task 3: Build a data set

In this procedure, you build a data set to indicate what data to extract from the Customers, OrderDetails, and Products tables.

1 In Data Explorer, right-click Data Sets, and choose New Data Set.

2 In New Data Set, type the following text for data set name:

Sales

3 Choose Next.

4 Use the following SQL SELECT statement to indicate what data to retrieve. Type the column and table names, or drag them from Available Items to the appropriate location in the SELECT statement.

```
SELECT Customers.state,
Orderdetails.quantityOrdered,
Orderdetails.priceEach,
Products.productline

FROM Customers INNER JOIN Orders ON Customers.customerNumber
   = Orders.customerNumber
INNER JOIN Orderdetails ON Orders.orderNumber =
   Orderdetails.orderNumber
INNER JOIN Products ON Orderdetails.productCode =
   Products.productCode

WHERE Customers.country = 'USA'
```

This SELECT statement joins four tables to get the required data.

5 Choose Finish to save the data set. Edit Data Set displays the columns specified in the query, and provides options for editing the data set.

6 Choose Computed Columns, then choose New to create a computed field that calculates extended prices by multiplying values from the QUANTITYORDERED and PRICEEACH fields.

7 In New Computed Column, specify the following values, as shown in Figure 20-2:

1 In Column Name, type

EXTENDED_PRICE

2 In Data Type, select Float.

3 In Expression, type

row["QUANTITYORDERED"] * row["PRICEEACH"]

Alternatively, open the expression builder to construct the expression by selecting the appropriate data set fields. Note that data set field names are case-sensitive. If you typed row["quantityOrdered"] in the Expression field, BIRT displays an error when you preview the results returned by the data set. The case requirement for data set field names is unlike the SELECT statement where you can type table field names in any case.

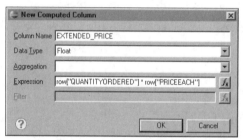

Figure 20-2   Computed field EXTENDED_PRICE

4 Choose OK to save the computed field.

8 Choose Preview Results to confirm that the query returns the correct data. Figure 20-3 shows some of the data rows that the data set returns.

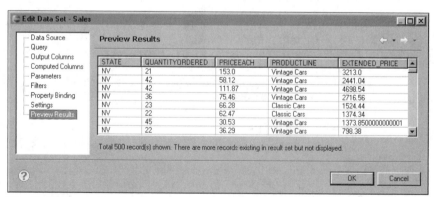

Figure 20-3   Preview of rows returned by the Sales data set

9 Choose OK to save the data set.

Task 4: Set up data for the cross tab

In this procedure, you set up the following items:

- A data group, or dimension, containing values to use as the cross tab's row headings

- A data group, or dimension, containing values to use as the cross tab's column headings

- A summary field, or measure, providing aggregate values to use in the cells of the cross tab

Data that you set up for a cross tab is stored in an entity called a cube.

1 In Data Explorer, right-click Data Cubes, and choose New Data Cube.

2 In Cross Tab Cube Builder, specify the following information:

- In Name, type

  ```
  Sales Cube
  ```

- In Primary dataset, select Sales.

3 Choose Groups and Summaries.

4 In Available Fields, expand Sales. Drag STATE and drop it on the following location, as shown in Figure 20-4:

  ```
  (Drop a field here to create a group)
  ```

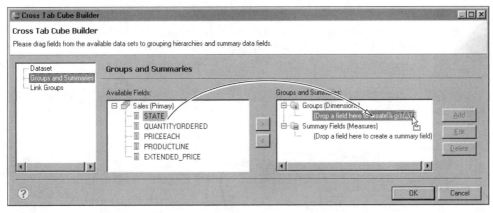

Figure 20-4   Adding a state group to the cube

5 In Add Group, use the default group name. Choose OK.

6 Drag PRODUCTLINE from Available Fields and drop it on the following location:

  ```
  (Drop a field here to create a group)
  ```

7 Use the default group name.

Cross Tab Cube Builder shows the STATE and PRODUCTLINE dimensions you created, as shown in Figure 20-5.

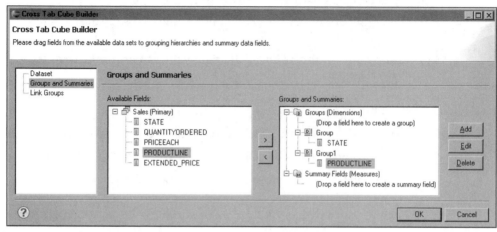

Figure 20-5   Cross Tab Cube Builder displaying two groups

8 Drag EXTENDED_PRICE from Available Fields and drop it on the following location:

(Drop a field here to create a summary field)

EXTENDED_PRICE(SUM) appears under Summary Field. SUM indicates that the SUM aggregate function is used to calculate the totals of the EXTENDED_PRICE values. The cube builder selects the SUM function by default. You can, however, select a different function to apply to a measure by selecting the measure, then choosing Edit.

Figure 20-6 shows the dimensions and measure you defined.

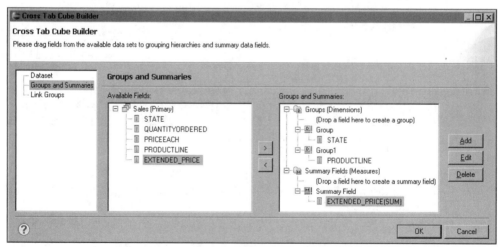

Figure 20-6   Cross Tab Cube Builder displaying two groups and a summary field

9 Choose OK to save the cube. The Sales cube appears under Data Cubes in Data Explorer.

10 Expand the Sales Cube to view its contents, as shown in Figure 20-7.

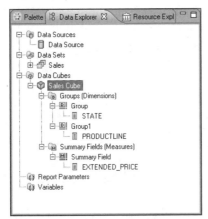

Figure 20-7 Data Explorer showing the Sales cube

Task 5: Add a cross tab to the report

In this procedure, you add a cross tab to the report, then you insert data from the cube into the cross tab.

1 Choose the palette, then drag a cross-tab element from the palette to the report. A cross tab appears in the report.

2 Choose Data Explorer. Under the first group in the Sales cube, drag STATE and drop it in the cross-tab area that displays the following text:

`Drop data field(s) to define rows here`

Figure 20-8 shows inserting STATE in this location.

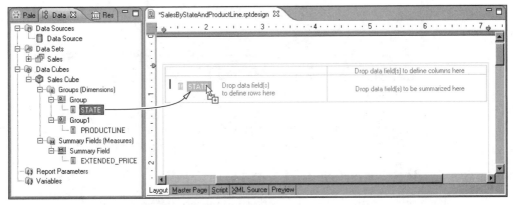

Figure 20-8 Inserting STATE data in the cross tab

3 From the Sales cube, under Group1, drag PRODUCTLINE and drop it in the cross-tab area that displays the following text:

```
Drop data field(s) to define columns here
```

4 From the Sales cube, under Summary Field, drag EXTENDED_PRICE and drop it in the cross-tab area that displays the following text:

```
Drop data field(s) to be summarized here
```

The cross tab should look like the one shown in Figure 20-9.

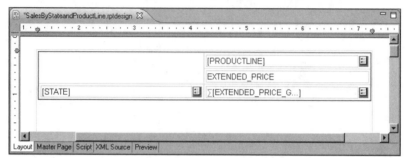

Figure 20-9   Cross tab design

5 Choose Preview. Figure 20-10 shows a portion of the data that the cross tab displays.

	Classic Cars	Motorcycles	Planes	Ships	Trains	Trucks and Buses
	EXTENDED_PR	EXTENDED_PR	EXTENDED_PR	EXTENDED_PR	EXTENDED_PR	EXTENDED_PR
CA	458563.64	162710.5699999	108632.2599999	66758.95	17965.32	167896.48
CT	89671.2800000	39699.67	41142.34	5936.68	9548.5299999	15671.4900000
MA	223366.59	91024.09	51924.57	71419.4	12184.49	58487.98
NH	69150.35					7922.29
NJ		35116.44	33308.4900000	4346.26		
NV	58718.89					
NY	260619.7299999	99514.8700000	24647.66		36219.6499999	15033.47	77996
PA	102856.2399999	39025.09	15889.79	4983.38	4862.02	37483.0899999

Refresh Report   **Note:** Current maximum number of data rows is limited to 5000. (Click to change Preview Preferences)

Figure 20-10   Preview of the cross tab data

The row headings display the states, the column headings display product lines, and the cells display the sales totals. The first cell displays 458563.64, which is the sales total of classic cars sold in California.

Task 6: Add grand totals

Each number displayed in the cross tab represents the sales total of a particular product for a particular state. In this procedure, you add grand totals to display the total sales of all products for each state, the total sales of each product, and the total of all sales across products and states.

1 Choose Layout to resume editing the cross tab.

2 Select the cross tab, if necessary, by clicking on the tab in the lower left corner of the cross tab. Make sure you select the entire cross tab, not just a part of it.

3 In Property Editor, choose the Row Area tab.

4 Choose Grand Totals, then choose Add.

5 In Grand Total, shown in Figure 20-11, use the default values, then choose OK.

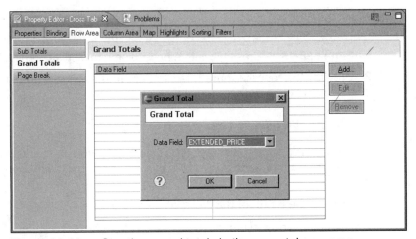

Figure 20-11 Creating grand totals in the cross-tab row area

A new row is added to the bottom of the cross tab, as shown in Figure 20-12. In this row is a label that displays Grand Total and a data element that displays Σ [EXTENDED_PRICE].

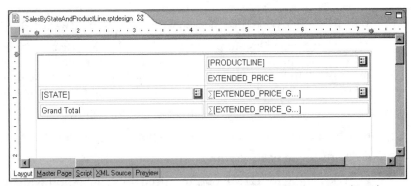

Figure 20-12 Cross tab including a new row to display grand totals

6 In Property Editor, choose the Column Area tab.

7   Choose Grand Totals, then choose Add.

8   In Grand Total, use the default values, then choose OK. A new column is added to the cross tab, as shown in Figure 20-13.

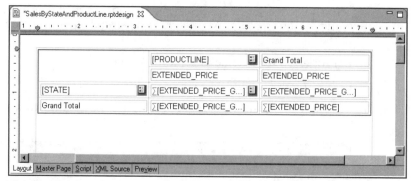

Figure 20-13   Cross tab with a new column to display grand totals

9   Preview the report. Grand totals appear in the last row and last column of the cross tab.

Task 7: Format the cross tab

Now that the cross tab displays the correct data, you can focus on improving the presentation of data in the cross tab. You perform the following tasks in this section:

- Expand the width of the cross tab to fit the data.

- Display a string in empty cells.

- Change the format of the numbers.

- Edit the column headings.

- Use darker lines around the cross tab and the cells.

Expand the width of the cross tab to fit the data

The default report layout preference, Fixed Layout, displays a cross tab with columns of equal size within a display area determined by the page size and margins set in the master page. In the report preview, notice that the EXTENDED_PRICE labels and some of the numbers are truncated.

To avoid losing content, you can do one of the following:

- Change the page orientation from portrait to landscape.

- Increase the page width.

- If designing for HTML output, specify that the report width expand automatically to fit the data.

The following procedure uses the third option.

1 Choose Layout to resume editing the cross tab.

2 In the layout editor, click on an empty area of the report page.

3 In Property Editor, under Properties, choose General.

4 Set Layout Preference to Auto Layout.

5 Preview the report. Figure 20-14 shows a portion of the data that the cross tab displays. Each column in the cross tab expands to accommodate its content.

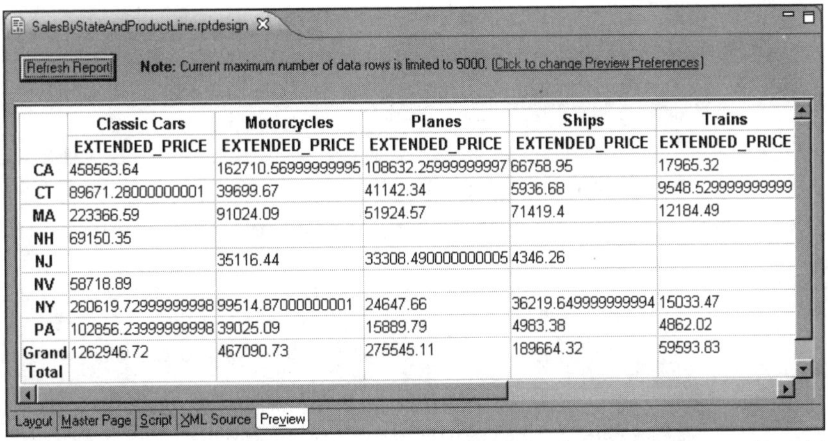

Figure 20-14 Preview of the cross tab when the layout preference is set to Auto Layout

Note that this auto-expand feature applies only to HTML output. In other output formats, the size of the cross tab is always constrained by the page dimensions.

Display a string in empty cells

If there are no sales for a particular product in a particular state, the cell displays nothing. Because an empty cell can be interpreted as missing data, you can display a string, such as 0.00 or --, to indicate that the value is zero.

1 Choose Layout to resume editing the cross tab.

2 Select the cross tab by clicking on the tab in the lower left corner of the cross tab.

3 In Property Editor, choose Properties, then choose Empty Rows/ Columns.

4 In the "For empty cells, show:" field, type the following text:

--

Figure 20-15 shows the Empty Rows/Columns properties.

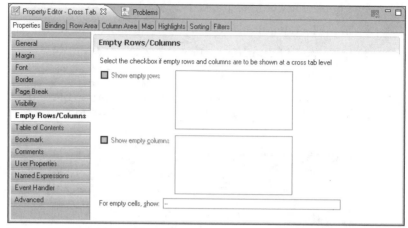

Figure 20-15 Empty Rows/Columns properties of the cross tab

5 Preview the report. Cells that were previously empty now display --, as shown in Figure 20-16.

	Classic Cars	Motorcycles	Planes	Ships	Trains
	EXTENDED_PRICE	EXTENDED_PRICE	EXTENDED_PRICE	EXTENDED_PRICE	EXTENDED_PRICE
CA	458563.64	162710.56999999995	108632.25999999997	66758.95	17965.32
CT	89671.28000000001	39699.67	41142.34	5936.68	9548.529999999999
MA	223366.59	91024.09	51924.57	71419.4	12184.49
NH	69150.35	--	--	--	--
NJ	--	35116.44	33308.490000000005	4346.26	--
NV	58718.89	--	--	--	--
NY	260619.72999999998	99514.87000000001	24647.66	36219.649999999994	15033.47
PA	102856.23999999998	39025.09	15889.79	4983.38	4862.02
Grand Total	1262946.72	467090.73	275545.11	189664.32	59593.83

Figure 20-16 Preview of the cross tab showing -- to indicate no data

Change the format of the numbers

To indicate that the numbers displayed in the cross tab are dollar amounts, use the currency format. It is also easier to read the numbers if they are aligned to the right.

1 Choose Layout to resume editing the cross tab.

2 Click in an empty area on the report page.

3 Choose Element→Style→New Style.

4 In Custom Style, type the following name for the new style:

```
crosstab_currency
```

5 Specify a currency format, using the following steps:

  1 Choose Format Number from the list of property categories.

  2 In Format As, select Currency from the drop-down list.

  3 In Currency Settings, specify the following values:

    ❑ Set Decimal places to 2.

    ❑ Select Use 1000s separator.

    ❑ In Symbol, select $.

    ❑ Use the default values for the other currency settings.

  Figure 20-17 shows the currency values you set.

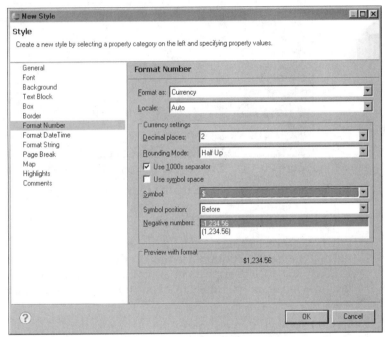

Figure 20-17   Format Number showing the currency settings

6 Specify the text alignment, using the following steps:

  1 Choose Text Block from the list of property categories.

  2 In Text alignment, select Right.

7 Choose OK to save the crosstab_currency style.

8 Apply the crosstab_currency style to the data elements, using the following steps:

  1 In the layout editor, select the four [EXTENDED_PRICE] data elements, as shown in Figure 20-18.

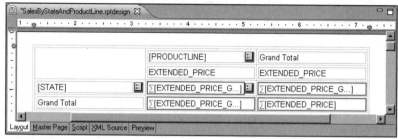

Figure 20-18 Data elements selected

2 In Property Editor, choose Properties, then choose General. In Style, select crosstab_currency, as shown in Figure 20-19.

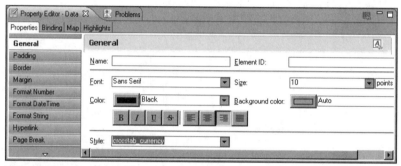

Figure 20-19 Style showing crosstab_currency selected

9 Preview the report to verify the formatting change.

Edit the column headings

When you insert a summary field or measure, BIRT adds a label that displays the field name as a column heading. In the generated cross tab, the heading EXTENDED_PRICE appears in every column, above the sales data. Because the cross tab displays values from one measure only, the heading is not necessary.

1 Choose Layout to resume editing the cross tab.

2 Select the cross tab.

3 In Property Editor, choose Properties, then choose General.

4 Select Hide Measure Header, as shown in Figure 20-20.

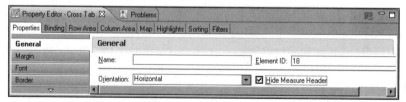

Figure 20-20 Hide Measure Header selected

5 Preview the report. The row that displays the measure headings is hidden. Figure 20-21 shows a portion of the generated cross tab.

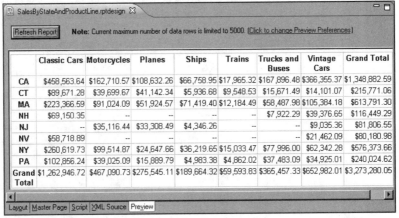

Figure 20-21 Preview of the cross tab with the measure header hidden

Use darker lines around the cross tab and the cells

BIRT uses two predefined styles, crosstab and crosstab-cell, to set the default appearance of the overall cross tab and the cells, respectively. To change any of the cross tab or cell formats, such as the width or color of borders, edit these styles.

1 Choose Layout to resume editing the cross tab.

2 Choose the Outline view, located next to Navigator.

3 Expand the Styles item to show the crosstab and crosstab-cell styles, as shown in Figure 20-22.

Figure 20-22 Outline view displaying the cross-tab styles

4 Right-click the crosstab style, then choose Edit Style.

5 In Edit Style, choose Border. The colors of the borders are set to Gray.

6 Change the color of all the borders to Black, as shown in Figure 20-23.

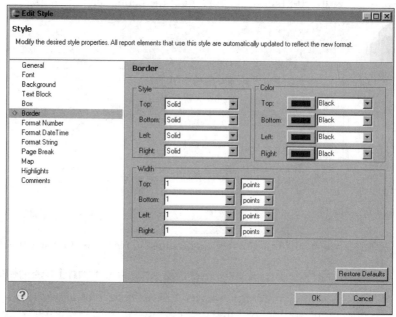

Figure 20-23   Border colors set to Black

7 Choose OK to save your change to the crosstab style.

8 In Outline, right-click the crosstab-cell style, then choose Edit Style.

9 In Edit Style, choose Border.

10 Change the color of all the borders to Black. Choose OK.

In the layout editor, the lines around the cells and around the cross tab appear in black, as shown in Figure 20-24.

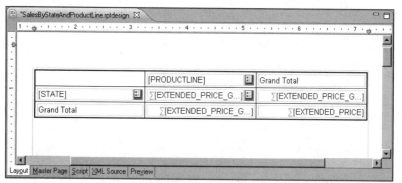

Figure 20-24   Cross tab design showing black borders

11 Preview the report. Figure 20-25 shows a portion of the generated cross tab.

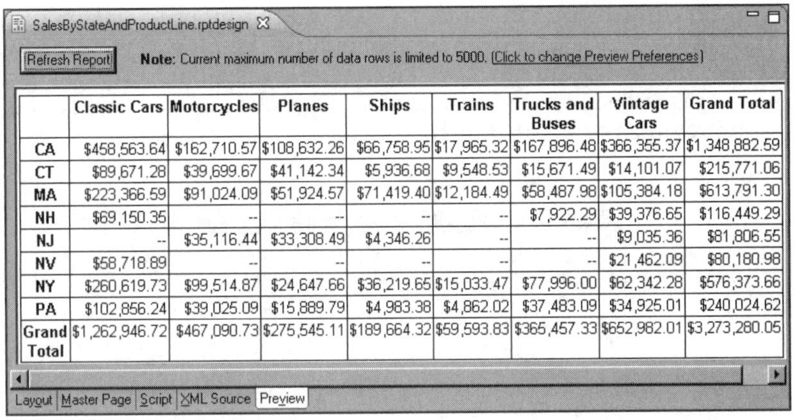

	Classic Cars	Motorcycles	Planes	Ships	Trains	Trucks and Buses	Vintage Cars	Grand Total
CA	$458,563.64	$162,710.57	$108,632.26	$66,758.95	$17,965.32	$167,896.48	$366,355.37	$1,348,882.59
CT	$89,671.28	$39,699.67	$41,142.34	$5,936.68	$9,548.53	$15,671.49	$14,101.07	$215,771.06
MA	$223,366.59	$91,024.09	$51,924.57	$71,419.40	$12,184.49	$58,487.98	$105,384.18	$613,791.30
NH	$69,150.35	--	--	--	--	$7,922.29	$39,376.65	$116,449.29
NJ	--	$35,116.44	$33,308.49	$4,346.26	--	--	$9,035.36	$81,806.55
NV	$58,718.89	--	--	--	--	--	$21,462.09	$80,180.98
NY	$260,619.73	$99,514.87	$24,647.66	$36,219.65	$15,033.47	$77,996.00	$62,342.28	$576,373.66
PA	$102,856.24	$39,025.09	$15,889.79	$4,983.38	$4,862.02	$37,483.09	$34,925.01	$240,024.62
Grand Total	$1,262,946.72	$467,090.73	$275,545.11	$189,664.32	$59,593.83	$365,457.33	$652,982.01	$3,273,280.05

Figure 20-25 Preview of the finished cross tab

You just learned how to build a basic cross tab that displays data from three fields. The rest of this chapter shows how to build more complex cross tabs.

Setting up data for a cross tab

As the tutorial demonstrates, when setting up data for a cross tab, you create at least one data source and one data set, just as you would to prepare data for other report elements. Unlike a table, a list, or a chart, however, you cannot insert a data set field directly in a cross tab.

To set up data for a cross tab, there is one additional step to perform: creating a cube. The data that you insert in a cross tab must come from a cube. As the tutorial also demonstrates, you build a cube using data from a data set. Figure 20-26 illustrates how the cross tab gets its data.

If you are wondering why there is an additional data entity, the answer is that the cube offers a far more powerful way to store numeric data for fast analysis.

About cubes

Commonly associated with online analytical processing (OLAP) technology, a cube is a multidimensional data structure that is optimized for analysis and reporting. A cube organizes data into dimensions and measures. Measures represent values that are counted or aggregated, such as costs or units of products. Dimensions are categories, such as products, customers, or sales periods, by which measures are aggregated. For example, a retail cube might contain data that supports viewing sales volume and cost of goods, which are measures, by store location, time period, and product lines, which are dimensions.

Dimensions can be hierarchical and contain multiple levels. For example, a region dimension can contain a region-country-state hierarchy. Similarly, a time dimension can contain a year-quarter-month-week hierarchy. Most cubes include a time dimension because, for most reports, showing measures by day, week, month, quarter, or year is essential to analyzing data. The time dimension is a special dimension. The cube groups dates stored in a field into any time period of your choice.

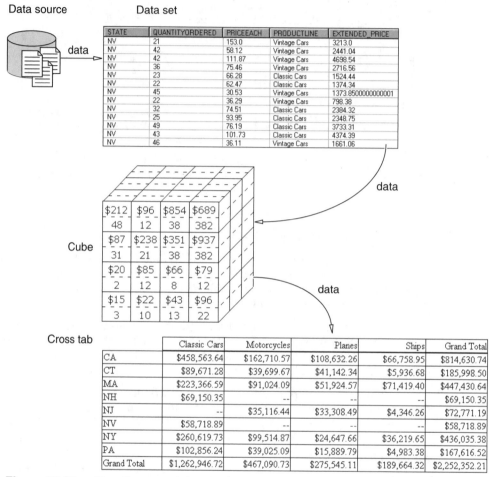

Figure 20-26   How the cross tab gets data

Planning the data

Before building a data set or a cube, think about the aggregate data you want to display in the cross tab, and how you want to categorize the aggregate data. For example:

■ Average score and high score by year by school district

■ Sales volume by month by product by store

- Call volume and average call time by support person by day and by call type

After deciding the information to display in the cross tab, you can identify which data fields to define as measures and dimensions in the cube. In the first example, the measures are average score and high score, and the dimensions are year and school district.

After identifying the contents of the cube, you know what data to retrieve from the data source. Figure 20-27 shows the data planning flow.

1. What data will the cross tab display?

	Classic Cars	Motorcycles	Planes	Ships	Grand Total
CA	$458,563.64	$162,710.57	$108,632.26	$66,758.95	$814,630.74
CT	$89,671.28	$39,699.67	$41,142.34	$5,936.68	$185,998.50
MA	$223,366.59	$91,024.09	$51,924.57	$71,419.40	$447,430.64
NH	$69,150.35	--	--	--	$69,150.35
NJ	--	$35,116.44	$33,308.49	$4,346.26	$72,771.19
NV	$58,718.89	--	--	--	$58,718.89
NY	$260,619.73	$99,514.87	$24,647.66	$36,219.65	$436,035.38
PA	$102,856.24	$39,025.09	$15,889.79	$4,983.38	$167,616.52
Grand Total	$1,262,946.72	$467,090.73	$275,545.11	$189,664.32	$2,252,352.21

2. What measures and dimensions are needed in the cube?

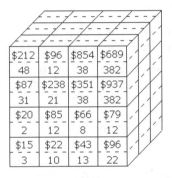

3. What data needs to be retrieved from the data source?

STATE	QUANTITYORDERED	PRICEEACH	PRODUCTLINE	EXTENDED_PRICE
NV	21	153.0	Vintage Cars	3213.0
NV	42	58.12	Vintage Cars	2441.04
NV	42	111.87	Vintage Cars	4698.54
NV	36	75.46	Vintage Cars	2716.56
NV	23	66.28	Classic Cars	1524.44
NV	22	62.47	Classic Cars	1374.34
NV	45	30.53	Vintage Cars	1373.8500000000001
NV	22	36.29	Vintage Cars	798.38
NV	32	74.51	Classic Cars	2384.32
NV	25	93.95	Classic Cars	2348.75
NV	49	76.19	Classic Cars	3733.31
NV	43	101.73	Classic Cars	4374.39
NV	46	36.11	Vintage Cars	1661.06

Figure 20-27 How to plan the data to display in a cross tab

Notice that the planning steps are in the reverse order of the implementation steps. Start with the end result and work backward to determine the best way to get the results you want. If you have control of the data source as well—the database, for example—you can go a step further and create a database schema that supports the queries to return data for a cube.

Most report developers, however, neither create nor maintain corporate databases or other information systems. The rest of this section provides some guidelines for designing data sets and cubes, given the typical ways databases are structured.

Designing the cube

In theory, it is possible to create a cube with any number of dimensions and measures. You might be tempted to create a cube that stores all measures against every combination of dimensions. This approach is not practical in real-world applications. The number of aggregations increases exponentially with the number of measures and dimensions. The higher the number of aggregations BIRT must calculate, the greater the amount of time and computer resources BIRT requires.

Therefore, for each cross tab you want to create, design a cube that provides only the data to display in that cross tab.

Observe the following rules:

- Cube data can be used in cross tabs and charts only. You cannot use cube data in a table or list.

- A cross tab or chart can use data from one cube only. This requirement is similar to tables, lists, and charts using data from one data set only.

The cube's data structure is symmetric to the cross tab's structure. The cube organizes measures by dimensions, and the cross tab displays aggregate data (measures) by any number of data groups (dimensions). This symmetry makes designing a cube intuitive and straightforward. Determine what your users want to see and how they want to see it, and define the measures and dimensions for the cube accordingly.

Designing data sets for a cube

This design phase requires more thought and planning. The data set must accomplish two key things. It must retrieve data from the source in a resource-efficient manner and also in a way that makes sense for the cube. How you write the SQL query to get the data depends on how the database is structured. When planning how to get data for a cube, you also have to decide whether to build one data set or multiple data sets.

BIRT supports the creation of cubes using data from a single data set or multiple data sets to support the different ways data sources can be structured, and report developers' different levels of expertise. In other words, the decision to build one or multiple data sets to get data for a cube depends on how the data source is structured, and also on your grasp of OLAP design principles.

The cube builder in BIRT is designed for report developers with varying OLAP expertise. You do not have to know much about OLAP to build a data set or a cube for a cross tab, but if you have the expertise, you can design data sets that apply OLAP design principles for optimal performance.

It is beyond the scope of this book to teach OLAP principles, but an introduction to the subject might help you decide whether it is worth exploring OLAP further.

Comparing OLTP and OLAP

Online Transaction Processing (OLTP) systems and Online Analytical Processing (OLAP) systems are two common database structures. Each serves a different purpose.

OLTP is the standard, normalized database structure designed for transactions, where data inserts, updates, and deletes must be fast. One of the ways OLTP systems optimize the entry or updates of records is by minimizing repeated data. For example, complete information about an order includes an order number, a customer name, a bill-to address, a ship-to address, and a payment method. The order details include a product number, a product description, the quantity ordered, and the unit price. In a flat structure, each order detail record would need all that information. That is a lot of repeated information, which is why OLTP systems use relational technology to link the information. The Classic Models sample database is an example of an OLTP database. Figure 20-28 shows a partial view of the Classic Models schema. Tables are linked to one another by keys.

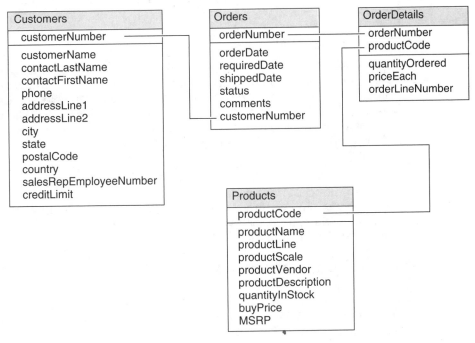

Figure 20-28   A partial view of the Classic Models schema

By contrast, OLAP is a database structure designed for performing analysis to reveal trends and patterns among data. This structure more closely represents the way people ask questions or want to view data. For example:

- What are the sales amounts for each product this month?

- Are product sales up or down compared to previous months?

- What products saw the greatest increase this quarter?

- In what regions did product sales increase this quarter?

Figure 20-29 shows an example of an OLAP structure.

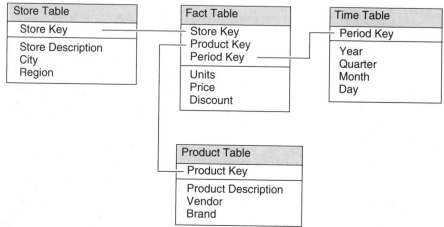

Figure 20-29 An OLAP schema

This particular OLAP structure is commonly referred to as a star schema because the schema diagram is shaped like a star, that is, one in which points radiate from a central table. The central table is called a fact table, and the supporting tables linked to it are dimension tables. As Figure 20-29 shows, the fact table contains the measures and keys to link to each dimension table. The dimension tables do not link to one another.

Many-to-one relationships exist between the keys in the fact table and the keys they reference in the dimension tables. For example, the Product table defines the products. Each row in the Product table represents a distinct product and has a unique product identifier. Each product identifier can occur multiple times in the Sales fact table, representing sales of that product during each period and in each store.

Designing a single data set

Design a single data set if:

- You are retrieving data from a database that uses an OLTP structure.

- You are well-versed in writing SQL joins. Because an OLTP structure minimizes repeated data, you typically have to join many tables to get all the data you need. The query you created in the tutorial joined four tables to get data for a cube that contained only two dimensions and one measure.

■ You find it too complicated to create data sets from a OLTP structure to resemble a star schema. This exercise can feel like fitting a square peg into a round hole.

The disadvantage of creating a single data set is that, typically, it must use multiple joins. These joins are complex to create and increasing the number of joins can slow queries.

Designing multiple data sets in a star schema

Create multiple data sets to retrieve data for a cube if:

■ You are retrieving data from a database that uses an OLAP star schema.

■ You are familiar with star schemas.

■ The number of joins required to get the data from multiple tables is too complex and degrades performance.

If the database uses a star schema, you can create data sets that mimic the structure, one data set for each fact table and dimension table in the star schema.

If the database uses an OLTP structure, you can also create one data set to retrieve the data to calculate the measures, and one data set for each dimension. Because you are trying to map data from an OLTP structure to data in a OLAP star schema, the mapping process is less intuitive, and you might also find that you still need to create multiple joins in each data set.

Building a multi-dataset cube

The tutorial earlier in this chapter walked through the steps for building a cube that used data from a single data set. In this section, you learn how to create a multi-dataset cube. Because the concepts and procedures are easier to understand with an example, this section walks through the steps for performing the following tasks:

■ Creating the data sets to retrieve data from the Orders, OrderDetails, and Products tables in the Classic Models sample database

■ Using data from the data sets to build a cube that contains a sales amount measure, a product line dimension, and a year dimension

How to create data sets for a multi-dataset cube

In this procedure, you create two data sets:

■ A fact data set, SalesTotal, to retrieve the data for calculating the sales totals

- A dimension data set, Productlines, to retrieve data about the product lines

Note that we are not creating a separate data set for the year dimension, as is typical in a star schema. It is sometimes too complicated to create a pure star schema design when working with data stored in an OLTP system.

1 Create a new data set named SalesTotals. Create the following query:

```
select CLASSICMODELS.ORDERDETAILS.PRODUCTCODE,
CLASSICMODELS.ORDERS.SHIPPEDDATE,
CLASSICMODELS.ORDERDETAILS.QUANTITYORDERED *
    CLASSICMODELS.ORDERDETAILS.PRICEEACH as "EXTENDED_PRICE"

from CLASSICMODELS.ORDERDETAILS, CLASSICMODELS.ORDERS
where CLASSICMODELS.ORDERS.ORDERNUMBER =
    CLASSICMODELS.ORDERDETAILS.ORDERNUMBER
and CLASSICMODELS.ORDERS.STATUS = 'Shipped'
```

The query does the following:

- Retrieves PRODUCTCODE data because it is the key to later link to the PRODUCTLINE dimension

- Retrieves SHIPPEDDATE data to use for the year dimension

- Creates a calculated column, EXTENDED_PRICE, used to aggregate values to calculate the sales totals

- Creates a join between the Orders and OrderDetails tables to get all the necessary data about the orders. Because the data set is retrieving data from an OLTP database, joins are unavoidable

- Defines a filter condition to retrieve order data for orders that have been shipped, and therefore, that have been paid

2 Create a new data set named ProductLines. Create the following query:

```
select CLASSICMODELS.PRODUCTS.PRODUCTLINE,
CLASSICMODELS.PRODUCTS.PRODUCTCODE
from CLASSICMODELS.PRODUCTS
```

The query does the following:

- Retrieves PRODUCTLINE data to use for the PRODUCTLINE dimension.

- Retrieves PRODUCTCODE data because it is the key that the SalesTotals data set will need to reference.

How to create a multi-dataset cube

1 In Data Explorer, right-click Data Cubes, then choose New Data Cube.

2 In the Dataset page of Cross Tab Cube Builder, supply the following information, as shown in Figure 20-30:

1 In Name, specify a descriptive name, such as Sales Cube, for the cube.

2 In Primary dataset, select SalesTotals. In a multi-dataset cube, the fact data set that retrieves the data to calculate measures is the primary data set.

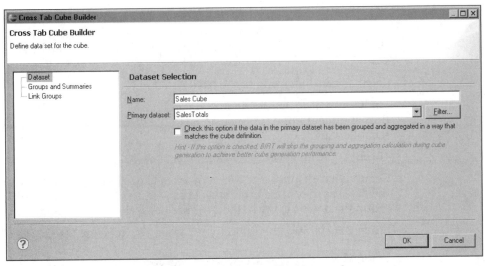

Figure 20-30   Name and primary data set specified for a cube

3 Choose Groups and Summaries to define the dimensions and measures for the cube. The Groups and Summaries page, shown in Figure 20-31, displays the available data sets and fields.

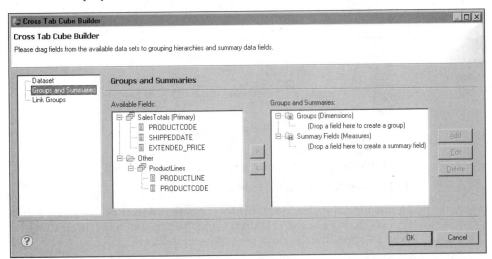

Figure 20-31   Groups and Summaries page shows the available data sets and fields

4 Define the product line dimension, using the following steps:

1 Under the Productlines data set, drag PRODUCTLINE and drop it under Groups (Dimensions) in the drop location that displays the following text:

`(Drop a field here to create a group)`

2 In Add Group, use the default group name.

3 Under the Productlines data set, drag PRODUCTCODE and drop it on the PRODUCTLINE dimension. This action creates a hierarchical relationship between PRODUCTLINE and PRODUCTCODE.

5 Define the year dimension of the cube.

1 Under the SalesTotals (Primary) data set, drag SHIPPEDDATE and drop it under Groups (Dimensions) in the drop location that displays the following text:

`(Drop a field here to create a group)`

Group Level displays the different ways to group the dates. To display the dates as they appear in the data source, select Regular Group. To group the dates by any of the time periods, select Date Group.

2 Select Date Group, then select year, as shown in Figure 20-32.

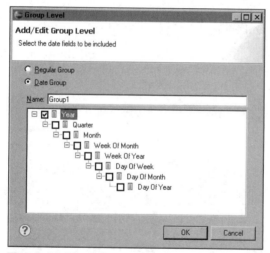

Figure 20-32   Group Level showing the year group selected

3 Choose OK to save the year dimension.

6 Define the cube's measure. Under the SalesTotals (Primary) data set, drag EXTENDED_PRICE and drop it under Summary Fields (Measures) in the drop location that displays the following text:

`(Drop a field here to create a summary field)`

The Groups and Summaries page, shown in Figure 20-33, displays the defined dimensions and measure.

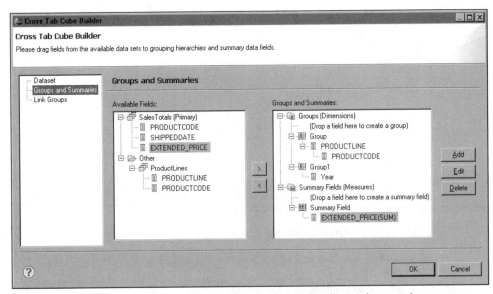

Figure 20-33   Groups and Summaries page shows the dimensions and measure

7 Link the data in the dimensions with the fact data set.

    1 Choose Link Groups. The Link Groups page displays the Productline dimension you created and the primary (fact) data set.

    2 Link the PRODUCTCODE field in both items, as shown in Figure 20-34.

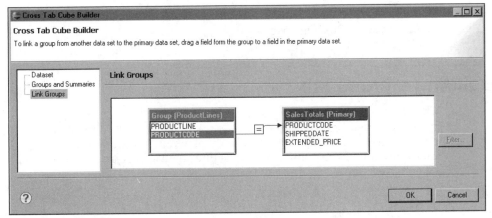

Figure 20-34   Link Groups page shows how the dimension and fact data sets are linked

    8 Choose OK to save the cube. You can now build a cross tab that uses data from this cube.

Figure 20-35 shows a cross tab that uses the year and PRODUCTLINE dimensions and the EXTENDED_PRICE measure from the cube.

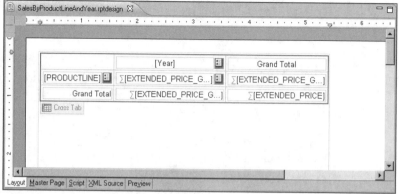

Figure 20-35   Cross tab design

Figure 20-36 shows the generated cross tab.

	2003	2004	2005	Grand Total
Classic Cars	$1,362,984.66	$1,682,980.21	$577,635.76	$3,623,600.63
Motorcycles	$344,998.74	$527,243.84	$212,684.55	$1,084,927.13
Planes	$284,773.21	$438,255.50	$109,701.56	$832,730.27
Ships	$201,044.48	$292,595.34	$62,989.19	$556,629.01
Trains	$65,822.05	$86,897.46	$22,311.26	$175,030.77
Trucks and Buses	$357,094.59	$448,702.69	$143,207.06	$949,004.34
Vintage Cars	$606,378.07	$823,927.95	$212,866.47	$1,643,172.49
Grand Total	$3,223,095.80	$4,300,602.99	$1,341,395.85	$8,865,094.64

Figure 20-36   Cross tab output

Building a cross tab

The tutorial earlier in this chapter walked through the procedures for building a basic cross tab. In this section, you learn how to create more complex cross tabs, including how to display multiple dimensions and measures, how to customize row and column headings, and how to create custom measures.

Areas of a cross tab

A cross tab consists of the following three areas, as shown in Figure 20-37:

- The row area
- The column area
- The detail area

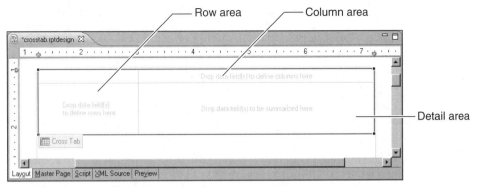

Figure 20-37   Cross tab row, column, and detail areas

The row and column areas are where you insert dimensions from a cube. The dimension values form the row and column headings of the cross tab. The detail area is where you insert a measure or measures from a cube to display aggregate data.

Displaying multiple dimensions in row and column areas

When building a cross tab, you typically group the aggregate data by at least two dimensions, for example, sales totals by year and product line, or sales totals by year and state. Often, report users want to view aggregate data by more than two dimensions.

The cross tab in Figure 20-38 shows the sales total by region, state, product line, and product. To create the cross tab, two dimensions (State and Year) are inserted in the row area, and one dimension (ProductLines) is inserted in the column area. The ProductLines dimension has two levels, ProductLine and ProductName.

SalesByProductLineAndProductAndStateAndTime.rptdesign

Refresh Report   **Note:** Current maximum number of data rows is limited to 0. (Click to change Preview Preferences)

		Classic Cars		Vintage Cars			Grand Total
		1968 Ford Mustang	1969 Ford Falcon	1903 Ford Model A	1912 Ford Model T Delivery Wagon	1932 Model A Ford J-Coupe	
East	2003		$7,121.52			$3,107.00	$10,228.52
	2004	$7,498.90	$10,121.80		$2,832.40		$20,453.10
North East	2003	$7,751.52	$11,912.67	$15,578.24	$2,745.60		$37,988.03
	2004	$9,242.00			$3,867.68	$11,296.39	$24,406.07
West	2003	$15,011.07	$7,720.18	$6,098.72	$5,975.28	$15,262.02	$50,067.27
	2004		$4,069.44	$5,285.99	$3,494.45	$3,467.97	$16,317.85
Grand Total		$39,503.49	$40,945.61	$26,962.95	$18,915.41	$33,133.38	$159,460.84

Layout | Master Page | Script | XML Source | Preview

Figure 20-38   Cross tab using multiple dimensions in the row and column areas

As the example shows, each additional dimension by which you group data appears as a column or row, and each additional dimension provides a more comprehensive and detailed view of the data. Just as you can define an unlimited number of dimensions for a cube, you can build a cross tab that displays aggregate data by as many dimensions as you want.

Calculating aggregate data by too many dimensions, however, can result in many empty cells, a problem commonly referred to as data sparsity. When designing a cube that contains more than two dimensions, make sure that processing time is not spent calculating zeros.

In addition, a cross tab that contains more than two or three dimensions in either the row or column area is difficult to read. Rather than display data by too many dimensions in a single cross tab, consider dividing the data into multiple cross tabs.

How to insert multiple dimensions in the row or column area

1 Drag a dimension from the cube and drop it in the row or column area of the cross tab.

2 Drop the second dimension either on the left or right side of the first dimension, depending on the order in which you want to display the data. Figure 20-39 shows placing the second dimension on the right side of the first dimension, as indicated by the position of the line cursor.

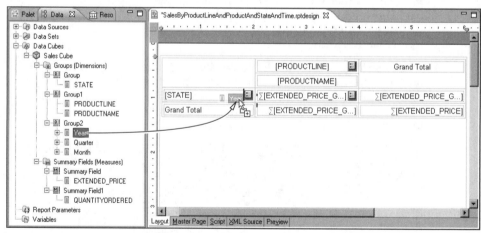

Figure 20-39   Dropping a second dimension in the row area of a cross tab

Displaying or hiding dimension levels

When you insert into the cross tab a dimension that contains multiple levels (for example, year, quarter, month), by default, the cross tab displays only the top level. You can, at any time, select additional levels to display. You can even skip levels. For example, in a year-quarter-month hierarchy, you can display the year and the month, and skip the quarter.

How to display or hide levels

1 Click the button next to the data element, as shown in Figure 20-40.

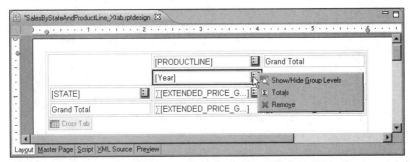

Figure 20-40 Displaying a menu for a selected element in the cross tab

2 Choose Show or Hide Group Levels.

3 In Show or Hide Group Levels, select the levels to display. Figure 20-41 shows an example of selecting all levels.

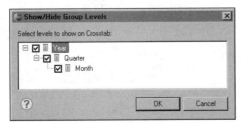

Figure 20-41 Show or Hide Group Levels

In the example, the time dimension has only three levels. If you want to display additional levels, such as week-of-month or day-of month, edit the definition of the time dimension in the cube builder.

4 Choose OK. BIRT creates a data element for each selected level, as shown in Figure 20-42.

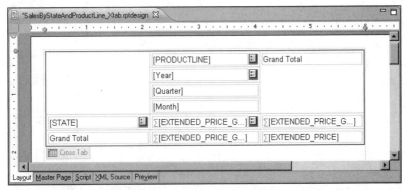

Figure 20-42 Cross tab displays a data element each for the year, quarter, and month levels

Displaying multiple measures

A cross tab can display any number of measures. For example, a cross tab that displays aggregate data by product line and state can show the sales total in dollars, the number of units sold, the number of customers, and so on. Figure 20-43 shows a cross tab that displays two measures, sales total amounts and total units sold.

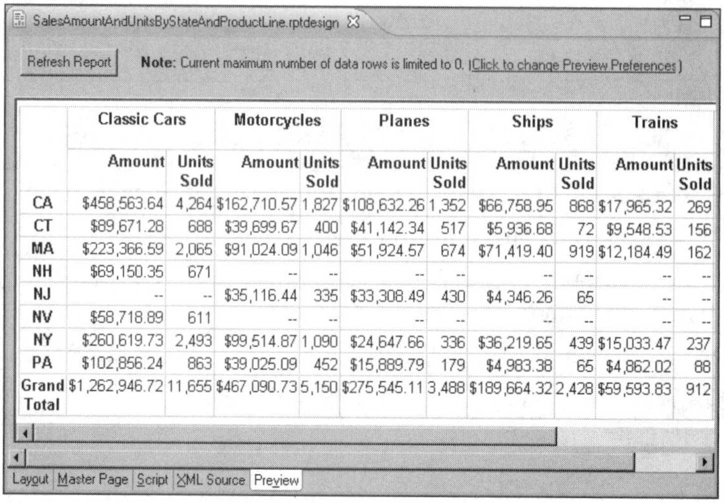

	Classic Cars		Motorcycles		Planes		Ships		Trains	
	Amount	Units Sold	Amount	Units Sold	Amount	Units Sold	Amount	Units Sold	Amount	Units Sold
CA	$458,563.64	4,264	$162,710.57	1,827	$108,632.26	1,352	$66,758.95	868	$17,965.32	269
CT	$89,671.28	688	$39,699.67	400	$41,142.34	517	$5,936.68	72	$9,548.53	156
MA	$223,366.59	2,065	$91,024.09	1,046	$51,924.57	674	$71,419.40	919	$12,184.49	162
NH	$69,150.35	671	--	--	--	--	--	--	--	--
NJ	--	--	$35,116.44	335	$33,308.49	430	$4,346.26	65	--	--
NV	$58,718.89	611	--	--	--	--	--	--	--	--
NY	$260,619.73	2,493	$99,514.87	1,090	$24,647.66	336	$36,219.65	439	$15,033.47	237
PA	$102,856.24	863	$39,025.09	452	$15,889.79	179	$4,983.38	65	$4,862.02	88
Grand Total	$1,262,946.72	11,655	$467,090.73	5,150	$275,545.11	3,488	$189,664.32	2,428	$59,593.83	912

Figure 20-43 Cross tab displays two measures side by side

When you insert multiple measures, by default, the cross tab displays the measures horizontally as shown in Figure 20-43. You can specify that the cross tab display them vertically instead, as shown in Figure 20-44.

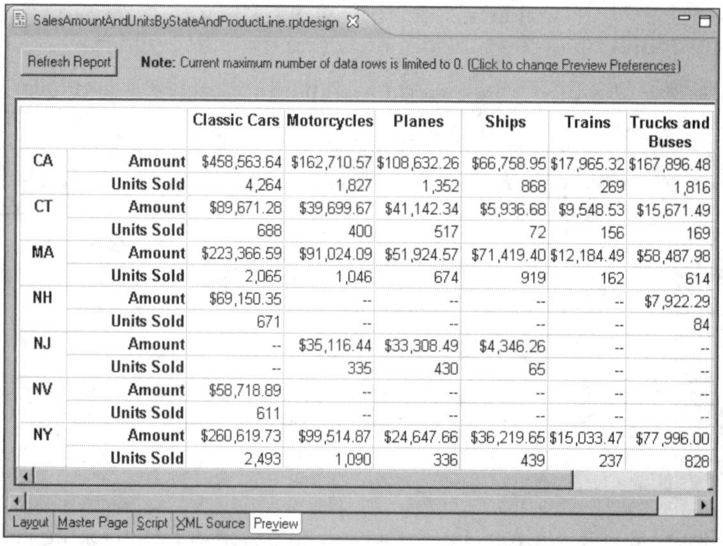

		Classic Cars	Motorcycles	Planes	Ships	Trains	Trucks and Buses
CA	Amount	$458,563.64	$162,710.57	$108,632.26	$66,758.95	$17,965.32	$167,896.48
	Units Sold	4,264	1,827	1,352	868	269	1,816
CT	Amount	$89,671.28	$39,699.67	$41,142.34	$5,936.68	$9,548.53	$15,671.49
	Units Sold	688	400	517	72	156	169
MA	Amount	$223,366.59	$91,024.09	$51,924.57	$71,419.40	$12,184.49	$58,487.98
	Units Sold	2,065	1,046	674	919	162	614
NH	Amount	$69,150.35	--	--	--	--	$7,922.29
	Units Sold	671	--	--	--	--	84
NJ	Amount	--	$35,116.44	$33,308.49	$4,346.26	--	--
	Units Sold	--	335	430	65	--	--
NV	Amount	$58,718.89	--	--	--	--	--
	Units Sold	611	--	--	--	--	--
NY	Amount	$260,619.73	$99,514.87	$24,647.66	$36,219.65	$15,033.47	$77,996.00
	Units Sold	2,493	1,090	336	439	237	828

Figure 20-44 Cross tab displaying two measures, one above the other

A comparison of the cross tabs in Figure 20-43 and Figure 20-44 shows that displaying measures vertically reduces the width of the cross tab and increases its height. So, besides your preference for reading the values horizontally or vertically, use this layout option to adjust the height and width of a cross tab.

How to insert multiple measures in a cross tab

1 Drag a measure from the cube and drop it in the detail area of the cross tab.

2 Similarly, insert the second measure next to the first measure.

   ▪ To display the second measure to the right of the first measure, drop the measure when the line cursor appears to the right of the data element for the first measure, as shown in Figure 20-45.

   ▪ To display the second measure to the left of the first measure, drop the measure when the line cursor appears to the left of the data element for the first measure.

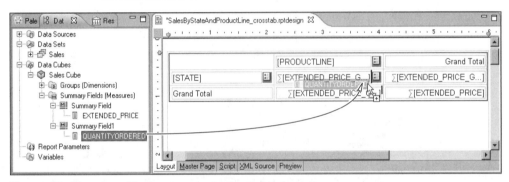

Figure 20-45   Inserting a measure to the right of another measure

How to display measures vertically

1 Select the cross tab.

2 In Property Editor, select General properties.

3 In Orientation, select Vertical. Figure 20-46 shows this option selected.

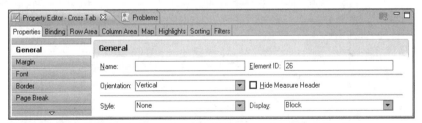

Figure 20-46   Select the option to display measures vertically

Adding a derived measure

Typically, measures are field values that are aggregated using one of the standard aggregate functions. You can also define a measure, called a derived measure, that involves a more complex calculation. For example, instead of displaying just sales totals by product line and by state, the cross tab can also display the product line sales totals as a percentage of the state total, as shown in Figure 20-47.

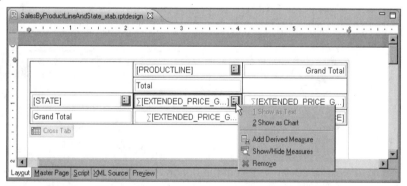

	Classic Cars		Trains		Trucks and Buses		Vintage Cars		Grand Total
	Total	Percentage	Total	Percentage	Total	Percentage	Total	Percentage	
CA	$458,564	45.37%	$17,965	1.78%	$167,896	16.61%	$366,355	36.24%	$1,010,781 43.18%
CT	$89,671	69.52%	$9,549	7.40%	$15,671	12.15%	$14,101	10.93%	$128,992 5.51%
MA	$223,367	55.92%	$12,184	3.05%	$58,488	14.64%	$105,384	26.38%	$399,423 17.06%
NH	$69,150	59.38%		0.00%	$7,922	6.80%	$39,377	33.81%	$116,449 4.97%
NJ		0.00%		0.00%		0.00%	$9,035	100.00%	$9,035 0.39%
NV	$58,719	73.23%		0.00%		0.00%	$21,462	26.77%	$80,181 3.43%
NY	$260,620	62.65%	$15,033	3.61%	$77,996	18.75%	$62,342	14.99%	$415,991 17.77%
PA	$102,856	57.10%	$4,862	2.70%	$37,483	20.81%	$34,925	19.39%	$180,126 7.69%
Grand Total	$1,262,947		$59,594		$365,457		$652,982		$2,340,980

Figure 20-47   Cross tab displaying two measures, one a derived measure calculating product line totals as a percent of the state total

How to create a derived measure

1 Click the button next to a data element that displays a measure, as shown in Figure 20-48.

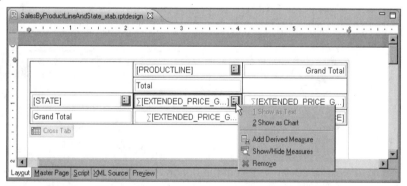

Figure 20-48   Displaying a menu for a selected measure in the cross tab

2 Choose Add Derived Measure.

3 In Derived Measure, specify the following information:

- In Name, type a name for the derived measure.

- In Data Type, select a data type appropriate for the data returned by the expression you specify next. For a derived measure, you typically select Float or Integer.

- In Expression, specify the expression that evaluates to the data to return. Use the expression builder to construct the expression. Figure 20-49 shows an example of an expression for calculating the product line sales total as a percentage of the state total. The expression uses column bindings defined in the cross tab.

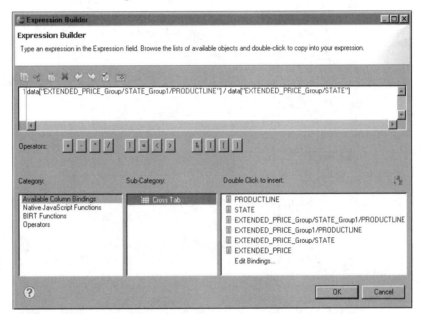

Figure 20-49   The expression builder showing an expression

Figure 20-50 shows an example of a complete definition for a derived measure.

Figure 20-50   Defining a derived measure in a cross tab

4 Choose OK to save the derived measure.

In the layout editor, the cross tab displays the derived measure next to the measure you selected in the first step.

Adding subtotals and grand totals

You can display totals for each dimension that you add to a cross tab, and for each level within a multilevel dimension. The cross tab in Figure 20-51 displays sales data by product line, state, year, and quarter. The rows and columns that display the subtotals and grand totals are highlighted.

BIRT does not create the subtotal and grand total rows and columns by default. You choose whether or not to display grand totals, and which subtotals to display.

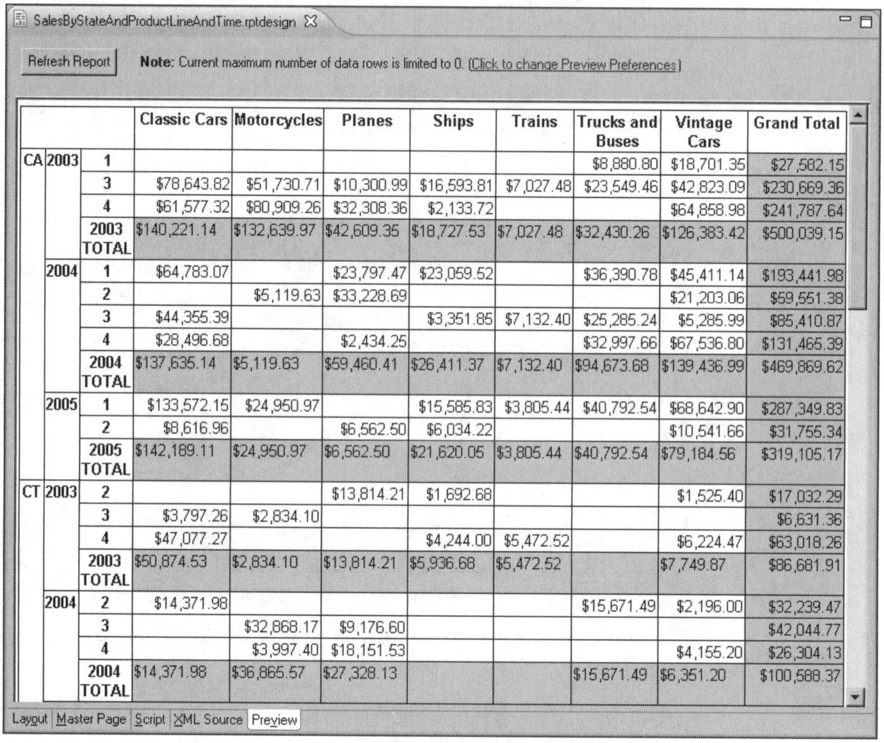

SalesByStateAndProductLineAndTime.rptdesign

Refresh Report | **Note:** Current maximum number of data rows is limited to 0. ([Click to change Preview Preferences])

			Classic Cars	Motorcycles	Planes	Ships	Trains	Trucks and Buses	Vintage Cars	Grand Total
CA	2003	1						$8,880.80	$18,701.35	$27,582.15
		3	$78,643.82	$51,730.71	$10,300.99	$16,593.81	$7,027.48	$23,549.46	$42,823.09	$230,669.36
		4	$61,577.32	$80,909.26	$32,308.36	$2,133.72			$64,858.98	$241,787.64
		2003 TOTAL	$140,221.14	$132,639.97	$42,609.35	$18,727.53	$7,027.48	$32,430.26	$126,383.42	$500,039.15
	2004	1	$64,783.07		$23,797.47	$23,059.52		$36,390.78	$45,411.14	$193,441.98
		2		$5,119.63	$33,228.69				$21,203.06	$59,551.38
		3	$44,355.39			$3,351.85	$7,132.40	$25,285.24	$5,285.99	$85,410.87
		4	$28,496.68		$2,434.25			$32,997.66	$67,536.80	$131,465.39
		2004 TOTAL	$137,635.14	$5,119.63	$59,460.41	$26,411.37	$7,132.40	$94,673.68	$139,436.99	$469,869.62
	2005	1	$133,572.15	$24,950.97		$15,585.83	$3,805.44	$40,792.54	$68,642.90	$287,349.83
		2	$8,616.96		$6,562.50	$6,034.22			$10,541.66	$31,755.34
		2005 TOTAL	$142,189.11	$24,950.97	$6,562.50	$21,620.05	$3,805.44	$40,792.54	$79,184.56	$319,105.17
CT	2003	2			$13,814.21	$1,692.68			$1,525.40	$17,032.29
		3	$3,797.26	$2,834.10						$6,631.36
		4	$47,077.27			$4,244.00	$5,472.52		$6,224.47	$63,018.26
		2003 TOTAL	$50,874.53	$2,834.10	$13,814.21	$5,936.68	$5,472.52		$7,749.87	$86,681.91
	2004	2	$14,371.98					$15,671.49	$2,196.00	$32,239.47
		3		$32,868.17	$9,176.60					$42,044.77
		4		$3,997.40	$18,151.53				$4,155.20	$26,304.13
		2004 TOTAL	$14,371.98	$36,865.57	$27,328.13			$15,671.49	$6,351.20	$100,588.37

Layout | Master Page | Script | XML Source | Preview

Figure 20-51 Cross tab displays sales subtotals and grand totals

How to display subtotals and grand totals

1 Select the cross tab.

2 In Property Editor, choose the Row Area tab or the Column Area tab to add a subtotal or grand total in the row area and column area, respectively.

Figure 20-52 shows the Row Area tab selected.

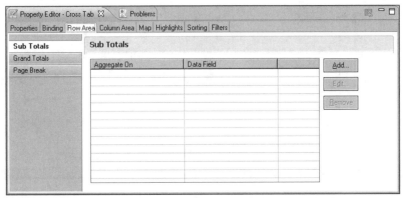

Figure 20-52   Adding a subtotal to a cross tab's row area

3   To create a subtotal, select Sub Totals, then choose Add. To create a grand total, select Grand Totals, then choose Add.

A cross tab can always include grand totals. If a row or column area consists of only one dimension, however, there can be no subtotals. The Add button is disabled if you cannot create a subtotal.

4   In Sub Total or Grand Total, specify the following information:

1   In Aggregate On, select the dimension or dimension level for which to display the total.

2   In Data Field, select the summary field for which to aggregate values.

Figure 20-53 shows an example of displaying subtotals for the year dimension.

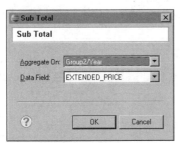

Figure 20-53   Specifying a subtotal in a cross tab

3   Choose OK.

A new row or column, which contains a label and a data element, is added to the cross tab. For the subtotal example shown in Figure 20-53, a label in the new row displays [year_TOTAL], and a data element displays Σ [EXTENDED_PRICE], as shown in Figure 20-54.

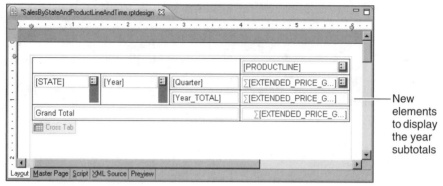

New elements to display the year subtotals

Figure 20-54   Elements that display year subtotals in a cross tab

Displaying totals before the detail data

In the report shown in Figure 20-51, the cross tab displays subtotals and grand totals after the detail data. If you prefer, you can display totals before the detail data. The cross tab in Figure 20-55 shows the same data as the cross tab in Figure 20-51, except that the grand totals appear in the first column and in the first row, and the year subtotals appear before the quarter values.

			Grand Total	Classic Cars	Motorcycles	Planes	Ships	Trains	Trucks and Buses	Vintage Cars
CA	2003	2003 TOTAL	$500,039	$140,221	$132,640	$42,609	$18,728	$7,027	$32,430	$126,383
		1	$27,582						$8,881	$18,701
		3	$230,669	$78,644	$51,731	$10,301	$16,594	$7,027	$23,549	$42,823
		4	$241,788	$61,577	$80,909	$32,308	$2,134			$64,859
	2004	2004 TOTAL	$469,870	$137,635	$5,120	$59,460	$26,411	$7,132	$94,674	$139,437
		1	$193,442	$64,783		$23,797	$23,060		$36,391	$45,411
		2	$59,551		$5,120	$33,229				$21,203
		3	$85,411	$44,355			$3,352	$7,132	$25,285	$5,286
		4	$131,465	$28,497		$2,434			$32,998	$67,537
	2005	2005 TOTAL	$319,105	$142,189	$24,951	$6,563	$21,620	$3,805	$40,793	$79,185
		1	$287,350	$133,572	$24,951		$15,586	$3,805	$40,793	$68,643
		2	$31,755	$8,617		$6,563	$6,034			$10,542
CT	2003	2003 TOTAL	$86,682	$50,875	$2,834	$13,814	$5,937	$5,473		$7,750
		2	$17,032			$13,814	$1,693			$1,525
		3	$6,631	$3,797	$2,834					
		4	$63,018	$47,077			$4,244	$5,473		$6,224
	2004	2004 TOTAL	$100,588	$14,372	$36,866	$27,328			$15,671	$6,351
		2	$32,239	$14,372					$15,671	$2,196
		3	$42,045		$32,868	$9,177				
		4	$26,304		$3,997	$18,152				$4,155

Figure 20-55   Cross tab displaying subtotals and grand totals before the measure values

How to display totals before the detail data

1 Click the button next to any data element that displays dimension values, as shown in Figure 20-56.

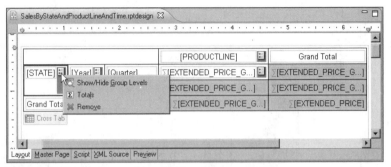

Figure 20-56 Accessing the Totals command

2 Choose Totals. Totals shows the subtotals and grand totals that the cross tab displays in the row area and the column area.

3 For each subtotal or grand total row or column that you want to display before the detail data, under Position, click After, then select Before, as shown in Figure 20-57.

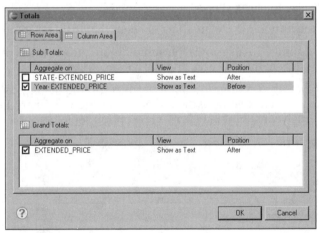

Figure 20-57 Totals displaying the cross tab's subtotals and grand totals

4 Choose OK.

Displaying totals as charts

If a cross tab consists of many rows and columns, users might find it difficult to read and compare totals. Displaying totals as charts can improve the readability of the data. Figure 20-58 shows a cross tab where the year totals appear as a chart. You can easily compare the sales totals of each product line for a given year.

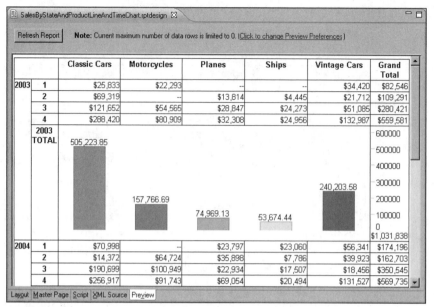

		Classic Cars	Motorcycles	Planes	Ships	Vintage Cars	Grand Total
2003	1	$25,833	$22,293	--	--	$34,420	$82,546
	2	$69,319	--	$13,814	$4,445	$21,712	$109,291
	3	$121,652	$54,565	$28,847	$24,273	$51,085	$280,421
	4	$288,420	$80,909	$32,308	$24,956	$132,987	$559,581
2003 TOTAL		505,223.85	157,766.69	74,969.13	53,674.44	240,203.58	$1,031,838
2004	1	$70,998	--	$23,797	$23,060	$56,341	$174,196
	2	$14,372	$64,724	$35,898	$7,786	$39,923	$162,703
	3	$190,699	$100,949	$22,934	$17,507	$18,456	$350,545
	4	$256,917	$91,743	$69,054	$20,494	$131,527	$569,735

Figure 20-58   Cross tab displaying year totals as a chart

How to display totals as charts

1 Click the button next to any data element that displays dimension values.

2 Choose Totals. Totals shows the subtotals and grand totals that the cross tab displays in the row area and the column area.

3 Select the subtotal or grand total that you want to display as a chart. Under View, click Show as Text, then select Show as Chart. Figure 20-59 shows the year subtotal with its View option set to Show as Chart.

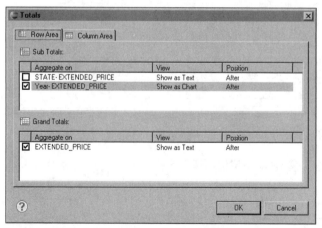

Figure 20-59   Year subtotal View option set to Show as Chart

4 Choose OK.

Displaying empty rows and columns

A cross tab displays one column or one row for each unique value in a field used as a dimension, if there is measure data to display. The cross tab in Figure 20-60 displays sales totals by product line, state, year, and quarter. Notice that these rows are missing: CA 2003 Q2, CA 2005 Q3, and CA 2005 Q4. The cross tab skips these rows because there is no sales data for those quarters.

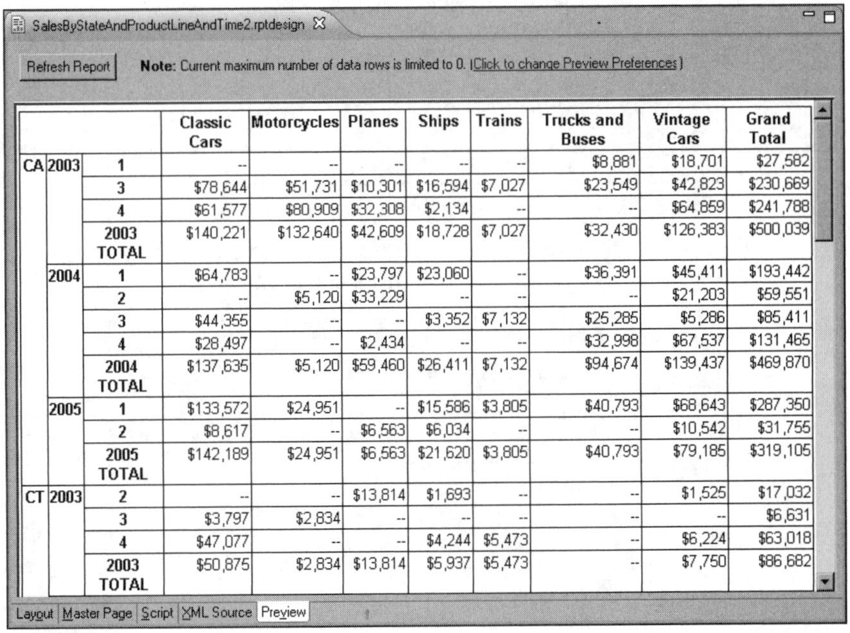

			Classic Cars	Motorcycles	Planes	Ships	Trains	Trucks and Buses	Vintage Cars	Grand Total
CA	2003	1	--	--	--	--	--	$8,881	$18,701	$27,582
		3	$78,644	$51,731	$10,301	$16,594	$7,027	$23,549	$42,823	$230,669
		4	$61,577	$80,909	$32,308	$2,134	--	--	$64,859	$241,788
		2003 TOTAL	$140,221	$132,640	$42,609	$18,728	$7,027	$32,430	$126,383	$500,039
	2004	1	$64,783	--	$23,797	$23,060	--	$36,391	$45,411	$193,442
		2	--	$5,120	$33,229	--	--	--	$21,203	$59,551
		3	$44,355	--	--	$3,352	$7,132	$25,285	$5,286	$85,411
		4	$28,497	--	$2,434	--	--	$32,998	$67,537	$131,465
		2004 TOTAL	$137,635	$5,120	$59,460	$26,411	$7,132	$94,674	$139,437	$469,870
	2005	1	$133,572	$24,951	--	$15,586	$3,805	$40,793	$68,643	$287,350
		2	$8,617	--	$6,563	$6,034	--	--	$10,542	$31,755
		2005 TOTAL	$142,189	$24,951	$6,563	$21,620	$3,805	$40,793	$79,185	$319,105
CT	2003	2	--	--	$13,814	$1,693	--	--	$1,525	$17,032
		3	$3,797	$2,834	--	--	--	--	--	$6,631
		4	$47,077	--	--	$4,244	$5,473	--	$6,224	$63,018
		2003 TOTAL	$50,875	$2,834	$13,814	$5,937	$5,473	--	$7,750	$86,682

Figure 20-60   Cross tab with missing rows for quarters in which no sales data exists

You can add those missing rows, as the cross tab in Figure 20-62 shows. Similarly, you can also add missing columns. Add missing rows and columns to make it clear that there is no data for certain categories. In this example, displaying all the quarters also makes the data appear complete and consistent. Use this feature judiciously. Adding missing rows and columns can result in a cross tab that shows too many empty cells.

How to display empty rows and columns

1 Select the cross tab.

2 In Property Editor, under Properties, choose Empty Rows/Columns.

   The Empty Rows/Columns page shows the dimensions for which empty rows and columns can be added.

3 Select Show empty rows or Show empty columns, or both.

4 In the last field, type the string to display in the empty cells.

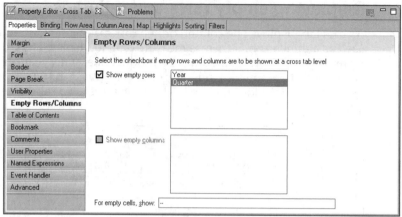

Figure 20-61 Selecting Show empty rows

5 Preview the report. Figure 20-62 shows an example of empty rows added for quarters that do not contain sales data.

			Classic Cars	Motorcycles	Planes	Ships	Trains	Trucks and Buses	Vintage Cars	Grand Total
CA	2003	1	--	--	--	--	--	$8,881	$18,701	$27,582
		2	--	--	--	--	--	--	--	--
		3	$78,644	$51,731	$10,301	$16,594	$7,027	$23,549	$42,823	$230,669
		4	$61,577	$80,909	$32,308	$2,134	--	--	$64,859	$241,788
		2003 TOTAL	$140,221	$132,640	$42,609	$18,728	$7,027	$32,430	$126,383	$500,039
	2004	1	$64,783	--	$23,797	$23,060	--	$36,391	$45,411	$193,442
		2	--	$5,120	$33,229	--	--	--	$21,203	$59,551
		3	$44,355	--	--	$3,352	$7,132	$25,285	$5,286	$85,411
		4	$28,497	--	$2,434	--	--	$32,998	$67,537	$131,465
		2004 TOTAL	$137,635	$5,120	$59,460	$26,411	$7,132	$94,674	$139,437	$469,870
	2005	1	$133,572	$24,951	--	$15,586	$3,805	$40,793	$68,643	$287,350
		2	$8,617	--	$6,563	$6,034	--	--	$10,542	$31,755
		3	--	--	--	--	--	--	--	--
		4	--	--	--	--	--	--	--	--
		2005 TOTAL	$142,189	$24,951	$6,563	$21,620	$3,805	$40,793	$79,185	$319,105

Layout | Master Page | Script | XML Source | Preview

Figure 20-62 Cross tab displaying rows for quarters in which no sales data exists

Displaying user-defined values in row and column headings

By default, the row and column headings in a cross tab display dimension values exactly as they appear in the data set fields. These values can sometimes be cryptic or ambiguous. You can replace such values with more descriptive terms.

Sometimes, certain values appear infrequently in a set of rows. Consider the example in which certain products sell very poorly. In a cross tab that displays sales data by product and month, rather than display a row for every product and show many empty cells, you can group all the unpopular products into one user-defined value named Others.

Compare the reports in Figure 20-63, Figure 20-64, and Figure 20-65. The report in Figure 20-63 shows sales by state and product line. The state values display exactly as they appear in the state field.

	Classic Cars	Motorcycles	Planes	Ships	Trains	Vintage Cars	Grand Total
CA	$458,563.64	$162,710.57	$108,632.26	$66,758.95	$17,965.32	$366,355.37	$1,180,986.11
CT	$89,671.28	$39,699.67	$41,142.34	$5,936.68	$9,548.53	$14,101.07	$200,099.57
MA	$223,366.59	$91,024.09	$51,924.57	$71,419.40	$9,695.99	$99,107.58	$546,538.22
NH	$69,150.35	--	--	--	--	$39,376.65	$108,527.00
NJ	--	$35,116.44	$33,308.49	$4,346.26	--	$9,035.36	$81,806.55
NV	$58,718.89	--	--	--	--	$21,462.09	$80,180.98
NY	$260,619.73	$99,514.87	$24,647.66	$36,219.65	$15,033.47	$62,342.28	$498,377.66
PA	$102,856.24	$39,025.09	$15,889.79	$4,983.38	$4,862.02	$34,925.01	$202,541.53
Grand Total	$1,262,946.72	$467,090.73	$275,545.11	$189,664.32	$57,105.33	$646,705.41	$2,899,057.62

Figure 20-63   Cross tab displays sales totals by state and product line

The report in Figure 20-64 shows the same data, except that the abbreviated state names are replaced with full state names.

	Classic Cars	Motorcycles	Planes	Ships	Trains	Vintage Cars	Grand Total
California	$458,563.64	$162,710.57	$108,632.26	$66,758.95	$17,965.32	$366,355.37	$1,180,986.11
Connecticut	$89,671.28	$39,699.67	$41,142.34	$5,936.68	$9,548.53	$14,101.07	$200,099.57
Massachusetts	$223,366.59	$91,024.09	$51,924.57	$71,419.40	$12,184.49	$105,384.18	$555,303.32
Nevada	$58,718.89	--	--	--	--	$21,462.09	$80,180.98
New Hampshire	$69,150.35	--	--	--	--	$39,376.65	$108,527.00
New Jersey	--	$35,116.44	$33,308.49	$4,346.26	--	$9,035.36	$81,806.55
New York	$260,619.73	$99,514.87	$24,647.66	$36,219.65	$15,033.47	$62,342.28	$498,377.66
Pennsylvania	$102,856.24	$39,025.09	$15,889.79	$4,983.38	$4,862.02	$34,925.01	$202,541.53
Grand Total	$1,262,946.72	$467,090.73	$275,545.11	$189,664.32	$59,593.83	$652,982.01	$2,907,822.72

Figure 20-64   Cross tab displays full state names

The report in Figure 20-65 shows sales data by regions instead of by state. The region values are not stored in a field. Rather, the region values are created using expressions that group states into user-defined regions. Grouping the data provides a different view of the data, and in this example, eliminates empty values from the cross tab. BIRT calculates the new sales totals according to the user-defined groups.

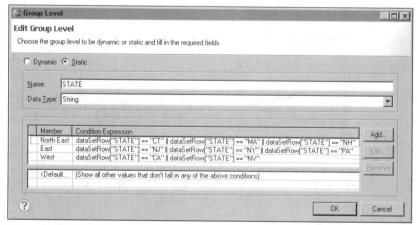

SalesByRegionAndProductLine.rptdesign ⊠

Refresh Report | **Note:** Current maximum number of data rows is limited to 0. (Click to change Preview Preferences)

	Classic Cars	Motorcycles	Planes	Ships	Trains	Vintage Cars	Grand Total
East	$363,476	$173,656	$73,846	$45,549	$19,895	$106,303	$782,726
North East	$382,188	$130,724	$93,067	$77,356	$21,733	$158,862	$863,930
West	$517,283	$162,711	$108,632	$66,759	$17,965	$387,817	$1,261,167
Grand Total	$1,262,947	$467,091	$275,545	$189,664	$59,594	$652,982	$2,907,823

Layout | Master Page | Script | XML Source | Preview

Figure 20-65 Cross tab displays sales totals grouped into regions

How to specify user-defined values for row and column headings

1 In Data Explorer, expand Data Cubes, and double-click the cube.

2 In the Cross Tab Cube Builder, choose Groups and Summaries.

3 Select the dimension to edit, then choose Edit.

4 In Group Level, select Static. This option indicates that this dimension displays static values that you define.

5 Create a member-expression entry for each value to display.

  ▪ In Member, type the value to display in the cross tab.

  ▪ In Condition Expression, type the expression that indicates the value to replace.

Figure 20-66 shows examples of member-expression entries to display the following values:

  ▪ North East in place of CT, MA, and NH

  ▪ East in place of NJ, NY, and PA

  ▪ West in place of CA and NV

Figure 20-66 Group Level showing user-defined dimension values

Choose OK to save the changes.

6 Choose OK to close the cross tab builder.

Sorting cross tab data

By default, a cross tab displays data sorted by dimension values. In other words, values displayed in the row and column headings are sorted in ascending order. If you wish, you can sort the dimension values in descending order.

A more common reporting requirement is to sort data by totals. Compare the cross tabs in Figure 20-67 and Figure 20-68. The cross tab in Figure 20-67 displays row and column heading values in the default ascending order. In the rows, the values are East–West. In the columns, the values are Classic Cars–Vintage Cars.

	Classic Cars	Motorcycles	Planes	Ships	Trains	Vintage Cars	Grand Total
East	$363,475.97	$173,656.40	$73,845.94	$45,549.29	$19,895.49	$106,302.65	$782,725.74
North East	$382,188.22	$130,723.76	$93,066.91	$77,356.08	$21,733.02	$158,861.90	$863,929.89
West	$517,282.53	$162,710.57	$108,632.26	$66,758.95	$17,965.32	$387,817.46	$1,261,167.09
Grand Total	$1,262,946.72	$467,090.73	$275,545.11	$189,664.32	$59,593.83	$652,982.01	$2,907,822.72

Figure 20-67   Data sorted by default

The cross tab in Figure 20-68 displays data sorted by product grand totals, in ascending order. The product line names in the column heading are not in alphabetical order. The product grand totals in both cross tabs are highlighted for easier comparison.

	Trains	Ships	Planes	Motorcycles	Vintage Cars	Classic Cars	Grand Total
East	$19,895.49	$45,549.29	$73,845.94	$173,656.40	$106,302.65	$363,475.97	$782,725.74
North East	$21,733.02	$77,356.08	$93,066.91	$130,723.76	$158,861.90	$382,188.22	$863,929.89
West	$17,965.32	$66,758.95	$108,632.26	$162,710.57	$387,817.46	$517,282.53	$1,261,167.09
Grand Total	$59,593.83	$189,664.32	$275,545.11	$467,090.73	$652,982.01	$1,262,946.72	$2,907,822.72

Figure 20-68   Data sorted by product line grand totals in ascending order

How to sort cross tab data

1 Select the cross tab.

2 In Property Editor, choose the Sorting tab.

3 In the Sorting page, choose Add.

By default, New Sort Key displays sort information for the first dimension in the column area, as shown in Figure 20-69. The default Key value, data["PRODUCTLINE"], indicates that the values in the PRODUCTLINE dimension are sorted by product line name in ascending order.

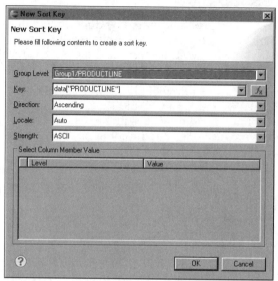

Figure 20-69   New Sort Key showing default sort values for the PRODUCTLINE dimension

4 In New Sort Key, supply the necessary sort information, as follows:

1 In Group Level, select the dimension on which to sort.

2 In Key, select the data on which to sort.

3 In Direction, select Ascending or Descending.

4 In Locale, select a language. The language determines the sorting, or collation, attributes that conform to local conventions. Select Auto to sort data according to the locale set on the user's machine.

5 In Strength, select a collation strength, also known as a collation level. The collation strength determines whether accent marks, case, or punctuation are considered when sorting strings.

For more information about locale-specific sorting and collation strength, see Chapter 11, "Sorting and Grouping Data."

6 Choose OK to save the sort definition.

Figure 20-70 shows an example of sorting on product line grand totals. This sort definition was created to generate the cross tab shown in Figure 20-68.

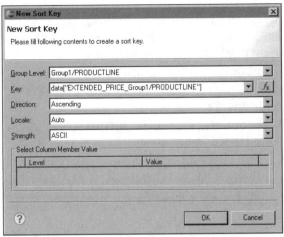

Figure 20-70 New Sort Key specifying sorting on product line grand totals

Limiting the amount of data the cross tab displays

When generating a report that contains a cross tab, BIRT creates one column or one row in the cross tab for each unique value in the dimensions that you insert in the cross tab. If a cross tab displays sales totals by products in the column area and months of a particular year in the row area, and there are 100 products in the data set, the cross tab consists of at least 100 columns, 12 rows and 1200 cells, not counting a row and column for the grand totals. This cross tab is obviously too wide to view on-screen or print. You can reverse the dimensions so that the product values appear as rows, and the month values as columns, but then the cross tab is much taller.

Although there is no limit to the amount of data that a cross tab can display, limiting the amount improves the usability of the data. After all, the main advantage of presenting data in a cross tab is the ability to compare and analyze information, preferably on a single page or screen.

As with any other type of report, you narrow the scope of data to include in a cross tab by creating filter conditions. If the data originates from a database, it is best, for performance reasons, to specify the filter condition in the SQL query. Alternatively, filter at the data set level, the cube level, and finally, at the cross tab level. The filtering option you select depends on whether other report elements or cross tabs are using the same data set or cube.

How to filter data at the cross tab level

1 Select the cross tab.

2 In Property Editor, choose Filters and choose Add.

3 In New Filter Condition, specify the following information:

    1 In Target, choose one of the following options:

❑ Choose Group level to filter data in a specific dimension, then select a group. For example, if the cross tab displays sales totals by product line and by year, you can create a filter to display data for certain product lines or for certain years.

❑ Choose Measure to filter measure data, then select a measure. For example, you can create a filter to display sales totals greater than a specific number.

❑ Choose Detail to filter on a field that is not used in the cross tab, but that is defined in the cube.

In Filter Condition, the first field displays the expression of the selected group or measure. You can change this value.

2 Complete the filter condition by specifying the following information:

1 In the first field, select a dimension or a measure, or a group total for which to evaluate values. Alternatively, choose the expression builder button to create an expression.

2 In the second field, select the operator that specifies the type of filter test.

3 In the third field, specify the value to search in the dimension or measure specified in the first field. You can type a value, or choose <Select value...> to display a list of values. You can also specify an expression that evaluates to a value.

Figure 20-71 shows an example of a complete filter condition. The filter limits the data to only the years where the annual sales exceed 2000000. The annual sales is calculated by the data field, EXTENDED_PRICE_Group1/year.

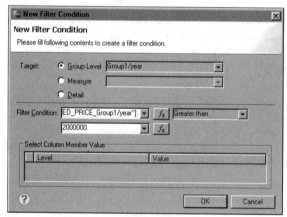

Figure 20-71   New Filter Condition showing an example of a complete filter condition

3 Choose OK to save the filter.

Presenting Different Views of the Same Data

A report can often be more effective when it highlights and reinforces key information. A common design technique is to present key data in both graphical and textual formats. Compare the reports in Figure 21-1.

Total Sales: $149,833.76

California $51,172.72   **34.15%**

Product Code	Total Units	Amount	% of Total Amount
S10_1678	**152**	**$12,652.59**	**24.73%**
Order 10145	45	$3,445.20	27.23%
Order 10159	49	$3,986.15	31.50%
Order 10168	36	$3,410.64	26.96%
Order 10201	22	$1,810.60	14.31%
S10_2016	**125**	**$13,044.24**	**25.49%**
Order 10145	37	$3,872.79	29.69%
Order 10159	37	$3,740.70	28.68%
Order 10168	27	$2,633.31	20.19%
Order 10201	24	$2,797.44	21.45%
S10_4698	**146**	**$25,475.89**	**49.78%**
Order 10145	33	$5,112.69	20.07%
Order 10159	22	$3,749.24	14.72%
Order 10168	20	$3,214.80	12.62%
Order 10201	49	$9,394.28	36.88%
Order 10362	22	$4,004.88	15.72%
Total:		$51,172.72	

Massachusetts $25,758.16   **17.19%**

Product Code	Total Units	Amount	% of Total Amount
S10_1678	**78**	**$6,821.58**	**26.48%**
Order 10285	36	$3,445.20	50.50%
Order 10388	42	$3,376.38	49.50%
S10_2016	**97**	**$11,145.67**	**43.27%**
Order 10285	47	$5,198.67	46.64%
Order 10388	50	$5,947.00	53.36%

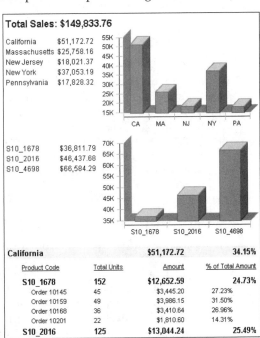

Total Sales: $149,833.76

California	$51,172.72
Massachusetts	$25,758.16
New Jersey	$18,021.37
New York	$37,053.19
Pennsylvania	$17,828.32

S10_1678	$36,811.79
S10_2016	$46,437.68
S10_4698	$66,584.29

California $51,172.72   **34.15%**

Product Code	Total Units	Amount	% of Total Amount
S10_1678	**152**	**$12,652.59**	**24.73%**
Order 10145	45	$3,445.20	27.23%
Order 10159	49	$3,986.15	31.50%
Order 10168	36	$3,410.64	26.96%
Order 10201	22	$1,810.60	14.31%
S10_2016	**125**	**$13,044.24**	**25.49%**

Figure 21-1   Comparison of reports displaying summary data in different formats

The report on the left shows the first page of a report that displays detailed sales data. Totals and percentages for each state are displayed prominently in each state group header, but it is difficult to compare the aggregate data among the states because the data appears on multiple pages.

The report on the right shows the same detailed sales data, and adds summary tables and charts to highlight the aggregate data. The summary tables and charts provide summary versions of the same sales data. Notice that each summary table and chart next to it show identical data. As this report illustrates, presenting different views of the same data draws attention to key information and also makes the report more compelling visually.

This chapter discusses the different ways for report elements to share and display the same data, and provides tips and examples for building a dashboard report, a type of report that exemplifies data sharing among report elements.

Ways to share data

As you learned in previous chapters, a data set can provide data for multiple report elements of different types, and a cube can provide data for cross tabs and charts. This section reviews these two ways of sharing data, describes a third way for report elements to share data, and provides guidelines for using the different data-sharing methods.

Sharing a data set

Report elements can use the same data set if the data set returns the right amount and type of data for each element. For example, two tables can use the same data set if one table displays detailed data, and the other table displays the summary version of the same data. In the second report shown in Figure 21-1, the two summary tables and the sales detail table use data from the same data set. Each report element that uses data from a single data set can sort, group, filter, or aggregate its data differently. For example, one table can sort sales data by country, and another table can sort the same data by sales total.

Sharing a cube

A cross tab must use data from a cube. A chart can use data from a data set or from a cube. If you create a cube for a cross tab and you want to display the same data in a chart, set up the chart to use the cube. Cube data is appropriate for a chart because a cube organizes data into dimensions (groups) and measures (aggregate data), which map well to a chart's category series and value series. A cross tab and a chart that use data from the same cube can sort and filter their data differently.

Sharing data defined in another report element

This method is ideal for displaying the same data in multiple report elements, and for using the same sorting, groups, filters, and aggregations in every element. One report element is the primary element that determines how data is processed, and other elements use the data in the primary element. Typically, the primary element is a table or a cross tab, and charts use the data in those elements.

Another common example is a series of charts showing the same data. For example, to display identical data in a bar chart, a pie chart, and a line chart, one chart can be the primary element, and the other charts share the primary chart's data. Data sharing among report elements is useful for building dashboard reports, described later in this chapter.

Guidelines for selecting a data-sharing method

Use the guidelines in Table 21-1 to decide whether to share data set data or report element data when creating multiple report elements to display the same data. Because a cube is limited to cross tabs and charts only, Table 21-1 does not include the cube-sharing method in the comparison.

Table 21-1   Guidelines for selecting a data-sharing method

When to share data set data	When to share report element data
The data set returns the necessary data for the different report elements.	The data set does not return data that can be summarized in a chart. With XML or text data, for example, you do not have the capabilities of a SQL query to group or aggregate data. In these cases, use a table to group and aggregate the data, then set up the chart to use the table data.
To sort, group, filter, or aggregate data differently in each report element, so that each element shows a different perspective of the data.	To sort, group, filter, or aggregate data identically in each report element to reinforce key data.

Building a dashboard report

A dashboard report provides a concise view of key metrics. Those metrics might include costs, sales, customer satisfaction, or other measures critical for monitoring goals and trends. A dashboard report has the look and functionality of a dashboard in a car or plane, displaying data as a set of graphic representations.

Figure 21-2 shows an example of a dashboard report.

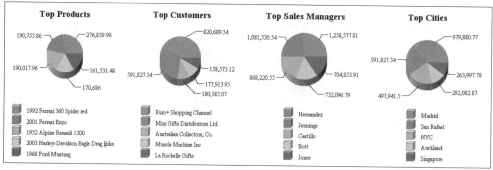

Figure 21-2   Example of a dashboard report

An effective dashboard report distills extensive detail data onto a single page, and highlights trends or potential problems. A typical dashboard report presents a series of charts to display data from different perspectives, for example, sales data by product, by customer, by sales manager, and by region, as shown in Figure 21-2.

A chart relies on data derived from typically hundreds, even hundreds of thousands, of data rows. If the data is stored in a database, you can write a query that groups, aggregates, and filters the data to return a small subset of the rows that can be used as summary data for a chart. If a dashboard report displays multiple charts, creating multiple data sets, each running a different query, can be resource-intensive.

To build a dashboard report, it is sometimes more efficient to create charts that reference, or reuse, data in another report element, typically a table or a cross tab. A data set you create for a table or a cross tab frequently returns a large number of data rows, which the table or cross tab then groups and aggregates to display the data in an organized, readable format. By using table or cross tab data, it is possible to create a single data set that multiple charts access through the table or cross tab.

A key point to remember when creating a chart that uses data from another report element is that the sorting, groups, aggregations, and filters defined in the report element also apply to the chart. You cannot sort, group, aggregate, or filter data differently in the chart. Rather than being a limitation, this behavior helps synchronize the data in various report elements.

For example, the report in Figure 21-3 shows a series of charts that use data from a cross tab. The cross tab defines a filter that enables the report user to specify at run time the quarters for which to get sales data. Each time the report runs with a different value, the cross tab and all the charts display sales data for the selected quarters. This report illustrates the primary advantage of using another report element's data—dynamic and consistent data updates.

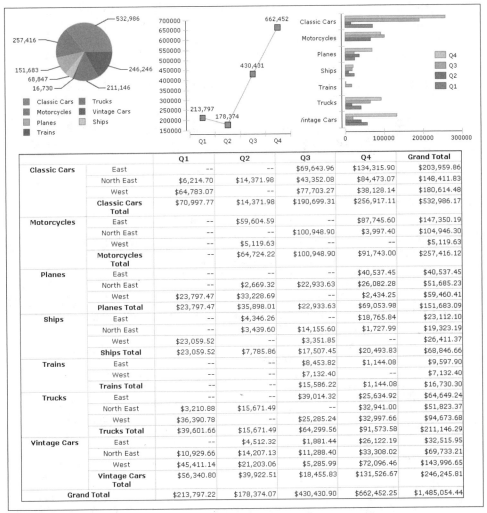

		Q1	Q2	Q3	Q4	Grand Total
Classic Cars	East	--	--	$69,643.96	$134,315.90	$203,959.86
	North East	$6,214.70	$14,371.98	$43,352.08	$84,473.07	$148,411.83
	West	$64,783.07	--	$77,703.27	$38,128.14	$180,614.48
	Classic Cars Total	$70,997.77	$14,371.98	$190,699.31	$256,917.11	$532,986.17
Motorcycles	East	--	$59,604.59	--	$87,745.60	$147,350.19
	North East	--	--	$100,948.90	$3,997.40	$104,946.30
	West	--	$5,119.63	--	--	$5,119.63
	Motorcycles Total	--	$64,724.22	$100,948.90	$91,743.00	$257,416.12
Planes	East	--	--	--	$40,537.45	$40,537.45
	North East	--	$2,669.32	$22,933.63	$26,082.28	$51,685.23
	West	$23,797.47	$33,228.69	--	$2,434.25	$59,460.41
	Planes Total	$23,797.47	$35,898.01	$22,933.63	$69,053.98	$151,683.09
Ships	East	--	$4,346.26	--	$18,765.84	$23,112.10
	North East	--	$3,439.60	$14,155.60	$1,727.99	$19,323.19
	West	$23,059.52	--	$3,351.85	--	$26,411.37
	Ships Total	$23,059.52	$7,785.86	$17,507.45	$20,493.83	$68,846.66
Trains	East	--	--	$8,453.82	$1,144.08	$9,597.90
	West	--	--	$7,132.40	--	$7,132.40
	Trains Total	--	--	$15,586.22	$1,144.08	$16,730.30
Trucks	East	--	--	$39,014.32	$25,634.92	$64,649.24
	North East	$3,210.88	$15,671.49	--	$32,941.00	$51,823.37
	West	$36,390.78	--	$25,285.24	$32,997.66	$94,673.68
	Trucks Total	$39,601.66	$15,671.49	$64,299.56	$91,573.58	$211,146.29
Vintage Cars	East	--	$4,512.32	$1,881.44	$26,122.19	$32,515.95
	North East	$10,929.66	$14,207.13	$11,288.40	$33,308.02	$69,733.21
	West	$45,411.14	$21,203.06	$5,285.99	$72,096.46	$143,996.65
	Vintage Cars Total	$56,340.80	$39,922.51	$18,455.83	$131,526.67	$246,245.81
Grand Total		$213,797.22	$178,374.07	$430,430.90	$662,452.25	$1,485,054.44

Figure 21-3   Report showing three charts displaying the same data as a cross tab

Using data from a table

A table is the most common element for displaying data. A table can display pages of detail data or just summary data. You can group data to show hierarchical views of the data, display aggregate information at any group level, and filter data at the table and group levels. Because you can manipulate data in a table in ways not possible at the data set level, the table is most often used as the source of data for charts, when presenting the same data in a table and a chart.

The report in Figure 21-4 shows four charts and four tables that display summary sales data in various categories. Each chart uses data from the table below it, for example, the Top Products chart displays the top products listed in the Top 5 Products table. When data in any of the tables is updated, the data in the corresponding chart is updated, too. Figure 21-5 shows the same report updated to display the top four performers in each category.

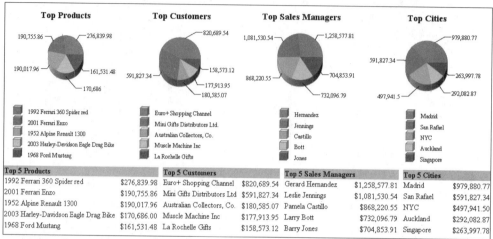

Figure 21-4 Report showing charts displaying the same top 5 data as the corresponding summary tables

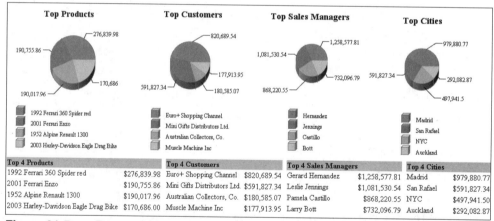

Figure 21-5 Report showing charts displaying the same top 4 data as the corresponding summary tables

The previous report showed how you can base a chart on a table that displays summary data. You can also base a chart on a table that displays detail data. The report in Figure 21-6 shows two charts and two tables. The table on the left displays detailed sales data grouped and aggregated by order number and country, and filtered to display only sales in the top three countries. The Top Countries chart uses data from this table to display the sales totals for the top three countries. The table on the right displays similar sales data, except by sales representative instead of country. The Top Sales Representatives chart uses data from this table to display sales totals for the top three sales representatives.

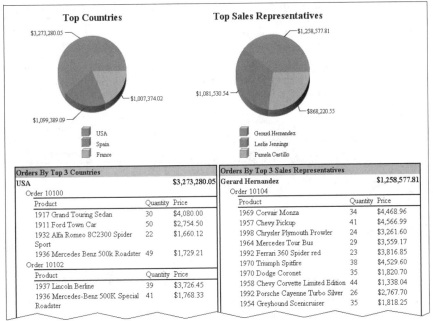

Orders By Top 3 Countries			
USA			$3,273,280.05
Order 10100			
Product		Quantity	Price
1917 Grand Touring Sedan		30	$4,080.00
1911 Ford Town Car		50	$2,754.50
1932 Alfa Romeo 8C2300 Spider Sport		22	$1,660.12
1936 Mercedes Benz 500k Roadster		49	$1,729.21
Order 10102			
Product		Quantity	Price
1937 Lincoln Berline		39	$3,726.45
1936 Mercedes-Benz 500K Special Roadster		41	$1,768.33

Orders By Top 3 Sales Representatives			
Gerard Hernandez			$1,258,577.81
Order 10104			
Product		Quantity	Price
1969 Corvair Monza		34	$4,468.96
1957 Chevy Pickup		41	$4,566.99
1998 Chrysler Plymouth Prowler		24	$3,261.60
1964 Mercedes Tour Bus		29	$3,559.17
1992 Ferrari 360 Spider red		23	$3,816.85
1970 Triumph Spitfire		38	$4,529.60
1970 Dodge Coronet		35	$1,820.70
1958 Chevy Corvette Limited Edition		44	$1,338.04
1992 Porsche Cayenne Turbo Silver		26	$2,767.70
1954 Greyhound Scenicruiser		35	$1,818.25

Figure 21-6   Report showing charts displaying the same data as tables with detail data

How to create a chart that uses data from a table

This procedure assumes you have already created the table that contains the data to share with the chart.

1   Specify a name for the table, using the following steps:

    1   Select the table. In Property Editor, under Properties, choose General.

    2   In Name, type a name for the table. Figure 21-7 shows the name, CustomerOrderTable, specified for a table.

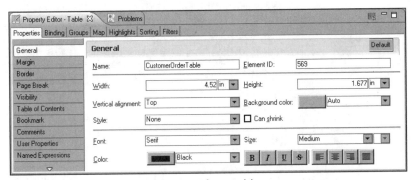

Figure 21-7   Name property set for a table

2 Insert a chart anywhere in the report, but do not place the chart inside the table.

3 In the chart builder, select a chart type suitable for displaying the data, then choose Select Data.

4 Select the data to display in the chart, using the following steps:

1 Under Select Data, select Use Data From, and click the down arrow to display a list of report elements from which data is available, as shown in Figure 21-8.

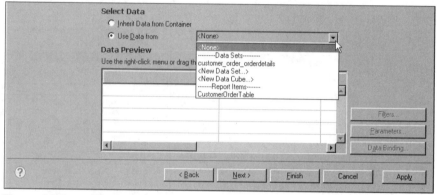

Figure 21-8   Displaying the list of elements from which a chart can use data

The list displays the report items from which you can use data below Report Items. Figure 21-8 shows the table, CustomerOrderTable, under this category.

2 Select the table from which to use data. Data Preview displays the data from the selected table, as shown in Figure 21-9. In addition to the data fields used in the table, Data Preview also displays the groups and aggregate data defined in the table. Groups and aggregate data are identified by special symbols next to the column binding names.

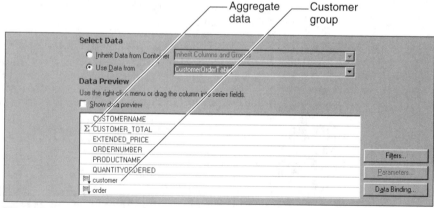

Figure 21-9   Data Preview displaying data from a selected table

3   Select a group from Data Preview to use as the chart's category series. You select data that is already grouped because you cannot group in a chart when using data from another report element.

4   Select aggregate data to use as the chart's value series. Figure 21-10 shows an example of data selected for a pie chart. The customer group is selected for the category series. The CUSTOMER_TOTAL aggregation is selected for the value series, or, in the case of a pie chart, the slice size definition.

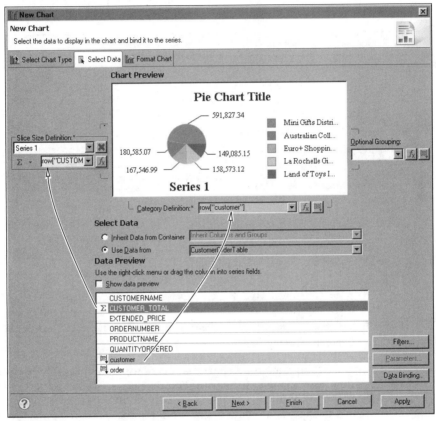

Figure 21-10   Data selected for a chart

5   Choose Finish to close the chart builder.

5   Preview the report to verify that the chart displays the correct data.

Using data from a cross tab

A cross tab is the ideal element for displaying aggregate data, or measures, by multiple categories. Many types of charts are also suitable for displaying aggregate data by different categories, although not by as many categories as a cross tab. To show aggregate data by x and by y, use a chart to present the data graphically and a cross tab to present the data in a compact row-and-column matrix.

To present the same data in both elements, it makes sense for a chart to leverage the data in the cross tab. After you define the initial measures in the cube and insert them in a cross tab, the cross tab calculates all the subtotals and grand totals and creates all the necessary column bindings. The report in Figure 21-3 shows three charts—order totals by product line, totals by quarter, and totals by product line and by quarter—based on a single cross tab. Figure 21-11 shows the column bindings that BIRT creates for each measure and dimension in that cross tab.

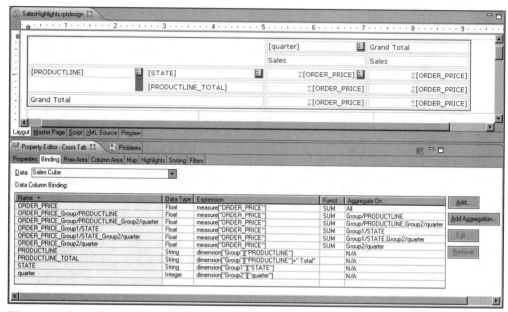

Figure 21-11   Column bindings defined for a cross tab

When specifying data for a chart that uses cross tab data, all you do is select a measure to use as the value series. You do not select a dimension for the category series because a measure already defines the category or categories by which the aggregate data is grouped. For example, the measure defined by the column binding ORDER_PRICE_Group/PRODUCTLINE returns the sum of order prices by product line groups. ORDER_PRICE_Group/PRODUCTLINE_Group2/quarter returns the sum of order prices by product line and by quarter.

Based on the measure you select, the chart builder assigns the appropriate dimension to the category series and, if applicable, to the optional Y series grouping as well. Figure 21-12 shows the measure ORDER_PRICE_Group/PRODUCTLINE_Group2/quarter selected for the value series. The chart builder assigns data["PRODUCTLINE"] to the category series and data["quarter"] to the optional y series grouping. As the Chart Preview shows, the chart displays order price totals by product line and by quarter.

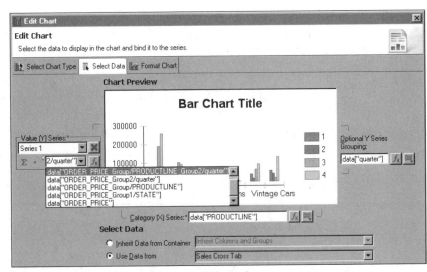

Figure 21-12   Cross tab data used in a chart

How to create a chart that uses data from a cross tab

This procedure assumes you have already created the cross tab that contains the data to use in the chart.

1 Specify a name for the cross tab, using the following steps:

  1 Select the cross tab and in Property Editor, choose the Properties tab.

  2 In General properties, in Name, type a name for the cross tab. Figure 21-13 shows the name, Sales Cross Tab, specified for a selected cross tab.

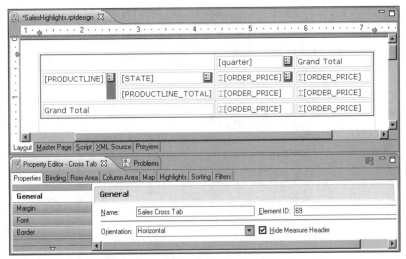

Figure 21-13   Name property set for a selected cross tab

2 Insert a chart in the desired location in the report.

3 In the chart builder, select a chart type suitable for displaying the data, then choose Select Data.

4 Select the data to display in the chart, using the following steps:

　1 Under Select Data, select Use Data From, and click the down arrow to display a list of items from which to get data.

　2 Under Report Items, select the cross tab that contains the data to use.

　3 Select a measure to use as the chart's value series. Under Value (Y) Series, below Series 1, click the down arrow to display the cross tab measures, then select one of the measures. Figure 21-14 shows an example of a list of measures.

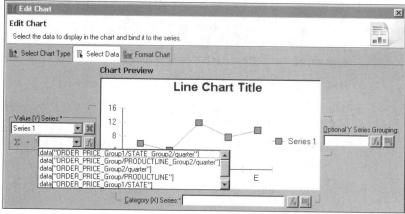

Figure 21-14　List of measures available for a value series

After you select a measure, the chart builder selects the appropriate data for the category series, and if applicable, the data for the optional Y series grouping. For example, if you select a measure that calculates the order totals by quarter, the chart builder selects the quarter data field for the category series, as shown in Figure 21-15.

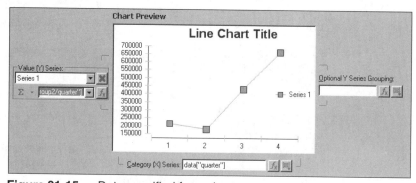

Figure 21-15　Data specified for a chart

4 Choose Finish to save the chart.

5 Preview the report to verify that the chart displays the correct data.

Using data from a chart

To display identical data in a series of charts, create one chart as the primary element, then create the other charts to use data from the first chart. Figure 21-16 shows an example of a bar chart, a pie chart, and a line chart displaying identical data, sales by product line.

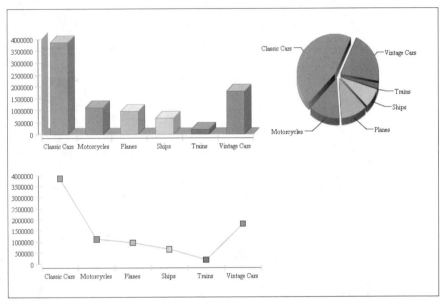

Figure 21-16   Three charts displaying the same data

In the example shown in Figure 21-16, the bar chart is the primary chart. The bar chart defines the data to use in the value and category series, and controls how the data is sorted, grouped, aggregated, and filtered. The other charts reuse this data; you cannot make any modifications to the data in the pie chart or line chart. To change the data that appears in all three charts, edit the bar chart.

Figure 21-17 shows the data definition for the bar chart. This chart uses data from a data set, Sales By Product Line. Value (Y) Series displays data from the TotalSales column, and Category (Y) Series displays data from the PRODUCTLINE column.

Figure 21-18 shows the data definition for the pie chart, which uses data from the bar chart. Notice that the data specified in Slice Size Definition and Category Definition is the same data specified in the bar chart and is read-only.

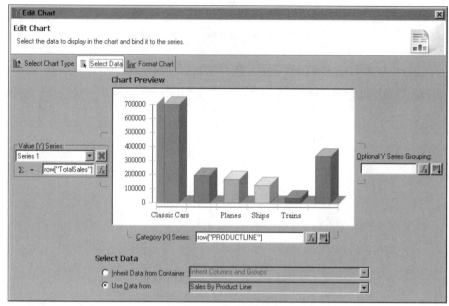

Figure 21-17 Data specified for a primary chart

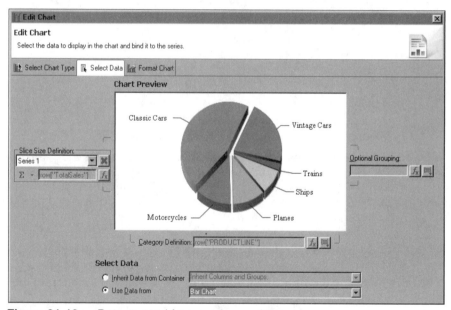

Figure 21-18 Data re-used from a primary chart

How to create a chart that uses data from another chart

This procedure assumes you have already created the primary chart.

1 Specify a name for the primary chart, using the following steps:

1 In the layout editor, select the chart. In Property Editor, choose the Properties tab.

2 In General properties, in Name, type a name for the chart.

2 Insert a second chart in the report.

3 In the chart builder, select a chart type suitable for displaying the same data as the primary chart, then choose Select Data.

4 Select the data to display in the chart, using the following steps:

1 Under Select Data, select Use Data From, and click the down arrow to display a list of items from which to get data.

2 Under Report Items, select the chart from which to use data.

The chart builder fills in the value and category series fields with the data defined in the primary chart.

5 Choose Finish to save the chart.

6 Preview the report to verify that the chart displays the correct data.

Enhancing Reports

22

Designing a Multipage Report

Most reports display and print on multiple pages. When designing a report, consider how a multipage report displays and prints. For example, you can design a report so that page breaks occur at logical places. For a report that contains a series of subreports, you can specify page breaks to start each subreport on a new page.

You can also design a page layout that enhances the report's appearance and usability. A page layout specifies the style of the pages that display report data. For example, you can specify that all pages display the report title in the top left corner, the company logo in the top right corner, a page number in the bottom right corner, and a report-generation date in the bottom left corner. You can also design special effects, such as a watermark that appears in the background. To design a page layout, customize the report's master page.

Planning the page layout

Before designing a page layout, preview the report in the desired output format, and decide what changes, if any, to make to the default page layout. Consider the following design issues:

- Decide for which output format you are designing a page layout. A report design renders differently in the different output formats.

  - For an HTML report, an important decision is whether the report appears on a single scrollable page or on multiple pages in the report viewer. A single page is typical for online viewing, but, if the report is very long, displaying the report on multiple pages in the report viewer might be more suitable. If you choose to display an HTML report on a single page, decide if a master page is necessary. For instance, it does not make sense to display a page number for a one-page report.

- For output formats that support pagination, such as PDF and DOC, decide the page dimensions, including paper size, margin sizes, header size, footer size, and page orientation. The default master page uses US letter size (8.5" x 11"). If developing a report for a locale that typically uses A4 paper, change the page size.

- Decide the design of the master page. The default page layout displays the report-generation date in the bottom left corner of every page. You typically customize the master page to reflect a corporate style or to provide additional information, such as a company logo or a confidentiality statement. You can design a different master page for different output formats by displaying elements for one output and hiding them for another. You can also design and use different master pages in a single report.

Controlling pagination

Pagination is the division of a document into pages of a specified size. It applies to the following output formats supported by BIRT: DOC, PDF, and PPT. In PPT, each report page is a PowerPoint slide. By default, reports in these formats display as much data as can fit on each page, up to 40 detail rows. This specification can result in key sections appearing in the middle or at the bottom of a page. For most paginated reports, a common approach is to start certain sections at the top of a new page or avoid breaking a section across two pages.

By contrast, an XLS report appears on a single Excel worksheet; page breaks that you specify in the report design have no effect. Similarly, an HTML report always displays on a single scrollable page when you preview a report in the layout editor or as HTML. The page breaks that you specify take effect when an HTML report is viewed in the report viewer.

Inserting page breaks

Reports that consist of a series of documents or distinct sections typically look more organized if each document or section appears on a separate page. For example, if a report consists of a cover letter, disclaimer information, and a summary report that is followed by a detailed report, you can insert page breaks to display each type of information on a separate page. Similarly, if a report groups sales data by state, then by customer, you can start the data for each state on a new page.

You can specify page breaks for the following elements:

- Top-level elements. These are elements that are not placed within another element.

- Second-level elements. These are elements that are placed in a top-level list, table, or grid. For example, if table A contains table B, and table B contains table C, you can specify a page break for table A and table B, but not for table C.

- Groups. You can specify page breaks for data groups defined in top-level and second-level tables or lists.

- Grid rows and detail rows in tables.

Specify page breaks using the Page Break Before and Page Break After properties. Table 22-1 describes the values you can select for these properties.

Table 22-1   Values for Page Break Before and After properties

Page Break Before, Page Break After value	Description
Always	Always insert a page break before or after the selected element.
Auto	Insert a page break before or after the element as necessary. Auto is the default value.
Avoid	Avoid inserting a page break before or after the selected element.
Always Excluding First	Applies only to groups and Page Break Before. Always insert a page break before each instance of the selected group, but not before the first instance.
Always Excluding Last	Applies only to groups and Page Break After. Always insert a page break after each instance of the selected group, but not after the last instance.

The rest of this section provides examples of inserting page breaks for various elements. For simplicity, the examples of the generated reports shown in this section are in PDF format. The other output formats that support pagination show similar results.

Inserting page breaks in a report with multiple sections and groups

Figure 22-1 shows a PDF report with default page breaks. In this report, the page break properties are set to Auto. Figure 22-2 shows the same report with page breaks after the Top Products and Top States reports and after each state group in the Sales By State and Product report. Notice in Figure 22-2 that the title, Sales By State and Product, repeats at the top of every page of that report. The Repeat Header option is set by default. To display the report header only once, at the beginning of the report, deselect the Repeat Header option.

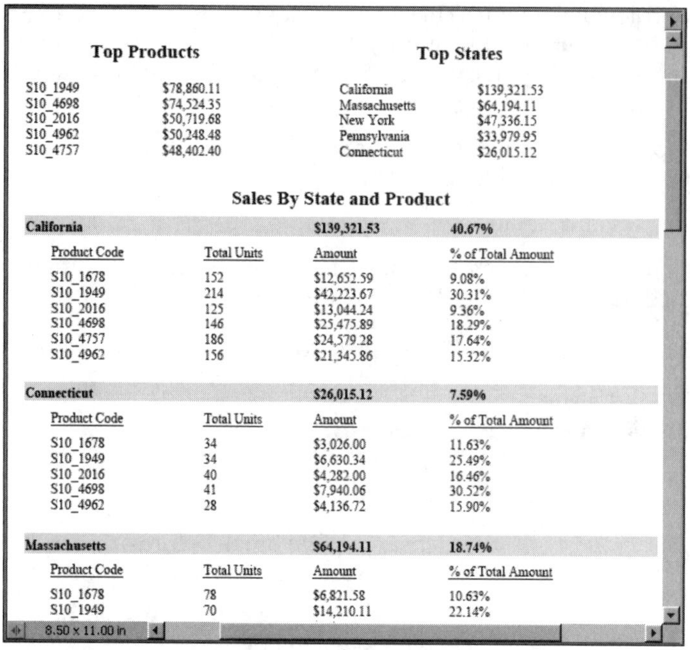

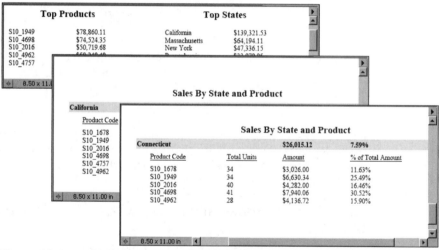

Figure 22-1   PDF report using default pagination

Figure 22-2   PDF report using custom pagination

Figure 22-3 shows the report design and indicates where and how page breaks are set. In this report design, page breaks are set as follows:

- The Page Break After property of the grid at the top of the report is set to Always, which inserts a page break after the grid. Alternatively, selecting the top-level table element that appears after the grid and setting its Page Break Before property to Always achieves the same result.

- The Page Break After property of the state group is set to Always Excluding Last. This setting inserts a page break after each state group, except for the last group. If the Page Break After property is set to Always, the report displays a blank page after the last group. Alternatively, set the state group's Page Break Before property to Always Excluding First. This setting inserts a page break before each state group, except for the first group, and prevents a blank page from appearing before the first group.

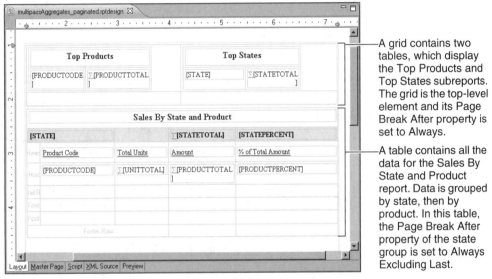

Figure 22-3   Page break property settings in a report design

Figure 22-4 shows a partial view of the group editor where you set the state group's Page Break After property.

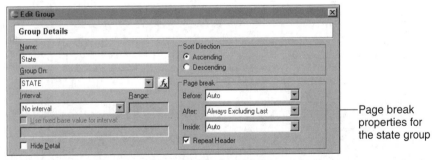

Figure 22-4   Page break properties for a group

Inserting page breaks in a master-detail report

In the next example, a report displays data with a master-detail relationship. An outer, top-level table contains two inner tables. The top-level table displays customer information. For each customer, the inner tables display order information and payment information, respectively. Figure 22-5 shows the PDF report that is paginated so that each customer's information starts on a new page.

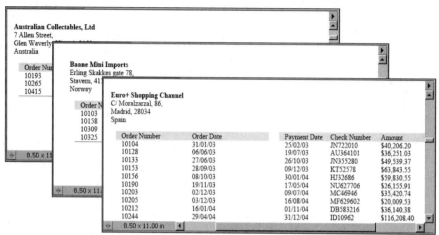

Figure 22-5   PDF output starting each customer's data on a new page

Figure 22-6 shows the report design and indicates where and how the page break is set. The Page Break After property of the second-level table is set to Always.

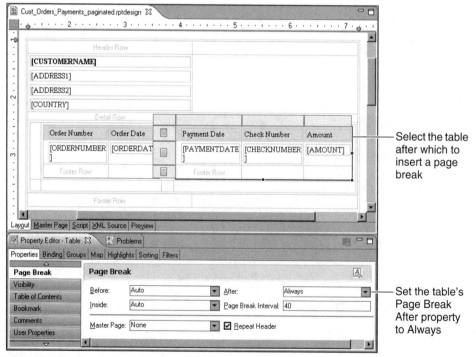

Figure 22-6   Report design that starts each customer's data on a new page

Avoiding page breaks in a section

In addition to specifying where page breaks occur, you can also specify that contents of a particular report section stay on the same page, when possible. Figure 22-7 shows a portion of a PDF report that groups items sold by order number and by customer. The figure shows the detail rows for an order split onto two pages.

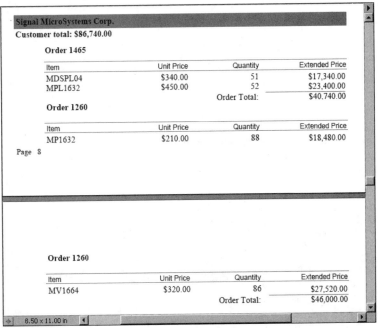

Figure 22-7   Detail rows of an order appear on two pages

You can keep the order details together by setting the Page Break Inside property of the orders group to Avoid, as shown in Figure 22-8.

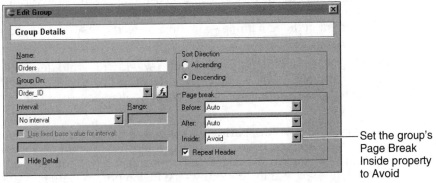

Figure 22-8   Page Break Inside set to Avoid for orders group

Figure 22-9 shows the results of setting the Page Break Inside property of the orders group to Avoid. All the detail rows for the order appear on the same page. To keep the rows together, BIRT starts the order on a new page.

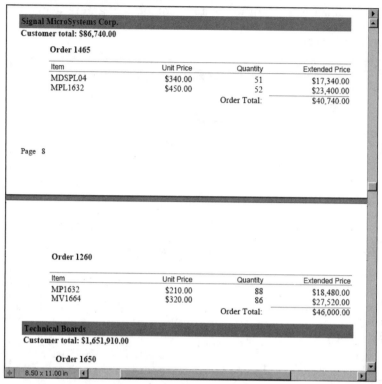

Figure 22-9   Detail rows that were previously split appear on the same page

To keep all the orders for each customer together, set the customer group's Page Break Inside property to Avoid. Figure 22-10 shows the results of setting the Page Break Inside property of the customers group to Avoid. The data for each customer stays together on the same page. If the data for a customer does not fit in the remaining space on a page, the customer record starts on a new page.

Setting an element's Page Break Inside property to Avoid does not guarantee that the contents of the section always appears on the same page. If the contents of a section exceed one page, the content has to appear on more than one page.

Use Page Break Inside sparingly. Computing where data should appear and where to insert page breaks is resource intensive. In addition, if some sections contain a lot of data, the pages of the generated report are likely to display a lot of white space at the bottom, as the PDF report in Figure 22-10 shows.

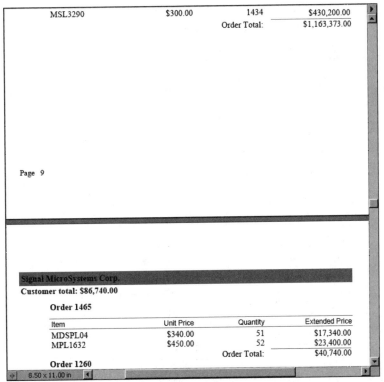

Figure 22-10   Customer data that was previously split appears on the same page

Specifying the number of rows per page

Specifying page breaks before or after selected sections or groups in a report is the typical way to control pagination. Another way is to insert a page break after a specified number of data rows. For example, in a simple listing report that does not contain groups or multiple sections, you could display twenty rows on each page.

While the typical case for specifying the number of rows per page is for a simple listing report, you can also apply this pagination method to a report that groups data.

Figure 22-11 shows two pages of a report that displays ten data rows per page in the report viewer. The report groups products sold by customer and by order number. Notice that only detail rows are counted. Group header and footer rows are not counted. As Figure 22-11 also shows, detail rows in a group can be split onto multiple pages, not a result you typically want.

Orders by Top Ten Customers		

Euro+ Shopping Channel   **$820,689.54**
   Order 10104

Product	Quantity	Price
1962 City of Detroit Streetcar	32	$1,705.92
Diamond T620 Semi-Skirted Tanker	33	$3,781.47
1950's Chicago Surface Lines Streetcar	49	$2,770.95
1954 Greyhound Scenicruiser	35	$1,818.25
1992 Porsche Cayenne Turbo Silver	26	$2,767.70
1958 Chevy Corvette Limited Edition	44	$1,338.04
1970 Dodge Coronet	35	$1,820.70
1970 Triumph Spitfire	38	$4,529.60
1992 Ferrari 360 Spider red	23	$3,816.85
1964 Mercedes Tour Bus	29	$3,559.17

Page: 1

Euro+ Shopping Channel   **$820,689.54**
   Order 10104

Product	Quantity	Price
1998 Chrysler Plymouth Prowler	24	$3,261.60
1957 Chevy Pickup	41	$4,566.99
1969 Corvair Monza	34	$4,468.96

   Order 10128

Product	Quantity	Price
The Mayflower	32	$2,328.00
1904 Buick Runabout	43	$3,321.32
Collectable Wooden Train	41	$3,307.47
1903 Ford Model A	41	$4,928.20

   Order 10133

Product	Quantity	Price
ATA: B757-300	27	$3,107.43
American Airlines: B767-300	24	$1,841.52
1930 Buick Marquette Phaeton	27	$1,001.43

Page: 2

Figure 22-11   Report pages displaying ten data rows per page

To specify the number of data rows per page, select the table element that contains the data and set the table's Page Break Interval property. The Page Break Interval property applies page breaks to all output formats, except HTML and XLS. Figure 22-12 shows the report design that generates the report shown in Figure 22-11. The selected table has its Page Break Interval property set to 10.

The default value for Page Break Interval is 40. For output formats that have a fixed page size, such as PDF and DOC, a page typically fits fewer than 40 data rows, so the default Page Break Interval value does not have any effect. Each page displays as many rows as will fit. Page Break Interval has a noticeable effect only if it is set to a number smaller than the number of rows that can fit on a fixed-size page. In that case, each page displays the specified number of rows followed by blank space.

When displaying the report in the report viewer, however, the Page Break Interval value is significant whether it is set to a low number or a high one. Unlike a report in PDF or DOC format, each page in the report viewer can display hundreds of data rows.

To display an entire report on one page in the report viewer, set Page Break Interval to 0. Note, however, that if the report is very long, a single page takes longer to generate than multiple shorter pages.

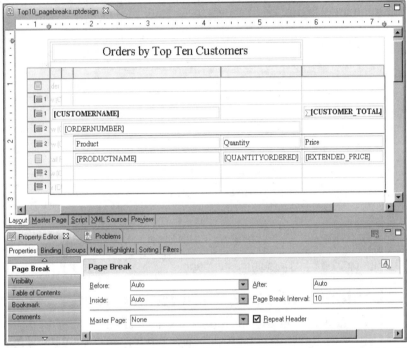

Figure 22-12   Table displaying its Page Break Interval property set to 10

Customizing the master page

The master page determines the dimensions and style of the pages on which report data appears. For example, you can specify that the page size is 7" x 9", the printable area is 6" x 8", the company logo always appears in the top right corner, and the page number appears in the bottom right corner.

The page size and margin settings apply primarily to reports in PDF, DOC, and PPT formats, where size dimensions matter, because these document types are page-oriented. For HTML reports that use the default fixed layout setting, the output appears the same as the PDF report. For HTML reports that use the auto layout setting, the layout of data adjusts to the size of the viewer or browser window.

Viewing the master page

When creating or opening a report design, the layout editor always shows the report layout. To view the master page, use one of the following options:

- Choose Page➜Master Page➜Simple Master Page.
- Choose the Master Page tab at the bottom of the layout editor.

You can view either the report layout or the master page but not both at the same time. Figure 22-13 shows the default master page.

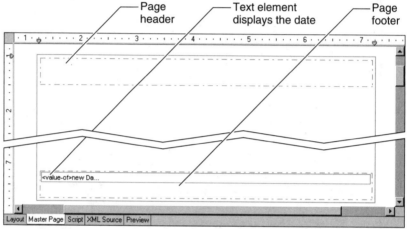

Figure 22-13   Default master page

Designing the page header and footer

The default master page includes a text element that displays the current date in the page footer. When previewing a report, the current date appears on the bottom left of every report page. You can delete or edit this text element. You can add other elements to the master page by dragging them from the palette and dropping them in the page footer or header.

Observe the following rules:

- You can place elements in the header and footer only. You cannot place elements in the report content area because the contents of those elements would overlap report data.
- You can place only one element directly in the header or footer. To place multiple elements, insert a grid, then insert the elements in the grid.

Displaying page numbers, the current date, and other text

Common header and footer information includes the page number, report-generation date, company name, author name, copyright information, and confidentiality statements.

As Figure 22-14 shows, BIRT Report Designer provides predefined text elements for displaying some of these common items, including the current date, page number, author name, and file name. These items are available on the palette when the master page is displayed.

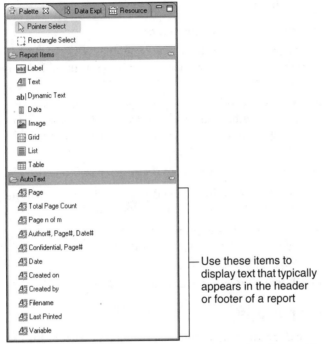

Use these items to display text that typically appears in the header or footer of a report

Figure 22-14   Text elements for common header and footer items

For example, the date element is a text element that contains the following dynamic value:

```
<VALUE-OF>new Date()</VALUE-OF>
```

After inserting a predefined text element in the page header or footer, you can edit the text to display different information. For example, you can edit the date element to display the date in a different format. By default, the report displays the date according to the locale that is set on the machine on which the report is generated. Use the format attribute to display the date in a custom format, as shown in the following expression:

```
<VALUE-OF format="MM-dd-yy">new Date()</VALUE-OF>
```

To display other text in the header or footer, use the other predefined text elements in the palette and edit the text content or insert a regular text or label element and type the text from scratch.

Remember, to display more than one element in the header or footer, you must first insert a grid, then insert the elements in the grid. The predefined Author#, Page#, Date# element creates a grid and three text elements, so it may be convenient to insert this element, then edit the individual text elements.

As with any text element, you can also customize the appearance of the predefined elements. For example, you can display text in a different style or color, or align text in the center or right of the page.

How to display text in the header and footer

1 In the layout editor, choose the Master Page tab. The layout editor displays the master page. The palette displays additional elements under AutoText, specifically for use in the master page.

2 To display a single text element in the header or footer, drag the desired element from the palette, and drop it in the header or footer. For example, to display the page number, insert either the Page element or the Page n of m element.

3 To display multiple text elements in the header or footer:

   1 Insert the grid element in the header. If inserting in the footer, delete the date element from the default footer first.

   2 In Insert Grid, specify the number of columns and rows for the grid. For example, to display two text elements on the same line, specify 2 columns and 1 row.

   3 Insert each text element in a grid cell.

Displaying an image

You can display dynamic and static images in a page header or footer. Insert an image in a master page the same way you insert an image in the report layout. The difference is that you cannot insert an image inside a table in the master page. Therefore, when you insert a dynamic image directly on the master page, the same image—the image in the first data row—appears on every page.

Specifying a header size

The size of the header in the generated report can be different when rendered in PDF and in HTML. For an HTML report, the header dynamically resizes to accommodate its contents, and the header always appears directly above the report content. In an HTML report, the header height property is ignored.

For a PDF report, the header also dynamically resizes to accommodate its contents. Unlike the HTML report, you can specify a fixed size for the header. If you specify a header size of one inch, and insert an image that is half an inch in height, the report displays half an inch of space between the image and the report data. If the header size you specify, however, is not sufficient to display a large image, the report overrides the specified header size and resizes the header to display the image in its entirety.

Increasing the header size is one way to increase the space between the header content and the report content. Because header size applies only to PDF output, however, this technique is not recommended when creating a master page that serves both PDF and HTML output equally well.

The preferred technique to add space between the header content and report content is to increase the padding at the bottom of the text or label element placed in the header. Alternatively, if you use a grid to organize multiple elements, add a row at the bottom of the grid and set the row size. Using either of these techniques, the extra space appears in both PDF and HTML output.

Specifying a footer size

Like the header, the size of the footer in the generated report can be different for PDF and HTML reports. In both types of reports, the footer dynamically resizes to fit its content. If you specify a footer size, the PDF report displays a footer section of the specified size, except when the contents exceed the specified size. The HTML report ignores the specified footer size.

How to specify a header or footer size

1 In the layout editor, choose the Master Page tab. The layout editor displays the master page.

2 In Property Editor, choose General properties. Property Editor displays the master page's general properties, as shown in Figure 22-15.

3 Specify a size for the header height, the footer height, or both.

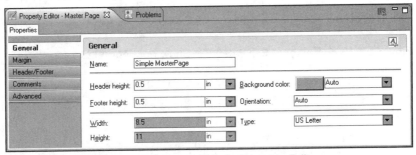

Figure 22-15 Master page properties in Property Editor

Excluding header content from the first page

It is common practice to display header content on every page except the first. For example, a report displays a title in bold and large font on the first page, but in a smaller font at the top of the other pages, as shown in Figure 22-16. To create this design:

■ Insert a text element in the report page to display the title on the first page.

- Insert a text element in the master page header to display the title on subsequent pages. An element in the page header appears, by default, on every page in the report.

- Turn off the Show header on first property. This property controls whether headers appear on all pages, or on all pages except the first.

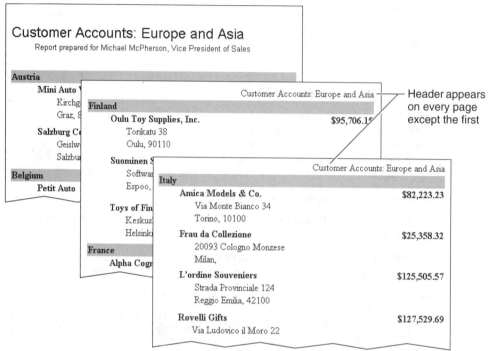

Figure 22-16 Report output when the Show header on first property is turned off

How to exclude header content from the first page

1 In the layout editor, choose Master Page. The layout editor displays the master page.

2 In Property Editor, choose Header/Footer. Property Editor displays the header and footer properties, as shown in Figure 22-17.

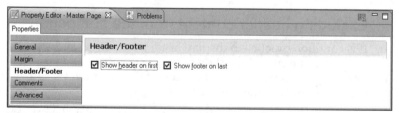

Figure 22-17 Header and footer properties

3 Deselect Show header on first.

4 Choose Preview to verify the report output. If the report contains more than one page, the header content appears on all pages except the first.

Displaying an image in the background

A page can contain an image that appears behind the report data. This effect is called a watermark. For example, a document in draft form can display the word Draft across the page. A government document can display a department seal in the background. Figure 22-18 shows examples of reports that include watermarks.

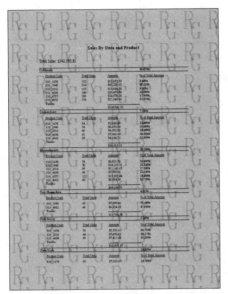 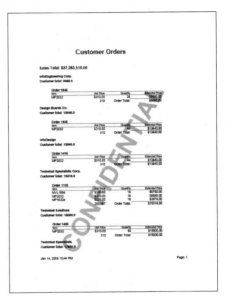

Figure 22-18   Reports including watermarks

When designing a watermark:

- Make sure the image recedes into the background and does not interfere with the readability of the report. For example, use very light-colored images.

- You can use a small image and repeat it so that it fills the entire page. In Figure 22-18, the report on the left shows this effect. Use this technique judiciously. As the example report shows, filling the page with colored images can reduce the readability of the report.

- You can use a large image that fills the page. In Figure 22-18, the report on the right shows this effect.

- Bear in mind that if any report elements in the report layout have background color, this color appears on top of the background image. Figure 22-19 shows this effect. If you want to display a watermark, limit the use of color in the report layout; otherwise the report readability is compromised.

Figure 22-19   Report using colors and a watermark

To use an image as a watermark, select the master page. In Property Editor, select Advanced, expand Simple Master Page, then expand Background, as shown in Figure 22-20. In Background image, choose the ellipses button to select an image file stored in the resource folder. Alternatively, type the URL of the image file, such as:

```
http://mysite.com/images/logo.jpg
```

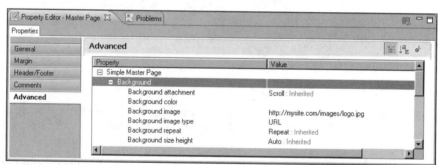

Figure 22-20   Property Editor showing advanced properties for the master page

You can specify a local file-system location, such as c:/images/logo.jpg. You should, however, use a local path for testing purposes only. When you deploy the report on a server, the report cannot find the image on the local machine.

Designing the appearance of the background image

By default, a background image repeats to fill the page. You can change this behavior by setting the value of the Background repeat property as follows:

- Specify No Repeat to display the image once.

- Specify Repeat X to repeat the image across the page horizontally.
- Specify Repeat Y to repeat the image across the page vertically.

Figure 22-21 shows the results of setting the Background repeat property to different values.

Background repeat = No Repeat   Background repeat = Repeat X   Background repeat = Repeat Y

Figure 22-21   Reports using different values for the Background repeat property

Positioning the background image

If you set the Background repeat property to No Repeat, Repeat X, or Repeat Y, you can reposition the image to display it on a different part of the page by using the Horizontal position and Vertical position properties. For Horizontal position, you can select the Center, Left, or Right values. For Vertical position, you can select the Bottom, Center, or Top values.

For both these properties, you can also specify a precise position or a percentage. For example, setting Horizontal position to 3 in displays the image 3 inches from the left of the page. Setting Vertical position to 25% displays the image at the top 25% of the page. Use Dimension Builder, as shown in Figure 22-22, to specify a precise position by inches, millimeters, pixels, and so on.

Figure 22-22   Dimension Builder

Figure 22-23 shows the results of setting the Background repeat, Horizontal position, and Vertical position properties to different values.

Background repeat = Repeat X
Vertical position = Center

Background repeat = Repeat Y
Horizontal position = 75%

Background repeat = No repeat
Horizontal position = Right
Vertical position = Top

Figure 22-23   Reports using different background property values

Displaying different content in different output formats

You can design a master page that differs for different output formats. Simply select the element or elements on the master page to display in a particular output format, then set the element's Visibility property accordingly. Figure 22-24 shows a picture element's Visibility property set to hide the picture in an XLS report.

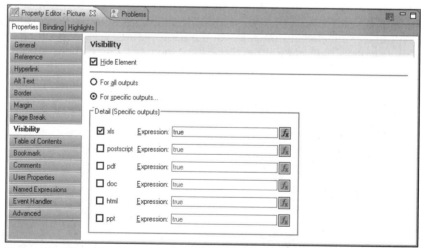

Figure 22-24   Hiding an element in XLS output only

You also have the option of disabling the master page for HTML reports. Sometimes, it makes sense to hide header and footer information for HTML reports, if the reports are set to display on a single page. For example, page numbers and report headers are not necessary for a one-page report. If the master page contains only these items, disabling the entire master page, rather than hiding individual elements on the master page, is more efficient.

To disable the master page for HTML reports, choose Window→Preferences, then choose Report Design—Preview, and deselect Enable master page content. Note that this option takes effect at the application level, not at the report level. The master page is disabled in all HTML reports.

Specifying page size, orientation, and margins

These page settings apply only to output formats, such as PDF and DOC, that use fixed page sizes. An HTML report set to auto layout displays directly in the report viewer and its size adjusts to the size of the viewer window. Report data in XLS format appears on a single worksheet.

The default master page uses the following settings:

- US letter size, 8.5" x 11"

- Portrait orientation

- Left, top, right, and bottom margins of 0.25"

You can change these page settings in Property Editor. Select the master page, then in the General page of Property Editor, shown in Figure 22-25, specify the page orientation, width, and height. To change the page margins, choose Margin.

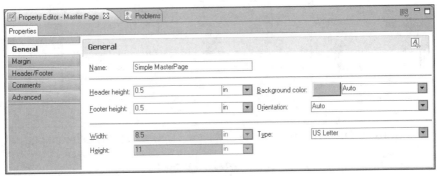

Figure 22-25   Master page general properties

If designing a report for PDF, specify the page settings before you begin laying out report data. For example, if you set the page width to a smaller size after laying out the report data, you probably have to adjust the report contents to fit in the new page size.

Using multiple master pages

You can use multiple master pages in a single report. A report can use different master pages to display, for example, one section of a report in portrait mode and another section in landscape mode. Using multiple master pages, you can also specify different background color, or different header and footer content for different sections of a report. Figure 22-26 shows a report that uses two master pages. The first page uses a master page that has portrait mode and a watermark. The second page uses a master page that has landscape mode and text in the footer.

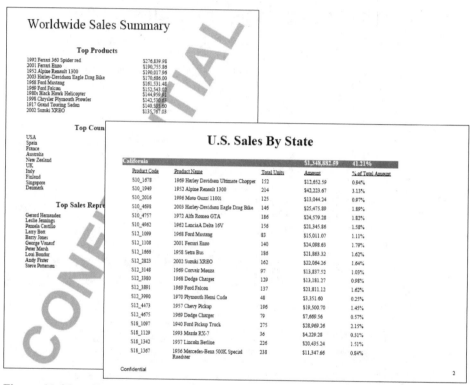

Figure 22-26   Report using two master pages to display different page styles

To use multiple master pages in a report:

- Create the master pages. You can create any number of master pages through the Outline view. Right-click MasterPages and choose Insert Element to add a new master page to the report design.

- Specify a page break for each report section that uses a different master page.

- Assign a master page to each report section.

For example, to design the report in Figure 22-26, two master pages, named Portrait and Landscape, are created. The Portrait master page is applied to the first report page, and the Landscape master page to the body of the report, using the following procedure:

- Select the report section to appear on the title page, and on Property Editor, choose Page Break. On the Page Break page, set the Master Page property to Portrait. Then, set the Page Break After property to Always. Figure 22-27 shows a grid selected, and its master page and page break properties set. The grid contains all the elements used to display data on the first page.

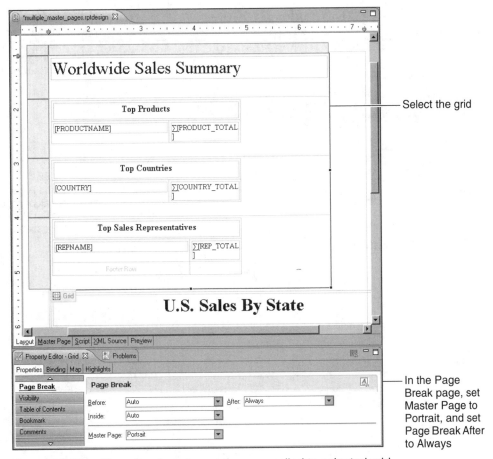

Figure 22-27   Page break and master page applied to selected grid

- Select the first element that appears on the body of the report, which starts on the next page. Set its master page to Landscape, as shown in Figure 22-28. The Landscape master page is used for the rest of the pages in the report.

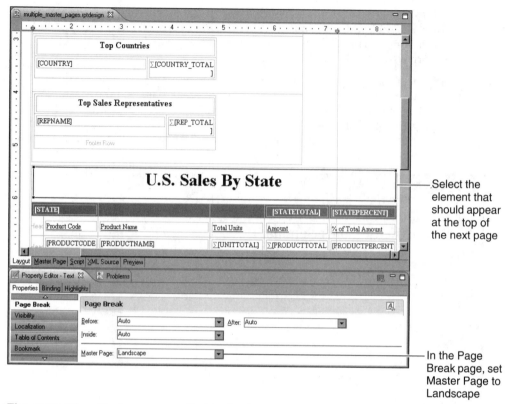

Select the element that should appear at the top of the next page

In the Page Break page, set Master Page to Landscape

Figure 22-28   Master page applied to the first element in the body of the report

23

Adding Interactive
Viewing Features

Some reports are long and complex, which can make it difficult for readers to
locate and use the information that they need. If these reports will be viewed
online, you can add interactive features that help users to navigate and
explore reports.

Hyperlinks and tables of contents offer different ways for a user to find
information or drill down to more detailed data. Interactive chart features
enable you to customize the data that a chart displays and provide links to
additional information. When designing an HTML report, you can add
interactive elements common to web pages, such as buttons and check boxes.

Not all report output formats support every interactive viewing feature.
Output formats, such as PPT, XLS, and DOC, provide limited support. For
example, interactive charts are available only in the BIRT report viewer; the
table of contents appears only in the report viewer and in PDF; interactive
web page elements apply to HTML reports only.

Creating hyperlinks

You can create a hyperlink that links one report element to another element,
either in the same report or in a different report. For example, a report can
contain a summary listing with hyperlinks to detailed information. Similarly,
a large report that consists of several subreports can contain a title page with
hyperlinks to each subreport.

The report element that acts as the hyperlink is called the source report
element. It must be a data, label, image, or chart element. The report element
to which you link is called the target report element.

Figure 23-1 shows two pages of a report in the BIRT report viewer, and how clicking a hyperlink on the first page jumps to content on the sixth page. The first page of the report displays sales summary information in a table and a chart. The state names in the table and the slices of the pie chart are hyperlinks. When the user clicks a hyperlink, the report viewer displays the detailed sales information for the selected state, as shown in Figure 23-1.

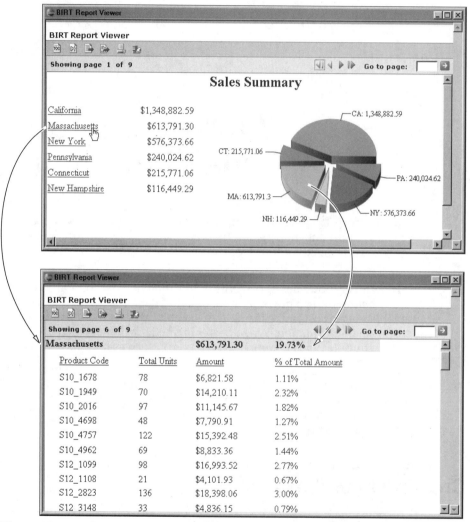

Figure 23-1   Clicking a hyperlink to go from one section in a report to another

Linking two sections in a report

To create a link from one report element to another element in the same report, use a bookmark and a hyperlink. First, define a bookmark for the target report element. Then, define a hyperlink for the source report element. Perform these tasks in this sequence because the hyperlink requires the bookmark information.

Defining a bookmark

As its name suggests, a bookmark is a marker for finding a place in a report. When defining a bookmark, you specify information that determines how BIRT generates the bookmark. The information can be one of the following:

- A name, such as "Bookmark 1" or "Bookmark for Sales Details Section". If you type a name, you must enclose it within double quotation marks, as shown in Figure 23-2.

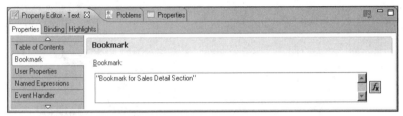

Figure 23-2   Using a name for the bookmark

Specify a name to link to a specific static location in the report. For example, to link to the beginning of a particular subreport in a report, select the label element that displays the title of the subreport, then create a bookmark using a name.

- An expression, such as row["STATE"], as shown in Figure 23-3.

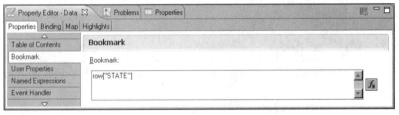

Figure 23-3   Using an expression for the bookmark

Specify an expression when you want to link to a location that is generated dynamically. The report shown in Figure 23-1 is such an example. In the Sales Detail section, the data element that displays the state name has a bookmark. The bookmark expression, row["STATE"], generates a dynamic bookmark for each state in the section.

How to define a bookmark

1 Select the target report element.

2 In Property Editor, under Properties, choose Bookmark.

3 In Bookmark, type the name of the bookmark, or create an expression. You can use any bookmark name that does not start with "__TOC_." This string is reserved for internal use by BIRT.

Figure 23-4 shows the bookmark definition for the example report shown in Figure 23-1.

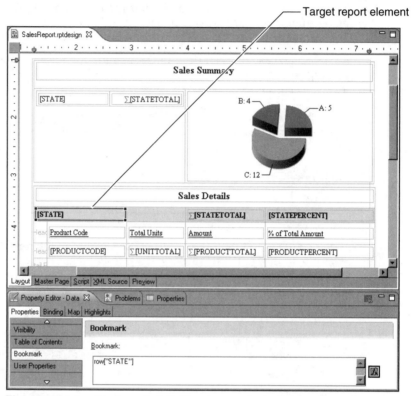

Figure 23-4   Bookmark definition for a selected data element

Defining a hyperlink

After creating the bookmark, define a hyperlink that goes to the bookmark. Specify the following information:

- The type of hyperlink. To link two sections within a report, use Internal Bookmark.

- The bookmark, or a link expression that changes the bookmark dynamically based on factors, such as report parameters, session values, or data values.

Use a link expression to link to bookmarks conditionally. For example, the details to which you link for each customer in a customer listing report may be different depending on the role of the person viewing the report. Someone in the sales department may need to see purchase order details, while someone in the shipping department may need to see bill of lading information. Adding a script to change the bookmark based on user role accomplishes this result.

A hyperlink can only be defined for a data, label, image, or chart element. The hyperlink options are the same for all these elements. The way in which you access the hyperlink options, however, differs for a chart and the other elements. For a chart, you use the interactivity editor in the chart builder to access the hyperlink options. For the other elements, you use the Hyperlink page of Property Editor.

How to create a hyperlink that links two sections in a report

1 Select the source report element, then perform one of the following tasks:

- For a data, label, or image element, In Property Editor, under Properties, choose Hyperlink. In the Hyperlink page, choose Edit to open Hyperlink Options. Figure 23-5 shows the Hyperlink page and the selected data element for the example report shown in Figure 23-1.

Figure 23-5   Selected data element and Hyperlink page

- For a chart, perform the following steps to open Hyperlink Options:

    1 Double-click the chart to open the chart builder.

2 Select Format Chart, then choose the chart element for which to define a hyperlink. The chart element can be a value series, the chart area, the legend, the *x*- and *y*-axis, or a title. Figure 23-6 shows an example of a pie chart's value series selected.

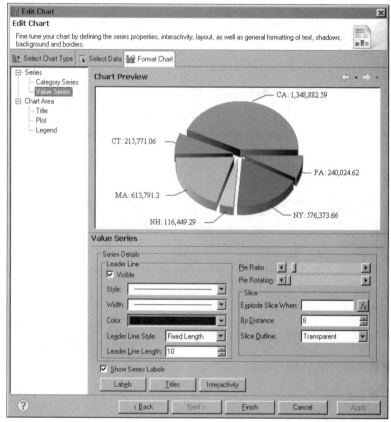

Figure 23-6   Edit chart displaying format options for value series

3 Choose Interactivity. In the interactivity editor, in Action, select Hyperlink. Choose Add.

4 Choose Edit Base URL to open Hyperlink Options, as shown in Figure 23-7.

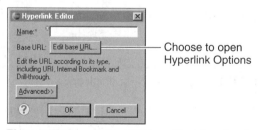

Figure 23-7   Interactivity editor showing hyperlink action selected

2 In Hyperlink Options, complete the following tasks:

　1 In Select Hyperlink Type, select Internal Bookmark.

　2 Choose one of the following procedures:

　　❏ In Bookmark, select a bookmark from the drop-down list. The list displays all the bookmarks defined for the report. The bookmark you select appears in both Bookmark and Linked Expression, as shown in Figure 23-8.

　　❏ In Linked Expression, choose the expression builder button, then build an expression.

　Figure 23-8 shows an example of a hyperlink definition that uses a bookmark value.

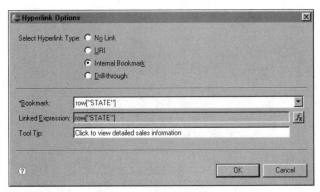

Figure 23-8　　Hyperlink Options

　3 Choose OK.

3 Preview the report and test the hyperlink. In the previewer and the report viewer, a data or label element with a hyperlink appears as blue underlined text, and an image has a blue border. For a chart, a hyperlink does not have a different appearance, but a cursor shaped like a hand appears when you hover the mouse pointer over a hyperlink.

Linking to a section in a different report

Creating a link from one report to a different report is similar to creating a link between elements in the same report. Begin by creating a bookmark in the target report. Then, create a hyperlink in the source report. This type of hyperlink is called a drill-through hyperlink, and requires additional information, including:

■ The name of the target report. The target report can be one of the following file types:

　■ Report design (.rptdesign). Specify a report design to run a report to display current data when the user clicks the hyperlink, or to generate a customized report based on a parameter value.

- Report document (.rptdocument). A report document is a previously executed report that contains cached data. Report document is the recommended target report type if the report is very large or if the report data changes infrequently.

- The bookmark in the target report to which to link. Alternatively, link to a table of contents entry in the target report. The table of contents, described later in this chapter, is another mechanism for navigating from one report section to another. If you do not specify a bookmark or a table of contents entry, the hyperlink goes to the beginning of the target report.

- Whether to open the target report in the same window or in a new window.

- The output format in which to display the target report.

Figure 23-9 shows an example of hyperlink options specified to link to a bookmark, row["STATE"], in a target report named SalesDetails.rptdesign.

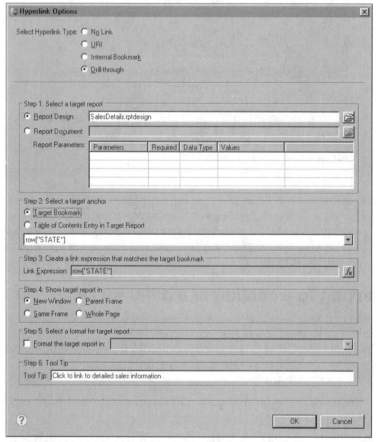

Figure 23-9   Hyperlink options for linking two reports

You can customize the data displayed by the target report and improve performance by using report parameters. For example, instead of generating a target report that shows sales details for all states, use a target report design that has a report parameter that filters data by state. The report displays sales details only for the state whose hyperlink the user clicks. Typically, generating a filtered report is faster than generating a report with all the data.

To generate such a report, perform the following tasks:

- In the target report, create a report parameter to get the state value at run time.

- In the source report, define a hyperlink that runs the target report and passes the selected state value to the target report's parameter. Figure 23-10 shows a hyperlink definition where the row["STATE"] value is passed to the report parameter, RP_State, in the target report SalesDetail.rptdesign. When the target report you specify contains report parameters, click the cell under Parameters in Hyperlink Options to view a list of the parameters.

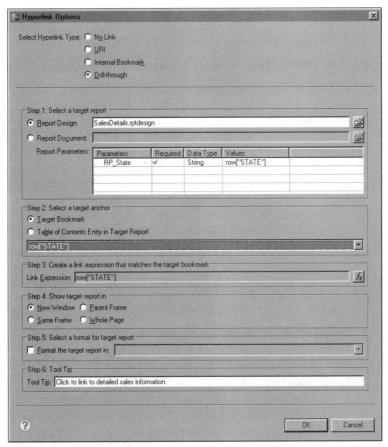

Figure 23-10   Hyperlink options for a link that passes a parameter

Linking to external content

You can use a hyperlink to open a document or a web page. These links provide users with easy access to additional sources of information, creating more interactive reports. For example, use a hyperlink to:

- Open a company web page when a user chooses a label.

- Open a text file that contains detailed copyright information when a user chooses a label that displays a copyright statement.

- Open an image file or play a movie clip when a user chooses a thumbnail image in the report.

This type of hyperlink uses a Uniform Resource Identifier (URI) to locate a document, image, or web page.

How to link to external content using a URI

1 Select the report element, such as a label or image, for which to define a hyperlink.

2 In Property Editor, under Properties, choose Hyperlink.

3 In the Hyperlink page, choose Edit.

4 In Hyperlink Options, specify the following values:

   1 Choose URI as the hyperlink type.

   2 In Location, specify the URI, using one of the following methods:

      ❑ To type a specific URI, choose the arrow button next to the expression builder button, and choose Constant. Type the URI. The following are examples:

```
http://www.mycompany.com
http://mysite.com/legal_notices/copyright.html
http://mysite.com/images/executives.jpg
file:/C:/copyright/statement.txt
```

      ❑ To specify an expression that evaluates to a URI at report run time, choose the expression builder button to construct the expression. Use an expression to construct a URI dynamically when the full URI is not known at design time or if the URI changes depending on data retrieved from a data source.

   3 In Target, specify where to open the target document. The choices correspond to the target attributes for an HTML anchor tag. Select Blank to open the target document in a new window. Select Parent, Self, or Top to open the target document in the same window.

   4 In Tool Tip, optionally type the text to display when the user hovers the mouse pointer over the hyperlink.

Figure 23-11 shows an example of linking to a web page.

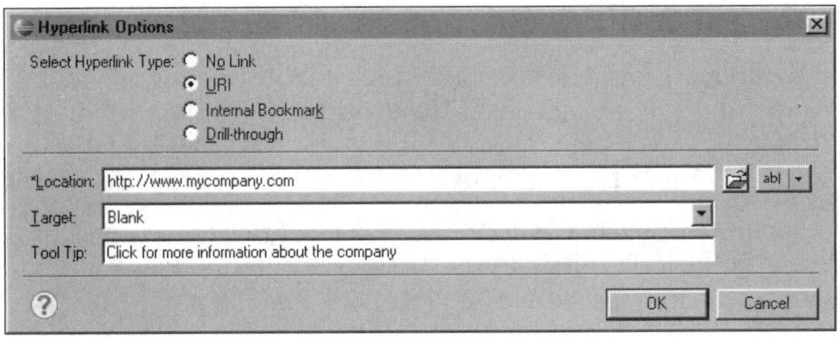

Figure 23-11   Hyperlink options for a URI

Creating a table of contents

Like hyperlinks, a table of contents provides an effective way for a report user to navigate to specific locations in a large report. A table of contents displays a list of items that reflect the organization of the report. These items are known as table of contents entries. These entries are active links to locations within the report. You can either use the default values for these entries or create custom values that are more meaningful to the report users.

Figure 23-12 shows a report, in the report viewer, that displays products by product line. The table of contents, which appears to the left of the report when the TOC button is selected, lists all the product lines in the report. When the user selects a product line, the report viewer displays the corresponding section of the report. When viewing the report in PDF format, the table of contents entries appear as bookmarks to the left of the report.

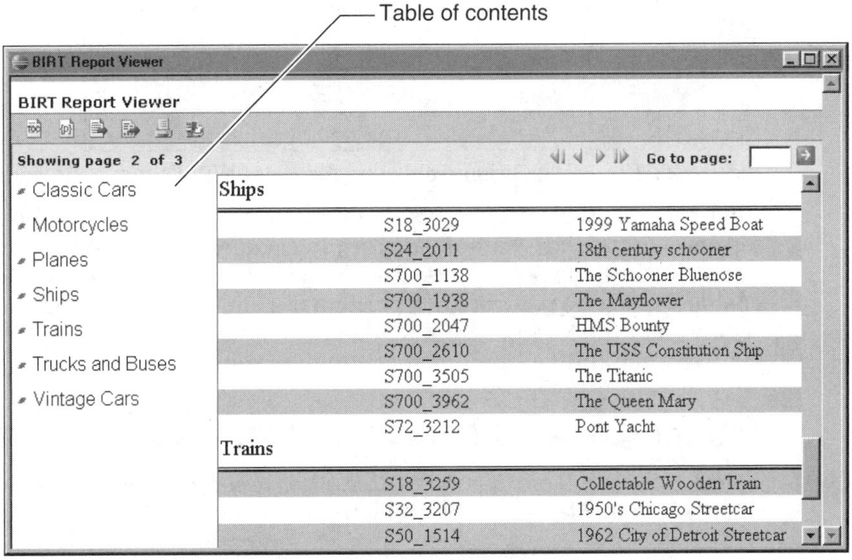

Figure 23-12   Report viewer displaying a table of contents next to a report

Using the default table of contents

By default, a grouped report includes a table of contents that displays the group values. For example, if the group key is a data set field named PRODUCTLINE, the table of contents displays all the values in the PRODUCTLINE field, as shown in the example report in Figure 23-12.

To generate this table of contents, BIRT defines the expression, row["PRODUCTLINE"], in the Table of Contents Item Expression option in the group editor, as shown in Figure 23-13.

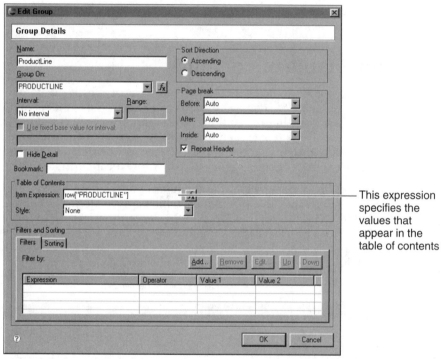

This expression specifies the values that appear in the table of contents

Figure 23-13   Edit Group displaying the default TOC item expression

BIRT creates a table of contents for every group in a report, not just for the top-level group. For example, if grouping order data by state, customers, and order ID, the table of contents displays a hierarchy of group values that enable the user to navigate to a particular state, customer, or order ID. To remove a group's values from the table of contents, simply delete the expression in the Table of Contents Item Expression in the group editor.

Defining a custom table of contents

You can create a table of contents for other report elements, such as dynamic images or data elements. Select the report element from which to use values in the table of contents, choose Table of Contents in Property Editor, then specify an expression that determines the values to display. For example, add a nested table of contents to the report shown in Figure 23-12 to display product codes under each product line. To create this table of contents, select the [PRODUCTCODE] data element and specify row["PRODUCTCODE"] as the expression for the Table of Contents property, as shown in Figure 23-14.

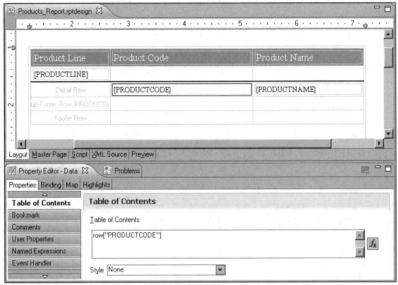

Figure 23-14   Table of Contents property for the selected data element

In the report viewer, the table of contents displays product codes within the product line entries, as shown in Figure 23-15.

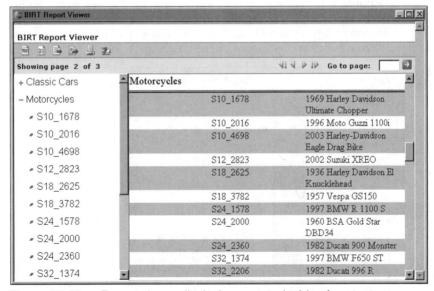

Figure 23-15   Report viewer displaying a nested table of contents

In some cases, you may not want the table of contents to display field values exactly as they are saved in the data source. For example, the values might be obscure. You can customize the table of contents expression to create a more informative table of contents entry. For example, to display a product name on a separate line after a product code, the table of contents expression would be as follows:

```
row["PRODUCTCODE"] + " \n" + row["PRODUCTNAME"]
```

You can provide any valid JavaScript expression as a table of contents expression. For example, to show that a product is obsolete, you can check the value of the OBSOLETE database field, as the following example shows:

```
if ( row["OBSOLETE"] == "yes" ) {
    row["PRODUCTCODE"] + " (Obsolete)"
} else {
    row["PRODUCTCODE"] + " \n" + row["PRODUCTNAME"]
}
```

Adding interactive chart features

You can bookmark or link to a chart or include a chart in the table of contents, as described earlier in this chapter. Use additional interactive features, available through the chart builder, to enhance the behavior of a chart in the report viewer.

An interactive chart feature supports a response to an event, such as the report user choosing an item or moving the mouse pointer over an item. The response can trigger an action, such as opening a web page, drilling to a detail report, or changing the appearance of the chart. For example, use a Tooltip to display the series total when a user places the mouse pointer over a bar in a bar chart, as shown in Figure 23-16.

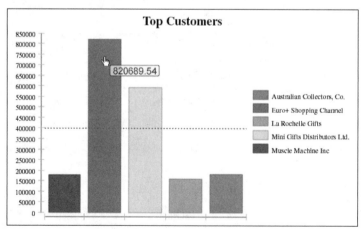

Figure 23-16 Chart showing a Tooltip

You can add an interactive feature to a value series, the chart area, a legend, marker lines, the *x*- and *y*-axis, or a title. Figure 23-17 identifies these elements.

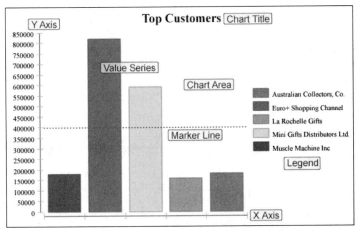

Figure 23-17   Elements selectable for chart interactivity

Start the process of adding interactivity to a chart by choosing Format Chart in the chart builder and selecting the chart element you wish to make interactive. Choose the Interactivity button, and the interactivity editor appears. Figure 23-18 shows the location of the Interactivity button for a chart legend.

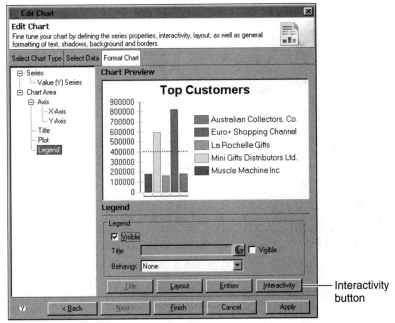

Figure 23-18   Accessing interactivity for a chart legend

The location of the button to invoke the interactivity editor varies by chart element. Table 23-1 lists the procedure used to invoke the interactivity editor for each element. Not all chart types have all elements listed in the table.

Table 23-1   Accessing chart interactivity options

Chart element	How to invoke the interactivity editor
Chart Area	Choose Interactivity in the Chart Area formatting page
Chart Title	Choose Interactivity in the Title formatting page
Legend Area	Choose Interactivity in the Legend formatting page
X-Axis and Y-Axis	Choose Interactivity in the X-Axis or the Y-Axis formatting page
Marker	Choose Markers in the X-Axis or the Y-Axis formatting page. Axis Markers appears. Choose Interactivity.
Value Series	Choose Interactivity in the Value (Y) Series page.

Defining interactivity events and actions

To make a chart interactive, specify the type of event that triggers interactivity for a selected chart element and indicate the action you wish to perform in Interactivity. For example, in a chart legend, you can use a mouse click to toggle the visibility of the associated data point. Figure 23-19 shows the event type and action in Interactivity required to accomplish this event.

Figure 23-19   Toggle visibility on legend with mouse click

There are a variety of event types that can be used to trigger interactivity. Table 23-2 lists the event types available in the interactivity editor, and describes the UI gesture associated with each.

Table 23-2   Event types

Event type	Description
Mouse Click	Click the selected chart element.
Mouse Double-Click	Double-click the selected element.
Mouse Down	Press and hold the mouse button down over the selected element.
Mouse Up	Release the mouse button above the selected chart element.
Mouse Over	Move the mouse pointer onto the selected element and leave it there.
Mouse Move	Pass the mouse pointer over the selected element.
Mouse Out	Move the mouse pointer off the selected element.
Focus	Put UI focus on the selected element with the mouse or tab navigation.
Blur	Remove UI focus from the selected element using either the mouse or tab navigation.
Key Press	Press a key while the mouse pointer is over the selected element.
Key Down	Press and hold a key down while the mouse pointer is over the selected element.
Key Up	Release a key while the mouse pointer is over the selected element.
Load	Load the chart in the viewer.

Table 23-3 lists the action options associated with each event type in the interactivity editor. A chart element can have multiple interactive features, but a particular event can produce only one action.

Table 23-3   Interactive features

Action name	Result
Hyperlink	Links to a web page, a document, or an image. Also used to link to another report.
Invoke Script	Invokes a client-side script inside the viewer.
Show Tooltip	Displays explanatory text over a chart element.
Toggle Visibility	Changes the visibility of a chart element, typically a series.
Highlight	Highlights a chart element, such as a data point.

Chart formats and supported actions

Not all actions are available in all chart output formats. Highlighting and Tooltips, for example, are not available to charts in JPG and BMP format. Only SVG charts support all the interactive features. In addition, to use the interactive features, the report user must view the report in a browser that has an SVG plug-in and that supports JavaScript. To see how an interactive feature works in a chart, preview the report in the report viewer.

Adding interactive elements to an HTML report

Using JavaScript, you can add interactive HTML elements to a report. Some common elements, used in many web pages, include pop-up windows, alert messages, drop-down menus, and buttons. For example, in an HTML report, you can add a button that, when clicked, expands or collapses a report section.

To add an interactive HTML element, perform the following tasks:

- Insert a text element and set its type to HTML.

- In the text editor, use the script tag to write JavaScript code that runs when an event, such as a mouse click, occurs.

Figure 23-20 shows a report design with a text element placed in the header row of a table that displays customer information.

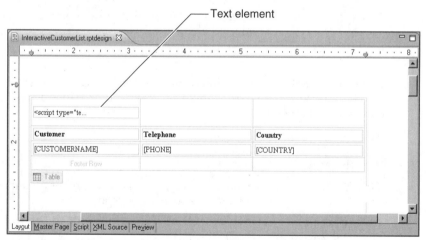

Figure 23-20   Report design that includes an HTML text element

Figure 23-21 shows an example of HTML text specified for the text element. Within the script tag is a user-defined function, showinfo( ), that displays the number of customer rows in a table. The last line of code creates a button that, when clicked, runs the showinfo( ) function.

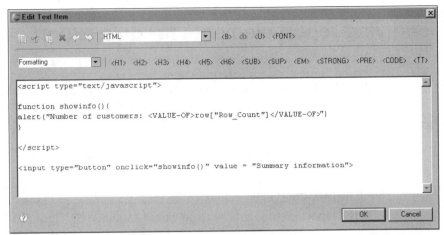

Figure 23-21 The text editor showing HTML text that includes a JavaScript function

Figure 23-22 shows the HTML output. A Summary information button appears at the top of the report. When the user clicks this button, a dialog appears and displays the information you specified.

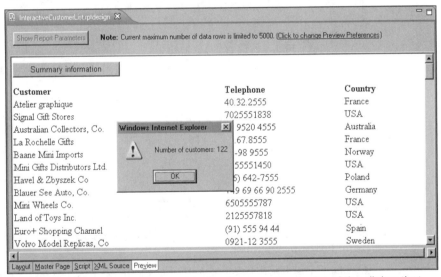

Figure 23-22 The previewer showing the report output and the dialog that appears when the Summary information button is clicked

Interactive HTML elements appear only in an HTML report. If a report is to be viewed in other formats, such as PDF, hide the text element that contains the JavaScript code in all formats, except HTML. Otherwise, the report displays the space occupied by the text element when viewed in a format other than HTML.

Identifying report elements for data export

A report user can export report data from the report viewer to a comma-separated values (.csv) file. Using the export feature, a user can extract some or all of the data from a report, then use this data in another document. For example, a user could export customer sales data from a report for a previous quarter, then use the numbers in a spreadsheet to create a forecast for an upcoming quarter.

As a report developer, you can provide report elements with descriptive names so that the user can easily find the information to export.

How to export report data

1 In the report viewer, choose Export data, as shown in Figure 23-23.

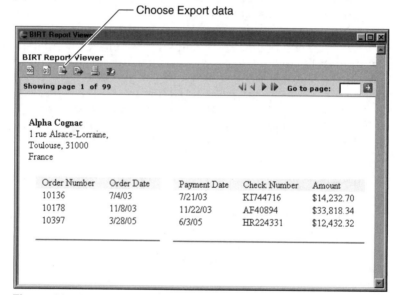

Figure 23-23   Export data button in the report viewer

2 When Export Data appears, as shown in Figure 23-24, select a result set from the drop-down list.

Available result sets lists the container elements, such as tables and charts, that contain data. By default, the names that are displayed in the list are internal names that begin with the prefix ELEMENT, for example, ELEMENT_50, ELEMENT_72, and so on.

3 Move the data that you want to export from Available Columns to Selected Columns.

4 Choose OK.

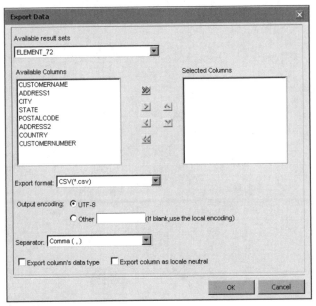

Figure 23-24 Export Data

5 In File Download, choose Save. In Save As, type a file name and select a folder in which to save the file.

How to identify a report element

To make it easier for a report user to identify the section of the report they wish to export data from, give each report element a more meaningful name in Property Editor. For example, to give a more meaningful name to the main table in a customer report, select the table in the layout editor, and in General properties, in Name, type "Customer Data", as shown in Figure 23-25.

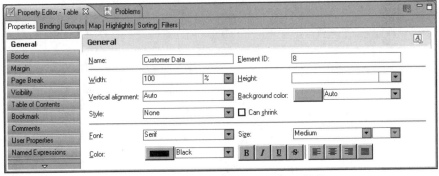

Figure 23-25 Giving an element a name in Property Editor

24

Building a Shared Development Framework

Previous chapters describe how to create and use data sources and data sets and lay out and format report items. A single report developer with a requirement for only a few reports can use these approaches effectively. For a larger project, either one with more developers or one that requires more reports, many designs need to use the same elements or layouts.

To support creating and maintaining standard formats, building reports in collaboration with other report developers, and avoiding error-prone, repetitious design tasks, BIRT uses the following file types:

- A library

  The main purpose of a library is to provide developers of report designs with a shared repository of predesigned report elements and styles. The file-name extension for a library file is .rptlibrary. BIRT locates libraries in the resource folder.

  A library is a dynamic component of a report design. When a library developer makes changes to a library, the report design synchronizes itself with the changed library. In this way, changes propagate easily within a suite of report designs.

  A library stores customized report elements, such as data sources, visual report items, styles, and master pages. Use a library in a report design to access the customized elements. You can use multiple libraries in a single report design. By using multiple libraries, you can separate the styles and functionality that different projects or processes need.

- A template

  The main purpose of a template is to provide a standard start position for a new report design. As such, the structure of a template file is identical to the structure of a report design file. The file-name extension for a template file is .rpttemplate. BIRT locates templates in the template folder.

A template is a static framework on which to build a new report design. A report design derived from a template modifies a copy of that template. For this reason, a report design can derive from only one template. Because report designs use copies of the template, when a template developer changes a template, report designs based on that template do not automatically reflect those changes.

A template provides a structure for a standard report layout. A template can contain visual report items that appear in the report's layout, data sources and data sets, and master page layouts. A template uses libraries in the same way that a report design does. BIRT Report Designer provides a set of standard templates, such as Simple Listing and Grouped Listing report templates.

- A CSS file

  This type of file provides styles for formatting items in a report, similar to the formatting of items on a web page.

Developing a library or a template uses skills similar to those used to develop report designs. All these file types use the same report elements from the palette, Data Explorer, and the Outline view in BIRT Report Designer.

Sharing report elements using a library

A library provides a straightforward way to share custom report elements and styles across an enterprise. When a library developer saves a customized element in a library, the element is available to any report design that uses the library directly. Because a report design can use multiple libraries, you can separate logical sets of report elements.

Figure 24-1 shows the structure of a report design that uses libraries. The expanded Libraries item shows the three libraries that the report design uses.

—Library name spaces

Figure 24-1   Outline view showing included libraries

Understanding dynamic library behavior

A library is dynamic. When a library developer changes an element in a library, the same changes occur in all report designs that use the library. For example, if the enterprise's preferred font changes from Arial to Book Antiqua, the library developer makes the changes to styles in a library. When a user generates a report from any design that uses styles from that library, or when a report developer opens or refreshes the design in BIRT Report Designer, the changes take effect. This dynamic behavior ensures that all report elements that derive from a library always use the current styles and properties.

When an enterprise implements a policy of using libraries, the best practice is for every custom element used by more than one report design to derive from a library element. Using an element directly from the palette and customizing it in the same way in multiple designs is error-prone and requires a report developer to update the element in each design if the enterprise's needs change.

Creating a library

BIRT Report Designer provides the following three ways to create a library:

- Creating a library from an entire report design

  Use this technique if a model report design exists that contains a strong base of report elements having a desirable structure, properties, and styles. In the Outline view, right-click the report design root, shown in Figure 24-2, and choose Export to Library. All report items in the Body slot in the report design now appear in the Report Items slot in the new library. The report design's custom styles appear in the defaultTheme theme in the library's Themes slot. Other elements appear in the same slot in the library as in the report design.

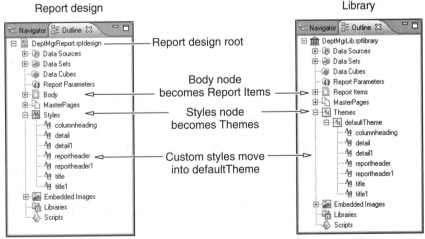

Figure 24-2   Comparing a report design outline and a library outline

- Creating an empty library

  Use this technique to develop a set of related report elements that do not depend on existing report designs. Choose File→New→Library. BIRT Report Designer creates the new library in a folder in the current workspace.

- Creating a library from individual report elements

  Use this technique if model report elements having desirable properties, structure, and style exist in multiple separate report designs. In the Outline view, right-click the report element and choose Export to Library. Provide a name for a new library or select an existing library in the resource folder.

Developing library report elements

After creating a library, you begin to build a library framework by adding report elements to the library. This process is similar to developing elements in a report design. To create or edit a data source, data set, data cube, or report parameter, use the same Data Explorer wizards and dialogs in the library as in a report design. To add a visual report item, drag an item from the palette to the layout editor. The new item appears both in Report Items in the Outline view and on its own page in the layout editor, as shown in Figure 24-3. To edit an existing report item in a library, select the item in Report Items in the Outline view.

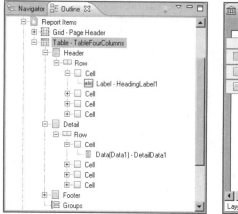
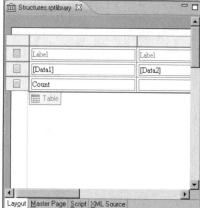

Figure 24-3   Library report item outline and appearance

Grouping library styles into a theme

A library provides a flexible way to share sets of styles by grouping styles into themes. Each theme supports the complete set of styles used in a report design. The Outline view of a library shows Themes where the outline of a report design shows Styles. In a newly created library, Themes contains one theme named defaultTheme. During the development of report items in a library, BIRT Report Designer displays the items using styles in this theme.

A library developer chooses the properties such as the set of colors to use in the styles in each theme. For example, first, he creates the report style that contains the background color, border, and font properties for all items. Next, he designs a table-header style using the same color palette so that each table's header stands out from the rest of a report but the appearance does not clash with the other report items.

To create a new theme, in Outline, right-click Themes and choose New Theme. For example, provide styles in defaultTheme for use in most report designs. Then, make special themes for financial and marketing report designs, as shown in Figure 24-4. A report design uses styles from only one theme. If some styles must be the same for all themes, copy the styles from one theme to the other themes that need those styles.

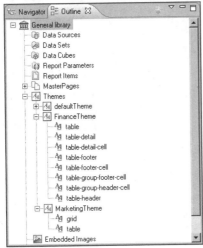

Figure 24-4   Multiple themes in a library

Comparing themes and CSS files

Both themes and CSS files provide shared styles. Use a CSS file when your company already has a standard set of styles in a CSS file or if your report developers are familiar with using CSS. Use a theme from a library instead of a CSS file to group related styles together or to use more style properties than BIRT supports in CSS.

Sharing a library with other report developers

BIRT Report Designer uses the resource folder to contain libraries and other resources used by files in a workspace. To share a library across a team of report developers, place the library in the resource folder. Each report developer must set the resource folder for a workspace to the same location. Typically, the resource folder is a directory on a shared network drive. The developer uses Resource Explorer to access report elements from the libraries in the resource folder.

To set the location of the resource folder, choose Windows→Preferences. Expand Report Design and select the Resource page, as shown in Figure 24-5. Browse to a folder within the workspace or file system, use an Eclipse variable, or type the name of the resource folder. Then, choose OK.

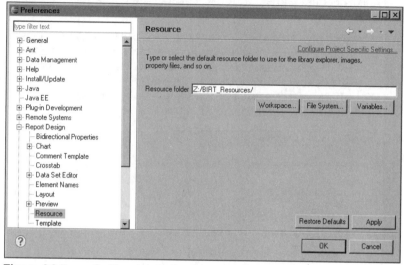

Figure 24-5   Setting up a resource folder

The contents of the resource folder appear in Resource Explorer, as shown in Figure 24-6.

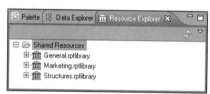

Figure 24-6   Resource Explorer

Placing a library in the resource folder

When you use BIRT Report Designer to share a library from your workspace, BIRT copies the library file to the resource folder. The original library file remains in your workspace. Make sure the shared library has a meaningful file name. BIRT Report Designer displays the name to report developers who use the resource folder.

How to share a library from your workspace

1   Open the library in BIRT Report Designer.

2   Choose File→Place Library in Resource Folder.

3 In Publish Library, shown in Figure 24-7, make changes to the file name and folder. To place the library in a subfolder of the resource folder, use Browse. Choose Finish. The library appears in Resource Explorer.

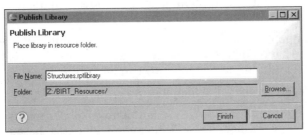

Figure 24-7   Sharing a library

Organizing resources

If an enterprise has many libraries, BIRT supports the following two ways to organize the files:

- Using subfolders to organize the libraries within a single, central resource folder. For example, \\SharedServer\Resource\General contains general libraries, and \\SharedServer\Resource\Finance contains libraries used by financial reports. Resource Explorer displays this file structure.

- Using project-specific settings to specify a resource folder for an individual project. Resource Explorer displays only the resources in the project-specific resource folder and does not show resources in the central folder specified for the workspace. To set a project-specific resource folder, use the Configure Project-Specific Settings option in the Resource preferences page.

Updating a shared library

After changing or adding a report item in a library, place the updated library in the resources folder. Other report developers refresh Resource Explorer to see the changes.

When a report developer opens a report design that uses the updated library, the changes take place immediately. To see the changes in an open report design that uses the library, expand the Libraries slot in the Outline view for the report design. Then, right-click the changed library and choose Refresh.

Designing libraries for a shared environment

A library is a key tool for achieving consistent appearance in a suite of report designs. To use libraries effectively, consider how to make the best use of their properties and functionality. Although you can use one library containing every custom component that all of your report designs need, this library would be large and confusing for other report developers.

One way to design a suite of libraries is firstly to make libraries containing elements common to all reporting projects. Secondly, for each reporting project, you create a project-specific library. These project-specific libraries can contain elements that are simple modifications of the standard report elements and complex elements, such as tables nested within grids or lists.

A library can refer to items in other libraries. For example, if a project library contains a grid for a report header that uses the company logo, you can include the logo from the general library in that grid.

For example, create the following libraries:

- A general library containing standard items that all projects use, such as themes, an image element for the company logo and master pages including standard page headers and footers

- A library containing complex items that all projects use, for example, a table element with predefined behavior, such as highlighting

- One or more libraries containing elements specific to each project, such as data sources

By building suites of libraries in this way, you provide the building blocks for a standard appearance for all reports, and package the behavior and appearance of report elements appropriate to each reporting project. Figure 24-8 shows an architecture for libraries and report designs.

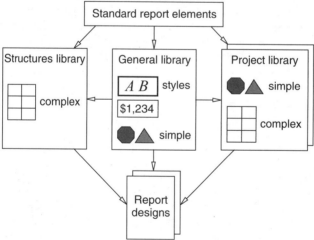

Figure 24-8   Project architecture using libraries

Designing a general library

A general library contains standard, simple items, such as a company logo image element or a text element that contains a confidentiality agreement. This library also contains a default theme that includes settings for predefined styles and any custom styles for all report designs. If multiple reporting projects need to use a different theme, place that theme in this library. You can also include common items such as master pages that use the other basic components in the library.

Designing a structures library

A structures library provides grids, lists, and tables to report designs. For example, most report designs use a table element. Initially, the table element in a structures library is identical in behavior to the table from the palette. Later, a need arises to alternate the row colors for every table in every report design. Make the change to the tables in the library and every report design that uses the table from the library now has the new feature. If the structures library did not contain table elements, report developers would have to make this change manually in every design.

Designing structure elements

When a report developer uses an item from a library in a report design, he can change any properties, but not the item's structure. For example, if the developer uses a table from a library, BIRT allows changes to the table's style or data binding, but not adding or removing cell contents, columns, or groups. A library structure has the maximum number of columns, rows, and groups available to a report design. To reduce the number of visible columns in a report, a report developer sets the width of a column to zero.

Figure 24-9 is an example of this approach. The table in the library has four columns. Cells in the header row contain labels, cells in the detail row contain data elements, and cells in the footer row contain a label and data elements. A report design uses two copies of the library table. One copy modifies the cell contents to show a list of customers in three columns and sets the width of the empty fourth column to zero. The other copy uses all four columns to display order information.

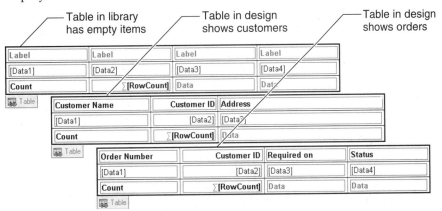

Figure 24-9 Customizing a table from a library

The developer of grid, list, and table elements in a library must consider the contents of the cells as well as the layout and behavior of the element itself.

The recommended practice is to place a report item in every cell in a grid, list, or table defined in a library. By changing the properties of the labels or data items after placing the element in a report design, report developers use the same structure to achieve many different results.

Designing data binding for library table elements

Designing the data binding at the same time as developing a table element in a library reduces the steps required to use the element in a report design. The most important task in the design process is to decide on a naming convention for columns in a data set. Both library and report developers must use this convention to set the alias of each column. For example, in the data set editor shown in Figure 24-10, each column in the data set has an alias that begins with Data. Each alias has a numeric suffix.

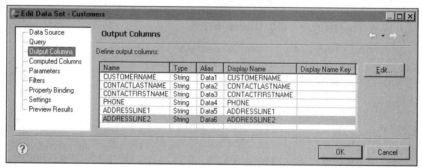

Figure 24-10   Standardized aliases for output columns in a data set

The library developer determines the desired structure for the table. For example, the diagram in Figure 24-11 shows a four-column table having a single grouping level. The table uses two data items in the first group header row and four data items in the detail row.

				——Table header row
	Data1	Data2		——Group header row 1
				——Group header row 2
Data3	Data4	Data5	Data6	——Table detail row
				——Group footer row
				——Table footer row

Figure 24-11   Layout of data items bound to fields in a library table

The library developer uses a dummy data set to prepare the data binding for the table. This data set has the same number of columns as data items required in the table. For example, the following query on the Customers table in the Classic Models sample database provides the six columns required for the table in Figure 24-11:

```
select
    CUSTOMERS.CUSTOMERNAME, CUSTOMERS.CONTACTLASTNAME,
    CUSTOMERS.CONTACTFIRSTNAME, CUSTOMERS.PHONE,
    CUSTOMERS.ADDRESSLINE1, CUSTOMERS.ADDRESSLINE2
from CUSTOMERS
```

Using the data set editor, define aliases conforming to the naming convention for the columns, as shown in Figure 24-10.

The library developer creates a table having the desired number of columns, rows, and groups. Next, he drags data fields from the data explorer into the desired cells in the table. This action binds the dummy data set to the table and uses the column aliases to assign the column bindings to the data items. BIRT also creates label items as column headings for each data item. Figure 24-12 shows the appearance of a table having the structure shown in Figure 24-11 and data items using the names shown in Figure 24-10 in the layout editor.

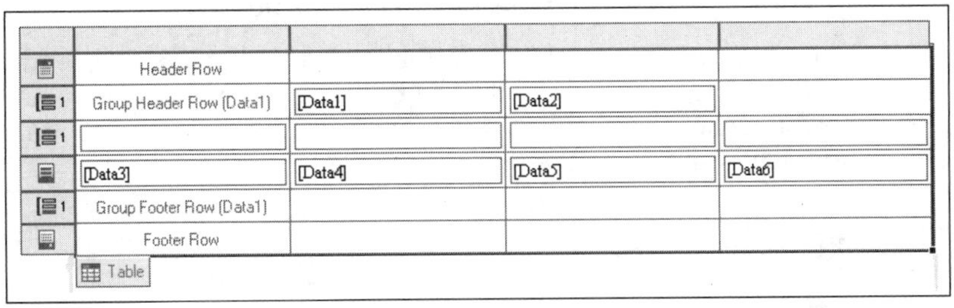

Figure 24-12   Library table containing data items and empty labels

The library developer removes the binding for the dummy data set from the table. To retain the data bindings used by the data items, do not clear the existing data field information when prompted. This data field information contains the standard names for data columns.

The library developer completes the structure of the table by adding report items to the remaining empty cells, for example label items for additional column and row headings and data items to contain aggregations for column totals. The developer does not provide bindings for the aggregation data items. The library table stores only bindings for data fields. The report developer must provide bindings for aggregations.

The library table is now ready for publishing to a library in the resource folder and for use in a report design.

How to set up a library table to use standardized data binding

1 Open or create a library.

2 Create a table having the desired number of columns, rows, and groups.

3 Create a data source of any type. For example, create a data source using the Classic Models Inc. Sample Database.

4 Create a data set using the data source. Define a query to provide the number of data fields required by the table.

5 In Edit Data Set, in Output Columns, edit each column. In Edit Column, type a standardized alias.

6 Set up the data structure of the table. After completing this step, a table matching the diagram in Figure 24-11 looks like Figure 24-12.

   1 In the Outline view, expand the Report Items node and select the table.

   2 From Data Explorer, drag columns from the data set into table cells.

   3 Move or delete the labels that appear in the group header row, as required. Delete the text from the labels.

   4 Select the table again. In Property Editor, select Groups. In Groups, select the group. Choose Edit. In Edit Group, in Group on, select a field. Then, choose OK. If a new data item that you do not need appears in the group header, delete the item.

7 Using the palette, add labels to the remaining header cells and data items to contain aggregations to the footer cells. For each data item, in New Data Binding, choose Cancel. A table matching the diagram in Figure 24-11 now looks similar to the one in Figure 24-13.

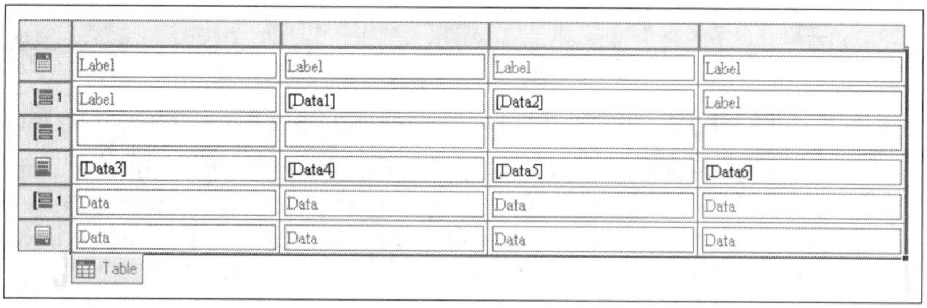

Figure 24-13   Library table containing all required items

8 Optionally, rename the labels and data items to have meaningful names.

9 Remove the temporary data elements from the library.

   1 Select the table.

   2 In Property Editor, select Binding. In Data Set, select None. To retain the data field information for the table, in Change Data Set, choose No.

   3 In Data Explorer, delete the data set and data source.

10 Save and publish the library. Choose File➤Save. Choose File➤Place Library in Resource Folder.

Defining a project library

The purpose of a project library is to provide customized report elements for report designs within a single reporting project. The most common elements specific to a project are data sources. Other simple elements contained in a project library are project-specific image elements and text elements having standard wording and formatting. A project library can also contain complex, structured elements, such as tables that have custom layout or behavior.

A project library can include data sets, but, for best report generation speed, a report design should use a data set developed for its specific needs. A data set from a library is often too general for optimum efficiency because it retrieves more fields from a data source than most report designs require.

There are two ways to set up a project library.

- Customizing every type of report element

  Report developers use only this library in every new report design for the project. Instead of using report items directly from the palette or the general libraries, they use report items from the project library. Use this technique if the project customizes many elements or if the project's requirements are likely to change frequently.

- Customizing only the project-specific report elements

  Report developers use this library and the general libraries in every new report design for this project. They use the report items from the project library or from the palette. Use this technique if the project customizes only a few elements or provides only complex structures to complement the elements from the palette.

Using a library

To add report elements and styles from a library to a report design, use the Resource Explorer view. Resource Explorer shows the elements in a library using the same tree structure as the Outline view. Figure 24-14 shows an example of how elements in a library appear in Resource Explorer.

Understanding libraries in Resource Explorer

Resource Explorer is a source for elements in a report design. You place elements from a library into a report design and then customize them. You do not use Resource Explorer to change or create elements in a library.

Resource Explorer does not check actively for changes to libraries. To update Resource Explorer to display changes to the list of available libraries or the items in an individual library, right-click and choose Refresh.

Using library report elements

Use report elements from a library in the same way as items from the palette or data elements from Data Explorer. In Resource Explorer, expand a library and the slots in the library to see the items available. Next, drag a component from the library to the place where you need it in your report design.

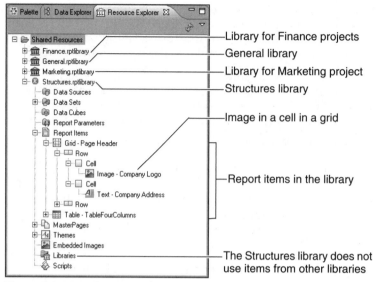

Figure 24-14 Resource Explorer showing elements in a library

For example, to use a visual report item, expand Report Items inside the library. Then, drag the report item to the layout of your report design. BIRT Report Designer adds the library to the report design. The library and library items appear in the Outline view as icons with a link, as shown in Figure 24-15. This illustration shows a report design using all three libraries shown in the Resource Explorer in Figure 24-14. The Structures library provides the TableFourColumns item and the PageHeader grid used by the master page. The other libraries provide the data sets.

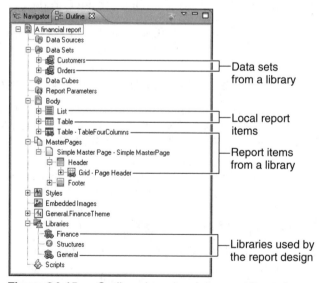

Figure 24-15 Outline view showing report items from a library

To identify the library defining an element, select the element in the layout or Outline. Property Editor displays the field, Library, as shown in Figure 24-16. This field shows the full path of the library that defines the element.

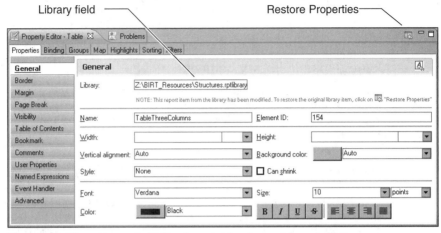

Figure 24-16   Property Editor for a table element from a library

If a report item in the library is a structure such as a grid, you must include the entire structure in your report design. You cannot select one piece of the structure, such as the image in a cell in a grid shown in Figure 24-14. For such an item to be available to a report design, the library must provide it as a separate item.

To add a data set from a library to a report design, drag the data set from Resource Explorer onto the Data Sets slot in the Outline view. The data set appears in Data Explorer as well as in Outline.

Understanding library name space

BIRT uses name space to identify the sets of report elements that each library contains. BIRT bases the name space on the file name of the library. For example, if the name of the library is FinanceProject.rptlibrary, the name space is FinanceProject. BIRT uses a separate name space for each library to support a report design using multiple libraries containing items of the same name. For example, if a grid named Page Header occurs in more than one library that the report design uses, BIRT uses the name space to select the one to display in the report.

The name space appears in the Libraries node in the Outline view for the report design, as shown in Figure 24-1, and in the names of themes and styles that the report design uses, as shown in Figure 24-22. The use of the name space in a style shows a report developer where the style is defined.

If a report design uses more than one library having the same file name space, BIRT Report Designer prompts for a name space for the second and subsequent libraries. In this case, provide a name space that distinguishes the library from the others but shows a relationship to the library's file name.

Modifying a library-based element

An element from a library provides a base for report development. Typically, you modify some of the element's properties when using a library element in a report design. For example, a report design contains many copies of a data item from a library. Each data item displays a different data value by using a different column binding.

Using dynamic library behavior

You modify a library-based report element in the same way as any other element in the report design. The report design stores only the changed properties. BIRT uses all other property values from the element in the library. In this way, BIRT both retains the dynamic nature of the library and supports local changes.

All properties of a simple report item, such as an image or text element are changeable. For a library structure such as a table, column bindings and grouping are changeable, as are expressions and values in labels and other report items inside the structure, but not the structure itself. For example, you cannot add or remove columns or groups in a grid, list, or table element from a library. To hide columns or rows, set the width of a column to zero, or use the visibility properties to hide the element.

Discarding modifications to a library-based element

Development of a report design is an iterative process. In some cases, the initial modifications to an element from a library do not produce the required result. To revert to the original properties of an element from a library, select the Restore Properties button on Property Editor's tool bar. Figure 24-16 shows the location of this button. When you select this button, BIRT Report Designer prompts you to confirm that you want to discard your changes.

Using a library table having standardized data binding

A library table having standardized data binding is more straightforward to use than a table without standardized binding. The report developer sets aliases on columns in a data set before binding the data set to the table. Using the aliases binds the data columns to the data items in the table. Without standardized binding, the report developer must modify each data item in the table separately.

After adding the library table to a report design, check the position of each data item in the table. Then, edit the data set to bind to the table. Ensure that each alias matches the required location in the table. For example, in a table having a structure matching Figure 24-13, the data fields in the group header bind to columns named Data1 and Data2. To display CUSTOMERNUMBER and STATUS columns in the group header, set the aliases to Data1 and Data2 respectively as shown in Figure 24-17.

After updating the data set, bind the data set to the table. BIRT updates the data types of the table's column bindings to match the data type of the columns in the data set. Then, add aggregations to the table's bindings and bind the aggregations to data items. For example, add an aggregation to display the number of records in a group.

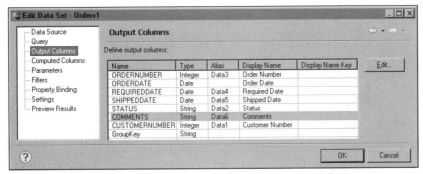

Figure 24-17   Data set using standardized aliases for output columns

Column bindings must exist for every data item in the table. If the report does not require as many data items as the library table provides, set the column bindings on the table for the unused data items to empty strings.

How to use a library table having standardized data binding

1 Drag the table from a library in Resource Explorer into the report design.

2 Create a data source and data set.

3 Add a standard alias to each column in the data set.

4 Select the table. In Property Editor, select Binding. In Data Set, select the data set. To retain the data field bindings, in Change Data Set, choose No.

5 Choose Add Aggregation to define calculations for data items in footers.

6 Double-click each data item in the footers. In Column Binding, open Expression Builder and select an aggregation from the available column bindings. Choose OK in Expression Builder and in Column Binding.

7 Edit the labels to display suitable headers.

8 Make any other changes, such as grouping and filtering. Figure 24-18 shows the grouped, four-column table element shown in Figure 24-13 customized to display customer information.

Customers by City	Label	Label	Label
City and Country	[Data1]	[Data2]	Label
Company		Credit Limit Contact	Phone
[Data3]		[Data4] [Data5]	[Data6]
[City Count Label] [City Count]		Data	Data
[Total Count Label] [Total Count]		Data	[Today]

Figure 24-18   Customization of the library table to show customers by city

Figure 24-20 shows the report produced by the table in Figure 24-18.

Customers by City

City and Country		Chatswood		Australia		
Company			Credit Limit	Contact		Phone
Souveniers And Things Co.			93,300	Adrian Huxley		+61 2 9495 8555
	City Count	1				

City and Country		Glen Waverly		Australia		
Company			Credit Limit	Contact		Phone
Australian Collectables, Ltd			60,300	Sean Clenahan		61-9-3844-6555
	City Count	1				

City and Country		White Plains		USA		
Company			Credit Limit	Contact		Phone
Mini Classics			102,700	Steve Frick		9145554562
	City Count	1				
	Total Count	122				August 17, 2010

Figure 24-19   Customers by city report using the customized library table

Figure 24-20 shows the same table element customized to display order information and the report produced by this table.

Orders by Status	Label	Label	Label
Customer:	[Data1]	[Data2]	Label
Order Number	Required by	Shipped on	Comments
[Data3]	[Data4]	[Data5]	[Data6]
Data	Data	Data	Data
Data	Data	Data	Data

Orders by Status

	Customer:	103		Status: Shipped	
Order Number		Required by		Shipped on	Comments
10123		May 29, 2003		May 22, 2003	
10298		Oct 5, 2004		Oct 1, 2004	
10345		Dec 1, 2004		Nov 26, 2004	
	Customer:	112		Status: Shipped	
Order Number		Required by		Shipped on	Comments
10124		May 29, 2003		May 25, 2003	Customer very concerned about the exact color of the models. There is high risk that he may dispute the order because there is a slight color mismatch

	Customer:	496		Status: Shipped	
Order Number		Required by		Shipped on	Comments
10138		Jul 16, 2003		Jul 13, 2003	
10360		Dec 22, 2004		Dec 18, 2004	
10399		Apr 12, 2005		Apr 3, 2005	

Figure 24-20   Customization of the library table to show orders by status

Using styles from a library

A report design supports use of a theme from a library to display report items using a complete set of predefined styles. A report design can use styles from a theme, from a CSS file, and from the report design itself. If any of these styles have the same names, BIRT uses the following rules to determine which style to use:

- If the report design defines a style, that style takes precedence over a style in a CSS file or a theme.

- A style from a CSS file takes precedence over a style in a theme.

- A style in a theme is used when there is no style defined in a CSS file or the report design itself.

To assign a theme to a report design, drag the theme from the library in Resource Explorer and drop it onto the report design. This action makes all the styles in that theme available to items in the report design. Any predefined styles in the theme, such as grid and table, take effect immediately on items in the design. Property Editor shows the theme that the report design is using, as shown in Figure 24-21.

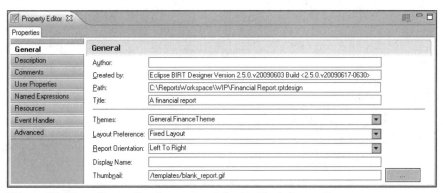

Figure 24-21   Properties for a report design that uses a theme

As shown in Figure 24-22, the styles in the theme appear in the Outline view in a new slot that has the same name as the theme.

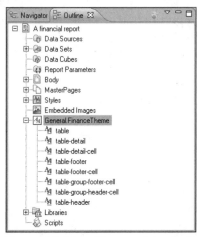

Figure 24-22   Theme styles in Outline

To revert a report design to use no theme, set the Themes property of the report design to None. After setting this property, the Outline view no longer shows a Themes item.

Because a library is dynamic, when a library developer adds styles to a theme, they become available to all report designs that use that theme. For example, consider a theme that does not have a style called table. Tables in a report design that uses this theme appear in the default style. Later, a library developer adds a style called table to the theme. Now the appearance of the tables in that design match the style defined in the theme. Figure 24-23 demonstrates the change in appearance of a table after a library developer adds a table style having a border to the theme in the library.

Order Number		Customer ID	Required on	Status
[Data1]		[Data2]	[Data3]	[Data4]
Count		Σ[RowCount]	Data	Data
🖫 Table				

— Table without a table style

Order Number		Customer ID	Required on	Status
[Data1]		[Data2]	[Data3]	[Data4]
Count		Σ[RowCount]	Data	Data
🖫 Table				

— Table after library includes a table style

Figure 24-23   Effect of new library styles on a report element

How to set a theme for a report design

1 In Resource Explorer, expand the library that contains the theme. Expand the Themes node in the library.

2 In the layout editor, click a blank area of the report. Then, drag a theme use from Resource Explorer and drop it in the layout editor.

How to drop a theme from a report design

To drop a theme, change the Theme property of the report root item.

1 In the Outline view, select the report root item, as shown in Figure 24-24. The report design's properties appear in Property Editor.

Figure 24-24   Report root item selected

2 In Property Editor, select None from the list in Themes, as shown in Figure 24-25.

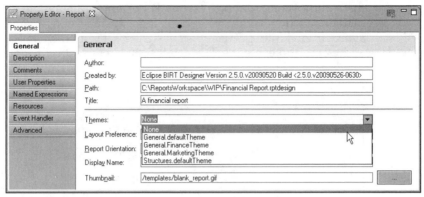

Figure 24-25   Dropping a theme in Property Editor

Trouble-shooting library problems

Sometimes, BIRT cannot apply changes from a modified library to a report design without additional action on the part of a report developer. The following list describes these situations:

- The name of the library changes or the library no longer exists.

- The library no longer contains an element that the report design uses.

- The name of the element in the library changes.

- The name of the element in the library refers to a different type of element from the element in the report design. For example, an image element in the report design derives from CompanyLogo in the library but the library element, CompanyLogo, is a text element.

If BIRT Report Designer opens a report design that has any of these problems, a warning message appears in the layout in place of the affected report element, as shown in Figure 24-26.

> Content of this report item is corrupted. If you wish to continue to work on this report, you should delete this item first. Failure to do so may further damage the report design file, and/or render the report designer unresponsive.

Figure 24-26   A report item that cannot access a library definition

To repair any of these conditions, you must add the missing library or correct the problem with the library. Alternatively, if you are familiar with XML, you can edit the XML source of the report design. If you choose to edit the XML, you should back up the report design first.

Sharing a report layout as a template

A template provides a custom layout and master pages for a suite of reports. Figure 24-27 shows how the library architecture extends to using templates. Libraries provide access to sets of report elements, and templates assemble them into a standard report layout. For example, a template for a bulk marketing letter can use a company logo, the marketing theme, and a data source from libraries. The report designs built from the template get addressees and content for the letter from a report-specific data set.

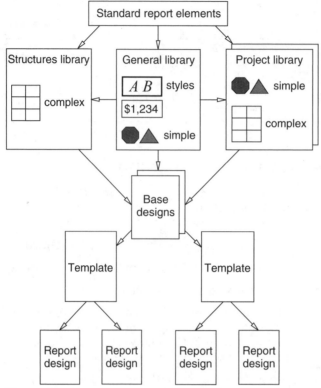

Figure 24-27   Project architecture using templates

Developing a custom template

A template can contain any report element, such as data sources, data sets, master pages, and any type of report item. BIRT Report Designer provides two ways to create a template. The creation options are

- Creating an empty template

  From the main menu, choose File➤New➤Template. Then, design the template in the same way as a report design. Use this technique if you have no existing report designs that have the required structure.

- Creating a template from an existing report design

  Open the report design. From the main menu, choose File➤Register Template with New Report Wizard. Use this technique if you have an existing report design that has the structure that you need.

When you create a template, BIRT prompts for template-specific properties. Figure 24-28 shows the properties and describes where they appear in the New Report wizard when a report developer creates a new report. The only required property is Display Name.

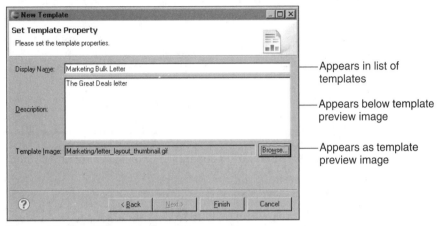

Appears in list of templates

Appears below template preview image

Appears as template preview image

Figure 24-28   Template-specific properties

When you create a template from a report design, the default image is the image from the template that you use to create the design. You can change the default image to a thumbnail by setting the template's Preview Image property in Property Editor.

Designing template report items

After you develop the structure of a template, you can choose to identify some or all of the items in the layout as template report items. When a report developer uses the template to create a report design, a template report item in the layout has a standard appearance and contains an informational message. Double-clicking the template report item activates the item as a standard report item and its appearance changes to match the properties that you set when you designed the template.

A template can contain both template report items and normal report items. Use template report items for items that you want the report developer to modify for the new report design. Use normal report items for items that the report developer does not need to change.

Typically, you first set simple report items, such as data elements inside a table element, to be template report items. Next, make the container into a template element, with overall instructions for the items inside it. To provide complex instructions for using a template, create a set of instructions for the template called a cheat sheet. Property Editor displays the Cheat sheet property in a template root's Advanced properties. To create a cheat sheet, use the Eclipse Plug-in Development Environment. For instructions, see the New Cheat Sheet Wizard topic in the Plug-in Development Environment Guide in the Eclipse online help.

How to create a template report item

1 Open or create a template.

2 Add a report item to the layout, or select an existing item in the layout. For example, Figure 24-29 shows a text item inside a table item and its appearance in the Outline view.

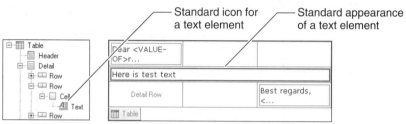

Figure 24-29 Standard appearance of text element and its icon

3 In the layout editor, right-click the report item, for example the text item. Choose Create Template Report Item.

4 In Create Template Report Item, type instructions to the report developer. These instructions explain how to use the report item. Figure 24-30 shows an example of some instructions.

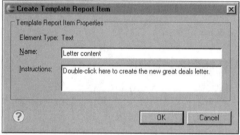

Figure 24-30 Providing instructions for a template report item

Choose OK. The report item now appears in the layout as a template report item. The template report item displays an icon appropriate to the type of report item and the instructions you provided and in Outline, the report item's icon changes to be a template item icon. Figure 24-31 shows how the text element shown in Figure 24-29 appears after conversion to a template report item.

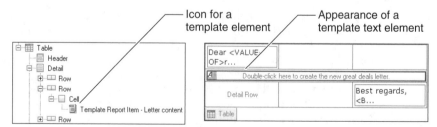

Figure 24-31 Text element as a template report item

Registering a template with the New Report wizard

BIRT Report Designer uses the template folder to contain custom templates. The default location of the template folder is the folder in the BIRT Report Designer user interface plug-in that contains the standard, built-in templates. Typically, this folder is not in a shared location, so each report developer in a team must define the same shared location as the template folder. Typically, the template folder is a directory on a shared network drive. When a developer chooses File→New→Report, BIRT Report Designer lists all templates in that folder as well as the standard BIRT templates.

To share a template across a team of report developers, publish the template to the template folder. To provide visual assistance to the report developer, associate an image, known as a thumbnail, with the template. This image appears in the preview area of the New Report wizard when the developer selects the template. The wizard displays both the templates in the shared template folder and the built-in templates.

How to set up a template folder

1 From the Eclipse main menu, choose Window→Preferences.

2 In Preferences, expand Report Design, and choose Template.

3 To navigate to the template folder, choose Select and select a folder. Then, choose OK.

4 In Preferences, choose OK.

How to publish a template

1 Open the report template.

2 Click in a blank area of the layout editor. The template's properties appear in the Property Editor.

3 To set the image that appears in the New Report wizard to a thumbnail or an image file on the file system, perform the following steps:

   1 In the Property Editor, next to Thumbnail, choose the ellipsis button.

   2 In Manage Thumbnail, specify the thumbnail for the template by performing one of the following steps:

      ❑ Select Generate from the report. Then, choose Generate.

      ❑ Select Browse from file system. Then, choose Browse. In Select an image file, navigate to and select the thumbnail image for the template. Then, choose Open.

      ❑ Select Import from shared resources. Then, choose Import. In Select an image file, navigate to and select the thumbnail image for the template, as shown in Figure 24-32. Then, choose OK.

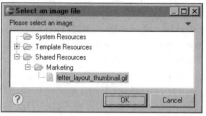

Figure 24-32   Choosing a thumbnail image from shared resources

The thumbnail image appears in Manage Thumbnail, as shown in Figure 24-33.

Figure 24-33   A thumbnail image selected for the template

3   In Manage Thumbnail, choose OK. The name of the thumbnail appears in the Thumbnail property in the Property Editor.

4   Save the report template.

4   Choose File➤Register Template with New Report Wizard.

5   In Publish to Template Folder, check the properties. Make any corrections to the display name and description, as shown in Figure 24-34.

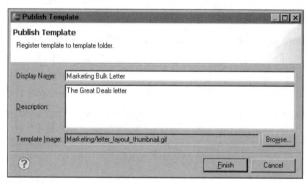

Figure 24-34   Publishing a template

6 To change the template image, choose Browse. Then, select an image from the available resources and choose OK.

7 Choose Finish.

Using a custom template

To use a custom template as a starting point for a report design, you must define the template folder. The New Report wizard includes all custom templates in the list of available templates. Figure 24-35 shows an example of a custom template that has a preview image and a description.

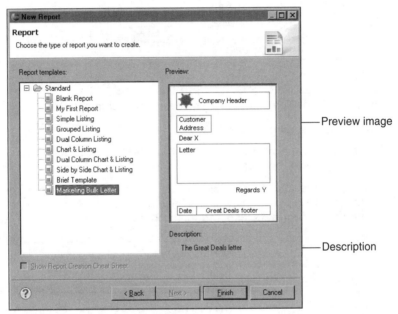

Figure 24-35   Using a custom template

If the template does not supply some of the optional template properties, the New Report wizard displays default values. Figure 24-36 shows how such a template appears. No description appears for this template. Because this template does not specify a preview image, BIRT Report Designer displays a thumbnail representation of the template's layout in Preview.

After you choose Finish in the New Report wizard, BIRT Report Designer displays the layout of the template in the layout editor. All the report elements in the template, such as data sources, data sets, and visual report items, are available for editing in the same way that you edit report elements in one of BIRT's predefined templates.

A template can include template report items in the layout as well as standard report items. You can see the appearance of a template report item in Figure 24-31, earlier in this chapter. To edit a template report item, follow the instructions displayed in the item.

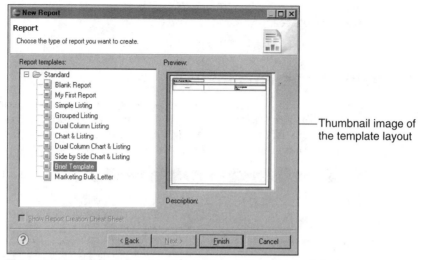

Thumbnail image of
the template layout

Figure 24-36 Template having no description or template image

How to use a template report item

1 Create a report design. In the New Report wizard, choose the Chart and
Listing predefined template.

2 Perform the steps in the cheat sheet adjacent to the layout editor. The final
instruction is to edit the chart. This template item appears in the layout
with an appropriate icon and instructional text, as shown in Figure 24-37.

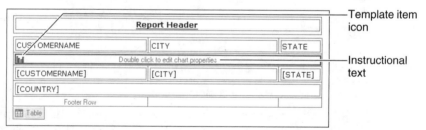Template item
icon

Instructional
text

Figure 24-37 Using a template report item

When you double-click the template report item, BIRT changes the
template report item to a standard report item. The chart now appears as a
standard chart element in the layout.

3 Double-click the chart element. The chart builder appears.

4 Set up the chart as described earlier in this book.

5 To discard the changes that you made to the chart, right-click the chart
element, and choose Undo Edit Chart.

6 Right-click the chart element again, and choose Undo Transfer to Report
Item. The chart now appears as the original template report item, as
shown in Figure 24-37.

Localizing Text

When inserting label and text elements, you typically type the text that you want the report to display. Use literal, or static, text if a report will always be viewed in one language or locale. If, however, a report will be translated into multiple languages or regional dialects, use resource keys rather than static text. The resource keys are translated, or localized, in resource files.

If you are not familiar with resource keys or resource files, think of resource keys as variables, and resource files as text files in which the variables are set to their values. If a report needs to appear in three languages, create three resource files to define text values for each language. When a report runs, BIRT uses the machine's current locale, the resource keys, and the resource files to find the appropriate text value to display. Figure 25-1 shows the functions of resource files and resource keys in a localized report.

Resource files for English, Spanish, and French locales. Each file contains the resource key, greeting, and the localized version.

Report design uses the resource key, greeting, in a label element.

Report output when run in English, Spanish, and French locales, respectively.

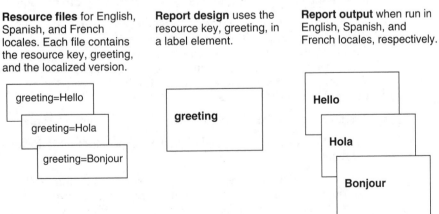

Figure 25-1   Resource keys in resource files, the report design, and the report

You can specify resource keys for the following items:

- Static text in label, text, and chart elements. For example, you can localize report titles, column headings, chart titles, and other static labels.

- Display names of data set fields or computed fields. These names appear in the report design.

- Text values that come from a data set field. Data values of date or number type do not need to be localized. BIRT automatically displays numbers and dates according to the locale to which the report user's machine is configured.

- Prompt text and help text associated with report parameters.

Overview of the localization process

The localization processes are similar for BIRT reports and for Java applications. This section provides an overview of the entire process. The steps that you perform using BIRT Report Designer are described in more detail in later sections in this chapter. The basic steps are as follows:

- Create the default resource file. The resource file is a text file with a .properties file-name extension. In this file, define all the resource keys in key=value format, as shown in the following examples:

```
hello=Hello
thanks=Thank you
```

  If you know the text strings that you want to localize, you can create the resource file in an external text editor and define the keys before building a report. Alternatively, create the resource file in BIRT Report Designer and define keys as you add label and text elements to the report.

- If you created the default resource file in an external text editor, place the file in the resource folder. If you create the resource file in BIRT Report Designer, the file is created in the resource folder. You specify the location of the resource folder in the Preferences page, which you access by choosing Window→Preferences from the main menu, then choosing Report Design→Resource.

- Assign the resource file to the report that you want to localize.

- For each report parameter, label, text, or chart element to localize, choose the resource key to use.

- When you finish defining the keys in the default resource file, create a resource file for each language that the report will support. The file name must include the language code and, if necessary, the region code. The file name must be in the following format:

```
<filename>_<ISO 639 language code>_
    <ISO 3166 region code>.properties
```

For example, MyResources_en_US.properties is for U.S. English, and MyResources_en_UK.properties is for British English. For a list of supported language and region codes, see the Java reference documentation at the following URL:

```
http://www.oracle.com/technetwork/java/index.html
```

- In the localized resource files, use the same set of keys that are defined in the default resource file, and set their values to the translated strings. A quick way to create the keys is to make a copy of the default resource file, then edit the values. Unless you are multilingual, this task is typically done by a team of translators.

  The following examples show resource keys and values that could appear in two localized versions of the same information:

```
MyResources_fr.properties:

   hello=Bonjour
   thanks=Merci
```

```
MyResources_es.properties:

   hello=Hola
   thanks=Gracias
```

- Use the native2ascii command to convert the localized resource files to a format that the Java platform can use. The command requires an input file name and an output file name, so copy the resource file to a temporary file, then use the correct file name as the output file name.

  The following example converts a Japanese resource file:

```
copy MyResource_ja.properties temp.properties
native2ascii -encoding SJIS temp.properties
   MyResource_ja.properties
```

  For more information about native2ascii and the list of supported encoding character sets, see the Java reference documentation at the following URL:

```
http://www.oracle.com/technetwork/java/index.html
```

- Place all the localized resource files in the resource folder. When a report runs, BIRT uses the appropriate resource file to find the localized text values to display. If BIRT cannot find a resource file for a specific locale, it uses the default resource file.

Assigning a resource file to a report

You can add as many resource files as needed to the resource folder. Different reports in a project can use different resource files, and you can assign multiple resource files to a report. Assign a resource file to a report by completing one of the following tasks:

- Select a resource file that currently resides in the resource folder.

- Create a new resource file in BIRT Report Designer, then assign it to the report.

If you select an existing file, you can assign the keys that are defined in that file to report parameters, label, text, or chart elements. If you create a new resource file, it contains no keys. You define the keys as you add report parameters, label, or text elements to the report.

How to assign a resource file to a report

1 In the layout editor, select the report by clicking in an empty area on the report page.

2 In Property Editor, under Properties, choose Resources. Property Editor displays the Resources page, as shown in Figure 25-2.

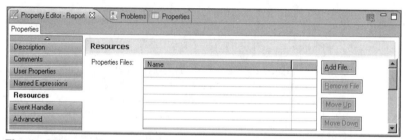

Figure 25-2   Property Editor displaying the Resources page

3 Choose Add File, next to Properties Files.

4 In Browse Resource Files, indicate which resource file to use by completing one of the following tasks:

- To use a resource file that currently exists in the resource folder, select the resource file displayed under Shared Resources.

- To create a new resource file using BIRT Report Designer, select a folder. In New File Name, type a name for the new resource file, such as CustomerReportResources.properties, as shown in Figure 25-3. You must type the .properties file-name extension.

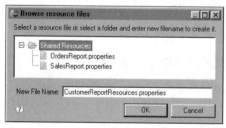

Figure 25-3   Browse Resource Files showing a new resource file

5 Choose OK.

The name of the resource file appears in Properties Files in the Resources page of Property Editor. The report uses the selected resource file. You can specify a different resource file to use at any time. You can also delete a resource file by choosing Remove File in the Resources page.

Assigning resource keys

After assigning a resource file to a report, localize text by assigning resource keys to the report elements that display text. The procedure varies depending on the report element. For most elements, you can select existing keys or create new keys.

Before creating a new key, review the list carefully. You do not want to define new keys if they are already available. For example, you do not want five different keys for the Customer Name label. To make maintenance and look-up of keys easier, use a consistent naming convention. For example, avoid ambiguous or inconsistently named keys, such as Name, customer name, and Name_Contact.

Assigning a resource key to a label or text element

Assign a resource key that you defined earlier, or define a new resource key, then assign it to the label or text element.

How to assign an existing resource key to a label or text element

1 In the layout editor, select the label or text element that contains the text to localize.

2 In Property Editor, under Properties, choose Localization, as shown in Figure 25-4.

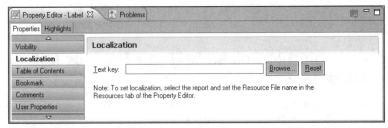

Figure 25-4   Property Editor displaying the Localization page

3 Choose Browse next to the Text key field. This button is enabled only if you have already assigned a resource file to the report.

Select Key displays the current list of keys and values that are defined in the resource file that the report uses, as shown in Figure 25-5.

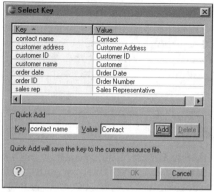

Figure 25-5   Select Key

4   Select the key to assign to the label or text element, then choose OK. In the layout editor, the label or text element displays the value that corresponds to the key.

How to define a new resource key

1   Select the label or text element that contains the text to localize.

2   In Property Editor, choose Localization.

3   Choose Browse next to the Text key field. This button is enabled only if you have already assigned a resource file to the report.

Select Key displays the list of keys and values that are defined in the resource file that the report uses.

4   If the key you want to assign is not in the list, add a new key as follows:

    1   In Quick Add, provide a key and value, then choose Add. The key is added to the resource file and appears in the list of keys.

    2   To assign the key to the label or text element, select the key from the list, then choose OK. In the layout editor, the label or text element displays the value that corresponds to the key.

Changing localized text in a label or text element to static text

If you change your mind about localizing a label or text element, remove the resource key and use static text instead.

How to remove a resource key from a label or text element

1   Select the label or text element.

2   In Property Editor, choose Localization. Property Editor displays localization information for the selected element, as shown in Figure 25-6.

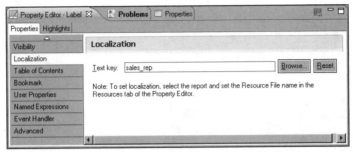

Figure 25-6   Localization properties for an element

3 Choose Reset. The label or text element displays either nothing or the default static text, if you specified any default text when you inserted the element.

Assigning a resource key to chart text

Localize static text in a chart, such as the chart title and axis titles, by assigning a resource key to the chart text. You can only select an existing key. If the key that you want to use for the chart text is not available, edit the resource file to add a new key. Information about this task appears later in this chapter.

How to assign a resource key to chart text

1 In the layout editor, double-click the chart element to open the chart builder, then choose Format Chart.

2 Navigate to the section for the chart part to localize. For example, to localize the chart title, navigate to the Chart Area section. To localize the *y*-axis title, navigate to the Y-Axis section. Figure 25-7 shows the portion of the chart builder that you use to work with the *y*-axis.

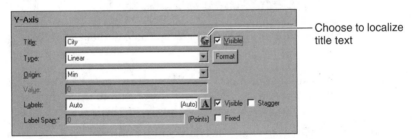

Figure 25-7   Localizing title text on the *y*-axis

 3 Choose the button that is next to the field to localize. For the example in Figure 25-7, choose the button at the right of the Title field.

Externalize Text appears, as shown in Figure 25-8. Lookup Key displays, by default, the first key in the resource file. Default Value displays the current text label applied to the chart element.

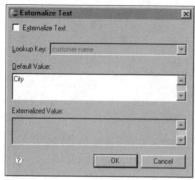

Figure 25-8   Externalize Text displaying default settings

4   Assign a resource key to the chart text as follows:

1   Select Externalize Text. The list of resource keys is enabled in the drop-down list that is next to Lookup Key.

2   From the drop-down list, select a key to assign to the chart text. The value that corresponds to the key that you selected appears in Externalized Value, as shown in Figure 25-9.

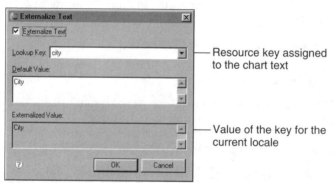

Resource key assigned to the chart text

Value of the key for the current locale

Figure 25-9   Resource key and its externalized value

3   Choose OK.

   The Title field in Edit Chart shows the title's display value. To use a different resource key, choose the button to open the Externalize Text dialog, and select a different key from the Lookup Key list.

5   Choose Finish to close the chart builder and return to the layout editor. In the report design, the chart text displays the value that corresponds to the key that you selected.

Changing localized chart text to static text

If you change your mind about localizing text in a chart, remove the resource key and use static text instead.

How to remove a resource key from chart text

1 Navigate to the Format Chart section for the chart part to change.

 2 Choose the Externalize Text Editor button that is next to the field to change.

Externalize Text displays the resource key that is assigned to the chart part, as shown in Figure 25-10.

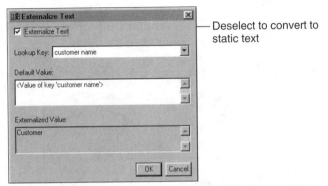

Figure 25-10 Externalize Text displaying the assigned resource key

3 Deselect Externalize Text.

4 In Default Value, type the static text to display for the chart part, then choose OK. The Title field in the chart builder shows the title's new display value.

5 Choose OK to return to the layout editor. In the report design, the chart displays the static text you typed.

Assigning a resource key to a data value

Localizing text data that originates from a data source requires that you know the data values at report design time because you map each data value to a resource key when you design the report. If you do not map a data value to a resource key, the report displays the original data value. Assuming the original values are in English, if you do not map every value in the data set field, the report displays unmapped values in English and mapped values in the language specified by the user's machine locale.

How to assign a resource key to a data value

1 In the layout editor, select the data element that displays the values to localize.

2 In Property Editor, choose the Map tab.

3 In Map List, choose Add to create a map rule.

4 In New Map Rule, specify the following information:

1 In the first field, select from the drop-down list, Value of this data item. The field displays the expression that refers to the data set field, which contains the values to localize.

2 In the second field, select an operator from the list. For example:

   Equal to

3 In the third field, specify the value to localize, using one of the following steps:

   ❑ Choose <Select value...> from the drop-down list, as shown in Figure 25-11. In Select Value, select a value.

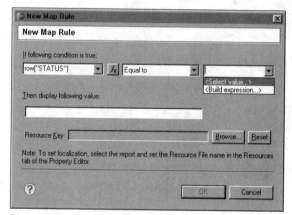

Figure 25-11   New Map Rule displaying the options for specifying the value to map

   ❑ Choose <Build expression...> to use the expression builder to write an expression.

   ❑ Type the value to replace. For example:

   "Shipped"

   You must enclose string values in quotation marks (" ").

4 Skip the next field, "Then display following value". Enter a value for this field only to map the data value to a literal text value.

5 Specify a resource key. Choose Browse to select a resource key. You can access resource keys only if you have assigned a resource file to the report.

   Select Key displays the current list of keys and values that are defined in the resource file that the report uses.

   1 Perform one of the following steps:

   ❑ Select an existing key to assign to the data value.

   ❑ Under Quick Add, create a new key and value, choose Add, then select the key from the list.

2 Choose OK to confirm the resource key selection. The resource key appears in the Resource Key field in New Map Rule. Figure 25-12 shows a completed map rule, which maps the value Cancelled to the localized value defined for the resource key cancelled.

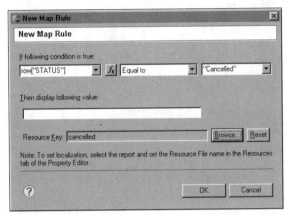

Figure 25-12   Map rule that maps a data value to a resource key

6 Choose OK to save the map rule. The rule appears in Map List.

5 Repeat steps 3 through 4 to create additional rules, one for each data value to replace. Figure 25-13 shows an example of six map rules created for a data element that displays order status.

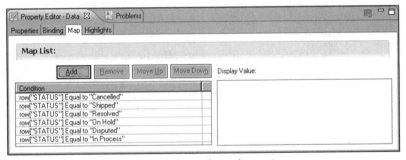

Figure 25-13   Six map rules for a data element

Assigning a resource key to a report parameter

You can localize the following items associated with a report parameter:

- The text that prompts report users to supply a value for a report parameter

- The help text provided for a report parameter

- The static values displayed in radio buttons, a list box, or a combo box

Figure 25-14 shows the dialog box, Enter Parameters, that displays report parameters to the report user. The figure also identifies the text that you can localize, including prompt text and values that appear next to radio buttons and in the list boxes. In Enter Parameters, a report parameter's prompt text appears next to the curly braces symbol, **{ }**.

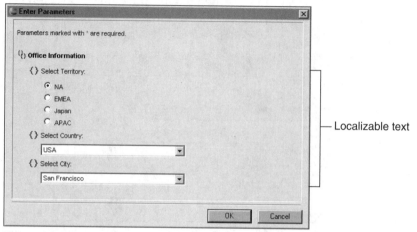

Figure 25-14   Text that can be localized in Enter Parameters

How to assign a resource key to a report parameter prompt text or help text

These instructions assume that you have already created the report parameters and assigned a resource file to the report.

1 In Data Explorer, under Report Parameters, select the report parameter to localize. Do not double-click the parameter, which opens the Edit Parameter dialog.

2 In Property Editor, choose Localization.

3 To localize the report parameter's prompt text, choose Browse next to the Prompt text key field. To localize the report parameter's help text, choose Browse next to the Help text key field.

Select Key displays the current list of keys and values that are defined in the resource file that the report uses.

4 Perform one of the following steps:

- Select an existing key to assign to the report parameter.

- Under Quick Add, create a new key, choose Add, then select the key from the list.

5 Choose OK.

How to assign a resource key to a report parameter value

These instructions assume that you have created the report parameter that displays a list of values in a list box, combo box, or radio buttons. The values must be static. Values that are derived dynamically at run time cannot be localized.

1 In Data Explorer, under Report Parameters, double-click the report parameter that contains the values to localize.

2 In Edit Parameter, in the Selection values table, select the value to localize, then choose Edit. Edit Selection Choice appears. Figure 25-15 shows an example of a radio button value (Shipped) selected for editing.

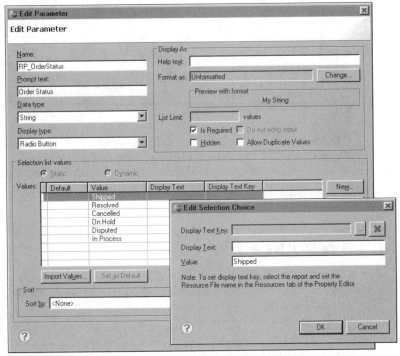

Figure 25-15   A parameter value selected for editing

3 In Edit Selection Choice, choose the ellipsis (...) button next to the Display Text Key field. This button is enabled only if you have already assigned a resource file to the report.

Select Key displays the current list of keys and values that are defined in the resource file that the report uses.

4 In Select Key, perform one of the following steps, then choose OK:

■ Select an existing key to assign to the report parameter value.

■ Under Quick Add, create a new key, choose Add, then select the key from the list.

5 Choose OK to apply the key to the report parameter value.

In Edit Parameter, the Selection values table displays the actual value, the display value that the user sees, and the resource key mapped to the display value. Figure 25-16 shows an example of a localized parameter value.

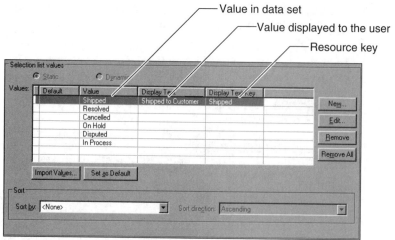

Value in data set

Value displayed to the user

Resource key

Figure 25-16   The Selection values table in the Edit Parameter dialog
displaying information about a localized parameter value

6   Repeat steps 2 to 5 to localize the remainder of the parameter values.

Editing a resource file

It is often necessary to change the values of keys or add new keys as you
design a report. You can accomplish these tasks through the localization
properties page of Property Editor for a label or text element, but it is easier
to edit the resource file directly.

When you edit the values of keys, the values in the report are updated
automatically. If you change a key name or delete a key, report text that uses
that key does not display a value because BIRT cannot find the key. It is best
to limit your edits to adding new keys or editing the values of the existing
keys.

When editing a resource file, to use spaces in the keys, precede the space with
a backslash (\). For example:

```
order\ ID=Order Number
```

When you add a key through the Select Key dialog, and you type order ID as
the key, BIRT adds the backslash, which you see when the resource file is
open.

Be aware that when you edit a resource file after it has been translated into
locale-specific resource files, those locale-specific resource files must be
updated also. Otherwise, the report does not display the intended text when
it runs in other locales. For this reason, you should create localized resource
files only after you have finalized the default resource file and finished
creating and testing the report.

How to edit a resource file

Choose File→Open File, navigate to the resource folder, then double-click the resource (.properties) file. The file that opens in the report editor displays the list of keys and their values, as shown in Figure 25-17.

Edit the file as needed, then save and close it.

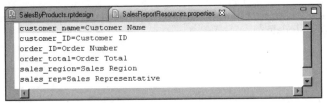

Figure 25-17   Resource file opened in the report editor

Previewing a report in different locales

After completing all the localization tasks, preview the report in all the locales that it supports to verify that the localized text appears properly. BIRT Report Designer provides an easy way to preview a report in any locale without changing your machine's locale. You can test the report in a different locale by setting the locale option in BIRT's preview preferences.

How to preview a report in a different locale

1   Choose Window→Preferences.

2   On the left side of the dialog, expand Report Design, then choose Preview. The preview properties appear, as shown in Figure 25-18.

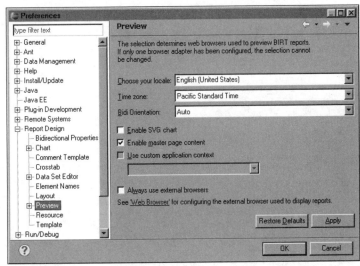

Figure 25-18   Preview preferences in BIRT Report Designer

3 In Choose your locale, select a locale in which to preview the report, then choose OK. The selected locale applies only to previewed reports. It does not change the locale that your machine uses, nor does it change the localized text that appears in the report design.

4 Preview the report. The localized text appears in the language for the selected locale.

5 To preview the report in another language, repeat the previous steps to select a new locale.

abstract base class

A class that defines the requirements and behavior of descendant classes by specifying methods and variables. An abstract base class does not support the creation of instances.

Related terms
class, descendant class, method, variable

Contrast with
object

abstraction

A technique that reduces duplication of program code. Abstraction provides a framework for related classes in an object-oriented system.

Related terms
class, object-oriented programming

aggregate function

A function that performs a calculation over a set of data rows. For example, SUM calculates the sum of values of a specified numeric field over a set of data rows. Examples of aggregate functions include AVERAGE, COUNT, MAX, MIN, and SUM.

Related terms
data row, field, function, value

Contrast with
aggregate row, aggregate value

aggregate row

A single row that summarizes data from a group of rows returned by a query. A SQL (Structured Query Language) query that includes an aggregate expression and a Group By clause returns one or more aggregate rows. For example, a row that totals all orders made by one customer is an aggregate row.

Related terms
data, group, query, row, SQL (Structured Query Language)

Contrast with
aggregate value, data row, SQL SELECT statement

aggregate value

The result of applying an aggregate function to a set of data rows. For example, a set of data rows has a field, SPEED, which contains values: 20, 10, 30, 15, 40. Applying the aggregate function MAX to dataSetRow("SPEED"), produces the aggregate value, 40, which is the maximum value for the field.

Related terms
aggregate function, data row, field, value

alias

An alternative name:

1 In a SQL SELECT statement, a name given to a database table or column.

2 A name given to a data-set column for use in an expression or in code in a script method.

Related terms
column, data set, database, expression, method, SQL SELECT statement, table

Contrast with
display name

analytics

The iterative process of analyzing data to inform and plan business decisions. Analytics uses drill-down and statistical techniques to examine the same information in both detail and overview forms. Analytics tools promote business intelligence goals by supporting inspection, cleaning, and transformation of data.

Related term
data

ancestor class

A class in the inheritance hierarchy from which a particular class directly or indirectly derives.

Related terms
class, inheritance, hierarchy

Contrast with
class hierarchy, descendant class, subclass, superclass

applet

A small desktop application that performs a simple task, for example, a Java program that runs directly from the web browser.

Related terms
application, Java

application

A complete, self-contained program that performs a specific set of related tasks.

Contrast with
applet

application programming interface (API)

A set of routines, including functions, methods, and procedures, that exposes application functionality to support integration and extend applications.

Related terms
application, function, method, procedure

argument

A constant, expression, or variable that supplies data to a function or method.

Related terms
constant, data, expression, function, method, variable

Contrast with
parameter

array   A data variable consisting of sequentially indexed elements that have the same data type. Each element has a common name, a common data type, and a unique index number identifier. Changes to an element of an array do not affect other elements.

Related terms
data, element, data type, string, variable

assignment statement

A statement that assigns a value to a variable. For example:

```
StringToDisplay = "My Name"
```

Related terms
statement, value, variable

attribute

A property of an element defined as a name-value pair. For example, in the following line, the attribute defines a Universal Resource Identifier (URI) that links to a web page:

```
<a href="http://www.eclipse.org">
```

Related terms
element, property, Universal Resource Identifier (URI), web page

Contrast with
Extensible Markup Language (XML)

base unit

A unit of time displayed on a time-scale axis in a chart.

Related term
chart

Contrast with
tick

bidirectional text

Text written in multiple languages, at least one of which reads from right-to-left (RTL) and one of which reads from left-to-right (LTR). When right-to-left text, such as Arabic, mixes with left-to-right text, such as English, in the same paragraph, each type of text is written in its own direction.

BigDecimal class

A Java class used for numeric calculations requiring decimal, floating point arithmetic. A BigDecimal value consists of an arbitrary precision integer and a 32-bit integer scale, for example 1024x10 to the power of 3. This class provides accessor methods that support getting and setting the value.

Related terms
class, Java, method, value

Contrast with
Double class, Float class, Integer class

BIRT

See Business Intelligence and Reporting Tools (BIRT).

BIRT extension

See Business Intelligence and Reporting Tools (BIRT) extension.

BIRT Report Designer

See Business Intelligence and Reporting Tools (BIRT) Report Designer.

BIRT technology

See Business Intelligence and Reporting Tools (BIRT) technology.

bookmark

An expression that identifies a report element. For example, a table of contents uses a bookmark to navigate to a topic.

Related terms
Business Intelligence and Reporting Tools (BIRT) technology, expression, report element, table of contents

Boolean expression

An expression that evaluates to True or False. For example, Total > 3000 is a Boolean expression. If the condition is met, the condition evaluates to True. If the condition is not met, the condition evaluates to False.

Related term
expression

Contrast with
conditional expression, numeric expression

breakpoint

In BIRT Report Designer, a place marker in a program being debugged. At a breakpoint, execution pauses so the report developer can examine and edit data values.

Related terms

Business Intelligence and Reporting Tools (BIRT) Report Designer, data, debug, value

bridge class

A class that maps the functionality of one class to the similar behavior of another class. For example, a Java Database Connectivity (JDBC)-open database connectivity (ODBC) bridge class enables an application that uses the standard JDBC protocol to communicate with a database through the ODBC protocol.

Related terms

application, class, database, Java Database Connectivity (JDBC), open database connectivity (ODBC), protocol

Business Intelligence and Reporting Tools (BIRT)

 An analytics and reporting platform built on Eclipse, the industry standard for open-source software development. BIRT provides a complete solution for extracting data and presenting the results in a formatted document.

Related terms

analytics, data, Eclipse, report

Contrast with

Business Intelligence and Reporting Tools (BIRT) extension

Business Intelligence and Reporting Tools (BIRT) Chart Engine

A tool that supports designing and deploying charts outside a report design. Using this engine, Java developers embed charting capabilities into an application. BIRT Chart Engine is a set of Eclipse plug-ins and Java archive (.jar) files. The chart engine is also known as the charting library.

Related terms

application, Business Intelligence and Reporting Tools (BIRT), chart, design, Java, Java archive (.jar) file, library, plug-in, report

Contrast with

Business Intelligence and Reporting Tools (BIRT) Report Engine

Business Intelligence and Reporting Tools (BIRT) Demo Database

A sample database used in tutorials for BIRT Report Designer and BIRT RCP Report Designer. This package provides this sample database in Derby, Microsoft Access, and MySQL Enterprise formats.

Related terms

Business Intelligence and Reporting Tools (BIRT), Business Intelligence and Reporting Tools (BIRT) Report Designer, Business Intelligence and Reporting Tools (BIRT) Rich Client Platform (RCP) Report Designer, database

Business Intelligence and Reporting Tools (BIRT) extension

A related set of extension points that adds custom functionality to the BIRT platform. BIRT extensions include

- Charting extension

- Rendering extension

- Report item extension

Related terms

Business Intelligence and Reporting Tools (BIRT), charting extension, extension, extension point, rendering extension, report item extension

Business Intelligence and Reporting Tools (BIRT) Report Designer

A tool that builds BIRT report designs and previews reports generated from the designs. BIRT Report Designer is a set of plug-ins to the Eclipse platform and includes BIRT Chart Engine, BIRT Demo Database, and BIRT Report Engine. A report developer who uses this tool can access the full capabilities of the Eclipse platform.

Related terms

Business Intelligence and Reporting Tools (BIRT), Business Intelligence and Reporting Tools (BIRT) Chart Engine, Business Intelligence and Reporting Tools (BIRT) Demo Database, Business Intelligence and Reporting Tools (BIRT) Report Engine, design, Eclipse platform, plug-in, report

Contrast with

Business Intelligence and Reporting Tools (BIRT) Rich Client Platform (RCP) Report Designer

Business Intelligence and Reporting Tools (BIRT) Report Engine

A component that supports deploying BIRT charting, reporting, and viewing capabilities as a stand-alone application or on an application server. BIRT Report Engine consists of a set of Eclipse plug-ins, Java archive (.jar) files, web archive (.war) files, and web applications.

Related terms

application, Business Intelligence and Reporting Tools (BIRT), chart, Eclipse, Java archive (.jar) file, plug-in, report, view, web archive (.war) file

Contrast with

Business Intelligence and Reporting Tools (BIRT) Chart Engine

Business Intelligence and Reporting Tools (BIRT) Rich Client Platform (RCP) Report Designer

A stand-alone tool that builds BIRT report designs and previews reports generated from the designs. BIRT RCP Report Designer uses the Eclipse Rich Client Platform. This tool includes BIRT Chart Engine, BIRT Demo Database, and BIRT Report Engine. BIRT RCP Report Designer supports report design and preview functionality without the additional overhead of the full Eclipse platform. BIRT RCP Report Designer does not support the Java-based scripting and the report debugger functionality the full Eclipse platform provides. BIRT RCP Report Designer can use, but not create, BIRT extensions.

Related terms

Business Intelligence and Reporting Tools (BIRT), Business Intelligence and Reporting Tools (BIRT) Chart Engine, Business Intelligence and Reporting Tools (BIRT) Demo Database, Business Intelligence and Reporting Tools (BIRT) extension, Business Intelligence and Reporting Tools (BIRT) Report

Engine, debug, design, Eclipse platform, Eclipse Rich Client Platform (RCP), extension, Java, report

Contrast with
Business Intelligence and Reporting Tools (BIRT) Report Designer

Business Intelligence and Reporting Tools (BIRT) Samples

A sample of a BIRT report item extension and examples of BIRT charting applications. The report item extension sample is an Eclipse platform plug-in. The charting applications use BIRT Chart Engine. Java developers use these examples as models of how to design custom report items and embed charting capabilities in an application.

Related terms
application, Business Intelligence and Reporting Tools (BIRT), Business Intelligence and Reporting Tools (BIRT) Chart Engine, chart, design, Eclipse platform, Java, plug-in, report, report item, report item extension

Business Intelligence and Reporting Tools (BIRT) technology

A set of Java applications and application programming interfaces (API) that support the design and deployment of a business report. BIRT applications include BIRT Report Designer, BIRT RCP Report Designer, and a report viewer web application servlet. The BIRT Java APIs provide programmatic access to BIRT functionality.

Related terms
application, application programming interface (API), Business Intelligence and Reporting Tools (BIRT), Business Intelligence and Reporting Tools (BIRT) Report Designer, Business Intelligence and Reporting Tools (BIRT) Rich Client Platform (RCP) Report Designer, design, Java, report, report viewer servlet

cascading parameters

Report parameters that have a hierarchical relationship, for example:

```
Country
   State
      City
```

In a group of cascading parameters, each report parameter displays a set of values. When a report user selects a value from the top-level parameter, the selected value determines the values that the next parameter displays, and so on. Cascading parameters display only relevant values to the user. Figure G-1 shows cascading parameters as they appear to a report user.

Related terms
hierarchy, parameter, report, value

cascading style sheet (CSS)

A file containing a set of rules that attaches formats and styles to specified HyperText Markup Language (HTML) elements. For example, a cascading style sheet can specify the color, font, and size of an HTML heading.

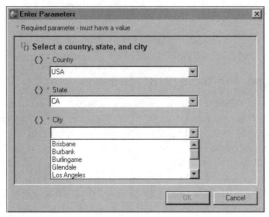

Figure G-1   Cascading parameters

Related terms
element, font, format, HyperText Markup Language (HTML), style

Contrast with
template

case sensitivity

A condition in which the letter case is significant for the purposes of comparison. For example, "McManus" does not match "MCMANUS" or "mcmanus" in a case-sensitive environment.

category

1 In an area, bar, line, step, or stock chart, one of the discrete values that organizes data on an axis that does not use a numerical scale. Typically, the x-axis of a chart displays category values. In a pie chart, category values are called orthogonal axis values and define which sectors appear in a pie.

2 A set of values that can be organized into a hierarchy.

Related terms
chart, data, hierarchy, value

Contrast with
series

cell   The intersection of a row and a column that displays a value in a cross tab, grid element, or table element. Figure G-2 shows a cell.

Related terms
column, cross tab, grid element, row, table element, value

character

An elementary mark that represents data, usually in the form of a graphic spatial arrangement of connected or adjacent strokes, such as a letter or a digit. A character is independent of font size and other display properties. For example, an uppercase C is a character.

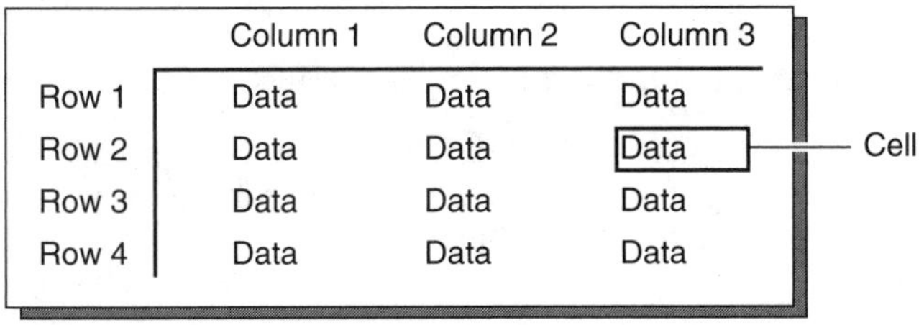

Figure G-2   Cells in a cross tab

Related terms
data, font, property

Contrast with
character set, glyph, string

character set

A mapping of specific characters to code points. For example, in most character sets, the letter A maps to the hexadecimal value 0x21.

Related terms
character, code point

Contrast with
locale

chart   A graphic representation of data or the relationships among sets of data, for example a bar, bubble, line, meter, pie, radar, or stock chart.

Related term
data

Contrast with
chart element

chart element

A report item that displays values from a data set in the form of a chart.

Related terms
chart, data set, report item, value

Contrast with
charting extension

chart engine

See Business Intelligence and Reporting Tools (BIRT) Chart Engine.

charting extension

An extension that adds a new chart type, a new component to an existing chart type, or a new user interface component to the BIRT chart engine.

Related terms
Business Intelligence and Reporting Tools (BIRT) Chart Engine, chart, extension

Contrast with
report item extension

charting library

See Business Intelligence and Reporting Tools (BIRT) Chart Engine.

class A set of methods and variables that defines the properties and behavior of an object. All objects of a given class are identical in form and behavior, but can contain different data in their variables.

Related terms
data, method, object, property, variable

Contrast with
subclass, superclass

class hierarchy

A tree structure representing inheritance relationships among a set of classes.

Related terms
class, inheritance

class name

A unique name for a class that permits unambiguous references to its public methods and variables.

Related terms
class, method, variable

class variable

A variable that all instances of a class share. An object-oriented environment makes only one copy of a class variable. The value of the class variable is the same for all instances of the class, for example, the taxRate variable in an Order class.

Related terms
class, object-oriented programming, value, variable

code point

A hexadecimal value in a character set. Every character in a character set is represented by a code point. The computer uses the code point to process the character.

Related terms
character, character set, value

column 1 A vertical sequence of cells in a cross tab, grid element, or table element. Figure G-3 shows a column in a cross tab.

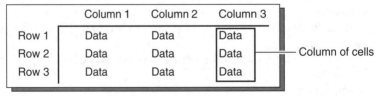

Figure G-3   Column in a cross tab

2 A named field in a database table or query. For each data row, the column can have a different value, called the column value. The term column refers to the definition of the column, not to any particular value. Figure G-4 shows the names of columns in a database table.

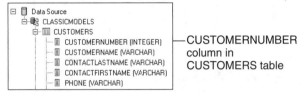

Figure G-4 Columns in a database table

Related terms
cell, cross tab, data row, database, field, grid element, query, table, table element, value

column binding

A named column that defines an expression specifying what data to return. For each piece of data to display in a report, there must be a column binding. Column bindings form a required intermediate layer between data-set data and report elements.

Related terms
column, data, data set, expression, report, report element

column key

An expression used to group data rows into columns and sub-columns in a cross-tab element.

Related terms
column, cross-tab element, data row, expression, group

Contrast with
row key

combination chart

A chart in which multiple data series appear as different chart types. In Figure G-5, for example, the data series for 2004 appears as a line, which stands out as the year of highest annual revenue.

Related terms
chart, data, series

Contrast with
chart element

comma-separated values (CSV) file

A flat file format that stores data in a tabular structure, separating the rows by new-line characters, the column values by commas, and delimiting the column values containing special characters by quotation marks.

Related terms
column, data, flat file, format, row, value

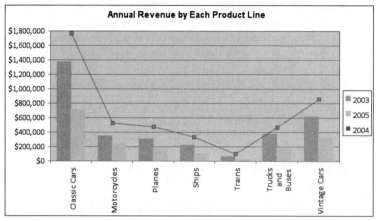

Figure G-5 Combination chart

computed field

A field that displays the result of an expression.

Related terms
expression, field

Contrast with
computed value

computed value

The result of a calculated expression. To display a computed value in a report, use a data element.

Related terms
data element, expression, report, value

Contrast with
computed field

conditional expression

An expression that returns value A or value B depending on whether a Boolean expression evaluates to True or False.

Related terms
Boolean expression, expression, value

conditional format

A format that applies to a cell when a specified condition is met.

Related terms
cell, format

configuration file

An Extensible Markup Language (XML) file containing the parameters and settings used to set run-time values in a program environment. For example, BIRT connection profiles and Eclipse plug-ins use configuration files.

Related terms
Business Intelligence and Reporting Tools (BIRT), Eclipse, parameter, plug-in, run time, value

Connection

A Java object that provides access to a data source.

Related terms
data source, Java, object

constant

An unchanging, predefined value. A constant does not change while a program is running, but the value of a field or variable can change.

Related terms
field, value, variable

constructor code

Code that initializes an instance of a class.

Related term
class

Contrast with
object

container

1 An application that acts as a master program to hold and execute a set of commands or to run other software routines. For example, an application server provides a container that supports communication between an application and an Enterprise JavaBean.

2 A data structure that holds one or more different types of data. For example, a grid element can contain label elements and other report items.

Related terms
application, data, Enterprise JavaBean (EJB), grid element, label element, report item

containment

A relationship among instantiated objects in a report. One object, the container, defines the scope of other objects, the contents.

Related terms
container, instantiation, object, report, scope

containment hierarchy

A hierarchy of objects in a report.

Related terms
hierarchy, object, report

content

See structured content.

converter

A tool that converts data from one format to another format. BIRT technology provides an Excel converter, PDF converter, PostScript converter, PowerPoint converter, Word converter, and an XML converter.

Related terms

Business Intelligence and Reporting Tools (BIRT) technology, data, Excel converter, format, PDF converter, PostScript converter, PowerPoint converter, Word converter, XML converter

cross tab

A report that arranges data into a concise summary for analysis. Data values appear in a matrix of rows and columns. Every cell in a cross tab contains an aggregate value. A cross tab shows how one item relates to another, such as monthly sales revenues aggregated by product line. Figure G-6 shows a cross tab.

Year/QTR/Month 2004		Classic Cars	Motorcycles	Planes	Ships	Trains	Trucks and Buses	Vintage Cars	Grand Total
1	1	$109,562	$39,987	$31,159	$26,310	$6,387		$42,909	$256,315
	2	$108,232	$45,694	$34,000	$24,894	$4,763	$35,749	$48,688	$302,021
	3	$99,512			$15,559	$9,879	$32,193	$45,252	$202,395
2	4	$89,998	$32,229	$33,882	$10,808			$33,352	$200,269
	5	$70,698	$47,873	$35,898	$3,440	$4,862	$31,729	$38,536	$233,036
	6	$46,025			$16,472		$41,967	$48,110	$152,574
3	7	$139,040	$65,156	$43,256	$20,260	$8,985	$36,967	$72,418	$386,082
	8	$140,458	$55,640	$32,083	$23,485	$7,132	$32,147	$65,019	$355,964
	9	$140,177	$6,515	$30,634	$23,114	$5,611	$37,720	$62,984	$306,755
4	10	$210,010	$69,147	$31,081	$40,881	$13,781	$68,620	$107,121	$540,642
	11	$397,834	$121,934	$97,607	$43,535	$12,148	$78,998	$183,657	$935,713
	12	$131,433	$43,069	$68,654	$43,838	$13,350	$52,612	$75,882	$428,838
	Total	$1,682,980	$527,244	$438,255	$292,595	$86,897	$448,703	$823,928	$4,300,603
Grand Total		$1,682,980	$527,244	$438,255	$292,595	$86,897	$448,703	$823,928	**$4,300,603**

Figure G-6   Cross tab displaying order totals

Related terms

aggregate value, cell, column, data, report, row, table, value

Contrast with

aggregate function, analytics, cross-tab element, grid

cross-tab element

 A report item that displays a cross tab. A cross tab displays aggregate values in a matrix of rows and columns. Figure G-7 shows a cross-tab element.

Related terms

aggregate value, column, cross tab, report item, row

Contrast with

analytics

cross-tabulation

See cross tab.

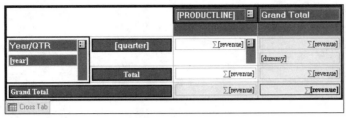

Figure G-7   Cross-tab element

CSS   See cascading style sheet (CSS).

cube   A multidimensional data structure that provides multiple dimensions and
multiple measures to access and analyze large quantities of data. BIRT uses a
cube to structure data for display in a cross-tab element.

Related terms
Business Intelligence and Reporting Tools (BIRT), cross-tab element, data,
dimension, measure, multidimensional data

Contrast with
analytics

custom data source

See open data access (ODA).

data   Information stored in databases, flat files, or other data sources.

Related terms
data source, database, flat file

Contrast with
metadata

data analysis

See analytics.

data binding

See column binding.

data element

A report item that displays a computed value or a value from a data set field.

Related terms
computed value, data set, field, report item, value

Contrast with
label element, Report Object Model (ROM) element, text element

Data Explorer

An Eclipse view that shows the data cubes, data sets, data sources, and report
parameters used in a report. Use Data Explorer to create, edit, or delete these
items. Figure G-8 shows Data Explorer.

Figure G-8   Data Explorer

Related terms
cube, data set, data source, Eclipse view, parameter, report

data point

A point on a chart that corresponds to a particular pair of x- and y-axis values.

Related terms
chart, value

Contrast with
data row, data set

data row

One row of data that a data set returns. A data set typically returns many data rows.

Related terms
data, data set, row

Contrast with
data point, data source, filter

data set

A definition of the data to retrieve or compute from a data source.

Related terms
data, data source

Contrast with
data element, data point, data row

data set parameter

A parameter associated with a data set column that restricts the number of data rows that a data set supplies to a report.

Related terms
column, data row, data set, parameter, report

Contrast with
report parameter

data source

1   A relational database or other data repository. For example, an Extensible Markup Language (XML) file, a flat file, or any other source of

information can be a data source. A report can include any of these types of data. This data source provides data rows to a report through a data source element.

2 A design construct that retrieves data rows from a relational database or other data repository.

Related terms
data, data row, database, Extensible Markup Language (XML), flat file, data source element, report

Contrast with
data set

data source element

An item containing connection information for a data source.

Related term
data source

Contrast with
data row, data set

data type

The structure of a value that constrains its characteristics, such as the information the values can hold and permitted operations. In report development, three processes use data types: accessing data, internal processing of data, and formatting output as a report.

Internal data types used by BIRT include Date, Double, Varchar, Time, and Timestamp. These data types map to the Java constants declared in Java.sql.Types, such as DATE, DOUBLE, INT, and STRING. BIRT maps the data types from supported data sources to these internal data types. To format values in a report, BIRT provides date-and-time, number, and string data types.

Related terms
Business Intelligence and Reporting Tools (BIRT), Date data type, date-and-time data type, double data type, Java, number data type, String data type, Time data type, Timestamp data type, value, Varchar data type

database

An integrated collection of logically related records that provides data for information application platforms, such as BIRT. The database model most commonly used is the relational model. Other typical models are entity-relationship, hierarchical, network, object, and object-relational.

Related terms
application, data

database connection

See data source.

database management system (DBMS)

Software that organizes simultaneous access to shared data. Database management systems store relationships among various data elements.

Related term
data, database, element

database schema

See schema.

Date data type

A Java data type used for date-and-time calculations. The base Date data type, java.util.Date, is a class that encapsulates a millisecond date value from January 1, 1970 00:00:00.000 GMT through the year 8099. This Date class provides accessor methods that support getting and setting the value.

Related terms
class, data type, Java, method, value

Contrast with
Time data type, Timestamp data type

date-and-time data type

A data type used to display date, date-and-time, or time values. Report items that contain expressions or fields having a date-and-time data type display the values in the report document. The appearance of these values depends on locale and format settings specified by your computer and the report design.

Related terms
data type, design, expression, field, format, locale, report, report item, value

Contrast with
Date data type, Time data type, Timestamp data type

debug

To detect, locate, and fix errors in a computer program. Typically, debugging involves executing specific portions of the program and analyzing the operation of those portions.

declaration

The definition of a class, constant, method, or variable that specifies the name and, if appropriate, the data type.

Related terms
class, constant, data type, method, variable

declarations section

That portion of Java code that contains constant, data type, and global variable declarations.

Related terms
constant, data type, declaration, Java, variable

deploy To bundle and distribute a software package, such as an Eclipse plug-in or a web application, to a run-time environment.

Related terms
application, Eclipse, package, plug-in, run time

derived class

See descendant class.

descendant class

A class that extends another class to provide additional functionality.

Related term
class

Contrast with
subclass, superclass

design A report specification or the act of creating a report specification. Designing a report includes selecting data, laying out the report visually, and saving the layout in a report design file.

Related terms
data, layout, report

Contrast with
file types

design time

The period of time in which a report developer creates a report specification.

Related term
report

Contrast with
design, run time, view time

DHTML (Dynamic Hypertext Markup Language)

See Dynamic HyperText Markup Language (DHTML).

dimension

In a cube, a category containing measures. For example, a dimension, such as orders, can include average cost and total units of products.

Related terms
category, cube, measure

Contrast with
analytics, multidimensional data

display name

An alternative name for a chart series, report parameter, table column, or user-defined Report Object Model (ROM) property. This name can contain any character, including punctuation and spaces. For example, BIRT Report Designer displays this alternative name as a column heading in a report.

Related terms

Business Intelligence and Reporting Tools (BIRT) Report Designer, character, chart, column, property, report, report parameter, Report Object Model (ROM), series, table

Contrast with

alias

document object model (DOM)

A model that defines the structure of a document such as an Extensible Markup Language (XML) or HyperText Markup Language (HTML) document. The DOM defines interfaces that dynamically create, access, and manipulate the internal structure of the document. The Uniform Resource Locator (URL) to the World Wide Web Consortium (W3C) document object model is:

www.w3.org/DOM/

Related terms

Extensible Markup Language (XML), HyperText Markup Language (HTML), interface, Uniform Resource Locator (URL), World Wide Web Consortium (W3C)

Contrast with

document type definition (DTD), structured content

document type definition (DTD)

A set of Extensible Markup Language (XML) elements and attributes that defines a schema describing the structure of an XML document.

Related terms

attribute, element, Extensible Markup Language (XML), schema

Contrast with

document object model (DOM), structured content

domain name

A name that defines a node on the internet. For example, the domain name of the Eclipse Foundation is eclipse. The Uniform Resource Locator (URL) is:

www.eclipse.org

Related terms

Eclipse, node, Uniform Resource Locator (URL)

Double class

A Java class that encapsulates the primitive data type, double. The class provides accessor methods that support getting and setting the value.

Related terms

class, data type, double data type, Java, method, value

Contrast with

BigDecimal class, Float class, Integer class, number data type

double data type

A Java data type that stores a double-precision 64-bit IEEE 754 floating point number, from 4.9065645841246544E-324 to 1.79769313486231570E+308 in value.

Related terms
data type, Java, value

Contrast with
Double class, float data type, int data type, number data type

driver An interface that supports communication between an application and another application or a peripheral device such as a printer.

Related terms
application, interface

Dynamic HyperText Markup Language (DHTML)

A HyperText Markup Language (HTML) extension providing enhanced viewing capabilities and interactivity in a web page. The Document Object Model (DOM) Group of the World Wide Web Consortium (W3C) develops DHTML standards.

Related terms
document object model (DOM), HyperText Markup Language (HTML), web page, World Wide Web Consortium (W3C)

dynamic text element

 A report item that adjusts its size to display varying amounts of HyperText Markup Language (HTML) or plain text. Figure G-9 shows a dynamic text element in a generated report.

Design Systems, Inc.   Accounts receivables are 180 days past due The account manager has not been able to get in touch with the customer. Suspend all P.O.s until further notice. —Dynamic text element expands to fit its contents

Figure G-9   A report displaying text in a dynamic text element

Related terms
HyperText Markup Language (HTML), report, report item

Contrast with
text element

dynamic variable

A variable that changes during program execution. The program requests the memory allocation for a dynamic variable at run time.

Related terms
run time, variable

Eclipse An open-source development platform, written in Java. The Eclipse platform consists of a plug-in framework, run-time environments, and tools.

Related terms
Eclipse platform, framework, Java, plug-in, run time
Contrast with
Business Intelligence and Reporting Tools (BIRT)

Eclipse launcher

A tool that supports testing an Eclipse project without the need to package the project as a JAR file. For example, the Eclipse Plug-in Development Environment provides a launcher to test new plug-ins.

Related terms
Eclipse, Eclipse Plug-in Development Environment (PDE), Eclipse project, Java archive (.jar) file, plug-in

Eclipse Modeling Framework (EMF)

A Java framework and code generation facility that uses a structured model to build tools and other applications. EMF uses Extensible Markup Language (XML) schemas to generate the EMF model of a plug-in. For example, a BIRT chart type uses EMF to represent the chart structure and properties.

Related terms
application, Business Intelligence and Reporting Tools (BIRT) technology, chart, Eclipse, Extensible Markup Language (XML), framework, Java, plug-in, property, schema

Eclipse perspective

A visual container that includes a set of views and editors. Eclipse Workbench provides a series of perspectives, such as the BIRT Report Designer, Java Development Environment, and Plug-in Development Environment (PDE). A developer can switch between perspectives to work on different tasks. Figure G-10 shows the Eclipse Java perspective.

Related terms
Business Intelligence and Reporting Tools (BIRT) Report Designer, Eclipse, Eclipse Plug-in Development Environment (PDE), Eclipse view, Eclipse Workbench, Java
Contrast with
Eclipse platform, view

Eclipse platform

The framework of the Eclipse application development system. The design-time environment provides user interfaces for specifying application components. The run-time environment provides an extensible system of plug-ins that load and run as needed.

Related terms
application, design time, Eclipse, framework, interface, plug-in, run time
Contrast with
Eclipse perspective, Eclipse view, Eclipse Workbench, extension

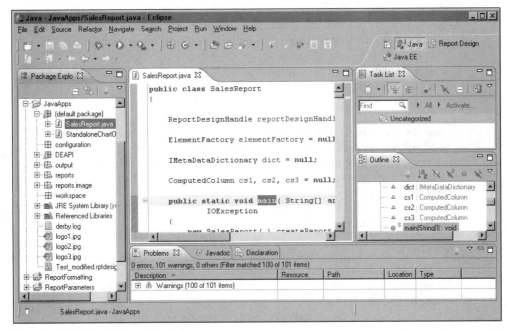

Figure G-10   Eclipse Java perspective

Eclipse Plug-in Development Environment (PDE)

An integrated design tool for creating, developing, testing, debugging, and deploying a plug-in. The Eclipse PDE provides wizards, editors, views, and launchers to support plug-in development. The Eclipse PDE supports design and run-time environments.

Related terms
debug, deploy, design, design time, Eclipse, Eclipse launcher, Eclipse view, plug-in, run time

Contrast with
Eclipse Modeling Framework (EMF), Eclipse platform

Eclipse project

A top-level directory within an Eclipse workspace. An Eclipse project contains folders and files used for builds, resource organization, sharing, and version management.

Related terms
Eclipse, Eclipse workspace, resource

Eclipse Rich Client Platform (RCP)

An Eclipse framework for supporting a client application that uses a minimal set of plug-ins. An Eclipse rich client application is typically a specialized user interface such as the report development tools in BIRT Rich Client Platform (RCP).

Related terms

application, Business Intelligence and Reporting Tools (BIRT) Rich Client Platform (RCP) Report Designer, Eclipse, framework, interface, plug-in, report

Contrast with

Eclipse platform

Eclipse view

A dockable window on the Eclipse Workbench. An Eclipse view can be an editor, the Navigator, a report item palette, a graphical report designer, or any other functional component that an Eclipse perspective provides. A view can have its own menus and toolbars. Multiple views can be visible at one time.

Related terms

design, Eclipse, Eclipse perspective, Eclipse Workbench, Navigator, Palette, report, report item

Eclipse Workbench

A graphical development environment containing perspectives used to create, edit, and view a project, such as the report design perspective.

Related terms

design, Eclipse, Eclipse perspective, Eclipse project, report

Contrast with

Eclipse platform

Eclipse workspace

A file system directory containing one or more projects used to manage resources in Eclipse Workbench.

Related terms

Eclipse project, Eclipse Workbench, resource

EJB   See Enterprise JavaBean (EJB).

element

1   A single item of data.

2   A logical structure in an Extensible Markup Language (XML) or HyperText Markup Language (HTML) document specifying a type and optionally one or more attributes and a value. For example, the following code specifies a ConnectionParam element that has three attributes, Name, Display, and Type, and no value:

```
<ConnectionParam Name="username"
    Display="User name"
    Type="string"
/>
```

Related terms

attribute, data, Extensible Markup Language (XML), HyperText Markup Language (HTML), value

Contrast with
report item, Report Object Model (ROM) element

ellipsis

 A button that opens tools that you use to perform tasks, such as navigating to a file or specifying localized text.

encapsulation

A technique that bundles related functions and subroutines. Encapsulation compartmentalizes the structure and behavior of a class so that parts of an object-oriented system do not depend upon or affect each other's internal details.

Related terms
class, function, object, object-oriented programming

enterprise

An integrated set of computers running on multiple platforms in a network environment. Typical software products in an enterprise environment include applications, browsers, databases, and servers that support an information warehouse.

Related terms
application, database, platform

Contrast with
enterprise reporting

enterprise archive (.ear) file

A compressed file format used to deploy Java EE web applications.

Related terms
application, Java Platform Enterprise Edition (Java EE)

Contrast with
Java archive (.jar) file, web archive (.war) file

Enterprise JavaBean (EJB)

A server component used to encapsulate application logic. A client application makes a remote procedure call (RPC) to the server to run an EJB. Enterprise JavaBeans (EJB) are a standard-based framework designed to provide persistence, security, and transactional integrity to enterprise applications.

Related terms
application, enterprise, framework, JavaBean

enterprise reporting

A system that delivers a high volume of complex structured documents that include data from a variety of data sources.

Related terms
data, data source

Contrast with
enterprise, structured content

event   An action external to a program that requires handling, such as a mouse click. An event handler in the program collects information about the event and responds.

Related term
event handler

Contrast with
event listener

event handler

A function or method that executes when an event occurs. Report items, data sets, and data sources have event handlers for which a developer can provide code.

Related terms
data set, data source, event, function, method, report, report item

Contrast with
event listener

event listener

An interface that detects when a particular event occurs and calls a function or method to respond to the event.

Related terms
event, function, interface, method

Contrast with
event handler

Excel converter

A module that converts a report or report data to a Microsoft Excel spreadsheet (.xls) file.

Related terms
converter, data, report

exception

An abnormal situation that a program encounters. The program handles some exceptions and returns a message to the user or application running the program. In other cases, the program cannot handle the exception, and the program ends.

Related term
application

executable file

A file that generates report output when run in a report designer or web application. For example, a BIRT report executable (.rptdesign) file generates BIRT report output.

Related terms
application, file types, report, report design (.rptdesign) file

expression

A combination of constants, functions, literal values, names of fields, and operators that evaluate to a single value.

Related terms
constant, field, expression builder, function, operator, value

Contrast with
regular expression

expression builder

A tool for selecting data fields, functions, and operators to write expressions. Figure G-11 shows the expression builder in BIRT Report Designer.

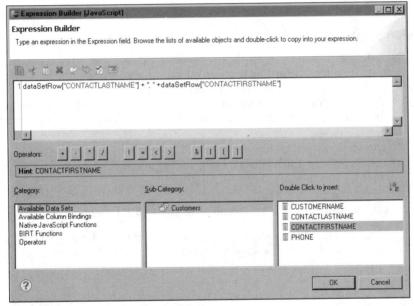

Figure G-11   Expression builder

Related terms
Business Intelligence and Reporting Tools (BIRT) Report Designer, data, expression, field, function, operator

Extensible Markup Language (XML)

A markup language that supports the interchange of data among applications and data sources. Using XML, a wide variety of applications, databases, and legacy systems can exchange information. The World Wide Web Consortium (W3C) specifies the standard for XML schema and documents. XML documents must be well-formed.

Related terms

application, data, data source, database, schema, well-formed XML, World Wide Web Consortium (W3C)

Contrast with

Dynamic HyperText Markup Language (DHTML), HyperText Markup Language (HTML)

extension

A module that adds functionality to an application. For example, BIRT consists of a set of extensions, called plug-ins, which add report development functionality to the Eclipse platform.

Related terms

application, Business Intelligence and Reporting Tools (BIRT), Eclipse platform, plug-in, report

Contrast with

Business Intelligence and Reporting Tools (BIRT) extension, extension point

extension point

A defined place in an application where a developer adds custom functionality. The application programming interfaces (API) in BIRT support adding custom functionality to the BIRT framework. In the Eclipse Plug-in Development Environment (PDE), a developer views the extension points in the PDE Manifest Editor to guide and control plug-in development tasks.

Related terms

application, application programming interface (API), Business Intelligence and Reporting Tools (BIRT), Eclipse Plug-in Development Environment (PDE), extension, framework, plug-in

Contrast with

Business Intelligence and Reporting Tools (BIRT) extension

field The smallest identifiable part of a database table structure. In a relational database, a field is also called a column. Figure G-12 shows a field in a table.

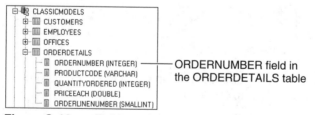

Figure G-12 Fields and tables displayed in a query editor

Related terms

column, database, query editor, table

field variable

In Java, a member variable having public visibility.

Related terms

Java, member, variable

file types

BIRT provides file types to store information used and created by report designs. Table 26-1 lists the report designer's file types.

Table 26-1 File types

Display name	File extension
BIRT Report Design	RPTDESIGN
BIRT Report Design Library	RPTLIBRARY
BIRT Report Design Template	RPTTEMPLATE
BIRT Report Document	RPTDOCUMENT

Related terms
library (.rptlibrary) file, report design (.rptdesign) file, report document (.rptdocument) file, report template (.rpttemplate) file

filter A mechanism that enables a user to reduce the number of items in a list.

flat file A file that contains data in the form of text.

Related term
data

Contrast with
data source

Float class

A Java class that encapsulates the primitive data type, float. The class provides accessor methods that support getting and setting the value.

Related terms
class, data type, float data type, Java, value

Contrast with
BigDecimal class, Double class, Integer class

float data type

A Java data type that stores a single-precision 32-bit IEEE 754 floating point number, ranging in value from 1.40129846432481707E-45 to 3.40282346638528860E+38.

Related terms
data type, Java, value

Contrast with
double data type, Float class, int data type, number data type

font A family of characters of a given style. A font contains information that specifies posture, typeface, type size, and weight.

Related term
character

footer   A logically separate unit of information that appears after the main body of content. For example, a page footer typically contains a page number. A group footer aggregates group data.

Related terms
data, group

Contrast with
header

format   1   A specification that describes layout and properties of rich information, such as HyperText Markup Language (HTML), PDF, PostScript, PowerPoint, RTF, or spreadsheet.

2   A set of standard options with which to display and print currency values, dates, numbers, strings, and times.

Related terms
data, HyperText Markup Language (HTML), layout, property, string, value

Contrast with
style

fragment

See plug-in fragment.

framework

A set of interrelated classes that provide an architecture for building an application, such as the chart engine.

Related terms
application, Business Intelligence and Reporting Tools (BIRT) Chart Engine, class

function

A code module containing a set of instructions that operate as a subroutine in a program. To invoke the function, include its name as an instruction anywhere in the program. BIRT provides JavaScript and other functions to support building expressions.

Related terms
Business Intelligence and Reporting Tools (BIRT), expression, JavaScript

Contrast with
method

global variable

A variable available at all levels in an application. A global variable stays in memory in the scope of all executing subroutines until the application terminates.

Related terms
application, scope, variable

glyph   1   An image that is the visual representation of a character.

2 A specific letter form from a specific font. For example, an uppercase C in Palatino font is a glyph.

Related terms
character, font

grandchild class

See descendant class.

grandparent class

See ancestor class.

grid

See grid element.

grid element

A report item that contains and arranges other report elements in a static row and column format. A grid element aligns cells horizontally and vertically. Figure G-13 shows a report title section containing an image and two text elements in a grid element. This grid element has one row and two columns.

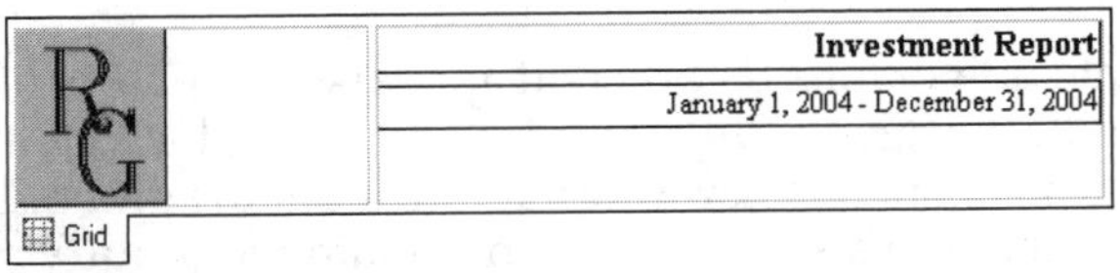

Figure G-13   Grid element

Related terms
cell, column, image element, report, report item, row, text element

Contrast with
list element, table element

group

A set of data rows organized by one or more common values. For example, in a sales report, a group consists of all the orders placed by a single customer.

Related terms
data row, report, value

Contrast with
group key, grouped report

group footer

See footer.

group header

See header.

grouped report

A report that organizes data by common values. Figure G-14 shows a grouped report organized by customer name.

Related terms
data, report, value

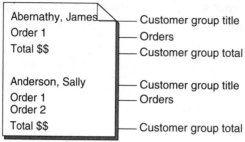

Figure G-14   Grouped report
Contrast with
group

group key

An expression that groups and sorts data. For example, a report developer can group and sort customers by credit rank.
Related terms
data, expression, group, sort

header   A logically separate unit of information that appears before the main body of content. For example, a page header typically contains a document title. A group header typically contains key information about the group. For example, a group header in a sales report can contain the country name.
Related terms
group, page
Contrast with
footer

hexadecimal number

A number in base 16. A hexadecimal number uses the digits 0 through 9 and letters A through F. Each place represents a power of 16. By comparison, base 10 numbers use the digits 0 through 9. Each place represents a power of 10.
Contrast with
character set

hierarchy

Any tree structure that has a root and branches that do not converge. Figure G-15 shows an example hierarchy of classes.
Related term
class

HTML   See HyperText Markup Language (HTML).

HTML element

See element.

HTTP   See HyperText Transfer Protocol (HTTP).

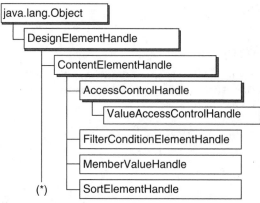

Figure G-15   Hierarchy of classes

hyperchart

A chart that supports linking to report data or other related information. For example, a pie chart segment representing the sales amount for the Boston office links to the report data for that office.

Related terms
chart, data, report

Contrast with
hyperlink

hyperlink

 An active connection in a online document that supports access to related information in the same document or an external source. The document can be an e-mail, PDF, report, spreadsheet, or web page. A change from the standard cursor shape to a cursor shaped like a hand indicates a hyperlink.

Related terms
report, web page

Contrast with
hyperchart

HyperText Markup Language (HTML)

A standards-based specification that determines the layout of a web page. HTML is the markup language that a web browser parses to display a web page. The World Wide Web Consortium (W3C) specifies the standard for HTML.

Related terms
layout, web page, World Wide Web Consortium (W3C)

Contrast with
Dynamic HyperText Markup Language (DHTML), Extensible Markup Language (XML)

HyperText Markup Language page

See web page.

HyperText Transfer Protocol (HTTP)

A standard that supports request-response communication between two applications on a network. The World Wide Web Consortium (W3C) specifies the standard for HTTP.

Related terms
application, request, World Wide Web Consortium (W3C)

Contrast with
protocol

identifier

A name assigned to an item in a program, for example a class, function, or variable.

Related terms
class, function, variable

image
A graphic that appears in a report. BIRT supports .gif, .jpg, and .png file types.

Related terms
Business Intelligence and Reporting Tools (BIRT), report

Contrast with
image element

image element

 A report item that adds an image to a report design.

Related terms
design, image, report, report item

inheritance

A mechanism whereby one class of objects can be defined as a special case of a more general class and includes the method and variable definitions of the general class, known as a base or superclass. The superclass serves as the baseline for the appearance and behavior of the descendant class, which is also known as a subclass. In the subclass, the appearance, behavior, and structure can be customized without affecting the superclass. Figure G-16 shows an example of inheritance.

Related terms
class, descendant class, method, object, subclass, superclass, variable

Contrast with
abstract base class, hierarchy, object-oriented programming

inner join

A type of join that returns records from two tables using specified values in the join fields. For example, joining customer and order tables where the customer IDs are equal produces a result set that excludes records for customers who have no orders.

Related terms
field, join, result set, table, value

Contrast with
outer join

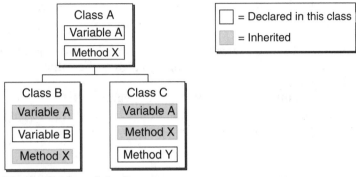

Figure G-16   Inheritance

Input Method Editor (IME) file

A Java class file that sets the keyboard mapping for a character set. BIRT uses this mechanism to support non-ASCII characters. Place the IME file in the jre\lib\ext directory to make it accessible to the Java environment.

Related terms
Business Intelligence and Reporting Tools (BIRT) Report Designer, character, character set, class, Java

input source

See data source.

instance

See object.

instance variable

A variable that other instances of a class do not share. The run-time system creates a new copy of an instance variable each time the system instantiates the class. An instance variable can contain a different value in each instance of a class, for example, the customerID variable in a Customer class.

Related terms
class, run time, value, variable

instantiation

In object-oriented programming, the process of creating an object in a run-time environment based on the class definition.

Related terms
class, object, object-oriented programming, run time

int data type

A 32-bit Java data type that stores whole numbers, ranging in value from -2,147,483,648 to 2,147,483,647.

Related terms
data type, Java, value

Contrast with
double data type, float data type, Integer class

Integer class

A Java class that encapsulates the primitive data type, int. This class provides accessor methods that support getting and setting the value.

Related terms
class, data type, int data type, Java, method, value

Contrast with
BigDecimal class, Double class, Float class

interface

A software component that supports access to computer resources. For example, in Java, a set of methods that provides a mechanism for classes to communicate in order to execute particular actions.

Related terms
class, Java, method

internationalization

The process of designing an application to work correctly in multiple locales.

Related terms
application, locale

Contrast with
localization

IP address

The unique node identifier on a TCP/IP network.

Related term
node

J2EE   See Java Platform Enterprise Edition (Java EE).

J2SE   See Java Platform Standard Edition (Java SE).

JAR   See Java archive (.jar) file.

Java   An object-oriented programming language used to develop and extend BIRT technology.

Related terms
Business Intelligence and Reporting Tools (BIRT) technology, object-oriented programming

Contrast with
JavaScript

Java 2 Enterprise Edition (J2EE)

See Java Platform Enterprise Edition (Java EE).

Java 2 Runtime Standard Edition (J2SE)

See Java Platform Standard Edition (Java SE).

Java archive (.jar) file

A compressed file format used to deploy Java applications.

Related terms
application, Java

Contrast with
web archive (.war) file

Java Database Connectivity (JDBC)

A standard protocol that Java uses to access databases in a platform-independent manner.

Related terms
database, Java, protocol

Contrast with
data element, schema

Java Development Kit (JDK)

A software development kit that defines the application programming interfaces (API) used to build Java applications. As well as software tools, the kit contains documentation and examples.

Related terms
application, application programming interface (API), Java

Contrast with
Java Platform Enterprise Edition (Java EE), Java Platform Standard Edition (Java SE), JavaServer Page (JSP)

Java Naming and Directory Interface (JNDI)

An application programming interface (API) that provides unified access to named components and directory services in an enterprise system.

Related terms
application programming interface (API), enterprise

Java Platform Enterprise Edition (Java EE)

A platform-independent development environment that includes application programming interfaces (API), such as Java Database Connectivity (JDBC), Remote Method Invocation (RMI), and web services. A programmer uses Java EE to develop a highly scalable, fault-tolerant, web-based application.

Related terms

application, application programming interface (API), Java Database Connectivity (JDBC)

Contrast with

Java Development Kit (JDK), Java Platform Standard Edition (Java SE), Java Virtual Machine (JVM)

Java Platform Standard Edition (Java SE)

A smaller-scale, platform-independent development environment defining the Java programming language and application programming interfaces (API) supporting interaction with file systems, networks, and graphical interfaces. A programmer uses Java SE to develop an application to run on a virtual machine.

Related terms

application, application programming interface (API), Java

Contrast with

Java Development Kit (JDK), Java Platform Enterprise Edition (Java EE), Java Virtual Machine (JVM)

Java Virtual Machine (JVM)

The Java SDK interpreter that converts Java bytecode into machine language for execution in a specified software and hardware configuration.

Related terms

Java, SDK (Software Development Kit)

JavaBean

A reusable, serializable, standards-based component that encapsulates application logic.

Related terms

application, encapsulation

Contrast with

Enterprise JavaBean (EJB)

JavaScript

An interpreted, platform-independent, scripting language used to embed additional processing in a web page or server. For example, BIRT uses JavaScript to support aggregate expressions and event handling.

Related terms

Business Intelligence and Reporting Tools (BIRT), event handler, web page, web server

Contrast with

aggregate function, Java

JavaServer Page (JSP)

A standard Java extension that supports the generation of dynamic web pages. A JavaServer Page combines HyperText Markup Language (HTML) and JSP tags in one document. A servlet container interprets a JSP tag as a call to a Java class. The servlet container compiles the Java classes to generate a web page.

Related terms
class, container, extension, HyperText Markup Language (HTML), Java, servlet, tag, web page

JDBC   See Java Database Connectivity (JDBC).

JDK   See Java Development Kit (JDK).

JNDI   See Java Naming and Directory Interface (JNDI).

join   A SQL (Structured Query Language) query operation that combines records from two tables and returns them in a result set based on the values in the join fields. Without additional qualification, join usually refers to the join in which field values are equal. For example, customer and order tables are joined on a common field such as customer ID. The result set contains combined customer and order records in which the customer IDs are equal.

Related terms
field, query, result set, SQL (Structured Query Language), table, value

Contrast with
inner join, join condition, outer join, SQL SELECT statement

join condition

A condition that specifies a match in the values of related fields in two tables. Typically, the values are equal. For example, if two tables have a field called customer ID, a join condition exists where the customer ID value in one table equals the customer ID value in the second table.

Related terms
field, join, table, value

joint data set

A data set that combines data from two or more data sets.

Related terms
data, data set

JSP   See JavaServer Page (JSP).

JVM   See Java Virtual Machine (JVM).

keyword

A reserved word that is recognized as part of a programming language.

label element

`abl` A report item that displays a short piece of static text in a report. Figure G-17 shows label elements used as column headings in a table header row.

Related terms
column, header, report item, row, table

Product Code	Product Name	Price Each	Quantity	Price

Figure G-17   Label elements in a table header row

Contrast with
data element, text element

layout   The designed appearance of a report. Designing a report entails arranging report items on a page so that a report user can analyze the information easily. A report displays information in a combination of charts, footers, headers, paragraphs, subreports, and tabular lists.

Related terms
chart, footer, header, report, report item, subreport

layout editor

A tool in a report designer in which a report developer arranges, formats, and sizes report items.

Related terms
design, format, report, report item

Contrast with
report editor

lazy load

The capability in a run-time environment to load a code segment to memory. By lazily loading a code segment, the run-time environment minimizes start-up time and conserves memory resources. For example, BIRT Report Engine builds a registry at startup that contains the list of available plug-ins, then loads a plug-in only if the processing requires it.

Related terms
Business Intelligence and Reporting Tools (BIRT) Report Engine, plug-in, run time

left outer join

See outer join.

library   **1**   A file used when creating or running a program. For example, Windows library files are dynamic link libraries. UNIX library files are shared libraries.

2   A collection of reusable and shareable report elements. A library can contain data sets, data sources, embedded images, JavaScript code, styles, and visual report items. A report developer uses a report designer to develop a library and to retrieve report elements from a library for use in a report design.

Related terms
Business Intelligence and Reporting Tools (BIRT) Report Designer, data set, data source, design, image, JavaScript, report element, report item, style, variable

> **Contrast with**
> file types

library (.rptlibrary) file

> In BIRT Report Designer, an Extensible Markup Language (XML) file that contains reusable and shareable report elements. A report developer uses a report design tool to create a library file directly or from a report design (.rptdesign) file.
>
> **Related terms**
> Business Intelligence and Reporting Tools (BIRT) Report Designer, design, Extensible Markup Language (XML), library, report design (.rptdesign) file, report element
>
> **Contrast with**
> file types

link

> See hyperlink.

listener

> See event listener.

list element

> A report item that iterates through the data rows in a data set. The list element contains and displays other report items in a variety of layouts.
>
> **Related terms**
> data row, data set, layout, report item
>
> **Contrast with**
> grid element, table element

listing report

> A report that provides a simple view of data. Typically, a listing report displays a single line for each data row. Figure G-18 shows a listing report.

Customer List		
Customer	Phone	Contact
ANG Resellers	(91) 745 6555	Alejandra Camino
AV Stores, Co.	(171) 555-1555	Rachel Ashworth
Alpha Cognac	61.77.6555	Annette Roulet

Figure G-18   Listing report

> **Related terms**
> data, data row, report

local variable

> A variable that is available only at the current level in an application. A local variable stays in memory in the scope of an executing procedure until the procedure terminates. When the procedure finishes, the run-time system destroys the variable and returns the memory to the system.

Related terms
application, procedure, run time, scope, variable

locale   A location and the currency format, date format, language, sorting sequence, time format, and other characteristics associated with that location. The location is not always identical to the country. There can be multiple languages and locales within one country. For example, China has two locales: Beijing and Hong Kong. Canada has two language-based locales: French and English.

Related term
format

Contrast with
localization

localization

The process of translating database content, printed documents, and software programs into another language. Report developers localize static text in a report so that the report displays text in another language that is appropriate to the locale configured on the user's machine.

Related terms
database, locale, report

Contrast with
internationalization

manifest

A text file in a Java archive (.jar) file that describes the contents of the archive.

Related term
Java archive (.jar) file

mashup

A web application that combines data and functionality from multiple sources into a single presentation. For example, the Google Maps® mashup combines maps and directions to assist a user in locating and traveling to a destination.

Related term
application, data

master page

A predefined layout that specifies a consistent appearance for all pages of a report. A master page typically includes standard headers and footers that display information such as a copyright statement, a date, or page numbers. The master page can contain report elements in the header and footer areas only, as shown in Figure G-19.

The master page's header and footer content appears on every page of the report in paginated formats, as shown in Figure G-20.

Related terms
footer, header, layout, report, report element

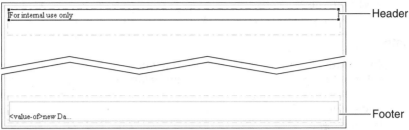

Header

Footer

Figure G-19   Master page layout

Contrast with
template

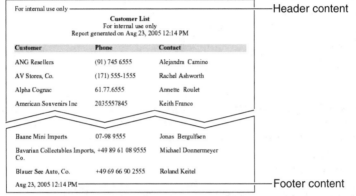

Header content

Footer content

Figure G-20   Master page header and footer in report

measure

In a cube, aggregated values, such as average cost or total units of products.

Related terms
aggregate value, cube

Contrast with
dimension

member

A method or variable defined in a class. A member provides or uses information about the state of a single object.

Related terms
class, method, object, variable

Contrast with
global variable, instance variable, static variable

member variable

A declared variable within a class. The member variables for an object contain its data or state.

Related terms
class, data, declaration, object, variable

metadata

Information about the structure of data enabling a program to process information. For example, a relational database stores metadata that describes the data type, name, and size of objects in a database, such as tables and columns.

Related terms
column, data, data type, database, object, table

method

A routine that provides functionality to an object or a class.

Related terms
class, object

Contrast with
data, function

modal window

A window that retains focus until explicitly closed by the user. Typically, dialog boxes and message windows are modal. For example, an error message dialog box remains on the screen until the user responds.

Contrast with
modeless window

mode

An operational state of a system. Mode implies that there are at least two possible states. Typically, there are many modes for both hardware and software.

modeless window

A window that solicits input but permits users to continue using the current application without closing the modeless window, for example, an Eclipse view.

Related terms
application, Eclipse view

Contrast with
modal window

multidimensional data

Any set of records that you can break down or filter according to the contents of individual fields or dimensions, such as location, product, or time. This data organization supports presenting and analyzing complex relationships.

Related terms
data, dimension, field, filter

Contrast with
analytics

multithreaded application

An application that handles multiple simultaneous sessions and users.

Related term
application

Navigator

In BIRT Report Designer, an Eclipse view that shows all projects, reports, and associated files within each project. Each project is a directory in the file system. Use Navigator to manage report files, for example, deleting files, moving files from one project to another, or renaming files. Figure G-21 shows Navigator.

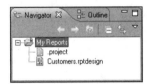

Figure G-21   Navigator

Related terms
Business Intelligence and Reporting Tools (BIRT) Report Designer, Eclipse project, Eclipse view, report

node

A computer that is accessible on the internet.

Contrast with
domain name

null

A value indicating that a variable or field contains no data.

Related terms
data, field, value, variable

number data type

A data type used to display numeric values. Report items that contain expressions or fields having a number data type display numeric values in the report document. The appearance of these values depends on the formats and locale settings specified by your computer and the report design.

Related terms
data type, design, expression, field, format, locale, report, report item, value

numeric expression

A numeric constant, a simple numeric variable, a scalar reference to a numeric array, a numeric-valued function reference, or a sequence of these items, separated by numeric operators. For example:

```
dataSetRow["PRICEEACH"] * dataSetRow["QUANTITYORDERED"]
```

Related terms
array, constant, function, operator, variable

Contrast with
Boolean expression

object   An instance of a particular class, including its characteristics, such as instance variables and methods.

Related terms
class, instance variable, method, variable

object-oriented programming

A paradigm for writing applications using classes, not algorithms, as the fundamental building blocks. The design methodology uses four main concepts: abstraction, encapsulation, inheritance, and polymorphism.

Related terms
abstraction, application, class, encapsulation, inheritance, polymorphism

Contrast with
object

ODA   See open data access (ODA).

online analytical processing (OLAP)

The process of analyzing, collecting, managing, and presenting multidimensional data.

Related terms
data, multidimensional data

Contrast with
analytics

online help

Information that appears on the computer screen to help the user understand an application.

Related term
application

open data access (ODA)

A technology that handles communication between a data source and an application. ODA provides interfaces for creating data drivers to establish connections, access metadata, and execute queries to retrieve data. ODA also provides interfaces to integrate query builder tools within an application designer tool. The Eclipse Data Tools Project plug-ins provide ODA to BIRT.

Related terms
application, Business Intelligence and Reporting Tools (BIRT), Connection, data, data source, Eclipse, interface, metadata, open data access (ODA) driver, plug-in, query

open data access (ODA) driver

An ODA driver communicates between a data source and an application. An ODA driver establishes a connection to a data source, accesses metadata about the data, and executes queries on the data source. In BIRT, ODA drivers are plug-in extensions to the Eclipse Data Tools Platform project.

Related terms
application, Business Intelligence and Reporting Tools (BIRT) technology, data, data source, driver, Eclipse, extension, metadata, open data access (ODA), plug-in, query

open database connectivity (ODBC)

A standard protocol used by software products as a database management system (DBMS) interface to connect applications and reports to databases.

Related terms
application, database, database management system (DBMS), interface, protocol, report

Contrast with
Connection, data source, Java Database Connectivity (JDBC)

open source

A software development methodology in which the community of programmers and users has complete access to the source code. For example, BIRT is an open-source project built on the Eclipse platform.

Related terms
Business Intelligence and Reporting Tools (BIRT), Eclipse platform

operator

A symbol or keyword that performs an operation on expressions.

Related terms
expression, keyword

outer join

A type of join that returns records from one table even when no matching values exist in the other table. The three types of outer join are left, right, and full outer join. A left outer join returns all records from the table on the left side of the join expression, even if no matching values exist in the table on the right side. A right outer join returns all records from the table on the right side of the join expression, even if no matching values exist in the table on the left side. For example, joining customers and orders tables on customerID with the customers table on the left side of the expression returns a result set that contains all customer records, including customers who have no orders. A full outer join is the union of the result sets of both left and right outer joins.

Related terms
join, result set, table, value

Contrast with
inner join

Outline   An Eclipse view that shows all report elements in a report design, report library, or report template. Outline shows the report elements' containment hierarchy in a tree-structured diagram. Figure G-22 shows Outline.

Figure G-22   Outline
Related terms
design, Eclipse view, hierarchy, library, report, report element, template

package

1   A set of functionally related Java classes organized in one directory.

2   A complete application, including all configuration files and programs.
Related terms
application, class, configuration file, Java

page   An area in a window that arranges and displays related information. A window can contain several pages, each of which is accessed by a tab.
Related term
tab

Contrast with
JavaServer Page (JSP), master page, web page

Palette   An Eclipse view that shows the report items used to display and organize data in a report. Figure G-23 shows Palette.

Figure G-23   Palette of report items

Related terms
data, Eclipse view, report, report item

parameter

1 A report element that provides input to the execution of the report. Parameters provide control over report data formatting, processing, and selection.

2 The definition of an argument to a procedure.

Related terms
argument, data, format, procedure, report, report element

Contrast with
cascading parameters, data set parameter, report parameter

parent class

See superclass.

password

An optional code that restricts user name access to a resource on a computer system.

pattern

A template or model for implementing a solution to a common problem in object-oriented programming or design. For example, the singleton design pattern restricts the instantiation of a class to only one object. The use of the singleton pattern prevents the proliferation of identical objects in a run-time environment and requires a programmer to manage access to the object in a multithreaded application.

Related terms
class, design, instantiation, multithreaded application, object, object-oriented programming, run time, template

PDF converter

A tool that converts a report to a PDF file.

Related terms
converter, report

perspective

See Eclipse perspective.

platform

The software and hardware environment in which a program runs. Linux, MacOS, Microsoft Windows, Solaris OS, and UNIX are examples of software systems that run on hardware processors made by vendors such as AMD, Apple, Hewlett-Packard, IBM, Intel, Motorola, and Sun.

Contrast with
Eclipse platform

plug-in **1** An extension used by the Eclipse development environment. At run time, Eclipse scans its plug-in subdirectory to discover any extensions to the platform. Eclipse places the information about each extension in a registry, using lazy load to access the extension.

2 A software program that extends the capabilities of a web browser. For example, a plug-in gives you the ability to play audio samples or video movies.

Related terms
Eclipse, extension, lazy load, run time

Contrast with
Eclipse Plug-in Development Environment (PDE)

plug-in fragment

A separately loaded plug-in that adds functionality to an existing plug-in, such as support for a new language in a localized application. The plug-in fragment manifest contains named values that associate the fragment with the existing plug-in.

Related terms
application, localization, manifest, plug-in, value

polymorphism

The ability to provide different implementations with a common interface, simplifying the communication among objects. For example, defining a unique print method for each kind of document in a system supports printing any document by sending the instruction to print without concern for how that method is actually carried out for a given document.

Related terms
interface, method, object

Contrast with
object-oriented programming

PostScript converter

A tool that converts a report to a PostScript (.ps) file.

Related terms
converter, report

PowerPoint converter

A tool that converts a report to a Microsoft PowerPoint (.ppt) file.

Related terms
converter, report

Contrast with
Excel converter, PDF converter, PostScript converter, Word converter, XML converter

previewer

A tool that supports displaying data or a report. A data previewer enables the report developer to review the values of columns returned by a query before designing the report layout. A report previewer enables the report developer to review and improve the report layout before delivery to the user.

Related terms
column, data, design, layout, query, report, value

Contrast with
viewer

procedure

A set of commands, input data, and statements that perform a specific set of operations. For example, methods are procedures.

Related terms
data, method, statement

process

A computer program that has no user interface. For example, the servlet that generates a BIRT report is a process.

Related terms
Business Intelligence and Reporting Tools (BIRT), interface, report, servlet

project   See Eclipse project.

Properties

A grouped alphabetical list of all properties of report elements in a report design. Experienced report developers use this Eclipse view to modify any property of a report element. Figure G-24 shows Properties.

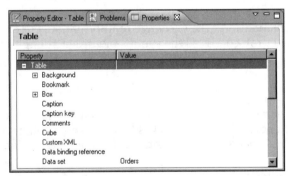

Figure G-24   Properties displaying a sample of table element properties

Related terms
design, Eclipse view, property, report, report element, table element

Contrast with
Property Editor

property

A characteristic of a report item that controls its appearance and behavior. For example, a report developer can specify a font size for a label element.

Related terms
font, label element, report item

Contrast with
method

Property Editor

An Eclipse view that displays sets of key properties of report elements in a report design. The report developer uses Property Editor to modify those properties. Figure G-25 shows Property Editor.

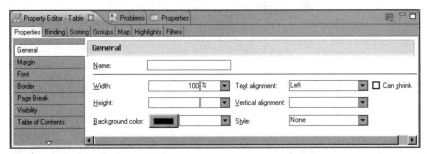

Figure G-25   Property Editor

Related terms
design, Eclipse view, property, report, report element

Contrast with
Properties

protocol

A communication standard for the exchange of information. For example, in TCP/IP, the internet protocol (IP) is the syntax and order through which messages are received and sent.

Related term
syntax

publish   To copy files to a shared folder to make them available to report users and developers. BIRT Report Designer publishes libraries and resource files to the resources folder. Published templates reside in the templates folder.

Related terms
library, report, resource file, template

query   A statement specifying the data rows to retrieve from a data source. For example, a query that retrieves data from a database typically is a SQL SELECT statement.

Related terms
data, data row, data source, database, SQL SELECT statement

query editor

A graphical tool used to write a statement that requests data from a data source.

Related terms
data, data source, statement

Contrast with
SQL SELECT statement

range   A continuous set of values of any data type. For example, 1–31 is a numeric range.

Related terms
data type, value

regular expression

A JavaScript mechanism that matches patterns in text. The regular expression syntax can validate text data, find simple and complex strings of text within larger blocks of text, and substitute new text for old.

Related terms
data, expression, JavaScript, string, syntax

rendering extension

A BIRT extension that produces a report in a specific format. For example, BIRT provides rendering extensions for Adobe PDF, Adobe PostScript, HyperText Markup Language (HTML), Microsoft Excel, Microsoft PowerPoint, and Microsoft Word.

Related terms
Business Intelligence and Reporting Tools (BIRT), Business Intelligence and Reporting Tools (BIRT) extension, extension, format, HyperText Markup Language (HTML), report

report   A category of documents that presents formatted and structured content from a data source, such as a database or text file.

Related terms
data source, database, format, structured content

report design (.rptdesign) file

An Extensible Markup Language (XML) file that contains the complete description of a report. The report design file describes the structure and organization of the report, the constituent report items, data sets, data sources, and Java and JavaScript event handler code. A report developer uses BIRT Report Designer to create the report design file and the BIRT Report Engine processes it to create a formatted report.

Related terms
Business Intelligence and Reporting Tools (BIRT) Report Designer, Business Intelligence and Reporting Tools (BIRT) Report Engine, data set, data source, design, event handler, Extensible Markup Language (XML), format, Java, JavaScript, report, report item

Contrast with
file types

report document (.rptdocument) file

A binary file that encapsulates the report item identifiers and values, and additional information, such as data rows, pagination, and table of contents.

Related terms
data row, report item, table of contents, value

Contrast with
file types

report editor

In BIRT Report Designer, the main window where a report developer designs and previews a report. The report editor supports opening multiple report designs. For each report design, the report editor displays these five pages: Extensible Markup Language (XML) source editor, layout editor, master page editor, previewer, and script editor.

Related terms
Business Intelligence and Reporting Tools (BIRT) Report Designer, design, Extensible Markup Language (XML), master page, layout editor, previewer, report, script editor

Contrast with
report design (.rptdesign) file

report element

A visual or non-visual component of a report design. A visual report element, such as a table or a label, is a report item. A non-visual report element, such as a report parameter or a data source, is a logical component.

Related terms
data source, design, element, label element, report, report item, report parameter, table element

report executable file

A file that contains instructions for generating a report document.

Related term
report

Contrast with
file types

report item

A report element that is a visual component of a report design. A report item displays content in the report output. For example, a data element displays data from a data set.

Related terms
data, data element, data set, design, report, report element

Contrast with
structured content

report item extension

A BIRT extension that implements a custom report item.

Related terms
Business Intelligence and Reporting Tools (BIRT) extension, report item

report library file

See library (.rptlibrary) file.

Report Object Model (ROM)

The abstract specification for BIRT technology. The ROM defines the visual and non-visual components of a report. The ROM specification is an Extensible Markup Language (XML) document. The complete ROM specification is at:

`http://www.eclipse.org/birt/ref`

Related terms
Business Intelligence and Reporting Tools (BIRT) technology, Extensible Markup Language (XML), report

Contrast with
Report Object Model definition file (rom.def), Report Object Model (ROM) element, Report Object Model (ROM) schema

Report Object Model definition file (rom.def)

The deployment file containing the Report Object Model (ROM) specification that BIRT technology uses to generate and validate a report design.

Related terms
Business Intelligence and Reporting Tools (BIRT) technology, design, report

Contrast with
Report Object Model (ROM), Report Object Model (ROM) element, Report Object Model (ROM) schema

Report Object Model (ROM) element

An Extensible Markup Language (XML) element in the Report Object Model (ROM) that describes a visual or non-visual component of a report. Visual elements include items appearing in a report such as a label, list, or table element. Non-visual elements include data sets, data sources, and report parameters.

Related terms
data set, data source, element, Extensible Markup Language (XML), label element, list element, report, report item, Report Object Model (ROM), report parameter, table element

Contrast with
report element, Report Object Model definition file (rom.def), Report Object Model (ROM) schema

Report Object Model (ROM) schema

The Extensible Markup Language (XML) schema defining the content, semantics, and structure of the components in the BIRT Report Object Model (ROM). The ROM schema is at:

```
http://www.eclipse.org/birt/2005/design
```

Related terms
Business Intelligence and Reporting Tools (BIRT), Extensible Markup Language (XML), Report Object Model (ROM), schema

Contrast with
Report Object Model definition file (rom.def), Report Object Model (ROM) element

report parameter

A report element that enables a user to provide a value as input to the execution of the report. Using a parameter to customize a report provides more focused information to meet specific needs. For example, parameters support selecting sales information by country and city.

Related terms
parameter, report, report element, value

Contrast with
cascading parameters, data set parameter

report template

See template.

report template (.rpttemplate) file

An Extensible Markup Language (XML) file that contains a reusable design providing a start position for developing a new report.

Related terms
design, Extensible Markup Language (XML), report

Contrast with
file types, library (.rptlibrary) file, report design (.rptdesign) file, report document (.rptdocument) file, template

report viewer servlet

A Java EE web application servlet that produces a report from a report design (.rptdesign) file or a report document (.rptdocument) file. When deployed to a Java EE application server, the report viewer servlet makes reports available for viewing over the web. The report viewer servlet is also an active component of the report previewer of BIRT Report Designer.

Related terms
application, Business Intelligence and Reporting Tools (BIRT) Report Designer, Java Platform Enterprise Edition (Java EE), previewer, report, report design (.rptdesign) file, report document (.rptdocument) file, servlet, web server

request

A message that an application sends to a component to perform an action.

Related term
application

reserved word

See keyword.

resource

An application component, such as a class, configuration file, image, library, or template.

Related terms
application, class, configuration file, image, library, template

Contrast with
resource file

resource file

A text file that contains the mapping from resource keys to string values for a particular locale. Resource files support producing a report having localized values for label and text elements.

Related terms
label element, locale, report, resource key, string, text element, value

Contrast with
localization, resource

resource key

A unique value that maps to a string in a resource file. For example, the resource key, greeting, can map to Hello, Bonjour, and Hola in the resource files for English, French, and Spanish, respectively.

Related terms
resource file, string, value

result set

Data rows from an external data source. For example, the data rows that are returned by a SQL SELECT statement performed on a relational database are a result set.

Related terms
data row, data source, database, SQL SELECT statement

Rich Client Platform (RCP)

See Eclipse Rich Client Platform (RCP).

right outer join

See outer join.

ROM   See Report Object Model (ROM).

row

1 A record in a table.

2 A horizontal sequence of cells in a cross tab, grid element, or table element.

Related terms
cell, cross tab, grid element, table, table element

Contrast with
data row

row key

An expression used to collect data rows into row groups and subgroups in a cross-tab element.

Related terms
cross-tab element, data row, group, expression

Contrast with
column key

RPTDESIGN

See report design (.rptdesign) file.

RPTDOCUMENT

See report document (.rptdocument) file.

RPTLIBRARY

See library (.rptlibrary) file.

RPTTEMPLATE

See report template (.rpttemplate) file.

run To execute a program, utility, or other machine function.

run time

The period of time in which a computer program executes. For example, a report executable generates a report during run time.

Related terms
report, report executable file

Contrast with
design time, view time

schema

1 A database schema specifies the structure of database components and the relationships among those components. The database components are items such as tables.

2 An Extensible Markup Language (XML) schema defines the structure of an XML document. An XML schema consists of element declarations and type definitions that describe a model for the information that a well-formed XML document must contain. The XML schema provides a

common vocabulary and grammar for XML documents that support exchanging data among applications.

Related terms
application, data, database, declaration, element, Extensible Markup Language (XML), object, table, well-formed XML

scope The parts of a program in which a symbol or object exists or is visible. The location of an item's declaration determines its scope. Scopes can be nested. A method introduces a new scope for its parameters and local variables. A class introduces a scope for its member variables, member functions, and nested classes. Code in a method in one scope has visibility to other symbols in that same scope and, with certain exceptions, to symbols in outer scopes.

Related terms
class, declaration, function, member, method, object, parameter, variable

script editor

In the report editor in BIRT Report Designer, the page where a report developer adds or modifies JavaScript for a report element.

Related terms
Business Intelligence and Reporting Tools (BIRT) Report Designer, JavaScript, page, report, report editor, report element

scripting language

See JavaScript.

SDK (Software Development Kit)

A collection of programming tools, utilities, compilers, debuggers, interpreters, and application programming interfaces (API) that a developer uses to build an application to run on a specified technology platform. For example, the Java SDK supports developers in building an application that users can download to run on any operating system. The Java Virtual Machine (JVM), the Java SDK interpreter, executes the application in the specified software and hardware configuration.

Related terms
application, application programming interface (API), Java, Java Virtual Machine (JVM), platform

section A horizontal band in a report design. A section uses a grid element, list element, or table element to contain data values, images, and text.

Related terms
data, design, grid element, image, list element, report, table element, value

select To highlight one or more items in a user interface, such as a dialog box or a layout editor. Figure G-26 shows selected items in a report design in the layout editor.

Related terms
data element, design, interface, layout editor, report

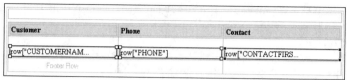

Figure G-26   Three selected data elements

SELECT

See SQL SELECT statement.

series   A sequence of related values. In a chart, for example, a series is a set of related points. Figure G-27 shows a bar chart that displays a series of quarterly sales revenue figures over four years.

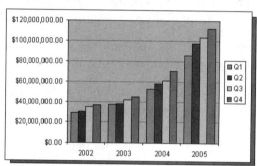

Figure G-27   Series in a chart
Related terms
chart, value
Contrast with
category

servlet   A small Java application running on a web server that extends the server's functionality.
Related terms
application, Java, run, web server

Simple Object Access Protocol (SOAP)

A message-based protocol using Extensible Markup Language (XML). Use SOAP to access applications and their services on the web. SOAP employs XML syntax to send text commands across the internet using Hypertext Transfer Protocol (HTTP).
Related terms
application, Extensible Markup Language (XML), HyperText Transfer Protocol (HTTP), protocol, syntax

slot   A construct that represents a set of ROM elements contained in another ROM element. For example, the body slot of the report design element can contain one or more of any type of report item. Figure G-28 shows a body slot.

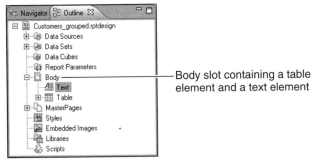

Body slot containing a table
element and a text element

Figure G-28   Body slot

Related terms
design, report, report element, report item, Report Object Model (ROM)
element

sort   To specify the order in which data is processed or displayed. For example,
customer names can be sorted in alphabetical order.

Related term
data

Contrast with
sort key

sort   An expression used to sort data. For example, if you sort data by country, the
key   country field is a sort key. You can sort data using one or more sort keys.

Related terms
data, expression, field, sort

SQL (Structured Query Language)

A language used to access and process data in a relational database.

Related terms
data, database, query

Contrast with
SQL SELECT statement

SQL SELECT statement

A query statement in SQL (Structured Query Language) that provides
instructions about the data to retrieve from a database. For example, the
following SQL query accesses a database's customers table and retrieves the
customer name and credit limit values where the credit limit is less than or
equal to 100,000. The SQL query then sorts the values by customer name.

```
SELECT customers.customerName,
customers.creditLimit
FROM customers
WHERE customers.creditLimit <= 100000
ORDER BY customers.customerName
```

Related terms
data, database, query, report, sort, SQL (Structured Query Language), statement, table

statement

A syntactically complete unit in a programming language that expresses one action, declaration, or definition.

Related term
declaration

Contrast with
SQL SELECT statement

static variable

A variable shared by all instances of a class and its descendant classes. In Java, a static variable is known as a class variable. The compiler specifies the memory allocation for a static variable. The program receives the memory allocation for a static variable as the program loads.

Related terms
class, class variable, descendant class, Java, variable

string

An array of characters.

Related terms
array, character

String data type

A data type that consists of a sequence of contiguous characters including letters, numerals, punctuation marks, and spaces.

Related terms
character, data type, string

Contrast with
string expression

string expression

An expression that evaluates to a series of contiguous characters. Parts of the expression can include a function that returns a string, a string constant, a string literal, a string operator, or a string variable. For example, "abc"+"def" is a string expression that evaluates to "abcdef".

Related terms
character, constant, expression, function, operator, string, variable

Contrast with
String data type

structured content

A formatted document that displays information from one or more data sources.

Related terms
data source, format

Contrast with
report

Structured Query Language (SQL)

See SQL (Structured Query Language).

style   A named set of formatting characteristics, such as alignment, borders, color, and font that report developers apply to a report item to control its appearance.
Related terms
font, format, report, report item
Contrast with
cascading style sheet (CSS)

style sheet

See cascading style sheet (CSS).

subclass

The immediate descendant class.
Related terms
class, descendant class
Contrast with
superclass

The immediate descendant class.

subreport

An item using data from a different data set or data source from other items in a report design. An outer report can contain multiple subreports, also called nested reports. In this case, the subreports typically use data values from the outer report to filter data rows for display. Alternatively, multiple independent subreports exist at the same level in the report design.
Related terms
data, data set, data source, design, report, value

superclass

The immediate ancestor class.
Related terms
ancestor class, class
Contrast with
descendant class, subclass

syntax   The rules that govern the structure of a language.

tab   The label above or below a page in a window that contains multiple pages. Figure G-29 shows tabs that access different Eclipse views in BIRT Report Designer.

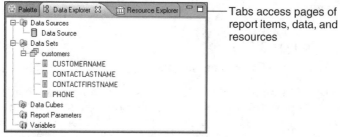

Figure G-29   Tabs in BIRT Report Designer

Related terms
Business Intelligence and Reporting Tools (BIRT) Report Designer, Eclipse view, page

Contrast with
label element

table   A named set of columns in a relational database. Figure G-30 shows tables in the query editor in BIRT Report Designer.

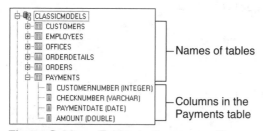

Figure G-30   Tables in the query editor

Related terms
Business Intelligence and Reporting Tools (BIRT) Report Designer, column, database, query editor

Contrast with
table element

table element

 A report item that contains and displays data in a row and column layout. The table element iterates through the data rows in a data set. Figure G-31 shows a table element.

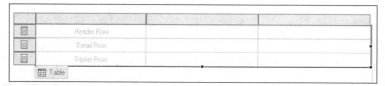

Figure G-31   Table element

Related terms
column, data, data row, data set, layout, report item, row

Contrast with
grid element, list element, table

table of contents

A hyperlinked outline of report contents.

Related terms
hyperlink, report

tag   An element in a markup language that identifies how to process a part of a document.

Related term
element

Contrast with
Extensible Markup Language (XML)

template

In BIRT Report Designer, a predefined structure for a report design. A report developer uses a report template to maintain a consistent style across a set of report designs and to streamline the report design process. A report template is a model for a complete report or a component of a report. BIRT Report Designer provides standard templates and supports custom templates.

In Figure G-32, New Report displays the available templates and Preview displays a representation of the report layout for the selected My First Report, a customer-listing report template.

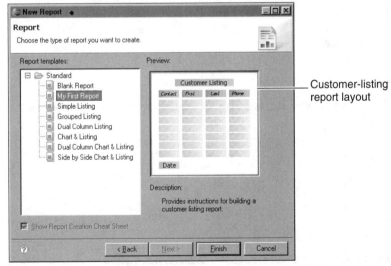

Figure G-32   Templates available for a new report design

Related terms
Business Intelligence and Reporting Tools (BIRT) Report Designer, design, layout, listing report, report, style

Contrast with
report template (.rpttemplate) file

text element

 A report item that displays user-specified text. The text can span multiple lines and can contain HyperText Markup Language (HTML) formatting and dynamic values derived from data set fields or expressions.

Related terms
data set, expression, field, format, HyperText Markup Language (HTML), report item, value

Contrast with
data element, dynamic text element, label element

text file See flat file.

theme A set of related styles stored in a library (.rptlibrary) file. A theme provides a preferred appearance for the report items in a report design. A library file can store multiple themes. A report design can use styles from a single theme as well as styles defined in the report design itself.

Related terms
design, library (.rptlibrary) file, report, report item, style

Contrast with
cascading style sheet (CSS)

tick A marker that occurs at regular intervals along the x- or y-axis of a chart. Typically, the value of each tick appears on the axis.

Related terms
chart, value

Contrast with
tick interval

tick interval

The distance between ticks on an axis. Figure G-33 shows a tick interval in a chart.

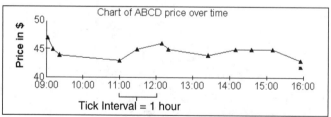

Figure G-33   Chart displaying multiple tick intervals
Related terms
chart, tick

Time data type

A Java data type used to represent time values in SQL (Structured Query Language) statements. The Time data type stores a time value as hour:minute:second.millisecond.

Related terms
data type, Java, statement, Structured Query Language (SQL), value

Contrast with
Date data type, Timestamp data type

Timestamp data type

A Java data type used to represent date-and-time values in SQL statements. The Timestamp data type stores a combined date and time (hour:minute:second.millisecond).

Related terms
data type, Java, statement, Structured Query Language (SQL), value

Contrast with
Date data type, Time data type

toolbar   A user interface component that provides access to common tasks. Different toolbars are available for different kinds of tasks.

Related term
interface

translator

See converter.

type   See data type.

Unicode

A living language standard managed by the Technical Committee of the Unicode Consortium. The current Unicode standard provides code points for more than 65,000 characters. Unicode encoding has no dependency on a platform or software program and thus provides a basis for software internationalization.

Related terms
code point, character, internationalization

Uniform Resource Locator (URL)

A character string that identifies the location and type of a piece of information that is accessible over the web. http:// is the indicator that an item is accessible over the web. The URL typically includes the domain name, type of organization, and a precise location within the directory structure where the item is located.

Related terms
character, domain name, HyperText Transfer Protocol (HTTP), string

Contrast with
Universal Resource Identifier (URI)

universal hyperlink

See hyperlink.

Universal Resource Identifier (URI)

A set of names and addresses in the form of short strings that identify resources on the web. Resources are items such as documents, downloadable files, and images.

Related term
image

Contrast with
Uniform Resource Locator (URL), string

URI See Universal Resource Identifier (URI).

URL See Uniform Resource Locator (URL).

value **1** The content of a constant, parameter, symbol, or variable.

2 A specific occurrence of an attribute. For example, blue is a possible value for an attribute color.

Related terms
attribute, constant, parameter, variable

Varchar data type

A data type used for string calculations. The Varchar data type stores a sequence of Unicode characters. The Varchar data type supports specifying a maximum character length for the string.

Related terms
character, data type, string, Unicode

variable

A named storage location for data that a program can modify. Each variable has a unique name that identifies it within its scope and contains a certain type of data.

Related terms
data, data type, scope

Contrast with
class variable, dynamic variable, field variable, global variable, instance variable, local variable, member variable, static variable

view A predefined query that retrieves data from one or more tables in a relational database. Unlike a table, a view does not store data. Users can use views to select, delete, insert, and update data. The database uses the definition of the view to determine the appropriate action on the underlying tables. For example, a database queries a view by combining the requested data from the underlying tables.

Related terms
data, database, query, table

Contrast with
Eclipse view, previewer

view time

The period of time in which a user examines a report.

Related term
report

Contrast with
design time, run time

viewer   A tool that supports basic viewing tasks, such as navigating a report, using a
table of contents, viewing parameter information, and exporting data.

Related terms
data, parameter, report, table of contents

Contrast with
previewer

web archive (.war) file

A file format used to bundle web applications.

Related terms
application, format

Contrast with
file types, Java archive (.jar) file

web page

A HyperText Markup Language (HTML) page containing tags that a web
browser interprets and displays.

Related terms
HyperText Markup Language (HTML), tag

Contrast with
page

web server

A computer or a program that provides web services on the internet. A web
server accepts requests based on the HyperText Transfer Protocol (HTTP). A
web server also executes server-side scripts, such as Active Server Pages
(ASP) and JavaServer Pages (JSP).

Related terms
HyperText Transfer Protocol (HTTP), JavaServer Page (JSP), request, web
service

web service

A software system designed to support interoperable machine-to-machine
interaction over a network. Web service refers to a client and server that
communicate using Extensible Markup Language (XML) messages adhering
to the Simple Object Access Protocol (SOAP) standard. A web service is
invoked remotely using SOAP or Hypertext Transfer Protocol (HTTP)-GET

and HTTP-POST protocols. The web service returns a response to the client in XML format. Any operating system that supports the SOAP protocol and XML can build and consume a web service.

Related terms
Extensible Markup Language (XML), HyperText Transfer Protocol (HTTP), protocol, Simple Object Access Protocol (SOAP)

Contrast with
request

well-formed XML

An Extensible Markup Language (XML) document that follows syntax rules established in the XML 1.0 recommendation. Well-formed means that a document must contain one or more elements and that the root element must contain all the other elements. Each element must nest inside any enclosing elements, following the syntax rules.

Related terms
element, Extensible Markup Language (XML), syntax

Word converter

A tool that converts a BIRT report to a Microsoft Word (.doc) file.

Related terms
Business Intelligence and Reporting Tools (BIRT), converter, report

workbench

See Eclipse Workbench.

workspace

See Eclipse workspace.

World Wide Web Consortium (W3C)

An international standards body that provides recommendations regarding web standards. The World Wide Web Consortium publishes several levels of documents, including notes, working drafts, proposed recommendations, and recommendations about web applications related to topics such as Extensible Markup Language (XML) and HyperText Markup Language (HTML).

Related terms
application, Extensible Markup Language (XML), HyperText Markup Language (HTML)

XML (Extensible Markup Language)

See Extensible Markup Language (XML).

XML converter

A tool that converts a report to an Extensible Markup Language (XML) file.

Related terms
converter, Extensible Markup Language (XML), report

XML element

See element.

XML PATH language (XPath)

XPath supports addressing an element or elements within an Extensible Markup Language (XML) document based on a path through the document hierarchy.

Related terms
element, Extensible Markup Language (XML)

XML schema

See schema.

XPath   See XML PATH language (XPath).

Z-order   The order in which a combination, multiple *y*-axis, or three-dimensional chart element displays the chart series. Series having a higher Z-order hide series having a lower Z-order. The example in Figure G-34 shows a bar series having a Z-order of 1 and area series having a Z-order of 0.

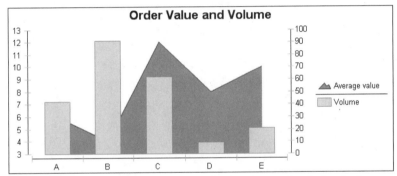

Figure G-34   Multiple *y*-axis chart having bar series in front of area series

Related terms
chart element, combination chart, series

blank fields 341
blank lines (delimited text files) 68
blank pages 581
blank report designs 26
blank rows and columns
   deleting 132
   generating output and 132
   spacing elements with 192, 395
blank space characters 40
blank values 341
block-level elements 39
Blur event type 617
BMP files 142
BMP format 422
bold text style 165
bookmark names 603, 604
Bookmark property 603
bookmarks 670
   creating 603–604
   linking report sections and 602, 604
   linking to external reports and 608
   selecting 607
Boolean expressions 204, 297–298, 670
Boolean values 255, 297
Border property 247, 525
borders
   adding to cross tabs 525
   cascading styles and 174
   formatting properties and 163
   grouping data and 230, 247
   resizing 194
Borders property 194
bottom *n* logic filters 309
bottom *n* summary reports 274
break reports. *See* grouped reports
breakpoints 670
bridge class 671
Browse Resource Files dialog 654
browsers. *See* web browsers
bubble charts
   See also charts
   creating 403
   formatting 456–457
   identifying bubbles in 438
   plotting data values for 431
bug reports 6
builds 5
bulleted lists 150

Business Intelligence and Reporting
   Tools 671
   See also BIRT
buttons
   assigning values to 333
   formatting values for 330, 332, 340
   localizing 661, 662
   selecting values and 319, 332
   setting default values for 331
   sorting values for 336
   specifying as display type 330
   testing values for 351

C

cache, clearing 84
cache conflicts 9
caching data 112
calculated data. *See* computed data
calculated fields. *See* computed fields
calculations
   aggregation and 253, 254, 260, 264, 265
   column bindings and 119, 122, 124
   computed fields and 108, 109
   date values and 140, 295, 296
   derived measures and 544
   incorrect results from 260, 278
   multiple dimensions and 540
   null values in 266
   operator precedence and 283
   percentages and 267–271
   prototyping reports and 52
   textual information and 149
   updating 119, 120
   verifying 108
calendar tool 296
call statements 92
candlestick markers (charts) 404, 468
candlesticks (charts) 438, 439, 441, 468
capitalization 279, 293
   See also case sensitivity
cartesian join 89
cascading parameters 344–350, 673
   See also report parameters
cascading style sheets
   See also styles
   defined 673
   linking to reports 177–180, 181
   renaming 178
   reusing 55, 176

EMF (defined) 688
EMF software 4
empty cells 521, 540
empty fields 341
empty lines (delimited text files) 68
empty pages 581
empty report designs 26
empty rows and columns
    adjusting spacing with 190, 192, 395
    deleting 132
    displaying 551
    generating output and 132
empty strings 284, 341
Enable Live Preview setting 410, 447
Enable master page content setting 597
encapsulation 691
encoding 71, 653, 733
Enter dynamic image expression
    property 146
Enter Parameters dialog
    displaying parameter groups and 342,
      344
    displaying user-selection elements
      and 332
    localizing text in 661
    selecting parameters from 318
Enter URI property 144
enterprise 691
Enterprise JavaBeans. *See* EJBs
enterprise reporting 55, 691
enterprise systems 691
environment settings 46
environments 715
error log view 84
error messages 24, 84, 282
error reports 84
errors 9, 24, 84
event handlers 692
    See also events
event listeners 692
event types 616
events 614, 616, 618, 692
example database. *See* Classic Models
    demo database
Excel converter 692, 716
Excel output formats 47
Excel spreadsheets 48, 190
    See also spreadsheet reports
exceptions 692

executable files 692
executing
    BIRT projects 18
    queries 319, 325
    reports 77, 81, 327
    stored procedures 92
experts. *See* wizards
Export Data dialog 620
Export data icon 620
Export to Library command 625, 626
exporting data 47, 620–621
expression builder 693
    accessing 280
    creating column bindings and 121, 124
    creating expressions and 141, 279–281
    defined 693
    generating computed values and 108,
      109
    selecting items in 124
    setting up run-time connections
      and 80, 82
expression builder button 280
expressions
    adding to reports 153
    aggregating data and 254, 260, 265
    binding connection properties to 78
    calculating percentages and 267, 269,
      270
    charting data and 409, 432, 433, 448,
      449
    combining dynamic and static values
      in 150, 151, 156, 157, 285
    combining values from multiple fields
      in 286
    comparing values and 297, 301, 308,
      315
    computing values and 108, 109, 119,
      140, 282, 309
    concatenating values and 40, 108, 140,
      255, 286, 287
    copying 251
    copying data elements and 123, 124
    counting unique values and 255, 267
    creating 141, 277, 278, 279, 280
    creating multiple sets of
      candlesticks 442
    creating multiple y-axis 442
    defined 693
    defining bookmarks and 603, 607

line break characters 68
line charts
   See also charts
   coloring data series for 502
   creating 401
   formatting 455–456
   plotting data values for 431
   plotting multiple sets of risers for 438
line colors
   axis lines 494
   candlesticks 468
   chart markers 492
   chart outlines 476
   curve-fitting lines 510
   pie charts 465
line markers (charts) 490, 491, 492
line styles
   axes lines 494
   candlesticks 468
   chart markers 492
   chart outlines 476
   curve-fitting lines 510
   leaders 465
line widths
   candlesticks 468
   chart markers 492
   chart outlines 476
   curve-fitting lines 510
   pie charts 465
linear axis type 496, 499
lines, drawing 247
link expressions 604, 607
linking fields (subreports) 370, 371
linking to
   charts 605
   external style sheets 178
   images 143
   report elements 601, 602, 605
   report sections 602–609, 611
   reports 367, 601, 603, 607
   subreports 369–372, 601, 609
     tutorial for 383, 387
   table of contents 608
   web pages 610
links. *See* hyperlinks
Linux servers 10
list boxes
   creating list of values for 332, 333,
     337–339

enabling blank or null values for 341
   formatting values for 330, 340
   localizing 661, 662
   selecting multiple values in 339
   setting default values for 330, 331, 340
   sorting values for 336
   specifying as display type 330, 332
   testing values in 351
list elements
   See also lists
   adding 129, 136–138, 379
   building subreports and 368, 370, 379
   defined 707
   placing in libraries 631
list layouts 136, 137, 368
list style (predefined) 172
list-detail style (predefined) 172
listeners. *See* event listeners
list-footer style (predefined) 172
list-group-footer-*n* style (predefined) 173
list-group-header-*n* style
  (predefined) 173
list-header style (predefined) 173
listing reports 24, 197, 253, 585, 707
lists
   See also list elements
   adding bulleted or numbered 150
   adding group headers or footers
     to 173
   applying styles to 172
   binding dynamic text elements to 154
   binding to data sets 138, 158
   creating 129, 134, 136–138
   displaying alternate values in 337, 338
   filtering data in 305, 312, 319, 327
   grouping data in 215, 226
   linking to charts and 429
   placing CLOB fields in 154
   placing report elements in 137
   placing textual elements in 154, 158
   selecting values from 319, 331, 337,
     339
   sorting data in 209
   specifying page breaks for 579
   standardizing 638
   updating 332
literal characters 166
literal spaces 286
literal text. *See* static text

limiting data returned by 87
matching text patterns and 309
previewing result sets for 31, 113
retrieving data with 30, 86, 114, 300, 319
sorting data with 209
query editor 719
Query page 30, 92
Query Text property 114, 115
queryText property 113, 114
quotation mark characters. *See* double quotation mark character; single quotation mark character

R

radio buttons
  assigning values to 333
  formatting values for 330, 332, 340
  localizing 661, 662
  selecting values and 319
  setting default values for 331
  sorting values for 336
  specifying as display type 330
  testing values for 351
randomly generated data 410, 447
range 719
  See also range of values
range fill colors 492
range filter conditions 302, 308
range markers (charts) 490, 491, 492
range of values
  defined 719
  highlighting in charts 402, 490, 491
  searching 302, 308
  setting axis scale for 499
  setting grouping intervals for 215, 219
Range setting 219, 220, 221
RANK function 256
RCP (defined) 689
  See also Rich Client Platforms
RCP Report Designer package 4
  See also BIRT RCP Report Designer
read-only styles 177
record-level elements (XML) 98
records 68, 299
  See also rows
referencing column names 36
referencing data set fields 141, 279
Refresh Report command 325

RegExp objects 290, 291
  See also regular expressions
region codes 652, 653
Register Template with New Report Wizard command 644, 648
regular expressions 290, 292, 719
relational databases 62
  See also databases
relational models 86
relational structures 86
release build 5
remote servers 99
removing. *See* deleting
renaming
  cascading style sheets 178
  column bindings 122
  columns 107, 407
  data sources 62
  report design files 233
  resource keys 664
rendering environments 53
rendering extensions 719
  defined 719
  See also output formats
Repeat Header property 133, 579
replace function 285, 287
replacing
  multiple strings 285
  null values 287
  specific characters 290, 292
  text 36, 285, 293, 589
report components. *See* report elements; report items
report descriptions 137
Report Design command 21
report design environments 19–20
  See also BIRT; Eclipse
report design file names 233
report design files 45
  defined 719
Report Design perspective 7, 8, 21
report design tasks 18, 44
report design tools 3
report design views 22–24
report design window 22
  See also report editor
Report Designer Full Eclipse Install package 4, 7
Report Designer package 4

U

underline text style 165
underscore (_) character 90
Undo Edit Chart command 650
Undo Transfer to Report Item
  command 650
ungrouped reports 208
Unicode code points 212
Unicode encoding 733
Unicode standard 733
Uniform Resource Locators. *See* URLs
unique values 255, 267, 330, 337
unit-spacing values 470
universal hyperlinks. *See* hyperlinks
Universal Resource Identifiers. *See* URIs
UNIX platforms 10
unpacking BIRT archives 8, 9
Update Manager 11
updating
  calculations 119, 120
  charts 445
  data formats 164
  data set parameters 323
  filter conditions 327
  libraries 625, 629, 635
  list of values 332
  projects 23, 45
  report designers 11–13
  resource files 664
  resource keys 664
upgrades 11
uppercase characters 35, 169, 212
Uppercase format type 169
URIs 144, 145, 610, 734
URL Template property 66
URLs
  defined 733
  image files and 144, 594
  JDBC connections and 63, 66
  localized reports and 11, 653
  web service data sources and 100
  XML data sources and 71
  XML schemas and 71
  XML specification and 71
Use CSS dialog 179
Use CSS File command 179
Use Data from setting 427, 429
Use fixed base value setting 220
Use identifier quoting setting 91

user IDs 293
user interface elements 161
User Name property 63
user names 63, 78, 80
user-defined formulas 118
user-defined values 552–554
user-named styles 175
users
  creating reports and 52, 54
  displaying data and 317
  prompting 104, 317, 318, 330, 342
  providing list of choices for 331, 336
  setting run-time filters 319, 320, 326
user-selection elements
  creating list of values for 333, 338
  importing values for 333
  providing descriptive labels for 335
  returning unique values for 330, 337
  setting default values for 340
  sorting values for 336

V

Value (Y) Series settings 431
value expressions 311
value series
  See also data series
  adding to charts 416
  adding to legends 505
  adding trendlines to 501
  assigning to meters 449, 451
  coloring 502, 504
  combining multiple 447
  displaying data as 430
  emphasizing 456
  exploding pie sectors and 466
  formatting 415, 456, 500
  grouping 430, 439
  hiding 501
  identifying 507
  plotting text data and 430
  selecting data for 430
  setting dial radius and 459
  setting interactive features for 616
  specifying chart type and 431
  stacking 501
value series definitions (charts) 448
value series expressions 439, 442, 448,
  451

Y

y-axis
  See also axes values
  adding a second 442
  adding acceleration lines to 456
  adding gridlines to 493
  arranging tick marks on 493
  building 430, 431, 432
  displaying data on 430, 431, 445
  grouping data for 438–442
  highlighting points on 491
  intersecting 498
  overlapping labels and 495
  rotating 469
  scaling 499
  transposing 443
y-axis labels 494, 496, 507
y-axis titles 489, 657

Z

z-axis 420
z-axis rotation settings 469
zero values 266, 284, 521
zip codes 104, 293
ZIP files. *See* archive files
z-ordering priority 448

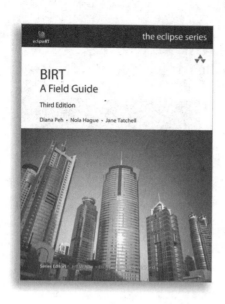